D1265462

Oxford Archaeological Guides

General Editor: Barry Cunliffe

England

Timothy Darvill is Professor of Archaeology in the School of Conservation Sciences at Bournemouth University. The author of over a dozen books, including *Prehistoric Britain* (Routledge, 1998) and *Prehistoric Britain from the Air* (Cambridge University Press, 1996), he has served as Chairman of the Institute of Field Archaeologists and Member of the Council of the National Trust.

Paul Stamper is an Inspector of Ancient Monuments for English Heritage, working in the west midlands. Formerly he was involved with the compilation of the Register of Historic Parks and Gardens in England. Before 1993 he was an editor with the Victoria County History of Shropshire. He has published widely on landscape history, and has served as Secretary of the Society for Medieval Archaeology.

Jane Timby is a freelance archaeological consultant specializing in pottery and post-excavation analysis. She has written a number of reports for county and national journals and books and is author of two excavation monographs. She is currently working on material from Britain, North Africa, and Italy.

Barry Cunliffe is Professor of European Archaeology at the University of Oxford. The author of more than forty books, including *The Oxford Illustrated Prehistory of Europe* (Oxford University Press, 1994), he has served as President of the Council for British Archaeology and the Society of Antiquaries, and is currently a member of the Ancient Monuments Advisory Committee of English Heritage.

Oxford Archaeological Guides

England

An Oxford Archaeological Guide to Sites from Earliest Times to AD 1600

Timothy Darvill, Paul Stamper, and Jane Timby

OXFORD
UNIVERSITY PRESS

OXFORD
UNIVERSITY PRESS

Great Clarendon Street, Oxford OX2 6DP

Oxford University Press is a department of the University of Oxford.
It furthers the University's objective of excellence in research, scholarship,
and education by publishing worldwide in

Oxford New York

Auckland Bangkok Buenos Aires Cape Town Chennai
Dar es Salaam Delhi Hong Kong Istanbul Karachi Kolkata
Kuala Lumpur Madrid Melbourne Mexico City Mumbai Nairobi
São Paulo Shanghai Singapore Taipei Tokyo Toronto
with an associated company in Berlin

Oxford is a registered trade mark of Oxford University Press
in the UK and in certain other countries

Published in the United States
by Oxford University Press Inc., New York

British Library Cataloguing in Publication Data
Data available

Library of Congress Cataloging in Publication Data
Data available
ISBN 0–19–285326–0 (hbk.)
ISBN 0–19–284101–7 (pbk.)

1 3 5 7 9 10 8 6 4 2

Designed by First Edition, London
Typeset by RefineCatch Limited, Bungay, Suffolk
Printed by Book Print S. L.
Barcelona, Spain

Series Editor's Foreword

Travelling for pleasure, whether for curiosity, nostalgia, religious conviction, or simply to satisfy an inherent need to learn, has been an essential part of the human condition for centuries. Chaucer's 'Wife of Bath' ranged wide, visiting Jerusalem three times as well as Santiago de Compostela, Rome, Cologne, and Boulogne. Her motivation, like that of so many medieval travellers, was primarily to visit holy places. Later, as the Grand Tour took a hold in the eighteenth century, piety was replaced by the need felt by the élite to educate its young, to compensate for the disgracefully inadequate training offered at that time by Oxford and Cambridge. The levelling effect of the Napoleonic Wars changed all that and in the age of the steamship and the railway mass tourism was born when Mr Thomas Cook first offered 'A Great Circular Tour of the Continent'.

There have been guidebooks as long as there have been travellers. Though not intended as such, the *Histories* of Herodotus would have been an indispensable companion to a wandering Greek. Centuries later Pausanias' guide to the monuments of Greece was widely used by travelling Romans intent on discovering the roots of their civilization. In the eighteenth century travel books took on a more practical form offering a torrent of useful advice, from dealing with recalcitrant foreign innkeepers to taking a plentiful supply of oil of lavender to ward off bedbugs. But it was the incomparable 'Baedekers' that gave enlightenment and reassurance to the increasing tide of enquiring tourists who flooded the Continent in the latter part of the nineteenth century. The battered but much-treasured red volumes may still sometimes be seen in use today, pored over on sites by those nostalgic for the gentle art of travel.

The needs and expectations of the enquiring traveller change rapidly and it would be impossible to meet them all within the compass of single volumes. With this in mind, the Oxford Archaeological Guides have been created to satisfy a particular and growing interest. Each volume provides lively and informed descriptions of a wide selection of archaeological sites chosen to display the cultural heritage of the country in question. Plans, designed to match the text, make it easy to grasp the full extent of the site while focusing on its essential aspects. The emphasis is, necessarily, on seeing, understanding, and above all enjoying the particular place. But archaeological sites are the creation of history and can only be fully appreciated against the *longue durée* of human achievement. To provide this, each book begins with a wide-ranging historical overview introducing the changing cultures of the country and the landscapes which formed them. Thus, while the Guides are primarily intended for the traveller they can be read with equal value at home.

Barry Cunliffe

Acknowledgements

We are very grateful to the Royal Commission on the Historical Monuments of England, English Heritage, and the Cambridge University Committee for Aerial Photography for permission to use plans and photographs from their collections. Several friends and colleagues have allowed Oxford University Press to base illustrations on their plans, provided information, and answered our queries; we are particularly grateful to Mick Jones, Neil Holbrook, Miles Russell, Paul Tyers, Bruce Induni, Nick Johnson, John Williams, Ian Hewitt, Philip Crummy, Michael Jones, David Viner, Mark Horton, and Alan Vince. We would also like to thank George Miller and Shelley Cox at Oxford University Press for their patience during the preparation of this volume, and Barry Cunliffe for his support.

Contents

Visiting archaeological sites

Some of the sites listed here are managed as tourist attractions, and while they may be easy to reach and provided with car parks, toilets, and gift shops, they frequently lose something of their atmosphere and mystery as a result. There is usually a charge made for entry. Others, probably the majority, are not managed in this way and are in a sense more authentic because they are uncluttered by the trappings of modern life. These sites can be slightly more difficult to find, but the rewards of visiting them are great.

Getting there

Sites promoted as tourist attractions are usually signposted from main roads; look out for brown-coloured 'tourist signs'. Others can be more difficult to find and it is often useful to take with you a map showing footpaths (1:50,000 scale or larger) or the street plan if in a town. To help you pinpoint the position of the monuments mentioned in this Guide on an Ordnance Survey map a standard National Grid Reference (NGR) is given for each entry.

All archaeological sites in England are owned by somebody. Many of those listed here are in the care of English Heritage, the National Trust, or a local authority, and are open to the public. Others lie in public open spaces, or can be seen from a public right of way. At the time of going to press, all the monuments in this book were open, accessible, or easily visible. Arrangements are, however, constantly changing, and if you are ever in doubt about access always ask permission from the landowner. The inclusion of a site in this Guide does not itself confer any right of access.

Many monuments can be visited at any reasonable time, but those under private management or in the charge of a custodian usually have restricted opening hours comprising the normal working day or some part of it. Further restrictions may apply on Sundays and Public Holidays; most are closed on Christmas Day, Boxing Day, and New Year's Day, some also at Easter. To avoid disappointment it is advisable to check opening times in advance if making a long journey; there is a list of useful contacts in the Reference section.

Appropriate footwear and clothing is always advisable. A torch is useful for barrows with accessible chambers or buildings which you can go inside; a candle is even more authentic!

Being there

Archaeological sites can be enjoyed in many different ways. They provide inspiring and challenging subjects for painting, sketching, photography, or writing; your imagination is the only constraint on what you can achieve.

When visiting a site try to visualize it as it might have been in earlier times. Capture in your mind's eye any ramparts or banks with vertical outer faces, and the dazzling brightness of bare earth, rock, and upstanding stones before any lichen, grass, or shrubs took hold. Contemplate how many people occupied or visited the site you are looking at. Who were they? Were they there all the time or did they only come for special occasions or in times of trouble? What was their mood? Did they live there, work there, retreat there out of fear, congregate there for ceremonies at special times, or was it only at funerals and solemn occasions that people came?

Think about how long it took to build the structures you see. Visualize if you can the countryside around about. Was the site deliberately placed to enjoy or exploit a particular view, for military, ritual, or aesthetic purposes? Above all, remember that no matter how isolated and remote a site may appear today, thousands of people have been there before you, creating, exploiting, or admiring the monuments and landscapes that you see.

Think of Others

When visiting archaeological sites always observe the Country Code. Never damage monuments by picking up stones, digging holes, lighting fires, taking bits away, or rubbing rock art or decorated stones. The unauthorized use of a metal detector on a protected monument in England is against the law; so too is the act of damaging or defacing one.

Think of others too while enjoying a site. Park sensibly if arriving by car, take away your rubbish, and don't presume an automatic right of access. Shamanistic rites or picnics in the centre of small monuments may be fun, but can be irritating to others. Always respect the sacred nature of ritual, ceremonial, burial, or religious sites.

How to use this Guide

This Guide cannot tell you everything. It is a starting point and as such serves as both an introduction and an index to what lies beyond. The aim of the Introduction is to set the scene with a general chronological account of England's past and some background information.

The main text lists sites to visit, arranged in twelve sections, each relating to a geographical region (Map 1) roughly ordered from north to south. Each regional section has a brief introduction to set the scene and pick out distinctive geographical and topographical features. The main list of sites is arranged alphabetically by name; a map at the start of each section shows the distribution of the places covered. Deciding which sites to leave out was more difficult than selecting which to include: some entries refer to other nearby places that are certainly worth visiting but we could not cover with full entries. Some sites have been given a star rating based on the state of preservation, interest, and accessibility (see alphabetical index at the end of the book). Two stars indicate sites that really must be visited; one star designates sites that should not be missed if you are in the area. The brief notes on how to find sites will be useful, but it is best to obtain the relevant Ordnance Survey Landranger map (scale: 1:50,000) and use the national grid reference to find the site and check the best approach to it. The pace of development and the rerouting of roads means that access arrangements are constantly changing. Don't give up; if at first you can't find a site ask others for directions.

Within the entries and in the Introduction, cross-references to other sites covered in the present Guide are shown in SMALL CAPITALS. Terms for which there are entries in the glossary (pp. 464–71) are indicated by means of a dagger (†). The following symbols are used on the maps at the head of each regional section: ■ Prehistoric site; ● Roman site; ▲ medieval site.

Recognizing that many readers will wish to follow up a visit that has interested them, background reading is given at the end of each entry. This is normally the report on any excavations or major surveys that have been carried out, although in some cases it is a synthesis of recent work. Some of these reports were compiled many years ago so the terminology and dating may need revising in the light of what you will find earlier in this section of the Guide. Some of references will take a bit of searching to find, but the chase is part of the fun of research! The Internet is fast becoming a major source of information about archaeological sites. We have included a few addresses as points of entry, but much more will be found by surfing around with your browser.

The reference section at the end includes a chronological summary, a glossary, and some general suggestions for further reading about

▲ Fig. 1 The twelve regions of the guide

1 Northumbria 2 The Lake District and north-west 3 Yorkshire and the Humber basin 4 East Midlands 5 The Midlands plain and Welsh borders 6 East Anglia 7 The Chilterns and Northampton borders 8 The Cotswolds and upper Thames valley 9 London 10 The Weald and downland of south-east England 11 Wessex and the west country 12 The south-west peninsula

archaeological methods, approaches, and the results of recent work. There is also a list of national, regional, and thematic museums that will be of interest to visitors, especially on days when getting out and about to see sites is hampered by poor weather. For those wishing to become more involved in archaeological interests we have included information about societies to join and periodicals that can be obtained on subscription.

Maps

Text boxes

Sites listed by archaeological period

Star-rated sites marked ★ and ★★

Palaeolithic

Boxgrove, W Sussex (R10)
Cheddar Gorge and the Mendip Caves, Som. (R11)★
Creswell Crags, Derby. (R4)★★
Kent's Cavern, Devon (R12)★
King Arthur's Cave, Herefordshire (R5)
Oldbury Rock Shelters, Kent (R10)
Victoria Cave, N Yorks. (R3)

Mesolithic

Cheddar Gorge and the Mendip Caves, Som. (R11)★
Creswell Crags, Derby. (R4)★★
King Arthur's Cave, Herefordshire (R5)
Star Carr, N Yorks. (R3)
Victoria Cave, N Yorks. (R3)

Neolithic

Addington Park, Kent (R10)★
Arbor Low, Derby. (R4)★★
Arthur's Stone, Herefordshire (R5)

Avebury, Wilts. (R11)★★
Ballowall Barrow, Corn. (R12)
Bant's Carn, Isles of Scilly (R12)
Belas Knap, Glos. (R8)★★
Birkrigg Common, Cumbria (R2)
Bridestones, Staffs. (R5)
Carn Brea, Corn. (R12)
Carrock Fell, Cumbria (R2)
Castlerigg, Cumbria (R2)★★
Chestnuts Long Barrow, Kent (R10)
Cissbury Ring, W Sussex (R10)
Coldrum Long Barrow, Kent (R10)
Combe Gibbet, W Berks. (R8)
Coombe Hill, E Sussex (R10)
Copt Hill, Tyne and Wear (R1)
Crickley Hill, Glos. (R8)★★
Devil's Arrows, N Yorks. (R3)
Devil's Lapful, Northumb. (R1)
Dod Law, Northumb. (R1)★★
Duggleby Howe, E Riding,Yorks. (R3)
Durrington Walls, Wilts. (R11)

Eskdale Moor, Cumbria (R2)
Five Wells, Derby.(R4)
Gardom's Edge, Derby. (R4)★
Gib Hill, Derby. (R4)
The Grey Mare and her Colts, Dorset (R11)
Grime's Graves, Norfolk (R6)★★
Hambledon Hill, Dorset (R11)★
Harrow Hill, W Sussex (R10)
Hasting Hill, Tyne and Wear (R1)
Hembury, Devon (R12)
Hetty Pegler's Tump, Glos. (R8)★
Hoe Hill, Lincs. (R4)
Hurlers, Corn. (R12)
Ilkley Moor, W Yorks. (R3)★
Innisidgen, Isles of Scilly (R12)
King Arthur's Round Table, Cumbria (R2)★
Kingston Russell, Dorset (R11)
Kit's Coty House, Kent (R10)★
Knowlton, Dorset (R11)★
Lambourn Seven Barrows, W Berks. (R8)
Lanyon Quoit, Corn. (R12)
Little Kit's Coty, Kent (R10)

Long Bredy, Dorset
(R11)
Long Meg and Her
Daughters, Cumbria
(R2)★
The Longstone, Corn.
(R12)
Long Stone, Glos. (R8)
Long Stone, Forest of
Dean, Glos. (R8)
Lordenshaws,
Northumb. (R1)★
Maiden Castle, Dorset
(R11)★★
Maumbury Rings,
Dorset (R11)
Mayburgh, Cumbria
(R2)
Merrivale, Devon (R12)
Merry Maidens, Corn.
(R12)
Mitchell's Fold,
Shropshire (R5)★
Nine Ladies, Derby.
(R4)
Nine Maidens Stone
Circle, Corn. (R12)
Nine Maidens Stone
Row, Corn. (R12)
The Nine Stones, Dorset
(R11)
Notgrove Long Barrow,
Glos. (R8)
Nympsfield Long
Barrow, Glos. (R8)
Oakley Down, Dorset
(R11)
Old Bewick, Northumb.
(R1)★
Porlock, Som. (R11)
Porth Hellick Down,
Isles of Scilly (R12)
Randwick Long Barrow,
Glos. (R8)
Rollright Stones, Oxon.
(R8)★★
Roughtor, Corn. (R12)
Roystone Grange Trail,
Derby. (R4)★

Rudston Monolith, E
Riding, Yorks.
(R3)★★
The Sanctuary, Wilts.
(R11)
Silbury Hill, Wilts.
(R11)★
Stanton Drew, Bath and
NE Som. (R11)★
Stonehenge, Wilts.
(R11)★★
Stoney Littleton, Bath
and NE Som. (R11)
Stowes Pound, Corn.
(R12)
Stripple Stones, Corn.
(R12)
Swinburn Castle Stone,
Northumb. (R1)
Swinside, Cumbria
(R2)★
Thornborough Circles,
N Yorks. (R3)
Tregiffian, Corn. (R12)
Trethevy Quoit, Corn.
(R12)★
The Trundle, W Sussex
(R10)★
Waulud's Bank, Luton
(R7)★
Wayland's Smithy,
Oxon. (R8)★
West Kennet Long
Barrow, Wilts.
(R11)★
West Rudham Long
Barrow, Norfolk (R6)
White Barrow, Wilts.
(R11)
Willerby Wold, N Yorks.
(R3)
Windmill Hill, Wilts.
(R11)
Windmill Tump, Glos.
(R8)
Woodhenge, Wilts.
(R11)
Zennor Quoit, Corn.
(R12)

Bronze Age

Afton Down, I.o.W.
(R10)
Alderley Edge, Ches.
(R5)
Arbor Low, Derby.
(R4)★★
Birkrigg Common,
Cumbria (R2)
Breamish Valley Trail,
Northumb. (R1)
Bully Hills, Lincs. (R4)
Danby Rigg, N Yorks.
(R3)
Eskdale Moor, Cumbria
(R2)
Five Barrows,
Northumb. (R1)
Flag Fen, Peterborough
(R6)★★
Flowerdown Barrows,
Hants. (R10)
Gardom's Edge, Derby.
(R4)★
Grimspound, Devon
(R12)★
Halangy Down, Isles of
Scilly (R12)
Hampstead Heath,
Greater London
(R9)
Harrow Hill, W Sussex
(R10)
Hob Hurst's House,
Derby. (R4)
Horridge Common,
Devon (R12)
Ilkley Moor, W Yorks.
(R3)★
Lambourn Seven
Barrows, W Berks.
(R8)
Mam Tor, Derby. (R4)★
Man-an-Tol, Corn.
(R12)
Merrivale, Devon (R12)
Nine Barrows, Dorset
(R11)

Nine Ladies, Derby.
(R4)
Norton Fitzwarren,
Som. (R11)
Oakley Down, Dorset
(R11)
Poor Lot, Dorset (R11)
Priddy Circles and Nine
Barrows, Som. (R11)
Rider's Rings, Devon
(R12)
Roughtor, Corn. (R12)
Shaugh Moor and
Upper Plym Valley,
Devon (R12)
Stonehenge, Wilts.
(R11)★★
Stowes Pound, Corn.
(R12)
Therfield Heath, Herts.
(R7)
Uffington White Horse
and Castle, Oxon.
(R8)★★
Victoria Cave, N Yorks.
(R3)
Windmill Hill, Wilts.
(R11)

Iron Age

Arbury Banks, Herts.
(R7)
Badbury Rings, Dorset
(R11)★
Bagendon, Glos. (R8)
Barbury Castle, Wilts.
(R11)
Beacon Hill, Hants.
(R10)★
Bindon Hill, Dorset
(R11)
Blackbury Camp, Devon
(R12)
Bokerley Dyke, Dorset
(R11)
Brackenbury Ditches,
Glos. (R8)

Bratton Camp and
Westbury White
Horse, Wilts. (R11)
Breamish Valley Trail,
Northumb. (R1)
Brean Down, Som.
(R11)
Bredon Hill, Worcs.
(R5)
Brent Knoll, Som. (R11)
British Camp,
Herefordshire (R5)★★
Burrough Hill, Leics.
(R4)
Bury Ditches,
Shropshire (R5)
Butser Hill, Hants.
(R10)
Caburn Hill, E Sussex
(R10)
Cadbury Camp, N Som.
(R11)
Caer Caradoc,
Shropshire (R5)
Caesar's Camp, Greater
London (R9)
Carn Euny, Corn. (R12)
Cerne Abbas Giant,
Dorset (R11)★★
Chun Castle, Corn.
(R12)
Chysauster, Corn.
(R12)★★
Cissbury Ring, W
Sussex (R10)
Cleeve Hill, Glos. (R8)
Colchester
(*Camulodunum*),
Essex (R6)★★
Conderton Camp,
Worcs. (R5)
Crickley Hill, Glos.
(R8)★★
Croft Ambrey,
Herefordshire (R5)
Crosby Garrett,
Cumbria (R2)
Danby Rigg, N Yorks.
(R3)

Dane's Dyke, E Riding,
Yorks. (R3)★
Dane's Graves, E Riding,
Yorks. (R3)
Danebury, Hants.
(R10)★
Ditchling Beacon, E
Sussex (R10)
Dod Law, Northumb.
(R1)★★
Dolebury, N Som. (R11)
Eggardon Hill, Dorset
(R11)
Eston Nab, Redcar and
Cleveland (R1)
Ewe Close, Cumbria
(R2)
Figsbury Ring, Wilts.
(R11)
Glastonbury Lake
Village, Som. (R11)
Grassington, N Yorks.
(R3)★
Great Hetha Camp,
Northumb. (R1)
Grim's Ditch, Oxon
(R8)
Grim's Ditch, Greater
London (R9)
Gurnard's Head, Corn.
(R12)
Halangy Down, Isles of
Scilly (R12)
Halliggye Fogou, Corn.
(R12)
Ham Hill, Som. (R11)
Hambledon Hill, Dorset
(R11)★
Haresfield Beacon, Glos.
(R8)
Heathrow Airport,
Greater London (R9)
Hembury, Devon (R12)
Hengistbury Head,
Bournemouth (R11)
Highdown Hill, W
Sussex (R10)
Hunsbury, Northants.
(R7)

Ivinghoe Beacon, Bucks. (R7)★

Kinver Edge, Staffs. (R5)

Long Man of Wilmington, E Sussex (R10)

Lordenshaws, Northumb. (R1)★

Lydney Park, Glos. (R8)

Maiden Castle, Ches. (R5)

Maiden Castle, Dorset (R11)★★

Mam Tor, Derby. (R4)

Midsummer Hill, Herefordshire (R5)

Milber Down Camp, Devon (R12)

Norton Fitzwarren, Som. (R11)

Old Bewick, Northumb. (R1)★

Old Oswestry, Shropshire (R5)★★

Old Sarum, Wilts. (R11)

Oldbury Camp, Wilts. (R11)

Oldbury Hill, Kent (R10)

Pilsden Pen, Dorset (R11)

Portfield Fort, Lancs. (R2)

Poundbury, Dorset (R11)

Rainsborough Camp, Northants (R7)★

The Ridgeway, Oxon. (R8)

Royston Grange, Derby. (R4)★

The Rumps, Corn. (R12)★

St Catherine's Hill, Hants. (R10)

South Cadbury, Som. (R11)

Stanwick, N Yorks. (R3)★

Staple Howe, E Riding, Yorks. (R3)

Therfield Heath, Herts. (R7)

The Trundle, W Sussex (R10)★

Uffington White Horse and Castle, Oxon. (R8)★★

Uleybury, Glos. (R8)

Wandlebury, Cambs. (R6)

Wappenbury, War. (R8)

Warham, Norfolk (R6)

Wheathampstead, Herts. (R7)

Worlebury, Weston super Mare (R11)

The Wrekin, Telford and Wrekin (R5)

Yeavering Bell, Northumb. (R1)

Romano-British

Ackling Dyke, Dorset (R11)

Aldborough (*Isurium Brigantium*), N Yorks. (R3)

Alice Holt, Surrey (R10)

Ambleside (*Galava*), Cumbria (R2)

Ancaster, Lincs. (R4)

Baginton, War. (R8)★★

Bancroft, Milton Keynes (R7)

Banks East, Cumbria (R2)

Bartlow, Essex (R6)★★

Bath (*Aquae Sulis*), Bath and NE Som. (R11)★★

Benenden, Kent (R10)

Benwell (*Condercum*), Tyne and Wear (R1)

Bignor, W Sussex (R10)★★

Binchester (*Vinovia*), Co. Durham (R1)

Birdoswald (*Camboglanna*), Cumbria (R2)★

Bitterne (*Clausentum*), Southampton (R10)

Black Carts Turret, Northumb. (R1)

Blackpool Bridge, Glos. (R8)

Blackstone Edge, W Yorks. (R3)

Bowes Fort (*Lavatrae*), Co. Durham (R1)

Bowes Moor, Co. Durham (R1)

Brading, I.o.W. (R10)★★

Bradwell (?*Othona*), Essex (R6)

Brancaster (*Branodunum*), Norfolk (R6)

Breage Church, Corn. (R12)

Brean Down, Som. (R11)

Brough (*Navio*), Derby. (R4)

Brough (*Verterae*), Cumbria (R2)

Brough-on-Humber (*Petruaria*), E Riding, Yorks. (R3)

Brougham (*Brocavum*), Cumbria (R2)

Brunton Turret, Northumb. (R1)

Burgh Castle (*Gariannonum*), Norfolk (R6)★

Caistor St Edmund (*Venta Icenorum*), Norfolk (R6)

Caistor-on-Sea, Norfolk (R6)

Canterbury (*Durovernum Cantiacorum*), Kent (R10)★

Carisbrooke, I.o.W
(R10)
Carlisle (*Luguvalium*),
Cumbria (R2)
Carn Euny, Corn. (R12)
Carrawburgh
(*Brocolita*),
Northumb. (R1)
Carvoran (*Magna*),
Cumbria (R2)
Castleshaw
(*Rigodunum*), Greater
Manchester (R2)
Cawfields, Northumb.
(R1)
Cawthorn Camps, N
Yorks. (R3)
Charterhouse-on-Mendip,
Som. (R11)
Chedworth, Glos. (R8)★
Chester (*Deva*), Ches.
(R5)
Chesterholm
(*Vindolanda*),
Northumb. (R1)★★
Chesters Bridge
Abutment,
Northumb. (R1)
Chesters Roman Fort
(*Cilurnum*)
Northumb. (R1)★
Chew Green,
Northumb. (R1)★★
Chichester (*Noviomagus
Regnensium*), W
Sussex (R10)
Chysauster, Corn.
(R12)★★
Cirencester (*Corinium
Dobunniorum*), Glos.
(R8)
Clacket Wood, Surrey
(R10)
Colchester
(*Camulodunum*),
Essex (R6)★★
Corbridge
(*Corstopitum*),
Northumb. (R1)★

Crofton, Kent (R10)
Crosby Garrett,
Cumbria (R2)
Denton, Tyne and Wear
(R1)
Dorchester
(*Durnovaria*) Dorset
(R11)
Dover (*Dubris*), Kent
(R10)★★
Ewe Close, Cumbria
(R2)
Exeter (*Isca
Dumnoniorum*),
Devon (R12)
Farley Heath, Surrey
(R10)
Filey, N Yorks. (R3)
Fishbourne, W Sussex
(R10)★
Fosse Way (R8)
Gloucester (*Colonia
Nervia Glevensium*),
Glos. (R8)
Goldsborough, N Yorks.
(R3)
Great Casterton,
Rutland (R4)
Great Stukely, Cambs.
(R6)
Great Witcombe, Glos.
(R8)
Greatchesters (*Aesica*),
Northumb. (R1)
Greta Bridge (*Maglona*),
Co. Durham (R1)
Hadrian's Wall,
Cumbria (R2)
Hadrian's Wall,
Northumb. and Tyne
and Wear (R1)
Hardknott Castle
(*Mediobogdum*),
Cumbria (R2)★
Hare Hill, Cumbria
(R2)
Harlow, Essex (R6)
Harrow's Scar,
Cumbria (R2)

Heddon-on-the-Wall,
Northumb. (R1)
Hembury, Devon (R12)
High Rochester
(*Bremenium*),
Northumb. (R1)
Holtye, E Sussex (R10)
Horncastle
(*Banovallum*), Lincs.
(R4)
Housesteads
(*Vercovicium*)
Northumb. (R1)★★
Ilchester (*Lindinis*),
Som. (R11)
Ilkley (*Olicana*), W
Yorks. (R3)
Irchester, Northants.
(R7)
Jordan Hill, Dorset
(R11)
Kenchester (*Magna*),
Herefordshire (R5)
Keynsham East
(Somerdale), Bath
and NE Som. (R11)
Keynsham West, Bath
and NE Som.
(R11)
Kings Weston, Bristol
(R11)
Kingston Lisle, Oxon.
(R8)
Kirby Hill, N Yorks.
(R3)
Lancaster, Lancs. (R2)
Lanchester
(*Longovicium*), Co.
Durham (R1)
Leicester (*Ratae
Coritanorum*), Leics.
(R4)
Leicester (The Raw
Dykes), Leics. (R4)
Lincoln (*Lindum*),
Lincs. (R4)
London (*Londinium*),
Greater London
(R9)★★

Anglo-Saxon and Viking

Barnack, Peterborough (R6)
Barton-upon-Humber (St Peter's), N Lincs. (R3)★
Battle, E. Sussex (R10)
Bradford-on-Avon, Wilts. (R11)★
Breamore, Hants. (R10)
Canterbury, Kent (R10)★
Corhampton, Hants. (R10)
Deerhurst, Glos. (R8)★★
Earls Barton, Northants. (R7)★
Gloucester, Glos. (R8)
Jarrow (St Paul's), Tyne and Wear (R1)
Lincoln, Lincs. (R4)★★
London, Greater London (R9)★★
Monkwearmouth (St Peter's), Tyne and Wear (R1)
Offa's Dyke (R5)
Repton, Derby. (R4)
Stone-by-Faversham, Kent (R10)
Sutton Hoo, Suffolk (R6)
Tintagel, Corn. (R12)
Wansdyke, Wilts. (R11)
Wareham, Dorset (R11)
West Stow, Suffolk (R6)
Wing, Bucks. (R7)
Wroxeter, Shropshire (R5)★
York, Yorks. (R3)★★

Early Medieval (C11–mid-C14)

Abbey Dore, Herefordshire (R5)★

Aldworth, W Berks. (R8)
Appleton-le-Moors, N Yorks. (R3)
Ashleworth, Glos. (R8)
Battle, E Sussex (R10)
Beeston, Ches. (R5)
Bentley Grange, W Yorks. (R3)
Beverley, E Riding, Yorks. (R3)
Bishop's Waltham, Hants. (R10)
Boothby Pagnall, Lincs. (R4)
Boston, Lincs. (R4)★
Bradford-on-Avon, Wilts. (R11)★
Bredon, Worcs. (R5)
Bristol City, Bristol (R11)
Bury St Edmund's, Suffolk (R6)
Bushmead Priory, Beds. (R7)
Canterbury, Kent (R10)★
Carisbrooke, I.o.W. (R10)
Carlisle, Cumbria (R2)
Castle Rising, Norfolk (R6)
Chester, Ches. (R5)
Chichester, W Sussex (R10)
Chillingham, Northumb. (R1)
Colchester Castle, Essex (R6)
Conisbrough, S Yorks. (R3)
Corbridge (The Vicar's Pele), Northumb. (R1)
Corfe Castle, Dorset (R11)
Dover, Kent (R10)★★
Dunstanburgh, Northumb. (R1)

Durham, Co. Durham (R1)★★
Ely, Cambs. (R6)
Exeter, Devon (R12)
Fountains Abbey and Studley Royal, N. Yorks. (R3)★★
Gainsthorpe, N Lincs. (R3)
Geddington and Hardingstone, Northants. (R7)
Glastonbury, Som. (R11)
Gloucester, Glos. (R8)
Goodrich, Herefordshire (R5)
Great Coxwell, Oxon (R8)
Greensted, Essex (R6)
Haddiscoe, and Haddiscoe Thorpe, Norfolk (R6)
Higham Ferrers, Northants. (R7)
Houndtor, Devon (R12)
Isleham, Cambs. (R6)
Kempley, Glos. (R8)★
King's Lynn, Norfolk (R6)
Launceston, Corn. (R12)
Leigh Court, Worcs. (R5)
Lincoln, Lincs. (R4)★★
London, Greater London (R9)★★
Longthorpe Tower, Peterborough (R6)
Longtown Castle, Herefordshire (R5)
Malmesbury, Wilts. (R11)
Middle Littleton, Worcs. (R5)
Norfolk Broads (R6)
Northampton, Northants. (R7)
Norwich, Norfolk (R6)★

Abbreviations

AA	Archaeologia Aeliana
ACamb	Archaeologia Cambrensis
ACant	Archaeologia Cantiana
Arch J	Archaeological Journal
AN	Archaeology North
Ant J	Antiquaries Journal
BAJ	Berkshire Archaeological Journal
BIA	Bulletin of the Institute of Archaeology (University of London)
CA	Current Archaeology
CoA	Cornish Archaeology
CWAAS	Cumberland and Westmorland Antiquarian and Archaeological Society
DAJ	Derbyshire Archaeological Journal
EAA	East Anglian Archaeology
EAH	Essex Archaeology and History
EHD ii	English Historical Documents, vol. ii: 1042–1189, ed. David Douglas (Eyre & Spottiswoode, 1953)
EHD iv	English Historical Documents, vol. iv: 1327–1485, ed. A. R. Myers (Eyre & Spottiswoode, 1969)
HA	Hertfordshire Archaeology
HBMCE	Historic Buildings and Monuments Commission for England
HBNC	History of Berwickshire Naturalists Club
HMSO	Her Majesty's Stationery Office
JBAA	Journal of the British Archaeological Association
KAR	Kent Archaeological Review
MA	Medieval Archaeology
NA	Norfolk Archaeology
PCAS	Proceedings of the Cambridgeshire Antiquarian Society
PCNFC	Proceedings of the Cotteswold Naturalists' Field Club
PDAES	Proceedings of the Devon Archaeological Exploration Society
PDAS	Proceedings of the Devon Archaeological Society
PDNHAFC	Proceedings of the Dorset Natural History and Antiquarian Field Club
PDNHAS	Proceedings of the Dorset Natural History and Archaeological Society
PHFCAS	Proceedings of the Hampshire Field Club and Archaeological Society
PIWNHS	Proceedings of the Isle of Wight Natural History Society
PLPLS	Proceedings of the Leeds Philosophical and Literary Society

PPS	*Proceedings of the Prehistoric Society*
PSAL	*Proceedings of the Society of Antiquaries of London*
PSAN	*Proceedings of the Society of Antiquaries of Newcastle-upon-Tyne*
PSANHS	*Proceedings of the Somerset Archaeological and Natural History Society*
PUBSS	*Proceedings of the University of Bristol Spelaeological Society*
PWCFC	*Proceedings of the West Cornwall Field Club*
RCHME	Royal Commission on the Historical Monuments of England
SAC	*Sussex Archaeological Collections*
SuAC	*Surrey Archaeological Collections*
TBAS	*Transactions of the Birmingham Archaeological Society*
TBGAS	*Transactions of the Bristol and Gloucestershire Archaeological Society*
TCNFC	*Transactions of the Cotteswold Naturalists' Field Club*
TCWAAS	*Transactions Cumberland and Westmorland Antiquarian and Archaeological Society*
TDAAS	*Transactions of the Durham Archaeological and Antiquarian Society*
TEHAS	*Transactions of the East Hertfordshire Archaeological Society*
TLCAS	*Transactions of the Lancashire and Cheshire Antiquarian Society*
TLMAS	*Transactions of the London and Middlesex Archaeological Society*
TNAS	*Transactions of the Norfolk Archaeological Society*
TPBAS	*Transactions and Proceedings of the Birmingham Archaeological Society*
VCH	Victoria County History
WANHM	*Wiltshire Archaeological and Natural History Magazine*
YAJ	*Yorkshire Archaeological Journal*

Introduction

Archaeology in England

Travelling around England is in many senses a journey backwards in time. On all sides, and sometimes even under the road or footpath itself, there are fragments of the ancient past side by side with the clutter of the modern world. Medieval villages, castles, ancient churches, and Roman villas are commonplace and take us back to the time of Christ. Far older, yet equally abundant, are the barrows, hillforts, stone circles, camps, standing stones, trackways, and other relics of prehistoric times that have survived for several thousand years.

This Guide is about all these ancient remains: the prehistoric, Roman and medieval sites which date from the time between the first appearance of people in what we now call England during the middle stages of the Pleistocene Ice Age around 500,000 years ago and the end of medieval times around AD 1600. Such sites range in size from small cairns of stones resulting from the clearance of fields for cultivation through to massive castles, monasteries, and historic towns. They vary in their visibility from low banks forming the boundaries of long-abandoned prehistoric fields to elaborate stone structures like HADRIAN'S WALL running coast to coast across the full width of northern England, or the wonderfully ornate churches built by the wool-traders of the Cotswolds in the Middle Ages. Some sites, like STONEHENGE (Wiltshire), are unique; others, like the round barrows of Bronze Age times or the Christian monasteries of medieval times, were constructed in considerable numbers. All monuments, large or small, modest or imposing, unique or commonplace, tell us something of the story of England's past.

The aim of this Guide is to describe for the visitor a selection of the best-known, most important, and easily accessible sites which illustrate the fortifications, homes, farms, work places, burial grounds, ceremonial centres, and sacred precincts of our distant ancestors. This is done in the main part of the Guide. Sandwiching that rich filling are two layers intended to help visitors before, during, and after their visits. This introductory section provides a background and context to the monuments that will be described. Attention is given to how sites are found and dated, and to their place within the long-term history of occupation in what is now England. A reference section at the back of the Guide provides definitions, further reading, information about relevant museum collections, and indexes.

Most visible archaeological monuments in England are found in the countryside. This is not because the areas which are now towns were unsuitable places for earlier communities to live in, but simply a result of recent occupation which has buried ancient sites deep beneath the pavements and buildings or destroyed them when foundations were dug. Many modern towns have historic cores and a selection is considered in this Guide.

Time, Calendars, and Dating the Past

Time is a strangely abstract dimension that is not fully understood. Our present calendar in England, shared by many countries in the Western Christian world and known as the Gregorian calendar, was introduced during the reign of George II by act of Parliament in AD 1752. Prior to this, back to at least the Council of Chelsea in AD 816, the Julian calendar had been used. This was eleven days different from the Gregorian calendar and the beginning of the year was what is now 25 March. During Roman times dates were determined either as years after the foundation of Rome, or as regnal years based on the anniversary of the Emperor's accession. What kind of calendar was used in pre-Roman times in England is simply not known.

To aid standardization, archaeologists working in England use chronology that is essentially a backwards projection of our own Gregorian calendar, recognizing of course that it had no meaning to anyone actually living before AD 1752! Thus dates are conventionally expressed in calendar years BC or AD. Arriving at fixed dates for particular events, structures, objects, and materials is, however, far from easy, especially for periods lacking written historical records. Radiocarbon dating provides the most widely used and reliable way of determining the age of ancient sites back to about 60,000 BC, but by no means all early sites have been dated in this way.

Absolute dates, whether from historical records, radiocarbon dating, or other kinds of scientific studies, provide a good way of thinking about time in the past. But there are other relevant approaches too. One in everyday use is the cultural-historical periodization of the past using things such as prevailing technologies (e.g. Stone Age; Bronze Age), dominant political regimes, or ethnic presence (Roman, Saxon, Viking), or the reign of particular leaders or rulers or dynasties (Hadrianic, Alfredian, Tudor, Elizabethan). These periods are not mutually exclusive, nor do they have very sharp beginnings and endings when absolute dates are applied. Some cultural-historical periods relate to a particular region, with little or no relevance to surrounding areas. They do, however, provide a convenient shorthand with which to discuss the past, and the chronological summary in the reference section attempts to relate those terms used in this Guide to each other and to an absolute chronology.

Changing Environments

England has not always been like it is today. The climate, tree and plant cover, wildlife, and even the form of the land itself has gradually changed, and will continue to do so.

The land area of England has diminished over the last 12,000 years or so. At the end of the last Ice Age, about 10,000 BC, the British Isles were connected to the European mainland and formed part of the great north European plain. As the ice melted, sea levels rose and the land returned to its former shape. Areas of low-lying dry land such as what is now the North Sea and the English Channel slowly flooded so that Britain became an island about 7000 BC.

Over the last 9,000 years the land has gradually changed shape as rivers have been tamed and erosion has washed soil off the hills and into adjacent valleys. The climate has oscillated between colder/wetter periods and warmer/drier phases, although the long-term trend over the last 10,000 years has been towards warmer and drier conditions. A major climatic maximum occurred about 4000 BC, but a decline followed to a low point about 700 BC when extensive peat bogs developed on high ground such as Dartmoor and the Pennines. Things improved before the Roman Conquest in the C1 AD before deteriorating again during the first few centuries AD. Amelioration followed with another optimum in the C13 AD, followed by a gradual deterioration to our own times.

Closely linked to climate is the range of trees and plants that grow, and the natural wildlife. In general the range of naturally occurring plant and animal species has decreased as the variety of domesticated and introduced species has increased. Particularly notable is the loss of large wild animals from the countryside: since prehistoric times brown bear, wild horse, boar, aurochs, and wolf have been amongst the most notable losses.

What is England?

England as a politically and geographically definable country is a recent construction. The origins of England can be traced back to the C8 AD, but there is no terminology to describe earlier arrangements let alone the many and diverse articulations of nationhood that history records in these islands over the last 1,500 years or so.

In this Guide we use the term 'England' to refer to the land area occupied by present-day England, back-projecting its borders into earlier times. For administrative purposes, England is divided into counties, unitary authorities, and, below this, parishes. The county, authority, and parish names used here are those obtaining in 2000, although again it should be emphasized that these are not static and that other names may be found in earlier and later maps and sources.

Monuments and Wider Worlds

This Guide inevitably highlights particular sites or places for the visitor to look at. These are important, but focusing on them leads one to forget their wider setting. As today, people in the past experienced their world as a totality. Certainly there are set places where they lived, worked, kept their animals, carried out ceremonies, communed with their gods, and buried their dead, but they moved about within and between these places in their wider environment. There may not be much archaeo-logical trace of this activity, but almost every patch of ground had some meaning and significance to someone. Moreover, the idea of distinguish-ing what today we call 'natural' from what is not natural is a wholly modern way of looking at the world. In ancient times an old tree, special rock formation, spring, or cave may have been revered and treated in a special way every bit as much as the structures communities built for themselves. Indeed places sometimes take on a special meaning because of what happened there long before a stone was raised or a structure built to celebrate the place. In looking at ancient sites, it is therefore important to think not just about the monument itself but its situation, orientation, shape, form, and place in relation to the wider world—the hills, valleys, mountains, rivers, springs, and woods around about.

Prehistory

Prehistory spans an almost inconceivably long time, perhaps as much as half a million years. Traditionally, it is subdivided into five main cultural-historical periods: Palaeolithic (before 10,000 BC), Mesolithic (10,000 BC–4500 BC), Neolithic (4500 BC–2000 BC), Bronze Age (2000 BC–800 BC), and Iron Age (800 BC–AD 50). Each broad period is further subdivided into smaller units. These provide a useful shorthand when referring to particular cultural or archaeological phases, much as we might speak of Victorian times or the Tudor period. As already indi-cated, however, the increasing application of scientific dating methods, especially radiocarbon dating, means that it is now possible to speak of actual millennia and centuries BC for traditions and events in the distant past.

In amongst the Ice (500,000–12,000 BC)

When people first visited or settled Britain is not precisely known. Best estimates currently suggest it was around half a million years ago, at a time when much of the northern hemisphere was gradually colonized by a hominid species known in scientific terms as *Homo erectus*. These people are best represented by their distinctive pear-shaped flint or stone handaxes, so-called Acheulian handaxes, of which several thousand have been found in Britain to date.

Working out how these early people lived, and how they looked after themselves, is made difficult because between about one million years ago and approximately 12,000 years ago the whole of northern Europe underwent a series of glaciations: the Pleistocene Ice Age. Of the four main European glacial phases (Günz, Mindel, Riss, Würm), the last three can be recognized in Britain (Anglian, Wolstonian, Devensian). Preceding and separating the cold glacial periods were three main interglacials (Cromerian, Hoxnian, and Ipswichian) when the climate was rather warmer. It is now recognized, however, that such a scheme is a gross oversimplification; work on the polar ice caps and deep-sea cores from the floor of the Atlantic Ocean suggests as many as eight major cold phases and intervening warm phases.

During cold periods ice-sheets and glaciers would have covered much of northern Britain, and on occasions pushed as far south as what is now the English Channel. One effect of extensive glacial action was to erase the remains of earlier occupation and settlement, effectively wiping the slate clean and jumbling up more robust remains such as tools and weapons by washing them into the gravels and moraines that accumulated in, under, on, and in front of active glaciers.

In warm periods, with the ice caps far to the north, as they are today, climatic conditions allowed exotic animals to roam freely across what at some times would have been a massive north European plain extending from the Ural mountains of Russia in the east to Brittany and Cornwall in the west, and from the Alps and Carpathians in the south to the Pennines and Kjolen mountains in the north. At times these plains were grass savannah, but for some periods they were more or less wooded. Communities adept at using these different environments pursued herds of wild horse, deer, bison, wild cattle, and elephant.

We shall never find the remains of the first visitors to Britain, but the oldest securely dated site so far known is BOXGROVE near Chichester (West Sussex). Here, by a fluke of preservation, it has been possible to excavate a land surface occupied about 500,000 years ago during the latest stages of the Cromerian Interglacial. A fragment of human leg bone (tibia) from the site represents the remains of the earliest European yet known.

Arrivals and Departures

There is some debate as to whether early hominids were scavengers living off the remains of animals brought down and killed by other beasts, or whether these groups were hunters in their own right. In fact, both means of survival probably played a part, supplemented by fishing and collecting edible plants, fruits, and tubers. So far as can be seen, communities were mobile, some perhaps with a long-distance cycle of migration taking them through a series of different environments during the course of a year or more. Other groups were more specialized: reindeer hunters following the herds which provided their means of survival, or fishing communities responsive to the seasonal abundance of different species on the coast or in rivers and inland lakes.

Acheulian tool-making traditions associated with *Homo erectus* persisted a long time. Remains are known from numerous sites, including Fordwich (Kent), dated to before the Wolstonian (200,000–170,000 years ago), and KENT'S CAVERN (Devon), dated to the early Hoxnian (*c.*275,000 years ago). In addition to the Boxgrove remains, human bones have also been found at Swanscombe (Kent), dating to about 325,000 BC.

The Neanderthals

By about 225,000 BC, the human population and the kinds of tools they used had changed. *Homo erectus* was succeeded by another hominid species, *Homo neanderthalensis* (Neanderthal Man), and the characteristic equipment of these communities belongs to what is known as the Mousterian tradition. Like their predecessors these people sometimes lived in caves, but, more commonly, they used temporary encampments beside rivers or lakes, as at Baker's Hole, Northfleet (Kent).

Neanderthal skeletal remains are known from two sites in the British Isles: Pontnewydd Cave in Clwyd, Wales, and La Cotte de Saint-Brelade on Jersey in the Channel Islands.

Moderns

Modern humans, *Homo sapiens*, are known in northern Europe from about 40,000 BC and are associated with new styles of flint and stone tools, known as the Aurignacian. How these Moderns related, in evolutionary or genetic terms, to earlier populations is currently a matter of great debate. Two theories have been suggested: the first, known as the 'out of Africa' scenario, suggests that Moderns developed in the equatorial zone and spread into other parts of the world, replacing existing populations. The alternative scheme is the 'multi-regional' scenario, which sees one major dispersal from Africa of hominid populations (i.e. *Homo erectus*) followed by broadly parallel evolution in different parts of the world to produce the modern populations.

The linkage between populations and their ways of life is important when reviewing these early periods, because one of the mechanisms that accounts for changes in the nature and distribution of populations is their biological suitability and physical ability to live successfully in different kinds of situation. Thus the spread into northern Europe of communities who appear to have been genetically identical with ourselves before the last main glacial phase is important, not least because in many ways we are today living in an interglacial period not so different from what would have prevailed 30,000 years ago. What separates that time from today, however, was the most recent glacial phase: the Devensian glaciations.

The Last Ice Age

Like earlier glacial periods, the Devensian comprised a series of glacial advances and retreats. At their most extensive, ice-sheets from Scandinavia extended as far south as a notional line between Milford Haven and Flamborough Head. Many of the people formerly living in the far north-west corner of Europe gradually moved south, occupying parts of central and southern France and Spain. But some remained, joined by hunters from further north and east for whom life in a cold environment was already second nature. Nothing remains of their activity on the ice-flows, but just off the ice-covered lands there is archaeological evidence for the existence of these groups; for example, a burial known as the Red Lady of Paviland (actually a man) was found covered in red ochre in a cave in South Wales. Bones from this burial have been radiocarbon dated to about 16,500 BC.

Recolonizing Britain (12,000–7,000 BC)

The last Devensian ice-sheets had left Britain by about 12,000 BC, apart from some relatively small remaining glaciers in central Scotland, which persisted perhaps as late as 10,000 BC. Extensive ice-sheets still existed away to the north, however, locking up vast amounts of water, which thawed only gradually. Because of this, the sea level in northern Europe was low, and the British Isles were once again just a peninsula of the north-western European land mass. The English Channel and the North Sea were dry land, crossed by a few rivers and interrupted at intervals by large lakes formed in hollows scooped out by earlier ice-flows. As the climate warmed, many species of plants and animals gradually recolonized the land according to a biological and vegetational succession that begins with barren tundra and gradually develops into woodland dominated by pine and birch. Human groups prospered too, and their return to the British Isles marked the beginning of a continuous occupation down to the present day.

Post-Glacial Populations

The extensive new hunting grounds created by the retreat of the ice-sheets seem to have been heavily exploited. In Britain, these groups have been defined as belonging to the Creswellian tradition after the sites at CRESWELL CRAGS (Derbyshire), where important collections of material have been recovered from occupied caves. Among the distinctive tools are large leaf-shaped flint points and barbed harpoons made of bone. Small worked flint blades known as microliths were perhaps the barbs of spears and harpoons with wooden shafts. Like their forebears, Creswellian groups continued to use caves as shelters where they were available (Figure 2).

By about 10,000 BC the transformation from open tundra to closed

▲ **Fig. 2.** The Victoria Cave, Settle, North Yorkshire (Photograph: Timothy Darvill)

pine and birch woodland was complete. The climate became warmer, and deep rich soils developed. New tools and weapons were invented to hunt the animals of the forests such as red deer, roe deer, wild boar, and cattle. Creswellian traditions were succeeded by the so-called *Feder-messergruppen* assemblages after about 10,000 BC, changes which traditionally mark the end of the Late Upper Palaeolithic (LUP) in Britain.

The period from 9000 BC through to about 7000 BC saw the continuation of hunter-gatherer traditions similar those already established. With the continued existence of a land bridge between Britain and the Continental mainland, it is hardly surprising that there are marked similarities between sites over large areas. The *Federmessergruppen*, characterized by shouldered flint points, gives way to the Maglemosian tradition with abundant microliths in distinctive convex-backed and triangular forms.

Living in the Woods (7,000–4500 BC)

Between about 8000 BC and 6000 BC rising sea levels severed the land bridge between Britain and the Continent. From then on, Britain developed its own traditions of hunter-gatherer lifestyles: the later Mesolithic. This was also a time when the native woodland underwent further changes, now covering most of the country in a relatively dense oak, elm, and birch forest: what is sometimes referred to as the 'wildwood'.

Mobile Bands Settling Down

The picture of life about 5000 BC is one of a fairly numerous but widely scattered population, dependent mostly on red deer, wild cattle, wild boar, plants, and, on the coast, marine resources. Cycles of seasonal movement between a base camp and temporary hunting camps are likely, although the distances covered by any one group became less as time went on. Few groups would have lived in the heart of the forests; most seem to have settled around the edges, continuing earlier practices of living beside rivers, lakes, or coasts, all of which represent natural margins. Some groups seem to have created small-scale clearances in the forest by burning it. This had three effects: creating artificial margins as suitable places for settlement, enhancing the attraction of the area for herds of wild animals, who preferred the succulent new shoots of regrowth to the tough fodder of old forest, and making hunting easier by concentrating the quarry and allowing them to be seen in open ground.

In other ways, life became more complicated. With less mobility, opportunities to collect suitable raw material for making tools and weapons decreased. As a result, small-scale trading networks developed to move both finished items and raw materials to areas devoid of flint or good stone. Especially impressive was the manufacture of tranchet axes around the chalkland of Wessex, and their movement to almost all areas of southern Britain. Portland Chert from the limited outcrops of Portland Bill was also traded, pieces finding their way to most parts of south-western Britain, even as far as Land's End.

Making the Land Pay (4500–3000 BC)

One of the biggest social changes in history took place in Britain between 4500 and 3000 BC. During that time, people's attitudes to the world in which they lived seem to have changed markedly, and with it many of their ways of life and the things they used (i.e. their material culture). It was not a rapid change, but rather a gradual process of reorientation, which happened more quickly in some areas than others. Collectively, the changes represented mark the beginning of Neolithic times.

Archaeologically, the most visible indication of these changes is evidence for the biological manipulation of plants and animals to control their production and reproduction and thereby provide a more predictable food supply: farming. The idea of doing this undoubtedly originated in the Near East and spread northwards across Europe. Whether it was adopted in Britain as a result of colonization by farming communities or by native hunter-gatherer groups emulating their Continental neighbours is difficult to say, although the most likely explanation involves a combination of both. What is clear is that for a time hunter-gatherers existed alongside early farmers.

Changes in the production of food reveal more deep-seated shifts in the way people saw their world. Increasing control was the key. For the first time, people began to dominate nature, domesticating the wild, and for the first time creating a set of oppositions between what was within the domain of the social and what was not.

The Changing Countryside

Early farming communities had a considerable impact on the countryside, most notably by clearing woodland, introducing cereals (wheat and barley), and establishing grassland to pasture cattle, pigs, and, to a lesser extent, sheep.

Not all areas were settled by early farming groups. Well-drained, easily cultivated land attracted most interest, especially major river valleys and downland in central southern Britain. The uplands were only used for hunting and as sources of stone for the manufacture of tools and weapons.

But there were other changes too. Settlements became more permanent and more substantial than before. Farmsteads comprising perhaps one or two rectangular wooden houses were dotted about the countryside. Around each farmstead would have been a few small fields or gardens carved out of the wildwood.

Throughout southern and eastern Britain there were a series of large ditched enclosures known as causewayed camps† (Figure 3). A few, such as CRICKLEY HILL (Gloucestershire), and CARN BREA (Cornwall), seem to have been defended settlements or small villages. Others, like WINDMILL HILL (Wiltshire), were seasonal camps or meeting places where communities from the neighbourhood could gather together for ceremonies, to exchange raw materials and things they had made, and to meet potential husbands and wives. All of these enclosures combined domestic activities with ceremony and ritual; in the minds of these early farmers everyday life and the supernatural were inextricably linked in a way that we find hard to comprehend in today's scientific age.

Burying the Dead

Burial monuments were built by early farming groups, the first time that formal structures had been made for this purpose. Indeed, Neolithic tombs represent the earliest style of architecture known in Europe.

At first burial monuments were small structures, usually of stone, although where no stone was available timber and earth was used. Different groups built in different styles. In the south-west, portal dolmens† are common (Figure 4): four or five upright stone slabs supporting a massive capstone as at TRETHEVY (Cornwall). Further east, simple passage graves were favoured: a round mound in the centre of which was a stone chamber approached from the outside of the mound by a short passage. Elsewhere, oval or round barrows† were built. In most areas, the

▲ **Fig. 3.** Windmill Hill, Wiltshire (Photograph: CUCAP AO-38)

burials made in these simple tombs were inhumations, although even at this early time skeletons were rarely left alone. Inside an oval barrow at WAYLAND'S SMITHY (Oxfordshire), for example, the burial area comprised a stone pavement covered by a timber structure supported at either end by large posts. The fragmentary remains of fourteen individuals were found scattered over the pavement, including one child aged about 10.

The Age of the Long Barrows

After about 3500 BC the traditions of building small simple tombs were replaced by a tendency to build very much larger monuments: long barrows†. These massive structures are up to 100 m. long and must have taken a long time to construct with only bone tools, baskets, and human muscle-power. One of the largest long barrows is at WEST KENNET (Wiltshire). This example has stone-built chambers, but where stone was not available timber was used instead.

▲ **Fig. 4.** The Whispering Knights Portal Dolmen, Rollright, Oxfordshire (Photograph: Timothy Darvill)

Several regionally distinct traditions of long barrow construction can be distinguished in the British Isles: for example the Cotswold–Severn tombs of the Cotswolds and lands flanking the Severn valley; earthen long barrows in Wessex and Yorkshire; and the Clyde–Carlingford type in south-western Scotland and Northern Ireland. These groupings, and others beside, represent in a rather crude way the major population groupings at the time.

In all cases, however, the burial rites which took place at long barrows were complicated and drawn out. They involved not just funerals but also ceremonies at which bones from partly decomposed corpses were moved about within the different sections of the chamber and entrance passage.

Marking the Land

Long barrows were more than just burial monuments; their great size and the fact that such small parts of them were used for burials suggest they had other uses too. One of these was probably as a territorial marker for the community which built and used it. Set away from settlements, often on a prominent hill, these markers are evidence for the links between people and their land—the domesticated as opposed to the wild, the living as opposed to the dead.

Other kinds of sacred place were sometimes defined by rectangular ditched enclosures known as long mortuary enclosures. In some areas it is possible that corpses were exposed in these enclosures before the bones were collected up to be deposited in long barrows.

Occasionally, highly visible rocks seem to have been singled out for special attention, as with some of the natural tors on Bodmin Moor. Elsewhere, large blocks of stone were set upright as standing stones, beginning a tradition that carried on for several thousand years. Simple designs, cup-marks†, and rings were chipped into some natural rock outcrops and boulders. Rivers and wet places began to attract attention too, and numerous stone axes of Neolithic date have been found in rivers as if deliberately thrown there.

New Inventions

Among the other changes associated with the development of farming was the introduction of pottery, and the manufacture of a wide range of new tools and weapons. Some of these are very fine and show a high level of craftsmanship, as for example with the polished stone and flint axes used for felling trees and carpentry.

Obtaining good stone for making tools posed something of a problem. Surface outcrops were used wherever they were suitable, but the best raw materials lay underground. Mines for flint were established all across the chalklands of southern Britain, for example at CISSBURY (West Sussex), and GRIME'S GRAVES (Norfolk). These were massive undertakings, an individual shaft perhaps needing twelve people for two months to dig, and yielding maybe 7–8 tonnes of flint. At Cissbury there are upwards of 100 shafts known. In the north and west quarries were opened up where stone suitable for tool-making was found.

Trade and Communications

Many parts of the British Isles lacked good sources of flint and stone, and accordingly there developed an exchange network, which allowed the movement of raw material and finished items between regions. In some cases this may have involved people travelling to established sources to get the stone they needed. Mostly, however, material was passed from group to group at seasonal gatherings and meetings, travelling great distances in a number of small steps. In this way, flint, stone, pottery, and probably other materials too were moved about between communities.

Not everything that was traded was for everyday use. Exotica were moved about too, including very fine non-utilitarian polished stone axes. The finest of all were jadeite axes made in northern Italy or Switzerland, which, through being passed from group to group, found their way into all parts of Britain.

The countryside must have been criss-crossed by a network of paths and tracks. These would mostly have been little more than the kind of footpaths we are familiar with today. In wet areas, however, something more was needed and in the Somerset Levels timber trackways were built so that people could cross the wetland in safety.

Conflict and Contested Land Rights

Early farming communities seem to have been moderately successful, and over a period of about 1,000 years expanded out from a small number of initial areas of settlement to cover most of southern Britain, some areas quite intensively. It cannot be assumed, however, that this was necessarily a peaceful time. Indeed there is evidence to the contrary. At some causewayed enclosures†, notably CRICKLEY HILL (Gloucestershire), and HAMBLEDON HILL (Dorset), there is evidence for large-scale attacks that led to the destruction of the settlements.

The Age of Stonehenge (3000–1700 BC)

By 3000 BC many parts of Britain which had previously been densely occupied went into a period of decline. Long barrows were no longer built and those still in use were deliberately blocked up. Causewayed camps were abandoned. Woodland grew back on land which had been cleared. Why this happened is not exactly known, but warfare and inter-necine conflict caused by a rising population may be at least partly to blame. Whatever the reason, the old order was replaced. New types of heavily decorated and rather crude pottery, known as Peterborough Ware, appeared. Settlement now focused on land that had previously been neglected, especially the major river valleys and regions with less fertile soils. The most visible signs of change, however, can be seen in the construction and use of ceremonial monuments.

Around the turn of the fourth millennium BC there seems to have been a special concern for extremely long narrow monuments. Long low mounds of soil and earth were built over the decayed boundaries of the causewayed enclosures on Crickley Hill (Gloucestershire), and MAIDEN CASTLE (Dorset). Elsewhere in Dorset massive so-called 'bank barrows' were built.

Examples of a new type of monument, the cursus†, were built in many areas. Perhaps representing a grossly exaggerated form of long mortuary enclosure, cursus monuments were long narrow enclosures bounded by a bank and outer ditch. They are frequently set across the grain of the countryside along a spring-line or somehow associated with a river. The example at Springfield near Chelmsford (Essex) is 700 × 40 m. and has been extensively excavated. Near the eastern terminal there were the remains of a timber structure and pits and scoops containing the remains of fires and burnt bone. The purpose of cursus monuments is unclear, but it is assumed they were used for parades or some kind of ceremony which involved processions. Springfield is by no means the largest: the Dorset Cursus on Cranborne Chase has a maximum length of 10 km.

Here Comes the Sun

The passion for linear monuments around 3000 BC may, however, represent the final throes of a dying tradition. Shortly afterwards, in all parts of Britain, there emerged a very clear interest in a range of circular monuments. Some of these represent developments of earlier traditions, as for example the round barrows and passage graves whose ancestry lies in the early Neolithic. Others are wholly new, for example henges†, enclosed cremation cemeteries, and stone circles†.

Uniting many of these structures was an increasing interest in the movements of the sun, especially the midsummer and midwinter rising and setting positions. Many late Neolithic and early Bronze Age monuments embody alignments and axes of symmetry which mark these events and allow them to be systematically observed from within the structure. This is not to say, however, that the monuments were built as observatories; the inclusion of these alignments is probably to do with determining the appropriate timing for particular ceremonies or events.

A new type of pottery is also widely associated with late Neolithic monuments: Grooved Ware. This ware, distinctive because of its decoration, which imitates the weave of a basket, became very widespread so that by 2800 BC it was being used in all parts of the country.

Round Barrows and Single Grave Burial

Round barrows are the most numerous and widely distributed class of prehistoric burial monument. They began to be built during early Neolithic times, and continue well into the Bronze Age. Determining their age from external appearances is almost impossible, but, as a general rule, early examples tend to be small, bowl-shaped in profile, and cover graves containing multiple burials. Later Neolithic round barrows are also bowl-shaped in profile, but tend to be larger and built in several phases, each being set over a single burial. Most cover inhumations, although in some parts of the country cremation was preferred. Grave goods are sometimes included with the deceased, perhaps a pot or some tools, and they were probably buried fully clothed to judge from the presence of items such as belt fittings, buttons, and flint knives.

Passage Graves and the Art of the Unnatural

A few regions of the British Isles developed the use of highly distinctive tombs in the later Neolithic. In West Penwith and on the Isles of Scilly a series of small, stone-built, tombs known as entrance graves are known. Circular in plan, these monuments are rarely over 4 m. across. The chamber is rectangular in plan, radially set so that it is accessible from the edge of the mound. Excavations at Bosilliack (Cornwall) revealed a primary burial comprising a partial cremation and a small pot.

In Anglesey and in Orkney there are particularly impressive groups of burial monuments known as Developed Passage Graves. Another group probably existed around the river Mersey but the only visible remains are the Calderstones now in Liverpool Museum. All the Developed Passage Graves are large, over 10 m. in diameter, and have a central stone-built chamber approached from the outside of the mound by way of a long passage. Some of the stones used in the construction of Developed Passage Graves are typically decorated with spirals, lozenges, and zigzag lines. This is the same kind of decoration as is also found on Grooved Ware pottery, and links monuments in Britain with similar structures in Ireland. Recent studies of the form of this 'megalithic art' suggest that it may derive from entopic images in the form of bright shapes and lines visualized in the mind while in a trance or subconscious state. It is possible that hallucinogens, for example fly agaric, were used to bring on this state of mind.

Henges, Circles, Rows, and Avenues

Among the new kinds of late Neolithic circular monuments the most distinctive structures are henges (Figure 5). These comprise a substantial ditch, outside which is a bank. Typically they have one or two entrances, occasionally as many as four as at the largest known example, AVEBURY

▼ **Fig. 5.** Avebury, Wiltshire (Photograph: Timothy Darvill)

(Wiltshire). Inside some henges archaeological excavations reveal post-holes† representing the remains of what must have been timber circles or structures. Elsewhere, again as at Avebury, the interior contains one or more stone circles. Grooved Ware pottery is associated with most henges. They are interpreted as ceremonial enclosures, perhaps associated with periodic meetings and festivals.

Stone circles are also found without accompanying henges; indeed the majority of known examples are free-standing. The earliest stone circles were generally small rings with closely set stones and clearly defined entrances, for example CASTLERIGG (Cumbria). A little later came large open circles with widely spaced stones such as the HURLERS (Cornwall) where there are four such circles in a line. When excavated, many stone circles are found to be replacements of timber circles. Like henges, the stone circles are interpreted as ceremonial meeting places; and since henges and circles sometimes exist together it is likely that they were used in much the same way.

Processions and alignments were important in henges and stone circles. Avebury, for example, is approached by a pair of avenues defined by parallel lines of standing stones. Other circles also have avenues defining an approach to them, while both circles and henges sometimes have standing stones† outside them perhaps to define significant axes or alignments (Figure 6).

Other Enclosures

Henges and stone circles are not the only late Neolithic enclosures known. Of similar size are the enclosed cremation cemeteries, which comprise circular areas bounded by a bank and ditch within which numerous cremations were deposited. One of the best examples is the early phase of STONEHENGE (Wiltshire), which, unusually, incorporated elements of both the henge and enclosed cremation cemetery traditions.

Larger enclosures are also known. In Wessex there are four massive structures, so-called henge-enclosures, constructed in the style of henges (with an external bank around a large ditch) but which are of irregular shape and are known to contain large timber buildings. All four sites lie beside rivers and may represent small enclosed villages with both domestic and ceremonial buildings within them.

International Links and the Development of Metalworking

Closely connected with the changes in ritual and ceremonial monuments at the end of the Neolithic was an increase in contact between people in Britain and those in Ireland and mainland Europe. Goods and ideas were regularly exchanged, and as part of this process the technological know-how to produce metal objects came to Britain from the Continent.

Gold and copper were the first metals to be worked, followed shortly

▲ **Fig. 6.** The Rudston Monolith, Humberside (Photograph: Timothy Darvill)

afterwards by bronze (an alloy of copper, tin, and lead). The introduction of metalworking about 2500 BC traditionally marks the start of the Bronze Age, but the new technology did little for the majority of the population as most of the early products were luxury items such as daggers, trinkets, and ornaments. Everyday tools and weapons were still manufactured in flint and stone, although there is an interesting development represented by the copying of some early metal items in stone.

Another product of the increasing international contacts was the arrival of Beaker pottery. This pottery is distinctive because of its high quality, fine decoration, and beautifully curved shapes. The appearance of Beakers was once explained as an invasion of Britain by people from the Continent (the Beaker Folk), but beakers can now be seen to have been introduced as part of more widespread trading and exchange systems. At first Beaker pottery circulated alongside Grooved Ware, but gradually it seems to have taken over from Grooved Ware as the main ceremonial vessel, and later as the inspiration for domestic wares too. It is possible that the spread of beakers was linked to changing ceremonial practices; perhaps, as the name suggests, beakers were drinking cups for a particular new kind of beverage such as beer or mead.

The Rise of the Elites and the Place of Warriors

Many features of late Neolithic society suggest that it was hierarchically organized and that various kinds of specialist were present. If some of the linear monuments are correctly associated with processions then it suggests that someone was at the head of the line, while the use of the circle suggests that someone was at the centre while all others around the outside were equal. More convincing, however, is the fact that burials of the period were often single inhumations and that some people seem to be buried with a lot of grave goods while others have nothing at all.

Some of the most distinctive sets of grave goods are items related to warfare, especially archery equipment and daggers that might signify a warrior class. Equipment for craft activities is present in some graves suggesting another group of high-status individuals, while it is also possible that shamen or magicians are represented by such items as pieces of deer antler and nodules of iron pyrites.

The wealth and prestige of the late Neolithic elites was probably based on their position within long-distance trading networks and their ability to acquire exotic goods in return for raw materials. In this, increasing interest in the reserves of copper, tin, and gold in the north and west of Britain was especially important, and these areas, together with places along natural routes of communications to the north and west, seem to have the greatest abundance of wealth.

The elites displayed their power not only through the objects they wore and used, but in the monuments and structures they coerced their communities to build. Making cursus monuments, henges, and stone circles required an immense amount of labour and the coordination of effort. It can be argued that only a ranked society could achieve this. Perhaps the greatest achievement of all from this period was the construction of the massive conical mound of SILBURY HILL near Avebury (Wiltshire), estimated to have required 1.5 million hours of work to complete. Exactly why it was built, however, remains unknown.

By implication, late Neolithic elites must have operated within relatively restricted geographical areas. This can be glimpsed archaeologically by the fairly regular spacing at intervals of about 40 km. of major ceremonial centres which variously combine henges, stone circles, enclosures of various sorts, cursus monuments, and groups of round barrows. It is easy to imagine that each of these ceremonial centres (e.g. DORCHESTER (Dorset); KNOWLTON (Dorset); Stonehenge (Wiltshire); Avebury (Wiltshire); Dorchester (Oxfordshire), etc.) was the focal point in the life of a particular community, the place where they periodically met together, buried their dead, and carried out seasonal ceremonies and celebrations.

People Everywhere and a Climatic Optimum (1700–1000 BC)

The pattern of society established in the later Neolithic continued through into the Bronze Age, if anything becoming more regionalized in its character and more extensive in its use of the countryside. Indeed, the period from 1700 BC down to about 1000 BC marks a zenith in the distribution of settlement, unsurpassed even down to modern times. Upland areas such as Dartmoor, the North York Moors, the Pennines, and the Cheviots were intensively farmed up to altitudes of over 250 m. above sea level, while the already occupied lowlands continued in use as well. The implication of these new land-takes is that the population was rising.

One reason for this expansion outwards from traditionally occupied territories was a short-lived improvement in the climate, characterized by dryer and warmer conditions. It was this which allowed communities to make use of higher ground, including growing crops well above what would now be regarded as marginal land. Because these areas have not been available for intensive settlement since the Bronze Age, the fields and farms created in prehistoric times still survive in remarkably good condition.

Reorganizing the Countryside

The most impressive aspect of the early Bronze Age expansion of settlement is not so much the fact that many previously under-exploited areas were brought into use, but the fact that, for the first time, much of the countryside was organized in a regular way (Figure 7).

Evidence from pollen cores in peat bogs and old lakes suggests that a great deal of woodland was cleared, in many areas creating a countryside as open as that of today. In these areas large regular field-systems, paddocks, and grazing areas were laid out. One of the best preserved on Dartmoor is at HORRIDGE COMMON, but this is only one of many known around the country.

Village-size settlements of anything up to fifty dwellings are known in upland areas, for example GRIMSPOUND and RIDER'S RINGS on Dartmoor, while smaller groupings representing the settlements of one or two extended families are more common in eastern and southern areas, as for example at Itford Hill (West Sussex). Across southern Britain there were also a few large ditched enclosures of middle Bronze Age date, possibly tribal meeting places or trading centres, as for example at NORTON FITZWARREN near Taunton (Somerset).

Death and Ceremony

Burial rites changed during the course of the Bronze Age, from the inhumation of complete corpses to a preference for cremations. Round barrows were used for most burials, and extensive barrow cemeteries developed. The traditional bowl barrow continued to be built, but a

▲ **Fig. 7.** Aerial view of the Bronze Age field-system at Smacam Down, Dorset
(Photograph: CUCAP AY-16)

whole series of so-called fancy barrow types were added to the reper-
toire: bell barrows, disc barrows, saucer barrows, and the rather curious
pond barrows, which have a hollowed-out form, sometimes with a central shaft. In upland areas, cairns rather than barrows are common, some
perpetuating the shapes of the fancy barrows (for example the platform
cairns of Cornwall are the same as the disc barrows of Wessex), while
others are rather different as with various styles of ring-cairn. In plan,
ring-cairns look like a doughnut, with an outer bank and central flat
area.

Beakers were replaced by new styles of pottery both in the domestic
context and for deposition in graves. In the north and west, pots known
as 'food vessels' became common, while all over the country 'collared
urns' became the main style. When urns were used to contain cremated
remains they usually had a cover tied over the top and were then
inverted when placed in the burial pit. Increasingly, individual barrows
were used several times over, the mound being extended each time to
accommodate the new burials.

Some of the ceremonial and ritual monuments of the later Neolithic
continue through into the second millennium BC, others such as henges
and cursus monuments were abandoned. Perhaps the most widely distributed ceremonial monument was the stone circle, which at this time
developed numerous local variations of the circle idea: generally small
monuments with relatively few closely set stones. Some of these late

circles include a recumbent stone. The overall patterns of change can be seen very clearly at Stonehenge (Wiltshire), where the earlier enclosure was abandoned and first a simple open circle and later more complicated circles and horseshoe-shaped settings came and went.

Stone rows† also appear during the early Bronze Age, often incorporating a stone circle or cairn. These rows may be short, as at the DEVIL'S ARROWS near Boroughbridge (North Yorkshire), with just four stones, or very long as at MERRIVALE (Devon), with over forty stones.

Common to many Bronze Age ceremonial monuments is the continuation of a concern for orientation and alignment. The focus of attention varied from one part of the country to another, but the rising and setting of the sun and moon seem to have interested many communities. Water was also of interest, and a good proportion of fine metal objects, especially weapons, continued to be deposited in wet places such as rivers and bogs.

Metalworking and Crafts

Bronze remained the principal metal worked during the second millennium BC, although gold was used for ornaments. The quality of craftsmanship displayed in bronze and gold objects was extraordinary. The grave goods from the Bush Barrow near Stonehenge (Wiltshire) illustrate very well the range and quality of what could be achieved: two flat bronze daggers, a bronze axe, a gold breastplate, gold belt hook, gold lozenge, and many small gold rivets and studs perhaps from the ornamentation of a wooden handle.

Most of the main metalworking techniques were well developed, including casting (in two piece and *cire perdue* (lost wax) moulds), alloying, annealing, sheet metalwork, riveting, wire-making, graving, and soldering. The chemistry of the process changed a little during the Bronze Age with the introduction of arsenic to the alloy to improve casting.

Britain was a major producer of metal ores. Copper mines on the Great Orme in North Wales are among the largest in Europe, and early mining is also known in mid-Wales and on ALDERLEY EDGE (Cheshire). Copper and tin-mining was undoubtedly practised in Cornwall too, but no certain traces have yet come to light.

The range of tools and weapons made in metal increased markedly during the second millennium BC to include daggers, dirks, rapiers, swords, flat axes, palstaves, socketed axes, chisels, razors, and a vast range of ornaments and trinkets. Smiths seem to have been working at two different levels: some operated locally, making mainly tools and ornaments in locally distinctive styles; others operated regionally making mainly weapons and very complicated ornaments, which often reflected changing Continental fashions.

Metalworking was only one of many crafts practised at this time.

Most metal objects were in fact parts of artefacts involving other materials too, for example wood and bone for handles and hilts. Leather was widely used, and woven textiles began to be made from the mid-second millennium BC onwards. Stone continued to be worked, the traditional Neolithic axes being replaced by finely polished tools with perforations for hafting, for example so-called battle-axes, axe-hammers, and mace-heads. Some of these may have been symbols of power and authority as much as functional weapons or tools. Stone was also used for making metalworkers' tools such as touch-stones, hammers, and cushions. Potting was practised by almost every community.

Trade and the Importance of the European Community

Throughout the second millennium BC links with mainland Europe and Ireland remained strong. Travel between southern Britain and France is evidenced by two wrecks just offshore, one near Dover (Kent) and the other near Torbay (Devon). In both cases the boats in question were taking metalwork across the channel. Indeed it was probably because of Britain's involvement in the Europe-wide trade in metal ores that strong links were maintained.

Metalwork provides the strongest evidence of trade and cross-channel links. New styles of ornaments such as central European spiral-head pins were soon circulating or copied in Britain, while innovations in weapon technology, again derived from developments in central Europe, were also soon being applied here. Sometimes actual objects moved as with the Bohemian palstave found in the field-system at Horridge Common on Dartmoor. Pottery was not immune from imitation either. Wessex bi-conical urns match the Hilversum urns from the southern Netherlands. Even barrows, especially those with internal post-settings, show similarities of style between the Netherlands and southern Britain.

Climax and Catastrophe—Abandoning the Uplands

The climatic optimum which permitted the expansion of settlement into upland areas began to fade around 1000 BC. Wetter and cooler conditions gradually took over. This had three effects. Soil quality declined as nutrients were washed away and mineral 'pans' built up in the soil profiles. Crops could not be grown so successfully at high altitudes. Blanket bog began to form, gradually inundating fields and the open areas between them.

Many areas on the high ground and places with especially sensitive soils had to be abandoned. Because of changes to the soil profiles and the reduction of vegetation cover, the natural succession of scrub and woodland did not take hold after abandonment and these areas became moorland and heaths. This was especially marked in what are now Dartmoor, Exmoor, Bodmin Moor, and the Dorset Heaths. Paradoxically, these areas are today regarded as natural and unspoilt countryside: actually they are the products of human over-exploitation and an environmental catastrophe born of climatic change in the Bronze Age.

Brothers in Arms (1000–300 BC)

The first few centuries of the first millennium BC were turbulent times. As upland fields and settlements were abandoned the population seems to have retreated to lower ground: there may even have been displaced populations to contend with. Even in southern Britain arable cultivation declined, and there is some evidence for the widespread adoption of cattle-herding. Whatever the reasons, it appears that the existing population had to be supported on a smaller land area, a situation which inevitably brought about social and economic stress. In this case, there were two very visible signs of this pressure.

First was the development of defended settlements, usually on hilltops or promontories that afforded natural defence. Two kinds can be recognized, the majority of them being in areas adjacent to the most populated uplands: eastern Devon, Somerset, all along the Cotswold escarpment and Welsh Marches, and across the southern Pennines.

One type is the hilltop enclosure: large hillforts†, which probably included fields and paddocks for livestock at times of trouble. A particularly good example is Nottingham Hill (Gloucestershire).

A second type, and more widespread, is represented by small heavily defended settlements. CRICKLEY HILL (Gloucestershire) is a thoroughly excavated example, constructed about 700 BC with a massive timber-laced stone rampart enclosing an area of 3.8 ha. Like other hillforts of its type there is good evidence from excavations that the site was attacked and overrun on several occasions.

The second line of evidence for tension in the later Bronze Age is the increasing use of linear boundaries to partition the landscape into defined blocks, which are taken to represent the territories of individual communities. Some of these boundaries are very impressive, massive bank and ditches running for many kilometres across the countryside. Some cut across earlier field-systems, others neatly skirt existing fields as if containing them in the newly identified territory.

Technology and the First Arms Race

The high technological competence of the later second millennium BC continued into the first millennium, supplemented by new types of tools, weapons, and ornaments. As in earlier centuries, contacts with Continental Europe provided the inspiration for many of these.

Most notable are developments and changes in weapon technology which amount to an early arms race. Shields and body armour first appear. Swords became more common, in two main types: thrusting swords for use in hand-to-hand combat, and slashing swords for use by warriors on horseback. This is the first time that horses appear to have been used in warfare, and soon after, from around 700 BC, wheeled vehicles appear too. Initially they are very simple carts or wagons, and since there were no roads they must have been next to useless except for ceremonial parades on flat ground. Indeed, many of the finest weapons of the late Bronze Age and early Iron Age would have been of little use in battle and must be regarded as ceremonial. But battles did occur and human skeletons with bronze weapons still embedded in them have been found.

From about 700 BC iron begins to be worked. Iron has the advantage that it is widely available in areas of Britain where other metals are scarce (for example in the south-east) and only requires raw material from a single source. Early iron products were simply copies of bronze implements like sickles and razors, but it was not long before iron-smiths got the feel of the new material and developed edged tools which were probably technically superior to similar things in bronze.

Settlement outside the Hillfort Zone

Outside the main zones of early hillfort construction the pattern of settlement was diverse and closely tied to the kinds of occupation site that had developed during the middle Bronze Age. Many sites were enclosed, and some show signs that their occupants replaced simple fences with increasingly robust boundary works. This is especially marked in the north, where a tradition of palisaded enclosures containing perhaps two or three structures is widespread from Yorkshire and Humberside up to the Scottish borders.

Changing Burial and Ritual

Round barrows ceased to be built after about 1000 BC, and for the next few centuries burials were instead deposited in flat cemeteries or inserted into the top of existing barrows. Most were cremations, and large pots were often used to contain the ashes of the deceased. A number of regional traditions of burial urn can be seen, for example the Deverel-Rimbury styles of southern Britain, the Trevisker group in the south-west, and the Stainsby group in Lincolnshire and Humberside. By about 700 BC, however, burials were very rarely deposited in these traditional ways. New methods of disposing of the dead which leave little or no archaeological trace must have been used.

Wet places such as bogs, rivers, and lakes attracted attention throughout prehistory, but from about 1000 BC onwards they seem to have become very important focal points. Indeed, they may well have been used for the disposal of the dead. Much of the very finest metalwork made at this time was deliberately deposited in rivers, lakes, and bogs perhaps as grave goods or as dedications to water gods.

The Problem of the Celts

Traditionally, the development of hillforts and new weapons in Britain in the early first millennium BC were linked to migrations or invasions of new people from mainland Europe. Amongst the latest of these migrating groups were peoples sometimes called the Celts. These people, it was believed, were responsible for spreading a distinctive art style, the so-called La Tène style, and a distinctive Indo-European language, which has come down to us as Welsh, Breton, and Gaelic.

This traditional model can now be seen to be at odds with the archaeological evidence. Critically, the development of hillforts and new weapons took place over a long period and was the result of the combination of local traditions with influence from overseas rather than the arrival of new people. Also, these changes happened two centuries before La Tène art styles became widespread. Finally, the link with the spread of new languages must be discounted too because it is now recognized that Indo-European languages were established much earlier than previously thought, perhaps as far back as the fourth millennium BC. It is now recognized that there were no such people as the Celts who spread out across Europe. Rather there are a series of related tribal groups who, by about 500 BC, shared a common art style and interacted closely with one another. Adjoining groups may well have been linked through alliances or kinship. Collectively, these individual groups can be referred to as Celts.

Celtic Times (300–50 BC)

During the middle Iron Age, the last few centuries BC, the climate was rather like that of today. The pattern of settlement and economy became markedly regional, with three distinct traditions.

Western Areas

In the west of Britain settlements were mostly defended farmsteads and small hamlets of various sorts. These include cliff castles† and courtyard houses in Cornwall and enclosed farmsteads in the north-west. Small field-systems and grazing plots often lay around the settlements. The economy relied heavily on livestock grazed on open ground, with crops cultivated in the small garden-sized plots near to the settlements. There may have been some transhumance to exploit the higher ground in summer months.

Central Regions and the Developed Hillforts

In south-central Britain, the Welsh Marches, parts of the Pennines, and the Scottish borders, a simple hierarchy of settlement can be glimpsed. Many of the early hillforts fell out of use about 400 BC, but a few were refashioned as much larger and more elaborate defended enclosures, the so-called developed hillforts (Figure 8). DANEBURY (Hampshire) is one

▲ **Fig. 8.** Iron Age hillfort on The Herefordshire Beacon, Hereford (Photograph: Timothy Darvill)

of the most completely known examples. Such hillforts occur at intervals of about 25–30 km., and it is suggested that they were the centres of emerging political units, each with a petty king or chief at the head. It is possible that these important people lived in the main hillfort together with their close supporters, craftsmen, priests, and others of rank. Alternatively, the hillforts may have been community storage facilities for grain and livestock, a trading centre, and perhaps a ritual focus, with the important people living round about.

Certainly, around the developed hillforts there were numerous smaller settlements represented by enclosures of different sorts and in some cases groups of unenclosed houses. Most were the farms and homes of the majority of population. Some, however, seem more elaborate, as for example a series of enclosures with a ground plan in the shape of a banjo. The elaborate entrance and long approach passage suggests that the designers of these structures were trying to impress visitors with the scale and character of the place. Similar motives might also have affected the way some developed hillforts were built as the highest quality of workmanship is always around the main entrance.

Fields and grazing plots surround the hillforts and other settlements, individual landholdings sometimes being demarcated by linear earthworks. Local variations in economy are apparent from the proportion of enclosed settlements without fields (mainly livestock-based) as against open settlements with fields (mainly arable agriculture).

Eastern and South-Eastern Britain

In the Midlands, south-eastern regions, and East Anglia hillforts were rare and here settlements include village-like groups of houses, and enclosures representing farmsteads and hamlets. The landscape was well ordered with fields defined by hedges and ditches, trackways linking settlements, and unenclosed grazing areas beyond the more intensively used enclosed land.

Burial and Ritual

Iron Age burials are very rare but rivers, lakes, and wet places perhaps continued to be important as places for the disposal of the dead. In the west country a few burials of this date in stone-lined cists† are known, and around the river Humber a localized tradition of inhumation burials under square barrows developed. Some contain the remains of a chariot and the pair of horses that once pulled it.

Living on the Edge of the Empire (50 BC–AD 43)

The pattern of regional diversity established from about 300 BC remained roughly constant until the Roman Conquest, although within each region there were notable developments. Everywhere, tribal groupings seem to have become stronger and larger, and certainly more visible in the archaeological evidence available. Styles of pottery, for example, show greater regional affinity.

Alliances between neighbouring groups can be suspected. One reason for this may be the fact that from about 50 BC the Roman Empire had expanded into Gaul and from this time onwards southern Britain at least was living in the shadow of what at the time was one of the world's superpowers.

The South-East

Not surprisingly, it was southern and south-eastern Britain that were most influenced by the proximity of the Roman Empire. Here, some communities were strongly influenced by the affluence and high-living of the Roman world, and tried to emulate Mediterranean customs by acquiring, through trade, fine eating and drinking equipment, wine, luxury food, and exotic goods. Coins came into use, again following Mediterranean practices, and large settlements known as *oppida*† developed as centres for trade and commerce in the years leading up to the conquest. The wealthiest members of society were buried with provisions for an afterlife: wine and luxury food especially.

The luxuries of the Roman world did not come cheap. Communities in the south-east were trading in such commodities as silver, iron, grain, hunting dogs, and slaves, all of which were in demand within the Roman Empire. Some of this was available in south-eastern areas, but much of it was probably obtained either by trade or less peaceful means from communities living further to the north and west.

Beyond the South-East

Outside the south-east of Britain there was rather less direct contact with the Roman world, although occasional fragments of *amphorae* and imported pottery suggests that some luxuries were occasionally enjoyed.

Most of the hillforts ceased to function in their traditional ways after about 50 BC, although people were still living inside them on a modest scale. Most of the population seem to have been living in their farm-steads and enclosed settlements. In the far west, the traditional pattern of small defended farmsteads and fortified enclosures continued as before.

Craftsmanship seems to have been a strong tradition among communities in the west, and in the last few decades before the Roman Conquest produced some of finest metalwork ever. The graves of a few male warriors and rich females have been found in central and southern Britain, but these were the exception rather than the rule.

Caesar's Visits to Britain in 55 and 54 BC

According to his own accounts, Julius Caesar, then a provincial governor, made at least two sorties across the channel into southern Britain in 55 BC and 54 BC. No certain archaeological evidence exists to attest these invasions, and there is still much uncertainty about the route taken and places visited. Exactly what was the purpose of these expeditions is not clear either, and one line of argument is that Caesar simply wished to make a political impact back in Rome. Full-scale conquest does not seem to have been on his mind. More likely the visits were to develop trading links and to form alliances in order to secure stability along the northern boundary of the Empire.

It is not known where exactly Caesar's army landed in 55 BC, but it was most likely somewhere on the Kent coast, perhaps the neighbour-hood of Walmer. According to the written sources, bad weather pre-vented the landing of the cavalry fleet, thus depriving Caesar of his full military complement. The result was that despite a victorious battle against hostile local tribes he was forced to withdraw to Gaul. Plans were made for a second campaign but renewed hostilities in Gaul delayed action until the following year.

The second expedition, on a much larger scale, took place in 54 BC, again perhaps landing on the Kent coast. Caesar marched inland and captured the first major defended settlement he encountered, generally thought to be the hillfort at Bigbury. Following a battle against the native tribes led by Cassivellaunus, leader of the *Catulvellauni*, Caesar led the victorious Roman army across the Thames and thence into north-east Essex and the territory of the *Trinovantes*. The young prince of the

Trinovantes, Mandubricius, had come to Caesar in Gaul as a political exile following the murder of his father by Cassivellaunus. Eventually the native tribes capitulated and Cassivellaunus' stronghold, thought to be the site of the *oppidum* at WHEATHAMPSTEAD (Hertfordshire), was captured. The summer marked the end of the campaigning season and having exacted some sort of tribute, taken hostages, and agreed some kind of alliance, Caesar returned to Gaul. Further Gaulish rebellions and then his appointment as consul in Rome meant that he was never to return to Britain.

Waiting for the Romans

Caesar's visits had a great impact on those tribes occupying the south and south-eastern part of Britain. Some chiefs or petty kings were granted Roman citizenship, amongst them Togidubnus, whose capital lay at CHICHESTER (*Noviomagus*) and where a surviving inscription calls him 'Great King of Britain'. Some tribes adopted Roman customs, including coinage. Some chiefs probably visited Rome itself and thus had contact with classical culture. Roman luxury goods such as fine ceramic tableware, metalwork, and the *amphorae* containing wine, olive oil, and other foodstuffs from the Mediterranean, continued to be brought into Britain. To facilitate this trade it is likely that Roman merchants took up residence at ports along the south coast.

In the ninety-seven years between Caesar's visits to Britain and the Claudian invasion of AD 43 the political situation in Britain was highly volatile. Leadership seems to have been contested and alliances came and went. For a while, the two largest tribes in southern Britain, the *Trinovantes* and the *Catuvellauni*, joined together. But this was relatively short-lived, and the general picture was one of increasingly strong kingdoms competing with each other for supremacy and control over international trade and the materials that were exchanged during such trade. It was this turbulent and always unpredictable situation that may have prompted the Roman Emperor Claudius to consider invading Britain.

Romano-British Times

A Roman army under the Emperor Claudius invaded Britain in AD 43 (Figure 9). Four legions of the Roman army were involved (Legio II Augusta, Legio IX Hispana, Legio XIV Gemina, and Legio XX Valeria), commanded by Aulus Plautius. Each legion comprised about 5,000 soldiers divided into ten cohorts, and accompanying them would have been many auxiliary troops. But the Roman army was not just a fighting machine, it was able to support itself in hostile territory and thus many legionaries had specialist skills: engineers, architects, doctors, and craftsmen from various trades.

The channel crossing was made in three divisions. Traditionally, it is

▲ **Fig. 9.** Bronze head of the Roman Emperor Claudius. Recovered from the River Alde, Colchester, Essex (Photograph: Trustees of the British Museum (copyright))

believed that the invasion force landed near RICHBOROUGH (Kent), where a Claudian camp has been discovered. However, the recent discovery of similar works at FISHBOURNE near Chichester in West Sussex and a reinterpretation of the historical accounts suggest that a more westerly landing could have been possible. Further research is needed, but at Fishbourne excavations have revealed a complex of buildings which include a military stores depot, a substantial residence, probably dating from the time of Nero (AD 54–68), and a later C1 palace. One theory suggests that the expulsion of a local leader, Verica, to Rome precipitated Claudius' invasion, and explains the strong military presence in Verica's former kingdom.

Capturing Native Capitals

Following a pitched battle, traditionally thought to have been at a crossing of the river Medway in Kent, the Romans advanced north and east to capture the tribal capital at COLCHESTER (*Camulodunum*). The British tribes surrendered and Claudius claimed victory. It was at Colchester that the temple of the Imperial Cult, dedicated to Claudius as founder of the British province, was built. Earthworks belonging to the entrance to

▲ **Fig. 10.** Tombstone of a Centurion of the Twentieth Legion from Colchester, Essex (Photograph: Colchester Museums)

the former tribal royal compound and religious enclosure were partially reused in the construction of a Roman fortress occupied by Legio XX. Six years later, in AD 49, Colchester was made a *colonia*† where legionary veterans were granted plots of land (Figure 10), and the community was given the rights of self-government, according to laws set out in a charter.

The Fosse Way

The FOSSE WAY was a major Roman road diagonally crossing the country linking Topsham in Devon with LINCOLN via CIRENCESTER and LEICESTER. Another road continued the link through to the Humber. The discovery of several forts in the Midlands led to the suggestion that the routeway fell into some sort of early frontier or military zone, dividing the south-eastern part of the country, where the Romans appeared to have greater control and the support of client kingdoms, from the hostile Welsh and more troublesome tribes to the north.

The concept of a military frontier at this time is not universally accepted. The road was not constructed as a single event and probably only became consolidated as a routeway at a later date. It may have loosely defined the geographical extent of the early province of *Britannia*.

Conquest and Change

The Roman Conquest was a military subjugation which produced massive changes in all spheres of social and economic life, much of which is reflected in the archaeological record. The Romans have long been perceived as a civilized race, bringing with them luxuries such as central heating, water supplies, baths, public buildings, sewage disposal, roads, wine, and penalties such as taxation. Many Roman towns, for example SILCHESTER and WROXETER, as well as villas such as BIGNOR, LULLING-STONE, and WOODCHESTER, were investigated by Victorian antiquarians who felt a great affinity with such a cultured civilization. More recent archaeological research has shown, however, that in reality the picture is very different; there was no instant transformation brought about by Roman rule.

In the south and south-east of the country annexation to the Roman

Empire could in many ways be seen as the natural consequence of deep-seated social and political changes traceable back into the early C1 AD. Not surprisingly, several towns soon developed here, some adjacent to or coincident with previously established tribal centres such as Silchester (*Calleva Atrebatum*), ST ALBANS (*Verulamium*), and Chichester (*Noviomagus*). LONDON (*Londinium*) became a port and the hub of a developing road system. It may have been the intention to make London, founded around AD 50, the seat of government and provincial administration.

In the north and west things were rather different and in some areas there was little or no evidence of Roman impact until well into the C2.

Rebellion

In the late 50s action to control Wales was taken by the then governor, Suetonius Paullinus. Having defeated the *Silures* in the south he was marching into North Wales towards Anglesey, a retreat of the Druids, when news arrived of a serious rebellion in the south. This was the famous Boudiccan revolt of AD 60. Following the death of her husband Prasutagus, king of the *Iceni*, the Icenian kingdom, hitherto allied but independent, was incorporated into the Roman province. The royal household had been ill-treated and the kingdom plundered by Roman centurions and others. The *Trinovantes* to the south were also unhappy with the Romans' rather peremptory dealings with them, particularly the reallocation of lands to the legionaries and the loss of the tribal religious centre at Gosbecks. The two tribes thus joined forces under Boudicca and, before Paullinus could return with his armies from Wales, the new Roman towns at Colchester, London, and VERULAMIUM were sacked. Boudicca was eventually defeated, probably in the Thames valley, and Roman rule re-established.

Paullinus later exacted his revenge by laying waste the territories of those British tribes that had joined or supported the rebellion. Supporters such as the pro-Roman client king, Togidubnus, possibly based at Fishbourne, were rewarded with further land. It has been suggested that this included property around BATH, where major new buildings were started, including the baths complex and the classical-style temple dedicated to Neptune and Minerva. A programme of new civic building works was commenced at the destroyed Roman centres, and public structures such as the forum† in London may date from this time.

Conquests in the West and North

With the accession of the Emperor Vespasian following the suicide of Nero, and a quick succession of Galba, Otho, and Vitellius in AD 68, a much firmer policy was adopted towards the new province, the aim being to conquer all of Britain. First, in the north, came the defeat of the *Brigantes*, initially an ally of Rome, but who had risen against their pro-Roman Queen Cartimandua. The governor, Petillius Cerealis, led Legio

IX into *Brigantian* territory to establish a new fortress at YORK. Cerealis was recalled and replaced by Julius Frontinus, who turned his attention to South Wales, setting up a system of garrison forts in the hostile territories including a base at Caerleon, in direct contact with the Bristol Channel, and in the latter part of his governorship started the construction of a fortress at CHESTER (Figure 11).

Several civic projects were probably initiated by Frontinus including the building of fora (market places) at Verulamium and Cirencester. He was succeeded around AD 77–8 by Agricola, who maintained his position through the reigns of the Emperors Vespasian, Titus, and Domitian. Agricola's first act was to complete the subjugation of the Welsh and to take Anglesey. In the following season he campaigned in the north and several new garrisons were established.

Agricola continued his campaign of adding new territory to the province by moving north in two arcs from CORBRIDGE across the Tyne and Tweed and via CARLISLE to meet south of the Tay. According to his son-in-law, the writer Tacitus, the climax of Agricola's career was his victory at the Battle of Mons Graupius, thought to have taken place somewhere in the Grampian range. The disappearance overnight of most of the British army, however, deprived the Romans of the capture or destruction of the enemy and thus a full victory.

▲ **Fig. 11.** Roman legionary soldier

Consolidating the Province

The city was regarded by the Romans as the focus of civilized life. Towns were needed as centres of local government as well as assisting the spread of education and Roman civilization. Archaeology suggests that many planned town centres and street systems were begun in the later C1 AD. Throughout the Flavian period and in part under Agricola's administration many civil building works were started, including baths, temples, fora, and private housing. Most Roman towns were furnished with a standard complement of public buildings. The forum usually comprised a courtyard surrounded on three sides by ranges of rooms often used as shops, with the basilica†, a substantial aisled building, on the fourth side.

This was the administrative centre similar to today's council offices with a council chamber, treasury, and a public hall. Other public structures might include a *macellum*† (market hall) and an amphitheatre or theatre for entertainment. Amphitheatres were usually located on the edges of towns, or outside the walls as at Silchester, Dorchester, and Cirencester. Consisting of an oval arena surrounded by tiered seating they were used for a variety of activities. Theatres, usually semicircular in plan with a stage, are less common in Britain, the only substantially visible one being at Verulamium. Support and finance for civic building works came from Vespasian's successor, Titus, and an inscription marking the completion of the basilica at Verulamium probably dates from his first year as Emperor.

Romans used bath-houses as centres for relaxation and social intercourse, and any major town, military installation, and many country houses had such an establishment. Evidence for bath-house structures is frequently found as they were usually constructed in stone to minimize fire risk. Many of the larger public baths, such as at Wroxeter, had exercise halls (*palaestra*†). Large quantities of water would have been required and several towns probably found it necessary to construct aqueducts†. In Britain open channels were favoured, as at Dorchester (Dorset), which supplied the baths and other buildings. Although evidence for aqueducts in Britain is sparse, a number of sewers and drains have been found, for example, at Lincoln, York, Bath, and London.

It has been suggested that the rapid growth of London in the late C1 resulted in its elevation to the status of a *municipium*†. The forum and basilica were first constructed in the Flavian period and a military fort built sometime after the AD 80s, an unusual provision in a city. By around AD 100 the basilica was being replaced by a structure larger than any other north of the Alps at the time.

Around the closing years of the C1 new, defended *coloniae*† for retired veterans were established at Lincoln and GLOUCESTER, both on the sites of former legionary fortresses. The construction of a massive triumphal arch at Richborough may have been commissioned by the Emperor Domitian (AD 81–96) to mark the end of the conquest of Britain and perhaps an intended Imperial visit.

The Five Good Emperors

Domitian's unpopularity led to his assassination in AD 96, and the period that followed, lasting from AD 97 to 180, is often referred to as that of the 'five good emperors'. The first brief reign was that of Nerva to be followed in AD 98 by Trajan. In the early C2 the withdrawal of troops from southern Scotland, initiated during Domitian's reign, continued and a new frontier established along the Stanegate, a road built by Agricola to run from Corbridge (Northumberland) to Carlisle (Cumbria). The famous site at *Vindolanda* (CHESTERHOLM) also on Stanegate frontier probably dates from this time. The three legionary fortresses at York, Chester, and Caerleon were entirely rebuilt, with stone structures replacing the earlier timber ones. Towards the end of Trajan's reign there was another serious uprising in the north. His successor, Hadrian, visited Britain and ordered a reorganization of the northern frontier to include a physical barrier just north of the Stanegate.

Hadrian's Wall

Hadrian's Wall was one of the most elaborate frontiers in the Roman world (Figure 12). Built to control the movement of people, it underwent several modifications in its design during construction. Originally built partly in stone and partly in turf, the Wall extended from the Tyne in the east to the Solway in the west. In addition to the Wall itself, the frontier incorporated an elaborate system of forts, milecastles†, turrets, a great external ditch, and a service road set within a controlled area marked by an earthwork known as the Vallum. At the west end the works continued along the Cumbrian coast. The history of the construction of the Wall is an extremely complex one, extending over a considerable period of time. Its presence led to settled conditions to the south, allowing the local economies to expand and prosper. The largest fort was at STANWIX at the western end. This area seems eventually to have developed into a civil *civitas*† with its city at Carlisle.

▼ **Fig. 12.** View of Hadrian's Wall near Housesteads (*Vercovicium*), Northumberland (Photograph: Jane Timby)

Roman Britain's Golden Age

Several other new developments followed Hadrian's visit, including the renewal of building works at Wroxeter (*Viroconium Cornoviorum*) and the completion of the forum. Other building programmes perhaps stimulated by his visit included the forum at Leicester and the rebuilding of the forum-basilica at London. Caistor St Edmund (Norfolk) was granted the status of a *civitas*. A more widespread adoption of Roman ways and fashions is reflected in the range of artefacts found in the archaeological record from this time (Figure 13). The introduction of a monetary economy and a complex system of local and central administration allowed the economy to expand and prosper. Service industries grew up around towns and many rural industries developed, based on raw materials such as clay, stone, iron, and other minerals.

From around this time there was also an expansion of settlement into the Fenlands of East Anglia. Natural changes may have led to the lowering of the water-table, making the fertile land available, but waterways, canals, such as at WATERBEACH (Cambridgeshire), and roads all indicate public works and considerable state investment.

In AD 138 Hadrian was succeeded by Antoninus Pius, who continued Hadrian's foreign policy of non-expansion—except in the case of Britain. He appointed a new British governor, Q. Lollius Urbicus, who instigated a programme of work at the military base at Corbridge, where Agricola's old road north crossed the Tyne. This was clearly preliminary

▼ **Fig. 13.** A selection of samian tableware imported from Central Gaul (Photograph: Verulamium Museum)

to a renewed attempt to expand into Scotland, and by AD 142–3 southern Scotland was reoccupied by the Roman forces. A new frontier, the Antonine Wall, was established across the Forth–Clyde isthmus.

Temporarily Hadrian's Wall became redundant; gates were removed from the milecastles, and parts of the Vallum were deliberately slighted to form additional crossings. In AD 154 another serious uprising in *Brigantian* territory necessitated the evacuation of the Antonine Wall and the movement of troops southwards. Following suppression of the uprising Hadrian's Wall was restored and work started on rebuilding old forts in *Brigantia*. A final brief sortie into Scotland was made around AD 159 but did not last long. Hadrian's Wall was reoccupied as the northern frontier and additional outpost forts built along Dere Street leading northwards from Corbridge.

Roads

The Romans were responsible for establishing a coherent network of roads across Britain, which continued in use for many centuries; in some cases, as with part of the Fosse Way, they are perpetuated in our present road system. All the main centres of Roman occupation, in particular the regional capitals, were linked by roads, with London acting as the main radial centre as it does today. Although not visually impressive, the road system is one of the most lasting monuments to Roman occupation. There is little contemporary information relating to the roads but one important document is the *Itinerary* of Antoninus compiled in the late C2 or C3. This lists places and the distances between them. The roads were laid out by trained surveyors and engineers. A distinctive feature is the use of straight alignments for new roads, often ignoring the terrain, as exemplified by the stretch still visible at BLACKSTONE EDGE, Rippondale (West Yorkshire). Older routeways were upgraded too, but were often less straight. Roads were usually laid on a well-constructed embankment (*agger†*) which was sometimes metalled with gravel or stone. In iron-working areas slag was used to construct the *agger* as at HOLTYE (East Sussex).

The Countryside

It was important for community leaders and other wealthy citizens to have homes in the town and in the countryside. Change in the countryside was less rapid than in the towns and many traditional farmsteads continued unaltered into the C2 and sometimes beyond. From the Hadrianic period a two-tier system developed, with simple native farmsteads or small agricultural communities continuing in many areas alongside the villas and large rural houses built in the Roman style at the centre of sizeable estates, for example, Bignor (West Sussex), GREAT WITCOMBE (Gloucestershire), NORTH LEIGH (Oxfordshire), and BRADING on the Isle of Wight. In other areas, notably the upland regions, pre-existing native farms and villages continued the traditional pre-Roman patterns of agricultural production. Domestic buildings perpetuated Iron Age architectural styles with circular structures and courtyard houses such as those at CHYSAUSTER and CARN BREA (Cornwall).

The acquisition of land not only gave social respectability but also wealth. Arable farming played a large part in the economy of Roman Britain and much of the landscape became intensively farmed. Most villas were situated less than a day's ride from a town or city, suggesting a symbiotic link between the two.

A particularly grand residence has been found at Fishbourne (West Sussex). This started as an early military establishment, which was replaced first by a timber-framed villa, and then in the 60s by a stone villa. Sometime after AD 73 this was superseded by a palace, built using many exotic imported materials and surrounded by gardens and land-scaped parkland. The size and grandeur of the building suggests it may have been designed for a member of the Imperial family, or a high-ranking official. It may have been built for the client king Cogidubnus.

Increased productivity required a number of agricultural innov-ations. Improved drainage meant that poorer soils such as clay could be brought into cultivation. Agricultural implements were improved, mechanical mills introduced, and corn driers constructed. The main crops grown were spelt wheat and barley. It is still a question of debate whether the Romans introduced the grape vine into Britain; the dis-covery of *Vitis vinifera* pollen from Wollaston (Northamptonshire) strongly supports the suggestion.

Industry

Britain was an important resource for various raw materials, in particu-lar metal ores, many of which were exported. Indeed it was probably the existence of these valuable ores that drew the Romans to Britain in the first place. Before the conquest Strabo listed cattle, hides, corn, hunting dogs, slaves, and metals (gold, silver, and iron) as the main exports from Britain. One of the earliest industries to be developed by the Romans, probably under military supervision, was lead-mining in the Mendips, where evidence can still be seen at CHARTERHOUSE-ON-MENDIP (Somer-set). Silver could also be extracted from the lead. Acquiring gold and silver was vital for coinage and, in the late Empire, for official payments in plate and ingots. It is known that gold was obtained from the mines at Dolaucothi in Wales. The iron industry was also important from the C1, rapidly expanding in the early C2. Activity for this was focused on the Weald (Kent), the Forest of Dean (Gloucestershire), and at outcrops along the Jurassic ridge from Somerset to Lincolnshire. The western areas appear to have been worked by free miners, but the Wealden indus-try was state controlled using the Roman fleet, the *Classis Britannica*, reflecting its strategic importance.

Stone was extensively quarried and used for buildings, monumental structures of all kinds, and roads. Limestone was one of the most widely used building stones and was frequently transported long distances away from its source. Monuments in London, for example, used stone from Kent. The Purbeck industries around Poole harbour, Dorset, produced limestone marble veneers used in numerous public buildings such as the basilica at Silchester, as well as mortars, pottery, and other manufactured items in shale. Timber, although less visible archaeologically, was originally very important for building, domestic items, tools, and fuel. Earlier traditions of woodland management continued to perpetuate this critical resource, although it is likely that by the end of Roman occupation the overall level of tree-cover in Britain had decreased as a result of heavy exploitation.

Turbulent Times and the End of the Golden Age

The relatively peaceful Antonine period came to an end in AD 161 when Antoninus was succeeded by Marcus Aurelius. From this point onwards the Roman Empire was under increasing pressure from attack by barbarian tribes, in particular along the Rhine and Danube frontiers. Almost constant warfare had serious consequences for Imperial finances, and the situation was not satisfactorily dealt with before Marcus' death in AD 180. Shortly after that war broke out in northern Britain and Hadrian's Wall was again the focus of hostilities.

It is around this time, and presumably in response to the barbarian threat, that many of the previously undefended urban centres across Britain were provided with earthwork defences. Some already fortified towns such as Gloucester, Lincoln, and Colchester were provided with stone walls. In the C3 many of the earlier fortifications were rebuilt in stone and several unprotected settlements acquired defences.

Civil War

In AD 192, after Decimus Clodius Albinus had been made governor of Britain, the Emperor Commodus was murdered and a contest for the throne developed, setting in motion a civil war. By 197 the two main surviving claimants, Septimius Severus and Clodius Albinus, met in battle near Lyons, from which Septimius emerged the victor. Inevitably the withdrawal of substantial troops from Britain by Clodius to support his campaign led to some disruption and upheaval. During the following Severan reign (AD 193–211) a succession of governors was sent to try to re-establish law and order particularly in the Pennine region where there was considerable unrest. A programme of repair and maintenance work was undertaken on parts of Hadrian's Wall.

Severus himself came to Britain in AD 208 with reinforcements to help stabilize the still unsettled situation in the north. SOUTH SHIELDS fort at the mouth of the Tyne was rebuilt as a supply depot to support his Scottish campaigns. Severus took his troops back into southern Scotland but, following a rather unsuccessful expedition, ill-health forced him to retire to York, where he died in AD 211. His elder son, Caracalla, was left to continue the battle. Caracalla negotiated a diplomatic settlement with the enemy and fighting ceased. Peace brought with it a period of prosperity in the north with the establishment of new farmsteads and the rebuilding of the forts.

It was probably under Caracalla's administration that Britain was rearranged into two provinces: the southern 'upper province' (*Britannia Superior*), with legions at Chester and Caerleon and administered from London, and the northern 'lower province' (*Britannia Inferior*) with its centre at York. This was partly to prevent further attempts on the throne by limiting the resources potentially available to a single provincial governor.

Around this time York was granted the title of *colonia*.

The Politics of the Early Third Century

The C3 saw many political changes across the Roman Empire and a rapid succession of emperors. Both Gaul and Germany suffered several barbarian attacks, and other calamities struck more distant parts of the Empire. Life in Britain continued relatively untouched by the problems experienced elsewhere, although disruption of trade is reflected by the decline and disappearance of imported Gaulish samian, and oil and wine *amphorae* in the archaeological record. Coin hoards are a notable feature of the period, again perhaps indicating instability.

Caracalla's policy of consolidating the northern frontier was successful. Restoration and maintenance work continued on Hadrian's Wall and some of the forts such as BEWCASTLE (Cumbria) were refurbished. New forts were established on abandoned sites such as HIGH ROCHESTER (Northumberland) and RISINGHAM (Northumberland) on Dere Street. Substantial civil settlements developed adjacent to the forts, perhaps directly the result of Severus' permission for serving soldiers to have lawful wives.

Political Reform in the Late Third Century

In AD 284 the Emperor Diocletian instigated several political and social reforms. He built up the army, which had fallen below strength by the late C3, and created a new elite cavalry unit. The Tetrarchic system of government was introduced whereby responsibility for the Eastern and Western provinces was divided between twin pairs of junior and senior emperors. More administrative staff were employed and a new tier of provincial administration known as the *diocese* (group of provinces) was introduced. Britain was reorganized into four provinces (*Britannia Prima, Britannia Secunda, Maxima Caesariensis,* and *Flavia Caesariensis*), which collectively formed one such diocese. The four new provincial capitals were probably York, Lincoln, Cirencester, and London. Diocletian appointed Maximian to be responsible for the defence of Italy and the Western provinces. Maximian in turn appointed the officer Carausius to assist in the battle against the Saxon and Frankish raiders attacking the north Gaulish coast. Carausius was based at Boulogne but he became ambitious and greedy and, colluding with the barbarian pirates, kept some of the recovered booty for himself. Maximian ordered his execution but the move backfired and Carausius responded by proclaiming himself Emperor in 286/7. Seizing Britain, he cut it off from the central Empire defending himself with the naval fleet he already commanded along with substantial land forces in Gaul. Carausius even minted his own coinage, which describes him as 'restorer of Britain'. Maximian, despite attempts including a lost naval battle in 289, could not immediately dislodge Carausius, who still held Boulogne in 293.

Flavius Julius Constantius was appointed as Maximian's junior to help inaugurate the new system of government in the West. Constantius was based at Trier and undoubtedly part of his remit was to recover the provinces of Britain usurped by Carausius. His first step was to take Boulogne, an event shortly followed by the assassination in 293 of Carausius by one of his associates Allectus. Allectus in turn became the usurper. In 296 Constantius successfully crossed the channel and defeated Allectus, returning Britain to the Empire (Figure 14).

Around the early C4 widespread rebuilding of several northern military installations reflect a period of instability and threat of invasion. York's defences underwent extensive modifications and the walls of the fortress were rebuilt with a series of multi-angular towers along the river frontage. Refurbishment of other military installations in the C4 has also been noted, for example HOUSESTEADS (Northumberland), WALLSEND (Tyne and Wear), and Chester (Cheshire). Several towns also acquired or modified their defences.

A general programme of work to improve military security involved the consolidation of the coastal defence system from a series of discrete forts into a coherent system. This project, probably initiated by Probus

▼ **Fig. 14.** Medallion of Constantius I, struck at Trier and found at Arras, North France showing the relief of London (after Liversidge)

and continued by Carausius in the later C3, may have been completed at this time.

In 305 Diocletian retired and, following the new constitutional laws, so did Maximian. Thus Constantius was made full Emperor Augustus. In 306 he returned to Britain with his son Constantine to launch new campaigns in the northern territories.

Following a successful campaign in northern Britain Constantius I returned to York, where he died in 306, his son Constantine being proclaimed Emperor by the troops. Political instability and contest for supremacy from various other parties prevented him from assuming the full title until 324. Constantine made several visits to Britain in the interim period, well documented by coins minted at the time.

Villas

Although villas had been a feature of the countryside from the late C1 AD, the climax of villa prosperity dates from the later C3 and early C4. Many existing villas show phases of major expansion and aggrandizement, and it is to this period that many of the most impressive surviving mosaics belong. Several stylistically distinct regional mosaic schools have been identified. Notable examples of their products can be seen at Bignor (West Sussex), Brading (Isle of Wight), Lullingstone (Kent), and CHEDWORTH (Gloucestershire). The areas around Bath and Cirencester saw a sudden proliferation of villas, suggested by some to be the result of selling off Imperial estates to raise money. Some of this new prosperity may have been the result of an influx of capital, and perhaps owners, to Britain after late C3 unrest in Gaul and Germany. The presence of such large villa estates undoubtedly stimulated the economy. By contrast, few new public building works seem to have taken place within the towns.

Later Roman Industry

The decline in the availability of imported fine tableware from the later C2 acted as a stimulus for the development of a number of regional British pottery industries, mainly producing colour-coated ware. Amongst the largest producers were the Oxfordshire and lower Nene valley potteries, joined in the C4 by those of the New Forest in Hampshire.

In the C3–C4 there was a resurgence in the lead industry with a demand for both pewter vessels and lead coffins. Connected with the rise in pewter production was a growth in demand for tin, resulting in renewed activity at a few British mines at this time.

Trade in British textiles also seems to have become important in later Roman times and there is evidence of increased sheep husbandry and wool production. British woollen products had acquired an Empire-wide reputation.

Religion and Death

There were four main spheres of religious belief in Roman Britain: the official Roman state religion; the Celtic cults; oriental beliefs, of which the most popular was Mithraism; and Christianity.

The official state religion was concerned with the worship of the spiritual power of the reigning Emperor and with that of his predecessors, who were often deified after death. Often, the cult of Imperial persons was associated with the three chief deities, Jupiter, Juno, and Minerva, known as the Capitoline Triad. The temple of Claudius at Colchester, a major centre for the Imperial Cult, was built shortly after the conquest. Worship to the Roman gods formed a daily part of army life and many military sites have dedicatory stones, such as those at Corbridge (Northumberland) or MARYPORT (Cumbria).

Various other Roman deities found worshippers in Britain too, including Diana, Apollo, Mars, and Hercules. All the large towns probably had at least one temple built in the classical style although actual remains are scarce. These temples would have housed the cult statue of the deity, for example the head of Minerva found at Bath, and were not used for congregational worship. Less ornate, but common in the south, were smaller, rather simple Romano-Celtic temples, found both in the towns and in the countryside, for example HARLOW (Essex), Maiden Castle (Dorset), and JORDAN HILL (Dorset). Many had pre-Roman origins.

Pagan Celtic religion was dominated by the veneration of natural phenomena. Gods and goddesses were often associated with natural features such as trees, springs, watery places, islands, or through shafts or wells linking the known and the unknown worlds. Celtic ritual was linked to fundamental aspects of life such as fertility, prosperity, war, and death. An important section of Celtic society were the Druids. The Romans went to great lengths to suppress these people, culminating in Suetonius Paullinus' attack on the last Druid stronghold in Anglesey in AD 60. Other aspects of Celtic belief were tolerated.

Such toleration also extended to oriental cults, one of the most prominent being that of Mithras, a Persian god who represented fair dealing and the victory of the soul after death. Three Mithraea have been excavated, at London, CARRAWBURGH (Northumberland), and Housesteads (Northumberland). Evidence for the worship of Mithras has also been found at other sites including Leicester, York, Chester, and Rudchester.

Christianity, also of oriental origin, spread through the Mediterranean world during the C1 probably reaching Britain by the C3. The last great persecution was by Diocletian in 303 who thought that the disasters in the Empire stemmed from a neglect of the traditional gods. Constantine, however, was an enthusiastic supporter of Christianity and in the early C4 it became the state religion within the Roman Empire.

The churches started to become very wealthy landowners, and substantial rights and privileges were granted to men in Christian orders. At this time many pagan sculptures and altars were destroyed, as seen at the Temple of Mithras at Walbrook (London), whilst other temples, such as Uley (Gloucestershire), were converted to function as Christian churches. Early churches have been identified at Richborough, Verulamium, CANTERBURY, and Silchester.

A range of portable items have been found bearing Christian motifs such as the chi-rho, alpha and omega, or the representation of a fish. Occasionally such Christian symbols occur in mosaics such as those from the villa at Hinton St Mary (Dorset) now in Dorchester Museum. A suite of rooms at Lullingstone Villa (Kent) has also been identified as a Christian chapel.

The Romans were very much concerned with ideas of the afterlife. The spirit was seen as passing on to another world but it was also important that the dead had been properly buried with accompanying ritual in a grave which they could, in theory, return to. In Britain in the C1–C2 the urban dead were usually cremated. Offerings of food and drink and other items were often buried with the remains. For reasons of hygiene it was against the law for anyone to be buried in a settlement, so cemeteries are usually found alongside roads outside towns. Infant burials were exempt and are often found close to, or concealed under, buildings. During the mid to later C2 there was a gradual change from cremation to inhumation, generally unaccompanied by grave goods. The change was not absolute and exceptions occur in both periods. Many inhumations were buried in wood, lead, or stone coffins. In exceptional cases mausolea were built, as perhaps at STONE-BY-FAVERSHAM (Kent). In areas where stone was readily available tombstones bearing inscriptions were erected, and examples are known from Gloucester, Cirencester, Bath, York, Chester, and Carlisle amongst other towns. Such monuments were extremely rare in small towns and even more scarce in the countryside.

In the C1–C2 there was also a brief fashion for placing burials under large earthen barrows such as those at Six Hills, STEVENAGE (Hertfordshire) or the BARTLOW HILLS (Essex). In late Roman times there was an increased diversity in burial practice and examples of both cremation and inhumation are found. The arrangement and orientation of graves within cemeteries varies, and some burials are furnished with grave goods. This variety may reflect the growing diversification of religious beliefs in later Roman times.

Saxon Shore Forts

The *Classis Britannica*, the Roman fleet, was established from the C2 primarily to act as a support arm, transporting troops and supplies. Occasionally it was used in campaigns. Various bases were established on the east and south coasts including Dover, where two lighthouses were constructed. In early Roman times the fleet was heavily involved in the control of the iron industry in the Weald. Such state involvement highlights the strategic importance of the resource, which may have been stimulated by the programme of building works started under Agricola. The fleet would have provided supplies and technical expertise and controlled the exportation of part-processed raw material. Numerous iron-working sites have been identified, including Beauport Park, Bardown, and Cranbrook (East Sussex).

From the C3 existing bases were refurbished and new military installations constructed in the south and east, commonly referred to as the 'Saxon Shore Forts'. These probably housed a cavalry or infantry unit along with a detachment of the fleet. Two examples built around this time adjacent to major river estuaries are RECULVER (Kent) and BRANCASTER (Norfolk). Both were constructed in C2 style without the external towers or bastions seen in the later forts. The complete system of forts established by the C4 under the 'Count of the Saxon Shore' is listed in a document known as the *Notitia Dignitatum*. Amongst the examples on the south coast are PEVENSEY, LYMPNE, PORTCHESTER, Dover, and Richborough, to which can be added BRADWELL and BURGH CASTLE on the east coast.

The Fourth Century and Beyond

Constantine died in 337 and eventually his three sons, Constantine II, Constantius II, and Constans took control, with Constantine II ruling Spain, Gaul, and Britain. The brothers fell out and Constantine II invaded Italy in 340, where he was killed and superseded by Constans. Constans was assassinated in 350 and was succeeded briefly by Magnentius, who in turn was defeated in battle by Constantius II just three years later. Constantius, an Arian and therefore technically a heretic, returned the Empire to a single rule. Magnentius had allowed pagan worship but Constantius closed down pagan temples, and the death penalty was introduced for anyone worshipping pagan gods.

A brief revival in paganism was introduced by Julian, cousin to Constantius, who was proclaimed Emperor in 360. His death in 363 marked the end of the house of Constantine. Valentinian I, another devoted Christian, was appointed Emperor.

The Barbarian Conspiracy of 367?

Since the later C2 the northern frontiers of the Roman Empire had been frequently under attack, and from the C3 Britain too may have become a target, hence the consolidation of the Saxon Shore forts. In the received history of Britain the date of 367 has been linked with a concerted barbarian attack involving the Picts from north of Hadrian's Wall, the Scots and the Irish from Ireland, the Attacotti from the Western Isles, and the Franks and Saxons from across the North Sea. These events, traditionally seen as a turning point in C4 history, have now been challenged by some scholars in the context of Roman Britain. It is possible that the disruptions caused by the barbarians have been exaggerated and that the crisis brought about in Britain at this time could have arisen from food shortages, particularly those supplying the army as a result of poor administration and unscrupulous dealings.

Valentinian dispatched Flavius Theodosius to restore order, which he successfully did. He also led a military campaign against the Saxons. Where these campaigns actually took place is currently under debate but is now thought by some scholars to be in Batavia. Meanwhile in Britain there appears to be some evidence of repair work to some of the forts and new defensive works were carried out along the north-east coast, with the construction of a series of watch-towers such as those at FILEY and SCARBOROUGH (North Yorkshire). Control of the signal stations may have been coordinated from MALTON or York.

The death of Valentinian I in 375 marked the end of an era of competent government with a moderately tolerant attitude in religious matters. Control fell to his sons Gratian and Valentinian II, but a massive defeat of the Roman army by Goths at the Battle of Adrianople on the Danube in 378 led Gratian to turn for assistance to Count Theodosius' son, also called Theodosius. In 379 Theodosius the younger was proclaimed co-ruler of the Eastern Empire. Theodosius the Great, as he became known, was a devoted Christian and the growth in the power of the Church was unchecked with the rise of his associates to powerful positions. There was at this time much military deployment across the Empire with the increasing use of barbarian allies alongside regular troops. This may have included the withdrawal of troops from Britain and there is evidence that some of the forts, including Chester, were abandoned at this time. Britain went through a period of instability and was twice moved out of the control of the central Imperial regime, first by Magnus Maximus (383–8) and secondly by Eugenius (392–4). In both cases Theodosius managed to regain control and just before his death in 395 he had managed to reunite the Empire.

The Collapse of Imperial Rule

Theodosius was succeeded by his sons Arcadius and Honorius, effectively dividing the Eastern and Western Empires. It was during Honorius' reign from 395 to 423 that the Western Empire fell into terminal collapse. At the time of Theodosius' death most of the field army was in the West under the command of Flavius Stilicho, a Vandal by birth but connected to the Imperial house through marriage. Stilicho became effective ruler of the West as Honorius' chief of staff from 395 to 408. He appears to have led a campaign against a possible barbarian attack on Britain in 398.

Around this time he undertook a considerable reorganization of the British coastal defences, which possibly fixed the Saxon Shore in the form in which it stands in the *Notitia*. The Visigothic threat to the Western Empire in 401 meant that Stilicho needed troops. The *Notitia* also lists a number of British units serving elsewhere in the Empire, which may be evidence of a substantial withdrawal of troops from Britain for this purpose. Although raised in Britain, these units may have been already mobile field armies distinct from the more static garrisons. However, a significant decline in coinage in Britain from 402 may reflect the scale of the withdrawal since most money went to the payment of troops. Alternatively, it may reflect a more general governmental cash shortage.

The period 406–10 saw continued political instability across the Empire with constant revolts, local civil wars, and increasing chaos, culminating with the sacking of Rome itself by the Goth Alaric in 410. At this point Honorius advised the *civitates* of Britain to look to their own defence. Evidence for life in Britain after this date is extremely limited and difficult to interpret. The revolt of 410 effectively marked the end of Roman Britain as no further attempt was made by the Romans to return it to Imperial rule.

After the Empire

After the withdrawal of Roman authority and troops in the early C5 Britain entered what has often been called 'The Dark Ages'. This reflected an intellectual darkness, which, it was believed, closed in at the end of the Roman period and lasted until the Renaissance. Much of that darkness—less pitch-black than was sometimes supposed—mainly reflected the poverty of written sources and the rarity of archaeological finds. Moreover, such histories as do survive were written not as objective records but from particular perspectives and with polemic aims. There are two main sources. The *Ruin of Britain* was written about 500, somewhere in south-western Britain, by an educated Christian cleric named Gildas. This compares his fellow Britons (i.e. the residual Romano-British population) with the biblical Israelites, and presents invasions by the barbarian Anglo-Saxons as punishments by God for the Britons' sins. Just over two hundred years later Bede, a monk at JARROW in Northumbria, wrote an *Ecclesiastical History of the English People*. His was an Anglo-Saxon viewpoint, critical of the British, and his story was that of his people's conversion to Christianity.

From these and other scraps came the long-accepted story of the Anglo-Saxon takeover of Britain: of raids by Angles, Saxons, and Jutes from north Germany and Denmark, followed by piecemeal settlement and conquest. In this scenario the invaders moved ever westward across southern Britain during the course of the C5–C7.

Since the 1930s archaeology has challenged, contradicted, occasionally confirmed, and increasingly expanded upon this traditional view of England's early history. Central to the development of a new understanding has been the process of tracking the collapse of Roman institutions, documenting the continuing development of indigenous populations, and examining the role and influences of other groups living around the Atlantic fringes of north-west Europe through trade, migration, and colonization.

Continuity and Collapse

By the mid-C5 Britain no longer had a monetary economy. Industrial production of goods such as pottery had ceased, and political and administrative institutions had become fragmented. An increase in the number of coin hoards is generally taken to indicate that the system of taxation had broken down. Roman villas seem, for the most part, to have been abandoned soon after 400, although archaeology has shown that in some towns, for instance Cirencester, London, and St Albans, occupation continued for many decades. Even at these places, however, the large cemeteries outside the town walls were abandoned.

The clearest evidence of the last phases of urban life has come from Wroxeter, although as this town lies deep in western Britain it was well away from early Anglo-Saxon settlement and may be exceptional. Here, however, the central baths–basilica complex continued in use during the C5, albeit in an increasingly dilapidated condition, until its roof was deliberately removed and its walls lowered in height. Thereafter the interior continued in use, perhaps as a market place with stalls and booths. Then, about 530–70, the basilica shell was levelled to enable the construction of several separate buildings, mostly timber-framed and some substantial and possibly multi-storeyed. The excavators have speculated about who might have ordered their construction. Historical sources mention 'tyrants', local king-warlords, at places such as Bath, Gloucester, and Cirencester, and such a figure or dynasty might have assumed authority at Wroxeter. Another possibility is that this was the seat of a local bishop, perhaps combining a spiritual role with that of City Prefect. Whichever is the case, Wroxeter remained a special place of some sort, even if not a town as the Romans would have recognized, until the mid-C7.

In some places urban life may have been finally ended by a pandemic which contemporary sources call the Great Death. Almost certainly this was a bubonic plague, which reached Britain around 547. We have no way of knowing how many it killed; its return in 1348–9 demonstrates its potential malevolence.

From the mid-C5 onwards there was also another factor to be considered: migrations, colonization, and raiding first by Germanic and later by Norse communities who had formerly lived outside the Roman

Empire. What is conventionally termed the Anglo-Saxon period takes its name from the most dominant settlers from the C5 onwards in Britain, people coming across the North Sea from what is now the Netherlands and northern Germany. However, the Anglo-Saxon period is by no means uniform, and may be subdivided into early (roughly 450–650), middle (650–800), and late (800–1066) times. These are rather crude divisions, further complicated from the late C8 onwards by raids and settlement involving Norse peoples from what is now Scandinavia.

Early Anglo-Saxon Times (450–650)

The incoming Germanic peoples were pagans and are most visible archaeologically by their distinctive burials and the grave goods that accompanied their dead into the afterlife (Figure 15). In eastern and northern areas the usual rite was cremation, after which the ashes of the deceased and whatever had been burnt with them (for men sometimes a horse) were buried in a clay urn, often highly decorated. Some of these cemeteries are very extensive; at Spong Hill (Norfolk), for example, over 2,000 urns were excavated. In central and southern Britain inhumation was normal, with men being accompanied, if wealthy, by weapons such as swords, spears, and shields, and women by artefacts including beads and

▼ **Fig. 15.** Anglo-Saxon inhumation from Empingham, Rutland (after Timby), and cremation urn from Sancton, East Riding of Yorkshire (after Myres & Southern)

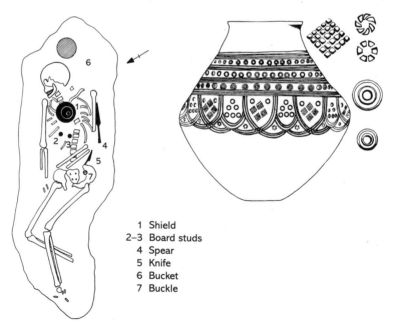

1 Shield
2–3 Board studs
4 Spear
5 Knife
6 Bucket
7 Buckle

brooches. The richest burial ever discovered, however, at SUTTON HOO (Suffolk), was something of a hybrid. Here an East Anglian king (or so it is assumed) was cremated and then his ashes buried in a ship sealed beneath a large earth barrow. Accompanying the burial was a fabulous array of goods including weapons, armour, jewels, and symbols of authority.

Settlements and Houses

Several Anglo-Saxon settlements have been excavated, and many more located. Most sites contain a mixture of post-built wooden halls and lesser, thatched structures with shallow storage cellars called *Gruben-häuser*. At WEST STOW, in Suffolk, buildings of both kinds have been reconstructed. Among these settlements are several interpreted, either on the basis of the buildings' size or historical evidence, as palaces: YEAVERING (Northumberland) and CHEDDAR (Somerset) are among them.

Middle Anglo-Saxon Times (650–800)

Despite the collapse of towns and most of the economy at the end of the Roman period, some long-distance trade, certainly in luxury goods, continued throughout the C5 and C6. Mediterranean pottery found on sites in western Britain presumably contained wine or oil. Then, about 700, coastal trading places (wics) began to emerge around the North Sea, at Ipswich (Suffolk), Hamwic (now SOUTHAMPTON, Hampshire), and near London and York. Further evidence of the revival of trade at this time is the re-emergence of coinage in the late C7.

Conversion to Christianity

Christianity never died out in western Britain, surviving as what is sometimes known as Celtic Christianity. In the east things were rather different and Christianity was introduced to Anglo-Saxon areas in 597 when Pope Gregory sent Augustine and a team of missionaries to Kent. Over the following half-century other kingdoms were converted. By about 700 the old pagan burial practices appear to have died out, suggesting that by this time Christianity was common at all levels of society. Many of the first purpose-built churches were minsters, home to communities of priests, who went out to preach the Gospel over wide territories. In time local churches were built within these territories, with cemeteries consecrated for the new burial rite of unaccompanied, east–west orientated inhumation. It is assumed that in many cases these churches were preceded by preaching crosses. Some carved stone examples have survived; completely lost is the wooden majority.

Scandinavian Raiding and Settlement (789 Onwards)

In 789 came the first recorded sea-borne raid by Scandinavians—the Vikings—with a landing on the ISLE OF PORTLAND (Dorset), followed in 793 by a dramatic attack on the island monastery of Lindisfarne. Attacks became more frequent from the 830s, and in time land was seized as well as booty. Norse colonies were established in north Britain, while a Danish 'Great Army' arrived on the east coast in 865, over-wintered, captured York in 866, and was only prevented from conquering the whole of southern Britain by the resistance of Alfred the Great, king of Wessex. Under him, and using a system of militia-manned fortified places known as *burhs*†—examples include WAREHAM (Dorset) and Cricklade (Wiltshire)—the Scandinavians were pushed back. After the Treaty of Wedmore (Somerset), concluded in 878, the Norse settlers were mainly confined to what became known as the Danelaw area, comprising eastern regions from the river Ouse northwards to the Tyne (Figure 16).

▼ **Fig. 16.** The political geography of England after the Treaty of Wedmore (after Reynolds)

The Scandinavian Presence

As with the Anglo-Saxons, it is unclear to what extent the Scandinavian takeover involved a mass folk movement as well as the replacement of one ruling elite by another. In so far as material remains are concerned, the archaeological evidence is limited. Most of the Scandinavian settlers in Britain were Christianized Danes, and the majority of the thirty known burial sites are single graves. The most celebrated exceptions are at REPTON, where the remains of 250 members of the Great Army which over-wintered there in 873–4 were discovered, and at nearby Ingleby, where there is a barrow cemetery, originally with fifty-nine mounds. In Yorkshire, especially, there are crosses which combine Christian and pagan iconography, while around York a distinctive type of 'hogback' grave marker is found. The most obvious evidence of a Scandinavian presence is preserved in place names, notably those ending in -by (e.g. Selby) or -thorpe (e.g. Fridaythorpe). In the old East Riding of Yorkshire ('riding' itself is a Scandinavian term, meaning a third part) nearly half of all today's place names exhibit Scandinavian influence.

Individual houses, however, have remained elusive, although it may be that they were little different from dwellings built by those who considered themselves Anglo-Saxon. One possible exception is from Goltho (Lincolnshire), where it has been suggested that a 24 m. long, bow-sided hall found in excavations beneath a castle is of a distinctively Danish form.

Late Anglo-Saxon Times and the Emergence of England (800–1066)

In the later C8 the midland kingdom of Mercia was the country's strongest. Under Offa (king 757–96) Kent and Essex were overrun, Wessex confined to south of the Thames, and the Welsh pushed back behind the great dyke that bears his name. At one point he was confident enough to call himself *Rex Anglorum*, translatable as 'King of England'. Northumbria, nevertheless, remained independent, although its king married Offa's daughter, thereby creating a close alliance.

The Viking invasions and the destruction of Northumbria and Mercia put an end to this nominal unity, but as Alfred and his successors drove back the Scandinavians the idea of a single state re-emerged. Under Alfred's son Edward (reigned 899–924) and daughter Aethelfleda (d. 918) land within the Danelaw was reconquered as far north as the Humber, while Edward's son Athelstan (reigned 924–39) received the submission of the rulers of the Scots, Welsh, and Cornish Britons. In 937 he was said to have been rowed on the river Dee near Chester by British, Welsh, and Scottish kings; a recognizable kingdom of England had been created.

Urban Revival

The Scandinavian settlement coincided with marked urban growth in England. Within Danelaw areas, for instance, Derby, Leicester, Lincoln, Nottingham, and Stamford all emerged (or were promoted) as places of trade and administration. Elsewhere in the north elements of Roman York, including its walls and some streets, were refurbished as the city was reoccupied about 870. In the great midland kingdom of Mercia King Offa and his successors founded *burhs* at places including Tamworth, Hereford, and Chester. In the south many of the *burhs* founded by King Alfred thrived in the C10 as they attracted permanent populations, traders, and manufacturers. By the end of the C10 WINCHESTER was so populous that traders and manufacturers had become grouped together, as is shown by contemporary street names such as Tanner Street, Fleshmonger Street, and Wheelwright Street.

Villages and Field-Systems

Across much of midland England wide-ranging changes took place in the countryside in the late Saxon period. Excavation at Raunds (North-amptonshire), and elsewhere, has shown that planned villages, with plots of the same size laid out in rows and sharing common boundaries, were being laid out from the early C10 onwards. The new nucleated settle-ments housed tenants whose farms were previously scattered in hamlets or as single holdings. At much the same time, and presumably as part of the same replanning, arable land was reorganized into the open fields, two or three great prairie-like corn grounds to each settlement, which remained such a distinctive feature of central England until the C18 or C19 when finally enclosed by Act of Parliament. What precipitated the reorganization of the countryside in the C10, and who was behind it, will never be known for sure. Almost certainly, however, it reflected the imposition of new taxes in an ever more hierarchical society, and the concept of tenants holding equal shares of a settlement's resources and paying in return equal shares of taxes.

The Spread of the Church

Although some of the best-known Anglo-Saxon churches—BREEDON-ON-THE-HILL (Leicestershire), REPTON (Derbyshire), Brixworth (Northamptonshire)—are of broadly middle Saxon date, the great majority are of the C10 and C11. This reflects the proliferation of local churches at this time, perhaps because for landowners a church was a status symbol. Churches and their priests were supported by a share (a tithe†) of the churchgoers' agricultural produce. The Domesday Book of 1086 records some 2,600 local churches, of which elements of about 500 still survive. In addition, it can be inferred there were perhaps several thousand more of which we know nothing.

Norman and Early Medieval England (1066–1200)

AD 1066 is perhaps the best-known date in English history; it was the year in which, on 14 October, the archers and heavy cavalry of William duke of Normandy (thereafter known as William the Conqueror) defeated the army of King Harold II near Hastings (East Sussex). William believed that he was the chosen and rightful heir to Edward the Confessor, king of England from 1042 until January 1066. On his deathbed, however, Edward promised the throne to Harold Godwinson, earl of Wessex, who had become the most powerful man in the country after the king himself. These political shenanigans provided the background to William's sea-borne invasion nine months later, depicted so graphically on the Bayeux Tapestry.

To help secure a hold on England, William constructed castles in major towns to overawe their populations and demonstrate authority. Houses were ruthlessly flattened to make way for them in Canterbury, EXETER, Shrewsbury, CAMBRIDGE, Huntingdon, and elsewhere. In NORWICH excavations found an Anglo-Saxon church which, along with ninety-eight houses (as Domesday Book records), was demolished in the course of constructing the castle. Prefabricated castles probably came with the invasion fleet. In addition the Normans reused existing defensive works such as the ruinous Saxon Shore forts, and also hastily constructed earthworks around camps and forts. As time permitted, larger, purpose-built earth and timber castles of motte† and bailey† plan, or ringworks†, were constructed (Figure 17). In a few places great stone keeps were begun, best known of which is the Tower of London. These were as much palaces and centres of government as strongholds.

William was correct in anticipating resistance from the English, and six years of hard campaigning followed the initial victory of 1066. Revolts flared in various parts of the country, to which the king's reaction was harsh, especially in his Harrying of the North, when, in the winter of 1069/70, his army systematically devastated Yorkshire, County Durham, and other adjacent areas. A high proportion of the population here was killed or became refugees, and the countryside was laid waste. According to one chronicler, the land remained untilled for nine years. Much of the infrastructure had to be rebuilt from scratch years later, and a number of the planned villages in northern England may date from this time. Wheldrake, outside York, for instance, seems to have been laid out with eight crofts† either side of the village street between 1066 and 1086.

Many of the leading Saxon landholders died at Hastings or in the revolts which followed, and in 1075 William decided on the need for a wholesale transfer of land and power from those who remained to his Norman French followers. By 1086 only two English tenants-in-chief (the main landholders) remained.

With the new aristocracy came a new language for government and

▲ **Fig. 17.** Launceston Castle, Cornwall. The motte and bailey castle as adapted about 1270 (after: Ball/English Heritage).

polite society: Anglo-Norman. There were also refinements, if not the introduction, of the system of landholding and social relations known as feudalism. In this lords supplied the king with a fixed number of knights in return for their landholdings.

At his Christmas court of 1085, held in Gloucester, William ordered the compilation of a comprehensive survey of landholdings in England. To contemporaries it seemed that here was all the information which would be needed on the Day of Judgement, and so the compiled results of the survey became known as the Domesday Book. The final volume records details of 45,000 landholdings in 14,000 places. The survey's main purpose was fiscal: to determine for the king who held what land, and what its value was.

Like their Anglo-Saxon predecessors, the post-conquest kings and queens had palaces, essentially comfortable manors on a grand scale, for example Clarendon (Wiltshire), where they could stay as they travelled around their kingdom giving governance and reinforcing their authority by their presence. Nevertheless, both for the Crown and for its aristo-cratic vassals, castles remained the real power centres throughout the early Middle Ages, combining the functions of stronghold, lordly residence, and barracks.

From about 1100 stone was increasingly used in castles, either as existing motte and baileys were remodelled in stone with the addition of a wall (shell keep) encircling the motte top and stone buildings in the bailey, or in entirely new structures. At Norwich, the Conqueror's youngest son Henry I (1130–5) built the first of a new class of square or rectangular keeps, influenced by what had been seen on crusade. Others followed at places including Portchester (Hampshire), Scarborough, Richmond, and Helmsley (all Yorkshire), and BROUGH (Cumbria).

Religious Life

In the years after the conquest, Normans, Flemings, Bretons, and other Frenchmen also took key posts as bishops and abbots in a Church which underwent major reform in the years after 1070. If castle-building emphasized and perhaps even exacerbated divisions between Norman and Saxon, church-building did, in some instances at least, give a common purpose. Enriched by the spoils of the conquest, the new aristocracy was able to embark on building works which both emphasized their piety and, through the presence of a clergy which they chose and supported, underpinned their authority. At Winchester, for instance, following the construction of a castle in 1067 and the doubling in size of the royal palace three years later, a complete rebuilding of the Anglo-Saxon minster church began in 1079. Where monasteries were founded or refounded some were independent Benedictine† houses, while more than thirty others were affiliated to the Burgundian abbey of Cluny which practised a more elaborate form of Benedictine observance, glorifying God through liturgy, music, architecture, and sculpture.

Early in the C12, in reaction to the success, worldliness, and wealth of the existing monasteries, new monastic orders were founded, among them the Savigniacs, Cistercians†, Grandmontines, Victorines, Premonstratensians†, Carthusians†, and Augustinians† (who followed the Rule of St Augustine), and military orders such as the Knights Hospitaller and the Knights Templar†. The Cistercians, the most successful, emphasized the role of manual work, austerity, and isolation for the religious. Accordingly, the sites they accepted for their new houses were usually in wild and uncultivated tracts of countryside, virgin sites which allowed the proper planning of standardized monasteries, at least initially stark and severe (Figure 18). Life for the early Cistercians was hard, deliberately so; the manual work was sapping, while within the monasteries diet was poor, there was little heating, and sleep was broken by the constant round of services. It has been calculated that about a dozen years of such asceticism was all a young man could sustain before it killed him; 28 was the average life expectancy.

There were, of course, also religious institutions for women. In Anglo-Saxon times they often coexisted alongside male monks in so-called 'double houses'. At Wimborne (Dorset), there were said to be 500 nuns in the early C8. The Scandinavian incursions of the C9 destroyed some of the double houses, and when monastic life revived in the C10

▲ **Fig. 18.** Fountains, Yorkshire, a major Cistercian abbey (Photograph: Paul Stamper)

single houses were preferred. By 1275 there were ten surviving Anglo-Saxon nunneries in England and Wales, together with 118 founded after the conquest. After 1275 only another ten were founded, albeit including England's most famous, at Syon beside the river Thames, endowed by Henry V in 1414. Some 125 nunneries survived to the Dissolution in the mid-C16, housing in all about 2,000 women.

The process of parish formation and definition continued after the conquest; in several north-western counties the number of parishes (and thereby churches) doubled between 1086 and 1250. In general, the century after 1066 saw a massive rebuilding of local churches, and a general replacement of timber manorial chapels with parish churches of stone. Excavations have shown that the first generation of stone churches were usually simple in plan, comprising one or two cells (units). They often included an apsidal east end. Sometimes a tower at the west end formed a third cell, although usually towers were later additions. While wall paintings and perhaps stained glass introduced colour to otherwise gloomy, ill-lit, interiors, furnishings were sparse. The font was the dominant internal structure. Services were conducted in Latin, and people stood in the nave while the priest went about his business. Seating was usually confined to a bench against the wall, reserved for the aged and infirm. Burial within the church was reserved for priests and patrons; everyone else was laid to rest in the surrounding churchyard.

Architecture

The style of architecture invariably adopted in building works was the Norman, or Romanesque, so called because it referred back to the classical forms used in Ancient Rome. Romanesque architecture occasionally appeared before the conquest in castles and in the early phases of Westminster Abbey built at the command of Edward the Confessor. It is characterized by heavy, load-bearing masonry, the round-headed arch and its derivatives, the groin, and barrel vaulting. Decoration is usually geometric and repetitive: lozenges, chevrons, and zigzags dominate.

About 1120 arches began to be made pointed, and from this grew the style known as Early English, the first phase of Gothic architecture in England. Salisbury cathedral, begun about 1220, is perhaps the finest example of the style, which is characterized by pointed arches, narrow lancet windows, and generally taller and architecturally lighter buildings.

High Medieval England (1200–1350)

Until the mid-C13 few people were literate. The use of writing for giving instruction or for record-keeping was extremely rare, limited to little more than certain types of royal communication and the chronicles and annals kept by some of the monasteries. Then, in the space of a few decades around 1250, during the long reign of Henry III (1216–72), it became routine. Estate accounts, legal proceedings, and title to land all began to be made in writing. It has been calculated that, in the C13 alone, some eight million charters (deeds) were drawn up for peasants, recording the sale or lease of plots of land, many of less than an acre (0.5 ha.). Rightly, this phase has been called the transition from memory to written record; the speed with which the new information technology was embraced and became commonplace is analogous with the spread of personal computers in the late C20. Not all, however, approved, and in the late C12 Henry II's Chief Justiciar commented that 'It was not the custom of old for every lesser knight to have a seal; they are proper only for kings and magnates'.

Population Growth and Rural Expansion

The C13 saw marked economic growth alongside a rapidly expanding population, which grew from about two million in 1086 to five or six million by 1300. Ever more marginal land including wetlands, heaths, and steep hillsides had to be brought into cultivation as the century progressed, much of it inherently unsuited to arable production. Lynchets† (cultivation terraces) in parts of Dorset, Wiltshire, and on the Cotswold scarps, for instance, are probably of this date. Some of this land was so poor or difficult that even during the ploughing-up campaigns of the First and Second World Wars it was left alone. Clearance of woodland and heath (assarting) continued, especially in the Weald of Kent and Sussex, in the Chiltern hills, and in the Arden district of

Warwickshire. Elsewhere the Crown allowed encroachment into woods at the core of hunting forests such as Rockingham (Northamptonshire), Melchet (Wiltshire), and Pamber (Hampshire) that had been established by the Norman kings. Inland wetlands were drained and converted either to arable or to rich pasture grounds, as with the Fenlands of East Anglia and the Somerset Levels, while low-lying coastal areas such as Romney marsh (Kent), the Essex marshes, the Pevensey Levels (East Sussex), and the south coast of Yorkshire, saw considerable investment in similar schemes. In upland areas, such as Dartmoor and Westmorland, some of the most climatically favourable conditions since the Bronze Age allowed settlement and cultivation to be pushed ever higher, and in Ryedale and Bilsdale (Yorkshire) studies have shown how secondary settlements were established on what had previously been upland pastures (Figure 19).

If the poorer peasantry were living at a bare subsistence level those with larger holdings, along with the landlords, were doing well from what has been described as a trade boom. Far more than in the past people looked to produce grain, wool, livestock, hay, fruit, and much else not only to feed their households but also to sell at market.

In the later C13 and C14 peasant houses became better built and more permanent. Where it was available, stone was used increasingly for footings or padstones, lifting structural timbers off the ground and slowing rot. In other areas, such as Kent and the West Midlands, increasingly

▼ **Fig. 19.** Houndtor. A Dartmoor village deserted in the 14th century (Photograph: Paul Stamper)

well-carpentered houses began to be constructed as peasants became sufficiently prosperous to pay professional carpenters rather than build their own houses. Landlords responded to rising prices by taking back in hand land which earlier had been leased out, and spent their wealth on stone manor houses, church-building, and deer parks. Many prudently invested in large new barns.

Towns and Trade

That the C12 and C13 were ones of growth is demonstrated most clearly by the expansion of towns and markets. The Domesday Book of 1086 recorded about 110 places as 'boroughs', which for present purposes can be taken as ones with urban characteristics. After about 1150 their number proliferated, increasing to 650 by 1310, by which time almost 20 per cent of England's population were town dwellers.

Markets, many in villages, saw rapid growth, and 1,200 places received a charter of authorization between 1227 and 1350. Not all were actually set up, but the purchase of the permission in itself indicates the economic vitality of the times, which contemporaries were aware of and wished to exploit. Another sign of this vitality was the amount of money in circulation. It has been estimated that over the course of the C13, circulating cash rose eightfold, from £125,000 to £1,100,000.

Some towns grew organically while others were deliberately promoted by their owners, attracted by the potential income from rents, tolls, and profits. Both lay and ecclesiastical interests were involved, and in the latter category come the six 'planted' towns of the bishops of Winchester, the five boroughs of the bishops of Hereford, and Stratford-upon-Avon, promoted by the bishop of Worcester. The element 'New' in a town's name (such as Newcastle, or NEWPORT) often indicates that it originated at this time, while the names of other foundations of the same period bespeak their origins and backers, as with Bishop's Castle (Shropshire), founded by the bishop of Hereford next to one of his castles.

As urban growth took off, new and distinctively urban types of house began to evolve. In major centres such as Southampton, Canterbury, and Lincoln, these were frequently built in stone, with one or two residential storeys above an undercroft used for storage and perhaps commerce.

Urban growth continued strongly until the early C14 when, reflecting most other aspects of the economy, it slowed. Not all towns, however, shared equally in the C13 prosperity. The most spectacular decline was that of Winchester, once the royal capital of Wessex and perhaps England's fourth largest town in the late C11. As it lost administrative functions its fortunes declined, and in 1334 tax records place it in fourteenth place. London, as always, headed the list, followed by York, BRISTOL, Norwich, Plymouth, COVENTRY, Lincoln, SALISBURY, KING'S LYNN, and

Colchester. Proximity of navigable water, enabling cheap and easy transport of goods, seems to have been the most recurrent factor in urban success.

Castles

By about 1200 the main defensive emphasis of castles was increasingly on the outer, curtain walls. In part, this stress on strong outer defences was a reaction to new and more powerful weapons, including crossbows and siege machines such as mangonels and trebuchets capable of throwing heavy rocks. Gatehouses became more important, while along the walls there were usually mural towers, designed as artillery platforms for archers and others as well as providing accommodation for knights and their attendant soldiers. New features included barbicans†, walls, and other outworks guarding the approach to an entrance. What are generally regarded as the military high points of castle-building are those built in Wales by Edward I (1272–1307) between 1277 and 1304, among them Caernarvon, Caerphilly, and Beaumaris. These are termed 'concentric', and are characterized by the way in which their many towers allowed overlapping fields of fire. In England itself there was nothing to match them.

Within the castle walls, at least at major castles, buildings multiplied, and became more sophisticated, in part reflecting an increasing degree of social stratification, and the likelihood that a castle would contain several different groups or households. Some became virtual palaces, largely abandoning any pretence of military effectiveness.

Religious Life

Despite their initial ideals of simplicity and poverty—or, rather, because of them, with patrons finding such idealism attractive—the reformed monastic orders prospered in the early Middle Ages. By the early C13 many of the new communities had acquired extensive estates and substantial endowments and had built monasteries which matched in scale anything constructed by those they had criticized. It was in reaction to this prosperity that yet further new reforming orders were established in the early C13, the friars. The main orders were the Friars Minor (Franciscans or Grey Friars, formed 1209) and the Order of Preachers (Dominicans or Black Friars, founded about 1214). Following the example of St Francis of Assisi these embraced absolute poverty, corporate as well as individual. The friars lived by begging, mostly in towns, where they were best placed to engage in their principal vocations, pastoral work and preaching. Preaching was sometimes undertaken in purpose-built churches, simple but with hangar-like preaching naves.

Architecture

The prosperity enjoyed by landowners in the C13 saw architectural expression through the development in about 1280 of the Decorated style. This was costly to construct, flamboyant, and characterized by ogee arches, flowing and inventive window tracery, and lighter vaulting. In churches the new style was applied to an ever-wider range of fixtures and fittings, which developed alongside and reflected an increasingly sophisticated liturgy. East-end ritual began to be conducted behind screens, and from the C14 most chancels had a rood screen†, piscina†, sedilia†, and aumbries†. Bishops began to have checklists of what every church should possess, from stone altars and fonts to images of the Virgin Mary and the patron saint.

Crisis and Calamity in the mid-C14

Those born in the early C14 who survived to old age would have witnessed a half-century as calamitous as any we have record of. After several centuries of intensive cultivation agricultural productivity had probably started to fall, living standards for most were declining, and population growth had ceased. Moreover, towards the end of the C13, the climate began to deteriorate. Areas of upland which had been brought into cultivation during the good weather of the climatic 'Little Optimum' of the C11 and C12, such as parts of Dartmoor, ceased to grow cereal crops as summers became shorter, colder, and wetter. In the second decade of the C14 a general agricultural crisis hit the country. Crop failures in 1315, 1316, and 1321, largely due to exceptionally wet summers, overlapped with catastrophic losses of animals as disease—'murrain'—devastated the nation's sheep flocks between 1313 and 1317 and its cattle 1319–21. There was also disease among the human population, including a typhoid-like epidemic in 1316. Crime rocketed as people starved.

This was as nothing to the horrors of a generation later. In June 1348 the pandemic plague known as the Black Death arrived at Melcombe Regis (now Weymouth, Dorset), previously having ravaged Asia, North Africa, and mainland Europe. By December 1349 it had spread throughout most of the British Isles. Its rapidity of spread and morbidity suggest that the plague was present in both bubonic and pneumonic forms. Contemporary accounts speak of repulsive-smelling, ashy-coloured swellings (buboes) in groin, neck, or armpit; 60 per cent of those presenting such symptoms would be dead ten days later. William Dene, a monk of Rochester, wrote that so great a multitude died 'that nobody could be found who would bear the corpses to the grave. Men and women carried their own children on their shoulders to the church and threw them into the pit.' This may have been the most deadly disease ever to hit Europe, and England's population fell from five to six million in 1347 to some three million in 1350. Plague returned in 1361 and in 1368–9, and the population level crept lower still, reaching a nadir in the later C15 at not much more than two million, the Domesday figure. Real recovery began only in the early C16.

Out of a time of tragedy came one of opportunity for those with spirit and resources. A shortage of labour led to higher wage levels, while landlords reduced rents to encourage the take-up of vacant land. Most was soon in production again, either taken on by previously landless families or amalgamated into existing holdings. Few villages were deserted as a direct result of the plague.

Late Medieval Times (1350–1530)

By 1348 urban growth had slowed dramatically, and the Black Death had taken up to 40 per cent of the country's townspeople. Squalor and the close proximity of urban living probably led to mortality rates as high as any. Thereafter most towns stagnated for a century or more, and urban growth only effectively revived under the Tudors in the C16. Queenborough, on the Isle of Sheppey (Kent), founded in 1368, seems to have been the last new town founded in the Middle Ages, and it never grew beyond a single street.

Even so, there were those who prospered, and in many towns— OXFORD, Bristol, Shrewsbury, York and many smaller places—the late Middle Ages saw the construction of ever-larger town houses, some private and some built as commercial speculations. In parts of the country where timber-framed building predominated, elaborately decorated and jettied structures appeared, some of three or more storeys. Sometimes the ground floor was given over to a series of small, lock-up shops with windows opening onto the street frontage, while on the floors above might be a hall or great chamber and the high-quality accommodation of a single family. Elsewhere upper floors were subdivided into lodgings.

The Countryside

In some parts of the countryside the demographic and social changes precipitated by the Black Death produced profound changes. Although few settlements were abandoned in 1348 itself, between 1300 and 1500 over 3,000 settlements (one-third of the total) disappeared, while in others the number of holdings was greatly reduced; villages became hamlets, and hamlets single farms. In midland, north-eastern, and south-eastern counties, numerous desertions and shrinkages followed changes in farming emphasis, from grain production to far less labour-intensive animal husbandry. Landlord graziers running sheep ranches over countryside occupied formerly by villages and fields attracted criticism in the early C16; they, however, were but the most visible manifestation of a broader and deeper trend. Another feature of the later C14 was that landlords no longer found it profitable to farm their demesnes (home farms) and instead returned to leasing them, increasing still further the amount of available land.

In villages, higher wages and larger holdings meant peasant incomes increased after the Black Death. Standards of living rose, diet improved, and more and more well-carpentered houses were constructed. Surprising numbers survive. In Kent, admittedly a county with a strong tradition of timber-framed building, there are still some 2,500 houses built between the late C13 and late C16, most of them post-dating 1370 when rebuilding began again after the disruption caused by the Black Death. Most were open-hall houses, with a living room open to the rafters and heated by a central hearth, with one- or two-storey cross wings with bedrooms, store rooms, and service rooms off one or both ends.

Church Life

The catastrophic plague losses of the Black Death helped fuel an obsession with the afterlife and to popularize chantries. These were endowments to pay for masses to be sung (Latin *cantare*, 'to sing'), usually near a tomb or effigy, for the repose of one or more souls in purgatory. Some were founded by individuals and some, for their members, by corporate bodies such as guilds or corporations, while poor parishioners might club together for a single annual obit (memorial mass). Well-endowed chantries were able to employ specific chantry priests, and to provide a chantry chapel, whether free standing or by screening off a section of a church aisle, where their duties could be performed. Large churches might have several chantries, cathedrals up to two dozen. Funerary monuments, especially figurative ones, generally repay study, and give identity to a past that is otherwise largely anonymous. It may be noted that tomb sculpture provides some of the most visible expressions of the Renaissance style in England in the first half of the C16, some (e.g. Henry VII's tomb in Westminster Abbey) produced by Italian masters such as Pietro Torrigiano.

Architecture

In about 1340, first at Gloucester cathedral, a new architectural style started to be used, the Perpendicular. So-called from the vertical lines of its window tracery and the similar effect of stone panelling used on walls, both houses and churches built in this style often have great expanses of glass and exceptionally airy and well-lit interiors. Also typical are ever more intricate types of vaulting, including 'fan' and 'pendant'. The Perpendicular was the last phase of Gothic architecture in England, and remained the predominant style until the mid-C16; the church of Bath Abbey, built 1501–39, was among the last major buildings where it was used.

Fortifications

The two centuries after 1400 saw new forms of defensive works develop in the wake of changes in the technology of warfare as gunpowder and heavy ordnance were introduced to battlefield and siege. At first, gunports were added to existing buildings (e.g. Quarr Abbey, Isle of Wight, and Southampton city walls), but from the C16 radically new types of fortifications began to be constructed to cope with artillery: forts or blockhouses that were low, squat, and with massive, absorbent earth banks, as seen in Henry VIII's coastal fortifications of the 1530s such as Hurst (Hampshire), Walmer (Kent), and PENDENNIS AND ST MAWES (Cornwall; Figure 20). Angle bastions, much seen on the Continent, were added to Portsmouth's defences in the 1540s and later to those of other dockyard towns. Little excavation has yet taken place on such sites, but at Camber Castle (East Sussex), one of the Henrician forts, it showed a rapid succession of plan changes, as engineers struggled to find a solution to the menace of artillery.

Dissolution, Reformation, and Beyond

There was no single end to the Middle Ages. Instead the concepts and institutions that had defined it each expired, some suddenly and others more gradually, to be replaced by the markers of a new age. Historians have generally taken the closing of the Wars of the Roses at the Battle of Bosworth in 1485 as the end of the Middle Ages. Archaeologists, more

▼ **Fig. 20.** St Mawes, Cornwall (Photograph: Paul Stamper)

concerned with the material world, look instead to the fundamental reforms of the Church, which took place from the 1530s.

From Monastery to Country House

Between 1536 and 1540 Henry VIII and his adviser Thomas Cromwell engineered the Dissolution of the Monasteries, an action which to contemporaries was profoundly controversial. There was no one reason for this radical action: the difficulties Henry was having in securing a divorce from Catherine of Aragon, his fundamental belief in his status as God's representative on earth, and an appreciation of the financial benefits which would follow, all played their part. A full-scale valuation, the *Valor Ecclesiasticus*, was made in 1535, while royal visitations conveniently revealed scandals and corruptions. In reality, complacency and inertia were probably the worst that most houses could be accused of. In 1536 all monasteries with an income of less than £200 were suppressed, followed in 1538 by smaller houses and friaries, and in 1539 the remaining great houses. All monastic cathedrals except Coventry were refounded as secular colleges, and some new cathedrals were established. Monks and nuns were pensioned off (few protested), while the Crown soon began to sell on monasteries and their lands to speculators. Asset-stripping was often rapid, with lead from the roofs and bells melted down, and stone and timber recycled. Not only was this profitable, it also helped to preclude any chance of a return to the old order.

At other sites at least a part of the complex was retained. Some monastic churches found a continued or a new lease of life as parish churches. Elsewhere new owners converted parts of monasteries into a country house. Most frequently it seems it was either the abbot's lodgings (or equivalent) or, as at Lacock Abbey (Wiltshire), some of the claustral buildings which were adapted. More ambitious were those schemes, as at Netley and Titchfield (Hampshire), where the monastic churches were included in the conversion. Whatever the individual solution, the claustral layout of the typical monastery was well suited as the basis for a fashionable Tudor mansion with its characteristic courtyard plan.

The mid-C16 fell in an age of transition for great houses, reflecting new lifestyles and new notions of status. The latter was no longer bound up with a communal life lived in and around a great hall, as it had been since Saxon times. Rather a person's standing was reflected more by their standards of behaviour and civility. The family became more important, the number of rooms—many now with special functions—multiplied, as did the range of their furnishings. The archetypal country house was rapidly evolving.

The Reformation of the Local Church

A decade after monasteries began to be suppressed, the reformers' attentions turned to parish churches. In the later 1540s the number of churches in major towns such as Stamford was far more than was required and many were ill-served by poorly paid clergy. To rectify this their number began to be reduced. In York, for instance, the corporation reduced the number of city churches to twenty, half of what it had been. In those that remained, many of the festivals, cult relicts, and shrines were done away with. Wall paintings were whitewashed over, statues, screens, and other fixtures stripped out, and fittings such as fonts and communion tables moved around to involve the congregation in the act of worship, now conducted in English. Churches bought Bibles published in English, and in 1549 the Book of Common Prayer appeared for the first time. Meanwhile, chantries were dissolved in 1547.

Reform ceased when Mary I came to the throne in 1553 (the Marian Reaction), and newly married priests had to return to saying masses in Latin. Under Elizabeth I (1558–1603), however, there was a return to communal worship in English, and fundamental texts such as the Creed and the Lord's Prayer began to be painted on church walls to assist the preaching of the Gospel. Over the chancel arch, in place of the terrifying vision of hell depicted by the late medieval doom paintings, there was likely to be the royal arms. At the same time, in many places, there was a return to a traditional arrangement of furnishings, a reintroduction of discarded screens and altars, and a renewed emphasis on the east end. The point has been made that in the end the Reformation saw a typical British compromise.

The Reformation, therefore, was not a single or seamless process, and to the ordinary parishioner it must have been confusing, and to many upsetting, to see the centuries-old orthodoxies cast aside, to be replaced, it must have seemed, by an uncertain modernity. Most ancient parish churches, apart from those which saw a ferocious restoration by a later, mid-C19 generation of reformers, have traces of the Reformation process: fragments of medieval wall paintings revealed beneath whitewash, or of the English texts which replaced them, empty statue niches, or holes in stone work where screens were wrenched out.

Archaeological sites arranged by region

Key to Fig. 21

1 Benwell (*Condercum*), Tyne and Wear
2 Binchester (*Vinovia*), County Durham
3 Black Carts Turret, Northumberland
4 Bowes Fort (*Lavatrae*), County Durham
5 Bowes Moor, County Durham
6 Breamish Valley Archaeological Trail, Northumberland
7 Brunton Turret, Northumberland
8 Carrawburgh (*Brocolita*), Northumberland
9 Cawfields, Northumberland
10 Chesterholm (*Vindolanda*), Northumberland
11 Chesters Bridge Abutment, Northumberland
12 Chesters Roman Fort (*Cilurnum*), Northumberland
13 Chew Green, Northumberland
14 Chillingham, Northumberland
15 Copt Hill, Tyne and Wear
16 Corbridge Roman Fort (*Corstopitum*), Northumberland
17 Corbridge (The Vicar's Pele), Northumberland
18 Denton, Tyne and Wear
19 Devil's Lapful, Northumberland
20 Dod Law, Northumberland
21 Dunstanburgh, Northumberland
22 Durham, County Durham
23 Eston Nab, Redcar and Cleveland

24 Five Barrows, Northumberland
25 Greatchesters (*Aesica*), Northumberland
26 Great Hetha Camp, Northumberland
27 Greta Bridge (*Maglona*), County Durham
28 Hadrian's Wall
29 Hasting Hill, Tyne and Wear
30 Heddon-on-the-Wall, Northumberland
31 High Rochester (*Bemenium*), Northumberland
32 Housesteads (*Vercovicium*), Northumberland
33 Jarrow (St Paul's church), Tyne and Wear
34 Lanchester (*Longovicium*), County Durham
35 Lordenshaws, Northumberland
36 Monkwearmouth (St Peter's Church), Tyne and Wear
37 Old Bewick, Northumberland
38 Piercebridge (*Morbium*), Darlington
39 Planetrees, Northumberland
40 Risingham (*Habitancum*), Northumberland
41 Sewingshields Wall, Northumberland
42 South Shields (*Arbeia*), Tyne and Wear
43 Swinburn Castle Stone, Northumberland
44 Warkworth, Northumberland
45 Wallsend (*Segedunum*), Tyne and Wear
46 Walltown Crags, Northumberland
47 Winshields, Northumberland
48 Yeavering Bell, Northumberland

1 Northumbria

This region covers the counties and unitary authorities of Northumberland, Tyne and Wear, Durham, Hartlepool, Darlington, Stockton-on-Tees, Middlesborough, and Redcar and Cleveland.

The north-east of England is a land where uplands and lowlands meet, and are never far apart. Climate, topography, and geology vary enormously over relatively short distances and these have inevitably influenced the type and disposition of archaeological sites.

▼ **Fig. 21.** Map of Region 1

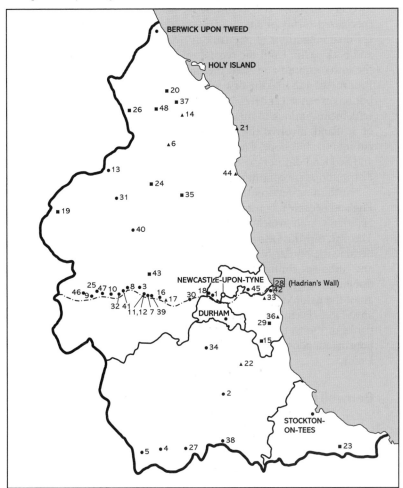

Along the coast from Loftus in the south to Berwick on Tweed in the north there is a coastal plain varying in width from just a few kilometres, where low hills meet the coast, to wide expanses around the major river valleys of the Tees, Wear, Tyne, Blyth, Wansbeck, Coquet, Aln, and Tweed. These are areas with a mild and relatively dry climate compared with that of the uplands to the west.

To the west, providing the headwaters of the many eastward-flowing rivers that join the North Sea, are some of the highest and most exposed uplands in England. In the far north are the Cheviot hills, dominated by the Cheviot rising to 816 m. above sea level. Further south is the spine of England: the Pennines. The highest peak is Cross Fell at 893 m. above sea level.

In prehistoric times it was the topography, geology, and climatic diversity that gave rise to distinctive patterns of settlement and rather specialized forms of site. In early prehistory there is evidence for the seasonal migrations of populations from the lowlands into the uplands and back again. Until the second millennium BC most people lived on the lower ground and used the uplands only occasionally. During the Bronze Age and into the first millennium BC, however, settlement distributions expanded and new habitations were created in the uplands. Some settlements, unique to this area and through into the southern uplands of Scotland, involved the construction of houses on levelled platforms cut into the hill slope. The present political boundary between England and Scotland did not exist in early times and thus many archaeological distributions are continuous between the rivers Tyne and the Forth.

In the first few centuries of the first millennium AD the north of England became a borderland. The Romans established a frontier along Hadrian's Wall which broadly follows the valley of the river Tyne. Through early historic times the land between the rivers Tyne and Tweed became the border between England and Scotland, a place of frequent and turbulent conflict. The presence of defended homesteads, fortified dwellings, and some of the most substantial castles anywhere in Britain attest the nature and longevity of the danger that people living in these areas faced. Eventually, by the C15 AD, the river Tweed and the northern flanks of the Cheviot hills provided the boundary between the neighbouring kingdoms, although not until 1707 was there a formal Act of Union.

Benwell (*Condercum*), Tyne and Wear   Roman fort, temple, and Vallum crossing on Hadrian's Wall

NZ 214647. Within suburbs of Newcastle S off A6115 at Benwell in Broombridge Avenue. Signposted. English Heritage. Figure 29 no. 4.

A fort bisected by the Newcastle to Carlisle road in 1751 and subsequently obliterated by a C19 reservoir and housing. Limited excavations in 1926–9 and 1930 found the underground storeroom of the *principia*† and other buildings.

Immediately south-east of the fort is a small C2 temple discovered in 1862. Fragments of a life-size statue, along with two ornate altars, all now in the Museum of Antiquities, Newcastle upon Tyne, show it was dedicated to Antenociticus, a youthful god with a neck torque. Three skeletons buried in cists† were found in the apse and three other altars recovered from nearby.

Nearby is the only remaining stone-built causeway across the Vallum controlled by a large gateway on the fort side.

F. Simpson and I. Richmond, 'The Roman Fort on Hadrian's Wall at Benwell', AA (4th ser.), 19 (1941), 1–43.

Binchester (*Vinovia*), County Durham   Roman cavalry fort

NZ 208314. On minor road N of A689 at Bishops Auckland, 1.5 km. N of Castle. Restricted opening. Admission charge.

A large cavalry fort occupied intermittently from AD 79 through to the C4. Part of the north and east ramparts are still visible. Excavations have revealed a hypocaust† system from a C4 bath-suite attached to the commandant's house. Recent work has exposed further rooms.

B. Dobson and M. Jarrett, 'Excavations at Binchester, 1955', TDAAS 11 (1958), 115–24.

Black Carts Turret, Northumberland   Roman turret and section of Hadrian's Wall

NY 885713. 3 km. W of Chollerford on B6318. English Heritage. Figure 29 no. 12.

A 460 m. length of restored Wall with the Narrow Wall built on Broad Wall foundations along with a turret.

P. Bidwell (ed.), Hadrian's Wall 1989–1999, CWAAS (1999), 120–2.

Bowes Fort (*Lavatrae*), County Durham   Roman fort

NY 990134. In Bowes village just S of A66, 6.5 km. W of Barnard Castle. Earthworks in a field behind the church accessible via public footpath.

Standing 9 km. west of GRETA BRIDGE, the Agricolan fort at Bowes guarded the east end of Stainmore Pass. Little of the original fort is exposed; the church covers the north-east corner, the cemetery the eastern half, and a Norman castle the north-west corner. However, the south and west ramparts are prominent as grassy banks.

R. Tomlin, 'The Roman Aqueduct at Bowes', YAJ 45 (1973), 181–4.

Bowes Moor, County Durham Roman signal station

NY 930125. 6.5 km. W of Bowes and a little E of Bowes Moor Hotel beside the A66. Lay-by on S side of road. Signal station N side of road 25 m. beyond fence.

The roughly square enclosure bounded by a turf rampart and ditch would have contained a timber signal tower in the C3–C4. Immediately north are traces of a small square camp. REY CROSS marching camp lies 3.2 km. to the west.

P. Robinson, 'The A66 Archaeology Project', CA 11/122 (1990), 62–6.

Breamish Valley Archaeological Trail, Ingram, Northumberland Prehistoric cairns†, settlements, and ancient fields

NU 008163. Waymarked circular walk of about 7 km. Starts at car park by Bulby's Wood W of Ingram Farm which is W of the Northumberland National Park Centre at Ingram, signposted W of A697 Powburn to Wooler road.

This toughish walk takes 4–5 hours, but leads through spectacular scenery. Trail guides are available from the National Park visitor centres and the numbered points noted below refer to those in the leaflet.

West of the car park mounds and hollows scattered across the hill slope are the remains of abandoned medieval and later farmsteads. At Point 3 is a Bronze Age settlement, a circular bank enclosing the stone foundations of buildings.

At the north-western corner of the trail is **Brough Law** (NT 998164), another prehistoric settlement, in this case defended by a substantial stone rampart. House foundations can be seen within the enclosure, probably of the later first millennium BC. South of the fort is a cross-ridge dyke, and in the area traversed by the path there are burial cairns and prehistoric field boundaries.

Three further prehistoric settlements are encountered in the middle section of the trail. **Middle Dean** (Point 7; NU 004147) is a substantially defended enclosure with several house foundations. **Cochrane Pike** (NU 007139) lies south of the trail and affords fine views, but defences and house foundations are indistinct. At **Wether Hill** (Point 9; NU 014145) a linear earthwork cuts off the approach to the hillfort†, as at Brough Law. Inside the fort are two kinds of house foundation: ring grooves probably for wooden structures, and stone foundations for later buildings. Nearby are areas of narrow rig and furrow (hand-cultivation using spades) from early farming.

The final section of trail passes through areas of ancient cultivation, of prehistoric, medieval, and later date. **Ingram Hill** (Point 11; NU 012159) is another prehistoric settlement. The circular enclosure boundary dates to about 300 BC. Rectangular stone structures built into the rampart are probably for medieval shepherds.

P. Topping, 'Excavation and Survey of Wether Hill', AN 14 (1997), 6–11.

Brunton Turret, Northumberland Roman turret and Hadrian's Wall

NY 923698. 0.5 km. N of Low Brunton village W of A6079. English Heritage. Figure 29 no. 9.

Restored turret: 60 m. of Wall flanks the turret with the Broad Wall running up to it on the west side while to the east the Narrow Wall stands on Broad Wall foundations.

J. Collingwood Bruce, Handbook to the Roman Wall, *13th edn. (Harold Hill, 1978), 104.*

Carrawburgh (*Brocolita*), Northumberland Roman fort and Mithraeum on Hadrian's Wall

NY 858710. 6 km. W of Chollerford on B6318. English Heritage. Car park. Figure 22; Figure 29 no. 13.

Traces of a fort built astride the Vallum with a late C3 temple to the south-west of the fort dedicated to the Persian sun god Mithras. Concrete facsimiles of the altars are present. The original temple was built around AD 205 and underwent several modifications before being destroyed. Bird and animal bones and pine cones from ritual activities were found. A reconstruction of the temple can be seen in the Museum of Antiquities, Newcastle upon Tyne.

▼ **Fig. 22.** The Roman Temple of Mithras, Carrawburgh (*Brocolita*), Northumberland (Photograph: Jane Timby)

West of the fort is **Coventina's Well**; C19 excavations yielded coins, jewellery, leatherwork, votive objects, and stone altars. Some are in the museum at CHESTERS.

L. Allason-Jones and B. McKay, Coventina's Well *(Trustees of the Clayton Collection, 1985); D. Breeze, 'Excavations at Carrawburgh', AA, 4th ser., 50 (1972), 81–144.*

Cawfields, Northumberland Roman milecastle†, turrets, camps, fortlet, on Hadrian's Wall

NY 716667. 2 km. N of Haltwhistle off B6318. English Heritage. Parking. Figure 29 no. 20.

Various Roman sites concentrated on consolidated stretch of Hadrian's Wall including an early fortlet. A temporary Roman camp lies east of the track to the milecastle. Here is also one of the best-preserved sections of Vallum earthwork and ditch.

D. Charlesworth, 'Recent Work on Hadrian's Wall, Cawfields', AA, 4th ser., 46 (1968), 69–74.

Chesterholm (*Vindolanda*), Northumberland Roman fort, settlement, milestone ★★

NY 771664. 2.5 km. SE of Twice Brewed on minor road off B6318. Restricted opening. Site owned by Vindolanda Trust. Site Museum. Car park and other facilities. Admission charge. Tel. 01434 344277. Website: www.vindolanda.com. Figure 29 no. 16.

An extensive programme of excavation and the discovery of some unique finds has made Chesterholm one of the more famous Roman sites in Britain. The fort, an Agricolan foundation established as part of the Stanegate frontier system, went through at least eight rebuilds. The best of the visible remains date to the C4. Of particular note is the headquarters building still showing parts of the ventilated floors, ornamental stone screens, and a pit for storing the pay chest. Many other remains are visible including the bath-house, *mansio*† (inn) and a replica section of the Wall itself.

Exceptional conditions have preserved many organic materials including numerous shoes and over 400 writing tablets, some on display in the Museum. Dating from around 100–20 the tablets include official reports, duty rosters, cash accounts, records of supplies and stores issued and requested, and personal letters, providing a fascinating insight into fort life.

In the museum gardens are several reconstructions including a Roman temple, shop, house, and Northumbrian croft†, all with audio presentations. The annual summer excavations have investigated the *vicus*† outside the defences as well as buildings in the fort.

P. Bidwell, The Roman Fort of Vindolanda *(Batsford and English Heritage, 1985).*

Chesters Bridge Abutment, Northumberland

Roman bridge abutment on Hadrian's Wall

NY 914700. Take signposted path alongside B6318 along a disused railway line on the opposite side of the river to Chester fort (below). English Heritage. Figure 29 no. 10.

Fragments of the bridge that carried Hadrian's Wall across the North Tyne are visible on each bank, the most impressive being on the east side. A short stretch of the Wall leads from the east abutment to a gatehouse tower.

P. Bidwell and N. Holbrook, Hadrian's Wall Bridges, *HBMCE Archaeological Report 9 (English Heritage, 1989).*

Chesters Roman Fort (*Cilurnum*), Northumberland
Roman fort on Hadrian's Wall ★

NY 912701. 1 km. W of Chollerford on B6318. English Heritage. Restricted opening. Admission charge. Car park and other facilities. Site Museum. Figure 23; Figure 29 no. 11.

Situated between the twenty-seventh and twenty-eighth milecastles†, Chesters is one of the Wall's best-preserved forts. It has a characteristic rectangular plan astride the Wall with a gate on each side. Foundations of internal buildings can be seen, including the headquarters building (*principia*†), the commandant's house, and three barrack blocks.

Originally the fort was garrisoned by a 500-strong Spanish cavalry unit—*ala II Asturum* (the Second Asturian Horse). The remains of the bath-house stands between the river and the fort.

The **Clayton Memorial Museum** displays artefacts from the fort and surrounding area.

J. Johnson, Chesters Roman Fort *(English Heritage, 1990) (Site Guidebook).*

Chew Green, Northumberland Roman camps ★★
NT 788085. Access is via a single-track no-through road leading N from A68 at Redesdale Camp. The track, some 12 km. long, winds through some remote but impressive countryside. Limited car-parking. Information board. Figure 24.

At 450 m. above sea level immediately south of the Scottish border, this is the northernmost Roman military installation in England. The access road follows the line of the Roman **Dere Street** for 6 km. and passes other Roman camps at **Sill Burn** (NT 824999), **Silloans** (NT 823007), **Featherwood East** (NT 8200570), and **Featherwood West** (NT 814057).

Chew Green itself is very complicated. Excavations in 1936 distinguished at least four partly superimposed, successive camps (I–IV).

The earliest and largest (I), an Agricolan marching camp of about AD

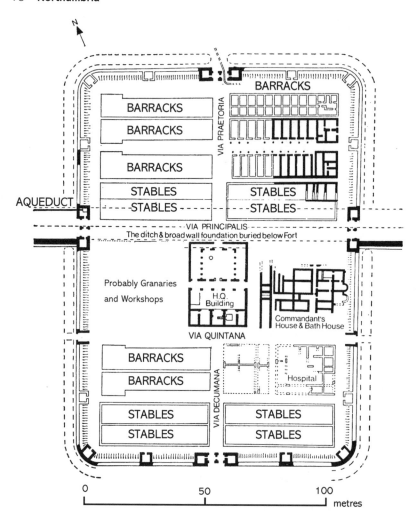

▲ **Fig. 23.** Plan of Chesters (*Cilurnum*) Roman fort, Northumberland (after Daniels 1978)

80, occupied the prime position on the hilltop. It could have held a full legion. The south and west sides only are preserved. Camp II, a mid-C2 temporary camp, lies to the north of Camp I. Camp III, also mid-C2, was built inside the earthworks of I but was a more permanent installation. Finally, Camp IV was built, a smaller permanent fortlet east of III. Two annexes were possibly wagon parks.

S. Frere and J. St Joseph, Roman Britain from the Air *(Cambridge University Press, 1983), 140–2.*

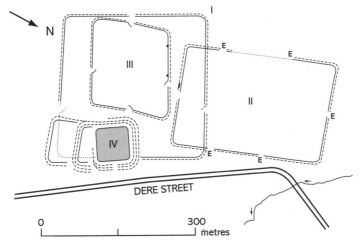

▲ **Fig. 24.** Plan of the Roman military earthworks at Chew Green, Northumberland (after Daniels 1978); E = entrance;

Chillingham, Northumberland Parkland, wild cattle

NU 062260. Signposted from Chillingham, 2.5 km. from Chatton, itself 8 km. from Wooler on B6348 to Bamburgh. Restricted opening (mainly during the summer). Figure 25.

Here is one of only four herds of so-called wild cattle, the other English example now being at Woburn (Bedfordshire). The ancestors of the

▼ **Fig. 25.** A Chillingham bull, 1789 (Thomas Bewick)

present herd were probably established here by the C13 when a royal licence was granted to crenellate the castle and to create a park. Today the only human interference is hay-feeding; no bulls were castrated in the C20 and the last culling was in 1918.

S. Hall and J. Clutton-Brock, Two Hundred Years of British Farm Livestock *(HMSO, 1989), 44–6.*

Copt Hill, Houghton-le-Spring, Tyne and Wear   Neolithic
round barrow†

NZ 353492. SE of Houghton-le-Spring, towards W end of a golf course S of B1404.

This tree-covered barrow stands about 2.4 m. high and is 20 m. in diameter. Excavations in 1877 revealed that below the mound was a crematorium containing the burnt remains of several individuals. This kind of burial is typical of the earlier Neolithic, about 4000 BC. Later in the early Bronze Age four inhumations and four cremations were added.

R. Young, 'The Copt Hill Round Cairn', AA, *5th ser., 13 (1985), 7–17.*

Corbridge Roman Fort (*Corstopitum*), Northumberland
Roman fort and settlement   ★

NY 982648. 1 km. NW of modern Corbridge on minor road, signposted. English Heritage. Restricted opening. Admission charge. Car park and other facilities. Site Museum. Figure 29 no. 7.

Agricolan fort, later the base for northern military campaigns. A succession of forts and a military depot stood on what was the main road northwards from YORK. The visible remains are mainly Severan and later, and include the main street, the Stanegate, and two large granaries. Workshops and administrative buildings can also be seen. The settlement became a market town active until the C5.

Nearby is **Hexham Herb Garden**, with reconstructed Roman herb and knot gardens.

M. Bishop and J. Dore, Corbridge: Excavation of the Roman Fort and Town 1947–80, *HBMCE Archaeological Report 8 (English Heritage, 1989).*

Corbridge (The Vicar's Pele), Northumberland   Medieval
tower house

NY 989644. In Corbridge, on A69 25 km. west of Newcastle upon Tyne. The pele is an information centre, open daily.

Pele towers are characteristic of the northern borderlands. Essentially they are tower houses, strong stone dwellings which offered some security against attack, albeit with little option for offensive return. Around them might be a palisaded enclosure into which stock could be driven. The Corbridge pele, built of reused Roman stonework, lies on the edge of the churchyard and was the vicar's house. It has three storeys. Unusually the door, reinforced with iron bars, is on the ground floor. This leads into a vaulted basement, lit by loopholes. Steps within the wall lead up to the living accommodation, a room with fireplace, garderobe†, and sink. On the third floor is a bedchamber, which may also have served as an oratory. At roof level is a wall walk. Built about 1300; the Scots burnt it out five times within its first fifty years. It remained in use until the C17.

R. Newton, The Northumberland Landscape (Hodder & Stoughton, 1972), 100–1.

Denton, Tyne and Wear Roman turret and Hadrian's Wall

NZ 198655. 6.5 km. W of Newcastle city centre at Denton on A69. English Heritage. Figure 29 no. 5.

The first turret known west of Newcastle. The foundations and a 65 m. section of restored Wall are visible. A platform base for a ladder would have given access to the parapet walk. Recent excavations noted a plaster render on the north face of the Wall.

P. Bidwell and M. Watson, 'Excavations on Hadrian's Wall at Denton, Newcastle upon Tyne', AA, 5th ser., 24 (1996), 1–56.

Devil's Lapful, Kielder, Northumberland Neolithic long

barrow†

NY 642928. In Kielder Forest to the N of Bakethin Reservoir. 1.5 km. SE of Kielder. Approached via forest tracks from Butteryhaugh. Figure 26.

A fine, typical Cheviot-region long barrow built of large rounded boulders. It is 58 m. long, 14 m. wide, and up to 2 m. high. The robbed north-east end probably had a pair of projecting horns† and a small forecourt. The better-preserved south-west terminal is rounded. Traces of the stone kerb can be seen on the east side. Modern sheepfolds obscure the north-west edge of the mound.

L. Masters, 'The Neolithic Long Cairns of Cumbria and Northumberland', in R. Miket and C. Burgess (eds), Between and Beyond the Walls (John Donald, 1984), 52–73.

Dod Law, Doddington (nr Wooler), Northumberland

Iron Age hillfort† and prehistoric rock art   ★★

NU 004317. On the hilltop 1 km. SE of Doddington village. Footpath from Doddington. Part golf course and part moorland. Figure 27.

Two later prehistoric hillforts stand on the edge of a steep slope with magnificent views westwards. Numerous decorated stones lie round about.

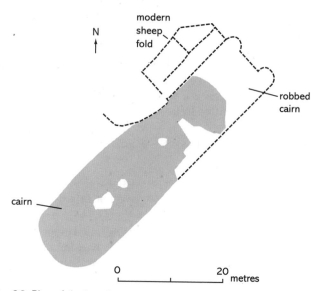

▲ **Fig. 26.** Plan of the long barrow known as the Devil's Lapful, Kielder, Northumberland (after Masters)

▼ **Fig. 27.** Rock art on a boulder at Dod Law, Doddington (nr Wooler), Northumberland (after Beckensall)

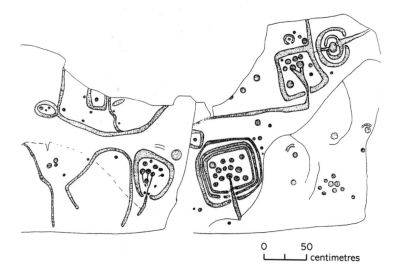

The western hillfort is the more impressive, and was probably a defended farmstead and stockyard. D-shaped in plan, it is bounded by a pair of concentric banks 6 m. wide and in places up to 2.7 m. high. Inside are at least ten circular houses ranging from 3.6 to 5.4 m. across. To the north-west is a small annexe delimited by a single bank which was perhaps a stockyard. North-east of the annexe is a circular house foundation with slight traces of two sub-rectangular structures to the east. Excavations identified three phases to the development of the main enclosure, beginning about 500 BC. The site continued in use until about AD 100.

The eastern hillfort is sub-rectangular in plan, about 0.6 ha. in extent, and bounded by a bank and outer ditch. The bank is about 3 m. wide and 0.5 m. high. There are entrances to the north-east and south-west, the latter being funnel-shaped in plan.

Between the two hillforts there are two good examples of decorated stones dating to the Neolithic or early Bronze Age. One is on the upper surface of a large earthfast boulder, the other on a natural outcrop of stone. Various motifs are visible. Other decorated stones are known in the area and some are indicated on Ordnance Survey maps; permission to visit should be obtained as most lie on private land.

C. Smith, 'Excavations at Dod Law West Hillfort', Northern Archaeology 9 (1990), 1–55.

Dunstanburgh, Northumberland Medieval castle

NU 258220. 10 km. NE of Alnwick, off A1. Approached via an easy 2 km. coastal walk from either Craster, to the S, or Embleton to the N. English Heritage. Restricted opening. Admission charge. Figure 28.

The castle's cliff-top setting was chosen for the security it offered by its builder Thomas, earl of Lancaster. When work began in 1313 Thomas, England's leading baron, faced two potential enemies: the Scots, who had again begun to raid south from the border 40 km. to the north, and the king, Edward II, whose unpopular homosexual paramour, Piers Gaveston, Lancaster had had judicially murdered in 1312.

The Scottish threat explains the castle's great extent (4.5 ha.): herein was refuge for the earl's tenants and their beasts. The main feature of the curtain wall is Lancaster's great early C14 twin-towered gatehouse. In the late 1380s it was succeeded as the main gate by John of Gaunt's gatehouse (now reduced to foundation level) and became the keep instead. Along the south curtain are three towers: the Constable's, occupied by the commanding officer; a small turret; and Egyncleugh's Tower, over the cliff-edge 'clough' or ravine. The most imposing tower, the Lilburn Tower, stands on the west curtain wall. This, some 18 m. tall, was built as a watch-tower, dominating the north-west approach, and as lodgings for soldiers.

Dunstanburgh saw action in 1385 when a Scottish attack was

1 Lilburn Tower	8 Constable's Tower
2 Sea Cliff	9 Thomas of Lancaster's Gatehouse
3 Outer Ward	10 Mantlet
4 East Curtain Wall	11 John of Gaunt's Gatehouse
5 Postern Gate	12 West Curtain Wall
6 Egyncleugh Tower	13 Inner Ward
7 South Curtain Tower	

▲ **Fig. 28.** Dunstanburgh Castle, Northumberland (after Ball/English Heritage)

successfully beaten off. Later, during the Wars of the Roses, it was a Lancastrian stronghold and was besieged in 1462 and 1464. Little used thereafter it was sold by the Crown to a private owner in 1604.

H. Summerson, Dunstanburgh Castle *(English Heritage, 1993) (Site Guidebook).*

Durham, County Durham Medieval city ★★

NZ 2742. Durham lies on the A1(M) 22 km. S of Newcastle upon Tyne.

From Norman times Durham was the principal centre of government in the north, with the bishop of Durham acting in most things as the king's representative. The city is dominated by the hilltop castle, built by the Conqueror in 1072 as a fortress for the bishop. In the mid-C12 a timber tower on four corner posts probably stood within a shell keep; the irregular octagonal keep which now rises from the motte† was largely rebuilt in 1840. Below it, in the bailey†, are the remains of chapel, halls, and domestic buildings. The cathedral, protected by the castle and high above the river Wear, is one of the finest of the great Norman churches. Already the resting place of St Cuthbert—his miraculously uncorrupted body was brought here to save it from the Danes in 995—it was rebuilt from 1093. To the initial phase belongs the chancel (or choir), while to the first thirty-three years of the C12 belong the nave with its drum piers deep cut with incised decoration, transepts, and west towers. The wonderful, lightly columned Galilee Chapel at the west end was added c.1170 to house the bones of the Venerable Bede, stolen from JARROW. The east end is C13, the central tower C15. Also post-Norman are most of the monastic buildings to the south, which in the Middle Ages were home to the monks who served the cathedral.

B. Roberts, Durham *(Batsford and English Heritage, 1994).*

Eston Nab, Guisborough, Redcar and Cleveland Iron Age hillfort†

NZ 568184. Approached by footpath from B1380 at Lackenby on the E outskirts of Middlesborough, or via one of numerous footpaths from the S.

This striking prehistoric promontory fort of about 400 BC lies perched on sandstone cliffs with a commanding view of the Tees estuary.

The 1.3 ha. hillfort is defined on the north-west side by a steep hill slope and cliffs partly eroded by C19 quarrying. Its south-east side is defined by a substantial earthwork about 400 m. long, comprising a bank, ditch, and counterscarp bank†. There was an entrance to the south-east; other causeways are recent additions.

Excavations revealed part of a round barrow†, about halfway between the ends of the ramparts; inside the hillfort were two successive later Bronze Age enclosures.

B. Vyner, 'The Hillfort at Eston Nab', Arch J, *145(1988), 60–98.*

Five Barrows, Holystone, Alwinton, Northumberland

Bronze Age barrow cemetery

NT 953020. Best approached from the W via footpath SW from Holystone.

Situated on a gentle hill slope south of Holystone is a small Bronze Age barrow cemetery, which, despite its name, comprises at least nine and perhaps as many as fourteen round barrows†. Some were excavated by Canon Greenwell in the 1870s. Both cremations and inhumations were found, and a range of grave goods including food vessels, collared urns, bone pins, and flint tools. Together these suggest a late Neolithic and early Bronze Age date for the cemetery.

South of the barrow cemetery is the **Five Kings** stone row† (NT 955001), said to represent five brothers, all kings. Stone rows are rare in the north of England, and this is probably the best preserved. Four stones are standing, and one is prostrate.

W. Greenwell, British Barrows *(Clarendon Press, 1877), 422–8.*

Round barrows

Round barrows are one of the most common kinds of prehistoric monument. They were built from the early Neolithic through to the middle Bronze Age, a period of more than 3000 years. All share two basic traits: a circular outline and a heaped mound over one or more burials. Details of the burial rites associated with round barrows vary enormously according to date and local traditions. (See Fig. A.)

Round barrows are traditionally classified according to their profile. Most common is the **bowl barrow**, a simple hemispherical mound like an up-turned pudding basin. Sometimes a kerb of stones or posts defines the edge of the mound and gives it more vertical sides. The more complicated kinds of round barrow are referred to as '**fancy barrows**'; there are four main types.

Bell barrows are usually surrounded by a ditch and outer bank separated from the mound by a narrow berm to give the impression that the mound is set on a platform. The mound has steep sides and a flange towards the bottom. Where ditches cannot be dug a platform and slight bank are made; these are **platformed barrows** or **rimmed platform barrows.**

Saucer barrows have a circular enclosure of bank and ditch or a platform, but the central mound is low, like an up-turned saucer. There is a berm between the mound and the surrounding earthwork or the edge of the platform.

Disc barrows are like saucer barrows but the mound is small in diameter as well as low in height.

Pond barrows are like inverted barrows. They have an enclosing bank and ditch, but instead of a mound in the middle they have a hollow or depression about 0.5 m. deep. In a few cases there is a deep shaft in the centre.

Other types of round barrow include **ring cairns** in upland areas where a circular area is defined by a low bank of stones, and **tor cairns** where a prominent stone or rock outcrop is surrounded by a bank of stones.

Greatchesters (*Aesica*), Northumberland   Roman fort on
Hadrian's Wall

NY 704667. To the W of Winshield milecastle†. 3 km. N of Haltwhistle off B6318. English Heritage. Parking. Figure 29 no. 19.

The remains of an infantry fort south of the Wall. The fort, measuring 128 × 102 m., has a blocked west gate. Details of the layout are unclear but a bath-house was found some 90 m. to the south which received water via an aqueduct from the head of Haltwhistle burn.

D. Breeze and B. Dobson, 'Fort Types on Hadrian's Wall', AA, 4th ser., 47 (1969), 15–32.

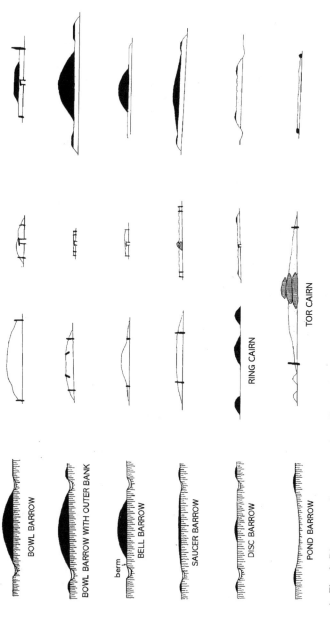

BOWL BARROW

BOWL BARROW WITH OUTER BANK

berm

BELL BARROW

SAUCER BARROW

DISC BARROW

POND BARROW

RING CAIRN

TOR CAIRN

▲ **Fig. A.** Diagrammatic cross-sections illustrating the range of round barrow types in England

Great Hetha Camp, Hethpool, Northumberland   Iron Age

hillfort††

NT 885274. Best approached along the bridleway beside the College Burn from Hethpool. Steep climb to Camp.

An oval hillfort (0.5 ha.) occupying a commanding position overlooking the College Burn. It is delimited by two roughly concentric banks, the inner one probably the remains of a wall. The hill slopes are less steep to the east and here the outer bank curves outwards to leave a substantial space between the two banks. Here is also a staggered entrance with the inner bank slightly in-turned. Traces of house foundations lie within the main enclosure, and between the two banks near the entrance are the remains of a two-cell stone structure. The site probably dates to the later first millennium BC. Many of the surrounding hills are also crowned with small circular or oval camps.

North-east of the camp on a level knoll west of College Burn is the ruinous **College Burn Stone Circle** [NT 892278]. Eight stones remain in what is best reconstructed as an open oval or U-shaped setting roughly 61 × 42 m. Three stones lie outside the circle to the north-east, the most southerly with possible ring-marks.

H. Honeyman, 'The Standing Stones of Hethpool', PSAN, 4th ser., 6 (1935), 116–17.

Greta Bridge (*Maglona*), County Durham   Roman fort

NZ 085133. 5 km. SE of Barnard's Castle, S of A66 by the river Greta. Turn off at the Morritt Arms Hotel towards Brignal. The fort site lies E of the road beside the river.

The hotel sits on top of the northern defences, but traces of the fort's ramparts can be seen as earthworks in the first field on the left. Originally, this fort formed part of the Stainmore Pass defensive system lying 8.7 km. east of BOWES FORT.

P. Casey and B. Hoffmann, 'Rescue Excavations in the vicus of the Fort at Greta Bridge, Co. Durham', Britannia, 29 (1998), 111–83.

Hadrian's Wall, Northumberland and Tyne and Wear

Roman frontier work

Hadrian's Wall is one of the most extensive archaeological monuments in England and is a World Heritage site. It stretches from Wallsend on the river Tyne in the E across to the Solway Firth in the W; parts are found in Regions 1 and 2 of this guide. Most extant parts of the wall are within reach of public transport. The Newcastle to Carlisle railway runs close by with numerous halts and stops along the way. Park and Ride Schemes and organized guided day trips are run by the Hadrian's Wall Bus Company from Hexham, Carlisle, and Tyneside during the summer—tickets

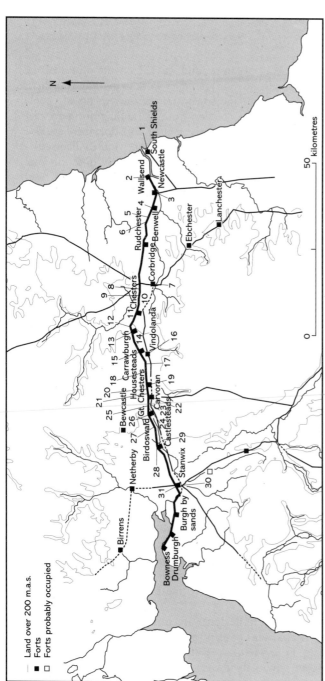

▲ **Fig. 29.** Map of Hadrian's Wall showing location of sites mentioned in the text. 1. South Shields; 2. Wallsend; 3. Newcastle Museum; 4. Benwell; 5. Denton; 6. Heddon-on-the-Wall; 7. Corbridge; 8. Planetrees; 9. Brunton; 10. Chesters Bridge; 11. Chesters fort; 12. Black Carts; 13. Carrawburgh; 14. Sewingshields; 15. Housesteads; 16. Chesterholm (Vindolanda); 17. Once Brewed; 18. Winshields; 19. Cawfields; 20. Greatchesters; 21. Walltown Crags; 22. Carvoran; 23. Poltross Burn; 24. Willowford; 25. Harrow's Scar; 26. Birdoswald; 27. Leahill and Piper Sike; 28. Banks East and Pike Hill; 29. Hare Hill; 30. Carlisle; 31. Stanwix.

available from Tourist Information centres at Carlisle, Haltwhistle, Once Brewed, Hexham, or the driver. There are car parks at intervals along the Wall, some of which make charges. A National Trail is being developed along the entire Wall. Figures 11 and 29.

Construction of the Wall began around AD 122 on the orders of the Emperor Hadrian for a frontier or boundary work to mark the northern limits of the Roman Empire and to control the movements of people and goods. It also provided protection from marauding northern barbarian tribes. The site acts as a military zone or corridor; there are also forts and supply stations, lines of communications, and civilian settlements. Some lie well south of the Wall itself. Nowhere does the Wall stand to its full height, and much of what is visible today has been restored. It is now generally accepted that there was originally a walkway along the top. We also know that in places at least the Wall was well finished, with plaster at DENTON and with whitewash at Peel Gap, a turret lying between WINSHIELDS and HOUSESTEADS.

It took about six years to complete the first 117 km. stretch from Wallsend-on-Tyne in the east to Bowness-on-Solway in the west. It was a massive undertaking: a wall up to 3 m. thick and 4.5–6 m. high was constructed partly in stone and partly in turf. A small fort or milecastle† was built every Roman mile, and between the milecastles were two turrets. These structures have been numbered by archaeologists in sequence from east to west.

Although the Wall was planned as a curtain wall, 3 m. thick, it was not always built to this width. Various lengths are referred to as the Broad Wall or the Narrow Wall reflecting the two main construction types. The 3 m. wide Broad Wall foundations form the base for much of the Wall's length; sometimes the Narrow Wall is built on these foundations. A third, even narrower, build has been identified in some parts, possibly C3. Immediately north of the Wall was a massive defensive ditch. A little way to the south of the Wall was another ditch, the Vallum, which defined a sort of military zone. Between the Vallum and the Wall lay the main roadway linking all the installations together and providing the main supply route. Several milestones survive from along this road.

Forts were constructed to garrison auxiliary troops, and to act as supply bases; in time these attracted civilian settlements. Other military outposts were constructed to the north. Inscriptions show that the soldiers on active duty on the Wall were drawn from all over the Roman Empire, mainly Gaul, Germany, Spain, the Balkans, and the Austrian Alps.

The main sites to visit in Region 1 are, from east to west (see Figure 29), SOUTH SHIELDS, WALLSEND, BENWELL, DENTON, HEDDON-ON-THE-WALL, PLANETREES, BRUNTON, CHESTERS BRIDGE, CHESTERS FORT, BLACK CARTS, CARRAWBURGH, SEWING-SHIELDS, HOUSESTEADS, WINSHIELDS, GREATCHESTERS, CAW-

FIELDS, and WALLTOWN CRAGS. To these should be added CHES-
TERHOLM (*Vindolanda*) and CORBRIDGE, on the Stanegate frontier
just S of the wall. These are described under individual entries. Some
have their own museums and displays; additional museums and visitor
centres for the Wall in Region 1 include: Museum of Antiquities, Newcastle upon Tyne, Tyne and Wear (on the University Campus near
Haymarket Metro. Figure 29 no. 3) and the National Park Visitor Centre
at **Once Brewed, Northumberland** (NY 753669. Figure 29 no. 17).

S. Johnson, Hadrian's Wall *(Batsford and English Heritage, 1989); R. Woodside and
J. Crow,* Hadrian's Wall: An Historic Landscape *(National Trust, 1999). See also the
Ordnance Survey's Outdoor Leisure Map 43 (1:25,000 scale), which shows the
wall with associated Roman sites.*

Hasting Hill, Offerton, Tyne and Wear Neolithic round
barrow†

*NZ 353544. E of the A19(T) on the outskirts of Sunderland. Best approached via
the unclassified road off A183 to Middle Herrington.*

Although now modest in appearance, this round barrow, with a mound
1 m. high and 12 m. across, was the centre of activity and reuse over
many centuries. Excavated in 1911, the primary burial dates to about
2500 BC and comprised a crouched inhumation in a cist† accompanied
by a beaker, bone pin, and flint tools. This lay off centre of the mound,
which was raised over it. Within and under the mound were human
bones from at least ten inhumations (three in stone cists and a fourth in
a rock-cut grave), flints, animal bones, and the parts of two Neolithic
pots.

In the early Bronze Age further cremation burials were added. Four
were contained in small stone-lined cists and two in collared urns. Finds
and reconstructions of some of the cists can be seen in Sunderland
Museum.

C. Trenchman, 'Prehistoric Burials', AA, *3rd ser., 11 (1914), 119–76.*

Heddon-on-the-Wall, Northumberland Section of Hadrian's
Wall

*NZ 137669. Immediately E of Heddon village, 1 km. S of A69, via B 6528 to
B6318. English Heritage. Figure 29 no. 6.*

A stretch of restored wall up to 3 m. thick. The remains of a circular
medieval kiln can be seen near the west end. The ditch of the Vallum is
seen in the hamlet of Heddon-on-the-Wall as a sunken lane parallel to
the main road.

J. Collingwood Bruce, Handbook to the Roman Wall, *13th edn (Harold Hill,
1978), 75.*

High Rochester (*Bremenium*), Northumberland   Roman fort

NY 833986. The fort can be reached via a minor road off A68 at S end of village by the war memorial. Limited parking inside fort. Access is by foot and onto private land; permission should be sought at the farm. A new archaeological reconstruction centre called Brigantium can be found in Rochester village. Leaflets from Northumberland National Park, Eastburn, South Park, Hexham NE46 1BS. Figure 30.

The porch of the house opposite the war memorial in the village is built from reused Roman stonework including stone gutters and two catapult balls. The fort is approximately 0.75 km. up the road, which passes through the rampart via what would have been the southern gate. Immediately left of the road at this point is a C4 interval tower with a clearly blocked doorway. The Roman road, Dere Street, lies to the east of the site. The first Agricolan fort was abandoned by about AD 100; most of what can be seen is C3 work when the fort was reoccupied.

From the centre of the fort access can be gained through farm gates to most of the defensive circuit. The gate to the left on a track cutting through the rampart leads to the massive stone block remains of the C4 west gate. Following the rampart line, further masonry can be found both to the left and right of the gate. Returning to the centre, access can be gained to the north-west corner; from here the playing-card shape of another fort, Birdhope, is visible on the facing slope. The multiple ditch system of High Rochester can then be followed round to the right to the east gate and then back to the centre.

R. Walton, 'The Roman Fort of Bremenium', HBNC 35/2 (1960), 104–11.

▼ **Fig. 30.** View of the West gate at High Rochester (*Bremenium*) Roman fort, Northumberland. The blocking is of more recent date (Photograph: Jane Timby)

Housesteads (*Vercovicium*), Northumberland Roman fort
and milecastle† on Hadrian's Wall ★★

NY 790688. 5 km. NE of Bardon Mill on B6318. English Heritage and National Trust. Museum and fort have restricted opening. Admission charge. Car park on main road approx 1 km. from site. Figure 29 no. 15.

The 2 ha. Roman fort occupies a commanding position on the cliffs of the Whin Sill. It was one of the twelve permanent forts built by Hadrian and is one of the most complete. Amongst the remains are four gates, the military headquarters, commandant's house, barracks, granaries, the only visible Roman hospital in Britain, and latrines with a flush system. A *vicus*† developed outside the gates. Numerous excavations have allowed a detailed picture of life in the fort. It was built to garrison an infantry cohort of some 800 men reinforced in the C3 by additional cavalry and infantry.

East of Housesteads is C3 **Knag Burn Gate**, one of only two isolated gates allowing alternative access through the wall. It has been partially reconstructed.

J. Crow, Housesteads *(Batsford and English Heritage, 1989).*

Jarrow (St Paul's), Tyne and Wear Anglo-Saxon monastery

NZ 3465. Jarrow is an eastern suburb of Newcastle upon Tyne, the principal road serving it being the A19. Within the city it is approached most easily by using the Metro, alighting at Bede or Jarrow. Figure 31.

A religious community was founded at Jarrow in 681–2 by Benedict Biscop, abbot of Wearmouth (*see* MONKWEARMOUTH), and the two were thought of as parts of the same monastery. The dedication stone over the chancel records the dedication of St Paul's Church in 685. This was the home of the scholar and historian Bede (d. 735) and the place where he wrote his *History of the English Church and People.*

Originally, as at so many Saxon monasteries, there were two churches here, positioned end-to-end. The smaller, more easterly, one survives as the chancel of the present church. There are three original windows, with tiny circular apertures for glass in the south wall, and a blocked door in the north. The other, western, monastic church was demolished in 1782; it was a much larger building with west porch, nave with chapels to either side, and a chancel. Its site is occupied by the nave and aisle of Sir George Gilbert Scott's church of 1866.

Domestic buildings lay to the south, and the foundations of what may have been a refectory and hall are laid out. Other buildings relate to the monastery refounded here after the Norman Conquest. Probably also of about the 1070s is the church tower, which originally linked the two monastic churches.

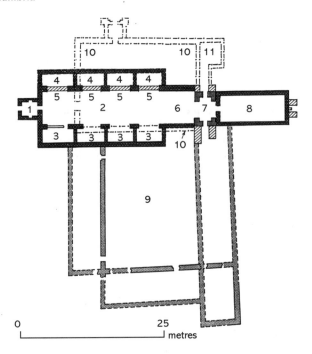

1 West porch
2 Nave
3 South chapels (1, 2, and 3: original main church
      demolished in 1782)
4 North chapels demolished before 1769
5 Four arches of north arcade shown in 1769 drawing
6 Probable area of the chancel of the main church
7 Connecting porch
8 Eastern chapel, originally separate, but joined quite early
      to the main church by the porch 7
9 Lawn of late eleventh-century cloister, still partially enclosed
      by remains of building of Aldwine's period
10 Outline of Scott's nineteenth-century nave
11 Vestry

▲ **Fig. 31.** Jarrow, Tyne and Wear (after Taylor & Taylor)

About 300 m. to the north is **Bede's World,** a museum with displays
and finds relating to the Saxon monastery.

J. Graham Campbell (ed.), The Anglo-Saxons *(Penguin, 1990), 74–5.*

Lanchester (*Longovicium*), County Durham Roman fort

NZ 158467. 13 km. NW of Durham on the A691. Take B6296 at Lanchester for Wolsingham. The site lies at the top of the hill S of road, 1 km. W of village.

A well preserved Antonine fort situated on Dere Street with BINCHES-TER 30 km. to the south and Ebchester 30 km. to the north. Inscriptions detail the garrisoning of the fort in the C2 and C3, including a cohort of Lingones, reinforced by a German cavalry unit who dedicated an altar (now in Lanchester church) to their Germanic goddess Garmangabis.

Most of the walls can be traced, and the fort platform stands 3–4 m. above its surroundings. Traces of a *vicus*† can be seen in earthworks east of the fort extending along Dere Street. A cremation cemetery has been located west of the fort.

Stonemason's workshops based at Chester-le-Street and Lanchester produced altars, mainly for the civilian market in the C3.

P. Casey et al., 'The Roman Fort at Lanchester', Arch J, 149 (1992), 69–81.

Lordenshaws, Rothbury, Northumberland Iron Age

hillfort† and prehistoric rock art ★

NZ 055993. On Garleigh Moor at the extreme NE end of Simonside Hills. Footpath from car park on N side of unclassified road NW from B6342 between Forestburn Gate and Rothbury. Within Northumberland National Park. Figure 32.

This small round hillfort has fine views over the valley of the river Coquet. Its full circuit can be traced on the ground when vegetation is low. There are two main enclosure boundaries, not necessarily contemporary. The inner circuit encloses an area about 60 m. across and comprises a simple bank preserved in places to a height of 2 m. Outside the inner enclosure are two rings of ditches and beyond this a further bank, ditch, and counterscarp bank†. There are entrances to the east and west, both narrow and constructed in the form of walled passages where they pass through the inner bank.

Within the enclosure are traces of circular house foundations probably dating to the later first millennium BC. Roughly in the centre is a larger house, perhaps occupied by the head family or perhaps a communal meeting house. Part of the south-east section of the boundary earthworks have been levelled for further circular houses. These may be Romano-British.

A linear earthwork†, traceable for nearly a kilometre, lies about 250 m. south-west of the fort; it is probably a later prehistoric land boundary.

Nearby are several decorated stones, two quite close by, possibly marking territories or routeways. One of the largest, immediately west of the fort, is over 4 × 3 m. and bears numerous complex motifs. South of

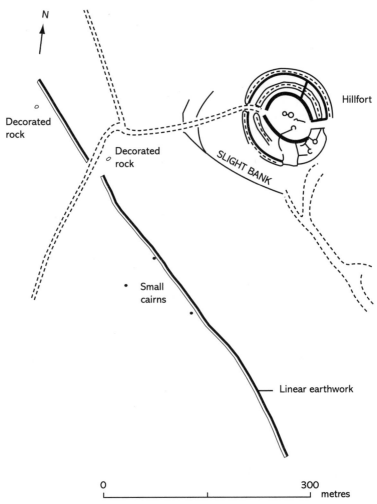

N

Decorated
rock

Decorated
rock

SLIGHT BANK

Hillfort

Small
cairns

Linear earthwork

0   300
                                            metres

▲ **Fig. 32.** Plan of the hillfort and other features at Lordenshaws Hillfort, Rothbury, Northumberland (after Hogg)

the fort is a group of small cairns†; three more lie to the east and there are scattered examples to the north. Some have a visible retaining kerb and one has an exposed stone cist†.

P. Topping, 'Lordenshaws Hillfort and its Environs', AA, 5th ser., 21 (1993), 15–27.

Monkwearmouth (St Peter's), Tyne and Wear Anglo-
Saxon monastery

NZ 3265. N of A185, access via minor road off roundabout junction of the A185.

About 673 Benedict Biscop, abbot of the monastery of SS. Peter and Paul at Canterbury, visited King Ecgfrith of Northumbria and was given land to establish a new monastery on the north bank of the river Wear, above a small harbour. Masons came from France to build a stone church, completed in 675, and glaziers to provide window glass.

What survives of that church is the west wall and its west porch, the latter forming the lower two storeys of the present church tower. The evidence suggests that the monastic church was narrow and tall like the well-known example at **Escomb**, County Durham (NZ 189302), with a chancel or chapel at its east end and a porticus (side chapel) on the north side of the nave (perhaps with a corresponding one to the south).

The monastery's domestic buildings lay south of the church, but nothing of these survives. The monastery was attacked by Vikings in 793 and abandoned in the C9.

The present church includes a C14 chancel, while the upper part of the tower is of the C11.

J. Graham Campbell (ed.), The Anglo-Saxons *(Penguin, 1990), 74–5.*

Old Bewick, Wooler, Northumberland Iron Age enclosures
and prehistoric rock art ★

NU 075216. Approached by footpath from Old Bewick village; it is advisable to follow the path around the foot of the hill to ascend from the E where the slopes are more gentle.

On a high westward projecting spur of Bewick Moor, overlooking the river Beamish, is a pair of enclosures. They may belong to the later first millennium BC. Both are D-shaped in plan, open on the straight side to the south where the steep slope provides a natural boundary. Each is defined on its curved side by a pair of massive banks with ditches between and on the outside. Traces of house foundations can be seen in the western enclosure, whilst the eastern one contains linear divisions, perhaps stock pens.

Immediately south-east of the enclosures are half a dozen decorated rocks, mainly earthfast boulders and exposed outcrops. One at NU 078216 in the next field to the north is particularly finely decorated.

J. Charlton, 'Report on a Trial Excavation at Old Bewick', PSAN, *4th ser., 6 (1935), 252–6.*

Piercebridge (*Morbium*), Darlington   Roman fort and bridge

abutment

NZ 214154. Piercebridge village is 6.5 km. W of Darlington on the B6275. Remains of the fort are accessible from the village centre opposite the green. Access to the bridge is from a car park and footpath from B6275 just before C18 road-bridge over R Tees, or by foot from the fort. English Heritage.

Piercebridge lies on Roman Dere Street connecting YORK with the north. A late C2–C3 fort was located here along with a substantial *vicus*†. The road originally crossed the Tees upstream from the present remains but the bridge was swept away in C2 and a replacement built downstream. The river migrated northwards, silting up the south end of the bridge, which was demolished and replaced with a causeway. Four piers survive on the south on top of a spillway of large flagstones. The southern abutment survives two courses high about 100 m. south of the present river.

The modern village lies mainly within the 4.4 ha. fort. Excavations have uncovered a C4 barrack block and bath-house. At the north end of the village beyond, and right of the Wheatsheaf Inn can be seen the north-east corner of the fort wall with an internal latrine.

A. Fitzpatrick and P. Scott, 'The Roman Bridge at Piercebridge', Britannia, *30 (1999), 111–32.*

Planetrees, Northumberland   Section of Hadrian's Wall

NY 935694. 1.5 km. SE of Chollerford on B6318. English Heritage. Figure 29 no. 8.

A 15 m. length of restored narrow wall on broad foundations extensively rebuilt in Roman times. The milecastle† has identical dimensions to the three preceding ones to the west.

J. Collingwood Bruce, Handbook to the Roman Wall, *13th edn (Harold Hill, 1978), 332.*

Risingham (*Habitancum*), Northumberland   Roman fort

NY 890862. On the A68 at West Woodburn, follow a farm track opposite minor road signposted for E. Woodburn and Monkridge. The fort is 0.75 km. along the track. For closer inspection seek permission at the farm. Figure 33.

A permanent fort guarding the river crossing was founded in the mid-C2. It lies on Dere Street where it crosses the marshy valley of the Rede some 20 km. north of the wall. Nothing is visible of the early fort, the extant remains dating from the C3 when it was rebuilt with polygonal towers flanking the south gate. The prominent grass mounds visible today cover the remains of the stone ramparts. In low light some interior features can be picked out in relief.

I. Richmond, 'Excavations at High Rochester and Risingham 1935', AA, *4th ser., 13 (1936), 184–98.*

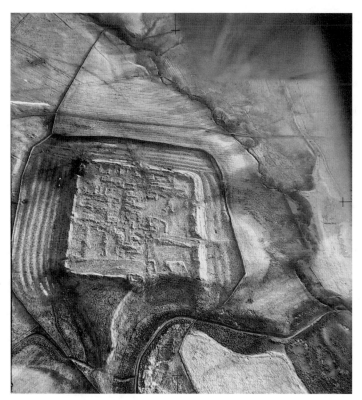

▲ **Fig. 33.** Risingham (*Habitancum*) Roman fort, Northumberland, from the air. Many of the visible earthworks within the defensive circuit are post-Roman (CUCAP AQO 90. Copyright reserved)

Sewingshields Wall, Northumberland   Roman milecastle†

and Hadrian's Wall

NY 813702. N of B6318, 2 km. E of Housesteads Fort. English Heritage. Figure 29 no. 14.

A largely unexcavated 3 km. stretch of Wall to the east of HOUSESTEADS, with remains of a recently excavated milecastle and a turret. A rare Roman stone cist† burial was found on the south side of the wall. **Grindon** (NY 814703) and **Coesike** (NY 821705) turrets are nearby.

D. Haigh and M. Savage, 'Excavations at Milecastle 35', AA, 5th ser., 12 (1984), 33–147.

South Shields (*Arbeia*), Tyne and Wear Roman fort

NZ 366678. Arbeia Roman Fort and Museum, Baring Street, South Shields, Tyne and Wear NE33 2BB. Well signposted from Tyne tunnel. Disabled access. Site museum. Tape tours available. Limited opening. A small charge to visit Time Quest, an archaeological resource centre. Figure 29 no. 1; Figure 34.

The Roman fort of *Arbeia* has a commanding view of the river Tyne. Although not actually on the line of Hadrian's Wall, the fort was an essential part of the frontier system controlling a main port and, in the later Roman period, acting as a military supply base.

Much of the site has been excavated and preserved and the visitor can see an impressive full-scale, accessible reconstruction of the west gate. The earliest fort has yet to be discovered but it is known that a new fort was built at around AD 160, coinciding with the reoccupation of Hadrian's Wall. The fort could have housed up to 480 foot soldiers and 120 cavalry at this time. In about 205–7, most of the buildings were demolished and the fort enlarged. Thirteen stone granaries were built, some visible as wall footings. Further expansion occurred in 222–35 with seven additional granaries and rebuilt accommodation. Following a fire in the late C3 or C4, extensive rebuilding took place and some granaries were converted to barracks. In the south corner was a large courtyard house, probably the commander's. The centre of the site shows the headquarters building which underwent several rebuilds. In the C4 the garrison was a unit of Tigris boatmen from Mesopotamia (Syria).

▼ **Fig. 34.** The reconstructed west gateway, South Shields (*Arbeia*) Roman fort, Tyne and Wear (Photograph: Jane Timby)

P. Bidwell and S. Speak, Excavations at South Shields Roman Fort, *Society of Antiquaries of Newcastle upon Tyne Monograph 4 (1994).*

Swinburn Castle Stone, Chollerton, Northumberland

Neolithic standing stone†

NY 935753. N of Coal Burn in the grounds of Swinburn Castle.

A fine monolith 3.6 m. high with deep weather-grooving down the sides. Possible cup-marks† can be seen on two faces near the bottom of the slab.

Nearby, beside the font in the church at **St John Lee, Acomb** (NY 935657) is another decorated stone found nearby in the 1970s; it may originally have been the cover slab of a cist† burial.

S. Beckensall, Northumberland's Prehistoric Rock Carvings *(Pendulum Publications, 1983), 221, 226–7.*

The Vicar's Pele, Corbridge *see* CORBRIDGE

Vindolanda see CHESTERHOLM

Wallsend (*Segedunum*), Tyne and Wear Roman fort and

bath-house on Hadrian's Wall   ★

SZ 305665. Take the A187 from Newcastle to Wallsend and the Tyne Tunnel. The site is just beyond the Industrial Estate. Restricted opening. Admission charge. Figure 29 no. 2.

Wallsend, the eastern end of Hadrian's Wall, is currently undergoing extensive excavations as part of the development of Segedunum Archaeological Park and Museum, which includes a working Roman bath-house. Excavations have uncovered two barracks housing cavalry troops (twenty-seven troopers and an officer in each), a forehall, granaries, and the remains of a hospital. Barrack blocks provide the first evidence of stables in Roman forts.

P. Bidwell (ed.), Hadrian's Wall 1989–1999 *(CWAAS, 1999).*

Walltown Crags, Northumberland Roman turret and

Hadrian's Wall

NY 674664. 5 km. from Haltwhistle railway station; 1 km. NE of Greenhead off B6318. English Heritage. Parking nearby. Figure 29 no. 21.

A well-preserved section of Wall passing along the crags to the turret (probably C2) on its summit. The turret was unusually built as a free-standing structure without wing-walls to join up with the curtain wall.

J. Collingwood Bruce, Handbook to the Roman Wall, *13th edn (Harold Hill, 1978), 186–7.*

Warkworth, Northumberland Medieval castle

NU 247058. Warkworth is on the A1068 10 km. SE of Alnwick. English Heritage. Restricted opening. Admission charge.

Warkworth Castle began as a motte† and bailey† castle commanding a loop of the river Coquet, to which stone curtain walls, towers, and a formidable gatehouse were added by the de Claverings who held it 1157–1332. It then passed to the Percys, was twice besieged in 1327 by the Scots, and then in 1405 was taken by Henry IV's army when the then Percy owner, the 1st earl of Northumberland, rebelled.

After restoration of the Percy estates by Henry V, Earl Henry laid out a huge chivalric fortress. On the old motte a great keep or tower house was raised, emblazoned with an imposing heraldic panel carrying the Percy Lion. Above its basement, ventilated by a central light well, are the main public rooms, with the great hall, kitchen, and the chapel's sanctuary rising through two storeys. Superficially thick walls are honeycombed with passages and chambers serving individual suites and lodgings. These, which include three single-chamber lodgings in the tall lookout tower, are skilfully planned, as are the arrangements for dealing with rainwater and for voiding garderobes†.

An unusual feature of the castle was a collegiate church† built, although probably never completed, across the bailey. Here it was intended that priests would say masses to speed the Percys' souls through purgatory.

Warkworth village runs downhill between the castle and the bridge over the river. This has a gatehouse, and is one of very few fortified bridges in Britain. Warkworth was promoted as a borough in the C12, and long but narrow burgage plots line the main street. St Lawrence's Church, near the river, has a fine C12 vaulted chancel.

H. Summerson, Warkworth Castle *(English Heritage, 1995) (Site Guidebook).*

Winshields, Northumberland Roman milecastles† and Hadrian's Wall

NY 759678. W of Steel Rigg car park on minor road off B6318. English Heritage. Figure 29 no. 18.

A rugged section of the wall following the crags of Whin Sill, including the highest point at Winshields Crag, 375 m. above sea level. The section has the remains of two milecastles. The foundations of a small barrack block can be seen on the west side of Castle Nick.

F. Simpson, Watermills and Military Works on Hadrian's Wall *(Titus Wilson, 1976).*

Yeavering Bell, Wooler, Northumberland Iron Age and
later hillfort†

NT 928294. Best approached from track leading SW from Old Yeavering on the B6351; the climb to the summit is long and steep. Figure 35.

High above the river Glen and its confluence with the river Till at the north-east end of the Cheviot hills is the conical hill of Yeavering Bell topped by one of the largest and most impressive hillforts in northern England. Yeavering Bell has several phases, the earliest being an undated palisaded enclosure around the eastern summit on which is a Bronze Age cairn†.

The main hillfort covers 5.2 ha. and is bounded by a single massive stone wall. There are four original entrances, which appear to have been simple gaps in the wall, although originally may have had timber gate structures. Inside the fort are over 130 circular house foundations and house platforms, mainly clustered around the two summits. Excavations

▼ **Fig. 35.** Aerial photograph of the hillfort on Yeavering Bell, Wooler, Northumberland (CUCAP G02. Copyright reserved)

in 1958 confirmed that occupation continued until the early first millennium AD. The focus of attention then shifted downhill into the adjacent valley with the establishment of a royal centre at **Old Yeavering** (NT 925305).

B. Hope-Taylor, Yeavering, *Department of the Environment Archaeological Reports 7 (HMSO, 1977).*

2 The Lake District and north-west

This region covers the counties and unitary authorities of Cumbria, Lancashire, Greater Manchester, Blackpool, and Blackburn with Darwen.

The north-west of England is dominated by the uplands of the Lake District and the western side of the Pennines. Separated by the valleys of the north-flowing river Eden and the south-flowing river Lune, these two uplands were inhospitable places for early settlement. Their climate did not help either, especially the higher than average rainfall caused by the high ground to the north and east.

The Lake District, now a National Park, forms a domed upland rising to 977 m. above sea level at Scarfell Pike. The radial drainage pattern flowing off it gives rise to the pattern of deeply incised valleys and their picturesque lakes. There is little soil-cover on the higher ground within the Lake District, much of it now open fell. Prehistoric and later settlement is slight, although during Neolithic times the fine igneous rocks available around Langdale Pikes were used to make stone tools. By Bronze Age times transhumance pastoralism was well established, this continuing until relatively recent times.

To the east, the Eden valley provides a fertile contrast, with abundant pasture land along the valley floor. Here were some of the largest complexes of early prehistoric ceremonial monuments in northern England, and by later prehistory the countryside was well divided up with long-lived farming villages. Eastwards again are the western slopes of the rugged Pennines offering opportunities for the valley dwellers to exploit the upland eastwards as well as west.

North of the Lake District is a broad coastal plain flanking the Solway Firth. Long considered an archaeological backwater, recent work shows that, like the Eden valley, the area was heavily used from early prehistory onwards. The Solway plain was the terminal of the Roman Frontier works connected to Hadrian's Wall. Roman settlement continued along the coastal plain west of the Lake District. South-east of the Lake District the narrow Lune valley separates the Cumbrian mountains from the Pennines. South of the Lune are two extensions of the Pennines: the forest of Bowland and the forest of Rossendale. Both were royal hunting grounds in medieval times, but earlier settlement is attested by later prehistoric farmsteads and occasional hillforts†.

Between the two forests the Ribble valley with its broad low-lying fertile coastal plain stretches from Manchester and Warrington northwards to Lancaster. Prehistoric settlement was sparse, but in Roman

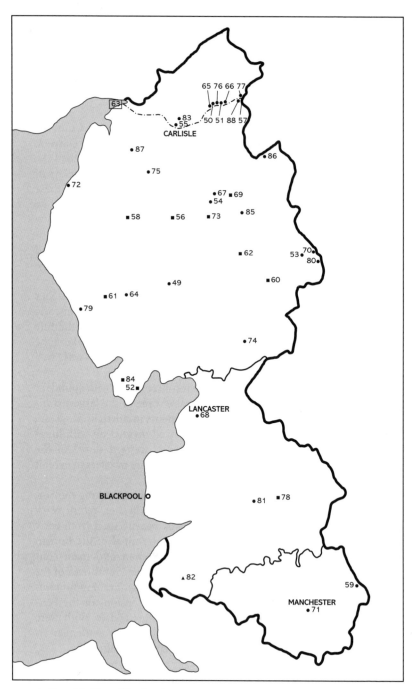

▲ **Fig. 36.** Map of Region 2

times major settlements were established for the area lay between the northern military zones and the predominantly civilian southern areas.

Ambleside (*Galava*), Cumbria Roman fort

NY 376033. 200 m. W of Waterhead car park, Ambleside. English Heritage and National Trust.

A Roman fort founded about AD 90 to guard the road from BROUGHAM to RAVENGLASS set at the north end of Windermere. Excavations in the early C20 located several large granaries. Finds displayed in the National Park Centre at **Brockhole** on the A591 (NY 393009).

A small cemetery east of the fort produced a tombstone recording a death of Flavius Romanus, killed by the enemy inside the fort, hinting at how unsettled the Lake District may have been in the C2 and C3. Masonry suggests a possible Roman jetty or harbour at the north end of Windermere.

R. Leech, 'The Roman Fort and vicus at Ambleside', TCWAAS 93 (1993), 51–74.

Banks East, Cumbria Roman turret on Hadrian's Wall

NY 575647. On minor road E of Banks village 6 km. NE of Brampton. English Heritage/Cumbria County Council. Figure 29 no. 28.

A well-preserved turret with adjoining stretches of Wall. Nearby is **Pike**

Key to Fig. 36.

Hill signal tower (NY 577648), unusually joined to the Wall at an angle of 45 degrees, presumably to facilitate long-distance signalling. The Turf Wall, ditch, and later Stone Wall all zigzag to accommodate its position.

I. Richmond, 'Excavations on Hadrian's Wall', TCWAAS 29 (1929), 303–15

Birdoswald (*Camboglanna*), Cumbria Roman fort and
Hadrian's Wall ★

NY 616663. 4 km. W of Greenhead, on minor road off B6318. English Heritage/ Cumbria County Council. Restricted opening. Admission charge. Figure 29 no. 26.

Birdoswald occupies a picturesque setting overlooking Irthing gorge. At no other point along the Wall can all the components of the Roman frontier system be found together in such a small area. The fort was to guard the bridge at WILLOWFORD, now replaced by a steel footbridge.

The Roman army

The legion was the basic formation of the Roman army. To join you had to be a Roman citizen. The legionaries were highly trained and disciplined infantry soldiers. Three, sometimes four, legions were stationed in Britain of which two, Legions II Augusta and XX, were permanent. By the late C1 bases were established at YORK, CHESTER, and Caerleon.

Each legion had between 5,000 and 5,300 men and was divided into ten cohorts. The first cohort had around 800 men, the remaining nine some 480 each. The latter cohorts were subdivided into six units of command known as centuries. The first cohort had five larger centuries. Each legion also had a small cavalry unit of around 120 men and horses, who were used for reconnaissance, escort duties, and as despatch riders.

A legionary was typically equipped with a short broad-bladed sword (*gladius*), a dagger (*pugio*), a throwing spear (*pilum*), and a rectangular metal-bound shield of laminated wood or leather. He would have worn protective body armour over a woollen tunic and a helmet on his head. The dress was completed by a studded belt, leather knee-breeches, a cloak, and hobnailed sandals. An auxiliary had slightly different equipment including a long sword (*spatha*) instead of the *gladius*, and an oval shield.

In addition to the legionaries there were also auxiliary troops, men who were not necessarily Roman citizens although they became so on discharge. Many auxiliary regiments were composed of newly conquered provincials who could provide a number of specialist duties, particularly the cavalry. An auxiliary unit was generally composed of 500 or 1,000 men. There were three types: cavalry named *ala*; infantry; and part-mounted cohorts.

From the north gate the Maiden Way runs to the fort at **Bewcastle** (NY 565745), 9.5 km. north of Birdoswald.

Initially designed for cavalry, the fort was garrisoned by an infantry cohort of 800 men in the C2. There is evidence of the fort walls, interval towers, and the south, west, and east gates. Inside the fort are granaries and ovens. In 1989 the remains of a basilican drill and exercise hall was discovered, so far unique among the auxiliary forts of the Roman Empire.

J. A. Biggins and D. J. A. Taylor, 'A Survey of the Roman Fort and Settlement at Birdoswald, Cumbria', Britannia, 30 (1999), 91–110.

Birkrigg Common, Aldingham, Cumbria Neolithic stone
circle† and Bronze Age barrow cemetery and enclosures

SD 292739. 3.5 km. S of Ulverston and 1 km. W of Bardsea, this area of open common land lies W of A5087 and is best approached via minor road from Bardsea to Great Urswick along the N side of the Common. Footpath access.

The prehistoric monuments scattered across Birkrigg Common provide a good range of well-preserved burial mounds, ceremonial structure, and enclosures dating from the later Neolithic through to the Iron Age.

In the south-eastern corner of the Common is the **Druid's Temple Stone Circle** (SD 292739). This, unusually, is a double circle. The inner comprises ten small limestone pillars in a ring 10 m. across while the less well-preserved outer circuit has fifteen pillars and is 23 m. in diameter. The outer ring may in fact be a kerb retaining a central paving or platform. In the south-east quadrant of the inner circle was a slab-covered pit containing cremated bone, while in the south-west quadrant were three small pits, again containing cremated bone, one covered by an inverted collared urn.

Between the Druid's Temple and the trig. point are at least nine well-preserved round barrows†. Four stand together in a group immediately east of the trig. point (SD 286742). Excavations have failed to reveal any traces of burials.

The most northerly barrow on the Common (SD 285744) is probably the biggest with a diameter of 12 m. and a height of just over 1 m. A large stone near the centre may be the displaced cover of a central cist†.

The most southerly barrow (SD 282740), a platform barrow, contained at least ten cremations. Some 15 m. across but only 0.3 m. high, it has a flat top with a kerb of larger stones. Two adjacent oval-shaped enclosures bounded by low banks can be seen near the centre of the Common (SD 288746). Inside are three depressions, probably house foundations. Both enclosures were probably small later Iron Age homesteads. Between them is a rather unusual rectangular mound 8 × 10 m.

and about 0.6 m. high. Excavations found seventeen cremations in the north-eastern sector. Three were accompanied by cordoned urns suggesting a date in the mid-second millennium BC, and thus pre-dating the enclosures.

J. Barnatt, Stone Circles of Britain, *British Archaeological Reports British Series 215 (1989).*

Brough (*Verterae*), Cumbria Roman fort

NY 791141. At Brough Castle (English Heritage), 12.8 km. SE of Appleby and 0.75 km. S of A66.

A Roman fort occupying a good defensive position above Swinedale beck, subsequently partly obliterated by a C12 castle. It is uncertain whether the impressive earthworks to the south are Roman or have been subsequently modified.

J. Charlton, Brough Castle *(English Heritage, 1988) (Site Guidebook).*

Brougham (*Brocavum*), Cumbria Roman fort

NY 537288. Immediately S of A66 approached via B6363, 2 km. SW of Penrith. Situated in a private field SE of Brougham Castle (English Heritage) by the river Eamont. Admission charge to castle.

Earthwork remains of a large fort, probably founded by Agricola, best seen from the medieval castle. Built to guard the river crossing on an important route to CARLISLE and thence into Scotland with a branch route to AMBLESIDE. A *vicus*† developed outside the defences, occupied until the end of the C4. Some Roman tombstones can be seen in the castle.

J. Charlton, Brougham Castle *(English Heritage, 1988) (Site Guidebook).*

Carlisle (*Luguvalium*), Cumbria Roman fort and town; medieval cathedral city

NY 4056. W of the M6; junctions 42, 43 or 44. Tullie House Museum, Abbey Street. Restricted opening. Admission charge. Figure 29 no. 30.

Carlisle was the most north-westerly town in the Roman Empire. Most of the Roman settlement lies under the modern city but finds are displayed in the Museum.

Recent excavations have revealed spectacular Flavian military remains in and around **Annetwell Street**, adjacent to Tullie House Museum. Further excavations at **Blackfriars Street** located an extensive C1 *vicus*† extending south from the fort. The Flavian fort had a timber gateway set in a wide rampart of turf and timber. Numerous coins date the foundation to about AD 79. The interior was completely refurbished in the late 80s or early 90s before it was demolished to make way for a rebuilt fort about 105. In the late C2 the fort was again rebuilt, this time in stone.

A large stone structure located near **Abbey Street** may be the forum†.

Carlisle's most significant medieval structure is the cathedral. Surviving from the Augustinian priory church from which it grew are two C12 bays of the nave, and the choir (1292 onwards) with C15 stalls and a screen of 1541. South and west of the church are the priory gatehouse, refectory, and prior's lodgings (now the Deanery).

A short distance north-west, up Castle Street, is **Carlisle Castle** (English Heritage). It has a C12 keep among mostly later military buildings. The best surviving length of the city's walls can be seen from the car park and gardens below West Walls.

D. Charlesworth, 'Roman Carlisle', Arch J, 135 (1978), 115–37.

Carrock Fell, Troutbeck, Cumbria   Prehistoric enclosure

NY 343337. 6 km. N of A66(T) on high open fells NE of Keswick. Best approached from the W by striking E from the Cumbria Way to the S of High Pike on the Caldbeck fells; the steep climb from the E is exhilarating!

Situated at nearly 700 m. above sea level this is one of the highest, and at 2.1 ha. also the largest hillfort† or hilltop enclosure in the region. Oval in plan, the enclosure is bounded by a single stone wall 2.7 m. thick. In a few places well-built stone faces can be seen. There are several gaps and one on the west and one on the south may be original entrances. Inside on the eastern summit are the remains of a heavily robbed cairn† with traces of a central cist†. The enclosure's date is uncertain; it may be later prehistoric, but features such as the discontinuous stone wall and isolated position might suggest an earlier date, perhaps even Neolithic (compare CARN BREA, Cornwall).

R. Collingwood, 'The Hillfort on Carrock Fell', TCWAAS 38(1938), 32–41.

Carvoran (*Magna*), Cumbria   Roman fort and Roman Army

Museum on Hadrian's Wall

NY 665658. On Hadrian's Wall NE of Greenhead. Only the NW angle is visible. Site of Carvoran Roman Army Museum run by the Vindolanda Trust. Restricted opening. Admission charge. Figure 29 no. 22.

A fort situated behind the Wall and Vallum guarding the Tipalt valley. Recent aerial photography has revealed an earlier, larger fort adjacent to the known Hadrianic fort. Excavation has located two military ditches, which produced late C1 and early C2 pottery. The history of the site is clearly complex and much awaits discovery.

C. Daniels, The Eleventh Pilgrimage of Hadrian's Wall (Society of Antiquaries of Newcastle upon Tyne, 1989), 41–3.

Castlerigg, Keswick, Cumbria Neolithic stone circle† ★★

NY 293236. About 2 km. E of Keswick, signposted via small lanes from A66(T) to the N and A591 to the S. Roadside parking. English Heritage and National Trust.

Possibly one of the earliest and certainly one of the most exquisitely placed stone circles in Britain. Located on a low hill above the confluence of the Naddle beck and the river Greta surrounded by high mountains.

The thirty-three slate pillars forming the main ring, 32 × 29 m. in extent, are graded in height. The two largest on the north side define the original 4 m. wide entrance. From the north side, the stones generally increase in height to the second focus on the south-east, marked by the tallest stone in the circuit which is set with its long axis radial to the circumference.

Inside the circle are several notable features. The most striking is a roughly rectangular setting of stones 3.4 × 7.7 m. on the east-south-east side. One side is formed by the perimeter of the circle, the other three sides by near contiguous stones. The inner face of the middle stone of the main circle that forms the east side of the rectangle is decorated with a large spiral. Other features include three low cairns† in the northern sector; three hollows in the interior; and, in the south-west quadrant, a slight bank 7.5 m. long immediately inside the ring of orthostats†. It is unclear whether these are original or result from modern investigations. In 1856 two stone axes were found in the circle, and in 1875 another was found nearby.

Surrounding the circle is medieval, or later, ridge and furrow† cultivation which has created a slight bank around the stones. A small single stone stands west-south-west of the ring; its antiquity is uncertain. In 1725 William Stukeley recorded a second circle at Castlerigg in the field west of the present ring. Nothing remains visible.

A. Burl, The Stone Circles of Britain, Ireland and Brittany (Yale University Press, 2000), 103–19.

Castleshaw (*Rigodunum*), Greater Manchester Roman forts

SD 998096. 9 km. NW of Oldham, N of A62 immediately N of the reservoirs at the head of Castleshaw valley in Saddleworth. Signed footpath off minor road to reservoir. Information panels.

Two superimposed military works comprising an Agricolan auxiliary fort with a smaller Trajanic fort constructed inside. The forts stand on the road connecting YORK with CHESTER.

Excavation has revealed the plan of the fortlet gateways, the development of the defences, and found a previously unknown outer ditch.

Internal timber buildings were also investigated, including two granaries and barracks. Occupation seems to have been brief.

J. Walker (ed.), Castleshaw: The Archaeology of a Roman Fortlet (Greater Manchester Archaeological Unit, 1989).

Crosby Garrett, Appleby, Cumbria Prehistoric settlements and field-system†

NY 719064. 1 km. N of Newbiggin-on-Lune and 2 km. S of Crosby Garrett, approached by footpath linking these two villages along the W side of Scandal beck. Figure 37.

This group of later prehistoric and early Roman settlements is the remnants of a much larger system of farmsteads and fields that once extended along the Scandal beck on the south-west side of Crosby Garrett fell, and indeed more widely along the Eden valley. The preserved sections comprise three distinct units, each of slightly different form.

In the south is the largest, and possibly the earliest. On the ground can be traced a series of six sub-rectangular compounds surrounded by a series of paddocks. There is a rectangular building with surviving stone doorposts on the south side. In plan, this settlement resembles a wheel; at the hub are the compounds with their houses and gardens, while radiating out from them are first paddocks and then larger fields. Two trackways run off to the west.

The second, smaller settlement lies about 700 m. north-east, separated by regular rectangular fields. This settlement is more nucleated with a cluster of perhaps seven or eight small compounds around a slightly elongated central area. Traces of houses can be seen within some compounds. A trackway leads into the settlement from the south-west. The settlement itself sits on a major east to west boundary, the land to the south being enclosed as a series of fields while to the north is open ground, perhaps pasture.

About 300 m. north-east of the second settlement is a third, different in character again. More rectangular in layout, here it is possible to trace two main compounds, each with two or three subdivisions in one of its corners. Again a trackway leads into the settlement from the west.

R. Lowndes, 'Celtic Fields, Farmsteads and Burial Mounds in the Lune Valley', TCWAAS 63(1960), 77–89.

Eskdale Moor (Burnmoor), Boot, Cumbria Neolithic and Bronze Age stone circles† and cairns†

NY 173025. Situated high on the open moors 3 km. S of Wast Water and SW of Burnmoor tarn. Best approached from S via footpath N up Gill Bank from Eskdale Mill at Boot. Hard walk. Partly National Trust.

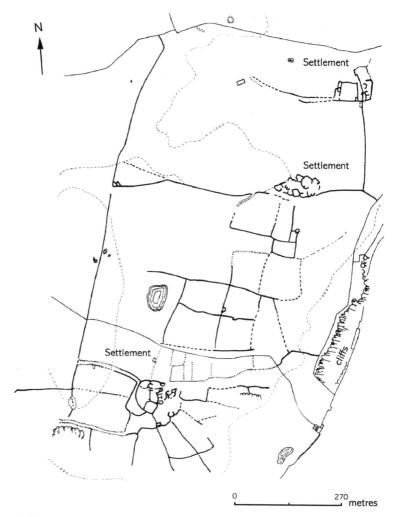

N

0   270 metres

▲ **Fig. 37.** Plan showing the layout of the settlements and field-systems at Crosby Garrett, Appleby, Cumbria (after B. Jones, 1975)

Five stone circles spread at intervals across open moorland. All are fairly low and can be difficult to locate. The largest, and the first encountered when approaching from the south, is **Brats Hill** (NY 173023). It measures 32 × 25 m. Some forty-two granite and porphyritic slate pillars can be seen on the circumference, most now fallen, the tallest at 0.9 m. being on the south side. Just outside the circle (about 10 m.) on the north side is a fallen outlier. Inside the circle are five small low cairns†, with stone kerbs†. Two opened in 1827 contained central stone settings covering human cremations, animal bones, and deer antlers.

About 130 m. north-west there are two smaller circles on **White Moss** (NY 172024). Both are about 16 m. in diameter and each contains a low centrally placed cairn. About 400 m. to the north again, and intervisible on a good day, is a further pair of circles at **Low Longridge** (NY 172028) also containing cairns.

Elsewhere on the moor it is possible to see a standing stone (west of White Moss), numerous hut platforms (at Boat How to the north of Low Longridge), and abundant small clearance cairns around and between the circles.

A. Burl, The Stone Circles of Britain, Ireland and Brittany *(Yale University Press, 2000), 124–5.*

Ewe Close, Crosby Ravensworth, Cumbria Later prehistoric and Romano-British settlement

NY 609135. On sloping ground 2 km. SW of Crosby Ravensworth village, approached by footpath leading SW from Town Head. Figure 38.

This extensive village, typical of many in the area, is preserved under grassland on a gentle, east-facing slope. The visible remains probably date to the first few centuries AD, but the original settlement is much earlier.

The complexity of walls and banks on the site takes a little time to sort out. The earliest part of the site seems to be the roughly square-shaped enclosure on the west side. In the centre is the foundation of a large circular house some 15 m. in diameter with its entrance to the south-east. A second rather smaller foundation lies just beyond. The square enclosure has its entrance on the south side adjoining a group of nine small structures built against the enclosure wall.

The south-east quarter of the square enclosure was demolished to accommodate a new focus, an oval enclosure more or less in the centre of the site. Within this enclosure are at least two circular buildings and perhaps as many as four compounds divided by internal walls. Roman finds from this area show continued occupation into the early first millennium AD.

Abutting the oval enclosure are several generally rectangular paddocks and yards, defined by stone walls with interspersed circular and rectangular buildings. Their relationship to the enclosure walls and to the occupation within the oval and the square enclosure is not clear.

The layout of the enclosures, paddocks, and yards suggests an emphasis on stock-raising. Around the farmstead are several other earthworks, mainly of later date. Immediately to the west is the hollowed out course of the Maiden Way, the main Roman road from Manchester

▲ **Fig. 38.** Aerial view of Ewe Close, Crosby Ravensworth, Cumbria, looking south-west over the site (CUCAP AQM04. Copyright reserved)

to Carlisle. The line of the road skirts the farmstead emphasizing its prehistoric origins.

W. Collingwood, 'Ewe Close', TCWAAS 9 (1909), 295–309.

Hadrian's Wall, Cumbria Roman frontier work

For a general introduction to this large monument see the main entry under Region 1. The principal sites to visit on the Wall in Region 2 are, from east to west (*see* Figure 29): CARVORAN, POLTROSS BURN, WILLOWFORD, HARROW'S SCAR, BIRDOSWALD, PIPER SIKE AND LEAHILL, BANKS EAST AND PIKE HILL, HARE HILL, CARLISLE, and STANWIX. Each is described individually.

Some sites have museums and displays; additional museums and visitor centres for the Wall in Region 2 include CARVORAN, Cumbria (NY 665657; Figure 29 no. 22).

Hardknott Castle (*Mediobogdum*), Cumbria Roman fort *

NY 218015. On minor road between A595 near Ravenglass to A593 near Ambleside. 14.5 km. NE of Ravenglass, at W end of Hardknott Pass. The fort stands immediately N of road. English Heritage and National Trust. Figure 39.

A well-preserved square Roman fort (1.3 ha.) strategically set with spectacular views. Immediately south of the fort is the Roman road. One of the earliest large-scale excavations in north-west England took place here in the 1890s. There was further work in the 1960s. The fort, founded in Hadrian's reign, was built to control the road from RAVEN-GLASS to AMBLESIDE. It was abandoned in the late Hadrianic/early Antonine period but reoccupied in the 160s. The walls survive to a height of 1.8 m. Visible remains inside the defences include the granaries, the headquarters building, and commandant's house. The fort has four gateways, three of which are double carriageways, the fourth (north) for pedestrians only. Outside the fort is the bath-house by the south gate and a flattened area 200 m. to the north-east used as a parade ground.

A fragmentary inscription suggests the fort was occupied at some

▼ **Fig. 39.** The Roman fort wall, Hardknott Castle (*Mediobogum*), Cumbria (Photograph: Jane Timby)

point by the Fourth Cohort of Delmations (from Yugoslavia). Fragments of leather found preserved in the peat included pieces from shoes typical of those worn by the auxiliary troops, shields, clothing, and a tent.

P. Bidwell et al., Hardknott Roman Fort *(CWAAS, 1999).*

Hare Hill, Cumbria　Hadrian's Wall and Roman turret

NY 562646. 1 km. NE of Lanercost, off minor road. English Heritage/Cumbria County Council. Figure 29 no. 29.

Short length of Wall standing 2.8 m. high. Hare Hill is a Turf Wall turret with the Narrow Wall brought up to its east and west sides and later covered by the medieval boundary wall of Lanercost Priory.

J. Collingwood Bruce, Handbook to the Roman Wall, *13th edn (Harold Hill, 1978), 223.*

Harrow's Scar, Cumbria　Roman milecastlet on Hadrian's Wall

NY 621664. 0.5 km. E of Birdoswald, on minor road off B6318. English Heritage and Cumbria County Council. Figure 29 no. 25; Figure 40.

Remains of a milecastle linked to BIRDOSWALD fort by a fine section of wall noteworthy because of the drainage channels which occur almost every 6 m. Originally a turf turret, rebuilt in stone.

J. Collingwood Bruce, Handbook to the Roman Wall, *13th edn. (Harold Hill, 1978), 197.*

King Arthur's Round Table, Eamont Bridge, Penrith, Cumbria　Neolithic henget　　　　　　　　★

NY 523284. 1 km. S of Penrith to the W of A6 at Eamont Bridge. Access from the B5320 where there is roadside parking. English Heritage.

This classic henge overlooking the river Lowther is one of three Neolithic ceremonial monuments between the rivers Lowther and Eamont. Visible today as a grass-covered earthwork, the site is slightly unusual in lying at the bottom of a slope.

The central area is flat with the slight remains of a low platform in the centre, possibly the remains of a barrow or cairn†. Around the central area is a ditch, which is effectively the result of later C19 attempts to landscape and restore the monument and need not represent the original form. Outside the ditch is a berm† about 7 m. wide, and beyond this the remains of the bank that once enclosed the site. Better preserved on the west side, the bank is up to 1.8 m. high and 13 m. wide at the base, but again there is evidence of landscaping and mutilation. Two opposed entrances give the site a rather unusual north-west to south-east axis. A

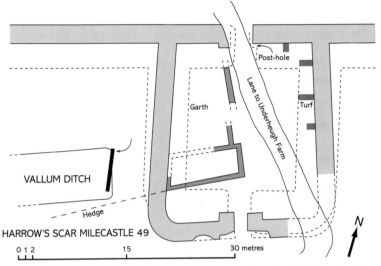

Post-hole

Lane to Underheugh Farm

Garth

Turf

VALLUM DITCH

Hedge

HARROW'S SCAR MILECASTLE 49

0 1 2   15   30 metres

N

▼ Fig. 40. Plan of the Roman milecastle at Harrow's Scar, Cumbria (after Daniels 1978)

sketch of 1664 by William Dugdale shows two standing stones outside the northern entrance, one either side. These had gone by 1725 when William Stukeley visited the site.

Excavations in 1937 and 1938 found a poorly preserved crematorium pit.

Standing in the centre of the monument looking north-westwards the bank of MAYBURGH henge about 155 m. away can be seen. At one time a third enclosure within this group, known as the **Little Round Table**, lay south of King Arthur's Round Table, intervisible with it, but nothing of this remains to be seen.

P. Topping, 'The Penrith Henges', PPS 58 (1992), 249–64.

Lancaster, Lancashire Roman fort and civilian settlement

SD 474620. W of the M6, access from junctions 33 or 34. Restricted opening. Roman remains signposted from the Castle and St Mary's Church. Information panel. The City Museum on Market Square has Roman finds.

Lancaster was originally the site of a succession of Roman forts with an adjacent civilian settlement. The forts were sited on Castle Hill overlooking the river Lune, now the location of the medieval castle and priory church. The only surviving fragment of the fort is a stub of C4 masonry in northern Vicarage Field known as the **Wery Wall** and probably representing part of a polygonal external corner bastion.

Excavations in 1973–4 exposed one wing of a courtyard building, perhaps a *mansio*† (inn), immediately outside the north wall of the fort. This contained a bath-suite of several rooms. Elements are still visible in Vicarage Field. The bath-house was demolished in 330–40 to make room for the C4 fort.

D. Shotter and A. White, Roman Fort and Town of Lancaster, *University of Lancaster Centre for North-West Regional Studies Occasional Paper 18 (1990).*

Leahill Turrett, Cumbria *see* PIPER SIKE, Cumbria.

Long Meg and Her Daughters, Langwathby, Cumbria Neolithic stone circle† ★

NY 571373. Signposted N from road between Little Salkeld and Gamblesby about 1 km. NE of Little Salkeld. Figure 41.

Situated on a wide flat sandstone terrace east of the river Eden, Long Meg is a tall standing stone† while Her Daughters are the stone pillars of an adjacent circle. Local folklore derives the strange name from the petrification by an indignant saint of a coven of witches.

This is the fourth largest stone circle in Britain. The slightly elliptical form (109 × 93 m.) is edged by sixty-eight massive igneous boulders. It is typical of the early circle-building tradition: crude in construction, low-lying, open aspect, wide spacing of the stones, the presence of an outlying standing stone, and the elaboration of the entrance. The entrance gap is slightly wider and marked by some of the largest stones in the circle. Two large stones also stand almost due east and west to mark the local equinoctial positions of the sun. A possible second entrance may lie on the north-west side marked by a wide gap with paired stones.

Cultivation of the site has not served it well. While the stones have survived, the antiquary John Aubrey records that two large cairns† once stood near the centre of the circle. Moreover, the flattened circumference on the north side is the result of constructing the circle against the perimeter of an earlier earthwork enclosure. In 1725 William Stukeley noted a second stone circle about 250 m. west of the main circle. No trace of this remains either.

Long Meg, a massive red sandstone pillar 3.7 m. tall, stands 18 m. outside the circle on the highest point of the slope on which the complex lies. On the flat south-east surface is a complicated series of rock art, dominated by three motifs: a cup and ring mark†, a spiral, and some concentric rings.

H. Burl, 'The Stone Circle of Long Meg and Her Daughters', TCWAAS 94 (1994), 1–12.

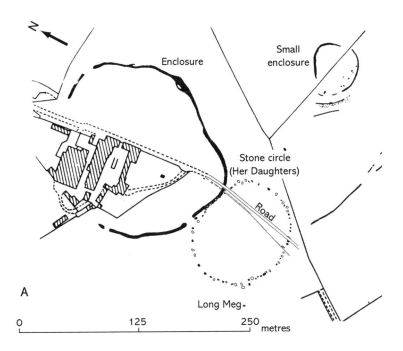

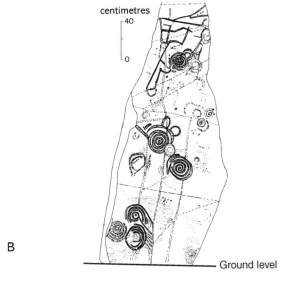

▲ **Fig. 41.** Long Meg and Her Daughters, Langwathby, Cumbria. (A) Plan of the site showing the position of the main visible features in relation to the adjacent enclosure. (B) Rock art on the south-east face of Long Meg (A after Soffe & Clare; B after P Frodsham)

Maiden Castle, Stainmore, Cumbria Roman fortlet

NY 872132. Lies immediately N of A66, 1.5 km., from Rey Cross. Difficult to access from busy road. Park on minor road S of A66 signposted to Kaber. Cross over A66 and follow the track. The route passes through a field gate and along a footpath to the fort and takes about ten minutes.

A small 0.1 ha. fortlet strategically set above the Eden valley and forming part of the Stainmore Pass defensive system linking BROUGH and BOWES. The fortlet is surrounded by a stone wall 1.8 m. thick and was occupied from the C2 to C4.

R. Collingwood, 'Maiden Castle', TCWAAS 27 (1927), 170–7.

Manchester (*Mamucium*), Greater Manchester Roman fort and town

Centred SJ 835975. Roman remains in area now known as Castlefield. Leaflet detailing archaeological trail available at Information Centre. Information panels. Archaeological material at the Manchester Museum, Oxford Road. Restricted opening.

An Agricolan timber fort was established here in AD 79 on the main route between CHESTER and YORK. Three subsequent forts were built on the site and a *vicus*† grew up around the walls to house families of the soldiers and members of the local tribe of the *Brigantes*. A Roman trail, taking around 45 minutes, starts in **Liverpool Road** (Castlefields) near the Museum of Science and Industry. Passing by the excavated foundations of three typical *vicus* buildings, a house, inn, and shop, the trail leads to the reconstructed North Gate and part of the C3 defensive system. The gate relates to the last fort phase dating to around AD 200. A painted mural in the railway viaduct leads through to the granary and part of the reconstructed west wall.

G. Jones, Roman Manchester (Manchester Excavation Committee, 1974).

Maryport (*Alauna*), Cumbria Roman fort and settlement

NY 038373. On private land adjacent to Senhouse Museum, Sea Brews, at N end of town at the end of Camp Street overlooking the sea. Museum has restricted opening. Admission charge. Figure 42.

Although there may have been an Agricolan fort here, the visible remains are Trajanic. Maryport formed part of the coastal defence system of

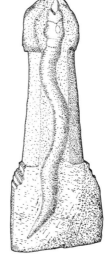

▲ **Fig. 42.** The Serpent stone, Maryport, Cumbria

mileforts† and signal towers with road links to CARLISLE and YORK. The fort earthworks can be seen from a ramp in the museum car park. Excavations recovered evidence of workshops and stabling and at least four building periods. C19 excavations recovered a remarkable collection of military altars from the parade ground and investigated other structures including a house, a shop, two temples, and a cemetery. Remains of a port have been found at the mouth of the river. The museum houses the Senhouse Collection, one of the oldest and largest collections of Roman antiquities from Britain dating back to the C16. It includes some very fine altars and other religious stones, all from Maryport.

R. Wilson (ed.), Roman Maryport and its Setting *(CWAAS, 1997)*.

Mayburgh, Eamont Bridge, Penrith, Cumbria Neolithic

henge† and four-stone setting

NY 519285. W of Eamont Bridge. Accessible via signposted lane leading N from B5320 about 300 m. W of its junction with the A6 S of Eamont Bridge. Roadside parking. English Heritage.

One of three Neolithic monuments in the Penrith complex beside the river Eamont (see also KING ARTHUR'S ROUND TABLE). Most impressive is the massive circular bank set on top of a natural glacial mound. Standing up to 4.5 m. high and 36 m. wide at the base, the bank is composed of water-worn river pebbles.

The level area enclosed by the bank is about 90 m. in diameter. A single entrance to the east allows a view to KING ARTHUR'S ROUND TABLE from the central area, the high banks excluding any other views. A single block of volcanic tuff nearly 3 m. high standing inside Mayburgh is probably the last stone of a setting known as a four-poster or four-stone circle. A drawing made by William Dugdale in 1664 shows all four stones, and also a pair of stones just outside the entrance, one on either side.

Although no internal ditch exists, the site is generally classified as a henge monument. As part of the Penrith complex, however, it might be better seen as a sacred enclosure connected with the use of the nearby henge, but separate from it.

P. Topping, 'The Penrith Henges', PPS *58 (1992), 249–64.*

Middleton Church, Burrow-in-Lonsdale,
Cumbria Roman fort and milestone†

SD 624859. In a field S of Middleton Church E of A683. Take the A683 from Kirkby Lonsdale N for 10 km. to Middleton, then take minor road W towards Sedbergh.

Several Roman forts underlie Burrow-in-Lonsdale. A milestone found in 1836 was re-erected near the Roman RIBCHESTER–CARLISLE road.

Etched into the stone are the Roman numerals LIII (53), the distance in Roman miles to Carlisle. The A683 follows the line of a Roman road connecting the fort at Burrow-in-Lonsdale (*Calacum*) with the north.

E. Hilyard, 'Excavations at Burrow-in-Lonsdale', TCWAAS 94 (1994), 66–101.

Old Penrith (*Voreda*), Cumbria Roman fort

NY 493385. 6.5 km. N of modern Penrith on private land immediately E of A6 between Carlisle and Penrith, 1.5 km. N of Plumpton Wall at Castlesteads.

The fort is visible in fields as a distinct rectangular platform 150 × 10 m. on a natural terrace by the river Petteril. Inscriptions and tombstones have been found. The east gate of the fort is visible, exposed in the C19 but formal investigation only took place in the 1970s. Geophysical survey has confirmed an extensive extra-mural settlement.

P. Austen, Bewcastle and Old Penrith (CWAAS, 1991).

Piper Sike and Leahill, Cumbria Roman turrets and Hadrian's Wall

NY 588653. On minor road 1.5 km. W of Birdoswald Fort. English Heritage and Cumbria County Council. Figure 29 no. 27.

Turrets on section of wall west of BIRDOSWALD, originally constructed for the Turf Wall. Both turrets were abandoned in the later C2. A rough hut was constructed in the ruins of Leahill in the later C4. Excavations in Piper Sike in 1970 revealed part of a cooking hearth and a flagged platform, perhaps a sleeping and eating area. Leahill, excavated in 1958, also contains a large platform against the north wall.

J. Collingwood Bruce, Handbook to the Roman Wall, 13th edn (Harold Hill, 1978), 219.

Poltross Burn, Cumbria Roman milecastle† and section of Hadrian's Wall

NY 634662. Immediately SW of Gilsland village by old railway station. English Heritage/Cumbria County Council. Figure 29 no. 23.

A well-preserved milecastle with a flight of steps and remains of gate-ways and barrack blocks. The walls were built to broad gauge, the Narrow Wall on broad foundations joining its wing-walls some 3.5 m. away either side.

J. Collingwood Bruce, Handbook to the Roman Wall, 13th edn (Harold Hill, 1978), 193–4.

Portfield Fort, Whalley, Lancashire Iron Age hillfort†

SD 745355. NE of A671 SW of Whalley, via lane between the A671 and Shabden.

Set on a spur overlooking the confluence of the Shabden brook and the river Calder this small 1.5 ha. fort has a commanding position. A single rampart runs all around the promontory, but the south-east and south-west sides are so steep that really it is superfluous; the main defences face north where there are three lines of ramparts visible.

Excavations have revealed a complicated history which, to judge from a hoard of metalwork found in the interior (now in Manchester University Museum), began in the later Bronze Age. The hoard contained a gold tress-ring, a gold bracelet, two bronze axes, a knife, a gouge, and a stud.

J. Forde-Johnson, 'The Iron Age Hillforts of Lancashire and Cheshire', TLCAS *72 (1962), 9–46.*

Ravenglass (*Glannoventa*), Cumbria Roman bath-house

SD 087961. Signposted via lane running S from a sharp bend on the minor road leading off the A595 to Ravenglass village. The site lies 0.75 km. down the lane. English Heritage. Figure 43.

Originally the location of a Hadrianic fort, built on the edge of a harbour immediately south of Ravenglass. The site has suffered from coastal

▲ **Fig. 43.** The Roman bath-house, Ravenglass (*Glannoventa*), Cumbria (Photograph: Jane Timby)

erosion and is bisected by a railway-line. The only visible remains are of the bath-house east of the fort. The structure is remarkably well preserved, partly due to its continued use as a domestic building into the Middle Ages. The walls, built of coursed red stone, stand almost 4 m. high with two doorways and five splayed windows. A niche probably held a votive statue.

Recent finds have linked with the site the *Cohors I Aelia Classica*, a part-mounted infantry unit from the naval fleet.

T. Potter, Romans in North-West England *(CWAAS, 1979).*

Rey Cross, Cumbria   Roman marching camp

NY 900124. On the A66 at the summit of Stainmore Pass, 8 km. W of Bowes, and approx. 1.5 km from Maiden Castle. The road passes through the site from E to W. Lay-by on S side.

Although incomplete, set at the summit of Stainmore Pass this is one of the most impressively defended marching camps in Britain. Originally some 8.1 ha. in size, the southern half of the western defences has been quarried whilst part of the north rampart has collapsed. The remaining stone-revetted ramparts average 1.8 m. in height but have no ditches because of the proximity of the bedrock. Nine of the original eleven gates survive. The Roman road crosses the camp, changing direction slightly as it leaves the east gate. The camp probably belongs to campaigns against the *Brigantes* in AD 72–3 and could have housed a legion.

I. Richmond and J. McIntyre, 'The Roman Camps at Rey Cross and Crackenthorpe', TCWAAS 34 (1934), 50–61.

Ribchester (*Bremetennacum*), Lancashire   Roman fort and settlement

SD 649349. Off the B6245 where it crosses the river Ribble in the modern village. Access to external remains any reasonable time. Museum has restricted opening. Admission charge. Nearby free public car park.

A C1 fort strategically placed between YORK and CHESTER. The fort was garrisoned by 500 cavalrymen, initially by Asturians from northern Spain. Important finds include a parade helmet and carved inscriptions, which can be seen at the adjacent museum. The remains of two granaries can be seen from a path at the back of the museum. A section of the north-west rampart and ditch can be observed along the footpath leading to the public car park. Excavations of the substantial extra-mural settlement revealed a rare example of veteran settlement.

Ruins of a bath-house are signposted from the museum and can be found near the **White Bull Inn** (open Easter to the end of October). The porch of the Inn is supported by Roman columns.

B. Edwards and P. Webster (eds), Ribchester Excavations *(University of Cardiff, 1985–8).*

Rufford Old Hall, Ormskirk, Lancashire Medieval manor
house

SD 463160. Rufford village is on the A59 8 km. NE of Ormskirk. National Trust; restricted opening. Admission charge. Figure 44.

Facing you as you approach is the great hall of 1530, which shows the elaboration of timber framing favoured in the north-west in the late Middle Ages. Externally what catch the eye are the closely spaced vertical timbers (close studding), quatrefoil decoration, and windows with moulded timber mullions. A large polygonal bay window (compare LITTLE MORETON) lights the high end where the Hesketh lords of Rufford had their dining table, while at the low end is the door into the hall. Inside the decoration is even more elaborate. The five-bay hammerbeam roof, resting on an embattled and moulded wall plate, has cambered collars, angels, and armorial bosses. Four purlins (the main longitudinal timbers) run along the roof, with quatrefoil wind braces between them. Between two carved and moulded spheres is a movable screen, richly carved, added in the early C16.

The contemporary service rooms and private chambers to either end of the hall have disappeared, replaced by wings of 1661 and later.

English Heritage properties in Cumbria include several castles: BROUGH (NY 791141); BROUGHAM (NY 537290); Penrith (NY 513299); and Piel (SD 233636); various monasteries: Furness (SD 218717);

▼ **Fig. 44.** Rufford Old Hall, Ormskirk, Lancashire (National Trust)

Lanercost (NY 556637); Shap (NY 548153); and Wetheral (NY 469542). In Lancashire the same organization has Salley Abbey (SD 776464), and the gatehouse of Whalley Abbey (SD 730360).

A. Emery, Greater Medieval Houses of England and Wales (Cambridge University Press, 2000), ii. 568–9.

Stanwix (*Petriana*), Cumbria   Roman fort on Hadrian's Wall

NY 402571. The fort lies within the northern suburbs of Carlisle mostly under modern development. The S ramparts are visible in the churchyard. Figure 29 no. 31.

The fort of Stanwix (*Petriana*), one of the largest on Hadrian's Wall, was built on the north bank of the river Eden opposite CARLISLE. Excavation in the car park of the Cumbria Park Hotel in 1984 revealed traces of the fort's northern defences.

J. Dacre, 'An Excavation on the Roman Fort at Stanwix, Carlisle', TCWAAS 85 (1985), 53–69.

Swinside, Broughton, Cumbria   Neolithic stone circle† ★

SD 172883. About 4 km. W of Broughton in Furness beside footpath running NW from Cragg Hall on minor road N of A595(T) 1 km. N of its junction with the A5093.

This ring with fifty-five porphyritic slate pillars is probably the best-preserved and most impressive stone circle in northern England. It is a classic example of the Cumbrian style with clearly defined entrances, and is early in the overall sequence of circle building in Britain.

Set on gently sloping ground ringed by hills, Swinside has its entrance on the south-west side, marked by a pair of 2 m. high stones forming a sort of porch.

Almost completely circular, Swinside is 28.7 m. in diameter. The tallest stone in the ring stands on the north side. Some stones have now fallen, but when originally standing the stones would have been almost contiguous. Excavations in 1901 failed to find any internal features but showed that the stones had been set in a layer of rammed pebbles.

C. Dymond, 'An Exploration at the Megalithic Circle Called Sunken Kirk', TCWAAS 2 (1902), 53–63.

Temple Sowerby, Cumbria   Roman milestone†

NY 6127. Village 10 km. NW of Appleby. The milestone is by a lay-by on the N side of the A66 heading E. Figure 45.

This uninscribed stone milestone, approximately 1.4 m. high and 0.3 m. in diameter, is now encased in an iron cage and is apparently in its original spot on the line of the Roman road from Kirkby Thore to BROUGHAM.

J. Sedgley, The Roman Milestones of Britain, British Archaeological Reports British Series 18 (1975).

▼ **Fig. 45.** The Roman milestone at Temple Sowerby, Cumbria (Photograph: Jane Timby)

Whitley Castle, near Alston, Cumbria Roman fort

NY 695487. Alston lies W of the A689 between Eamont Bridge and Langwathby. From Alston take the Bampton road (A689) for 3 km. to a narrow bridge over a stream. Immediately after is a track on the left leading to Whitlow Farm. Permission is required to visit the site which is just N of the farm. Figure 46.

A Roman fort set high in the Pennines, famous for its series of well-preserved ditches. The fort (1.2 ha.) lies 19 km. south of the fort of CARVORAN on Hadrian's Wall on the Maiden Way, a Roman road connecting it with Kirkby Thore (*Bravoniacum*). The fort has an unusual rhomboid shape. A bath-house excavated in the early C19 lies outside the north-east corner of the fort.

N. Shaw, 'Excavations at Whitley Castle', AA, 4th ser., 37 (1959), 191–202.

Wigton (Old Carlisle) (*Olenacum*), Cumbria Roman fort

NY 260465. Take B5304 S of Wigton for 1.5 km. and then minor road to Old Carlisle. The site lies in a field between the A595 and the minor road overlooking the Wiza beck. Figure 47.

The platform of a large cavalry fort, 1.82 ha. in size, is clearly visible as an earthwork with well-defined ditches on the west side. The fort was strategically placed on a road network linking it with HADRIAN'S WALL, CARLISLE, and OLD PENRITH. Throughout most, if not all its existence

▲ **Fig. 46.** Whitely Castle Roman fort, Cumbria, looking south (Photograph: CUCAP BEW 17. Copyright reserved)

the garrison was an *ala* of cavalry 500 strong. The fort had an extensive *vicus†*.

R. Collingwood, 'Old Carlisle', TCWAAS 28 (1928), 103–19.

Willowford Wall, Cumbria Roman turrets, bridge, and Hadrian's Wall

NY 625665. On minor road 1 km. W of Gilsland. English Heritage. Access to the bridge is via Willowford Farms. Admission charge. Figure 29 no. 24.

A stretch of some 910 m. of Wall, including two turrets, leading to bridge abutment on what was originally the east bank of the river Irthing. This is one of just three examples in northern Britain where Roman bridge remains have been preserved, the others being CHESTERS and PIERCEBRIDGE. The superstructure would have been of timber.

P. Bidwell and N. Holbrook, Hadrian's Wall Bridges, HBMCE Archaeological Report 9 (English Heritage, 1989).

▲ **Fig. 47.** Old Carlisle (*Olenacum*) Roman fort, Wigton, Cumbria, looking east (Photograph: CUCAP DS 58. Copyright reserved)

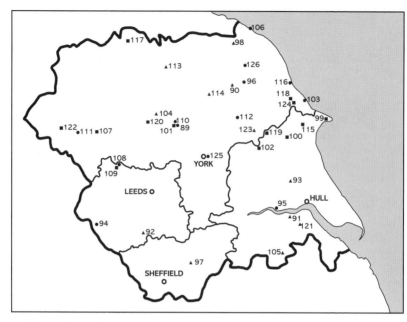

▲ **Fig. 48.** Map of Region 3

Key:

89 Aldborough (*Isurium Brigantium*), North Yorkshire
90 Appleton-le-Moors, North Yorkshire
91 Barton-upon-Humber, North Lincolnshire
92 Bentley Grange, West Yorkshire
93 Beverley, East Riding of Yorkshire
94 Blackstone Edge, West Yorkshire
95 Brough-on-Humber (*Petruaria*), East Riding of Yorkshire
96 Cawthorn Camps, North Yorkshire
97 Conisbrough, South Yorkshire
98 Danby Rigg, North Yorkshire
99 Dane's Dyke, East Riding of Yorkshire
100 Dane's Graves, East Riding of Yorkshire
101 Devil's Arrows, North Yorkshire
102 Duggleby Howe, East Riding of Yorkshire
103 Filey, North Yorkshire
104 Fountains Abbey and Studley Royal, North Yorkshire
105 Gainsthorpe, North Lincolnshire
106 Goldsborough, North Yorkshire
107 Grassington, North Yorkshire
108 Ilkley (*Olicana*), West Yorkshire
109 Ilkley Moor, West Yorkshire
110 Kirby Hill, North Yorkshire
111 Malham Moor, North Yorkshire
112 Malton (*Derventio*), North Yorkshire
113 Mount Grace, North Yorkshire
114 Rievaulx Abbey, North Yorkshire
115 Rudston, East Riding of Yorkshire
116 Scarborough, North Yorkshire
117 Stanwick, North Yorkshire
118 Star Carr, North Yorkshire
119 Staple Howe, East Riding of Yorkshire
120 Thornborough Circles, North Yorkshire
121 Thornton, North Lincolnshire
122 Victoria Cave, North Yorkshire
123 Wharram Percy, North Yorkshire
124 Willerby Wold, North Yorkshire
125 York (*Eboracum*), York
126 Wheeldale Road, North Yorkshire

3 Yorkshire and the Humber basin

This region covers the counties and unitary authorities of North York-shire, West Yorkshire, South Yorkshire, York, East Riding of Yorkshire, North-East Lincolnshire, North Lincolnshire, and Kingston upon Hull.

A region of great contrasts and one that for much of its past boasted a distinctive identity. On the west are the Pennines, with numerous eastward-flowing rivers that cut deep into the hard rocks: the Swale, Ure, Nidd, Wharfe, Aire, and Calder. The Yorkshire Dales National Park covers much of the upland in North Yorkshire, now isolated and dominated by grassland and fell. These uplands preserve some astonishing Roman and prehistoric remains, especially field-systems. Medieval times are well represented by monastic estates established in isolated and harsh landscapes to reflect austere spiritual regimes.

East of the Pennines is the extensive and low-lying Vale of York, connected to the coast by the Vale of Pickering in the north and the Humber lowlands in the south. In Roman times the lower ground around the Humber in particular was completely inundated by the sea, and really only became used for settlement and agriculture following drainage operations in medieval and later times. Inland, settlement of the low ground goes back into early prehistoric times, and includes a very fine range of ceremonial centres that can perhaps be related to trade and exchange across the Pennines. Roman occupation was extensive too, with a major Roman settlement at York.

On the east side of the region are two further groups of hills. North of the Vale of Pickering is the North York Moors, now a National Park, rising to over 400 m. above sea level around Danby Moor. Heavily occupied in the Bronze Age, this area preserves dense concentrations of burial monuments. South of the Vale of Pickering is the Yorkshire Wolds, an area of chalk upland. The Wolds meet the sea at Flamborough Head with some impressive chalk cliffs. This region too was well settled from Neolithic times, and preserves remarkable burial sites and ceremonial monuments. Being slightly lower than the North York Moors, the Wolds remained in heavy usage through later prehistoric, Roman, and medieval times. Numerous deserted villages attest the scale of medieval settlement, three or four times denser than today. Sadly, since the C18, the Wolds have been returned to intensive arable agriculture, which has damaged many archaeological sites.

The coastal region of the Humber estuary is low-lying and gradually eroding inland. Although many sites lie buried under the ground there are few visible monuments.

Aldborough (*Isurium Brigantium*), North Yorkshire Roman town

SE 405661. 1.25 km. SE of Boroughbridge, on minor road off B6265 within 1.5 km. of junction of A1 and A6055. English Heritage. Restricted opening. Admission charge. Figure 49.

Aldborough was the capital of the *Brigantes*. In the C1 the Romans established a fort here for their IXth Legion which subsequently developed into a Roman town and *civitas†* capital. Parts of the C2 town wall by the north gate, with its defensive towers, can be seen behind the museum. Excavations have revealed several mosaic pavements from wealthy town houses; two are on view, signposted from the Museum Garden. Others are in Leeds City Museum including a famous one depicting the legend of Romulus and Remus.

M. Bishop, Finds from Roman Aldborough *(Oxbow Books, 1996); J. Wacher,* The Towns of Roman Britain *(Batsford, 1995), 398–404.*

▼ **Fig. 49.** A Roman mosaic from Aldborough (*Isurium Brigantium*), North York-shire, depicting the story of Romulus and Remus and the wolf (Leeds City Museum)

Appleton-le-Moors, North Yorkshire Medieval village

SE 7387. On minor road N of A170 from Pickering to Thirsk.

Planned 'estate' villages of the C18 and C19 are well enough known. Less so are their predecessors of the C10 to C12, of which Appleton, on the southern fringe of the North York Moors, is an excellent example. The village houses, each within its own house plot or 'toft', face each other across the broad main street. At the north end of the village, on either side of the road, are the church and Appleton Hall. Extending behind the houses are their 150 m. long, straight, gardens or 'crofts', in which animals might be kept or vegetables grown. Back lanes run along the rear of the crofts parallel with the main street, giving access to fields. The present field boundaries date from the parish's enclosure of about 1710, but fossilize earlier medieval strip boundaries. As these boundaries continue the alignment of the tofts and crofts it seems likely that the whole landscape was laid out anew in a single act of replanning.

Three kilometres to the north is **Lastingham** [SE 7391], whose church has an Anglo-Saxon crypt. In the market town of **Pickering** [SE 8085], 7 km. to the south-east, is a good castle (English Heritage) and a church with a series of mid-C15 wall paintings.

A Quiney, 'Appleton-le-Moors', Arch J, 154 (1997), 270–4.

Barton-upon-Humber (St Peter's), North Lincolnshire Anglo-Saxon church ★

TA 0322. The church is in E part of town, N of A1077. The town stands on S bank of the river Humber, on the A15. English Heritage; restricted opening.

The tower of St Peter's is one of the finest Anglo-Saxon structures in the country, and with its rendered rubble walls divided up with decorative pilaster strips, long-and-short quoins, and doors to north and south, it has close similarities to that at EARLS BARTON (Northamptonshire). The lower two storeys are C10, the third, of dressed limestone, perhaps of the mid-C11. The tower originally stood between west and east annexes, of which the former still survives. That may have been a baptistery†, with the tower serving as nave and the lost east annexe as chancel. The site of the last is now occupied by the nave of the parish church, a large aisled structure of medieval date.

Barton's other ancient church, **St Mary's**, has Norman to Perpendicular work.

G. F. Bryant, The Early History of Barton-upon-Humber, 2nd edn (Workers' Educational Association, Barton-upon-Humber, 1994)

Bentley Grange, Elmley, West Yorkshire Medieval mining
remains

SE 266131. Elmley village lies 3 km. W of A636, 10 km. SW of Wakefield. Mining remains visible from minor road running E of the village to join A636.

Here in the C13 and C14 ironstone was mined and smelted for Byland Abbey, some 80 km. away, of which Bentley was an outlying grange or farm. Rings of mining spoil 2 m. high surround the sites of individual shafts, many now sheltering a thorn tree. Once each 'bell pit' (so-called because underground the shaft bellied out as the ironstone was extracted) became unsafe to work it was abandoned, and a new shaft sunk. Just how methodical, and by implication well managed, the exploitation was can be seen from the regular spacing of the mounds. The spoil heaps spread across, and therefore post-date, ridge and furrow†. This represents arable land abandoned to the more profitable iron industry in the C13. Mining had ceased by the C16.

M. Beresford and J. St Joseph, Medieval England: An Aerial Survey, *2nd edn (Cambridge University Press, 1979), 256–7.*

Beverley, East Riding of Yorkshire Medieval town
TA 0439. 10 km. NW of Hull and 40 km. SE of York. Figure 50.

Beverley prospered from the wool and cloth trades, becoming the largest town in the East Riding by the later Middle Ages. That prosperity was invested in building works. At the south end of the historic town is **Beverley Minster**—before the Reformation a collegiate church†—whose fittings, in particular, reflect its former prosperity. Rebuilding after a fire began in the 1220s at the east end; the main transepts and the first bay of the nave were up by 1260. Those were in the Early English style. When building restarted in 1308 the Decorated style had become fashionable, while by the time the east window, the north porch, and the twin-towered west front were finished in the mid-C15 the Perpendicular had long been in vogue. Inside see the musicians carved between the decorated wall canopies of the nave. The black marble font is C12, its huge cover of 1713. In the choir and transepts black marble shafts are striking detail, while the intricately carved choir stalls of 1520 have tip-up misericord† seats decorated with secular scenes. The C14–C15 tombs of the Percy family are grouped around the north-east transept which contains their chantry chapel†.

At the north end of town is **St Mary's Church**. The central tower collapsed in 1520, and much of the church dates from the subsequent rebuilding. Fortunately the chapel of St Michael in the north aisle of the chancel survived, dated about 1330–40 and in the late Decorated style.

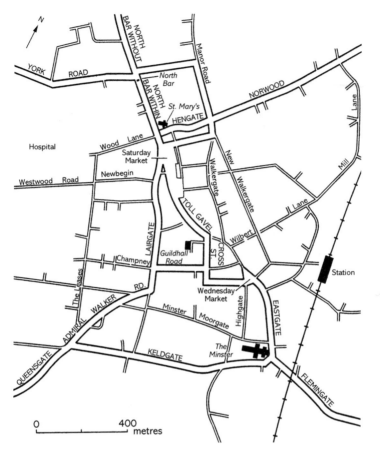

▲ **Fig. 50.** Beverley, East Riding of Yorkshire (after Clifton-Taylor)

St Mary's lies on North Bar Within, and at the north end of that street is the 'bar' or **town gate** itself. It is of 1409, and is an exceptionally early example of the use of brick. It is the only one of five gates to survive, gates which were connected by a town ditch but never a defensive wall. It was at these that tolls were collected from the medieval traders in wool and cloth, whose presence is still recalled in street names such as **Walkergate** (after the fullers who 'walked' the cloth to cleanse and thicken it), **Dyer Lane**, and **Flemingate**, on the route followed by Flemish traders.

K. Miller et al., Beverley, RCHME Supplementary Series 4 (HMSO, 1982).

Blackstone Edge, Rippondale, West Yorkshire Roman
road

SD 973170. From Littleborough take the A58. About 1.6 km. E the road takes a U-bend before climbing upwards. At the bottom of the hill a public footpath E of road follows the Roman road. Access also from car park at the top of the hill by the White House public house. Follow the Pennine Way footpath opposite car park for about 15–20 minutes. The Roman road crosses this path just before a stile. Figure 51.

From the base of the hill part of the Roman road running between Manchester and Ilkley cuts a straight line up the steep slope. Towards the top stone block paving approximately 5 m. wide is visible with a worn central channel presumably to facilitate braking and, if turfed, to provide

▼ **Fig. 51.** The Roman road at Blackstone Edge, West Yorkshire (Photograph: Barnaby's Picture Library)

better purchase for animal hooves. This flattens out where the road levels off at the top.

I. Margary, Roman Roads in Britain (John Baker, 1967), 404.

Brough-on-Humber (*Petruaria*), East Riding of Yorkshire Roman fort and town

SE 937267. Brough village is 16 km. W of Hull on N bank of river Humber. The Roman site is E of modern village.

Little is visible today. A Flavian fort was built here which fell out of use in the C2 and a civilian town developed in the later C2. Identification of the site as the *civitas*† capital of the *Parisi* is based on an inscription found when the theatre site was excavated. Some believe *Petruaria* was elsewhere; debate continues.

H. Ramm, The Parisi (Duckworth, 1978).

Cawthorn Camps, Pickering and Cawthorn, North Yorkshire Roman camps

SE 783898. 6.5 km. N of Pickering off minor road (signposted Keldy Bridge) between Cropton and Newton-on-Rawcliffe. Car park with signboard and marked trail. Booklet available from local villages. Figure 52.

A unique group of three exceptionally well-preserved Roman military fortifications built around AD 100. The site is in a good strategic position

▼ **Fig. 52.** Plan of Cawthorn Roman Camps, North Yorkshire (after RCHME)

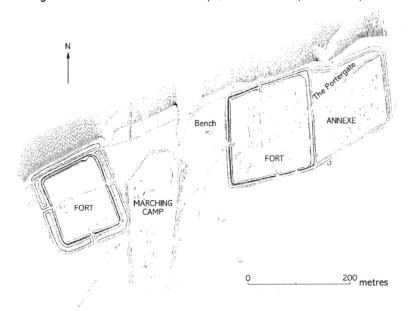

on the northern scarp edge of the Tabular hills. Recent survey work has concluded that Site C is the only true camp of the group. Sites D and A are currently thought to be forts with B forming an annexe to fort A, suggesting more permanent occupation. The coffin-shaped form of the marching camp, C, is unusual, as are the gateway arrangements with three on one side, and may be the result of earlier phases of activity. The two forts lie to the east and west of the camp respectively and their defences are much more pronounced. The easterly fort was enlarged by adding an annexe on the east side, whilst the westerly fort has a more complex defensive sequence.

RCHME, Roman Camps in England. The Field Archaeology *(HMSO, 1995), 137–42.*

Conisbrough, South Yorkshire Medieval castle

SK 515989. The castle stands NE of the town centre off A630. English Heritage. Restricted opening. Admission charge.

The castle stands on a scarped hill surrounded by strong counterscarp banks† except to the west where there is a small, curved bailey†, with a gatehouse to the south and small, half-round buttress-towers. The bailey contains a single-aisled hall, built against the wall, with lodgings to its south, which included a first-floor solar with fireplace. At the other end of the hall was the kitchen. The cylindrical, limestone ashlar keep of about 1180 was probably built by Hamelin Plantagenet, fifth Warenne earl of Surrey, who held the castle 1163–1202. Inside, there are four floors, the keep being entered at first-floor level through a door defended by bar-holes and with traces of drawbridge pivots. The basement contains the castle well; access was via a trapdoor in the centre of the vault. From the first floor stairs within the wall lead up to the second floor, a circular room with a fireplace, basin, window seats, and a latrine at the end of a zigzag wall passage. The third floor has the principal apartment, with a richly decorated chapel built into the thickness of the wall, its chancel set back into a buttress. The topmost floor has been destroyed, but enough survives to show there were two fighting lines around its edge, a covered walk with wall walk above.

S. Johnson, Conisbrough Castle *(English Heritage, 1984) (Site Guidebook).*

Danby Rigg / Danby High Moor, Danby, North Yorkshire Prehistoric cairns† and boundaries

NZ 710065. Upland to the S of Danby. Approached from the N, take minor road S of Danby across the river Esk via Ainthorpe to Bramble Carr. Proceed on foot uphill following available paths. Figure 53.

The upland moor of Danby Rigg preserves a wide range of prehistoric features, many connected with Bronze Age agriculture when the climate

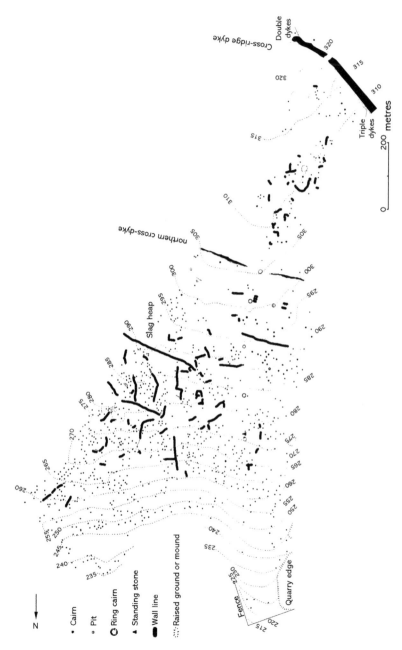

▲ **Fig. 53.** Plan showing the main archaeological features on Danby Rigg, North Yorkshire (after Harding)

N

- • Cairn
- ◦ Pit
- ⊙ Ring cairn
- ▲ Standing stone
- ▬ Wall line
- ⋯ Raised ground or mound

Fence

Quarry edge

Slag heap

northern cross-dyke

Cross-ridge dyke

Double dykes

Triple dykes

0   200 metres

was better. Two earthworks cut across the spur; the more southerly, known as **Double Dyke**, in fact comprises three banks and two ditches and dates to the later first millennium AD. The more northerly is a single stone bank, of unknown date. Between these two earthworks is a small banked enclosure, about 20 m. in diameter, and a number of stone cairns, some perhaps burial cairns.

At the north end of the hill, there are more than 800 small stone clearance cairns, testament to the determination of prehistoric farmers.

A. Harding, 'Prehistoric and Early Medieval Activity on Danby Rigg', Arch J, 151 (1994), 16–97.

Dane's Dyke, Flamborough, East Riding of Yorkshire Prehistoric linear earthwork† ★

TA 216694. 2 km. W of Flamborough, bisected by the B1229 and the B1255. Car park S of B1255 near Dane's Dyke Farm.

Dane's Dyke runs across Flamborough Head for 4.25 km. cutting off about 4 km. of the eastern part of the peninsular. It comprises a bank up to 5.4 m. high and a ditch up to 18 m. wide on the west (inland) side. A smaller second bank lies outside the ditch. For much of its course the earthwork is set to the east of a natural valley, which at the south end becomes a ravine.

There is one possible original entrance towards the north end; a second may be utilized by the modern Bridlington to Flamborough road.

Undated, the boundary is believed to be of the C1 BC but may be earlier. Its purpose is not known, although it may have been a defensive work. In Neolithic times Flamborough Head was one of the few sources of good quality workable flint in northern England.

H. Ramm, 'Dane's Dyke', Arch J, 141 (1983), 37–9.

Dane's Graves, Driffield, East Riding of Yorkshire Iron Age barrow cemetery

TA 018633. 4 km. W of Kilham, E of the B1249, mainly in woodland S of Westfield Farm.

Formerly a very extensive Iron Age cemetery with about 500 square-shaped barrows. The 200 or so remaining barrows range in size from 3 m. to 10 m. across and stand up to 1 m. high. Some have surrounding ditches.

The barrows belong to the late Iron Age Arras Culture tradition. Over 100 of the mounds have been excavated at various times, mainly by J. R. Mortimer in the late C19. The burials were found to be crouched inhumations in centrally placed grave pits typically buried with grave goods such as jewellery and food offerings in a pot. The quantity of grave goods varied, suggesting that rank and status were represented in death. Some graves contained dismantled chariots; others imports from Europe.

Finds are in the Yorkshire Museum, York, and the British Museum, London.

W. Greenwell, 'Early Iron Age Burials in Yorkshire', Archaeologia, 60 (1907), 251–324.

Devil's Arrows, Boroughbridge, North Yorkshire Neolithic stone row†

SE 391666. 1 km. W of Boroughbridge, immediately E of A1(T). Access from the narrow lane leading W from Boroughbridge to Roecliffe.

This line of three massive pillars of millstone grit set over a distance of 175 m. are the remains of a longer line of four or perhaps five stones. Their name derives from folklore that the Devil was hurling arrows at the town of Boroughbridge, but missed!

The pillars were clearly carefully selected and transported from at least 15 km away. The grooves in the stones are from natural erosion.

A. Burl, 'The Devil's Arrows', YAJ 63 (1991), 1–24.

Duggleby Howe, Kirkby Grindalythe, East Riding of Yorkshire Neolithic round barrow†

SE 881669. Immediately E of B1254 Duggleby to Sledmore road, 200 m. S of Duggleby.

This massive round barrow is one of about a dozen late Neolithic bowl barrows scattered across the Yorkshire Wolds and one of the largest in Britain. Its great hemispherical mound is 38 m. in diameter and 6 m. high.

Excavations by J. R. Mortimer in 1890 revealed a complicated and convoluted history to the site. Initially a shaft was dug into the chalk into which an adult male was interred. The filling of the shaft contained the remains of two further individuals and a separate skull. More burials were added to the top of the shaft and a second, rather less-deep shaft was dug next to the first to receive another inhumation. After this the primary mound was raised over the shafts, a further eight burials being added to the mound as it grew. Later, fifty-three cremations were inserted into the crest of the mound before the mound itself was enlarged to something like the structure we see today.

In 1971 air photography showed that the mound lay in the centre of a ditched enclosure roughly 370 m. across.

I. Kinnes et al., 'Duggleby Howe Reconsidered', Arch J, 140 (1983), 83–108.

Filey, Carr Naze, North Yorkshire Roman signal station

TA 132815. The waymarked 3.2 km. Nature Trail in Filey Country Park on the path between Filey Brigg and Carr Naze passes close to original site of the signal station. Now mostly destroyed by cliff erosion. Figure 54.

A late C4 signal station now partly destroyed by cliff erosion (see also GOLDSBOROUGH and SCARBOROUGH). Excavations discovered five stone bases thought to support a wooden watch tower. One of the bases decorated with a hound hunting a stag can be seen in the grounds of the public library.

P. Ottaway, 'Excavations on the Site of the Roman Signal Station at Carr Naze, Filey, 1993–94', Arch J 157 (2000), 79–199.

▼ **Fig. 54.** Reconstruction of a late 4th-century Roman signal station on the Yorkshire coast (Copyright Royal Archaeological Institute)

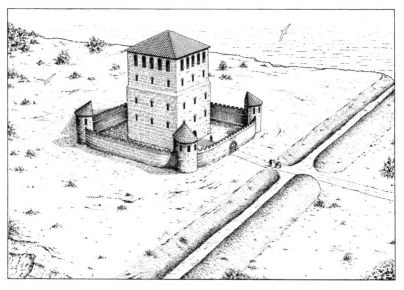

Fountains Abbey and Studley Royal, Ripon, North Yorkshire Medieval abbey ★★

SE 271683. 6 km. W of Ripon off B6265. National Trust and English Heritage. Visitor centre and small museum. Admission charge for the Abbey and Water Garden. Restricted opening. The Deer Park open at any reasonable time. World Heritage Site. Website: www.fountainsabbey.org.uk.

Fountains Abbey is one of the noblest and most extensive monastic sites in Europe. It stands in Skelldale, where, in 1132, a small group of monks chose to found a house following the austere Cistercian† rule. The support of wealthy patrons and expert management of their industrial and farming enterprises—Fountains was the largest producer of wool in the north—underpinned the house's expansion, and in the C13, at the height of its fortunes, there were about 120 monks and perhaps 400 lay brethren and servants here.

One of the latest additions to Fountains is Abbot Huby's great bell-tower, built in the late C15. Externally it is decorated with statues of saints and painted biblical texts, still partly visible. The church itself, begun in the 1150s, has an eleven-bay nave of finely cut ashlar masonry, the seven westernmost bays for lay brothers and those to the east for choir monks. At the east end of the church is the Chapel of Nine Altars, built in the C13 to allow the growing number of monks who were also priests to say mass. The west range, running south from the church, comprises at first-floor level the lay brothers' 91 m. long dormitory with at its end their latrine block, built over the river Skell. Beneath the dormitory is a vaulted undercroft†, used for storage and as the lay brothers' refectory. The east range includes the choir monks' dormitory, next to which, in the south range, is the warming house, where from 1 November to Good Friday fires were kept in the fireplaces. The monks' refectory lies at right-angles to the south range, a typical Cistercian arrangement.

Other monastic buildings within the precinct, which is 1000 m. long and 400 m. wide, include a watermill and guest houses.

In the earlier C18 the ruins were made the focus of John Aislabie's spectacular water garden, attached to his house of Studley Royal.

G. Coppack, Fountains Abbey *(Batsford and English Heritage, 1993).*

Gainsthorpe, North Lincolnshire Deserted medieval village

SK 955012. Access from minor road W of A15 S of Hibaldstow, 8 km. SW of Brigg. English Heritage.

The earthworks show two main, parallel, hollow-ways, one running west from the farmhouse, the other 70 m. to its north. The two are connected by a third former road, which is bisected by the modern track about 80 m. west of the farmhouse. Earthworks of houses and barns abound along the hollow-ways, while to all sides can be seen banks and ditches defining the former village's closes.

M. Beresford, The Lost Villages of England *(Lutterworth Press, 1954), 94–5.*

Goldsborough, North Yorkshire Roman signal station

NZ 835152. On Goldsborough–Kettleness footpath leading N from Goldsborough.

One of the five known stations on the Yorkshire coast (see also FILEY and SCARBOROUGH). Built during Theodosius' reign, Goldsborough had thick stone walls surrounded by ditches. The walls had rounded angles with semicircular projecting bastions for artillery with an entrance on the south side. The internal courtyard contained a well and a stone tower

14 m. square and perhaps originally 25–30 m. high. The site is now covered by a mound of soil with no visible stonework.

W. Hornsby and J. Laverick, 'The Roman Signal Station at Goldsborough', Arch J, 89 (1932), 203–19.

Grassington, North Yorkshire Prehistoric and later settlements
and field-systems ★

SD 9965. N of Grassington village, best approached from the Dales Way footpath running N from village. Figure 55.

Grassington is high in the limestone hills of the Pennines. Walking out onto the grassy hillsides post-medieval stone walls are clear enough, but equally obvious are the remains of earlier fields and paddocks surviving as upstanding banks, lynchets†, and soil-covered walls. The best groups lie immediately north of Grassington village, around **Sweet Side** (SE

▼ **Fig. 55.** Aerial photograph of the early field-systems at Grassington, North Yorkshire (CUCAP K17 AC 26)

004655), around **Lea Green** (SD 995665), and west of **Nook** (SD 992677).

Three main kinds of field plot can be seen. Most numerous are rectangular plots with their long axis running parallel to the contours. The second group are square-shaped. Finally, there are small paddocks or yards, generally less than 15 m. across, mainly near buildings or farmsteads. Trackways are also visible as pairs of parallel banks with a hollow between. An Iron Age to Roman date for the features seems likely. A few round barrows† attest to earlier activity.

J. St Joseph, 'Air Reconnaissance: Recent Results 32', Antiquity, 47 (1973), 296–7.

Ilkley (*Olicana*), West Yorkshire Roman fort and Museum

SE 116478. 16 km. N of Bradford. The Roman focus lies around the parish church. Manor House Museum next to the church. Restricted opening.

A series of forts were constructed close to the river Wharfe in the Agricolan, Antonine, and Severan periods. A *vicus*† developed nearby. Ilkley lies on the roads linking YORK with RIBCHESTER and MANCHESTER with ALDBOROUGH. Little remains of the Roman walls, which were extensively robbed. The parish church, which lies within the fort, contains much Roman stone including two altars recut to make window-heads in the Anglo-Saxon church. A stretch of wall can be seen behind the museum.

B. Hartley, 'The Roman Fort at Ilkley', PLPLS 12/2 (1966), 23–72.

Ilkley Moor (Rombalds Moor), Ilkley, West Yorkshire Neolithic stone circles†, cairns†, and rock art ★

SE 1044. Open moorland S of Ilkley, N of Bradford, encircled by the A65(T), A6034, A629, A650, and A6038. Criss-crossed by footpaths.

This relatively small area of moor contains an abundance of stone circles, cairns, and, most unusual of all, a concentration of carved rocks running all around the edge of the upland.

Most carved stones are flat-topped outcrops of the local millstone grit. One good group around **Addingham High Moor** on the north-west side (SE 080470), includes the Swastika Stone (now within a fenced pen) showing the double outline of a swastika with a cross-shaped arrangement of hollows in it. This design is so different from the others on the moor that it may be of a later period. There are more stones around **Green Crag Slack** on the north-east side (SE 140455) including the **Pancake Stone** which is rich in cup and ring marks†. Some of the best stones have been removed to safety, including the elaborately carved **Panorama Stone**, now in the public gardens opposite St Margaret's Church, Ilkley. There are also some casts of stones from Rombald's Moor in Leeds Museum.

Rock art

Although it has long been known that prehistoric communities cut symbols and images into rock surfaces, it is only in the last twenty years or so that the wide distribution and early date of these images has been realized. Three common situations can be identified: outcrops of living rock or the surfaces of boulders (open-air panels); small movable blocks (mobiliary panels); and on the component stones of monumental construction (monument-based panels). They were cut during Neolithic and early Bronze Age times, and form part of a far more widespread tradition found over many parts of Europe.

Several techniques of decorating rock surfaces were used. The most common are pecking, scratching, grinding, and engraving.

The images appear simple and, in our terms, rather abstract. The most common is the **cup-mark**, a small circular hemispherical depression. Sometimes several cups are joined together to form an oval depression. Cups are also widely associated with **rings** which comprise more or less concentric circles with the cup-mark at the centre. However, even the apparently simple cup and ring marks can be used to create complicated panels of decoration. Other common motifs include circles, rings and radial grooves, spirals, boxes, zigzag lines, lozenges, ladder patterns, axes, daggers, footprints, and hand-prints. Very occasionally animals are drawn in outline, and sometimes individual motifs are arranged to look vaguely humanistic, although whether this was the intention is not known.

The **Twelve Apostles Circle** lies on the north side of the moor (SE 126451) and has twelve stone pillars forming the ring, now all fallen; the stones are set at irregular intervals suggesting that once there may have been more. The **Grubstones Circle** (SE 136447) is smaller at about 10 m. in diameter but is almost perfectly circular with twenty surviving stones. The **Horncliffe Circle** (SE 134435) is oval in plan with its forty-six remaining stones set close together. Traces of a smaller central circle suggests that a burial monument was added later.

South-east of the Grubstones Circle there are several well-preserved cairns including **The Skirtful of Stones** (SE 141447), 26 m. in diameter and 2 m. high.

J. Hedges (ed.), The Carved Rocks on Rombald's Moor *(West Yorkshire Metropolitan County Council, 1986).*

Kirby Hill, North Yorkshire Anglo-Saxon church with Roman masonry

SE 394686. 3.2 km. N of Aldborough on B6265.

All Saints' Church is a complex structure, in part late Anglo-Saxon, and incorporating Roman masonry. The Saxon work is in the nave; see the typical side-alternate quoins at both original corners on the south side, and the truncated remains of the Saxon south door. This has an impost with interlace carving. Within the church, parts of the Saxon north wall can be seen above the Norman arcade.

The Saxon builders used, in part, stone robbed from nearby Roman buildings. Most prominent is a large dressed sandstone block in the bottom course of the south-west corner of the tower, possibly a statue base, and a small Roman altar built into a niche in the porch.

H. and J. Taylor, Anglo-Saxon Architecture *(Cambridge University Press, 1965).*

Malham Moor, North Yorkshire Roman marching camp

SD 916655. On minor roads N and W of A65 about 8 km. from Settle. Mastiles Lane crossing Malham Moor follows the field wall, which cuts across the centre of the camp.

A well-preserved large (8.2 ha.) marching camp clearly visible as low earthworks either side of Mastiles Lane. The camp is of legionary size and is defended by an earthen rampart and an incomplete ditch. There are four gates. A monastic cross base lies north of the lane near the centre of the camp.

RCHME, Roman Camps in England *(HMSO, 1995), 143–5.*

Malton (*Derventio*), North Yorkshire Roman fort and town

SE 791718. 27 km. NE of York. Roman sites in area of Orchard Fields, a public space on E side of Malton on the Malton–Pickering road (B1257). Museum in Old Town Hall.

Earthworks marking the site of a series of Roman forts and associated civilian settlement. A bank marks the complete length of the east rampart along with part of the north and south sides. The fort, used by the IX Legion, was first established in AD 79. A *vicus*† developed between the fort and the river Derwent whilst the Roman town was centred south of the river. In the C4 a cavalry force was based here. Finds from excavations can be seen in Malton Museum.

L. Wenham and B. Heywood, Malton (North Yorkshire): The 1968–1970 Excavations in the vicus *(Yorkshire Archaeological Society, 1998).*

Mount Grace, North Yorkshire Medieval priory ★

SE 449985. E of the A19 12 km. N of Thirsk, 7 km. N of Northallerton. English Heritage; restricted access. Admission charge. Figure 56.

Mount Grace is the best surviving example of a Carthusian† monastery (or charterhouse) in Britain; its setting captures the remoteness and tranquillity sought by its founders in 1398. Apart from the outer court,

▼ **Fig. 56.** Mount Grace, North Yorkshire: the priory church as it would have been in the 1530s (after English Heritage)

which contained the farm buildings and guests' accommodation, its precinct survives almost complete, with an inner court for the service buildings and a great cloister with the church and monks' cells. On the hillside to the east are three conduit houses, which fed a large and sophisticated water tower in the centre of the cloister and also a channel to the rear of the gardens which drained the latrines. The church was begun about 1400, with the bell-tower being added in the 1420s and various side chapels somewhat later. The short west section was for the monastery's lay brothers, the longer east part for the monks' choir, where they would gather for matins, mass, private mass, and vespers. Generally speaking, this was the only time the brethren met, for what most marked the Carthusians apart was that they lived not communally but in isolation, each in his own cell. Each cell—and there were eventually seventeen—comprised a two-storey house set in a private vegetable garden, with a four-roomed ground floor (entry, living room, bedroom-cum-oratory, and study) and a second-floor workroom, for every Carthusian had a trade. Each garden was bounded by two corridors: one was a private cloister for study and meditation, while the other led to the garden and latrine.

One of the cells has been reconstructed.

G. Coppack, Mount Grace *(English Heritage, 1996) (Site Guidebook).*

Rievaulx Abbey, North Yorkshire   Medieval abbey

SE 577849. 4 km. W of Helmsley on the B1257. English Heritage; restricted opening. Admission charge. Figure 57.

Rievaulx was the first Cistercian† abbey founded in Yorkshire in 1132 in a section of the Rye valley so narrow that the complex had to be rotated to face not east but south-east. It became one of the largest Cistercian houses, with 140 monks, 240 lay brothers, and at least as many again servants. Of the mid-C12 is the long lay brothers' nave, its piers square and austere. This part of the church is ruinous, but standing to full height are the central transepts, the third storey of which was added about 1225, and the choir† and presbytery† range east of that, superb Cistercian Early English architecture. The refectory is in a similar style. East of it is the warming house of about 1200. On the east of the cloister is the chapter house; there were daily readings from the order's rules. An unusually large secondary cloister, which served the infirmary, reflects the large community.

Above the monastery, and giving a fine view of it, is **Rievaulx Terrace** (National Trust). Here are two mid-C18 temples, part of the landscaping of Duncombe House.

G. Coppack and P. Fergusson, Rievaulx Abbey *(English Heritage, 1994) (Site Guidebook).*

Rombalds Moor, Ilkley, West Yorkshire *see* ILKLEY MOOR.

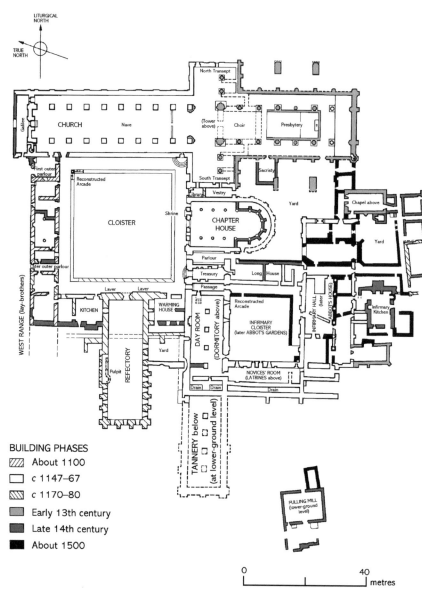

▲ **Fig. 57.** Rievaulx Abbey, North Yorkshire (after English Heritage)

Rudston Monolith, Rudston, East Riding of Yorkshire
Neolithic standing stone† and four associated cursus†
monuments. ★★

TA 097677. Within Rudston churchyard in the centre of village off the B1253, 8 km. west of Bridlington. Figure 58 and Figure 5.

The enormous gritstone block, 1.8 m. wide, 0.7 m. thick and soaring 7.8 m. out of the ground, is the largest standing stone in Britain. Its situation on a low hillock overlooking the Gypsey Race is impressive.

▼ **Fig. 58.** Plan of the cursus monuments in relation to the monolith at Rudston, Yorkshire (after Stoertz)

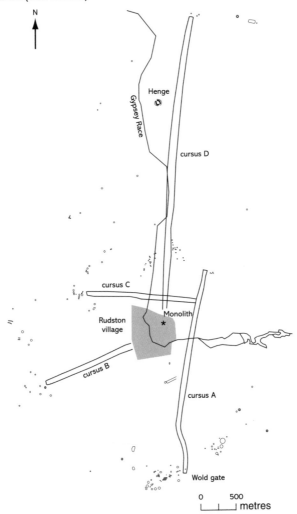

The Rudston Monolith is not local stone; it must have been carried from Cayton or Carnelian Bays over 16 km. to the north. The protective lead cap is modern.

Aerial photography has revealed four later Neolithic cursus monuments converging on the hillock with the monolith, effectively boxing it in. Such an arrangement is unique in Britain, but sadly almost all of the cursus monuments have been levelled by recent cultivation. Only one fragment survives, the south terminal of the southernmost cursus (A) which appears as a grassy bank in the field at **Wold Gate** immediately north of the minor road from Kilham to Bridlington, just west of its junction with the minor road leading down to Rudston (TA 099658).

C. Stoertz, Ancient Landscapes of the Yorkshire Wolds *(RCHME, 1997), 25–30.*

Scarborough, North Yorkshire Roman signal station

TA 052892. In grounds of Scarborough Castle. English Heritage; restricted opening. Admission charge.

One of five known stations along the North Yorkshire coast, the others being at Huntcliff, GOLDSBOROUGH, Ravenscar, and FILEY. Built in the later C4 as part of a defensive measure against barbarian invaders, the towers would have been topped with beacons. The tower stood within a small defended compound partly lost through cliff erosion.

P. Ottaway, Romans on the Yorkshire Coast *(York Archaeological Trust, 1995).*

Stanwick, Eppleby, North Yorkshire Iron Age *oppidum*†   ★

NZ 178124. E of B6274 between Forcett and Stanwick-St-John. Signposted from the A66(T) and A67. English Heritage. Figure 59.

This massive sprawling set of earthworks and enclosures covering about 300 ha. may have been the tribal capital of the *Brigantes* in the last few centuries BC, and up to and after the Roman Conquest. Excavations and surveys show a long and complicated development.

Stanwick is not defensively well positioned, but is at a good communications point. It probably originated as a series of unenclosed settlements amid fields and paddocks.

The massive defences were mainly built in the mid-C1 AD. The focus appears to have been around the present-day church, in the Tofts, and in the northern part of the site. A section of rampart uncovered during excavations can be seen on the north side (signposted). Standing in the Tofts, it is possible to see most of the outer circuit of defences, much of which can be walked following footpaths.

The north-west entrance (near where the present road running east from Forcett cuts through the ramparts) into the main occupation area was elaborate and massive. This, coupled with the presence of imported Roman goods (including wine *amphorae* and tableware) suggests that the *Brigantian* elite at this time were powerful and well connected.

▲ Fig. 59. Plan of the enclosures and defences at Stanwick, North Yorkshire (after Welfare, Topping, Blood & Ramm)

By the late C1 AD the site had been abandoned, historically coinciding with the Roman conquest of the region. Excavation finds are in the Yorkshire Museum, York, and the British Museum, London.

C. Haselgrove et al., 'Stanwick, North Yorkshire', Arch J, 147 (1990), 1–15.

Staple Howe, Knapton, East Riding of Yorkshire Iron Age settlement

SE 898749. 12 km. E of Malton and 2 km. SW of West Heslerton, the site lies S of A64(T) in Knapton Plantation about 2 km. E of the junction with B1258. A path leads to the site.

Staple Howe is a fine example of what, during the mid-first millennium BC, was a typical settlement site in this area. Situated in a commanding position on a natural chalk hillock, this was home to one or two extended families and their livestock.

Excavations between 1951 and 1958 demonstrated that the site started around 500 BC with a single oval house 10 × 6 m. The walls were made of stone and rammed chalk, and it had a gabled roof. The house was surrounded by yards and defended by a wooden palisade around the edge of the hill.

Around 400 BC the house was replaced by a pair of round houses and a granary now marked out with concrete posts. The second-phase houses had wooden walls and conical roofs supported by central posts, typical of the middle and later Iron Age houses. The entrances both faced south-east for maximum light and shelter from the weather. Both houses had hearths and ovens, and one had an upright loom for weaving cloth.

T. Brewster, The Excavation of Staple Howe (The East Riding Archaeological Research Committee, 1963).

Star Carr, Seamer, North Yorkshire Mesolithic settlement

TA 027810. 3 km. S of Seamer, W of the A64(T). Take footpath E of Staxton to Seamer Road (A64T) at TA 020811. The site is near the S bank of the river Hertford W of Star Carr bridge.

Although nothing remains to be seen on the surface, Star Carr is important because it is one of few well-explored Mesolithic settlements in Britain.

About 7500 BC the Vale of Pickering around what is now Star Carr was a shallow lake surrounded by fairly well-wooded countryside. At Star Carr, next to the lake, was a small seasonal settlement occupied by hunter-gatherers of the Maglemosian tradition.

Excavations between 1949 and 1951 revealed a settlement built on a brushwood platform. A wooden paddle shows that the occupants of the site used boats or canoes. Hunting provided most food: deer, wild cattle, elk, wild pig, pine martens, red fox, and beavers. Bones of a domesticated dog, the earliest yet known in Britain, were also found.

P. Mellars and P. Dark, Star Carr in Context *(McDonald Institute for Archaeological Research and Oxbow Books, 1998).*

Thornborough Circles, Ripon, North Yorkshire Neolithic henges†

SE 285795. 2 km. E of West Tanfield on NE side of the river Ure. Best approached from the N along minor road that heads S from the B6267 at Nosterfield. Visible from the road.

Situated on the north side of the river Ure this site comprises a linear arrangement of three henges spread at roughly equal intervals over a distance of 1.5 km. It is one of the largest and most complete of a series of Neolithic ceremonial foci in north-eastern England.

All three henges have the characteristic bank with an inner ditch, here with an outer ditch. Each henge has opposing pairs of entrances through the earthwork on a north-west to south-east axis, which is also the axis on which the three individual monuments were set out.

The entrances are wide and the ditch terminals at the entrances slightly expanded with square ends. The diameter of the interiors vary slightly from 90 m. Excavations in 1952 revealed that the banks, at least in the case of the central circle, had been covered in a layer of gypsum crystals, perhaps in imitation of more southerly sites like AVEBURY in Wiltshire.

Between the southern and central henges is the circular ring-ditch of a ploughed-out bowl barrow known as 'Central Hill'. Excavations in 1870 revealed a primary inhumation burial accompanied by a food vessel, a flint scraper, and a flint knife suggesting a date slightly later than the henges.

N. Thomas, 'The Thornborough Circles', YAJ 38 (1955), 425–45.

Thornton, North Lincolnshire Medieval abbey

TA 115190. Beside a minor road 6 km. NE of Immingham. English Heritage. The Abbey Grounds are accessible at any reasonable time; the Gatehouse has restricted opening.

A house of Augustinian canons was founded here in 1139, and although mostly only foundations survive it has one of the most elaborate surviving gatehouses of any monastic house. Its construction was licensed in 1382, supposedly a frightened response by the isolated community to the Peasants' Revolt of 1381. However, while it has arrow slits and a portcullis gateway, it is hard to think it was seriously intended for defence; rather the architectural vocabulary of the castle and palace has been borrowed for a very deliberate piece of structural show-boating.

The gatehouse is largely brick built—a very early use—with elaborate stone turrets and statue niches to the first floor. Inside were splendid quarters, probably for the abbot. The gatehouse is approached via a brick barbican†, a defensive outwork furnished with arrow slits and end turrets. This may post-date the dissolution of the abbey in 1539 and instead be associated with the later but short-lived mansion on the site.

G. Coppack, Thornton Abbey (English Heritage, 1993) (Site Guidebook).

Victoria Cave, Langcliffe, North Yorkshire   Occupied cave

SE 838650. 3 km. NE of Settle in W facing cliff known as Langcliffe Scar. From the B6479 at Langcliffe take minor road E towards Overclose. After a steep climb out of Langcliffe continue on foot using the lane that runs S from Clay Pits Plantation and then footpaths running S along Langcliffe Scar. (Fig. 1.)

This shallow cave or rock shelter in the limestone cliffs has a wonderful view westwards towards the Ribble valley. It has yielded evidence of occupation dating back to the last Ice Age. Three important finds have been made: part of an antler point of Upper Palaeolithic type and an antler point of Mesolithic type were found just outside the cave mouth, while a second Upper Palaeolithic point decorated with wavy lines was found inside the cave.

T. Dearne, The Romano-British Archaeology of Victoria Cave, British Archaeological Reports British Series 273 (1998).

Wharram Percy, North Yorkshire   Deserted medieval village

SE 859645. Site car park at Bella Farm, a short distance S of Wharram-le Street (which has a fine late Saxon church) off the B1248 10 km. SE of Malton. From the car park there is a stiff 1 km. walk before the church is glimpsed. English Heritage. Figure 60.

The deserted village of Wharram Percy in the high chalk Wolds was for forty years the scene of annual excavations under Maurice Beresford and John Hurst.

The village divides into two parts. The visitor will be drawn first to the church of St Martin, which stands in the bottom of a small valley, along with a short row of brick cottages, and the reconstructed millpond. The church survived the village, serving the surrounding settlements until 1949. Thereafter it fell into disrepair, and a project was initiated to excavate the entire parish church.

The church apparently began in the C10 as a small timber structure of nave† and chancel†. Before the Norman Conquest this had been rebuilt in stone, the local lords being buried beneath stone slabs south of its chancel. Early in the C12 the church was enlarged, and provided with a fashionable apsidal chancel. Between then and the early C15 the church expanded greatly, with the addition of south and north aisles, a

▲ **Fig. 60.** Wharram Percy, North Yorkshire. The earthworks of the village's West Row lie along the valley crest above the church (Photograph: Paul Stamper)

west tower, an even longer, square ended chancel, and a north chapel. Subsequent contraction, with both aisles demolished and the chancel foreshortened by the early C17, followed Wharram's desertion.

South of the churchyard is the reconstructed pond of the village's south mill. From here the visitor should retrace his steps to the cottages. These represent conversion of part of the 'improving' farm, established here as arable farming returned to the Wolds in the later C18.

With his back to the gable end of the cottages the visitor should climb the valley side to the site of the village houses. Here are to be found the fine earthworks of the long West Row of medieval peasant houses and their surrounding tofts† and crofts†. At the north end of this row of houses are the earthworks of the North Manor, home of the Percys, who gave their name to the village.

To address the questions of when and why the village was deserted— having some fifty houses and a likely population of 300 or more at its peak in the C13 and earlier C14—it seems likely that in the C15 the absentee lord chose to change from labour-intensive arable farming to almost labour-free sheep-rearing. As families left, no new tenants were sought for their holdings, and by the early C16 only the parson and the shepherd may have been left.

M. Beresford and J. Hurst, Wharram Percy: Deserted Medieval Village *(Batsford and English Heritage, 1990).*

Wheeldale Road, North Yorkshire Roman road

SE 805975. Signposted from Egton Bridge 11 km. to the N. Site off minor road crossing Wheeldale Moor N to S. English Heritage.

A 1.2 km. stretch of Roman road known as Wade's Causeway can be seen on Wheeldale Moor, near Goathland. The road connected MALTON with Whitby via CAWTHORN. The surface of stone slabs visible today originally formed the foundation for a finer layer of metalling. Kerbstones and drainage culverts with capstones occur at intervals.

R. Hayes and J. Rutter, Wade's Causeway *(Scarborough and District Archaeological Society, 1964).*

Willerby Wold, Staxton, North Yorkshire Neolithic long barrow†

TA 029761. 10 km. S of Scarborough and 3 km. SSE of Staxton. Take B1249 S from Staxton; turn E along minor road to Fordon; barrow is S of road at a sharp bend. Visible from road.

A Neolithic long barrow, typical of the dozen or so examples found in and around the Yorkshire Wolds. Excavations revealed that originally the barrow was 37 m. long by 10 m. wide, with a trapezoidal ground plan. Side ditches provided the white chalk rubble used in constructing the mound.

At the eastern end is a concave forecourt in which ceremonies and rituals took place. At the back of the forecourt was an entrance into a small timber chamber built into the end of the mound. Corpses were taken into the chamber to decay. After the accumulation of at least six bodies the eastern end of the barrow was set on fire. It was abandoned shortly after.

T. G. Manby, 'The Excavation of the Willerby Wold Long Barrow', PPS *29 (1963), 173–205.*

York (*Eboracum*), York Roman legionary fortress, *colonia*†, and medieval city ★★

SE 600520. E of A1, N of A64. Figures 61 and 62.

Largely unscathed by damage during the Second World War and later C20 redevelopment, York today retains many stone and timber-framed medieval structures interspersed with red-brick Georgian ones. Beneath street level are deep, well-stratified archaeological deposits. The York Archaeological Trust pioneered the display and interpretation of arch-aeological discoveries with its Jorvik Viking Centre in Coppergate (**1**), and its hands-on Archaeological Resource Centre in St Saviour's Church in St Saviourgate (**2**). See, too, the Yorkshire Museum in Museum Gardens (**3**). For the medieval city, The York Story, in the redundant church of St Mary, Castlegate (**4**), provides a good introduction.

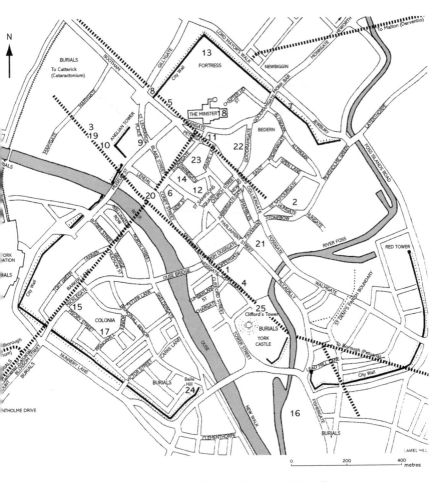

▲ **Fig. 61.** Plan of York (*Eboracum*) showing Roman and later sites

The confluence of the rivers Ouse and Fosse was a naturally attractive site to the military mind. In AD 71 a square, 20 ha. fort was built by
the IXth Legion on the east bank of the river, while west of the river was
the civilian *colonia*. From the end of the C1 York was the military capital
of Britain. From the late C2 York was one of the four *coloniae* of Britain
(see also GLOUCESTER, COLCHESTER, and LINCOLN).

The original earthen defences of the town were rebuilt in the early
C3 when York was made a provincial capital. The Emperor Constantius I
died in York in 306 and his son Constantine was acclaimed Emperor
here. Early in the C4 the fort was remodelled and provided with six
interval towers and two angle towers. Several elements of the later
fortification can be seen around the city.

▲ **Fig. 62.** View along a Roman sewer, York. Discovered in 1972 under buildings adjacent to Swinegate (Photograph: York Archaeological Trust)

South-east of Monk Bar part of an interval tower and the rounded remains of the east corner tower, the Aldwark Tower, can be seen (**5**). The medieval city wall north-west of Monk Bar overlies the Roman fortress wall. Two of the main streets through the fort are perpetuated by the modern-day Stonegate and Petergate (**6, 7**). Bootham Bar (**8**) marks the location of a Roman gateway, part of which is preserved in a modern underground building adjoining the Bar. A further section of fortress wall can be seen in St Leonard's Place (**9**). Constantine was probably responsible for the polygonal Multangular Tower at the south-west corner of the fortress and now visible in the Museum Gardens (**10**). The Roman wall butts onto a Norman archway in which there are Roman coffins and a stone-lined cistern, originally part of the public water supply. North-east of the Multangular Tower is another stretch of Constantinian wall and the base of the Anglian tower, a late or post-Roman feature.

Little remains of other buildings inside the fortress. Part of the *principia†* can be seen in the Undercroft Museum in York Minster (**11**). A section of a C4 bath house can be seen in the cellars of the Roman Bath Inn in St Sampson's Square (**12**). A column base and road cobbles are preserved under the Treasurer's House (National Trust) (**13**). A vaulted sewer at the corner of Swinegate and Church Street (**14**) can be seen by prior arrangement at the museum.

The Roman civilian town lay across the river Ouse in the Micklegate/Bishophill area. The settlement was given its own defences in the C3. Many churches have reused Roman masonry and part of a Roman tomb relief is in St Martin-cum-Gregory, Micklegate (**15**).

In the post-Roman centuries York remained an important town and mercantile centre. Then known as *Eorforwic* (**16**), it had a royal palace; it became the seat of a bishop in 625 and of an archbishop in 736. Predictably it was a target for the Vikings, and was captured by them in 866. Thereafter, for almost a century (until 954) Jorvik had Anglo-Scandinavian kings. It was during that time, as its population expanded, that much of the modern topography of the city was established. The most important pre-conquest monument (most structures were wooden) is the Anglo-Saxon tower of St Mary, Bishophill Junior (**17**).

How much of the medieval and later fabric of York you can see will depend on the time available. An excellent option for a quick visit is one of the free walking tours offered by the Association of Voluntary Guides departing from Exhibition Square. Of York's post-conquest buildings only a selection can be offered here. The Minster (**18**)—the cathedral of St Peter—has transepts of about 1220–55 (see the tomb of Archbishop Walter de Gray, about 1255, in the north transept), a chapter house of the late C13, nave of 1291 onwards with west window completed about 1335, Lady Chapel begun 1360, central tower of the early C15, and west towers of the mid- to late C15.

York also has many parish churches with medieval fabric, while west of the Minster are the remains of St Mary's Abbey (**19**); it stood outside the city walls and had its own defensive wall, crenellated in the early C14 as a result of Scottish raids.

Much of the ecclesiastical building was funded by mercantile success, evidenced further by the Guildhall (off Lendal) (**20**), and especially by the Merchant Adventurers' Hall (**21**) off Fossgate with its superb C14 hall. Many medieval houses survive, and while often concealed behind later stucco, some can be identified from their jettied (overhanging) upper stories. Lady Row, Goodramgate (**22**), built in 1316, is the earliest group of secular buildings still in use in York. Barley Hall, in Coffee Yard (**23**), is a spectacularly restored example of an important C14 and C15 house.

Two castles were begun by William the Conqueror in 1068, one on either bank of the Ouse. The motte† of that to the south, the Old Baile (**24**), survives by the city wall, while on top of the other is Clifford's Tower (English Heritage; **25**), a quadrilobate, limestone, shell keep of the mid-C13. The earlier castle was burnt in 1190 when Jews taking shelter there were massacred. The medieval city walls enclosed an area about five times the area of the Roman legionary fortress, with the circuit being closed by chains across the river Ouse at Skeldergate and Lendal. Along the surviving 3.2 km. length of walls are four main gates ('bars') raised and elaborated in the C13 and C14, three posterns, and thirty-nine towers. One of the finest ways to see York is to follow the wall-top walk, with breathtaking views over the pantiled roofs to the Minster.

P. Ottaway, Roman York (Batsford and English Heritage, 1993); R. Hall, York (Batsford and English Heritage, 1996).

4 East Midlands

This region covers the counties and unitary authorities of Lincolnshire, Nottinghamshire, Derbyshire, Leicestershire, Leicester, Rutland, Derby, and Nottingham.

The East Midlands marks the transition from highland England to the lowlands in a dramatic and distinctive way that is also reflected in its archaeology. To the west the Peak District includes some of the highest land in England; to the east is some of the most low-lying land, some below sea level.

The southern end of the Pennines appear in Derbyshire and Nottinghamshire as the Peak District, now a National Park. To the north is the High or Dark Peak, where gritstones and hard dark-coloured rocks predominate. Kinder Scout is the highest peak hereabouts at 633 m., famous because of the 1932 mass trespass for the right to roam. In the south of the Peak District is the White Peak, so called because of its dominantly limestone geology. Both areas were heavily occupied from the Bronze Age onwards, and contain ceremonial and burial monuments from the Bronze Age itself and some early Iron Age hillforts†. The White Peak also contains a fine group of Neolithic burial monuments in round and rectangular mounds.

The main eastwards-draining rivers of the Peak District, mainly the Derwent and the Manifold, join with the Trent to flow through eastern Nottinghamshire and northern Leicestershire heading northwards to the Humber estuary. In south-western Leicestershire are the undulating hill and vale lands which eventually join to the Northamptonshire heights. This is an area with abundant later prehistoric hillforts and enclosures of various kinds.

East of the Trent valley is the edge of the fen country in Lincolnshire and its borders with the Wash and east coast. Prehistoric land surfaces are known in this area, but they are generally well below the present ground level, sealed by layers of alluvium and peat that have developed over thousands of years as the sea level rose to gradually flood and inundate the land. From the C14 AD this trend was reversed as reclamation works dried out the land to produce high-quality farmland. In the C17 Dutch engineers were very much involved in the work, and part of south Lincolnshire is still known as Little Holland.

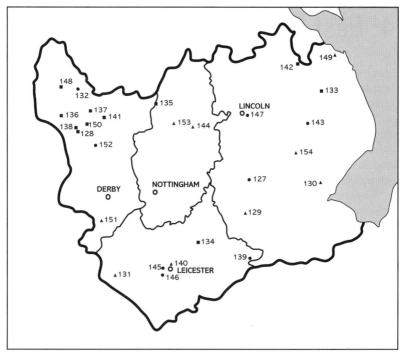

▲ **Fig. 63.** Map of Region 4

Key:

127 Ancaster, Lincolnshire	142 Hoe Hill, Lincolnshire
128 Arbor Low, Derbyshire	143 Horncastle (*Banovallum*), Lincolnshire
129 Boothby Pagnall, Lincolnshire	144 Laxton, Nottinghamshire
130 Boston, Lincolnshire	145 Leicester (*Ratae Coritanorum*),
131 Bosworth Field, Leicestershire	Leicestershire
132 Brough (*Navio*), Derbyshire	146 Leicester (The Raw Dykes),
133 Bully Hills, Lincolnshire	Leicestershire
134 Burrough Hill, Leicestershire	147 Lincoln (*Lindum*), Lincolnshire
135 Creswell Crags, Derbyshire	148 Mam Tor, Derbyshire
136 Five Wells, Derbyshire	149 Marshchapel, Lincolnshire
137 Gardom's Edge, Derbyshire	150 Nine Ladies, Derbyshire
138 Gib Hill, Derbyshire	151 Repton, Derbyshire
139 Great Casterton, Rutland	152 Roystone Grange Trail, Derbyshire
140 Hamilton, Leicestershire	153 Sherwood Forest, Nottinghamshire
141 Hob Hurst's House, Derbyshire	154 Tattershall, Lincolnshire

Ancaster, Lincolnshire   Roman town

SK 984435. The B6403 follows the line of Ermine Street as it approaches Ancaster from the S. The SE corner of the defences lie in field opposite church and N of A153 (Grantchester-Sleaford) where it crosses Ermine Street.

A defended Roman small town†, strategically located for communications, which developed on the site of an Iron Age settlement. Little is known about the internal layout although both Roman and Saxon cemeteries are known close by. A C1 fort and late Roman cemetery lie below the modern cemetery. Two Roman limestone coffins lie by a cemetery path. Roman finds from Ancaster can be seen in Grantham Museum.

B. Burnham and J. Wacher, The Small Towns of Roman Britain *(Batsford, 1990), 235–40.*

Arbor Low, Youlgreave, Derbyshire Neolithic henge† ★★

SK 161636. 5 km. W of Youlgreave. Signposted from A515 via minor road between Parsley Hay and Bakewell. The site is S of road approached through a farmyard. English Heritage. Figure 64.

Arbor Low, one of the best-preserved henge monuments in England, is defined by a partly silted-up ditch, 10 m. wide, and an external bank over 2 m. high and 76 m. across. Access to the interior is via opposing entrances to the north-west and south-east, with causeways across the ditch.

Within the henge is a circle of limestone slabs and a central setting of a kind known as a cove†. Today, the stones lie flat and it is uncertain whether they were ever upright; excavations in 1901–2 failed to reveal any sockets. It is possible, therefore, that the monument was never completed. A human burial was found beside the cove.

Beyond the south-eastern entrance is a large round Bronze Age cairn†. When excavated in 1845 it was found to contain cremations, a bone pin, and two pottery food vessels, all within a stone cist†. Finds from the site are in Sheffield Museum, the British Museum, and Buxton Museum. About 350 m. to the south-west is GIB HILL.

The nearby henge known as **The Bull Ring** at Dove Holes (SK 078782) is similar to Arbor Low, but with no central stones remaining.

H. St G. Gray, 'On Excavations at Arbor Low', Archaeologia, *58 (1903), 461–98.*

Boothby Pagnall, Lincolnshire Medieval hall

SK 9730. Village on B1176 6 km. SE of Grantham. Figure 65.

For whatever reason, perhaps the association of height with prestige, 'upper halls' found favour after 1066. The key feature was the location of the main hall, the formal dining and living room, on the first floor of what was usually a two-storey building. Here the late C12 Jurassic limestone example has a first-floor hall, heated, and with a secondary room off one end. Access, as usual in such halls, is via an external staircase. Beneath is a similar pair of rooms.

Originally the hall was a part of a wider complex set of buildings, all within a protective earth and timber ringwork†, later flattened.

N. Pevsner and J. Harris (rev. N. Antram), The Buildings of England: Lincolnshire *(Penguin, 1989).*

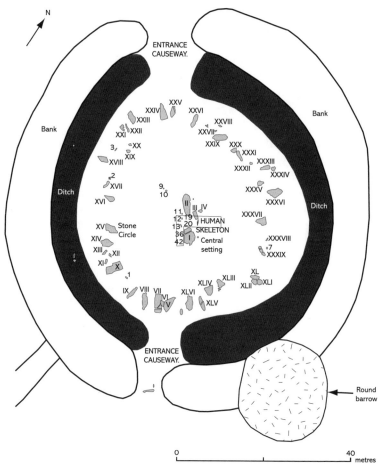

▲ **Fig. 64.** Plan of the late Neolithic henge at Arbor Low, Youlgreave, Derbyshire (after H St G Gray)

Boston, Lincolnshire Medieval town and port ★

TF 6320. At the junction of A52 and A16, 45 km. SE of Lincoln.

In the C13 the port of Boston was exporting more wool than either London or Southampton. Coming in was wine, cloth, and furs from northern Europe, and spices, silk, glass, and wax from the Mediterranean. Each year, on 17 June, merchants from all over Europe would come to Boston for the town's Great Fair, held on its triangular market place. This still survives, as does the restored late medieval **Shodfriars Hall** at its south end and the C15 brick **Guildhall**. Looming over all is the Stump, the colossal tower of **St Botoloph's Church**, visible for 70 km. around. Rebuilding of the body of the church was begun in 1309 in

▲ **Fig. 65.** The Manor House, Boothby Pagnall, Lincolnshire (Turner)

the Decorated style and was complete a century later. The sixty-two misericords† or priests' seats, carved with everything from lions to scenes of everyday life, are believed to be of 1390. The tower was raised in stages over the course of the C15, despite the slump in the town's fortunes after the Black Death of 1348.

Through the great tower, and the church's guild priests, the townsmen gave glory to God; and, it was hoped, avoided another terrible visitation of the plague.

N. Pevsner and J. Harris (rev. N. Antram), The Buildings of England: Lincolnshire (Penguin, 1989), 153–71.

Bosworth Field, Leicestershire Medieval battlefield

SK 401001. Battle of Bosworth Country Park, 20 km. W of Leicester, W of A447 Hinckley to Measham road. Well signposted. Visitor and interpretation centre with restricted opening and battlefield trail.

Here on 21 August 1485, Richard III's 8,000-strong army was defeated by the smaller force of the returning exile Henry Tudor. Richard had been king for two years, since he seized the Crown from his nephew Edward V. This and other cut-throat political manoeuvrings contributed considerably to Richard's defeat at Bosworth.

Richard positioned his forces on the high ground of Ambion Hill. When Henry Tudor's army attacked, Richard's main supporter, the duke of Norfolk, soon fell. Still, for an hour or more, the fight was evenly

The Black Death 1348–9

'Then the dreadful pestilence penetrated through the coastal regions from Southampton and came to Bristol, and almost the whole strength of the town perished, as if overcome by sudden death; for few there were who kept their beds for more than two or three days, or even half a day. Then this cruel death spread everywhere, following the course of the sun. At Leicester, in the small parish of St Leonard's there perished more than 380 people, in the parish of Holy Cross, 400, in the parish of St Margaret's Leicester, 700; and so in every parish a great multitude ... And there was a great cheapness of all things for fear of death, for very few took any account of riches or of possessions of any kind. A man could have a horse which was formerly worth forty shillings for half a mark (6s 8d), a big fat ox for four shillings, a cow for 12d, a heifer for 6d, a fat wether for 4d, a sheep for 3d, a lamb for 2d, a large pig for 5d, and a stone of wool for 9d. Sheep and oxen strayed through the fields and among the crops, and there was none to drive them off or collect them, but they perished in uncounted numbers throughout all districts for lack of shepherds, because there was such a shortage of servants and labourers! There was so great a scarcity of priests everywhere that many churches were left destitute, lacking divine offices, masses, matins, vespers, and sacraments. A chaplain could scarcely be obtained to serve any church for less than £10 or 10 marks, and whereas when there was an abundance of priests before the plague, a chaplain could be obtained for 5 or 4 marks or even 2 marks with his board, at this time there was scarcely one who would accept a vicarage at £20 or 20 marks. Within a short while, however, a great multitude of men, whose wives had died in the plague, flocked to take orders, many of whom were illiterate, and almost laymen, except that they could read a little but without understanding.' (*EHD* iv. 89–90)

matched, until Lord Stanley and his 4,000-strong host, who had been expected to support the king, joined battle on Henry Tudor's side. Richard led a brave counter-attack, but was hacked down in the melee, allegedly dying with the cry of 'Treachery!' on his lips. He was the first English king to die on a battlefield since Harold in 1066. According to legend—and Shakespeare—the crown was found in a thorn bush and placed on the victor's head, who became thereby Henry VII.

East of the battlefield, in **Sutton Cheney church**, is a memorial to Richard III. Here, on the eve of battle, he heard his last mass.

P. Foss, Field of Redemore: Battle of Bosworth, 1485 *(Kairos Press, 1998).*

Brough (*Navio*), Derbyshire Roman fort

SK 181827. Short signposted walk from roadside parking in Brough, a short distance after turning to Bradwell from Hathersage to Hope Road.

Two forts on the same site, visible as earthworks, lie immediately south-east of MAM TOR. The earlier, larger fort was occupied from AD 75–120 and the smaller fort from around the mid-C2 through to the mid-C4. Excavations have revealed principal buildings and barrack blocks in the interior, and baths and an extensive *vicus*† outside the fort to the south and east.

G. Jones and J. Wild, 'Excavations at Brough-on-Noe', DAJ 89 (1970), 99–106.

Bully Hills, Tathwell, Lincolnshire Bronze Age barrow cemetery

TF 330827. 4.5 km. S of Louth, W of A16(T) Louth to Skegness road. 1 km. E of Tathwell N of the minor road to Haugham. Visible from road.

A cemetery of seven bowl barrows in a neat line, six close together and the seventh a little apart. Well preserved for this part of the country, they are set along a skyline and make an impressive sight. Nothing is known of the date or content of these barrows.

J. May, Prehistoric Lincolnshire, History of Lincolnshire Committee 72 (1976).

Burrough Hill, Melton Mowbray, Leicestershire Iron Age hillfort†

SK 761119. 7 km. S of Melton Mowbray, 2 km. NW of Somerby within Burrough Hill Country Park. Parking off minor road from Somerby to Burrough on the Hill.

A massive polygonal Iron Age hillfort on a steep-sided spur overlooking the southern edge of the Eye valley. The fort is defended by a single massive bank, ditch, and counterscarp bank†.

The entrance lies in the south-east corner where the ramparts turn sharply inwards to form a passage nearly 46 m. long. At its inner end was a pair of guard-chambers to protect the main gate.

Established in the C2 BC or earlier, the site must have been one of the strongholds of the *Coritani* tribe, whose territory included Leicestershire and Lincolnshire.

M. Todd, The Coritani (Duckworth, 1973).

Creswell Crags, Derbyshire/Nottinghamshire
Palaeolithic and later caves and rock shelters   ★★

SK 535742. 1 km. E of Creswell with visitor centre accessible from the B6042 E of Creswell. Signposted from A616 and A60. Derbyshire County Council. Restricted opening.

Creswell Crags is a short river gorge, approximately 400 m. long, cut through a Magnesian limestone outcrop. The near-vertical sides are fissured, and twenty-four caves and rock shelters are known. The centre of the gorge is occupied by a lake, but a circular walk allows visitors to view the main caves.

Exploration began in the later C19. Initially, work was at **Pin Hole Cave**, the entrance to which lies towards the western end of the north side of the gorge. Other caves explored soon after included **Robin Hood's Cave**, **Mother Grundy's Parlour**, and **Church Hole**.

The archaeological remains span a very long period of time starting in the Middle Palaeolithic, probably between about 120,000 BC and 60,000 BC, when groups using Mousterian flintworking technologies occupied Pin Hole and Robin Hood's Cave. In the early part of the Upper Palaeolithic about 25,000–30,000 BC, Pin Hole and Robin Hood's Cave were again the focus of attention.

Later Upper Palaeolithic occupation was more extensive, involving Church Hole Cave, Mother Grundy's Parlour, Robin Hood's Cave, Yew Tree Shelter, and Pin Hole. Among the finds of this period are pieces of decorated bone carrying images of animals similar in style to those of the famous painted caves of southern France and Spain.

The flint tools and weapons of early post-glacial times from Creswell Crags, spanning the period 12,000 BC to about 8,000 BC, are sufficiently distinctive to be regarded as an exemplary assemblage; the area gives its name to the Creswellian tool-making tradition recognized throughout Britain.

R. Jenkinson, The Archaeological Caves and Rock Shelters in the Creswell Crags Area, *Creswell Crags Visitor Centre Research Report 1 (1978)*.

Five Wells, Taddington, Derbyshire Neolithic passage grave

SK 124711. 7 km. E of Buxton, S of A6(T) accessible via footpaths from the Limestone Way running S from A6 to the W of Taddington at SK 133714.

An oval-shaped stone barrow 21 × 19 m. covering two separate burial chambers set back to back with entrances to the north-east and south-west respectively. The cairn† is edged by a dry-stone revetment† wall. The south-west chamber is rather ruined, but the north-east one is fairly complete. Both chambers are passage graves: a wedge-shaped chamber approached by a narrow passage. Notice the portal slabs defining the junction between the passage and chamber. Originally, both chambers would have been roofed with limestone slabs or corbelling†.

C19 excavations found the remains of at least twelve individuals together with Neolithic pottery and flint tools. The finds are in Sheffield Museum.

J. Ward, 'The Five Wells Tumulus', Reliquary and Illustrated Archaeologist *(1901)*, 229–42.

Gardom's Edge, Baslow, Derbyshire Neolithic enclosure,
cairns†, and field-system† ★

SK 273730. 2 km. NE of Baslow. Access by footpath (to Nelson's Monument) N from car park on N side of A619 Chesterfield to Baslow road at SK 280721 (near the Robin Hood). The main area of archaeological interest NW of Nelson's Monument.

Gardom's Edge is part of the gritstone scarp which forms the eastern side of the Derwent valley. Behind the edge is a broad shelf, now covered in moorland, on which more than 2000 separate archaeological features have been recognized. Since 1995 the area has been the focus of a major survey and excavation programme. The preliminary results show two main phases to the visible archaeological remains.

The earliest centres on a massive stone-built enclosure, roughly ellip- tical, and probably Neolithic in date. This is situated on the highest part of the shelf and is bounded on the east by a rubble bank, which can be traced for over 600 m. and on the west by a precipitous natural scarp. There are at least two entrances through the boundary. Much of the interior of the site is strewn with boulders, but on the scarp towards the southern part of the enclosed area is a well-preserved barrow.

Just beyond the enclosure to the north-east is a large earthfast slab decorated with cup and ring marks† and other designs (the visible stone is a replica). Two other similarly decorated stones have been found on the moor.

A second phase of activity, probably later prehistoric in date, can be seen overlying some of the early features. Most prominent are stone house foundations, clearance cairns, linear boundaries†, and lynchets†. A series of small rectangular fields can be recognized in the central part of the moor.

S. Ainsworth and J. Barnatt, 'A Scarp Edge Enclosure at Gardom's Edge', DAJ 118 (1998), 5–23. See also www.shef.ac.uk/uni/projects/geap/

Gib Hill, Youlgreave, Derbyshire Neolithic oval barrow

SK 161636. Near ARBOR LOW, 5 km. W of Youlgreave. Signposted from A515 via minor road between Parsley Hay and Bakewell. The site is S of road approached through a farmyard. English Heritage.

Gib Hill appears as a large round barrow† 4.5 m. high, which on closer inspection shows two main periods of construction. When first built the tomb was an oval barrow 40 m. by 22 m. This can be seen forming the lower part of the present barrow. Excavations by Thomas Bateman in 1848 failed to find any burials from this period.

Later, during the early Bronze Age, a large round mound was added to its eastern end. Bateman found a stone cist† in this part, which contained a single cremation and a small pottery urn.

Immediately north-west of Gib Hill are slight traces of a ditched enclosure, about 55 m. in diameter, with a bank outside the ditch. It may be another henge†. ARBOR LOW lies about 350 m. to the north-west.

T. Bateman, Vestiges of the Antiquities of Derbyshire *(John Russell Smith, 1848), 64–6.*

Great Casterton, Rutland Roman town

TF 002090. The Roman town lies beneath and E of the modern town, the earthworks being the only visible feature. From the village follow minor road signposted Ryhall and Essendine; earthworks on the right after a farm. Figure 66.

▼ **Fig. 66.** Plan of the Roman town at Great Casterton, Rutland (after Burnham & Wacher adapted from Corder & Todd)

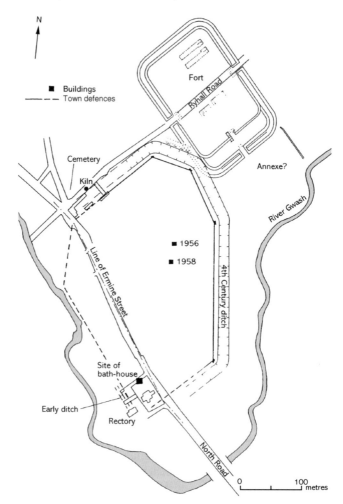

A small Roman town sited in a loop of the river Gwash north of the Ermine Street crossing. Originally a C1 fort, which developed into a defended town. In the late C4 rectangular bastions were added to the C2 stone walls and the ditch system was modified. The wide single late ditch and low rampart of the north-east corner can be traced along its eastern line in fields alongside the Gwash. Roman and Saxon cemeteries have been found outside the settlement.

M. Todd, The Roman Fort at Great Casterton, Rutland *(University of Nottingham, 1968).*

Hamilton, Leicestershire Deserted medieval village

SK 643073. On NE fringe of Leicester. The Barkby Thorpe to Scraptoft road bisects the site; a footpath leads off it across the earthworks.

In the C12 and C13 there were perhaps twelve to fifteen families living in the small village here, whose earthworks survive under permanent pasture. Ditches mark the divisions between individual tofts† and crofts†, while around the south and east sides of the earthworks can be seen the village's boundary bank. The most prominent platform, in the south-east corner, is probably where the manor house stood. Nearby was presumably the chapel of St John. This had already disappeared by 1477 and it may be that by that date the whole village had been deserted.

Adjoining the village earthworks is ridge and furrow†, once part of Hamilton's open field land.

R. Hartley, The Medieval Earthworks of Central Leicestershire, *Leicester Museums Publication 103 (1989).*

Hob Hurst's House, Baslow, Derbyshire Bronze Age barrow

SK 287692. 10 km. W of Chesterfield, S of A619 Baslow to Chesterfield road. Signposted access from minor road running W from B5057 at SK 316667. English Heritage.

Hob Hurst's House is a large mound, 10 m. in diameter and 1.2 m. high. More square than round, it has a ditch running round it and an outer bank beyond. A stone cist† with no capstone† was found in the centre of the mound containing cremated human remains.

Other barrows and a stone circle† can be seen 1 km. south-west of Hob Hurst's House near Hell Bank Plantation (SK 281685).

J. Barnatt and J. Collis (eds), Barrows in the Peak District *(Department of Prehistory and Archaeology, University of Sheffield, 1996).*

Hoe Hill, Binbrook, Lincolnshire Neolithic long barrow†

TF 215953. 1 km. N of Binbrook, W of B1203 between Binbrook and East Rayendale.

This fine middle Neolithic long barrow, now partly covered in beech trees, is typical of many in this part of eastern England, being constructed of earth, rubble, and timber in the earthen long barrow tradition. The mound measures 55 m. long by 18 m. wide, and is orientated approximately east to west. A dip near the mound centre may be the result of collapse or robbing.

Until recently there was a second long barrow at Hoe Hill only 65 m. to the north-west. This has now disappeared.

About 2.4 km. north of Hoe Hill on the opposite side of the valley of the Waithe beck is the **Ash Hill Long Barrow** (TF 209961). This is also wedge-shaped, about 39 m. long and 16 m. wide.

P. Phillips (ed.), Archaeology and Landscape Studies in North Lincolnshire, British Archaeological Reports British Series 208 (1989).

Horncastle (*Banovallum*), Lincolnshire   Roman town

TF 258695. 29 km. E of Lincoln at junction of A158 and A153. The Tourist Information Centre, Spilsby Road, displays Roman finds.

A small defended Roman town, located at the base of the Lincolnshire Wolds near the river Bain. Now beneath the modern town, little is known about the Roman plan. The church and market place lie within the sub-rectangular walled area of the Roman town (see signboard in Market Place) and a section of wall is visible within the library in Wharf Road. Other sections can be seen in the south-west corner of St Mary's churchyard and in Dog Kennel Yard off Lawrence Street, the latter with part of a bastion. A fourth section is visible on the south-west side near the school building (community centre).

B. C. Burnham and J. Wacher, The Small Towns of Roman Britain (Batsford, 1990), 240–5.

Laxton, Nottinghamshire   Relict medieval field-system†

SK 722670. Access by minor roads, 6 km. E of Ollerton, and 15 km. NW of Newark-on-Trent. Visitor centre in village (restricted opening).

In the Middle Ages farmers held their land in numerous allotment-like strips scattered across two or more prairie-like open fields. Each year one of these fields would be left uncultivated, 'fallow', in order to provide grazing land and to allow the ground to be rested and fertilized. At Laxton, although consolidation of lands in 1903–7 did away with the scattered strips, the sweeping bends of its South, West, and Mill field boundaries (the East or Town Field is long gone) are still basically medieval.

A walk around the village, whose north and east parts are largely the result of medieval replanning, can also encompass the de Caux's Norman motte† and bailey† castle north of the main street, fishponds to the south of the church, and Hollowgate Lane leading west from the village to the West Field.

J. Beckett, A History of Laxton *(Blackwell, 1989).*

Leicester (*Ratae Coritanorum*), Leicestershire Roman

civitas† capital

SK 583042. NE of the M1, access from junctions 21 and 22. Jewry Wall Museum, St Nicholas Circle is on W side of City, S of the railway station. The only extant Roman remains lie in the Museum grounds.

Although the Roman *civitas* capital of the *Coritani,* developed from a major local native centre, there is little to see today. The Jewry Wall, located in the grounds of the Museum, survived through being incorporated into a Saxon church. This piece of masonry, 7.3 m. high, formed part of the *palaestra†* of the public baths, the plan of which is laid out in front of the Museum. The Museum includes several mosaic panels.

J. Wacher, The Towns of Roman Britain *(Batsford, 1995), 335–57.*

Leicester (The Raw Dykes), Leicestershire Roman canal

SK 584026. Approximately 1.5 km. S of Jewry Wall Museum, on the Aylestone Road (A426) near its junction with Saffron Lane, north of railway bridge.

Part of an impressive earthwork, approximately 30 m. long with a wide ditch. Originally interpreted as part of an aqueduct† this is now thought to be a section of a Roman canal perhaps leading to a docks installation. The earthworks were reused as a gun redoubt during the Civil War.

J. Wacher, TheTowns of Roman Britain *(Batsford, 1995), 350–52.*

Lincoln (*Lindum*), Lincolnshire Roman fortress, *colonia†,* and

medieval cathedral city ★★

SK 970710. NE of the A1 at the junction of A46 and A15. Figures 67 and 68.

A fortress was constructed here by the IXth Legion in about AD 60 on a spur of high ground overlooking the river Witham. In the late C1 the abandoned fortress was converted into a *colonia* (see also GLOUCESTER, COLCHESTER, and YORK). In the early C2 the legionary earthen defences were rebuilt in stone enclosing 26.6 ha. A section of the defences can be seen at East Bight. Stone interval towers were later added, one of which is also visible here. The Newport Arch (**1**) is one of three surviving gates and probably dates to the C3. Following the line of the defences to the East Gate, the principal entrance to the *colonia,* another stretch of wall (**2**), 4.3 m. high, stands next to the Eastgate Hotel. In front of the hotel is the base of the north tower of the Roman east gate (**3**). Remains of the upper west gate are also visible (**4**). Lincoln was served by Ermine Street,

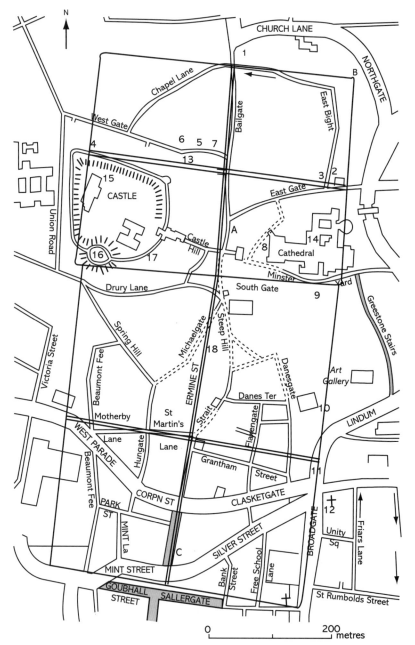

▲ **Fig. 67.** Plan of the modern town of Lincoln showing location of visible Roman and later remains

▲ **Fig. 68.** Excavations at the Roman Westgate, Lincoln (Photograph: Michael Jones, Lincoln Archaeological Trust)

the Fosse Way, and an artificial waterway linking the Wash with the river Witham.

Little is known of the internal streets and buildings. In Bailgate pavement settings mark the forum† colonnade (**5**). The basilica† lay to the north and part of its wall, 5.5 m. high and 21 m. long, survives as the Mint Wall, in West Bight near the Castle Hotel (**6**). A small church found in the courtyard of the forum is marked out in the ground (**7**). Part of a Roman mosaic can be seen under a stairway leading off the north-east corner of the cloisters in the cathedral precinct (**8**). Lincoln possessed a particularly well-developed sewerage system. The principal north–south stone-built sewer was found in Bailgate (**A**). Part of its aqueduct has also been investigated (**B**).

In the mid-C2 the settlement expanded into the 'lower town', which received its own stone defences and gates. A stretch of the eastern lower town wall is visible in the grounds of the medieval Bishop's Palace (English Heritage) (**9**). Sections of the ditch can be seen in the gardens of the Usher Art Gallery, Lindum Road (**10**). The west gate of the lower town is preserved in the medieval one (**11**). A large octagonal stone foundation in the High Street may have been part of a fountain (**C**). Several tombstones have been found and cemeteries are known outside the gates. The church of St Swithin's (**12**) has a Roman altar on display.

Lincoln probably remained important beyond the Roman period. In the 1980s excavations on the site of the church of St Paul in the Bail (that is, the castle bailey†) **(13)** found a church dating back to the C5 or C6. Within was a 'founder grave' with a high-quality bronze hanging bowl. Bede records that St Paulinus came to Lincoln about 628 and converted an official called Blecca, and then built a church of remarkable workmanship. Lincoln was clearly a major early centre of Christianity; indeed, it has even been suggested that in the Saxon period the whole of the walled upper town was an ecclesiastical enclosure.

Today Lincoln is dominated by the cathedral† **(14)**, an episcopal see being founded here by the Normans soon after the conquest. The new cathedral church was completed in 1092 and the core of the west end of this building, sufficiently strong to be used by King Stephen in 1140 as a temporary castle, is encapsulated in the west front of the modern cathedral. Rebuilding had to begin again after an earthquake in 1185, with the central tower being added in 1311. South of the cathedral are the ruins of the C12 Bishop's Palace (English Heritage), while to the west is Lincoln Castle, founded in 1068 and badly damaged in a siege of 1216 **(15)**. Unusually it has two mottes†, the Lucy Tower in the south-west corner **(16)**, and the later, mid-C12, Observatory Tower to the south-east **(17)**.

From the castle and cathedral Steep Hill leads down to the Lower City, passing several early houses including the so-called **Jew's House** of about 1170 **(18)**. On the High Street further into the south part of the city St Mary-le-Wigford and St Peter-at-Gowts both have Anglo-Saxon fabric including fine west towers.

J. Wacher, The Towns of Roman Britain *(Batsford, 1995), 120–37.*

Mam Tor, Castleton, Derbyshire Bronze Age settlement and Iron Age hillfort†† ★

SK 128837. 3 km. E of Castleton, N of A625. Parking areas and picnic sites N of Windy Knoll N of A625 about 6 km. E of Chapel-en-le-Frith. A steep climb to the very exposed hillfort. National Trust. Figure 69.

Rising to over 500 m. above sea level, Mam Tor is one of the highest hills in England. The ramparts of the hillfort enclosing most of the summit have a commanding view over the Vale of Eden and the river Noe.

The single rampart has a circumference of 1100 m. and comprises a ditch and inner bank. It encloses 6.4 ha. The main entrance is on the north while another to the south is used by a modern track. The gap in the west side is probably modern.

Numerous hollows inside the fort, particularly on the west slope, are house platforms. Their average diameter is about 7 m. Finds date them to the early first millennium BC; earlier occupation is known too.

D. Coombs, 'Mam Tor', CA 3/27 (1971), 100–2.

▲ **Fig. 69.** Aerial photograph of Mam Tor, Castleton, Derbyshire (CUCAP BAW 09)

Marshchapel, Lincolnshire Medieval salterns

TF 360988. E of A1032 Cleethorpes to Mablethorpe road. 15 km. SE of Grimsby. Figure 70.

On the north Lincolnshire coast, north-east of the villages of Marsh-chapel, Tetney, North Coates, and Grainthorpe, are low mounds known locally as 'the fitties'. These are the remains of medieval salterns, where sea water was evaporated to make salt. The coastal villages where the salt makers lived stand on islands or peninsulas of firm ground, with marshes and fens on their inland side and salt marshes on the seaward. Sea water would be collected in clay-lined pits called 'floors' in which mud would settle out and some of the water evaporate before the brine was transferred to lead or latten pans heated over fires for the final evaporation. It is the debris of these operations—mud, burnt clay, and ashes—which formed the fitties. After about 1600 salt making declined, and land reclamation has left the salterns 400 m. to 2,000 m. inland.

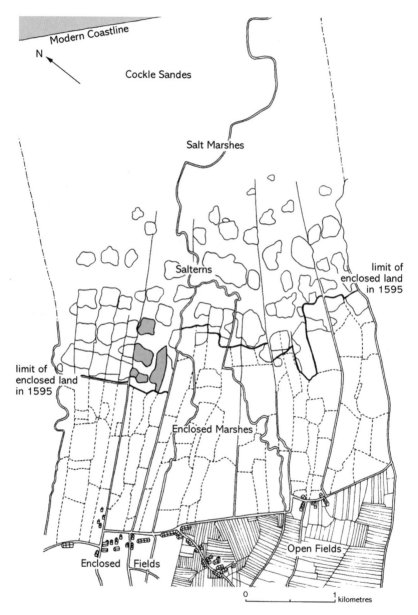

▲ **Fig. 70.** Marshchapel, Lincolnshire. Salterns shown on a (redrawn) map of 1595. The thick line shows the limit of reclaimed land. The stippled mounds remain unploughed (after Beresford)

Other good earthworks of salterns of about 1500 lie 1 km. south of Wainfleet All Saints, Lincolnshire (TF 495744).

R. Bewley (ed.), Lincolnshire's Archaeology from the Air, Occasional Papers in Lincolnshire History and Archaeology 11 (RCHME, 1998), 81–95.

Nine Ladies, Stanton Moor, Derbyshire   Neolithic stone

circle†

SK 253635. 6 km. SE of Bakewell, on upland moor W of A6(T) and the river Derwent. Signposted access from lane between Birchover and Stanton Lees. English Heritage and National Trust. Figure 71.

▼ **Fig. 71.** Plan of the barrows, cairns and enclosures on Stanton Moor, Derbyshire (after Thomas)

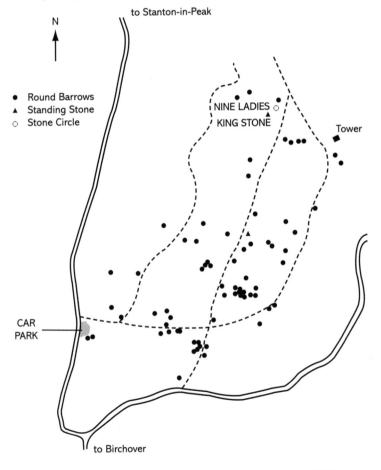

At the northern end of Stanton Moor is the Nine Ladies stone circle. It is about 10 m. across and comprises nine stones set on a low bank. In the centre are the remains of a small cairn†, and to the south-west is a single upright stone known as the King Stone.

Other remains on the moor include over seventy round barrows†, at least three ring cairns†, and several small enclosures. Overall it is an extremely rich concentration of late Neolithic and Bronze Age funerary monuments.

C. Hart, 'Stanton Moor, Derbyshire: Burial and Ceremonial Monuments', in D. Spratt and C. Burgess (eds), Upland Settlement in Britain, British Archaeological Reports British Series 143 (1985), 77–110.

Repton, Derbyshire Anglo-Saxon church

SK 303272. E of A38, 10 km. SW of Derby and 6 km. NE of Burton upon Trent. Figure 72.

Standing above the river Trent is St Wystan's Church, much of which is of the mid-C14 and C15 including the tower and spire, clerestory†, and roof. Parts, however, are much older, and a monastery was founded here by the Mercian royal family in the later C7. Although nothing of the earliest building survives, there is much work of the C8 and C9, comprising the chancel (notwithstanding the later windows) and, beneath, a crypt or mausoleum. This has a vaulted ceiling supported on round arches and four round columns carved with raised spiral strips or bands. In each of the four walls there is a recess, although only that to the west survives in anything like its original state. Precisely how the structure developed and functioned is still not clear, but it seems to have been built as a mausoleum for King Ethelbald of Mercia, murdered in 757 at

▼ **Fig. 72.** Repton, Derbyshire. Viking period features revealed by excavation (after Biddle & Biddle)

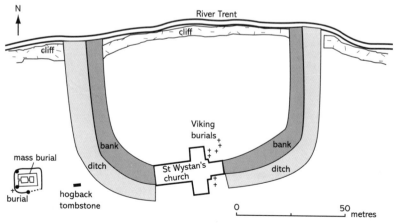

Seckington, 18 km. away, taking on its present form in the years before 839 as his grandson King Wiglaf adapted it as a magnificent burial place for himself. In 849 Wiglaf's own grandson Wystan was martyred, and after his burial it ceased to be a private vault and became instead a focus for pilgrimage, with access cut from the west to allow the saint's relicts to be venerated.

The *Anglo-Saxon Chronicle* records how in 873–4 the invading Danish army over-wintered at Repton. Excavations found D-plan Viking defences looping back from the church to the river Trent. East of the church were Viking burials, while outside the enclosure, 50 m. west of the church, a Saxon mortuary chapel had been levelled and used as the burial place of some 249 individuals, apparently members of the Danish army who died not from violence but from disease.

About 11 km. south-east of Repton, at **Breedon-on-the-Hill** (SK 405234), is a major Anglo-Saxon monastery church, with remarkable stone friezes.

H. Taylor, 'St Wystan's Church', Arch J, 144 (1987), 205–45; M. Biddle and B. Kjolbye-Biddle, 'Repton and the Vikings', Antiquity, 66 (1992), 36–51.

Roystone Grange Trail, Matlock, Derbyshire Multi-period
landscape   ★

SK 1958. 10 km. W of Matlock, S of A5012. Trail begins in Minninglow car park (SK 195582) off minor road from Pikehall on A5012 to Parwich. Leaflets obtainable from National Park Information Centre. Display boards on trail.

This trail through part of the White Peak follows paths for about 6.5 km. It takes at least two hours to complete.

The whole area was heavily settled in prehistoric times. The Neolithic barrow of Minninglow can be seen from the trail, and near Roystone Grange is a Bronze Age round barrow†. Prehistoric fields have also been recorded.

In Roman times there was a small settlement near the valley bottom associated with two large enclosures. A stretch of C2 field wall excavated near Ballidon demonstrates the continuity of many of the extant boundaries, from Roman times through to the present day.

Also on the trail are the remains of a medieval grange and a post-medieval brick works.

R. Hodges, Wall to Wall History (Duckworth, 1991).

Sherwood Forest, Nottinghamshire Medieval forest

SE 621682. Visitor centre at Edwinstowe, on W side of Ollerton 25 km. NE of Nottingham. Marked trails allow exploration of the forest landscape.

Sherwood Forest, a medieval royal hunting forest, is best known as the home of the outlaw Robin Hood. Whether or not he was real, later medieval sources place his activities not here but further north, in West Yorkshire.

Notwithstanding its dubious legendary associations, this is a special place, and a rare survival of a type (or types) of landscape now rarely found. Stag-headed oak trees mark areas of wood pasture (notably near Birkland where there are several hundred) where animals might be grazed. Best known of the trees is the Major Oak. Elsewhere birches (from which Birkland takes its name) predominate. The fact is, contrary to the popular image of a medieval forest, Sherwood was a varied landscape of heaths and woods.

O. Rackham, The History of the Countryside *(Dent, 1986), 293–7.*

Tattershall, Lincolnshire Medieval castle and church

TF 209575. On A153 W of Conningsby. National Trust; restricted opening. Admission charge.

Although by no means attractive, Tattershall's brick keep impresses by its sheer mass as it rises from the fenland. Built between 1432 and 1448 by Ralph, Lord Cromwell, High Treasurer of the Realm, certain features, such as the machicolations† below the battlements, may derive from Continental precedents. Built of still-novel red brick with decorative diaper work in darker brick and stone dressings, the keep is a tower with four main storeys over a basement and with an octagonal tower at each corner. On the ground floor was the Treasurer's parlour, on the first floor his hall, above it an audience chamber, and beneath the roof his bedchamber.

In 1440 construction began with a collegiate church† and an alms-house attached. The church, funded by Cromwell, was to have a staff of twenty, whose prayer would speed the founder's soul through purgatory. The cruciform church has huge Perpendicular windows, which until the C18 retained their medieval stained glass. Inside are the original screen and pulpit.

M. Thompson, Tattershall Castle *(The National Trust, 1974) (Site Guidebook).*

5 The Midlands plain and Welsh borders

This region covers the counties and unitary authorities of Merseyside, Cheshire, Staffordshire, Shropshire, West Midlands, Herefordshire, Worcestershire, Telford and Wrekin, Warrington, Stoke-on-Trent, and Hatton.

The West Midlands is an area of contrasts. The Midlands plain to the north is a low-lying area of generally rather heavy clay lands from Shrewsbury and Telford in the south to Chester and Northwich in the north. The headwaters of the east-flowing river Trent can be found around Stoke-on-Trent, but the majority of rivers in the area, including the Weaver, Dee, and Dane flow north-west to the Irish Sea. There are also wetlands and mires, many now dried up, especially in north Shropshire and southern Cheshire. Archaeologically, this is one of the least well-explored regions of England, although the Roman presence was strong and from early medieval times it was an important salt-producing area.

Southwards of Shrewsbury and running downwards through Kidder-minster and Worcester is the Severn valley. Relatively narrow here compared with the valley further south, none the less it is a dominant topographical feature and an important communications routeway. Archaeological evidence suggests that although the area was visited by early prehistoric communities it was not until later Bronze Age times that it was comprehensively cleared of natural woodland and opened up for agriculture. There are extensive Iron Age settlements all along the valley, and numerous hillforts† on the higher ground. Roman settlement is also widespread.

West of the Severn valley and the north midland plain is the Welsh Marches, classic hill and vale country with small areas of upland separated by deeply incised valleys. Like many upland fringes, and here it is important to remember that these lands lie on the eastern edge of upland Wales, the Marches are dominated in early prehistory by clusters of ceremonial monuments and in later prehistory by defensively positioned hillforts. These are part of a belt of such sites that continues southwards along the Cotswolds and down into Wessex. It remained a fought-over border region until the late C13 and beyond, and a high proportion of medieval villages have a castle of some sort.

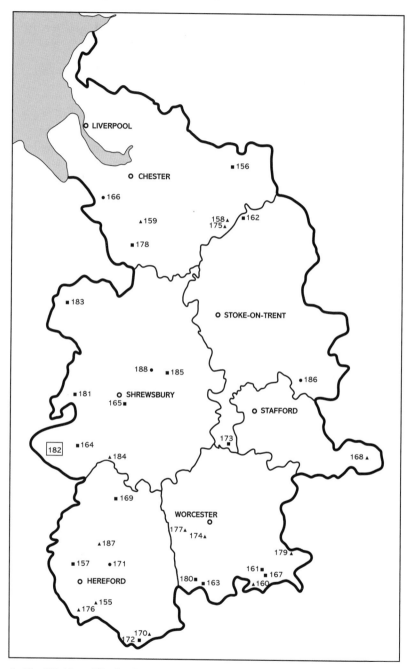

▲ **Fig. 73.** Map of Region 5

Abbey Dore, Herefordshire Medieval church ★

SO 388300. 16 km. SW of Hereford, on B4347, N of its junction with A465(T), between Pontrilas and Hay-on-Wye.

Cistercians† founded a church here in 1147. Between about 1170 and 1220 Abbey Dore was rebuilt and it is that work, mostly still standing, which makes it one of the best examples of Cistercian architecture in the country.

Rebuilding began with the choir in the late 1170s. Almost immediately the plan was modified to include side aisles and a vaulted ambulatory†, to reflect the plan of the new church under construction at Cîteaux, the order's mother church. What survives today as the parish church is the crossing, transepts, presbytery†, and ambulatory. To the west, extending into the modern graveyard, are parts of the nave and choir, while north of the church is the site of the twelve-sided chapter house and the cloisters.

In 1633 John Abel, later celebrated as 'King's Carpenter', restored the abbey as a parish church. His work includes the magnificent screen surmounted with the arms of the Scudamore patrons, the Stuarts, and Archbishop Laud, which greets the visitor, and the ceiling. There is much else to interest the visitor—the west gallery, C17 window glass, and wall paintings—and so much of it is of high quality.

Six km. to the east is Kilpeck, whose mid-C12 church has some of England's finest carved stonework.

R. Shoesmith and R. Richardson (eds), A Definitive History of Abbey Dore (Logaston, 1997).

Alderley Edge, Cheshire Prehistoric hillfort†, metal-extraction site, and later settlements

SJ 860775. 1 km. SE of Alderley Edge, N of B5087. Parking at the Wizard signposted off the B5087 at SJ 859774. National Trust.

The prominent sandstone escarpment known as Alderley Edge was worked for copper in post-medieval times. Traces of workings of this period are visible amongst the trees. However, the extraction of copper ore goes back much further. Although surface traces have apparently been obliterated, underground are remains of early workings associated with stone tools. Antiquarian researches in the C19 recovered over 100 primitive-looking tools. In 1875 a wooden shovel was found at Brindlow some 4 m. down in old workings subsequently radiocarbon dated to 1888–1677 BC.

A. Garner et al., 'The Alderley Edge Shovel', CA 12/137 (1994), 172–5.

Arthur's Stone, near Bredwardine, Dorstone, Herefordshire Neolithic long barrow†

SO 319431. 1 km. N of Dorstone accessible by signposted minor roads from B4348 at Dorstone or B4352 at Bredwardine. Roadside parking. English Heritage. Figure 74.

▼ **Fig. 74.** Plan of the Neolithic long barrow known as Arthur's Stone, near Bredwardine, Dorstone, Hereford and Worcester (after Hemp)

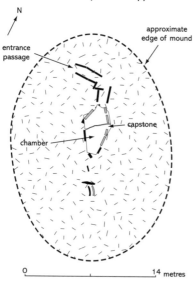

This partly restored middle Neolithic long barrow, constructed in the Cotswold–Severn tradition, lies on the northern edge of a narrow upland ridge with commanding views. The mound, orientated roughly north to south, is today partly obscured by the modern road; originally it would have been over 26 m. long and up to 3 m. high.

The chamber, now exposed, has nine orthostats† forming the walls and supporting the massive capstone†. Two stones south of the chamber may be the remains of a peristalith† around the former mound. A short passage provides access to the chamber from the north-west; between the passage and chamber, and bridging the different orientations of the two parts of the structure is a small

Long Barrows

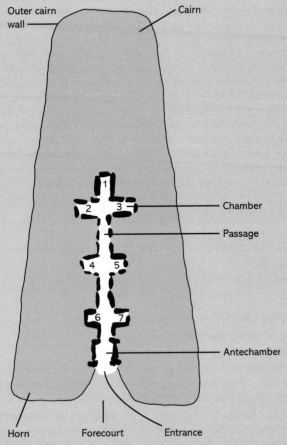

Long barrows, most of which were built and used between about 3800 BC and 3000 BC, are the most widespread and ubiquitous monuments of the middle Neolithic period. They represent one of the earliest traditions of architecture in Britain. Apart from obvious difference in construction caused by the local availability of materials—stone in the west as against timber and rubble in the east—a number of regional styles can be identified.

Typically, the burial chambers inside long barrows account for less than 5 per cent of the total monument. This has led to the suggestion that these structures are not simply burial places but some kind of territorial marker: a community literally engraving its existence and identity on the landscape. Whether or not this was so, there is also the problem of explaining the strange and very deliberate shape of these structures.

> The form of long barrows has been looked at in terms of two general ideas about the symbolism embodied in its design. First is the possibility that long barrows represent houses of the dead. This is based on analogies between the trapezoidal form of the mounds and the rather similar ground plans of timber houses constructed on the mainland of Europe in the later sixth and early fifth millennia BC. However, no such houses have yet been found in Britain and the analogy therefore hinges on the perpetuation of a memory of what the 'ancestral' homes were actually like.
>
> The second idea sees the tomb as a metaphor for the human body, and in particular the lower torso. Viewed or visualized in plan the analogy is clear: the horns are the tops of the legs, the cairn the abdomen and trunk. The back of the forecourt has a special significance whether the structure is seen as male or female, the latter being more likely if it is postulated that the deceased were being returned to the womb to be born again. The position of the chambers and the swelling of the cairn at its widest point support this idea.

antechamber. No traces of the roofing arrangements for passage or ante-chamber survive.

W. Hemp, 'Arthur's Stone', ACamb, 90 (1935), 288–92.

Astbury, Cheshire Medieval church

SJ 846615. On the A34 2 km. SW of Congleton.

Astbury is one of the most exciting of many good Perpendicular churches in Cheshire. Seven bays long, and with no division between nave† and chancel†, it has piers which rise to be continued as shafts which frame four-light clerestory† windows. The roofs are low-pitched and have camber beams, richly decorated with bosses carrying monograms, Symbols of the Passion, and openwork pendants. It is probably late C15 in date. Broadly contemporary is the unusual, three-storeyed west porch and the chancel and parclose screens†. There is much else to discover: from part of a C11 Anglo-Danish cross shaft to a good set of C14 and later monuments. The detached tower and spire were funded by Roger Swettenham, who willed money for their construction in 1366.

N. Pevsner and E. Hubbard, The Buildings of England: Cheshire (Penguin, 1971), 65–7.

Beeston, Cheshire Medieval castle

SJ 537593. 15 km. SE of Chester. English Heritage; restricted opening. Admission charge. Figure 75.

The rock of Beeston stands over one of the three gaps in the hills which encircle CHESTER, dominating the Cheshire Plain. *Castellum de Rupe*, 'the Castle of the Rock', as it was called in medieval documents, was started in 1225 by Ranulf, earl of Chester. The idea of a castle dependent, at least in part, for its strength on deep, rock-cut ditches may have owed much to fort-resses seen by Ranulf in Syria and the Holy Land while crusading. At Beeston the end of the hilltop crag was cut off by a ditch to create an inner bailey†, around the inner lip of which a wall was built. Lower down the hill an outer wall closed off a massive outer bailey. Towers, mostly D-plan, were built at regular intervals along the walls, the most massive to form gatehouses. These were concepts of castle defence only to be fully developed at the end of the C13 in Edward I's great castle-building campaign following the final conquest of Wales at Beaumaris, Rhuddlan, and his other 'concentric' castles†.

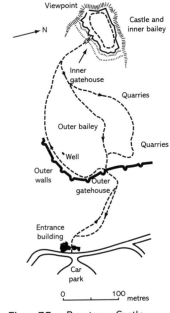

▲ Fig. 75. Beeston Castle, Cheshire (after English Heritage)

Beeston never had palatial buildings, and throughout the C13–C14 it remained a military base, spartan but potentially effective. A siege in the Civil War of the 1640s proved its strength and only potential starvation caused its defenders eventually to surrender.

J. Weaver, Beeston Castle *(English Heritage, 1995) (Site Guidebook).*

Bredon, Worcestershire Medieval barn

SO 919370. 5 km. NE of Tewkesbury on B4080. National Trust; restricted opening. Admission charge. Website: www.ntrustsevern.org.uk.

In the Middle Ages Bredon was owned by the bishops of Worcester, who, about 1340, funded the construction of a great stone barn. Some 44 m. long with nine aisled bays, it has a steeply pitched stone slate roof well supplied with ventilation holes. Two porched entrances project forward. Above one is the reeve's office, equipped with fireplace (note outside the unusual stone chimney cowl) and built-in cupboard; he was the official responsible for overseeing the stacking of sheaves and the threshing of grain. Major restoration followed a serious fire in 1980.

F. Charles, The Great Barn of Bredon *(Oxbow Books, 1997).*

Bredon Hill (Kemerton Camp), Eckington, Worcestershire Iron Age hillfort†

SO 958402. On the NW side of Bredon Hill 2 km. SW of Elmley Castle. Best approached by footpath from Elmley Castle.

This substantial strong fortress, strategically situated on a spur of Bredon Hill, overlooks the river Avon. It makes use of natural slopes on the north-west and north-east sides; two lines of constructed ramparts secure the remaining sides.

Excavations revealed a detailed picture of the fort's history. The first defence, built perhaps in the C6 BC, is now the outer rampart. The bank, 13.5 m. wide at the base and over 3 m. high, was faced with dry-stone walling on the outer face, but had a sloping back face. In front of the rampart was a berm†, beyond which was a V-profile ditch 10 m. wide and 4.5 m. deep. The area enclosed was 7.1 ha., room aplenty for a substantial settlement. No entrances are known for this phase.

Later, perhaps in the C2 BC, the inner rampart was added. Built in the glacis† style, there is no berm but a continuous 11 m. slope from the ditch bottom to the bank top. There was probably a timber breastwork along the top. A single entrance near the centre of the circuit was modified several times and ended up as visible today with in-turned rampart terminals creating a narrow entrance passage originally walled and gated. The area enclosed is half that of the earlier phase.

At the same time as the inner rampart was constructed two new entrances were built in the outer rampart. Although damaged by landslips these are still visible near the cliff edge at either end.

The excavations also discovered sixty-four bodies in the entrance passage through the inner rampart. Hacked to pieces and left where they fell, these were the remains of a massacre in the early C1 AD if not before. Six human skulls by the gateway were perhaps the remains of severed heads displayed above the gate. Just 2 km. to the south-west is another hillfort†, CONDERTON CAMP.

T. Hencken, 'The Excavation of the Iron Age Camp on Bredon Hill', Arch J, 95 (1937), 1–111.

Bridestones, Congleton, Staffordshire Neolithic long barrow†

SJ 906622. 4 km. E of Congleton, N of minor road leading from the A527 at Dane in Shaw to the A523 at Ryecroft Gate. Figure 76.

Although only the chamber of this middle Neolithic long barrow survives, originally it was over 90 m. long and 12 m. wide. Orientated east to west, the visible chamber is rectangular in plan, and divided into two parts by a slab (now broken) pierced by a circular hole known as a 'porthole'.

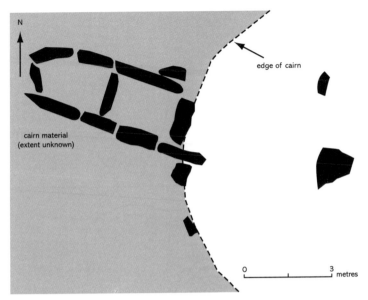

N

edge of cairn

cairn material
(extent unknown)

0   3
metres

▲ **Fig. 76.** Plan of the Neolithic long barrow at Bridestones, Congleton, Staffordshire (after Daniel)

East of the chamber is a semicircular forecourt, the edges traced by large stones. Two further chambers are said to have been destroyed when the mound was removed in the C18.

M. Dunlop, 'A Preliminary Survey of the Bridestones', TLCAS 53 (1938), 14–31.

British Camp, Herefordshire Beacon, Little Malvern, Herefordshire and Worcestershire Iron Age hillfort† ★★

SO 760399. Midway along the Malvern hills where the A4104 crosses the range. Roadside parking at Wynds Point; footpaths lead from here across open land to the hillfort. Figure 77 and Figure 7.

Occupying a prominent peak on the central Malvern hills, this massive Iron Age hillfort commands extensive views. Although never excavated, it is probably multi-phase. The earliest earthworks are those at the centre of the site which enclose 3.2 ha., largely following the natural contours. Originally comprising a single bank and ditch with entrances to the north-east and south-west, part of the circuit has been obliterated by the C12 castle which crowns the hill.

Late in the Iron Age the fort was expanded to enclose the whole ridge, an area of nearly 13 ha. On the west side these later defences merge with the earlier ones, but elsewhere they are quite distinct, lying outside the inner line. There are four entrances to the later Iron Age fort. Within

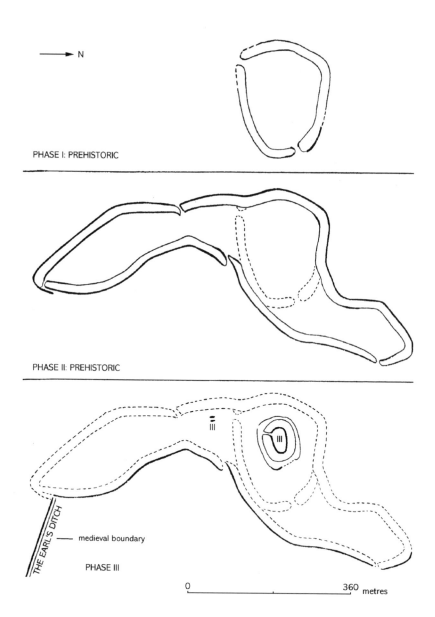

N

PHASE I: PREHISTORIC

PHASE II: PREHISTORIC

III

III

THE EARL'S DITCH

— medieval boundary

PHASE III

0   360 metres

▲ Fig. 77. Phase plans of the main stages in the evolution of the British Camp, Herefordshire Beacon, Little Malvern, Hereford and Worcester (after Wheeler)

the defences are numerous platforms, presumably the sites of houses and other buildings.

In the C12 AD a small ringwork† was added to the summit of the hill. The most recent earthwork is the Shire Ditch, built about AD 1290 by Gilbert de Clare, earl of Gloucester, to mark the boundary between Malvern Chase and the lands of the bishop of Hereford. The dyke runs along the crest of the Malverns for most of their length, but uses the eastern rampart of the hillfort for this section of its course.

R. Wheeler, 'The Herefordshire Beacon Hillfort', Arch J, 109 (1952), 146–8.

Bury Ditches, Clun, Shropshire   Iron Age hillfort††

SO 327836. 4 km. NE of Clun, approached by footpath from (SO 335844) W of minor road from Brockton on B4385 to Clunton on B4368.

Oval in plan, this fort stands on a spur where steep natural slopes add to the constructed defences all around apart from the north-east. On the south side there are two banks and a ditch, on the north and north-west sides there are four banks and ditches, while to the north-east there are five banks.

Two entrances provide access to the interior. That to the north-east is elaborate with a deeply in-turned inner rampart. The south-west entrance has a pair of ramparts deeply in-turned on the south side but on the opposite side the inner rampart stops short and the outer rampart is out-turned. This creates an obliquely angled entrance passage.

S. Stanford, 'The Function and Population of Hillforts in the Central Marches', in F. Lynch and C. Burgess (eds), Prehistoric Man in Wales and the West (Adams & Dart, 1972), 307–20.

Caer Caradoc, Church Stretton, Shropshire   Iron Age hillfort††

SO 477953. 3 km. NE of Church Stretton, E of A49(T) to Shrewsbury. Accessible by a steep climb from A49 or less energetically from the minor road E of A49 at Comley.

Caer Caradoc is situated on a prominent spur at 403 m. above sea level overlooking a deep river valley. The defended area covers about 2.3 ha. and is bounded on all sides by a single massive stone rampart with an outer ditch and counterscarp bank†, while the west, north, and east sides are further strengthened by a second and locally third rampart widely spaced on the west side and closely set on the north side.

There are two entrances, east and west, both clearly visible, and both with internal passages formed by in-turning the inner rampart.

Six or more house foundations are visible as round platforms in the interior. A collapsed shaft near the centre of the fort may be the remains of a well.

VCH, Victoria County History of Shropshire, vol. i (Institute of Historical Research, 1908), 362–3.

Chester (*Deva*), Cheshire Roman fortress, and Roman and medieval town

Centred SJ 405665. At the SW end of M56; also accessible from M53. The Grosvenor Museum, Grosvenor Street, Dewa Centre, Pierpoint Lane off Bridge Street, and the Heritage Centre, Bridge Street, provide good starting places for a visit. Figures 78 and 79.

It is difficult to walk around Chester and not be aware of its Roman origins. A legionary fortress, initially occupied by Legio II Augusta, was constructed between AD 76 and 80. It was strategically placed at the lowest crossing of the river Dee. After AD 87 the fort was garrisoned by Legio XX Valeria Victrix. In the C2 the fort defences were rebuilt in stone and a large civil settlement had become established. The medieval walls, amongst the most complete in Britain, broadly follow the line of the Roman defences and can be used as the basis of a trail around the Roman town. The complete circuit is about 3 km. and takes one to two hours.

In Newgate Street (**1**) foundations of the south-east angle of the fortress wall and interval tower are visible. Immediately north of the medieval Eastgate (Kaleyard Gate) (**2**), which lies over its Roman predecessor, are the foundations of the fortress wall outside the present city wall. Remains of the north fortress wall with a moulded cornice, rebuilt in C4, can be best seen from the towpath or the canal bridge on George Street (**3**) just outside the Northgate. Through an alleyway leading from Northgate Street to Hamilton Place/Goss Street (**4**) on the right are the excavated foundations of the strong room or treasury of the legionary fortress.

Other visible remains include the Roman amphitheatre†, the largest in Britain although only half is exposed (English Heritage). This is outside the south-east corner of the defences in St John's Street opposite the Visitor Centre (**5**). Open any reasonable time. Entry free.

Following St Johns Street opposite Newgate Street (**1** above) are public gardens (**6**) containing columns, a reconstructed hypocaust† and various building fragments. Further building remains form a commemorative feature in Northgate Street near junction with Princess Street outside Coach and Horses public house (**7**).

A unique Roman shrine can be seen by taking Lower Bridge Street to Handbridge (**8**). Over the bridge to the south of the river Dee, the shrine can be found immediately to the right in public gardens. This is the only known example of an *in situ* Minerva, here carved into the face of a Roman quarry.

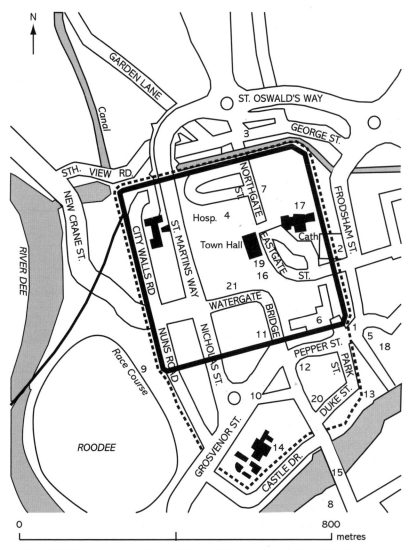

▲ **Fig. 78.** Plan of modern Chester. The solid line marks the line of the Roman city wall, the dashed one the medieval

The Roman and medieval harbour lay in the area of the Roodee racecourse (**9**). Remains of the quay wall beyond south-west corner of fortress can be seen.

The Grosvenor Museum, Grosvenor Street (**10**) contains finds from excavations in the city. A Roman experience can be visited at the Dewa Centre (**11**) with a walk through a Roman galley, a cellar excavation, finds displays, and a children's activity room. Further background on

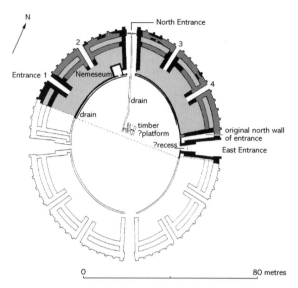

▲ **Fig. 79.** Plan of the amphitheatre at Chester (*Deva*) (after Fulford. Crown copyright)

the historical development of Chester can be sought at the Heritage Centre on the corner of Bridge Street and Pepper Street (**12**).

Chester remained important in Saxon times. Following a Viking raid, it was made a *burh*† in 907, gained a mint, and became one of the most important trading ports serving the Irish Sea.

The Roman city walls were extended south to the river Dee in and after the 1120s (**13**); today Chester is the only completely walled town in England. The north and east lengths follow exactly the Roman lines, and incorporate Roman material. At the north-east corner is King Charles Tower (where Charles I watched the defeat of his army at Rowton Moor in 1645) and at the north-west Bonewaldesthorne's Tower. This is connected by a spur wall to the Water Tower, completed in 1325 to protect the city when it was a major port. The medieval extension of the wall circuit took in the medieval castle (**14**) (largely replaced in the late C18), which overlooked what was then the harbour and the medieval Old Dee Bridge (**15**) (C15, widened in 1826).

The principal streets, forming an offset cross, meet at the Cross (**16**) at the town centre. From this point several examples of the 'Rows' can be seen, the walkways which pass above street-level shops giving access to a second level of shops at Row (first-floor) level. Normally separating the walkway from the street frontage are sloping stalls or stallboards, above the steps leading from the street into the lower shops, which occupy what are in fact undercrofts†. The Rows remain in commercial use; about twenty-five of the undercrofts are medieval.

The cathedral (17) (its church dedicated to St Werburgh) in the north-east quarter of the city was a Benedictine† abbey until the Dissolution. North of the church it has one of England's most complete groups of monastic buildings. The frater, or refectory, retains its wall pulpit from which the monks were read to while they ate in silence.

Of the town's medieval churches St John's (18), outside the city walls, was the cathedral church of Mercia 1075–95 before the see moved to Lichfield. The lower storey of the church dates from its time as a cathedral, the upper from the late C12. St Peter's (19), at the Cross, is of the C14 and C15; in the Middle Ages it was closely associated with the civic authorities. St Mary's began as the castle chapel, and was later rebuilt as St Mary on the Hill immediately outside the castle. It has a notable timber nave roof and several tombs of leading citizens. Of the town's other medieval churches St Olave's (20), Lower Bridge Street, is an interesting aisleless building, while Holy Trinity and St Michael's were rebuilt in the C19 and are now respectively the Guildhall (21) and a Heritage Centre (see 12 above). Apart from St Werburgh's, Chester's medieval religious houses are now remembered principally by street names such as White Friars and Black Friars.

P. Carrington, Chester *(Batsford and English Heritage, 1994)*.

Conderton Camp, Beckford, Worcestershire Iron Age
hillfort†

SO 972384. S side of Bredon Hill, 2 km. NE of Overbury, accessible by footpath from lane leading N from Overbury.

The smaller of the two hillforts on Bredon Hill (see also BREDON HILL). Roughly oval in shape, the fort is set on a spur utilizing steep slopes on all but the north side.

Excavations in 1958–9 revealed that the site was originally a corral for livestock. The outer defences were constructed to enclose 1.2 ha. with a simple bank and ditch and in places a counterscarp bank† beyond. There were two entrances, one in the centre of the north side, the other at the south end.

In the C1 BC the site was modified through the addition of a bank dividing off the north end. As can be seen today, there was no ditch associated with this subdivision. Within the sectioned-off area was a substantial village of round houses. House platforms can still be seen on the ground as hollows.

N. Thomas, 'The Excavations at Conderton Camp', TCNFC 33 (1959), 100–6.

Coventry, West Midlands Medieval town

SP 335790. W of Birmingham, S of M6.

Coventry's woollen textile industry was already well established in the C12, by when there were at least twelve fulling mills along the river Sherbourne. By 1300 the town's cloth merchants, whose houses were concentrated in Earl Street in the town centre, were trading with Flanders. Above all, prosperity depended on the celebrated 'Coventry blue' cloth with its non-fading qualities.

Despite the damage the city suffered in 1940 and the subsequent redevelopment, evidence of this medieval prosperity is still to be found in its buildings, both secular and religious. The most poignant reminder of the 1940 raid is the skeletal ruins of the old cathedral, which began life as the parish church of St Michael. Alongside is St Mary's Guildhall, begun in 1340 and enlarged in 1400, with hall (note the stained glass) and vaulted undercroft†. Facing the cathedral precinct is the church of Holy Trinity, with C15 pulpit and eagle lectern. Another surviving religious building, south-east of the city centre, is the eleven-bay dormitory of the Carmelite Friary; the basic structure dates from soon after the house's foundation in 1343, while the roof is C16. Also extant is the east range of the cloister, with the chapter house flanked by warming room and parlour. Details of the cathedral-like church, with nine-bay nave, have been revealed by excavation. Beneath the choir stalls metre-square resonance passages were found, intended to enhance the quality of the friars' singing.

Among secular buildings (beware that some have been moved from their original positions) is a row of C14 timber-framed terraced houses in Spon Street. Six were apparently a speculative development; unusually the houses are Wealden-type with an open, ground-floor hall to the left and a jettied first-floor solar to the right.

T. Slater, A History of Warwickshire *(Phillimore, 1981), 58–61.*

Croft Ambrey, Mortimer's Cross, Herefordshire Iron Age
hillfort†

SO 444668. On hilltop 1 km. E of Yatton, E of A4110 and N of B4362. Accessible by footpath from Leinthall Earls, Yatton, or the Croft Castle. National Trust.

Set on a spur overlooking the valley of the river Lugg, this site affords excellent views to the north-west. Extensively excavated between 1960 and 1966, the fort saw intensive occupation over a long period and many phases of construction and reconstruction.

The earliest fortification, probably of C6 BC date, was in the central part of the hill around the highest point. Originally defined by a rampart and outer ditch, the rampart was later removed and only the remains of the ditch are now visible. The 2.2 ha. enclosure contained rows of timber buildings, possibly for grain storage. There were entrances to the east and west, and at least five periods of reconstruction and modification are represented.

About 390 BC the original ramparts were levelled and a new 3.5 ha. enclosure built. This was defined by what is now visible as the inner rampart and two external banks separated by a pair of ditches. A new east gate was constructed. A hollow-way leading from this gate downhill to the east represents the approach route to the fort. New gates were added to the south-west. Through the C1 BC and early C1 AD the fort was intensively occupied. An annexe was added to the south of the fort, defined by a pair of banks and ditches. This may have been to protect livestock during times of hostility.

The fort was probably taken by the Romans in about AD 49. Many of the huts had been burnt when the site was abandoned. In the C2 AD a round mound was built outside the fort within the area of the annexe, perhaps a temple or sanctuary. Much later five pillow mounds were built in the annexe for farming rabbits.

Finds from the excavation are in Hereford City Museum, with a small selection on display in Croft Castle.

S. Stanford, Croft Ambrey *(Leominster: privately published, 1974).*

Goodrich, Herefordshire Medieval castle

SO 579199. 8 km. S of Ross-on-Wye off A40. English Heritage; restricted opening. Admission charge.

The castle stands high above a crossing point of the river Wye, an area taken from the Welsh by the Normans only in the late C11. The earliest fabric is the small, square keep, probably of the early to mid-C12 (note the original first-floor entrance, later reduced to a window). In the 1280s and 1290s this was incorporated into the quadrangular castle which we see today by William de Valance, a half-brother of Henry III, during Edward I's final conquest of Wales. The sophisticated ranges of halls and chambers may largely be the work of William's son Aymer, who succeeded in 1307. The most striking features of the castle are the round corner and gatehouse towers, tapering upwards from massive square bases set on the bottom of the 27 m. wide and 8 m. deep dry moat. The gatehouse, which incorporates the castle chapel, is approached by a bridge from the barbican†, which probably also dates from the late C13, as does the outer ward along the castle's north and west sides wherein stood stables and other service buildings.

Goodrich was besieged in the Civil War of the 1640s, and in 1646 was partially demolished.

A. Emery, Greater Medieval Houses of England and Wales, *vol. ii (Cambridge University Press, 2000), 537–40.*

Kemerton Camp, Eckington, Worcestershire *see* BREDON HILL.

Kenchester (*Magna*), Herefordshire Roman town

SJ 440428. 7 km. W of Hereford along A438 and via minor road to the N. The Roman site is located in fields off a minor road 1.6 km. SW of modern village.

A once important Roman town strategically placed in the Wye valley close to the Iron Age hillfort† of Credenhill. Little is now visible above ground, but in dry conditions cropmarks can be seen crossing the fields under which the former town lies, showing streets and buildings. The settlement was surrounded by a defensive stone wall forming an irregular hexagonal outline, preserved as a slight bank mirrored by the modern field edges. Excavations have revealed houses with mosaic floors, paved roads, and burials.

B. Burnham and J. Wacher, The Small Towns of Roman Britain *(Batsford, 1990), 70–6.*

King Arthur's Cave, Whitchurch, Herefordshire Palaeolithic and later occupied cave

SO 545155. In woodland 6 km. NE of Monmouth, E of A40(T). Approached by footpaths from minor roads running S from Great Doward. Car park at SO 547157.

Situated some 90 m. above the present river Wye, this cave was intermittently occupied from Upper Palaeolithic times until Roman times.

The cave comprises two chambers, the larger over 16.7 m. deep. Both are approached by short passages leading from a broad entrance area containing a natural pillar of rock. In front of the entrance is a broad platform.

Excavations in 1870–1 revealed that the earliest occupation was deep inside the cave. The bones of mammoth, woolly rhinoceros, lion, bison, and great Irish elk were found. These suggest that the cave was in use during a cold period, perhaps during the onset of the Devensian glaciation about 30,000 BC.

During the later part of the Upper Palaeolithic occupation seems to have been mostly confined to the entrance area and the outer platform. Tools and weapons of Creswellian tradition were found associated with hearths. Traces of later activity have also been recorded.

North-west of the cave is the wooded **Little Doward** hillfort (SO 540160). Inside is a fine round barrow†.

H. Taylor, 'King Arthur's Cave', PUBSS *3/2 (1928), 59–87.*

Kinver Edge, Kinver, Staffordshire Iron Age hillfort†

SO 835832. In woodland SW of Kinver, 8 km. SW of Stourbridge. Approached by footpath from S side of Kinver village. National Trust.

This 3 ha. Iron Age promontory fort lies in light woodland at the north end of a narrow sandstone ridge with wonderful views of the Clent hills to the east and Wenlock Edge to the west. Steep slopes provide natural defence on the north-west and south-east sides, a single massive rampart crosses the ridge to form the south side of the enclosure. No trace of an entrance remains.

Below the hillfort on the north side, at Holy Austin Rock, is a series of houses burrowed out of the soft sandstone. Some may be prehistoric in origin, but most are more recent, some being occupied as houses until the 1950s—apparently the last troglodyte dwellings in this country. Holy Austin Rock itself was a hermitage until the Reformation.

J. Forde-Johnston, Hillforts of the Iron Age *(Liverpool University Press, 1976).*

Leigh Court, Worcestershire   Medieval barn

SO 783535. Leigh is 8 km. W of Worcester, on minor road off the A4103. English Heritage; restricted opening.

Crucks, great curving oak trunks arching from ground level to the apex of a building, were one of the classic ways in the Middle Ages of providing a basic framework for a building, and a means to support its roof. Arguably the greatest of all cruck-framed buildings is Pershore Abbey's barn at Leigh Court, which dates from about 1300. Its crucks—nine full pairs and a pair at each end cut off halfway to form the half-hipped roof—are 10 m. long, with a scantling (dimension) of 0.53 m. and a span of 10.2 m. If anything the builders over-reached themselves, for later the pressure of the crucks made the sandstone sill walls they sit on splay outwards, requiring buttresses to be constructed. Also cruck-framed are the two porches on the south side. The side walls, which in a cruck building have little structural role, are timber-framed. Not only is this a large building, it is one with sophisticated carpentry and rich design: see the carved bargeboards of the porches. The nearby dovecote (or pigeon house) is unusually capacious, with 1,380 nesting holes.

F. Charles, The Great Barn of Bredon *(Oxbow Books, 1997), 2–4.*

Little Moreton Hall, Cheshire   Medieval manor house   ★★

SJ 832589. Little Moreton is 4 km. S of Congleton, E of A34. National Trust; restricted opening. Admission charge. Figure 80.

In the mid-C16 men of local standing in the north-west were still building timber-framed houses, by now of extraordinary external complexity and elaboration. At Little Moreton William Moreton (d. 1563) employed the carpenter Richard Dale to add turret-like bay windows (dated in carved inscriptions 1559) to the hall and withdrawing room of a mid-C15 timber-framed house. Windows wrap around the bays, flooding in light and, as glass was still expensive, proclaiming his wealth. The peerless south gatehouse range, multi-jettied and rising above the moat to

▲ **Fig. 80.** Little Moreton Hall, Cheshire, the 1559 bay windows (Photograph: Paul Stamper)

greet the visitor, is of about 1565, and also by Dale. Along its top attic floor is a wonderful long gallery, panelled and with arch-braced roof trusses designed to give maximum headroom. The gardens have been partly re-created, with box-hedged knots; two raised prospect mounds are original features.

A. Emery, Greater Medieval Houses of England and Wales, *vol. ii (Cambridge University Press, 2000), 555–6.*

Longtown Castle, Herefordshire Medieval castle and planned town

SO 784534. 22 km. SW of Hereford, on minor road running N off the A465. Castle: English Heritage.

Longtown had an early Norman castle; its location, below the eastern slopes of the Black Mountain, is both spectacular and strategic. Towards the end of the C12 the castle was rebuilt, with a strong round tower on the motte† top. One of three cylindrical buttresses contains the spiral stair, which gave access to the main, first-floor chamber. Another buttress has a fireplace recess, while a corbelled-out garderobe† adjoins the third. External sockets near the wall top were for the supports of an external timber gallery. The motte stands at the north-east corner of a square, subdivided bailey†, the inner portion of which is partly walled and has a gate.

Longtown belonged to the Lacys. Below the castle, at about the time they were rebuilding it, they laid out a planned town. Outside the castle defences are the borough's chapel (largely rebuilt in Victorian times) and the old town street, on either side of which are the house plots of the townsmen or 'burgesses'. Initially the town thrived, and by about 1310 there were a hundred properties. Later it declined, and is today little more than a village.

Other round towers in the Marches and Wales include Bronlyss (about 1176), Pembroke (about 1200), Tretower, and Skenfrith (the last both early C13).

M. Beresford, New Towns of the Middle Ages *(Lutterworth Press, 1967)*, 451.

Lower Brockhampton, Herefordshire   Medieval manor and chapel

SO 688560. 16 km. W of Worcester and 4 km. E of Bromyard, down a signposted track off A44. National Trust. Admission charge for house and car park. Access to the estate is possible at any reasonable time. Website: www.ntrustsevern.org.uk.

In the Middle Ages there was a village here, set in the secluded valley which gives the settlement its name: Brockhampton means 'brook settlement'. Today all that remains is a ruined Norman chapel and an early C15 manor house surrounded by a water-filled moat. While many of the manor's lesser buildings have been lost—the detached kitchen, stables, and other agricultural buildings—what survives gives a very good idea of a typical manorial complex. The house is timber-framed, and comprises a hall range with a cross (or solar) wing at one end; originally there was also one at the other end, giving an H-plan building. The hall, where meals would have been taken and perhaps manorial courts held, remains open to the roof as it was in the Middle Ages (a later inserted floor has been removed). A little two-storey gatehouse of about 1600, also timber-framed with close studding, guards the crossing over the moat.

A. Emery, Greater Medieval Houses of England and Wales, *vol. ii (Cambridge University Press, 2000)*, 558–9.

Maiden Castle, Bickerton, Cheshire   Iron Age hillfort†

SJ 497529. On NW side of Bickerton Hill 6 km. N of Malpas, E of A41(T) and S of A534. Best approached by footpath from Brown Knowl or Bickerton village.

Oval in plan, about 130 × 55 m. and covering 0.5 ha., this relatively small fort is defended by an artificially improved cliff on the west side and by two parallel banks to the east. Later the outer rampart was heightened by the addition of rubble dug from between the defences, thus creating the shallow ditch about 0.5 m. deep that is still just visible today.

There was only one entrance through the outer rampart, a simple gap that can still be seen in the east side. The inner rampart had a more elaborate entrance. Excavations revealed a massive timber gate about halfway along the passage allowing access to be controlled.

W. Varley, 'Further Excavations at Maiden Castle', Liverpool Annals of Archaeology and Anthropology, 23 (1936), 101–12.

Middle Littleton, Worcestershire Medieval barn

SP 080471. 5 km. NE of Evesham, E of B4085. National Trust; restricted opening. Admission charge. Website: www.ntsevern.org.uk.

Each of the trio of Littleton villages, South, North, and Middle, is attractive. In the last, next to a three-gabled C16 manor house, is an early C14 tithe† barn, built when the manor belonged to Evesham Abbey. It is of blue lias, with Cotswold stone dressings, and originally had four porches, in opposed pairs; sadly the eastern porches were demolished a hundred years ago. Its roof is supported by eleven pairs of raised base crucks. These great curved oak timbers spring from high in the stone walls to meet a collar near the roof apex. This mode of construction allowed the barn floor and working space to be entirely unencumbered by posts. That having been said, there is an aisled truss at either end.

This is the only survivor of 'eight magnificent granges' built between 1296 and 1316 by Abbot John de Brockhampton. He also rebuilt many churches, and even constructed canals.

F. Charles, The Great Barn of Bredon (Oxbow Books, 1997), 5–7.

Midsummer Hill, Hollybush, Herefordshire Iron Age hillfort††

SO 761375. On the S end of the Malvern hills immediately N of the A438 Tewkesbury to Hereford road. Car park N of A438 at SO 759369; a footpath leads N to the site. National Trust.

This large hillfort of 7.6 ha. includes two hilltops and is defined by a single bank and ditch with slight traces of an outer bank beyond the ditch in places. The remains of a shallow quarry ditch can be seen on the inside of the main bank. Excavations suggest a C5 BC date.

The main entrance is to the south-west in the valley between Midsummer and Hollybush hills. Excavation revealed over seventeen phases of construction and reconstruction during its life, most featuring a long entrance passage with a metalled road running into the fort. Within the fort there is evidence for dense occupation. About 250 scoops into the hillside can be seen on the surface, many of them platforms for round and rectangular houses.

The long mound between the two hills is a pillow mound used for post-medieval rabbit farming.

S. Stanford, Midsummer Hill *(Leominster: privately published, 1981).*

Mitchell's Fold, near Chirbury, Shropshire Neolithic stone
circle† ★

SO 306984. On moorland 2 km. NE of Priestweston, W of A488. Accessible by signposted track and footpath running N from minor road between Chirbury and Hyssington. English Heritage.

This stone circle lies on open ground towards the south-western end of Stapeley Hill with extensive views to both east and west.

Fourteen dolerite pillars remain standing, all less than 2 m. tall and most under 1 m. The circle has a diameter of about 25 m. but the remaining stones are irregularly spaced; two larger stones to the south-east may have been portals flanking an entrance.

About 75 m. to the south-east is a very weathered stone set on a small cairn†.

Approximately 3.2 km. south of Mitchell's Fold, but clearly visible, is **Corndon Hill** (SO 3096). Fine volcanic rock known as Hyssington picrite was used here in late Neolithic and early Bronze Age times to make polished tools and weapons.

W. Grimes, 'The Stone Circles and Related Monuments of Wales', in I. Forster and L. Alcock (eds), Culture and Environment *(Routledge, 1963), 93–152.*

Offa's Dyke, Cheshire, Shropshire, Herefordshire, and
Gloucestershire Anglo-Saxon frontier earthwork
This frontier work can be explored using the well-signposted long-distance Offa's Dyke footpath. Figure 81.

'There was in Mercia in recent times a certain valiant king called Offa, who was feared by all the kings and kingdoms around, who ordered a great dyke to be built from sea to sea between Britain and Mercia.' Thus, at the end of the C9, King Alfred's biographer Asser looked back a century or so to the time when Offa was ruler (759–98) of the great midland kingdom of Mercia, and there was endemic warfare between it, Northumbria, and Powys.

The dyke extends along a 240 km. frontier between England and Wales, from just east of the point where the river Wye joins the Severn estuary to its north end near Treuddyn in south Flintshire. Excavations show it to have comprised a 2 m. deep ditch with a bank or rampart on the west side, rising about 7.5 m. from the ditch bottom. The dyke is not continuous, and about 140 km. is upstanding. Some, certainly, has been destroyed, but there are other stretches where the dyke never existed. Its function remains uncertain: it may have been conceived as a defensible

▲ **Fig. 81.** Offa's Dyke crossing Llanfair Hill, south Shropshire. The English side of the Dyke is to the left (Photograph: CPAT 85-16-29, copyright)

barrier, or, more probably, as a well-defined frontier between two countries. The Dyke's life as a frontier was probably short, for in 822 the Mercians invaded North Wales and established a rule which was to last two generations.

Some of the best-preserved sections are in Shropshire, around Oswestry in the north-west of the county and around Clun in the southwest, notably where it crosses the bleak upland of Llanfair Hill, 5 km. to the south of Clun [SO 2579].

D. Hill, 2000, 'Offa's Dyke: Pattern and Purpose', Ant J, 80 (2000), 195–206.

Old Oswestry, Shropshire   Iron Age hillfort†   ★★

SJ 295310. 1 km. N of Oswestry. Access via signposted minor road N from A5(T) running out of Oswestry town centre. Also signposted from Oswestry bypass. English Heritage.

Old Oswestry is one of the most outstanding monuments in the Welsh Marches with fine views over the valley of the river Dee.

The visible earthworks coupled with the results of excavations in 1939–40 allow something of its complicated development to be understood. The earliest settlement, probably of the first half of the first millennium BC, was an open settlement with timber-built round houses. This was abandoned and the hill subsequently reoccupied and defended in the C5 BC. The defences were typical of the range of middle Iron Age hillforts in the Welsh Marches: an enclosure of 5.3 ha. defended by a single rampart with two fortified entrances.

In the C3 BC, Old Oswestry seems to have developed as a regional centre of some kind, most evident archaeologically in the elaboration of the defences. Existing structures were enhanced and new ones added. The inner rampart was expanded, to change the vertically faced design into the 'glacis' style of rampart popular from the C4 BC onwards. The inner and second rampart were similarly altered while, lower down, the naturally steep slopes of the hill were enhanced to create two outer lines of ramparts.

These final-phase additions left wide gaps between the defensive lines in some areas. A similar feature occurs around the edge of other developed hillforts, and at DANEBURY, Hampshire, Barry Cunliffe has suggested that these areas may have been used to protect and shelter livestock. Rather strange at Old Oswestry, however, is that north of the western entrance the area between the inner and outer ramparts is subdivided by substantial cross banks. These may have been built to hold livestock, or may have been tanks of some kind, perhaps to store water.

The site was abandoned during Roman times, although it was reused in early post-Roman times when it became associated with the legendary King Arthur and is regarded as the home of Gogyrfan, father of Guinevere. OFFA'S DYKE runs around the fort, connecting with it on two sides.

G. Hughes, 'Old Oswestry Hillfort', ACamb, 143 (1996), 46–91.

Stokesay Castle, Shropshire Fortified medieval manor house★★

SO 436817. Off the A49 10 km. NW of Ludlow. English Heritage; restricted opening. Admission charge. Figure 82.

Strictly speaking, Stokesay is not a castle but a fortified manor house; one of the best preserved and scenic defended houses surviving from medieval England.

In the late C13 the manor was purchased by Laurence of Ludlow, who had become rich through the wool trade. Stokesay was intended, it seems, as his country house, a place to entertain and to impress. To that end, in 1291 he obtained from the king a licence to crenellate Stokesay, and, in theory at least, make it defensible against the king. Laurence's concerns, however, were probably more with the Welsh.

The licence came at the end of a major rebuilding campaign spanning 1284–91. The great hall, spanned and supported by three huge pairs of crucks, is lit by six tall windows whose upper halves were glazed but the lower only shuttered. The walls were originally plastered, white-washed, and with some painted decoration. Heating was provided by a

▲ **Fig. 82.** Stokesay Castle, Shropshire, showing north tower (left), great hall and south tower (Photograph: Paul Stamper)

central hearth. The 'high' end of the hall, where the de Ludlows would have sat at a table, was at the far end from the draughty main door.

The rebuilding provided high-quality accommodation off both ends of the hall, reflecting the needs of a family which probably did much entertaining. At the south high end of the hall is a solar block, from the principal first-floor chamber of which two small windows either side of the fireplace look down into the hall. This was probably always one of the main private rooms in the castle; its impressive panelling is mid-C17. Beyond is the south tower, which has a complex geometric plan and has arrow loops piercing the crenellations. Despite its military posturing its main function was to provide comfortable accommodation.

From the 'low' end of the hall a medieval wooden staircase ascends to the private chambers in the north tower. The lower, stone-built part of the tower had probably been built as an essentially defensive structure in the mid-C13, but in 1284–91 it was converted to take on a more residential character with heated chambers. The most important of those is a light and airy room on the first floor, timber-framed and jettied over the moat.

The latest building in the complex is the timber-framed gatehouse of 1640–1. Carved figures adorn individual timbers.

Only the key buildings have survived at Stokesay; missing are the kitchen, stables, and other buildings which originally stood within the walled area.

The visitor approaches the castle via Stokesay churchyard. The church itself, rebuilt in the C17 after the Civil War, is worth visiting for its interior: wall paintings, squire's pew, and west gallery.

In general south Shropshire is rich in medieval sites of the first rank. Ludlow is a grid-plan town with a major castle and wool church. Other castles include Clun and Acton Burnell, while among the monasteries are Much Wenlock, Buildwas, and Haughmond (all five sites English Heritage).

J. Munby, Stokesay Castle *(English Heritage, 1993) (Site Guidebook).*

Wall (*Letocetum*), Staffordshire Roman town

SK 099067. N of A5 midway between its junctions with the A461 to the W and A5127 to the E. English Heritage and National Trust; restricted opening. Admission charge. Adjacent site museum.

A small Roman settlement lying on Watling Street, which began as a series of military establishments associated with the advance of the Roman army into Wales. Excavations have revealed the remains of buildings, first constructed in timber in the Neronian period, rebuilt in the Flavian period, and then replaced by a stone structure in the early–mid-C2. The remains of the later building, interpreted as a *mansio*† for travellers, with an adjacent public bath-house, are visible today.

P. Ellis, Wall: Roman Site *(English Heritage, 1999) (Site Guidebook).*

Weobley, Herefordshire Settlement with many medieval timber-framed houses

SO 402516. 12 km. SW of Leominster, access by turning S off A4112 onto B4230 which runs through the village.

In the Welsh Marches timber-framing remained the predominant means of building until relatively recent times. In and around the small town of Weobley is an excellent concentration of such buildings. Down both sides of Broad Street are houses, mostly late C14 and C15, which allow the various structural components of timber-framed buildings to be easily seen, notably cruck and box frames, and jettied overhangs.

St Peter and St Paul's Church, largely of the late C13 and early C14, is at the north end of the street, while at the south are the earthwork remains of the castle of the de Lacys of Ludlow.

About 6 km. to the north is **Pembridge**, whose church has a detached bell-tower. At the tower's core is a massively strong timber frame, which dendrochronology has recently dated to between 1207 and 1216 with rebuilding using many of the old timbers in 1668–9.

N. Pevsner, Herefordshire *(Penguin, 1963), 266–9, 311–15.*

The Wrekin, Wellington, Telford and Wrekin Iron Age

hillfort†

SJ 630083. On a high hill 15 km. E of Shrewsbury, S of A5, 3 km. S of Wellington. Accessible by footpath running S of minor road running from Little Wenlock to Cluddley on the A5. Figure 83.

The Wrekin is a distinctive steep-sided hill, 407 m. above sea level, and dominating the relatively low-lying Severn valley all around. A small Bronze Age round barrow† stands on the highest point and seems to have been respected when a massive hillfort was built, beginning perhaps as early as the C10 BC.

The earliest defences are probably the outer ring, defining an oval area of about 8 ha. Most of the circuit is a double rampart, but on the south side this reduces to a single line along a slight terrace, while at the east and west ends, around the two main entrances, there are three

▼ **Fig. 83.** Plan of The Wrekin, Wellington, Shropshire (after Hogg)

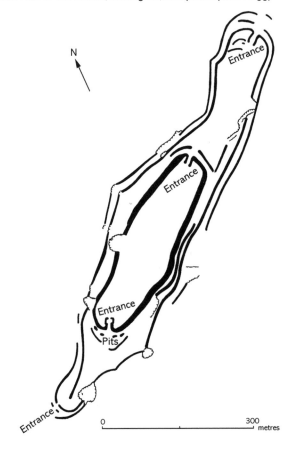

parallel lines of rampart. The gates have simple gaps in the outer ramparts with in-turned inner ramparts. Houses and storage structures were found within the outer fort, apparently destroyed and burnt down in the mid-C5 BC.

Around 420 BC the fort was reoccupied and the inner defences constructed to enclose an area of 2.6 ha. The ramparts are most impressive where they cross the hill; along the sides they appear more as terraces. The gates comprised in-turned ramparts to create entrance passages. These can still be traced on the ground with traces of guard-chambers leading off the inner passages.

The fort was probably the principal settlement of the *Cornovii* tribe who lived in the central Marches at the time. Following the Roman Conquest the tribal capital was moved to *Viroconium Cornoviorum* (modern WROXETER) 5 km. to the west.

S. Stanford, 'The Wrekin Hillfort', Arch J, *141 (1984), 61–90.*

Wroxeter (*Viroconium*), Shropshire   Roman *civitas*† capital   ★

SJ 568088. 8 km. E of Shrewsbury, 1.5 km. S of A5 on the B4380. English Heritage; some areas accessible at any reasonable time, but the remainder and site museum have restricted opening. Admission charge. Figure 84.

▼ **Fig. 84.** The 'Old Work', Wroxeter (*Viroconium*), Shropshire. This Roman wall formed part of the entrance from the exercise hall (*palaestra*) into the baths (Photograph: Paul Stamper)

Wroxeter, the fourth largest city in Roman Britain and tribal capital of the *Cornovii*, lies below the WREKIN, an Iron Age hillfort†. Excavations over many decades revealed the remains of a legionary fortress, a forum colonnade, public baths, and post-Roman occupation. The site was first occupied by the XIVth Legion later replaced by the XXth Legion. Around AD 88 the army relocated to CHESTER and Wroxeter developed as a civilian town. Like SILCHESTER it is one of the few Roman towns not subsequently built over and much of it lies under fields. Amongst the visible remains is an impressive isolated piece of standing masonry, known as the 'Old Work', which originally formed the south wall of the *palaestra*† belonging to the Hadrianic bath-house. A viewing platform allows the marked-out remains to be seen more clearly.

Near the site museum is a row of truncated columns, part of the colonnade of a portico belonging to the forum†. An important find in the 1920s was a Hadrianic inscription recording the building of the forum by the *civitas Cornoviorum* in 130.

Other columns have been reused as gate piers on the edge of Wroxeter churchyard. Large blocks of Roman masonry are incorporated in the church itself, part of the nave of which is Anglo-Saxon.

R. White and P. Barker, Wroxeter *(Tempus Publishing, 1998).*

▼ **Key to Fig. 85**

189 Barnack, Peterborough
190 Bartlow, Essex
191 Blythburgh, Suffolk
192 Bradwell (?*Othona*), Essex
193 Brancaster (*Branodunum*), Norfolk
194 Burgh Castle (*Gariannonum*), Norfolk
195 Bury St. Edmunds, Suffolk
196 Caister-on-Sea, Norfolk
197 Caistor St Edmund (*Venta Icenorum*), Norfolk
198 Cambridge, Cambridgeshire
199 Castle Rising, Norfolk
200 Cley, Norfolk
201 Coggeshall, Essex
202 Colchester (*Camulodunum*), Essex
203 Colchester Castle, Essex
204 Ely, Cambridgeshire
205 Flag Fen, Peterborough
206 Great Stukely, Cambridgeshire
207 Greensted, Essex
208 Grime's Graves, Norfolk
209 Haddiscoe, and Haddiscoe Thorpe, Norfolk
210 Harlow, Essex
211 Hatfield Forest, Essex

212 Isleham, Cambridgeshire
213 King's Lynn, Norfolk
214 Lavenham, Suffolk
215 Long Melford, Suffolk
216 Longthorpe Tower, Peterborough
217 Mersea Island, Essex
218 Norfolk Broads
219 Norwich, Norfolk
220 Orford, Suffolk
221 Orton Longueville, Peterborough
222 Pleshey, Essex
223 Sutton Hoo, Suffolk
224 Swaffham Prior, Cambridgeshire
225 Temple Cressing, Essex
226 Thaxted, Essex
227 Warren Lodge, Norfolk
228 Wandlebury, Cambridgeshire
229 Warham, Norfolk
230 Waterbeach (Car Dyke), Cambridgeshire
231 Water Newton (*Durobrivae*), Cambridgeshire
232 West Rudham Long Barrow, Norfolk
233 West Stow, Suffolk
234 Widdington, Essex

6 East Anglia

This region covers the counties and unitary authorities of Norfolk, Suffolk, Essex, Cambridgeshire, Thurrock, Southend, and Peterborough.

By the standards of most of England, East Anglia is a low-lying and relatively flat region, but there is in fact much variability in topography and even low hills form clear local eminences. Three main zones can be identified, each with distinctive archaeology.

In the north-east, from Cambridge north to the coast around the Wash is an area of fenland, low-lying and peat or alluvium-covered. Like the adjacent areas of the East Midlands, this land has been brought into

▼ **Fig. 85.** Map of Region 6

relatively recent agricultural usage as a result of drainage schemes. Apart from occupation on ancient islands (e.g. the Isle of Ely) in the wetland, and around the margins, most traces of prehistoric and Roman settlement lie underneath the peat. This cover-deposit provides excellent preservation, however, and sites such as FLAG FEN provide unique insights into life in the distant past and exceptional collections of waterlogged material.

In the centre of East Anglia, around Thetford, is the Breckland, sandy heaths and glacial deposits that are generally rather hostile for intensive settlement. Below this overburden lies chalk, in which is good quality flint. GRIME'S GRAVES in the middle of the Breckland, is the largest prehistoric flint-mine complex in England.

The third region comprises a broad arc of land from the eastern shore of the Wash in the north round the coast to the Thames estuary in the south. This is more than a coastal plain; it is a large and variable tract of land dominated by eastward-draining rivers such as the Bure, Wensum, Yare, Waveney, Gipping, and Stour. In the north are the low greensand and chalkland hills, in the south is high Suffolk with sand-covered chalk. These areas are good for cultivation and have seen abundant settlement since prehistoric times. Anglo-Saxon occupation seems to have been especially extensive, and in this area are some very rich cemeteries. Later, in the Middle Ages, East Anglia became one of the most prosperous, and populous, regions of the country.

Barnack, Peterborough Saxon church

TF 079050. On B1443 5 km. SE of Stamford.

Barnack's oolitic limestone (rag) was used in some of eastern England's greatest churches: Peterborough, ELY, and NORWICH cathedrals. South of the village in a field called the 'Hills and Holes' are the grassed-over stone quarries. Quarrying had begun (or recommenced) by the C9 AD, and although the stone was transported by road and water over long distances—there was a quay on the river Welland nearby—two of the most impressive examples of Saxon churches with Barnack stone stand close by: **Wittering** (TF 056020), where the stone was used in the long-and-short quoins, and Barnack itself.

Here, in the tower of St John the Baptist's, it was used for the quoins, for the cornices, and for the pilaster strips. The tower, probably late C10 or early C11, is richly ornamented. Inside, too, is Saxon work: note especially the west arch to the tower and the seat and windows within, the six remaining stones at the east end of the north arcade of the nave from an arch leading into a side chapel, and on the north wall of the aisle a remarkable carved figure, probably of Christ in Majesty. Its date is uncertain, but close to the conquest (1066).

The rest of the church is later. The belfry and short spire were added about 1200. The aisled nave and south porch are mainly of the C12 and C13 (with mainly C14 windows), the chancel C14, and the large and beautiful Lady Chapel south of the chancel added about 1500.

M. Beresford and J. St Joseph, Medieval England, 2nd edn (Cambridge University Press, 1979), 254–5.

Bartlow, Essex   Roman burial mounds   ★★

TL 586448. 2 km. S of A604 on the Essex–Cambridgeshire border. In the village take the Ashdon road; a footpath is signposted on the left after a former railway bridge. This gives access to three barrows; a fourth lies on private land but is visible from the others. Information panel.

A group of Romano-British burial mounds known as the Bartlow Hills. Originally comprising two rows of three and four barrows, only the latter have survived. This includes the largest extant Roman barrow in Britain, 44 m. across and 14 m. high. C19 excavations exposed cremations accompanied by rich burial goods of late C1–mid-C2 date. The finds, many of which were accidentally destroyed last century, included wooden chests containing bronze, glass and pottery vessels, an enamelled casket, a folding iron stool, and iron lamps. Some surviving artefacts are in Saffron Walden Museum.

J. Rokewood, 'The Recent Discovery of Roman Sepulchral Relics in one of the Greater Barrows at Bartlow, in the Parish of Ashdown, in Essex', Archaeologia, 26 (1836), 300–17, 462–3.

Blythburgh, Suffolk   Medieval church

TM 450753. On A12 17 km. SW of Lowestoft.

High above the coastal marshes stands the church of Holy Trinity. Flint built, and with a clerestory† rising above a pierced parapet, the church is dominated by the great ranks of identical windows, which light the interior. Inside is much high-quality woodwork, including eighteen bench ends of about 1475 carved with the Seven Deadly Sins, the occupations of the months, and angels holding crowns.

N. Pevsner and E. Radcliffe, The Buildings of England: Suffolk (Penguin, 1974).

Bradwell (?*Othona*), Essex   Roman Saxon Shore fort

TM 031081. 3 km. NE of Bradwell-on-Sea, which lies E of B1021 12 km. NE of Burnham-on-Crouch. The site is approached via the line of the original Roman road to the coast.

The site of a poorly preserved late Roman Saxon Shore fort set on the Blackwater estuary. The south wall, south of the church, still stands 1.2–1.5 m. high and fragments of the north and west sides survive but the east side has been destroyed by the sea. On the line of the west wall is the chapel of St Peter-on-the-Wall, probably mid-C7, with much reused Roman masonry.

H. Carter, The Fort of Othona *(Provost and Chapter of Chelmsford, 1967).*

Brancaster (*Branodunum*), Norfolk Roman Saxon Shore fort

TF 783430. On the coast 6 km. W from Burnham Market (A149). The site is 800 m. E of Brancaster crossroads. Take the side road to the N of A149 at E end of village. The site lies within an area of salt marsh. National Trust. Roadside parking. Information panel.

The site of the most eastern of the late Roman Saxon Shore forts, now almost 1.6 km. from the coast. Little is visible, apart from some humps and bumps. Excavations recently located the foundations of a C3 square building with bastions at the corners.

J. Hinchcliffe et al., Excavations at Brancaster 1974 and 1977 *(East Anglian Archaeology, 1985).*

Burgh Castle (*Gariannonum*), Norfolk Roman Saxon Shore fort★

TG 476046. Take the A143 out of Great Yarmouth and the signposted road to Burgh Castle. The fort is at W end of Breydon Water on an unclassified road 5 km. W of Great Yarmouth. Park near church. English Heritage.

Now set back from the sea overlooking the river Waveney, this late Roman Saxon Shore fort probably once occupied a peninsula commanding a tidal estuary. Three sides of the impressive fort walls remain, 3.4 m. wide at the base and up to 4.6 m. high, with projecting pear-shaped bastions. One surviving bastion on the south side has a socket traditionally interpreted as a ballista† support. Alternatively the socket may have supported a central roof timber. Only one gate survives in the east wall. The fort was destroyed in the mid-C4. The walls were later used as the bailey† of a Norman castle.

E. Martin, Burgh: Iron Age and Roman Enclosure *(East Anglian Archaeology, 1988).*

Bury St Edmunds, Suffolk Medieval town and abbey

TL 8564. Approximately midway between Cambridge and Ipswich, on A14.

A grid-plan town, laid out at the end of the C11 by Baldwin, abbot of St Edmundsbury Abbey.

Most interest focuses on the remains of the abbey (English Heritage), to which the relics of King Edmund, killed by the Danes in 869, were translated in 1095. The abbey church was destroyed after the abbey was dissolved in 1539, but its ruins remain in the monastic precinct whose walls run down to the river Lark. One gatehouse, erected in the 1130s, faces what was the west front of the church. Another, the Great

Gate (opposite the end of Abbeygate Street), which gave access to the outer court with its stables and service buildings, is a superb example of Decorated work of the years after 1327. It has a portcullis and, concealed behind its statues, arrow loops.

Within the precinct are two parish churches: St James's, C16 and later, which became a cathedral† in 1914, and St Mary's, begun about 1425 and one of England's finest Perpendicular churches.

The town was laid out with five streets parallel to the west front of the precinct; Churchgate Street, the third of these, continues the central axis of the abbey church, emphasizing the overall plan concept. There was already a market place on Angel Hill, but a large new one was laid out, which survives, much encroached upon, as Butter Market and Cornhill. On the north-east corner is Moyse's Hall, a flint and rubble building with Norman origins, perhaps as a monastic guest house with living quarters over a vaulted undercroft†. Now the local museum, its collections include finds from WEST STOW Anglo-Saxon village. Guildhall Street leads south from the south-west corner of Butter Market, the C15 Guildhall lying only a little way down it. The other main medieval structure is the Abbot's Bridge across the Lark.

D. Lloyd, Historic Towns of East Anglia *(Gollancz, 1989)*, 70–7.

Caister-on-Sea, Norfolk Roman fort and settlement

TG 518125. On W side of minor road joining A1064 to Acle on the W edge of Caister-on-Sea, 4.8 km. N of Great Yarmouth. English Heritage.

Possibly originally a fort, excavations discovered a small defended Roman town and port here. Just inside the south gate a large courtyard building, interpreted as a seaman's hostel, was built in the late C2. Parts of the foundations of this building and a section of the town wall and gateway are visible.

J. Ellison, 'Excavations at Caister-on-Sea', NA 33/1 (1962), 94–107.

Caistor St Edmund (Caistor-by-Norwich) (*Venta Icenorum*), Norfolk Roman town and *civitas*† capital

TG 230035. About 5 km. S of Norwich. Immediately S of the junction of A140 and A47 take the B1113 to Markshall and first right after Markshall. Caistor church stands within the SE corner of the Roman defences and is the only accessible point. Adjacent car park. Figure 86.

A small, walled Roman town, tribal capital of the *Iceni*, was established here around AD 70 after their famous leader, Queen Boudicca, led a revolt against the Romans in 60–1. Although no internal buildings are visible, being under agricultural land, traces of the defences can be followed, represented by a ditch and a rampart fronted by a flint stone wall on the north side. A marked footpath follows the line of the walls and

▲ **Fig. 86.** Photograph showing the remains of the north Roman defences, Caistor St Edmund (*Venta Icenorum*), Norfolk (Photograph: Jane Timby)

takes about an hour to complete. The defences are probably C3 with C4 bastions. Aerial photography has revealed many details of the internal plan including the location of the forum† and the public baths. The church of St Edmund is largely built out of Roman masonry. A large Saxon cemetery has been found nearby.

J. Wacher, The Towns of Roman Britain *(Batsford, 1955).*

Cambridge, Cambridgeshire Medieval university town ★

TL 4458. At the junction of A10 and A14, also accessible via the M11 (junctions 11–14). Figure 87.

Cambridge takes its name from a crossing point over the river Cam, which even now divides the town and its ancient colleges from the Backs, the colleges' parkland. The Cam seems first to have been bridged in Roman times on a predecessor of Magdalene Bridge, and a Roman camp and later town grew up nearby: the town ditch rampart is still to be seen at Mount Pleasant. The town re-emerged in later Saxon times when, politically, it was part of the Danelaw, and by the late C10 was a flourishing inland port and town.

In 1068 William the Conqueror raised a motte† and bailey†—still partly visible—on Castle Hill. Otherwise the conquest had little impact and the place continued to prosper, its reputation as a trading place being greatly enhanced by the annual town-edge Stourbridge Fair. This, then, was the place to which a group of Oxford scholars migrated in

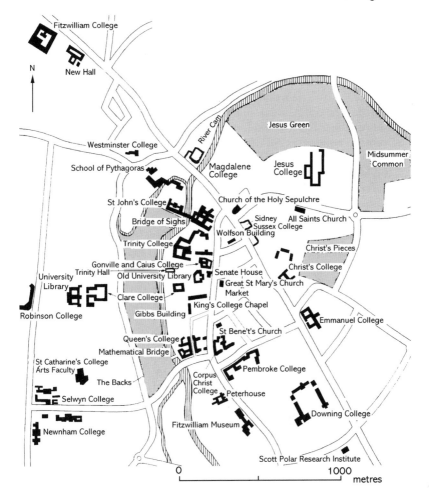

▲ **Fig. 87.** Cambridge (after Cligman & Crowe)

1209, unwittingly founding what became one of the world's greatest universities.

What became Peterhouse was founded in the C13, being joined in the early C14 by a number of other colleges. Michael House (later absorbed into Trinity College) was set up in 1324, Clare College in 1326, and Trinity and Gonville Hall soon after. As these expanded, they grew over land along the river formerly occupied by warehouses and quays. These earliest foundations were joined in the mid-C14 by Pembroke and Corpus Christi colleges, and in the C15 by King's and Queen's colleges. Effectively the whole of the western part of the old town was displaced by the university. Foundations at the end of the Middle Ages—Jesus

College in 1496, and ending with Sidney Sussex in 1594—had less impact on the topography as they were all on the site of earlier religious foundations.

The town has a wealth of colleges, churches, and other delights to explore. It would be invidious to choose just one to highlight, but Cambridge's most celebrated building is King's College Chapel, off King's Parade. The college was founded in 1446 by Henry VI, and his intention was that the chapel would form one side of a court. This grandiose plan came to nothing, as did Richard III's attempt to finish the chapel. It was his successor, Henry Tudor, who completed the job after 1508. The final building was far more elaborate than originally intended with displays of carved Tudor badges. Inside is the glorious high vault, like the latter phase of the exterior the work of the East Anglian architect John Wastell. The building is one of the late high points of the Perpendicular; Henry VIII's screen and stalls mark the arrival of Renaissance styles.

A. Taylor, Cambridge: The Hidden History *(Tempus, 1999).*

Castle Rising, Norfolk Norman castle and church

TF 666246. 6 km. NE of King's Lynn off A149. English Heritage; restricted opening. Admission charge. Figure 88.

Although termed a castle, and certainly massive, strong, and capable of defence, William d'Aubigny's great house of about 1140 is more a fortress-palace. After the death of Henry I in 1135 William married his widow, Adela of Louvain, and became earl of Arundel. William 'would

▼ **Fig. 88.** Castle Rising Castle, Norfolk (after English Heritage)

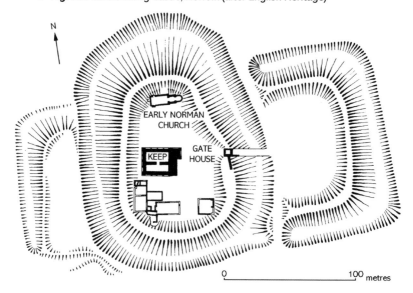

recognise no-one as his peer', and his house reflected his wealth and new status.

Standing within a huge earthen ringwork† (and, as excavation showed, on top of a late Saxon bow-sided hall) the palace-keep is entered via a richly decorated forebuilding, from which stairs ascend to an ante-chamber, which opens onto the great hall. On the same level is the earl's private chamber with its service room, kitchen, garderobes†, and chapel.

Alongside his castle d'Aubigny laid out a grid-plan town, the defences of which are traceable in parts. In the Middle Ages this was a port, accessible to small vessels via the Babingley river. The green west of the church was then the market place, and the market cross, standing on five steps, is a rare survival. The most important surviving component of the town is St Lawrence's Church, the west front of which is richly decorated with blind arcading and zigzag work. It is of much the same date as the castle.

R. Allen Brown, Castle Rising *(English Heritage, 1978) (Site Guidebook).*

Cley, Norfolk Medieval church

TG 040435. On A149 coastal road, 10 km. W of Sheringham

Cley, like many other north Norfolk coastal villages such as Salthouse, Wiveton, Burnham, and Blakeney, was once a busy port. Now standing inland, most of these villages have buildings of interest, and several possess churches whose size and richness attest to the prosperity that the medieval export of wool and agricultural produce brought.

The south transept of St Margaret's, Cley, was already ruinous by about 1600. The church stands in Newgate, south of the present settlement. A large and complex structure, the church is in a mixture of the Decorated and Perpendicular styles of the high to late Middle Ages.

The observant visitor to the Norfolk coast can hardly fail to notice its abundant Second World War defences, especially pillboxes. Increasingly these are being recognized as archaeological monuments and valued, passive reminders of the time when the country faced the very real prospect of invasion.

N. Pevsner, The Buildings of England: North-East Norfolk and Norwich *(Penguin, 1962), 113–16.*

Coggeshall, Essex Medieval clothier's house and Great Barn

TL 8422. On A120 between Braintree and Colchester. Paycocke's House is on S side of West Street, about 300 m. from the town centre [TL 848225]. The Great Barn is about 1 km. from town centre off A120 next to the Fleece Inn [TL 848225]. Both National Trust; restricted opening. Admission charge.

In the later Middle Ages, following the Black Death, small towns often thrived while larger, older, commercial centres declined. THAXTED is one example of the former, and another is Coggeshall. Here, **Paycocke's House** is probably the county's best-known town house, and when new-built about 1500 for wealthy clothiers it was bang up to date. Instead of the old medieval great hall, open to the roof, it was of two storeys throughout, with a first-floor parlour over a ground-floor central hall. This was a show house, generously lit with oriel windows, which gave the long street façade an almost symmetrical appearance. The external carved decoration, notably the bressumer (the main horizontal beam supporting the first floor) with the initials TP and the window transoms, is extravagant, while inside is panelling and further carving.

Largely hidden beneath later plaster, brick, or stucco, there are many other medieval buildings to be seen in Market Hill, Stoneham Street, and Church Street.

Other local buildings of note include **Coggeshall Grange Barn** (mid- to late C12), probably the oldest timber-framed barn in Europe. Originally it was a part of the Cistercian† monastery of Coggeshall. That lay east of the barn, along Abbey Lane.

Outside the site of the monastery gate is St Nicholas's Chapel, built about 1225. Bricks were used in its construction, one of the earliest uses of the material since Roman times.

C. Platt, The National Trust Guide to Late Medieval and Renaissance Britain (George Philip, 1986), 104–5, 211.

Colchester (*Camulodunum*), Essex Late Iron Age burial
ground, *oppidum*†, and Roman city   ★★

TM 0025. S of A12. The earlier sites are centred on TL 963240, on W side of modern Colchester, mainly S of A604. Some signposted. English Heritage. Figure 89. Gosbecks Archaeological Park. The later, Roman remains are centred on TM 0000253. Colchester Castle Museum, Castle Park, and Colchester visitor information centre, 1 Queen's Street, are good starting points. Figure 90.

Camulodunum is the largest and best-known later Prehistoric dyke-system *oppidum* in Britain. The huge site, covering about 4000 ha., was defended along the western side by a massive series of curving dykes. The area enclosed comprised a series of interrelated focal areas surrounded by fields and paddocks. The pattern was complicated and little has been investigated by excavation. This may have been the main residence of Cunobelin, king of the *Catuvellauni* tribe, and an influential ruler from the late C1 BC through to the Roman Conquest.

Several sections of the dykes system can be seen on the ground today, notably **Gryme's Dyke** (TL 960248–TL 964234) and its southwards continuation (TL 960231–TL 957221), **Chest Wood dyke** (TL 965218), **Triple Dyke** (TL 965245), **Lexden Dyke** (TL 974252–TL 974246), and the **Moat Farm Dyke** (TL 975264–TL 973258). Except the Triple Dyke, all comprise a stout bank and outer ditch.

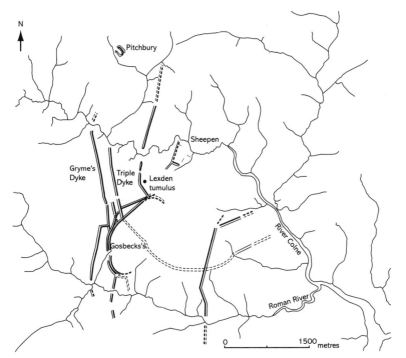

▲ **Fig. 89.** Plan of *Camulodunum* and the Lexden Cemetery, Colchester, Essex (after Cunliffe)

Excavations suggest that the main focus of settlement from about 10 AD onwards was east of the **Sheepen Dyke** (not now visible), west of the modern Sheepen Farm and mainly south of the A604. Numerous buildings of wattle and daub construction and evidence of various industrial activities were found including metalworking, enamelling, pottery manufacture, and possibly salt-making. A mint produced gold, silver, and bronze coins of Cunobelin. Many imports from Gaul and the Mediterranean were also found.

Between Sheepen and Gosbecks is the Lexden cemetery of the tribal aristocracy, which includes flat graves and barrows. The largest barrow is the **Lexden Tumulus** (TL 975247) of the late C1 BC. Located in Fitzwalter Avenue, about 2 km. from the town centre along the A12, Ipswich road, the barrow mound has a diameter of 23 m. When it was excavated, a central pit containing a single cremation was found, believed to have been Prince Addedomarus or one of his close family. There were also the smashed and broken remains of many prized personal objects and imports.

The importance of *Camulodunum* may have been the reason why the Roman army headed here in AD 43; it surrendered to the Emperor

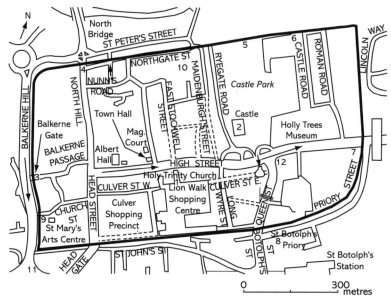

▲ **Fig. 90.** Colchester: modern street plan showing the location of the Roman defences and other sites

Claudius in the same year. The fortress of the XXth Legion was here, and although nothing is visible today, Lion Walk and Culver Street (**1**) lie in its centre.

In AD 49 the legion moved on. Soon after, a *colonia*† was founded, the *Colonia Claudia Victricensis*, on the south bank of the river Colne immediately east of Sheepen. This city was modelled on classical lines and was the embodiment of Roman colonial power in the newly annexed province. The Iron Age settlement was levelled and abandoned.

Although some streets and buildings of the earlier legionary fortress were reused, the defences were demolished to make room for the expansion of the *colonia* and the construction of public buildings. Of particular note was a classical-style temple dedicated to the Emperor Claudius. The temple was constructed over a series of dug concrete foundations now visible below the Norman Castle (**2**), which also houses the Museum.

The lack of defences probably contributed to Colchester's destruction in the Boudiccan revolt of AD 60. The burnt ruins of a fully stocked pottery and glassware shop have been excavated in the south-west corner of Insula 19. Once the Romans had regained control a triumphal arch was built over the main route from London into the town.

In the early C2 stone town walls were built and the triumphal arch integrated into the Balkerne Gate (**3**). Much of the defensive circuit, probably the first free-standing town walls in Britain, survives intact and takes about an hour to follow. Certain areas have been much repaired or modified in medieval times. Of six original gateways, the most famous is the Balkerne Gate. The line of the wall can be followed northwards up Balkerne Hill and round into Northgate Street, where the North Gate was originally located (**4**). A further stretch of wall occurs along Park Follet, visible from inside Castle Park (**5**). At the north-east corner of Holly Trees meadow the remains of the north-east postern gate are visible and, beyond the wall, part of the external ditch (**6**). Passing through a modern arch down Roman Road into East Hill a section of wall with a drain port can be seen in an alley beside St James's churchyard (**7**). The site of the East Gate lies under East Hill. The defences can then be followed around into Priory Street. The bastions here are medieval, using Roman masonry. St Botolph's Priory, C11, incorporates reused Roman masonry (**8**). The route then passes along Vineyard Street and Crouch Street and across Head Street. Head Gate at the end of Head Street was probably originally Roman although no longer extant. The wall can be picked up again in Balkerne Hill and in the wall on the north of St Mary's Steps part of the arch of a postern gate can be seen (**9**).

Numerous excavations have taken place; more mosaics have been recorded than in any other Roman town. Of the public buildings, other than the temple, only the theatre in Maidenburgh Street (**10**) is positively known. Part of the masonry is incorporated into St Helen's Chapel and an adjacent building. The foundations of a C4 building, probably a church, are laid out next to the Butt Road police station (**11**).

Outside the town were several cemeteries, some with richly furnished burials including a doctor's grave at Stanway, which contained medical equipment. Several Romano-Celtic temples and shrines are also known outside the town, particularly towards Sheepen Farm and Gosbecks Farm, 3 km. south-west along the Maldon Road (B1022). Gosbecks Archaeological Park located at the junction of Cunobelin Way and Oliver's Lane has a visitor centre and various interpretation panels explaining the history of the site.

P. Crummy, City of Victory *(Colchester Archaeological Trust, 1997).*

Colchester Castle, Essex Medieval castle

TL 998252. Close to the modern town centre, on N side of High Street. Figure 91.

Colchester Castle ranks with London's White Tower as a supreme example of William the Conqueror's ability to build a palace which also functioned as a stronghold sufficient to control an urban population. The keep, begun about 1074–6, incorporates much Roman masonry and was raised on the concrete podium of the Roman temple. It rose eventually to three storeys and 25 m. high. Battlements still visible at first-floor level record an intermediate halt to the Norman building work.

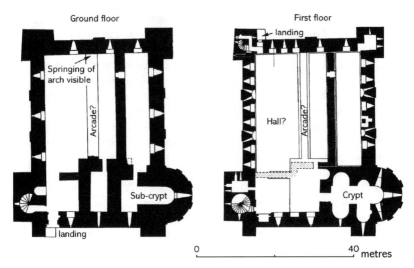

Ground floor

Springing of
arch visible

Arcade?

Sub-crypt

landing

First floor

landing

Hall?

Arcade?

Crypt

0   40 metres

▲ **Fig. 91.** Colchester Castle (after Drury)

Like the White Tower, Colchester was a hall-keep, with most of the
available space occupied by a great hall. The ground-floor entrance, an
early C12 modification, was originally protected by a forebuilding.
Projecting from the south-east corner of the keep (again as at the
White Tower) is an apsidal chapel, of which only the vaulted undercroft†
survives complete. About 1100 the castle received additional defences
when the High Street was diverted and an encircling rampart and ditch
constructed.

In 1683 the keep was sold for demolition, and the top stage was
destroyed, along with one of the two main internal cross-walls and the
main floors. The shell received a new roof in the 1930s.

*P. Drury, 'Aspects of the Origin and Development of Colchester Castle', Arch J, 139
(1982), 302–419.*

Ely, Cambridgeshire Medieval cathedral†

TL 541801. 20 km. NE of Cambridge on A10(T).

Ely was one of several C7 Benedictine† foundations destroyed by the
Danes in the C9 but refounded in the C10 during the monastic revival.
Rebuilding began at the east end in 1093, and during the C12 progressed
westwards. An exceptionally long nave was constructed, which ended
with a massive west-work completed in the early C13; the west porch or
galilee was remodelled soon afterwards. Inside and outside the church
rise tiers of arcading. Between 1234 and 1252 Bishop Northwold added
the Gothic east end, designed to house St Etheldreda's shrine, while the
Decorated Lady Chapel was begun in 1321. In 1322 the Norman central

tower collapsed and construction of a radical replacement was begun, the octagon, a broad and graceful tower which introduces a well of light into the centre of the church. The mid-C14 choir stalls, famed for their carved misericords†, originally stood here. The octagon's roof was designed by the king's carpenter, William Hurley; its timber vault poses as stone. Later additions include the late C15 and early C16 chantry chapels of Bishops Alcock and West, the latter with early Renaissance motifs, which stand at the east end of the cathedral.

In 1539 Ely's monastery was dissolved and, although the cloister was pulled down, the King's School incorporates many of the monastic structures including the early C14 Prior Crauden's Chapel, which has a rare mosaic pavement.

Ely's setting in the flat fenlands remains dramatic, and before C17 drainage works, it would have been far more so. Ely was then an island, surrounded by shallow water and marshes, which provided rich grazing for the abbey's sheep.

N. Coldstream and P. Draper (eds), Medieval Art and Architecture at Ely Cathedral (British Archaeological Association, 1976).

Flag Fen, Peterborough Bronze Age settlement ★★

TL 227989. 2 km. E of Peterborough town centre. Approached via signposted minor roads E of eastern ring road. Visitor centre. Restricted opening.

The Bronze Age settlement was a huge artificial island covering over 0.8 ha., set within what was then a lagoon, and linked to the dry land by a timber walkway. After its abandonment the site became flooded and covered in peat, which has preserved the wooden remains.

Since its discovery in 1982, about 2 per cent of the island has been excavated to reveal the roof supports and timber walls of a large rectangular building over 18 m. long with occupation debris on the floors. Sand had been spread on the floor in Bronze Age times to counteract the damp.

Excavations continue. A cover-building stands over the Bronze Age structure and a large-scale model of the site can be seen in an artificial pond. There are guided tours of the excavation area. Reconstructions of part of a Bronze Age field-system† and various round buildings can also be seen.

F. Pryor, Flag Fen (Batsford and English Heritage, 1991).

Great Stukely, Cambridgeshire Roman barrow

TL 219747. N of Huntingdon, on N side of B1043 in Great Stukely in children's playground adjacent to the Three Horseshoes public house.

A pair of well-preserved, albeit overgrown, large conical barrows adjacent to the Roman road (Ermine Street) which are thought to be of Roman date.

R. Collingwood and I. Richmond, The Archaeology of Roman Britain *(Methuen, 1971), 166–74.*

Greensted, Essex Medieval timber church

TL 538030. On minor road 1 km. W of Chipping Ongar, S of A414 from Harlow to Chelmsford.

St Andrew's is a unique survival of the sort of wooden church which was the norm until the widespread adoption of stone around the time of the Norman Conquest.

The nave† walls are formed of upright trunks of oaks from trees less than a century old when felled, split in half and set with the curved face to the outside. One of the original corner posts survives, a three-quarter log. The chancel was rebuilt in post-medieval times. Dendrochronology dates the church to the later C11. The use of timber, rather than stone, may reflect the fact that the manor was held by a lord who was non-resident, perhaps interested in no more than minimal investment in church building.

S. Pearson, 'Tree-Ring Dating', Vernacular Architecture, *28 (1997), 25–39.*

Grime's Graves, Norfolk Neolithic flint mines ★★

TL 818898. 8 km. NW of Thetford, 4 km. NE of Brandon. Signposted access along minor road from A1065 between Brandon and Mundford. English Heritage; restricted opening. Visitor centre and access to one of the mines by ladder.

Set amongst the conifer plantations of the Breckland, this is the largest group of Neolithic flint mines in Britain, and the only site where you can enter a mine.

Grime's Graves was worked for flint between about 3000 BC and 1900 BC, and traces of over 350 shafts are known within an area of about 9 ha. Some seventeen shafts have been excavated, and found to be up to 14 m. deep to obtain the highest-quality flint which lies at this depth.

The mine shafts are visible today as saucer-shaped depressions, 6 m. to 20 m. in diameter and up to 7 m. deep. They intercut one another in confusing fashion, the spoil heaps from one shaft being spread over the part in-filled remnants of an earlier adjacent shaft.

Shaft 1, excavated in 1914, is open for visitors to descend. It is about 9 m. deep, and once at the bottom you can see galleries radiating out from the main shaft.

Calculations suggest that 1,000 tons of overburden was removed to create a single shaft, which yielded approximately 8 tons of nodular flint. The exploitation of the mine could have been undertaken over a period of two to three months by a workforce of fifteen to sixteen people. If all the flint won from the mine was converted into axes in an efficient manner something like 10,250 blades could have been produced; even at worst over 6,000 axes could have been made. The whole site may have produced between 2.5 and 5 million axes during its working life. In fact, analysis of the working debris shows that axes and knives were the main products.

R. Mercer, Grime's Graves, Norfolk. Excavations 1971–2, vol. i, Department of the Environment Archaeological Reports 11 (HMSO, 1981).

Haddiscoe, and Haddiscoe Thorpe, Norfolk Medieval churches

TM 4496. On the A143 7 km. N of Beccles.

Between about 1050 and 1150 most of England's parish churches were rebuilt in stone. These already show distinct regional schools of crafts-manship, as well as the emerging preference for the Romanesque (Nor-man) style of architecture. In Norfolk, between Beccles and Yarmouth, are two churches with round, flint, towers, typical of so many Norfolk churches built before or immediately after the Norman Conquest. In fact, of the 143 round church towers standing at the last count, 125 are in Norfolk, mostly in the county's south-east corner.

St Mary's, Haddiscoe, consists of a narrow, circular west tower, nave with north aisle and south porch, and aisleless chancel. The tower is four-staged, the topmost with four double belfry windows with triangular heads and mid-wall shafts.

Just 2 km. to the north-west is **St Matthias's, Haddiscoe Thorpe**, which also has a round west tower. Here the rest of the church com-prises a small, aisleless nave and a thatch-roofed chancel of brick. The rest of the church is of flint.

N. Pevsner, The Buildings of England: North-West and South Norfolk (Penguin, 1962), 181–2.

Harlow, Essex Roman temple

TL 468124. At Harlow Mill roundabout on main road (A1169) turn into Edin-burgh Way. Signposted from 'Roman' roundabout. The site is along river Way on the right-hand side, set back from the modern road towards the railway line. Figure 92.

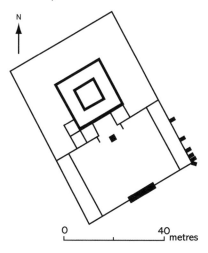

▼ Fig. 92. Plan of Harlow Roman temple, Essex (after France & Gobel)

N

0   40 metres

The plan of a small classic Romano-Celtic temple of C1–C3 date can be seen laid out as paving slabs on a raised mound. Excavations between 1962 and 1971 revealed details of the temple layout which had an inner square cella (shrine) surrounded by an ambulatory† and an outer *temenos*† wall. Finds, which can be seen in Harlow New Town Museum, included large quantities of Iron Age and Roman coins.

N. France and B. Gobel, The Romano-British Temple at Harlow *(West Essex Archaeological Group, 1985).*

Hatfield Forest, Essex　Historic woodland

TL 547208–546199. Hatfield can be reached off junction 8 of the M11, and lies S of the A120 between Great Hallingbury and Takeley. National Trust. Admission charge for car park, but otherwise accessible at any reasonable time. Figure 93.

Oliver Rackham, the country's leading woodland historian, says Hatfield is 'the only place where one can step back into the Middle Ages to see, with only a small effort of imagination, what a forest looked like in use'. Technically, from the time it was introduced to this country by the Normans, a forest was a tract of countryside—not just woods, but sometimes settlements and their fields as well—under not only the Common Law but also Forest Law. The latter gave specific protection to the vert (undergrowth) and venison (deer) in order to preserve extensive, and exclusive, royal hunting territories. Penalties were imposed for transgressors, which in theory could be draconian with execution and mutilation among the possibilities.

Hatfield Forest today extends to 400 ha. (1,000 acres). Its interest is that within it survive all the elements of a medieval forest: great timber trees, coppice woods, pollards, scrub, grassland and fen, deer and cattle, and a rabbit warren. It also has Forest Lodge (thought to be the only forest lodge with surviving above-ground medieval fabric) and Warren Lodge (a C17 brick rabbit-keeper's cottage). Generally speaking, the forest divides between plains, used for grazing, and coppice woods. In the latter oak, ash, hazel, hornbeam, and other naturally regenerating trees are managed by being cut off at ground level at intervals of, in theory, eighteen years. There are also about 600 pollards of eight different species, including mature oaks, hornbeams, and hawthorns, cut on a regular cycle at about 3 m. above ground level, that is, above the reach of grazing animals. In fact, most have not been cropped in this way for over a hundred years and are among the most visually impressive aspects of the forest.

O. Rackham, The Last Forest: The Story of Hatfield Forest *(Dent, 1989).*

Isleham, Cambridgeshire　Medieval church

TL 642744. 11 km. N of Newmarket, on the B1104.

Isleham's village-centre cruciform church, of flint and pebble rubble,

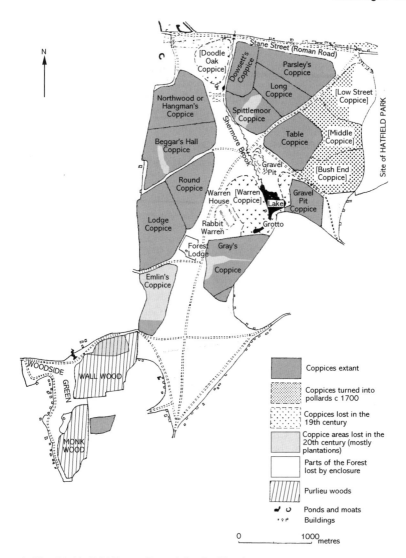

▲ **Fig. 93.** Hatfield Forest, Essex (after Rackham)

has a largely C14 core. Its main glory, however, is C15 work, a century which saw the remodelling of the church by the Peyton family, whose shields appear in the spandrels of the C14 arches above the nave piers. Especially notable is the C15 clerestory† and roof. The church's fittings and furnishings are very good and include Perpendicular font and *sedilia*, chancel stalls with misericords† of about 1400, carved bench ends, and a brass eagle lectern found in the C19 in the fen where it had presumably been hidden at the Reformation. The tombs and memorials are of an equal standard and include several of the Peytons.

On the north side of the village is a much simpler ecclesiastical building. It is the chapel of Isleham's alien priory, a simple three-cell structure of about 1090 comprising nave, chancel, and apsidal sanctuary, the last originally vaulted with a half-dome. The Benedictines of Saint-Jacut-de-la-Mer in Brittany established the priory here but had abandoned it by 1254 after merging it with their associated cell at Linton. The chapel is an English Heritage property.

N. Pevsner, The Buildings of England: Cambridgeshire (Penguin, 1970), 413–16.

King's Lynn, Norfolk Medieval town and seaport

TF 625200. Small town 5 km. S of the Wash, at the junction of the A10(T), A149, A47(T), and A17. Figure 94.

King's Lynn was once a prosperous sea port; an echo survives in its buildings. The town was promoted as a commercial venture in the C12 by the bishops of Norwich (it was then called Bishop's Lynn) when a grid of streets was laid out alongside the river Ouse, with town walls (traces remain, along with the South Gate) on the landward side. The Saturday Market Place was soon joined by the Tuesday Market Place. Public buildings include St Margaret's Church on the Saturday Market, built with a huge, twin-towered west front; St Nicholas's, in St Anne's Street, with its superb early C15 Perpendicular porch; the Red Mount Chapel, the Walk, built in 1485 to serve Walsingham-bound pilgrims; two guildhalls (Holy Trinity of 1421, facing the Saturday Market, and St George (now the Ferney Centre) of about 1406 in King Street), and the Custom House of 1683 on Purfleet Quay. Less magnificent than the last, but of greater historical significance, are the surviving houses and warehouses of the medieval and later merchants who carried on the town's international trade across the North Sea. On King Street, until reclamation the river frontage, a C12 timber-framed structure survives among the predominantly Georgian buildings. Among the warehouses is the timber-framed Hanseatic Warehouse of 1428 in St Margaret's Lane and several of C16 and C17 date in Kings Staithe Lane.

V. Parker, The Making of King's Lynn (Phillimore, 1965).

Lavenham, Suffolk Medieval town   ★★

TL 917494. On the A1141, 16 km. SE of Bury St Edmunds.

Lavenham is one of Suffolk's finest late medieval 'cloth' towns. While many of its C15 and C16 houses have had their façades plastered over or cased in brick and stone, their plans and jettied elevations give away their age. Little Hall (open, as the headquarters of the Suffolk Preserva-

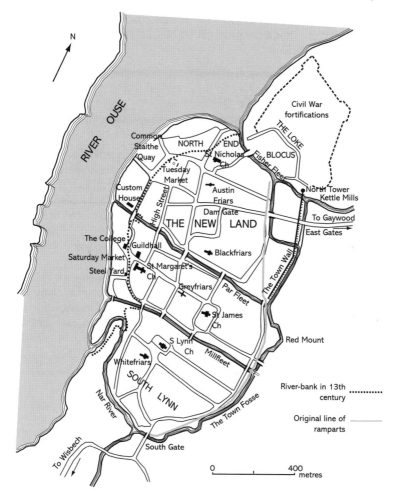

▲ **Fig. 94.** King's Lynn, Norfolk (after Dymond)

tion Society), which has been stripped to reveal a Tudor shop front, hints at the likely quality of the hidden timber-framing.

In the C15 the cloth industry here expanded, and there were thirty or more manufacturers. The townsmen invested in communal halls, one for each of the four guilds, which served social, charitable, and religious purposes. The 'Guildhall' at the corner of the Market Place and Lady Street—of 1528–9, and spacious and elaborately decorated—was actually that of the Guild of Corpus Christi (the Body of Christ). Another guildhall, the Wool Hall, built for St Mary's Guild, is incorporated in the Swan Hotel.

Large sums were also expended on the parish church of SS Peter and

Paul, on the western edge of the town. This contains the tomb of the weaver-clothier Thomas Spring, in 1524 England's wealthiest commoner outside London.

A. Betterton and D. Dymond, Lavenham Industrial Town *(Terence Dalton, 1989).*

Long Melford, Suffolk Medieval town

TL 865467. 5 km. N of Sudbury on former A134 (the present A134 bypasses Long Melford to the E).

Long Melford, like LAVENHAM, was a wealthy late medieval wool town. As well as private expenditure on timber-framed private houses, much investment went into the parish church of Holy Trinity, which stands on the green at the head of the long main street to which the place name prefix alludes (the suffix comes from the 'mill ford', now bridged, between street and green).

Although the church has C14 fabric, it was rebuilt between 1460 and 1496, and numerous inscriptions record the names of clothier patrons. Chief among those were members of the Clopton family, who are shown in stained glass in the north aisle and whose tombs occupy a chantry†, its roof with verses painted by the monk John Lydgate of Bury (d. 1440).

At nearby **Clare** (TL 769455), another wool town, are priory remains, a largely late C15 parish church, and a priest's house of 1473. A good view of the town is from the C11 motte† and bailey†.

D. Lloyd, Historic Towns of East Anglia *(Gollancz, 1989), 99–101.*

Longthorpe Tower, Peterborough Medieval tower with wall paintings

TL 163983. 3 km. W of Peterborough. English Heritage; restricted opening. Admission charge. Figure 95.

This externally austere, three-storeyed residential tower, with two upper chambers supplied with garderobe† and fireplace above a storage basement, was constructed 1300–10. What makes Longthorpe special is the almost complete scheme of wall paintings in the vaulted first-floor chamber, which is of international importance. The scheme, generally dated to the 1320s or 1330s, contrasts the worldly and the spiritual, and includes the Nativity and Apostles' Creed, the Three Living and the Three Dead, the Labours of the Months, the Ages of Man and, above the fireplace, the Wheel of the Five Senses with the king, as Reason, ruling over the physical senses represented by a monkey (taste), a vulture (smell), a spider's web (touch), a boar (hearing), and a cock (sight).

E. Clive Rouse, Longthorpe Tower *(English Heritage, 1989) (Site Guidebook).*

▲ **Fig. 95.** Longthorpe Tower, Peterborough (Turner)

Mersea Island, Essex   Roman barrow

TM 023144. Immediately after entering Mersea Island via the B1025 take the left fork, the East Mersea Road for 800 m. The barrow stands behind rails on the left.

An apparently isolated barrow, measuring some 34 m. in diameter and 6.7 m. in height. Excavations found a brick-vaulted burial chamber containing a small lead casket in which was a glass vessel with cremated remains of an adult. Finds now in Colchester Museum.

G. M. Benton, 'Roman Burial Group Discovered at West Mersea', Ant J, 4 (1924), 267–8.

Norfolk Broads   Medieval peat cuttings

TG 4015. Centred about 20 km. NE of Norwich accessible from A149 and B1152. Figure 96.

In east Norfolk, on the middle reaches of the rivers Waveney, Yare, and Bure, inland from the vast expanses of the Halvergate marshes, are the thirty or so lakes known since the Middle Ages as 'broads'. The Broads were originally thought to be natural features and it was only in 1960 that research demonstrated that these were flooded peat cuttings, representing extraction on a huge scale. The industry was probably at its peak between the C12 and C14. In all, some 30 million cubic yards of peat were extracted. By the early C15, however, as the climate deteriorated and the sea level rose, the cuttings had become flooded and digging ceased.

T. Williamson, The Norfolk Broads (Manchester University Press, 1997).

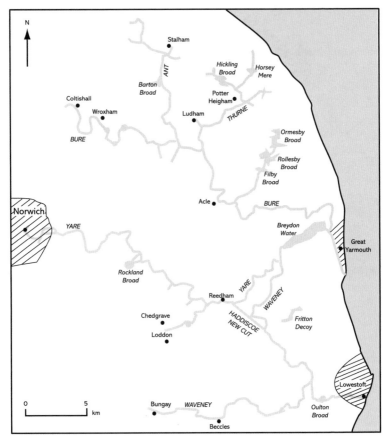

▲ **Fig. 96.** The Norfolk Broads

Norwich, Norfolk Medieval city   ★

TG 2208. County town of Norfolk between King's Lynn and Great Yarmouth.

In 1066 Norwich was one of the greatest towns of east England. It was surrounded by rich agricultural land, while the river Wensum gave opportunities for trade with Europe.

The town's continued growth led in 1094 to the translation here by Herbert de Losinga of his bishopric's cathedral from Thetford. The Cathedral Close dominates Tombland, the Saxon market place, which extends as far as the Wensum, where at Pulls Ferry, near the Watergate, the white Caen stone of Normandy was unloaded for rebuilding the cathedral. Losinga's plan for his cathedral priory was hugely ambitious in scale, with a fourteen-bay nave, transepts, and apsidal east end with radiating two-storey side chapels. By the time of his death only the first four easternmost bays of the nave had been completed, and it was left to his successors to complete the work.

South of the cathedral are the cloisters, rebuilt in the years before 1430. To its west, at the entrance to the outer court, is the Erpingham Gate of about 1420, built by Sir Thomas Erpingham, an Agincourt veteran.

There is much to see in Norwich. The Normans built a castle here, entailing the destruction of ninety-eight houses. By 1100 one of the largest and strongest stone keeps in the country had been raised. Restored by the Victorians, it now houses a museum. The town's late Saxon importance and wealth is reflected in part by the fifty or so churches. Of particular note is St Peter Hungate (now an ecclesiastical museum) and St Peter Mancroft on the edge of the market place. A good concentration of old houses can be found in King Street; it includes the mid-C15 Dragon Hall (now Norfolk Heritage Centre), built by the wool merchant Richard Toppes. Little remains of Norwich's medieval defences, but along the Riverside Walk, east of the cathedral, is the Cow Tower. This massively powerful circular brick tower with twelve 'shotholes' was built 1398–9 and is England's earliest gun-tower.

N. Pevsner, The Buildings of England: North-East Norfolk and Norwich *(Penguin, 1962), 204–82.*

Orford, Suffolk Medieval castle

TM 419499. In Orford on B1084, 25 km. NE of Ipswich. English Heritage; restricted opening. Admission charge.

Orford Castle, built for Henry II between 1165 and 1173, has a unique design: externally polygonal, internally circular, and with three projecting turrets. The lowest, basement, level of the castle, accessible only from within, contains the well. Two circular halls lie above, while the turrets contain two self-contained suites for the household. Over the entrance vestibule is a chapel with priest's chamber.

Orford was held by a royal constable, and was built next to what was at the time a major port. It gave Henry control of an area where, at least at the start of his reign, rival magnates such as Hugh Bigod, earl of Norfolk, posed a serious threat to his authority. His suspicions were well founded, and in 1173 Orford had an important part to play in putting down a rebellion led by the Bigods.

D. Renn, Framlingham and Orford Castles *(English Heritage, 1997) (Site Guidebook).*

Orton Longueville, Peterborough Roman camp and villa

TL 149977. Take the A605 W of Peterborough towards Alwalton and then minor road left to Nene Park Country Park, Ferry Meadows, about 1 km. W of Orton Longueville. Information centre.

Excavations in the 1960s and 1970s uncovered part of a C1 military fort and a C3 aisled building belonging to a small villa. The plan of the latter is now marked out in the recreation grounds near the information centre and car park. The corner of the military ditch is also visible. Across the river Nene at Longthorpe was a large legionary base now under a golf course.

G. Dakin, 'A Romano-British Site at Orton Longueville', PCAS 54 (1960), 50–67.

Pleshey, Essex Medieval castle

TL 660140. 4 km. E of A130, 9 km. NE of Chelmsford. Private ownership; restricted opening.

Pleshey is a classic Norman motte† and bailey† castle, the conical motte being connected by a brick bridge of about 1400 to the kidney-shaped bailey which wraps around a third of its circumference. The bailey is embanked, and a broad, water-filled moat runs around its exterior and that of the motte. These defences represent a refortification of the 1170s, right at the end of the earthwork tradition in castle-building, by William de Mandeville, third earl of Essex, of an earlier castle slighted in the 1140s.

On the north side of the motte, opposite the bailey, a hedge-line demarcates the semicircular perimeter of the defended borough founded here sometime in the early Middle Ages. Although it retained a market, the town never flourished. Immediately outside the western defences is a Victorian rebuilding of a collegiate church† founded in 1393, which in time became the parish church.

F. Williams, Pleshey Castle, Essex (XII–XVI century): Excavations in the Bailey, 1959–63, British Archaeological Reports British Series 42 (1977).

Sutton Hoo, Suffolk Anglo-Saxon barrow cemetery

TM 2848. It is reached via a turning off the A12 from Ipswich, as it bypasses Woodbridge, to Melton village. Sutton Hoo lies beyond the village, over Wilford Bridge. Open during the summer months, with guided tours. Visitor centre planned. National Trust. Figure 97.

Perhaps the most dramatic discovery ever made in British archaeology came in 1939 during excavations in a barrow cemetery above the estuary of the river Deben about 10 km. north-east of Ipswich. Three mounds opened in 1938 had proved to be robbed, but when the cemetery's largest (Mound 1) was opened the exact impression of a 27.4 m. long and 4.2 m. wide clinker-built ship, with each of its iron rivets still in place, was revealed.

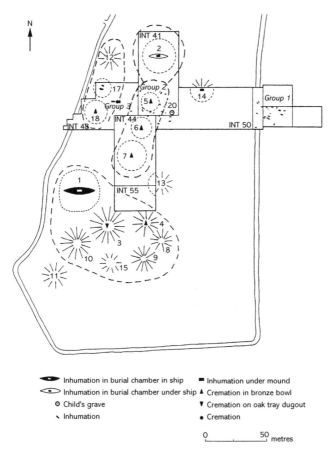

▲ **Fig. 97.** Sutton Hoo, Suffolk, showing the results after excavations (after Carver)

Dating to soon after AD 600 this must have been the burial of one of the kings of the emergent East Anglian kingdom. His remains, placed amidships in a coffin in a textile-hung chamber, were surrounded by the most ostentatious of grave goods: a whetstone sceptre, weapons, armour, including a magnificent crested helmet and parade shield, gold jewellery of the highest quality, drinking vessels, musical instruments, and silverware from the eastern Mediterranean, all now on display in the British Museum.

In all there are eighteen barrows in the cemetery, and in the 1980s a major campaign of research was launched. Among the discoveries was the rich burial of a young man, buried with weapons, vessels of wood and bronze, and horse harness, his horse buried alongside in a separate grave. There was clear evidence of a second ship burial, along with several cremations. Most had been robbed, but all the finds suggest the royal or at least aristocratic status of the person commemorated. Dating suggested all had been buried in the late C6 or early C7. Also found were thirty-nine graves, some contemporary with the rich burials and others of later Saxon date, of criminals who had been executed on a gallows (whose postholes† were located). The acidic sand had destroyed most of the bone, but the body shapes remained as eerie brown 3-D 'sandmen', well enough defined to show broken necks and decapitations.

After the excavation, the mounds were rebuilt to the height they were in 1983, with the exception of Mound 2, which was rebuilt to its original dimensions, and now stands 4 m. high, visible from Melton across the river.

M. Carver, Sutton Hoo: Burial Ground of Kings? *(Sutton Publishing, 1998).*

Swaffham Prior, Cambridgeshire   Medieval churches

TL 5764. On the B1102, 12 km. NE of Cambridge.

Most parish churches were founded by lords of manors and, accordingly, church and manor house frequently stand side by side. Equally, where a settlement was divided between two distinct manors and owners it could end up with two separate churches. Despite rationalization over the centuries, examples still survive of double-church villages. East Anglia has the greatest concentration of these (Norfolk even has triple-church villages), and Swaffham provides a good example with its two churches, dedicated to St Mary, and to SS Cyriac and Julitta. They stand side by side, with their west towers dominating the mounded churchyard above the village street.

The more impressive of the two is St Mary's with a tower lit by Norman, C12 windows. The church of SS Cyriac and Julitta is in the care of the Churches Conservation Trust.

E. Everitt and R Tricker, Swaffham: Two Churches *(Swaffham: privately published, 1996).*

Temple Cressing, Essex   Medieval barns   ★★

TL 7920. 2 km. SE of the Braintree bypass. The site is owned by Essex County Council, and is open to the public.

The great timber-framed Wheat and Barley Barns formed part of the farm at the heart of the manor of Cressing, given in 1137 to the Knights Templar† by Matilda, King Stephen's queen. Long appreciated for their sheer size, dendrochronology showed that these were constructed not, as had been thought, about 1500, but much earlier: the Barley Barn about 1220 and the Wheat Barn between 1273 and 1285. Key components of what has been argued were technologically innovative buildings include aisled trusses stiffened with long passing braces, while the survival of the latter's east-end wall and adjoining lengths of the side walls is remarkable.

The C16 granary to the south was refurbished in 1623. It may once have housed the manorial court.

D. Andrews (ed.), Cressing Temple: A Templar and Hospitaller Manor in Essex (Essex County Council, 1993).

Thaxted, Essex Medieval guildhall

TL 610310. On B184 10 km. SE of Saffron Walden. Restricted opening (mainly Bank Holidays and Sundays from Easter to September).

Medieval Thaxted—cloth and cutlery were its staples—had at least three guilds. These were social and religious fellowships, and the town's Guildhall belonged to one of them. Tree-ring dating shows it was built between 1430 and 1460. After the mid-C16 Reformation, when religious guilds were dissolved, it was used as a market cross and as a moot (court) hall. The arcaded ground floor is constructed around a massive central post from which dragon beams run out to support the three-sided jettying. The lock-up at the rear was inserted in the C18, at the same time that the rooms above became home to a grammar school. The building was enthusiastically restored in the medieval style in 1911.

With its dramatic, three-tiered profile, the Guildhall dominates the Town Street market place. From this the cobbled Stony Lane, lined with timber-framed houses, leads to the churchyard. The church of St John the Baptist is mainly of about 1340. The market place itself is long and rectangular; at its south-east end is a block of buildings, now separated by Orange Street and Mill End, which represents an encroachment onto it.

D. Lloyd, Historic Towns of East Anglia (Gollancz, 1989), 154–7.

Wandlebury, Cambridge, Cambridgeshire Iron Age hillfort†

TL 494534. 6 km. SE of Cambridge, 3 km. NE of Great Shelford. Situated immediately NE of A1307 between Cambridge and the junction with the A604 and A11(T).

Standing on the chalk ridge of the Gog-Magog hills, this roughly circular fort covers 6 ha. Originally defined by two concentric banks and ditches, it has only one circuit now visible; the inner rampart was flattened when the grounds of the house were laid out for Lord Godolphin in the C18. The original entrance to the south-east now carries a road to stable blocks.

There were two main phases. In the first, around C3 BC, the outer ditch was dug and the outer rampart raised. The bank was timber faced; the ditch was steep-sided and flat bottomed. In the C1 BC/AD the site was refortified on a larger scale. An inner bank and ditch were added to give the defences greater depth. The rampart was faced with timber. At the same time the outer ramparts were refurbished.

Within the fort there was fairly intensive occupation from the C3 BC through to the Roman Conquest. C17 and later accounts suggest that within or near Wandlebury Camp was the hill-figure of a Giant, perhaps like the CERNE ABBAS GIANT in Dorset. No traces of this remain.

B. Hartley, 'The Wandlebury Iron Age Hillfort', PCAS 50 (1957), 1–27.

Warham, Fakenham, Norfolk Iron Age hillfort†

TF 945409. 3.5 km. SE of Wells-Next-the-Sea, 1 km. S of Warham. Access via track/footpath running W from minor road between Warham and Wighton.

The best-preserved Iron Age hillfort in Norfolk. Almost exactly circular in plan, an area of 1.4 ha. is enclosed by two massive ramparts which are continuous except where cut by the river Stiffkey which was diverted to its present course in the C18 AD.

H. St G. Gray, 'Trial Excavations in the so-called "Danish Camp" at Warham, near Wells, Norfolk', Ant J, 13 (1933), 399–413.

Warren Lodge, Thetford, Norfolk Medieval gamekeeper's house

TL 839841. 4 km. west of Thetford, off the B1107. English Heritage. Figure 98.

Standing on the southern edge of the Breckland this is an excellent example of a defensive house belonging to a warrener. His duties included the care and management of the warren, a securely fenced area for rabbit burrows. Of C15 date, the Lodge comprises a two-storey stone tower, with living accommodation above a store room. An internal spiral staircase connected the two, while around the top would have been a parapet providing a wide field of view. The reason why the warrener required such secure housing reflected two things. First, especially in the early Middle Ages (the rabbit was introduced by the Normans), the high value of rabbit meat and fur made it attractive to poachers. Warrens, like deer parks, were also the focus of symbolic, but potentially still violent, protest by those with a grievance against the lord who owned it—in this case Thetford's **Cluniac Priory** (TL 865836. English Heritage).

F. Raby and P. Ballie Reynolds, Thetford Priory (English Heritage, 1979) (Site Guidebook).

Waterbeach (Car Dyke), Cambridgeshire Roman canal

TL 478680 to TL 496643. Wet ditch largely parallel to the A10 (Cambridge to Ely road) S of Waterbeach and past Waterbeach airfield.

The Car Dyke has more historic interest than visual impact. The Romans realized the rich agricultural potential of the Fens and a complex of

▲ **Fig. 98.** Thetford Warrener's Lodge, Norfolk (Photograph: Tony Baggs)

canals were dug, the Car Dyke being one, to drain the land and make it usable.

D. Hall and J. Coles, Fenland Survey: An Essay in Landscape Persistence, *English Heritage Archaeology Report 1 (1994).*

Water Newton (*Durobrivae*), Cambridgeshire   Roman town

TL 122968. 1 km. N of A1 and E of Water Newton on line of Ermine Street, where it deviates N from the A1.

Although it was once a thriving defended Roman town on the river Nene, there is today little to see of *Durobrivae* apart from some earthworks surrounding the site and the *agger†* of Ermine Street branching north-west from the bend in the A1.

The town probably originated as a *vicus†* outside a fort. It was one of the sites of a thriving pottery industry based in the Lower Nene valley in the C2–C4 producing widely traded colour-coated wares. The site gained notoriety in 1975 with the chance discovery of the Water Newton treasure, now in the British Museum. The group, one of the earliest

Christian silver hoards known from the Roman Empire, contained several silver vessels and plaques inscribed with Christian motifs.

B. Burnham and J. Wacher, The Small Towns of Roman Britain *(Batsford, 1990).*

West Rudham Long Barrow, near Harpley,
Norfolk Neolithic long barrow†

TF 810254. 3 km. SW of West Rudham, 3 km. SE of Harpley. N of a plantation E of Cross's Grave on minor road from Harpley to Harpley Common. Figure 99.

A Neolithic earthen long barrow, one of very few which survive in East Anglia. The mound, now partly under woodland, is almost oval in plan, 64 m. long by 21 m. wide. Excavations in 1937–8 revealed that the core of the mound was of turf, covered with gravel quarried from the surrounding ditch. Under the mound was a platform on which human bodies were cremated.

A. Hogg, 'A Long Barrow at West Rudham', TNAS *27 (1940), 315–31.*

West Stow, Suffolk Reconstructed Anglo-Saxon village

TL 8072. W of West Stow modern village, off the A1101 10 km. NW of Bury St Edmunds. St Edmundsbury Borough Council; restricted opening. Admission charge. Figure 100.

Close to where the Roman Icknield Way crosses the river Lark was an Anglo-Saxon hamlet. The site was fully excavated between 1965 and 1972. A sand dune had covered the site in the C13, protecting it and leading to excellent preservation.

The site was occupied from the early C5–early C7, and most of the low hill was covered at some stage during this period by timber buildings. Overall seven post-built 'halls' were found but of different dates, and at most only four were occupied at the same time. Around these were large numbers (some sixty-nine) of smaller satellite buildings, represented by rectangular hollows usually some 4 m. long, above which there would have been a building supported by end posts. Several buildings have been reconstructed and West Stow now functions as an open-air museum.

The families who lived here were buried in a cemetery 300 m. away. Unfortunately this was looted in the C19.

A. Selkirk, 'West Stow', CA *4–5/40 (1973), 151–8.*

Widdington (Prior's Hall Barn), Essex Medieval barn

TL 538319. Widdington lies off B1383 10 km. NE of Bishop's Stortford. English Heritage; restricted opening.

The fine timber-framed barn at Prior's Hall Farm was probably built as an investment in the property soon after Widdington became part of the

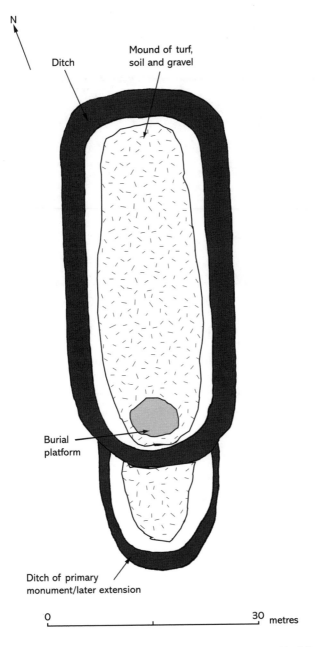

N

Ditch

Mound of turf,
soil and gravel

Burial
platform

Ditch of primary
monument/later extension

0   30 metres

▲ **Fig. 99.** Plan of the West Rudham Long Barrow, near Harpley, Norfolk (after Hogg)

▲ **Fig. 100.** West Stow Anglo-Saxon village, Suffolk (Photograph: Paul Stamper)

original endowment of New College, Oxford. Tree-ring dating has not been successful, but a date around 1380 is fairly certain. The barn has ten bays, gabled entries to either end and a crown-post roof supported on free-standing aisle posts. The barn has a tiled roof, is weatherboarded, and has a flint plinth.

C. Hewitt, The Development of Carpentry 1200–1700 *(David & Charles, 1969)*.

7 The Chilterns and Northampton uplands

This region covers the counties and unitary authorities of Northampton-shire, Buckinghamshire, Hertfordshire, Bedfordshire, Milton Keynes, and Luton.

This region is dominated topographically by two ranges of hills, separated by the valley of the river Ouse, that run broadly south-west to north-east. These ridges—one is of limestone while the other is chalk—lend structure and form to the area.

To the north are the Northamptonshire uplands, the most north-easterly extension of the broad band of limestone that runs diagonally across England and is best exposed as the Cotswold hills. In Northamptonshire the limestone is iron-rich, outcropping as dark honey-coloured or brown stone and lending these same hues to the stone-built architecture of the area. The area is drained by several major rivers: the Welland and the Nene which flow north-eastwards to the Wash; the Avon running south-westwards to join the Severn; and the Sence running north to join the Trent. This pattern means that the area is naturally linked to many surrounding regions and acts as something of a crossroads in the patterns of population movements, trade, and commerce from prehistoric times onwards.

To the south are the Chilterns rising to over 260 m. above sea level around Wendover. This great chalk ridge is a north-eastwards extension of the Wessex downlands, with ancient routeways such as the Ridgeway and the Icknield Way providing direct communications with the south-west. There are good communications to the south too as the area is drained by north-bank tributaries of the river Thames, for example the Rib, Lee, Ver, Gade, and Chess.

Archaeologically the region is rich, although modern development is making the visibility and appreciation of its ancient monuments increasingly more difficult. In early prehistoric times much of the settlement was along the major river valleys, with occasional enclosures and burial sites on the higher ground. By later prehistory, however, all the area was intensively occupied, with hillforts† on the higher ground. In Roman times the Chilterns in particular were dotted with well-appointed villas and farms reflecting the agricultural wealth of the area. Major settlements such as *Verulamium* carry through the location of earlier trading and political centres. In medieval times too the area was a major region of agricultural production, with a high density of small villages and hamlets. Many of those

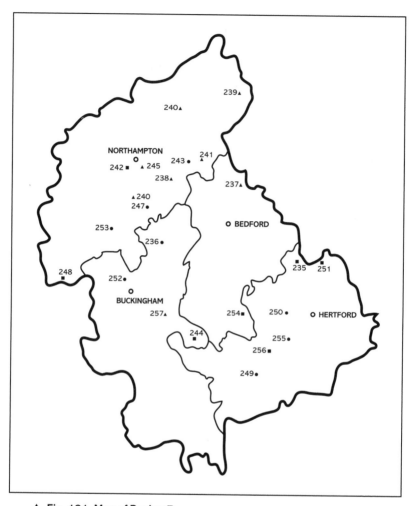

▲ Fig. 101. Map of Region 7

235 Arbury Banks, Hertfordshire
236 Bancroft, Milton Keynes
237 Bushmead Priory, Bedfordshire
238 Earls Barton, Northamptonshire
239 Fotheringhay, Northamptonshire
240 Geddington and Hardingstone, Northamptonshire
241 Higham Ferrers, Northamptonshire
242 Hunsbury, Northamptonshire
243 Irchester, Northamptonshire
244 Ivinghoe Beacon, Buckinghamshire
245 Northampton, Northamptonshire
246 Northamptonshire (Ridge and furrow)

247 Piddington, Northamptonshire
248 Rainsborough Camp, Northamptonshire
249 St Albans (*Verulamium*), Hertfordshire
250 Stevenage, Hertfordshire
251 Therfield Heath, Hertfordshire
252 Thornborough, Buckinghamshire
253 Towcester (*Lactodurum*), Northamptonshire
254 Waulud's Bank, Luton
255 Welwyn, Hertfordshire
256 Wheathampstead, Hertfordshire
257 Wing, Buckinghamshire

settlements were deserted by the C18; those that survived are our modern towns and villages.

Arbury Banks, Ashwell, Hertfordshire Iron Age hillfort†

TL 262387. 2 km. SW of Ashwell village, N of A505, E of A1(T) 5 km. NE of Baldock. Visible from footpaths SW of Ashwell and the Icknield Way path S of Ashwell.

Now ruinous banks and silted-up ditches representing the remains of a large oval-shaped hillfort or enclosure covering about 5 ha. Best preserved on the south-west and west sides. Excavations in the C19 revealed storage pits in the interior and showed that the boundary ditch was V-shaped and over 4 m. deep. More recently, aerial photography has located buildings within the enclosure.

J. Beldam, 'A Memoir on Some Excavations at the Arbury Banks nr Ashwell, Hertfordshire', PSAL, 1st ser., 4 (1859), 285–91.

Bancroft, Milton Keynes Roman villa

SP 827403. From A5 (Watling Street) take A422 E at Bradwell. Turn left at the second roundabout into Millers Way and second left into Constantine Road, signed for Bancroft Park. Villa remains lie in parkland. Signboard.

First discovered in 1967, the villa, a winged corridor house along with several ancillary buildings, has been extensively excavated. The ground plan of the main C3–C4 house is visible. Three of the rooms originally had C4 geometric mosaics and there were two bath-suites. Of particular note is the reconstructed rectangular fishpond in the villa garden. Evidence of earlier occupation was also found. Excavations at a second Roman site discovered 300 m. away at **Blue Bridge** found amongst other things a Romano-Celtic temple-mausoleum, a late Roman shrine, and cemeteries.

R. Williams and R. Zeepvat, Bancroft: A Late Bronze Age/Iron Age Settlement, Roman Villa and Temple-Mausoleum, Milton Keynes Archaeological Unit Monograph 7 (1994).

Bushmead Priory, Bedfordshire Medieval priory

TL 115607. Beside minor road 5 km. W of St Neots. English Heritage; restricted opening. Admission charge.

Bushmead, founded about 1195, was a house of Augustinian† Canons, known as the Black Canons from the colour of their habits. It comprised a small community of ordained priests, probably never more than six and drawn from local families, who lived together in poverty, celibacy, and obedience.

The refectory, or dining hall, probably of about 1250, is the most substantial portion of the priory to survive, with its west window (the tracery is of 1980), lavatorium in the south wall (now pierced by a door) for washing, and six-bay crown-post roof. Inside are traces of late medieval wall painting.

D. Sherlock, Bushmead Priory *(English Heritage, 1985) (Site Guidebook).*

Earls Barton, Northamptonshire Saxon church ★

SP 852638. Off the A45, 8 km. E of Northampton.

Rising high above Earls Barton is the Anglo-Saxon tower of All Saints' Church. Probably of about 1020, this rises in four stages, with long-and-short quoins at the corners and stone pilaster strips dividing it vertically; similar stone strips provide round-arched and lozenge-shaped decoration. Not all of its various openings are explicable. Straightforward enough are the west door, the baluster-shafted bell openings of the top storey, and the windows, which are in various different forms. But what of the first-floor door on the south side (there was originally one on the west too)? As much as anything this was a bell-tower; the lower chambers, however, may have been for priests, patrons, or both; the only other element of the church originally may have been a narrow chancel. The rest of the church is later, and includes some good Norman work, notably in the chancel.

Behind the church the churchyard wall loops over a mound, which is a wide- and deep-ditched fortification. It is probably a Norman (or C12 Anarchy period) castle motte†.

About 3 km. to the south is **Whiston** 'on the hill', its church (which includes a memorable west tower) exceptional for its early C16 date and high quality. It was built by the Catesbys, later to be implicated in the Gunpowder Plot.

M. Audouy et al., 'The Tower of All Saints' Church', Arch J, 152 (1995), 73–94.

Fotheringhay, Northamptonshire Medieval church and castle

TL 059931. 5 km. NE of Oundle on minor road NW off A605.

Fotheringhay Castle, where Mary Queen of Scots was executed in 1587, survives today only as earthworks. Alongside, however, is the magnificent church of St Mary and All Saints, at which Edward Plantaganet, duke of York, established a college with Master, twelve fellows, eight clerks, and thirteen choristers in 1411. Their role was to say requiem masses for his soul after his death, which came just four years later when he fell at Agincourt, as one of Henry V's captains. Its chancel and domestic buildings were pulled down after the suppression of the college in 1548, but what remains, mainly of the 1420s and 1430s, is Perpendicular work of the highest quality. The nave is broad and airy, being lit with closely spaced four-light windows both along its aisles and along the clerestory†, the two being linked by narrow flying buttresses. The aisles run either side of the west tower, the upper part of which is octagonal. Inside is a fan vault of 1529, an especially fine roof, and monuments to the second and third dukes of York of 1573.

N. Pevsner and B. Cherry, The Buildings of England: Northamptonshire *(Penguin, 1973), 219–21.*

Geddington and Hardingstone, Northamptonshire Eleanor Crosses

Geddington (SP 896830) is on A43 5 km. NE of Kettering. The Cross is in the village centre. Hardingstone (SP 754583) is now a suburb on S edge of Northampton. The Cross stands on E side of A508. Figure 102.

From the time she married the later Edward I in 1254 Eleanor of Castile was rarely apart from him, and between 1255 and 1284 bore him at least fifteen children. Edward was with her when, on 28 November 1290, she died of fever at Harby, near Lincoln. Her viscera were buried in Lincoln cathedral but the body was returned to Westminster, and at each of the twelve places where the funeral cortège rested Edward had a memorial cross erected.

▼ **Fig. 102.** Hardingstone, Eleanor Cross, Northamptonshire (Photograph: Paul Stamper)

Only three now survive, one at Waltham, Essex, and two in North-amptonshire. That at Geddington, where there was a royal hunting lodge, is the best preserved and most modest, although when erected all would have been brightly painted. The cross comprises a triangular pier on a stepped base, its elaborate gothic carving climaxing in the niches which contain statues of the queen. After staying at Geddington the party moved on to Delapré Abbey, near the village of Hardingstone on the main Northampton road. This cross, one of five contracted to John of Battle, is an octagonal pier in three tiers on a stepped base; the shaft at its top was installed in a restoration of 1840. The lowest tier is decorated with royal heraldry and with open books, presumably once with painted inscriptions. Above are four statues of the queen, set in elaborate can-opied tabernacles. The carving is notable for its innovative adoption of forms which blurred the line between sculpture and architecture. It is one of the first major expressions of the Decorated style of architecture.

J. Steane, The Archaeology of the Medieval English Monarchy (Batsford, 1993), 50–3.

Higham Ferrers, Northamptonshire Medieval church, grammar school, bede house, and college

SP 960687. On A6 3 km. N of Rushden. English Heritage and East Northampton District Council.

Although less picturesque than Oundle and Thrapston to the north, Higham Ferrers is an attractive small town with at its heart a remarkable group of buildings testifying to late medieval piety. The church of St Mary is large and grand, presumably reflecting the wealth of its patrons in the later C13 and C14, the dukes of Lancaster. The nave, south aisle, and tower are of about 1250–80, the splendid spire, north aisle, chancel windows, chancel aisle, and Lady Chapel probably of the 1330s and 1340s. Inside fittings again testify to the town's religious life in the Middle Ages, notably the twenty stalls for the members of Chichele College at the east end of the north aisle and an unusual number of medieval monumental brasses. They include members of the family of Henry Chichele, a native of the place, Archbishop of Canterbury 1414–43 and founder of All Souls College, Oxford.

Close to the church's west door is the three-bay chantry-like build-ing which until 1907 housed a grammar school. Already in existence by 1391 the school was refounded in 1422 by Chichele, and it was presum-ably he who paid for its rebuilding. Eight great windows light the plain interior; a mural stair towards the east end suggests the former presence of a screen here. The simplicity, almost austerity, of this building is as notable as the church's splendour, and demonstrates how markedly the Perpendicular of the later C14 and C15 differed from the earlier more flamboyant styles of architecture.

On the south side of the churchyard is Chichele's Bede House, refounded by the archbishop in 1429 as a home for twelve old men and a woman attendant. Of banded ironstone and limestone, internally there was a chapel at the east end and twelve sleeping cubicles, all heated by a large fireplace in the south wall.

Some 100 m. away on the main road are the remains of the college founded by Chichele in 1431 to house a master, seven chaplains, four clerks, and six choristers. What survives is the south range, possibly with chapel at the east end, and parts of the east (gatehouse), and west (?hall) ranges.

N. Pevsner and B. Cherry, The Buildings of England: Northamptonshire *(Penguin, 1973), 253–9.*

Hunsbury, Northampton, Northamptonshire Iron Age

hillfort†

SP 737584. 3 km. SW of Northampton immediately S of A45 southern bypass, W of A43(T). Access from minor road W of junction of the A43 and A45.

Hunsbury Camp now appears as a round enclosure, 1.7 ha. in area, defended by a single bank 20 m. wide and 6 m. high, flanked on the outside by a ditch originally 6.7 m. deep. The original entrance opens to the south-east.

Excavations in 1952 revealed a complicated sequence of construction. The first hillfort was probably constructed in the C4 BC. Its bank was revetted by vertical timbers, the ditch in front separated from the bank by a narrow berm†. Later clay was added to make the front of the rampart slope at the same angle as the inner face of the ditch. Traces of an outer ditch were discovered in 1903, but nothing of this is now visible.

The interior was heavily disturbed by iron-mining last century and the ground surface was lowered by 2.4 m. Numerous storage pits, many stone-lined, were discovered. A large and important collection of pottery, metalwork, and other objects was amassed, much of it now in Northampton Museum.

C. Fell, 'The Hunsbury Hillfort', Arch J, *93 (1936), 57–100.*

Irchester, Northamptonshire Roman town

SP 917666. N of A45 Cambridge–Northampton road and N of the modern village close to the river Nene.

The only visible remains of this small Roman town are traces of a bank and ditch on the north in fields visible from the public footpath. The area was occupied from the Iron Age and later became a walled Roman settlement. Excavations have located a cemetery, and traces of many buildings including a temple.

B. Burnham and J. Wacher, The Small Towns of Roman Britain *(Batsford, 1990), 142–8.*

Ivinghoe Beacon, near Dunstable, Buckinghamshire

Iron Age hillfort† ★

SP 960169. 9 km. SE of Leighton Buzzard, 1.5 km. NE of Ivinghoe village. S of B489 between its junction with the A4146 and Ivinghoe village. Some signposting. National Trust.

This small Iron Age hillfort of about 2.2 ha occupies a prominent spur on the Chilterns. Although set in a highly defensible position with extensive views north and west, the hillfort was probably only used for a short time in the C6 or C7 BC, and the defences were probably never completed.

Although heavily eroded, it is possible to make out the ditch of the defences on the north and east sides surviving as a level platform. A double platform representing the remains of the ramparts can be seen on the west side. The entrance was in the east corner.

Excavations between 1963 and 1965 demonstrated that the ramparts were composed of chalk rubble with timber revetments. Inside the fort were structures including round houses and granaries. This was one of the earliest hillforts to be built in the area.

M. Cotton and S. Frere, 'Ivinghoe Beacon', Records of Buckinghamshire, *18 (1968), 187–260.*

Northampton, Northamptonshire Medieval town

SP 7561. County town of Northamptonshire beside the river Nene, N of the M1 (junctions 15 or 16). Figures 103 and 104.

Northampton suffered terribly from development in the 1970s, losing much of its charm along with many good buildings. Nevertheless, gems survive, among them two churches which serve as reminders of the town's importance in the early Middle Ages: it was much visited by royalty (thirty times by John alone) and saw various acts of state including Archbishop Thomas Becket's trial in 1164. That took place in the royal castle (obliterated in 1879 by the railway station), whose proximity to St Peter's, in Marefair, may explain the architectural quality of that church. Externally St Peter's is interesting enough, with a low but ornate west tower (rebuilt in the C17), and long nave and chancel along which runs blind arcading. Internally the decoration is of a type and standard more usually encountered in abbeys and cathedrals. Note the tower arch, the former west doorway, and the arcades, sumptuously zigzagged arches rising off decorated capitals set on alternating drum and multiple piers. The date is probably about 1150. Even more remarkable is Holy Sepulchre, in Sheep Street, which was built at about the same time but with a circular plan: this was something which crusaders like Simon of Senlis, earl of Northampton, had seen in Jerusalem at the church of the Holy Sepulchre during the First Crusade, although the immediate model may have been the round churches of north Italy. The church was later much

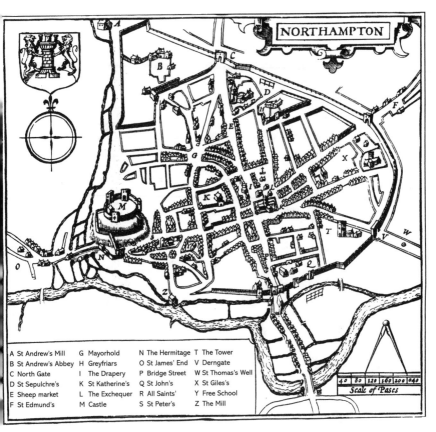

A St Andrew's Mill	G Mayorhold	N The Hermitage	T The Tower
B St Andrew's Abbey	H Greyfriars	O St James' End	V Derngate
C North Gate	I The Drapery	P Bridge Street	W St Thomas's Well
D St Sepulchre's	K St Katherine's	Q St John's	X St Giles's
E Sheep market	L The Exchequer	R All Saints'	Y Free School
F St Edmund's	M Castle	S St Peter's	Z The Mill

▲ **Fig. 103.** John Speed's 1610 map of Northampton. Holy Sepulchre (D) is near the North Gate, St Peter's (S) near the castle

enlarged. Inside the space is stunning, opening from the circular nave (now baptistery†) into the four parallel spaces of nave, south aisle, north aisle, and an outer north aisle. A narrow chancel originally lay east of the nave and parts of its north wall can still be seen, pierced by the arcade between the nave and the north aisle.

RCHME, An Inventory of the Historical Monuments in the County of Northampton, *vol. v:* Archaeological Sites and Churches in the County of Northampton *(HMSO, 1985).*

Northamptonshire Ridge and furrow†

This part of Midland England preserves some of the best and most visible ridge and furrow. Three good examples can be found in central Northamptonshire within a half hour's drive, all easily accessible from the A14.

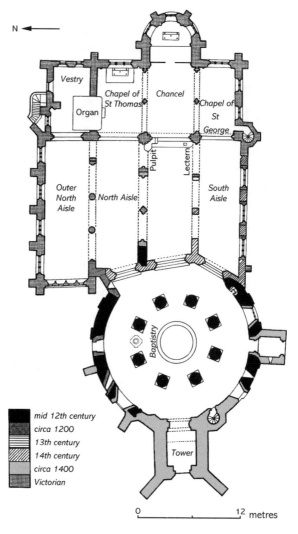

N ←

Vestry

Chapel of St Thomas

Chancel

Chapel of St George

Organ

Outer North Aisle

North Aisle

South Aisle

Pulpit

Lectern

Baptistry

Tower

mid 12th century
circa 1200
13th century
14th century
circa 1400
Victorian

0   12 metres

▲ **Fig. 104.** Northampton, church of the Holy Sepulchre (after Leleux)

In the Middle Ages much of England's heavier arable land was ploughed in linear, parallel ridges and furrows. Where it survives, fossilized as earthworks in permanent pasture, it resembles outsize corrugated iron, with each ridge between 5 m. and 15 m. wide. The main purpose was drainage, to allow heavy rain to run off the fields via the furrows. Only in the mid-C19 did cheap clay drainage pipes appear, and the practice of ridging cease. Huge amounts of ridge and furrow have been lost since the early 1970s as arable farming intensified.

Harrington (SP 7280). At the north-west end of the village are the terraced earthworks of a great formal garden of about 1700. At the bottom of the garden are huge embanked fishpond bays. All around, and especially to the north of the pond bays, is ridge and furrow. The site is in countryside stewardship, and a right of way passes through it.

Great Oxendon (SP 7484). The village is a rectangular, double-row, planned village of the early Middle Ages, with the church lying isolated 300 m. to the north on the Market Harborough road. From the church car park (St Helen's, including C13 and C14 work) large amounts of ridge and furrow can be seen, and more survives west, south, and east of the village.

Lilbourne (SP 5577). To the immediate north-east of the church (All Saints', C13 and later) is a fine earthwork motte† and bailey† castle. West of the church is a large field of ridge and furrow with access via public footpath across it to a second castle site. Inclosure here was in 1671.

D. Hall, The Open Fields of Northamptonshire *(Northamptonshire Record Society, 1995).*

Piddington, Northamptonshire Roman villa

SP 803545. Site on outskirts of modern village of Piddington just off B526 S of Northampton. Museum being established in village.

Ongoing excavations of a Roman farmstead comprising a late C3–C4 courtyard villa with bath-house into which a later tile kiln has been inserted. The settlement has Iron Age antecedents and was used as a cemetery in early medieval times.

A. Selkirk, 'Piddington', CA *13/2 (146) (1996), 57–64.*

Rainsborough Camp, Newbottle, Northamptonshire

Iron Age hillfort†   ★

SP 526348. 2 km. NE of Aynho, 6 km. W of Brackley, NE of A41(T). Accessible from footpath leading N from minor road between Aynho and Charlton.

This modest 2.5 ha. hillfort has a large bank with an outer ditch and counterscarp bank†; an outer ditch is now filled. The main entrance is near the middle of the west side. In plan the fort is trapezoidal, with rounded corners.

The basic fort was built as a single operation to an elaborate and sophisticated design in the C5 BC. The rampart was a compact structure with a stone-fronted stepped bank flanked by a steep-sided ditch, and outer rampart and ditch beyond. The total width of the defences was about 40 m. The gateway on the west consisted of a narrow passage through the bank. The sides of the passage were lined with upright timbers, and may have tunnelled through the rampart. At the inner end were two large guard-chambers, and beyond these massive double timber gates opening into the interior.

These defences were maintained for perhaps a century before a major overhaul. Soon after, the gateway, entrance passage, and parts of the ramparts were attacked and heavily burnt. The remains of a defender were found in one of the guard-chambers.

The site was then abandoned until the C2 BC when the defences were refurbished in a simple way and reoccupied for a short time. There was some reuse in Roman times, and it is possible that a temple was built somewhere in the immediate vicinity. In the C18 the site was landscaped and the stone walls, visible along the inner rampart, added for dramatic effect.

M. Avery et al., 'Rainsborough, Northants, England: Excavations 1961–5', PPS 33 (1967), 207–306.

St Albans (*Verulamium*), Hertfordshire Roman and
medieval town ★★

TL 135067. Ten minutes' drive from junction 21A on M25 or junctions 9, 7, or 6 on the M1. Follow signs for Roman Verulamium. Roman remains can be seen in a public park: Verulamium Park. Verulamium Museum, St Michael's (adjacent to Park) is a good starting point. Car park adjacent to museum. Restricted opening to the theatre; admission charge. Website: www.daysout.co.uk/colourapore/IA107.html. Figure 105.

Founded near a pre-Roman settlement (see Beech Bottom Dyke, ST ALBANS, and Devil's Dyke, WHEATHAMPSTEAD), *Verulamium* was the third largest Roman city in Britain and the only one granted the self-governing status of *municipium*†. It lies astride Watling Street and was about one day's march from *Londinium*. Established around AD 49 the settlement suffered two devastating fires, one caused by the revolt of Queen Boudicca in 61, the other in 155 during the reign of Emperor Antoninus Pius. The city was rebuilt each time and continued to thrive into the early C5. Alban was martyred here in the C3.

The defences enclosed some 81 ha.; about half is accessible in Verulamium Park. Amongst the remains are parts of the defences and city walls, the theatre, a hypocausted building, and ground plans of excavated shops and town houses. The course of the late C3 wall can be traced for most of its circuit (3.6 km.). The best-preserved stretches are adjoining the London Gate and at St Germain's Block. The mid-C2 theatre is one of only six theatres believed to have existed in Roman Britain.

The site of the basilica† and forum†, the main administrative and economic centre of the city, lies in the vicinity of St Michael's Church. Roman red tiles can be seen reused in the walls of the church. A large cemetery has been partly excavated outside the south-west gate alongside the road (King Harry Lane) to SILCHESTER. This contained burials of Iron Age, Roman, and Saxon date.

▲ **Fig. 105.** The *Verulamium* bronze Venus. Height c.20 cm. From an early 4th-century pit in Insula XIV, St Albans, Hertfordshire (Photograph: Verulamium Museum)

The Museum houses an extensive collection of finds along with several fine mosaics, wall paintings, and re-created Roman rooms.

The shrine of St Alban, one of the earliest British martyrs, was covered by a church from the C4. In the C11 St Alban's cathedral was constructed over the site of the shrine as the church of a Benedictine† abbey, and some of the Anglo-Norman work survives. Much of the monastic precinct was destroyed after the Dissolution†, and by the C19 substantial parts of the building were in ruin. Extensive restoration took place, mainly of the exterior, whilst much of the interior remained intact, notably the impressive collection of C13–C14 wall paintings.

S. Frere, Verulamium II, *Reports of the Research Committee of the Society of Antiquaries of London 41 (1972).*

Stevenage, Hertfordshire Roman burial mounds

TL 237237. On W side of London Road, Stevenage, adjacent to road and just W of the roundabout at junction of London Road and Six Hills Way.

Six C1 AD barrows, one of the finest surviving groups of Roman burial mounds. Excavations revealed single cremated burials in each, perhaps the members of a local, wealthy aristocratic Roman family.

H. Andrews, 'The Six Hills', TEHAS 3 (1906), 178–85.

Therfield Heath, Royston, Hertfordshire Neolithic and
Bronze Age barrow cemetery

TL 342402. 1.5 km. SW of Royston, S of A505, on Therfield Heath golf course. Visible from public footpaths across the golf course. Figure 106.

The earliest feature in this barrow cemetery is the long barrow† situated at its western end, one of the few still visible in this part of England. Excavations revealed that the east–west mound was about 38 m. long and was surrounded by a ditch. The mound is still over 2 m. high with a typical slightly trapezoidal outline. One burial is known towards the east end, and other graves were later dug into the mound; it is not certain, however, whether the excavators ever uncovered the main burials.

Immediately north of the long barrow is a cluster of eight round barrows†, all of the simple bowl-barrow type and between 6 m. and 21 m. in diameter. The largest is nearly 4 m. high. Antiquarian excavations show the barrows contained a variety of inhumations and cremations; they date mainly to between about 2000 BC and 1500 BC.

C. Phillips, 'A Re-examination of the Therfield Heath Long Barrow', PPS 1 (1935), 101–7.

Thornborough, Buckinghamshire Roman barrows

SP 732333. Beside A421 near Thornborough bridge E of Buckingham. Car park nearby.

Two impressive Roman burial mounds close to the junction of five major roads. When excavated in 1839–40 one was found to have already been plundered but the other produced a rich assemblage including gold and bronze ornaments, pottery, and glass dating to about 200 AD. A glass urn contained cremated remains. Traces of a Roman settlement and temple have been found nearby. The mounds are located alongside a 7 km. circular walk around Thornborough parish which also takes in an Iron Age camp, earthworks from a medieval village, and a nature reserve alongside the disused Buckingham canal.

J. Liversidge, 'The Thornborough Barrow', Records of Buckinghamshire, 16 (1954), 29–32.

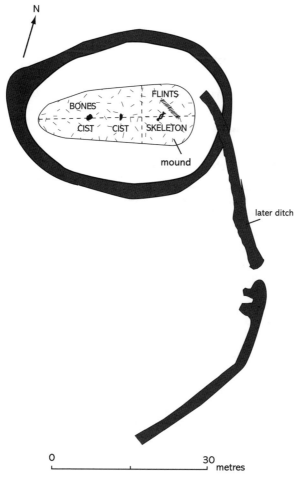

▲ **Fig. 106.** Plan of the Therfield Heath long barrow, Hertfordshire (after Phillips)

Towcester (*Lactodurum*), Northamptonshire Roman town

SP 694484. On Watling Street (A5) where it crosses the A43, S of the river Tove.

A Roman small town† set astride Watling Street now almost completely hidden by the modern town. Excavation suggests the settlement was well established by the mid-C2. The only visible remains relate to the defences with a single broad, very overgrown ditch in the north-west corner behind the police station. Accessible via a footpath (Grafton Way) between the police and fire stations at the N end of town on the A43.

B. Burnham and J. Wacher, The Small Towns of Roman Britain *(Batsford, 1990), 152–60.*

Waulud's Bank, Luton Late Neolithic enclosure   ★

TL 062246. In a public park off Sundon Road in the Limbury district of NW Luton, 4 km. from town centre. Access by minor road leading E of B579 Toddington road.

One of very few late Neolithic enclosures known in eastern England. A grassy bank standing 2 m. high in places represents the north, east, and south sides of this 7.2 ha. enclosure. The river Lea, which rises within the site, defines the west side.

J. Dyer, 'Waulud's Bank', CA 3/30 (1972), 173–6.

Welwyn, Hertfordshire Roman bath-house

TL 23541607. Beneath the A1(M) at its junction with the A1000 just off the central roundabout of the Welwyn bypass. Signposted. Administered by Welwyn Hatfield Museum Service; restricted opening. Admission charge.

A bath-house belonging to a C3 Roman villa (Dicket Mead) excavated in advance of road construction in the 1970s is preserved in a steel vault within the motorway embankment. The compact, simple and well-preserved bath-house contains all the basic facilities explained by attractive information boards. Related archaeological finds on display.

T. Rook, 'The Roman Villa Site at Dicket Mead', HA 9 (1987), 79–175.

Wheathampstead, St Albans, Hertfordshire Late Iron Age
oppidum†

TL 185135. 7 km. NE of St Alban's town centre, 1 km. SE of Wheathampstead. S of B653 on SE outskirts of Wheathampstead, partly cut by the bypass. Figure 107.

During the reign of King Cassivellaunus (d. 40–35 BC) the capital of the *Catuvellauni* may have been at Wheathampstead. On raised ground in the valley of the river Lea are the remains of a small *oppidum* of 35–40 ha. enclosed by earthworks; two sections remain visible, known locally as the Devil's Dyke and the Slad. The site has been investigated several times, most notably by Sir Mortimer Wheeler in 1932.

Devil's Dyke lies on the west side of the site under a line of trees (TL 184135) at the end of the modern village. **The Slad** lies on the east side, also in a line of trees (TL 188134), and is of comparable scale. The line of the boundary between these earthworks can tentatively be identified in field boundaries. It is assumed that the river Lea formed the northern boundary.

Excavations and aerial photography have failed to reveal much indication of occupation. It is possible that within the loosely defined enclosure there were smaller foci separated by open areas.

This may have been where, according to his *Gallic Wars*, Julius Caesar defeated the Catuvellaunian forces in 54 BC. There is no evidence that Wheathampstead continued in use far into the C1 AD, and indeed it

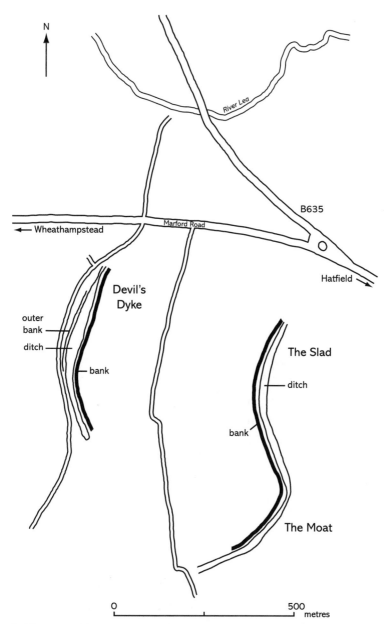

▲ **Fig. 107.** Plan of Wheathampstead, Hertfordshire (after Saunders & Havercroft)

may well have been superseded by a dyke-system *oppidum* at *Verulamium* (now St Albans) 8 km. to the south-west.

R. and T. Wheeler, Verulamium: A Belgic and Two Roman Cities, *Reports of the Research Committee of the Society of Antiquaries of London 11 (1936).*

Wing, Buckinghamshire Anglo-Saxon church

SP 880225. On the A418 10 km. NE of Aylesbury. Figure 108.

The first striking feature of the church of All Saints is its polygonal apse (compare DEERHURST), tall, and with decorated stone strips (pilasters, or lesnes) arranged to form a blind arcade with corner pilasters and gabled motifs above. Around its base three windows, one enlarged to form a door, light a vaulted crypt. As at Brixworth (Northants.), this has an ambulatory or ring passage, with side recesses and a central shrine for relics.

The basic structure is probably C7, with substantial modification in the C10. The nave, with surviving north aisle, certainly seems C7 with its massive arcades and, above the western arches, blocked doorways which gave access to a western gallery.

▼ **Fig. 108.** Wing church, Buckinghamshire, showing the polygonal apse with its pilaster strips (Photograph: Paul Stamper)

The rest of the church is later: the south aisle C14, and the tower, porch, and clerestory† C15. Among the monuments is the tomb in the north aisle of Sir Robert Dormer, a rare example of early Renaissance work, dated 1552.

H. and J. Taylor, Anglo-Saxon Architecture *(Cambridge University Press, 1965), ii. 665–72.*

8 The Cotswolds and upper Thames valley

This region includes the counties and unitary authorities of Gloucester-shire, Warwickshire, Oxfordshire, West Berkshire, Reading, Wokingham, Bracknell Forest, Windsor and Maidenhead, and Slough.

A topographically diverse region dominated by the Cotswold hills, a limestone ridge running south-west to north-east with a steep escarpment to the west. The hard white and cream-coloured limestone, ideal as building stone, was widely used from around 4000 BC onwards. The Cotswolds rise to about 320 m. above sea level at Cleeve Cloud near Cheltenham. Many small valleys cut into the upland, notably north bank

▼ **Fig. 109.** Map of Region 8

tributaries of the river Thames such as the Cherwell, Glyme, Windrush, Leach, Coln, and Churn. The Thames itself rises near Kemble.

In these valleys are some exceedingly picturesque villages, many dating back to the C11 AD or before. Roman villas, including some of the grandest examples in England, can also be found here. Indeed, in Roman times the Cotswolds were probably the wealthiest part of *Britannia*. Prehistoric settlement was intense too, with Mesolithic occupation along the rivers. Early farming communities built numerous causewayed enclosures† and long barrows†, and the barrow-building tradition was strongly represented during the Bronze Age too. During the Iron Age striking hillforts† were constructed along the escarpment.

West of the Cotswolds are the low-lying valleys of the Severn and Warwickshire Avon, only extensively cleared in the later Bronze Age. In the far western part of the region is the Forest of Dean and Wye valley, an upland about which little is known.

East of the Cotswolds is the extensive Thames valley, low-lying clayey land with gravel islands. These islands have always been settlement foci. Sadly there is little to see except the upstanding remains of medieval and

---

▼ **Key to Fig. 109**

258 Aldworth, West Berkshire
259 Ashleworth, Gloucestershire
260 Bagendon, Gloucestershire
261 The Lunt, Warwickshire
262 Belas Knap, Gloucestershire
263 Blackpool Bridge, Gloucestershire
264 Brackenbury Ditches, Gloucestershire
265 Chedworth, Gloucestershire
266 Cirencester (*Corinium Dobannorum*), Gloucestershire
267 Cleeve Hill, Gloucestershire
268 Combe Gibbet, West Berkshire
269 Coughton Court, Warwickshire
270 Crickley Hill, Gloucestershire
271 Deerhurst, Gloucestershire
272 Eton, Windsor and Maidenhead
273 Ewelme, Oxfordshire
274 Fairford, Gloucestershire
275 Fosse Way
276 Gloucester (*Colonia Nervia Glevensium*), Gloucestershire
277 Great Coxwell, Oxfordshire
278 Great Witcombe, Gloucestershire
279 Grim's Ditch, Oxfordshire
280 Haresfield Beacon, Gloucestershire
281 Hetty Pegler's Tump, Gloucestershire
282 Kempley, Gloucestershire
283 Kingston Lisle, Oxfordshire
284 Lambourn Seven Barrows, West Berkshire
285 Long Stone (Minchinhampton), Gloucestershire
286 Long Stone (Staunton), Gloucestershire
287 Lydney Park, Gloucestershire
288 Northleach, Gloucestershire
289 North Leigh, Oxfordshire
290 Notgrove Long Barrow, Gloucestershire
291 Nympsfield Long Barrow, Gloucestershire
292 Oxford, Oxfordshire
293 Randwick Long Barrow, Gloucestershire
294 Rollright Stones, Oxfordshire
295 Spoonley Wood, Gloucestershire
296 Sudeley Castle, Gloucestershire
297 Tewkesbury, Gloucestershire
298 The Ridgeway, Oxfordshire
299 Uffington White Horse and Castle, Oxfordshire
300 Uleybury, Gloucestershire
301 Wadfield, Gloucestershire
302 Wappenbury, Warwickshire
303 Warwick, Warwickshire
304 Wayland's Smithy, Oxfordshire
305 Windmill Tump, Gloucestershire
306 Windsor, Windsor and Maidenhead
307 Woodchester, Gloucestershire
308 Wotton-under-Edge, Gloucestershire

later settlement. Aerial photography and excavation in advance of gravel extraction reveal the below-ground evidence.

South of the Thames valley in southern Oxfordshire and Berkshire is the northern edge of the chalk downs, which at this point run broadly parallel to the Cotswold hills. Like the Cotswolds, the downs also have a steep escarpment to the north-west, here overlooking the upper Thames valley, where similar kinds of archaeology are represented.

Aldworth, West Berkshire Medieval church

SU 554794. On the B4009 5 km. W of Goring.

St Mary's Church has a rich collection of C14 monumental effigies, of the de la Beche family. The oldest is that of Sir Robert, knighted in 1278. Next to him is Sir Philip; at his feet is a dwarf, allegedly taken by him to court to better show off his height. The third of the tombs is of Philip's son John, who died in the Black Death of 1348–9, with his wife Isabella.

B. Kemp, English Church Monuments *(Batsford, 1980), 21–2.*

Ashleworth, Gloucestershire Medieval barn

SO 818252. Ashleworth is 1 km. E of A417, 7 km. N of Gloucester. The barn (National Trust) is by the river Severn SE of village. Restricted opening.

Ashleworth church, barn, and Court comprise an excellent example of an Augustinian rectorial manor. The church was granted to the Augustinian† abbey at Bristol in 1154, and the tithe barn was erected by Abbot Newland (1481–1515). Here would have been gathered, stored, and processed the grain crops gathered by the monks as their tenth share (tithe) of the villagers' output. The ten-bay, 38 m. long barn is of limestone with freestone dressings and diagonal buttresses. The queen post roof trusses support a stone slate roof. Access is via two gabled porches.

Ashleworth Church has a nave of about 1100 and a C13 chancel. Other elements date to the C14, C15, and C16.

Ashleworth Court, of about 1460 and little changed since its construction, was built as a manor house.

Ashleworth Manor, 0.5 km. to the north, was supposedly built by Abbot Newbury as a summer residence, also about 1460. After the Dissolution it became the vicarage.

D. Verey, The Buildings of Gloucestershire: The Vale and the Forest of Dean *(Penguin, 1980), 88–91.*

Bagendon, Perrott's Brook, Gloucestershire Late Iron Age

oppidum†

SP 017060. W of A435 4 km. N of Cirencester, N of A417(T) and partly cut by it. Best approached from Perrott's Brook. Figure 110.

Bagendon was the capital of the *Dobunni* tribe at the time of the Roman

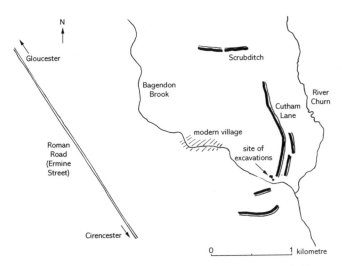

▲ **Fig. 110.** Plan of the *oppidum* at Bagendon, Perrott's Brook, Gloucestershire (after Clifford)

Conquest. The 80 ha. site is best viewed from the well-preserved boundary dykes, forming the eastern side of the *oppidum* beside Cutham Lane. East of the road is a 270 m. length of bank and ditch standing 75 m. forward of the main dyke.

Bagendon lies where the Bagendon brook joins the Churn valley, the brook representing the central axis of the *oppidum*. The dyke system runs down into the valley to cross the brook—perhaps the original entrance—before winding up the opposite slope. Multiple lines of earthwork exist in some areas.

Excavations show settlement was confined to a few specific areas within the enclosure, implying that sectors were open ground or in agricultural use. Industrial activity included a mint which struck coins bearing the names of *Dobunni* kings: ANTED, EISU, EPATICCU, and BODVOC. Various imported Roman luxury goods were also found.

Bagendon appears to have been abandoned around 70 AD when settlement shifted to the newly founded town of *Corinium Dobunnorum*, modern-day CIRENCESTER.

E. Clifford, Bagendon: A Belgic oppidum *(Heffers, 1960)*.

Baginton, The Lunt, Warwickshire Roman fort ★★

SP 346752. 3 km. S of Coventry E of A444, restricted opening. Site museum. Admission charge. Figure 111.

The Lunt Roman fort, on a spur overlooking the river Sowe, was

▲ **Fig. 111.** The reconstructed *gyrus* at The Lunt Roman fort, Baginton, Warwickshire (Photograph: Jane Timby)

completely excavated 1965–73. Subsequently reconstructions were made of the gateway, part of the defences, a granary, and a circular arena.

The Lunt is atypical of an average fort. The earliest fort appears to have been constructed very quickly around AD 60, coinciding with Boudicca's rebellion. This was later replaced by the main fort, occupied from the early 60s to about 80 when it was abandoned and demolished. The eastern defences, instead of being straight, curve around a large circular arena enclosed by a substantial wooden fence. This has been interpreted as a *gyrus,* or training ground, where the Roman cavalry trained their horses. In the south-east quadrant a large complex building was suggested to be the accommodation (*praetorium*) of a high-ranking officer. In the centre of the fort is the headquarters (*principia*). Other buildings uncovered include the barrack blocks, stabling blocks for the horses, equipment sheds, workshops (*fabrica*), and granaries (*horrea*).

B. Hobley, 'The Lunt Roman Fort and Training School for Roman Cavalry, Baginton, Warwickshire. Final Report: Excavations (1972–73) with Conclusions', TPBAS 87 (1975), 1–56.

Belas Knap, Gloucestershire   Neolithic long barrow†   ★★

SP 021254. 3 km. S of Winchcombe on NE side of Cleeve Hill, best approached along signposted lanes from the main A46 SW of Winchcombe. The lane is immediately SW of Winchcombe Hospital. Steep (signposted) footpath leads to the hilltop site about 1 km. away. English Heritage.

Belas Knap lies on a gentle hill slope overlooking a steep-sided river valley. The name derives from the Old English words *bel* meaning a beacon and *cnaepp* meaning a hilltop.

It displays classic features of the Cotswold–Severn long-barrow tradition. The wedge-shaped mound is over 50 m. long and stands nearly 4 m. high. At the north end is a deep forecourt between two rounded horns, and in the back of the forecourt is an H-shaped setting of stones, perhaps the remains of a portal dolment. The ditch, which seems to define the mound, is a product of reconstruction works after the 1930s excavations.

Three chambers, heavily restored, open into the mound from its long sides, while a fourth (roofless) chamber opens from the narrow southern end. The remains of about thirty people were found in the burial chambers.

A low round barrowt is visible in the ploughed field to the west of the long barrow.

J. Berry, 'Belas Knap Long Barrow Gloucestershire: Report of the Excavations of 1930', TBGAS 52 (1930), 123–50.

Blackpool Bridge, Forest of Dean, Gloucestershire Ancient road

SO 653087. Minor road N off B4431, beyond former railway bridge.

Paved road with curb edging and marks of wheeled transport. Traditionally thought Roman, it is now thought to be associated with the later Forest of Dean ironworking industry.

B. Walters, The Archaeology and History of Ancient Dean and the Wye Valley (Thirnhill Press, 1992).

Brackenbury Ditches, Wotton-under-Edge, Gloucestershire Iron Age hillfortt

ST 747948. NE of B4060 between Wotton-under-Edge and North Nibley, best approached by footpath from the N, parking in North Nibley and walking along the Cotswold Way past the Tyndale Monument.

Now shrouded in trees, Brackenbury Ditches is one of the best-preserved hillforts on the Cotswolds. Set on a small spur, it commanded extensive views over the Vale of Berkeley. Construction probably began about 650 BC.

In plan Brackenbury is D-shaped, with two lines of substantial ramparts forming the flat face running across the neck of the spur. The remainder of the outline is formed by a single line of ramparts around the spur edge. There is an entrance gap about 6 m. wide towards the south end.

E. Lindley, 'Brackenbury Ditches', TBGAS 76 (1957), 150–6.

Chedworth, Gloucestershire Roman villa ★

SP 053134. Accessible via minor road W off A429 (Fosse Way) at Fossebridge (signposted) towards Yanworth. National Trust; restricted opening. Admission charge. Site museum. Figure 112.

Chedworth Roman villa was discovered and excavated in 1864, since when it has been on display. It stands in a wooded coomb with a natural spring at its head. The house, started around 120, evolved into an opulent C4 mansion. The buildings occupy three sides of a courtyard. The principal range contains the dining room (*triclinium*), living rooms, and a bath-suite. The ante-room to the *triclinium* had a fine mosaic floor of which three panels survive, showing the seasons spring, summer, and winter. The service rooms on the south side include a latrine and possibly an estate office.

In the north-west corner is the *nymphaeum*†, a small shrine with an octagonal pool, which housed the spring and water supply to the villa. Two rim fragments were inscribed with the Christian chi-rho symbol.

The north wing had a bath-suite later converted to a *laconicum*†

▼ **Fig. 112.** Part of a floor mosaic showing the figure of Winter, Chedworth Roman villa, Gloucestershire (Photograph: National Trust)

with cold plunges. The fourth side was enclosed originally by a wall and later a colonnade with an elaborate entrance.

About 800 m. south-east of the villa is a small square temple overlooking the river Coln. A hunting relief from this structure is in the site museum.

R. Goodburn, The Roman Villa, Chedworth (The National Trust, 1972) (Site Guidebook).

Cirencester (*Corinium Dobunnorum*), Gloucestershire Roman *civitas*† capital and medieval market town

SP 0202. 11 km. SE of Cheltenham and 25 km. W of Oxford. Signposted. Corinium Museum, Park St; restricted opening. Admission charge. The amphitheatre (English Heritage) has open access.

A C1 fort here developed into the second largest town in Roman Britain. It is set on five important roads including the Fosse Way and Ermine Street, and a river crossing. The fort was dismantled around AD 75 and the town expanded, becoming the tribal administrative centre for the *Dobunni*. A grid of streets was laid out, many still perpetuated in the modern street system, for example Lewis Lane and Watermoor Road. The town had all the standard Roman public buildings, a forum† and basilica†, temple and amphitheatre, as well as a possible theatre and a *macellum*†. Shops and town houses have been excavated as well as a cemetery beyond the town walls.

Little of the Roman town is now visible. A section of C3 town wall is preserved in the Abbey Gardens. The defences are visible as a bank along the east side of the town, beside Beeches Road and City Bank. North of London Road a stretch has been conserved, reached via the housing estate of Corinium Gate opposite the end of Beeches Road. The apse of the basilica is marked out in a cul-de-sac, which opens off the Avenue opposite Tower Street and the forum is underneath and east of Tower Street.

The amphitheatre (signposted from the bypass on the south-east part of the town) has banks standing 7.6 m. high above the arena floor.

Immediately north of Cirencester two substantial round barrows† (Tar Barrows), visible north of the A433, are perhaps Roman burial mounds.

The medieval town was mainly focused in the north-east quarter of the earlier town. Rising above the long, broad Market Place is the bell-tower of St John's, one of England's finest Perpendicular churches (C15 and early C16). Note especially the three-storey south porch of about 1490 and the tall nave of 1516–30. Fittings include a stone pulpit with open tracery of the C15, the lower part of a rood screen† of about 1530, and some medieval glass.

At the east end of Thomas Street is St Thomas's Hospital, an almshouse founded in 1483 for four impoverished weavers. Nearby, in Spitalgate Lane, is St John's Hospital and Chantry, founded in 1133 by Henry I as a place of rest for travellers and a home for the destitute. What survives is part of its arcaded hall. While nothing of the main body of Cirencester Abbey remains, its C12 north gateway stands beside the A417 on the town edge.

T. Darvill and C. Gerrard, Cirencester: Town and Landscape (Cotswold Archaeological Trust, 1994).

Cleeve Hill, Cheltenham, Gloucestershire Iron Age hillfort† and linear boundary

SO 985255. On open common land partly used as a golf course 5 km. NE of Cheltenham and 4 km. SW of Winchcombe. Public footpaths cross the Common.

Cleeve Hill is the highest point on the Cotswold hills at about 300 m. above sea level. The steep western face is most impressive, although heavily quarried from medieval times onwards.

Cleeve Camp, an Iron Age hillfort perched right on the escarpment edge, is itself about half quarried away (SO 985254). Two ramparts can be seen, the outer with a golf green cut into it, and ditches over 10 m. wide.

To the north is a series of dispersed, smaller settlements broadly contemporary to the hillfort. The most obvious is a small roughly circular earthwork enclosure, known as **The Ring** (SO 985265).

Between the hillfort and the dispersed settlement is a **linear boundary**† (SO 985263), which follows a sinuous course. As with other cross-ridge dykes it starts on the edge of a steep slope. The preserved section runs for 0.5 km. and has a bank 4.5 m. wide and 0.9 m. high with a ditch to the south (down-slope) side.

RCHME, Ancient and Historical Monuments in the County of Gloucester, vol. i: Iron Age and Romano-British Monuments in the Gloucestershire Cotswolds (HMSO, 1976), 106–9.

Combe Gibbet, Inkpen Beacon, West Berkshire Neolithic long barrow†

SU 365621. 7 km. SE of Hungerford. Beside bridleway following the Berkshire Ridgeway (Wayfarer's Walk) between Walbury Hill and Inkpen Hill. Parking at viewpoint on Walbury Hill.

Overlooking the Kennet valley, this magnificently preserved long barrow stands on the edge of the Berkshire downs. The mound is 61 m. long, 23 m. wide, and 2 m. high. Flanking ditches run either side.

To the south-east (SU 374617) is **Walbury Hillfort**, an Iron Age enclosure covering 33 ha. and incorporating the highest chalk hill in England (297 m. above sea level). The fort is trapezoidal, bounded by a single bank and ditch, with entrances to the south-east and north-west.

P. Ashbee, The Earthen Long Barrow in Britain, 2nd edn (Geo Books, 1984).

Coughton Court, Warwickshire Late medieval country house

SP 080604. 3 km. N of Alcester on A435. National Trust; restricted opening. Admission charge.

Rising at the centre of the main façade is a three-storeyed, turreted gatehouse. It was built soon after 1518 by Sir George Throckmorton, Under Treasurer of England, and was unusual in being integrated with the wings to either side (although the façades you see today are of the 1780s). It is a fine example of the so-called prodigy buildings built by the richest and most intellectually advanced men. Mullioned turret and oriel windows running across the first and second storeys create a wall-of-glass effect from the exterior and light and airy chambers within.

It was here that on the night of 5 November 1605 a group, which included the wives of the conspirators, gathered to hear the result of the Gunpowder Plot. It dispersed when news of the Plot's miscarriage arrived.

Coughton Court (The National Trust, 1979) (Site Guidebook).

Crickley Hill, Gloucestershire Neolithic enclosures, long mound, and Iron Age hillfort† ★★

SO 928161. 6 km. S of Cheltenham, within the Crickley Hill Country Park. Access is from B4070 near the Air Balloon roundabout. National Trust and Gloucestershire County Council.

This multi-phase hilltop enclosure was used intermittently from about 4000 BC down to the early centuries of the first millennium AD. The hilltop spur has stunning views across the Severn valley. Excavations from 1969 to 1993 have revealed some of its complex history.

The earliest occupation was Neolithic with a causewayed enclosure† (4000 BC), later remodelled as a defended settlement. The ramparts of this second phase of Neolithic enclosure can be seen partly reconstructed in the middle of the hilltop: a low bank and slight traces of the ditch.

Following an attack on the enclosure, the site was abandoned, and not resettled until about 650 BC. There is slight evidence for Beaker occupation as a long mound of earth was built across the line of the earlier boundary, with its western end set over what appears to have been a small shrine or ceremonial focus. The long mound can be traced for about 100 m. on the ground towards the western end of the hilltop and running along the bottom of a shallow valley.

In the C7 BC the first of a succession of hillforts was built. The remains of these still survive extremely well as a massive bank and ditch cutting off the spur towards the eastern end of the hilltop. A wooden observation platform has been built over the rampart beside the original main entrance. At its most impressive in the C4 BC the defences comprised a massive stone wall with a vertical outer face and perhaps walkways along the top. Outside was a deep flat-bottomed rock-cut ditch. The main entrance had stout wooden gates and a defended passage. The fort was abandoned in the C3 BC.

Several other sites can be seen from Crickley Hill, including the Neolithic settlement site on **The Peak** (SO 925149) and the Bronze Age barrow cemetery in **Emma's Grove** (SO 935159). Some late Iron Age burials at **Barrow Wake** lay on the brow of the hill to the south.

P. Dixon, Crickley Hill, vol. i: The Hillfort Defences (University of Nottingham, 1994).

Deerhurst, Gloucestershire Saxon churches ★★

SO 869298. 4 km. SW of Tewkesbury. Figure 113.

St Mary's is one of the largest Saxon churches in England, second only to Brixworth (Northamptonshire). Already by 804 there was a minster at Deerhurst, a church with priests who went out to spread the Gospel. The nave, the lower part of the west porch, and the two pairs of two-storey porticus (side chapels) were standing by the C9. Of the C10, when the

▼ **Fig. 113.** Odda's chapel, Deerhurst, Gloucestershire (Photograph: Paul Stamper)

church saw rebuilding after Viking incursions in the region, are the upper storeys of the west tower, the ruined chancel with its elongated polygonal apse, and some of the elaborate interior arched openings. The west porch, originally two-storeyed, had a third floor added about the C9, with a double, triangular-headed window looking into the nave. Lower down is an asymmetrically placed door of similar date, presumably leading to a wooden gallery. Fittings include a possibly C9 font, and various pieces of Anglo-Saxon sculpture.

Close to St Mary's is Priory House (not open to the public, but visible), a mainly C14 building.

About 200 m. south-west of St Mary's is another Saxon church, **St Odda's Chapel** (English Heritage), a relatively simple structure of nave and chancel attached to one end of a farmhouse. An inscription records that Earl Odda ordered the chapel to be built for the soul of his brother Aelfric in 1056—the only Anglo-Saxon structure with an inscribed date. It fell into disuse in the mid-C16 at the Reformation.

P. Rahtz et al., St Mary's Church, Deerhurst *(Boydell & Brewer, 1997).*

Eton, Windsor and Maidenhead Medieval college

SU 967779. The College is on the NE edge of Windsor, at N end of Eton High Street.

Eton College was founded in 1440 by Henry VI. A magnificent church was to be constructed, where masses could be said for the soul of the founder and to which pilgrims would journey. Henry's intention was that services would be led by a college of clerics, with prayers augmented by twenty-five almsmen and twenty-five scholars. While the number of almsmen soon fell, that of scholars rose, and in time Eton became England's leading public school.

In the event, only the choir of Henry's church was built, now the school chapel. It is lit by huge Perpendicular windows; the glass is modern, as is the roof. The important wall paintings above the stalls of 1479–88 show scenes from the miracles of the Virgin. The college buildings, of red brick with blue diaper patterning, are grouped around two courtyards. The School Yard is entered via a range dating to 1689–91 which houses Upper School. The chapel is to the right, Lower School to the left. Opposite is a range rebuilt in the early C16 with central tower with octagonal turrets and two-storey oriel. Its archway leads to the cloisters where the clerical fellows lived. Their lower, brick part is C15, the ashlar top storey of 1725–9.

Most evocative are the schoolrooms and, above Lower School, Long Chamber. Now partitioned, this once slept all seventy scholars.

N. Pevsner, The Buildings of England: Buckinghamshire *(Penguin, 1960), 116–31.*

▲ **Fig. 114.** Ewelme church, Oxfordshire (Photograph: Paul Stamper)

Ewelme, Oxfordshire Late medieval church, almshouse, and school

SU 646914. 8 km. NE of Wallingford. Figure 114.

This outstanding group of early brick buildings, of 1437–50, bears witness to the piety of Alice Chaucer, the celebrated writer's granddaughter, and her husband William de la Pole, earl of Suffolk. Not only did they rebuild the church (retaining only the C14 tower) in the Perpendicular style—Alice's alabaster effigy is within—but close by they erected almshouses and a school. The almshouses are arranged college-style around a courtyard, and thirteen poor men had board and lodging. Supervision was by two chaplains, one of whom taught grammar in the nearby two-storey school.

J. A. A. Goodall, God's House at Ewelme *(Ashgate, 2001)*

Fairford, Gloucestershire Medieval church

SP 1501. On the A417 14 km. E of Cirencester. Figure 115.

Fairford's prosperity came from the late medieval wool and cloth trades. St Mary's was rebuilt about 1480 by John Tame, a wool merchant, and completed by his son. Externally it has rich late Perpendicular stonework, inset with sculptures including a hand holding a scourge, a griffin, Christ, and armorials.

Inside, too, is fine carved work—at the east end a triple *sedilia*†, angel corbels, canopies, and niches for rood sculptures, an octagonal

▲ **Fig. 115.** Fairford, Gloucestershire (Photograph: Paul Stamper)

font (C15)—as well as wall paintings and woodwork including choir and parclose screens, stalls with misericords†, a Holy Table of 1626, and tombs and brasses including that of Sir Edmund Tame (d. 1534) and his wives. The window glass was painted by Flemish craftsmen.

S. Brown, Life, Death and Art: The Medieval Stained Glass of Fairford Parish Church *(Sutton Publishing, 1998)*.

Fosse Way, Gloucestershire/Warwickshire Roman road

A major Roman road running from Exeter to Lincoln, now followed by the A303, A37, A367, A433, A429, and various minor roads and tracks.

By around AD 47 the Romans had occupied an area south and east of a line from the Severn to the Humber. A putative frontier zone linked the two rivers and extended beyond into the south-west. The Fosse Way was constructed along the frontier zone and parts of this survive. A good stretch passes through CIRENCESTER, forming the county boundary for 11 km. Lengths of *agger*† off the modern road (A429) are visible at Stow-on-the-Wold (SP 1899 2543), and in the parish of Batsford (NNE from SP 205328).

I. Margary, Roman Roads in Britain *(John Baker, 1973)*.

Gloucester (*Colonia Nervia Glevensium*),

Gloucestershire Roman *colonia*† and medieval cathedral city

Centred SO 830180. The City Museum, Brunswick Road, holds many finds from excavations. Figure 116.

Gloucester, one of the four *colonia* established in Britain, was founded AD 96–8 (see also LINCOLN, COLCHESTER, and YORK). Parts of several public buildings have been investigated, including the forum† basilica†. Although little of the Roman defences remain, much of the circuit, along with the main roads, is preserved in the present street pattern. The gates of the Roman town lie approximately in the same places as the later medieval north, south, east, and west gates. Remains of the Roman walls are only visible in three places, at the east gate outside Boots' store (1)

▼ **Fig. 116.** Gloucester: modern street plan showing the location of the Roman defences and other remains.

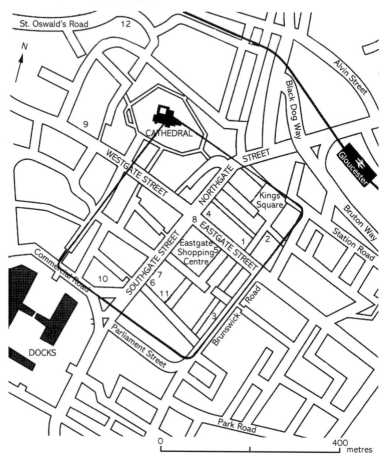

visible from the street and via an underground chamber; below the pavement in King's Walk shopping precinct (**2**) and in the City Museum in Brunswick Street (**3**). Other remains include fragments of mosaic in the National Westminster Bank, Eastgate Street (**4**) and in Eastgate Market Hall (**5**) and the crypt of the Friends' Meeting House, Crypt Lane (**6**). Little is known about the cemeteries although a large burial ground lies to the north and military tombstones have been found at Wotton.

Gloucester's cathedral was rebuilt after the Norman Conquest, and most of the church consecrated in 1100 survives today. Major rebuilding took place after the murdered Edward II was buried here in 1327 as his relics attracted visitors—and money. This work is in the Perpendicular style. Especially important are the fan-vaulted monastic cloisters (1350s–1412), the east window of fourteen lights (1350), and the crossing tower (mid-C15).

St Mary's Gateway, leading into the precinct, is C13. In the city beyond, churches of note include St Mary de Crypt (**7**) (Southgate Street), largely rebuilt in the late C14 by Llanthony Priory; St Michael's (**8**) (Eastgate Street), of which the tower of about 1465 survives from the medieval church; and St Nicholas's (**9**) (Lower Westgate Street), whose west tower is early C15.

The Blackfriars (**10**), off Southgate Street, is an exceptionally complete friary (English Heritage). The ruins of the Greyfriars (**11**) lie in the south-east quarter of the city, while off Lower Westgate Street is part of the church of St Oswald's Priory (**12**), founded in the early C10 by Aethelflaeda, daughter of Alfred the Great; the large stone blocks in the upper part of the wall are part of her church.

Among the city's surviving domestic buildings see the New Inn (**13**) in Northgate Street, built about 1450 by Gloucester Abbey for poorer pilgrims. The galleried courtyard is typical of medieval inns.

D. Verey, The Buildings of England. Gloucestershire: The Vale and the Forest of Dean *(Penguin, 1970), 198–254.*

Great Coxwell, Oxfordshire Medieval barn

SU 269940. 3 km. SW of Faringdon. National Trust. Figure 117.

Beaulieu Abbey, Hampshire, was given the Oxfordshire manor of Great Coxwell by King John in 1204. About 1246, below the fields sloping up to Badbury's ancient hillfort†, the Cistercians† constructed a massive limestone barn for grain crops, its walls pierced with holes to ventilate and cool the stored produce. It has single projecting cart bays to either side, the larger incorporating what was probably an office for the farm bailiff while the other has nesting boxes for doves. The roof is of Cotswold stone slates, and is of huge weight. Inside, massive timber aisle posts

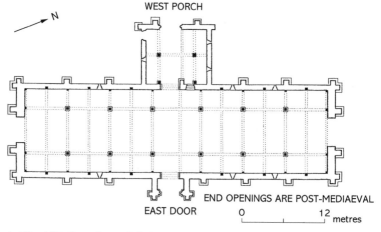

WEST PORCH

END OPENINGS ARE POST-MEDIAEVAL

EAST DOOR

0   12 metres

▲ **Fig. 117.** Great Coxwell, Oxfordshire (after Horn & Born)

alternate with a form of base crucks of the type to be seen at BRADFORD-ON-AVON.

Great Coxwell's other buildings, at the Dissolution a hall, chambers, and chapel, have been lost.

F. Charles, The Great Barn of Bredon (Oxbow Books, 1997), 14–16.

Great Witcombe, Gloucestershire Roman villa

SO 899143. 8 km. SE of Gloucester, off A417 at the base of Crickley Hill. Take a single-track road signposted for Great Witcombe. Villa remains 300 m. beyond car park. English Heritage. Figure 118.

The Roman villa discovered here in 1818 has some unusual architectural features. The house, built around three sides of a courtyard and land-scaped into a slope, looks out towards the Cotswold scarp. Unstable ground necessitated heavy buttressing of what was a two-floored build-ing. Most of the remains are mid-C3. The dominant feature is an octagonal room in the middle, interpreted as a dining room. The east wing contained a kitchen with an oven and a latrine whilst the west wing largely comprised a bath-suite. Three niches and a small central cistern in Room 1 in the west wing have been attributed a ritual use. The fragmentary surviving mosaics show an aquatic theme with fish and geometric patterns. These are preserved under modern buildings with part of the hypocaust system† (open only on certain days).

P. Leach, Great Witcombe Roman Villa, Gloucestershire, British Archaeological Reports British Series 266 (1998).

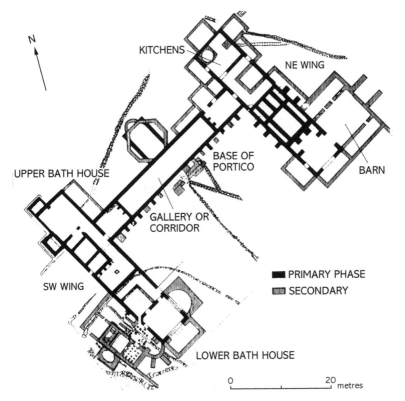

▲ **Fig. 118.** Plan of Great Witcombe Roman villa, Gloucestershire (after McWhirr)

Grim's Ditch, Oxfordshire Prehistoric linear earthwork†

SU 495839 to SU 418842. Berkshire/Oxfordshire county boundary 3 km. SW of Chilton, W of A34(T).

The rolling Berkshire downs south-east of Wantage preserve some fine stretches of linear earthwork, many known as Grim's Ditch. Most follow the edge of the downs, but with abrupt changes in direction, which suggest not all are contemporary. Where excavated, the ditch is generally V-shaped in profile and about 1.5 m. deep. One good section south-west of Chilton comprises a simple bank and ditch which twists and turns along the edge of the downs. Several Bronze Age barrows and field-banks lie on or very near the earthwork. Another well preserved section is near **Aldworth** (SU 546785 to SU 570792). Investigations of these meandering earthworks, sometimes called 'ranch boundaries', show a late Bronze Age or Iron Age date (mainly C8–C5 BC), a time when large tracts of downland were parcelled up for agriculture or pasture.

About 10 km. to the north of Grim's Ditch is the later Iron Age *oppidum*† of Dyke Hills just outside Dorchester on Thames (SU 574933). Accessible by footpath leading southwards from the modern town, there is a spectacular earthwork. It defines one side of a roughly rectangular promontory, edged on a further two sides by the river Thames, and on the fourth side by the river Thame. This was probably the precursor of the Roman town of Dorchester.

S. Ford, 'Fieldwork and Excavation on the Berkshire Grim's Ditch', Oxoniensia, 47 (1982), 13–36; D. Miles, 'Iron Age and Roman Dorchester', Arch J, 135 (1978), 288–9.

Haresfield Beacon, Little Haresfield, Gloucestershire   Iron Age hillfort†

SO 825090. 10 km. S of Gloucester, 5 km. NW of Stroud, via a partly signposted lane between Haresfield and Edge that bisects the site. National Trust. Figure 119.

Haresfield Beacon projects south-westwards from the Cotswold escarpment with extensive views into the Severn valley.

The western part of the hill, **Ring Hill**, has a single rampart, easily traceable on the ground. The main circuit lies south-west of the lane through the site and encloses about 4 ha. The boundary comprises a simple bank with no external ditch. There are five gaps; the two on the north and one to the south-east are probably original entrances.

East of the road are **The Bulwarks** (SO 829091), a massive bank and ditch which cuts off the spur on which Ring Hill is set.

RCHME, Ancient and Historical Monuments in the County of Gloucester, vol. i: Iron Age and Romano-British Monuments in the Gloucestershire Cotswolds (HMSO, 1976), 62–4.

Hetty Pegler's Tump, Uley, Gloucestershire   Neolithic long barrow†   ★

SO 790000. W of B4066 between Stroud and Uley. Signposted with some roadside parking. Approached by marked footpath. English Heritage.

The name of this fine long barrow comes from Henry Pegler, and his wife Hester, who owned the site in the C17 AD.

Built in the Cotswold–Severn tradition, the mound is trapezoidal, 36.5 m. long by 25.9 m. wide, and orientated roughly east to west. Two horns flank the narrow east forecourt, in the back of which is the chamber entrance. Once under the massive portal stone it is possible to stand up in the central passage. On the south are two side chambers, but two to the north have been blocked up for safety. Another chamber lies at the passage end.

Being inside the dark chamber with only a candle makes it easy to imagine a ceremony or burial ritual here 6,000 years ago. While in the

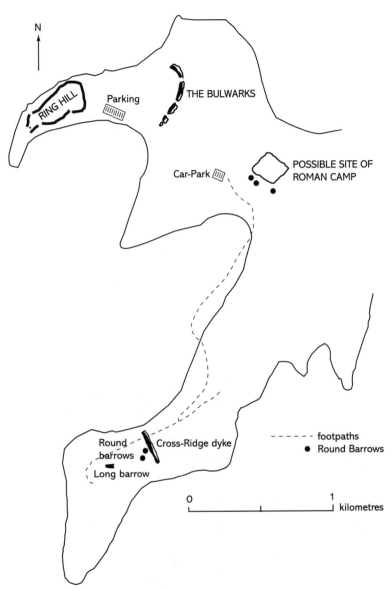

▲ **Fig. 119.** Plan showing the archaeological sites around Haresfield and Randwick, Gloucestershire (after RCHM(E))

chamber, notice the roof construction, the use of dry-stone walling to fill the gaps between the orthostats† forming the chamber walls, and consider the difficulties of moving corpses about in the confined space. When it was excavated in 1821 at least fifteen disarticulated skeletons were found, and a further eight or nine in 1854.

E. Clifford, 'Hetty Pegler's Tump', Antiquity, 40 (1966), 129–32.

Kempley, Gloucestershire Medieval church with wall paintings ★

SO 670312. On minor roads 7 km. NE of Ross-on-Wye. English Heritage; restricted opening. Figure 120.

Kempley's isolated church of St Mary's is an exceptional survival, its interior providing a wonderful idea of the vibrant, painted church interiors which before the Reformation were commonplace. The nave and vaulted chancel are generally considered to be of about 1110–25. Of like date is the south door with its original C12 ironwork and its surround, which includes a tympanum carved with the Tree of Life. The squat west tower is of about 1276.

The wall paintings came to light in 1872, having been whitewashed over in the mid-C16 Reformation. In the chancel are frescos dated to 1130–40. In the nave are other tempera paintings including a C14 scheme depicting the ten stages of man. Over the chancel arch is a fresco chequer pattern, probably C12.

▼ **Fig. 120.** Kempley, Gloucestershire, looking east to the chancel arch (Photograph: Paul Stamper)

Unseen above the ceiling of the nave, inserted in 1670–1, is Kempley's second exceptional feature, its roof of trussed rafter construction. Tree-ring dating placed it between 1120 and 1142. One other point of note is that the churchyard is circular, intimating its possible antiquity, going back to the earliest days of Christianity or before. To date, however, there has been little scientific testing of this theory, and certainly not at Kempley.

B. Morley, 'The Nave Roof of the Church of St. Mary, Kempley, Gloucestershire', Ant J, 65 (1985), 101–11.

Kingston Lisle, Oxfordshire   Roman barrow

SU 328882. On E side of minor road. 1 km. NNE from Kingston Lisle.

The form and position of this barrow suggest that it is of Roman date.

R. Collingwood and I. Richmond, The Archaeology of Roman Britain (Methuen, 1969).

Lambourn Seven Barrows, Lambourn, West Berkshire   Neolithic and Bronze Age barrow cemetery

SU 323834. 3.5 km. N of Lambourn, W of B4001. Approached by minor road running W from B4001 at SU 331810 through to B4507 at SU 325871. The barrows lie either side of the minor road near Sevenbarrows House. Figure 121.

In total this extensive barrow cemetery contains over forty mounds in two rows. Only those north of the road are accessible and visible.

Several kinds of round barrow† are represented: saucer, disc, bowl, and bell barrows. Some have been excavated. The more distinctive include Barrow 38, a saucer barrow with a small low mound. Barrow 10 comprises two bowl barrows within a single oval ditch. Barrows 11 and 12 are also bowl barrows, number 13 a disc barrow less than 0.5 m. high, 20 m. in diameter and enclosed within a ditch about 30 m. in diameter. Barrow 4 is another disc barrow, numbers 5, 6, and 7 bowl barrows, and number 8 another double bowl barrow enclosed by a single ditch. Barrow 9 is again a bowl barrow; excavations revealed a sarsen† stone cist† containing a collared urn and the cremated remains of a woman.

The best bell barrow is number 18, partly covered by trees beside the road. Excavations revealed a sarsen stone cist containing a cremation burial accompanied by a bronze awl and a jet pendant.

A long barrow† lies to the north-west at the south end of **Wescot Wood** (SU 323834). Excavations found a rough stone chamber-like feature towards the east end with a female burial, bones from various other individuals, and a necklace of dog whelk shells.

H. Case, 'The Lambourn Seven Barrows', BAJ 55 (1956–7), 15–31

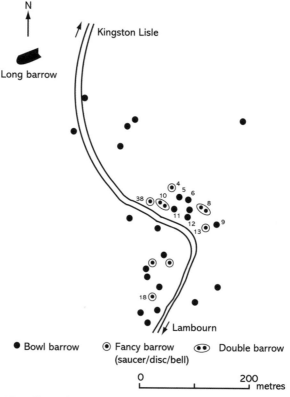

▲ **Fig. 121.** Plan of the barrow cemetery at Lambourn Seven Barrows, Lambourn, Berkshire (after Case)

Long Stone, Minchinhampton, Gloucestershire Neolithic

standing stone†

ST 884999. 2 km. E of Minchinhampton village N of road to Avening at Hampton Fields. Private ownership: visible from road.

One of several standing stones on the Cotswolds which were probably markers for Bronze Age cemeteries. This example, of local limestone, is over 2.1 m. tall. It is said that when the stone hears the village clock strike midnight it dances. A second stone can be seen in the field boundary to the west.

T. Darvill, Prehistoric Gloucestershire *(Alan Sutton and Gloucestershire County Library, 1987), 109–10.*

Long Stone, Staunton, Forest of Dean,
Gloucestershire Neolithic standing stone†

SO 559120. 1 km. E of Staunton village immediately N of A4136 Gloucester to Monmouth road.

A pillar of local sandstone over 2.5 m. high.

C. Hart, Archaeology in Dean *(Gloucester: privately published, 1967).*

Lydney Park, Gloucestershire Iron Age hillfort† and Roman temple

SO 616027. The Roman remains lie in Lydney Park, a private deer park. The entrance is on the A48 between Lydney and Aylburton. Open days between April and June. Museum.

Excavations 1928–9 by Sir Mortimer Wheeler on a promontory where Roman remains were known discovered a hillfort constructed during the C1 BC. Subsequent Roman occupation was probably linked with iron-working, and two mines have been found, one of which can still be accessed. The site is famous for its wealthy religious complex, built in the C4 and comprising a temple with guest house and a detached bath-suite. The temple, parts of which still remain, was set within a *temenos*†, and entered via a flight of steps. It originally had ten chapels and mosaic floors (no longer surviving), one of which carried a legend dedicating it to the Celtic god Nodens, a local deity connected with healing, sun, and water. Many votive offerings were found, including bronze dogs and models of limbs suggesting a healing cult.

R. and T. Wheeler, Report on the Excavation of the Prehistoric, Roman, and Post-Roman Site in Lydney Park, Gloucestershire, *Reports of the Research Committee of the Society of Antiquaries of London 9 (1932).*

Northleach, Gloucestershire Late medieval church

SP 112147. Close to the intersection of A429 from Cirencester, 14 km. to the SW, and A40 from Cheltenham, 18 km. to the NW.

The church of St Peter and St Paul stands on a rise close to the market place in this Cotswold town. Wealth from the late medieval woollen and cloth industries facilitated the rebuilding of the church on such a scale and with such high craftsmanship in the C15. The four-stage tower, topped by battlements, was probably completed soon after 1400. Other architectural elements include the fine south porch (early C15) and the aisled nave rebuilt about 1450. Internally there is a stunning collection of wool merchants' brasses.

D. Mclees, 'Northleach', Arch J, *145 (Supplement) (1988), 41–3.*

North Leigh, Oxfordshire Roman villa

SP 397154. 3 km. N of North Leigh, 16 km. W of Oxford off A4095. Pedestrian access only via trackway (about ten minutes). English Heritage. Figure 122.

A substantial C4 courtyard villa on a west-facing slope overlooking the river Evenlode, excavated in 1813–17 and several times in the C20. The ground plan of two of the original three wings is visible. A geometric mosaic belonging to the Cirencester mosaic school can be viewed under cover. Aerial photography has located further buildings.

P. Ellis, 'North Leigh Roman Villa, Oxfordshire: A Report on Excavation and Record-ing in the 1970s', Britannia, 30 (1998), 199–245.

▼ **Fig. 122.** Plan of the Roman villa at North Leigh, Oxfordshire (after Wilson)

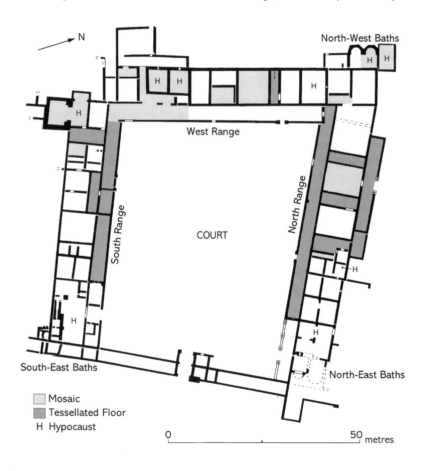

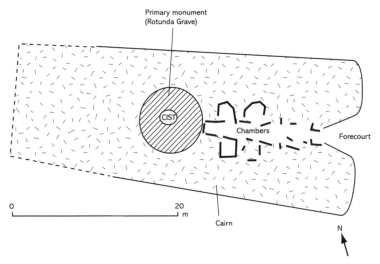

Primary monument
(Rotunda Grave)

▲ **Fig. 123.** Plan of the Notgrove long barrow, Gloucestershire (after Clifford)

Notgrove Long Barrow, Gloucestershire Neolithic long barrow†

SP 096211. 7 km. E of Andoversford, 6 km. W of Bourton-on-the-Water. Situated immediately S of B4068 (formerly A436) NW of Notgrove village. English Heritage. Figure 123.

Excavated in 1934–5 this site became a favourite long barrow to visit. However, in 1974, following deterioration, the site was covered with soil to protect it. The result is a strange-looking long barrow.

The barrow is a typical Cotswold–Severn example, with a neat trapezoidal mound 48 m. long by 24 m. wide at the east end. A forecourt flanked by small horns† opened to the east, in the back of which was the entrance to a central passage giving access to four side chambers and a small end chamber. Excavations yielded the remains of at least six adults in the chambers, together with fragmentary remains of children.

Below the long barrow was an earlier simple bowl barrow or rotunda grave with a central cist† containing a single adult male.

E. Clifford, 'Notgrove Long Barrow, Gloucestershire', Archaeologia, *86 (1936), 119–61.*

Nympsfield Long Barrow, Gloucestershire Neolithic long barrow†

SO 795014. Within Coaley Peak Country Park on the B4066 between Stroud and Dursley. 6 km. from Stroud. English Heritage and Gloucestershire County Council.

Nympsfield Long Barrow is similar in plan and situation to the nearby

HETTY PEGLER'S TUMP, but smaller and with only one pair of side chambers. The absence of capstones†, removed long ago, allows an appreciation of the layout and design of the chambers.

The plan is trapezoidal, 27 m. long and 18 m. wide. Originally it would have been much higher at the east end. The forecourt faces east, and gives access to a central passage leading to a pair of side chambers and a small end chamber. Constricting stones subdivide the passage and restrict access to the chambers. Excavations recovered the remains of between twenty and thirty individuals, together with pottery and flint weapons. In the forecourt were the remains of hearths and a small pit suggesting funerary rituals had taken place here.

2.4 km. north is another long barrow: **The Toots**, on Selsey Common (SO 827031). This has not been excavated, but is superficially similar to NYMPSFIELD and HETTY PEGLER'S TUMP.

A fine late Neolithic round barrow† known as **The Soldier's Grave** (SO 794015) lies near Nympsfield Long Barrow, in woodland behind the public lavatories at the northern end of Coaley Peak Country Park. This barrow is 17 m. in diameter and in its centre (marked by a hollow) excavations in 1936 revealed a boat-shaped cist† containing the remains of at least twenty-eight individuals.

A. Saville, 'Further Excavations at the Nympsfield Chambered Tomb', PPS 45 (1979), 53–92.

Oxford, Oxfordshire   Medieval city and university   ★

SP 5405. E of the river Thames near its confluence with the river Cherwell, 90 km. W of London S of M40.

Oxford had a monastery from at least the C8. It became a riverside *burh*† about AD 900, part of the West Saxons' scheme of national defence. The grid-plan layout of its streets originated at that time; St Michael's Church on Cornmarket, the tower of which with its balustered belfry openings is mid-C11, stands at what was the north gate into the town; one of its upper doorways could have led onto the town's wall walk. The later C13 town walls with semicircular bastions survive best along their eastern line, in New College gardens and alongside Merton Field. In 1071 Robert D'Oilly erected a castle on the west edge of the town, and its earth motte† looms over New Road. Within the adjoining late C18 prison, but visible from the encircling streets (which mark the line of the bailey†), is St George's Tower, probably added in 1074. Several medieval parish churches survive, as does the priory church of St Frideswide (now the chapel of Christ Church), which in 1546 became a cathedral. Begun in the later C12, it is one of the most remarkable Augustinian† churches to survive.

Oxford's origins as a place of learning began with the movement here in 1167 of English scholars expelled from the University of Paris. At first, students boarded in lodgings, later in halls supervised by masters. Tackley's Inn, behind 106–7 High Street, is an early C14 example. In the C13 and C14 colleges developed, some devoted to the education of the secular clergy and civil servants, while others were founded by individual monastic orders to provide a place of study for its members. St John's College, for instance, was founded in 1437 for Cistercians†, and architecturally this is the finest of the surviving monastic colleges. Others include Worcester (originally Gloucester) College, founded in the late C13 by the Benedictines†, and Trinity (originally Durham) College, set up about 1286 for Benedictines from the Northern Province.

Of the non-monastic foundations Merton gives the best impression of a medieval college. Behind its chapel is the C14 Mob Quad (the origin of the name is unknown), two sides of which are formed by a library, England's oldest and containing treasures including Chaucer's astrolabe.

J. Steane, Oxfordshire (Pimlico, 1996).

Randwick Long Barrow, Randwick, Gloucestershire Neolithic long barrow, Bronze Age round barrows, and cross-ridge dyke

SO 825069. 3 km. NW of Stroud, W of A4173. Approached by minor road from Whiteshill to Edge, turning W at Scottsquar towards Haresfield. Car park at SO 833087, from where footpaths lead S into Standish Wood. National Trust. (Fig. 119.)

This rectangular, wooded promontory overlooking the Severn valley and the river Frome, contains a range of well-preserved early prehistoric monuments.

Starting at the north end, a low 180 m. long cross-ridge dyke runs across the neck of the promontory. Although traditionally dated to the Iron Age, many such dykes have been shown to be Neolithic or Bronze Age in origin, defining sacred or ceremonial areas. This is exactly the case at Randwick. West of the dyke is a pair of ditched bowl barrows. Each is 12 m. in diameter, and 0.6 m. high.

Further west still is a long barrow† (SO 825069) constructed in the Cotswold–Severn tradition. About 56 m. long by 26 m. wide it stands 4 m. high at the north-east end. Excavations in 1883 found a forecourt here giving access to a chamber of one cell containing disarticulated human remains. Additional burials were found adjacent to the barrow on the south-west side.

G. Witts, 'The Randwick Long Barrow', PCNFC 8 (1883), 156–60.

The Ridgeway, Berkshire Downs, Oxfordshire Prehistoric and later trackway.

SU 567812 Near Streatley (Berkshire) to SU 110623 near Alton Priors (Wiltshire). Mainly bridleway or public footpath, in places waymarked, with occasional sections on minor roads and tracks.

Winding its way along the northern edge of the rolling Berkshire downs is an ancient track known as the Ridgeway, part of the great Icknield Way that ran from near King's Lynn in East Anglia to Salisbury plain in Wiltshire. Almost certainly it has been used since prehistoric times.

A good stretch is near UFFINGTON CASTLE (SU 297864), where there are panoramic views over the upper Thames valley and the Vale of the White Horse.

The wide track that forms the Ridgeway for much of its course today was created in the C18 AD, when low banks were erected on either side to preserve the right of way from encroachment by ploughing; the breadth was fixed at 1 chain (20.11 m.). At that time, it was used to move animals 'on the hoof' from west-country pastures to the markets of London and surrounding towns.

O. Crawford, Archaeology in the Field *(Phoenix House, 1953), 79–80.*

Rollright Stones, Little Rollright, Oxfordshire Neolithic

stone circle†, standing stone†, and portal dolmen† ★★

SP 296308. On upland ridge 6 km. N of Chipping Norton, SW of A34(T) and NE of A44. Access along minor road towards Little Rollright between the A34(T) and the A44. English Heritage; access to the King's Men by courtesy of the landowner, who may levy a charge.

The Rollright Stones comprise three elements: the King Stone, King's Men, and the Whispering Knights. Folklore has it the stones are the petrified remains of a king and his followers. In fact, all three monuments are of different dates, their existence on the hill reflecting the sacred importance of the place.

The **Whispering Knights** (SP 299308) is the remains of a portal dolmen-type burial chamber of about 4000 BC. Four stones stand upright, while a fifth, probably the capstone, lies fallen. The stones would never have been covered by a mound; rather they projected out of a low flat-topped platform that surrounded the setting.

The **King's Men** (SP 296308) is a fine stone circle broadly dating to 2670 BC to 1975 BC. The circle, on a hilltop setting, is nearly perfectly round, with a diameter of 33 m. In 1882 the circle was restored and new stones replaced missing ones. Of the seventy-three stones present today at least one-third were repositioned.

Rollright has been seen as some kind of prehistoric astronomical observatory. However, there are very few meaningful alignments represented, a view of the midsummer sunset being the only one that stands out as potentially significant.

The **King Stone** (SO 295309) is a large block of limestone about 2.5 m. high and now tipped at a rakish angle. This was the marker stone for an early Bronze Age cemetery. Several small cairns† containing cremations were discovered around the stone during excavations in 1979. The unusual shape of the stone is in part the result of early visitors chipping pieces off to use as talismans or for curative purposes.

G. Lambrick, The Rollright Stones: Megaliths, Monuments and Settlements in the Prehistoric Landscape, *HBMCE Archaeological Report 6 (English Heritage, 1988).*

Spoonley Wood, Sudeley, Gloucestershire Roman villa

SP 045257. From Charlton Abbots (5 km. S of Winchcombe off the A46) take the minor road W to Guiting Power. At Roel Gate crossroads turn left (signposted Winchcombe); 1 km. on, a lane leads to Spoonley Farm. The second right-hand track after the farm enters a wood, and continues as a public footpath past the villa site. Permission to visit should be sought at Charlton Abbots Manor. Figure 124.

An eerie setting for what must have once been a fine Roman villa. C19 excavations revealed a courtyard villa with ranges of rooms on three sides. Mosaic pavements were exposed, one of which (reconstructed) is visible. Very overgrown walls, largely restored in the C19, can be traced in places. Other earthworks hint at more extensive remains.

H. O'Neil, 'Spoonley Wood Roman Villa, Gloucestershire', TBGAS 71 (1952), 162–6.

▼ **Fig. 124.** Plan of the Roman villa at Spoonley Wood, Gloucestershire (after RCHME)

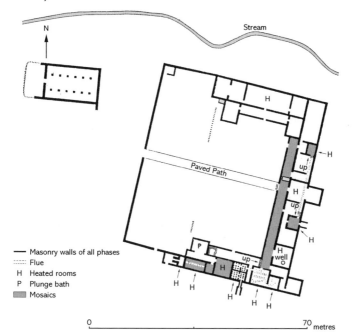

Sudeley Castle, Gloucestershire   Late medieval great house

SP 030275. S of Winchcombe, 10 km. NE of Cheltenham.

Sudeley Castle was largely built by Ralph Boteler, Treasurer of England (1443–6) and war captain, who held it until 1469, while its most magnificent elements were added by its next owner, the duke of Gloucester, later Richard III. Sudeley (slighted in 1649) was a castle in name only, and was in fact a typical late medieval great house arranged (just as if it were a monastery or college) around one or more courtyards. Here there are two, first a North or Outer Court, largely remodelled *c.*1572 but retaining Boteler's Gateway of about 1442. The South or Inner Court is missing its south range but has at its south-west corner Sudeley's strong point, a residential tower. On the east side of the Inner Court is a ruinous two-storey building of the later C15, expansively fenestrated. This is the royal suite built by Richard of Gloucester, the room lit by bay windows being the Presence Chamber with beyond (now Queen Katherine Parr's Room) private chambers communicating by a cloister to the private pew in the household's chapel.

That chapel was built about 1460. As well as a place of worship it was intended to serve as the family mausoleum. Of ashlar, at five bays long it is as big as a small parish church.

West of the approach from the north are the walls of a barn of the mid-C15, once of eleven or twelve bays.

C. Platt, Medieval Britain from the Air *(George Philip & Son, 1984), 186–9.*

Tewkesbury, Gloucestershire   Medieval town

SO 890324. W of the M5, access from junction 9. Figure 125.

Tewkesbury's Benedictine† abbey (consecrated 1121) attracted wealthy benefactors throughout the Middle Ages. In the 1340s the church's presbytery†, off which radiate six chapels, was rebuilt by the widow of Hugh le Despenser the Younger, who was executed for treason in 1326. Intended to serve as a dynastic mausoleum, it houses one of England's most dazzling collections of aristocratic tombs. Among them is that of Hugh's grandson Edward le Despenser (d. 1375), whose effigy kneels on top of his chantry chapel† facing the altar, and the Beauchamp chapel (begun 1422). The church is also the burial place of Edward, Prince of Wales, killed in the battle of Tewkesbury on 4 May 1471 as the Lancastrians were routed settling the Wars of the Roses.

South of the church, in Church Street, are Abbey Cottages. Jettied and timber-framed, these represent what survives of a row of twenty-four houses with shops, built by the abbey as a rent-earning speculation in the late C15. One, the Little Museum, has been restored to its original condition.

D. Verey, The Buildings of Gloucestershire: The Vale and the Forest of Dean *(Penguin, 1980), 357–79.*

▲ **Fig. 125.** Tewkesbury, Gloucestershire, showing the radiating eastern chapels (Photograph: Paul Stamper)

Uffington White Horse and Castle, Uffington, Oxfordshire Iron Age hillfort† and chalk hill-figure ★★

SU 301866. 4 km. E of Ashbury, approached by signposted minor roads leading S from B4507 road between Ashbury and Wantage. Car-parking at Woolstone Hill and at Uffington Fort. English Heritage and National Trust. Figure 126 and cover.

The Uffington White Horse is probably the best known and most ancient of the numerous hill-figures in southern England. It measures 111 m. from the tip of the tail to the end of the foremost ear. Facing right, the horse appears to be in galloping or jumping poise. The head, represented square in shape with a single eye in the centre, has two ears pointing forward. Less explicable are the two lines of a 'beak' on the front of the head and the short 'spur' on the front leg attached to the body.

The date and origin of the horse has caused debate and controversy for many years. There are two main views. First, that it is Saxon, perhaps carved to celebrate King Alfred's victory over the Danes at the Battle of Ashbury (an early name for Uffington Castle). This is best regarded as folklore. The second is that the horse was carved in the Iron Age and represents a tribal emblem. Excavations in 1990 added weight to the idea that the horse dates from later prehistory as deposits of fine silt in the beak were scientifically dated to the early first millennium BC. The best view of the horse at ground level is from further north on the B4508

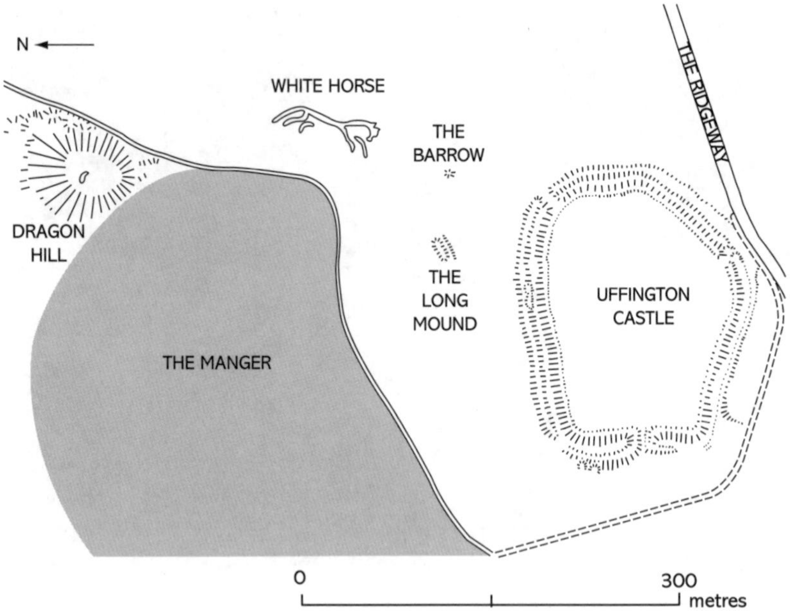

▲ **Fig. 126.** Plan of the Uffington White Horse and Castle, Uffington, Oxfordshire (after Miles & Palmer)

between Fernham and Longcot. In late Iron Age times this territory was probably occupied by the *Dobunni*† tribe, the area to the south by the *Atrebates*†. Thus it is possible that the White Horse was a territorial indicator signalling to anyone approaching that they were moving into the lands of another tribe.

Among C19 references are the stories of scouring and the associated fairs in 1813 and 1825 recorded by Hughes in his book *Tom Brown's Schooldays*.

The flat-topped hill below the horse is **Dragon Hill**. According to legend this was the place where St George slew the dragon.

About 200 m. south-west of the White Horse is **Uffington Castle** (SU 299864), an Iron Age hillfort of 3.2 ha. dating from the C7 BC.

D. Miles and S. Palmer, 'White Horse Hill', CA 12/142 (1995), 372–8.

Uleybury, Uley, Gloucestershire   Iron Age hillfort†

ST 784989. On Cotswold escarpment 2 km. N of Uley village, 8 km. SW of Stroud. Situated beside B4066 at the top of Crawley Hill leading N from Uley village. Roadside parking. Figure 127.

Uleybury is an impressive Cotswold hillfort. Constructed about 400 BC, the ramparts and defences can easily be traced on the ground. An inner

▲ **Fig. 127.** Aerial photograph of Uleybury, Uley, Gloucestershire (CUCAP AlO-15)

rampart runs around the edge of the hilltop enclosing 13 ha. Outside the natural hill slope has been scarped back in glacis style to create a steep slope which leads down to an artificial terrace some 20 m. wide, which runs all around the hill. The outer edge of the terrace has been strengthened by the construction of a second rampart. Outside this second circuit the natural slope has again been scarped to create a steep fall of about 10 m., at the bottom of which is a third, rather less substantial, rampart.

There are three outer entrances, but, rather unusually, two gaps in the outer ramparts do not have corresponding gaps in the inner line. Thus access into the fort must have involved going round the terrace to the north-east gate.

Uleybury is of a type known as 'developed hillforts' because of their size and the complexity of their defences and boundary systems. On the

Cotswolds such hillforts are regularly spaced at intervals of about 20 km., each one set within a putative territory defined topographically through the juxtaposition of rivers and hills.

Just beyond the fort (ST 790996) was a ritual and religious site known as the **Uley Temple**. Nothing remains visible today, but excavations revealed a sequence which began with a sacred enclosure in later prehistoric times, continued through Roman times as a temple to Mercury, and ended in the C7 AD or later after the site was used as a Christian baptistery† or cell. Nearby is HETTY PEGLER'S TUMP.

A. Saville (ed.), Uley Bury and Norbury Hillforts, *Western Archaeological Trust Monograph 5 (1979), 1–24.*

Wadfield, Sudeley, Gloucestershire Roman villa

SP 024261. Take the A46 from Winchcombe to Cheltenham and after 1 km. take minor road on the left signposted Charlton Abbots and Brockhampton. Beyond the sign to BELAS KNAP, *take the public footpath on the left. The site lies in a small copse in the middle of an arable field. Permission to visit needs to be sought at Charlton Abbots Manor, 1.6 km. further along the road.*

A small courtyard villa excavated in the C19. The ground plan of the villa is visible although overgrown, and appears to be three wings around a courtyard with a bath-suite in the south range. One room had a red tessellated floor and the main reception room a geometric mosaic, partly restored.

E. Brock, 'The Excavation of a Roman Villa in the Wadfield', JBAA (NS) 1 (1885), 242–50.

Wappenbury, Warwickshire Iron Age hillfort†

SP 377693. On W side of Wappenbury village, 7 km. NE of Leamington Spa, S of B4453 Leamington to Rugby road.

Set immediately above the river Leam, this fort is roughly rectangular and rather unusual in having such a low-lying position. The presence nearby of two fords may account for its location; possibly its inhabitants were involved in riverine trade.

The boundary ramparts comprise a single bank and ditch, with a possible entrance to the east. Excavations have shown that the rampart was originally perhaps 3 m. high and the external V-shaped ditch up to 4 m. deep. Finds suggest a C1 BC date. Its position just west of the Roman FOSSE WAY may suggest later occupation too.

M. and B. Stanley, 'The Defences of the Iron Age Camp at Wappenbury, Warwickshire', TBAS 76 (1958), 1–9.

Warwick, Warwickshire Medieval town and castle ★

SP 282650. 15 km. SE of Birmingham, N of M40 with access from junction 15. Figure 128.

Warwick is one of the finest late medieval castles in England, an oval, stone-walled enclosure studded with towers of strength and sophistication and with a great hall and state rooms rising above the river Avon. The visitor should first go to the exterior of the late C14 gatehouse at the east end of the castle, where the approach is via a barbican†. Embattled walls lead the visitor to the gatehouse proper, which has three residential storeys above the entrance.

The approach would have been hard to breach, with the long, narrow entrance passage defended, in addition to gates, portcullises, two drawbridges, and 'murder holes', by fire from triple battlements. Flanking the gatehouse, at the castle's two eastward corners, are the late C14 Guy's Tower and Caesar's Tower. The view from within the Inner Ward east to these towers remains uncannily like that painted by Canaletto in

▼ **Fig. 128.** Warwick Castle, Warwickshire (after Tussauds Group)

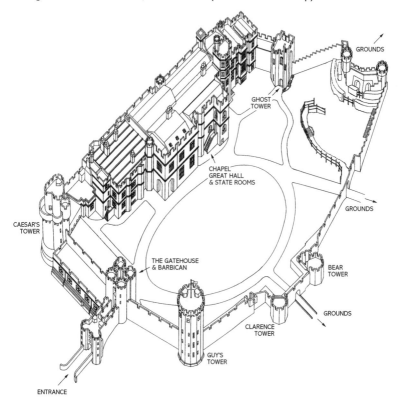

The advent of artillery

The explosive character of gunpowder—a mixture of sulphur, saltpetre, and charcoal—was apparently discovered in the C13. It is in two English manuscripts written by Edward III's clerk Walter de Milemete in 1326 that seven guns are first illustrated—flask-shaped, laid on trestles, and apparently firing arrow-like projectiles. By the Crecy campaign of the 1340s they were in use so successfully that Edward III wrote asking that all available guns in the Tower of London be shipped out to assist in the siege of Calais. By the 1350s and 1360s town and castle walls were being adapted for artillery; well before the end of the C14 fortifications were being designed both to resist gunshot and to provide gun platforms for offensive fire, throwing shot weighing up to 200 pounds. The castle was rapidly becoming redundant.

1748. At the opposite end of the castle, between the Norman motte† and the end of the hall range, is the water gate (the Ghost Tower). In the later C15 Richard of Gloucester (the future Richard III) began the construction of a mighty tower house on the north walls with an octagonal turret at each of its four corners. However, in 1485 Richard was killed at the Battle of Bosworth and building stopped. Bear and Clarence Towers represent the forward towers of this unrealized ambitious project.

It was the Beauchamps, earls of Warwick, who were responsible for the castle's transformation in the later C14, and their influence is to be seen, too, in St Mary's Church, whose tower dominates the town centre. In the Middle Ages the church, served by a college of priests, had an impressive collection of relics, from a fragment of Moses' burning bush to St Brandon's frying pan. In 1544 the church passed to the town's burgesses, except for the Beauchamp chapel. That is among the finest burial chapels in England, and was built in 1443–64 by Richard Beauchamp, whose gilded effigy lies at its centre. This is stunning, but was not modelled from life or a death mask. In fact the sculptor began work fifteen years after the earl's death and his brief was to produce a figure of a nobleman in armour.

Much of the church and town was lost in a fire in 1694. Some timber-framed buildings survived around the periphery, for instance in West Street, High Street, and Mill Street, east of the castle. Adjoining the West Gate is Lord Leycester's Hospital, an almshouse founded in 1571 for old soldiers but incorporating the premises of two earlier guilds. Among the structures rebuilt in the generation after the fire should be noted those by the architect Francis Smith: the former Court House in Jury Street, and no. 10, Market Place, built in 1714 for his father-in-law.

Just north of Warwick is Kenilworth, with one of England's greatest late medieval castle-palaces (English Heritage).

A. Clifton-Taylor, Six More English Towns *(BBC Books, 1981), 9–45.*

Wayland's Smithy, Oxfordshire Neolithic long barrow† ★

SU 281854. Beside the Ridgeway, 2 km. E of Ashbury. Can be approached from W along the Ridgeway from its junction with the B4000 at SU 274843 (about 1.5 km. walk), or from E by parking at the UFFINGTON WHITE HORSE (about 2 km. walk). English Heritage.

Now restored, Wayland's Smithy is the best and most accessible long barrow along the Berkshire Ridgeway. In its final form it is a classic Cotswold–Severn-style long barrow, but excavations have shown a long and complicated history.

About 3500 BC a mound over a wooden mortuary chamber was enlarged to what we see today. A monumental mound some 55 m. long edged with sarsen† slabs was built, the material for its construction being quarried from a pair of large flanking ditches (now filled in). Six great sarsen slabs, which average over 3 m. high, were set across the front of the mound to provide an impressive façade.

At the same time, a cruciform chamber roofed with large capstones† was constructed at the wider, higher end of the enlarged mound. This can still be entered. When excavated it contained the remains of at least eight people, including a child. When the tomb fell out of use, perhaps about 3000 BC, the chamber and passage were filled with chalk rubble and soil to seal the burial deposits and protect them.

Legend holds that an invisible smith lived here and that a horse left with a penny would be well shod by the time the owner returned to collect it. The coins, it seems, had to be left on the roofstone of the right-hand burial chamber, known traditionally as 'The Cave'.

A. Whittle, 'Wayland's Smithy, Oxfordshire: Excavations at the Neolithic Tomb in 1962–63 by R J C Atkinson and S Piggott', PPS 57/2 (1991), 61–101.

Windmill Tump, Rodmarton, Gloucestershire Neolithic long barrow†

ST 933973. N of the A433, 5 km. NE of Tetbury. Access by footpath from minor road between A429 and Rodmarton village, SW of the village. English Heritage.

Windmill Tump shares many features with other Cotswold–Severn-style long barrows. Instead of a chamber opening from the back of the fore-court it has a false entrance in the forecourt and lateral chambers opening from the sides of the mound, as at BELAS KNAP. The mound is about 61 m. long by 21.3 m. wide. It is enclosed by a modern stone wall.

Excavations revealed two lateral chambers, one opening from each side of the mound. The north chamber contained the remains of ten adults and three children, the south chamber an unknown number of disarticulated individuals. Both chambers were unusual in being set below the natural surface of the ground, with steps in the outer passage, and carefully made jambs in which a circular hole or 'porthole' allowed access to the chamber itself. Sadly, none of these details is visible today, although the position of the chambers can be seen.

In 1987 gales brought down a beech tree on the barrow revealing a third chamber. Others may await discovery.

E. Clifford and G. Daniel, 'The Rodmarton and Avening Portholes', PPS 6 (1940), 133–65.

Windsor, Windsor and Maidenhead Medieval castle and royal palace ★

SU 970770. Windsor is about 35 km. W of central London, S of the M4 with access from junction 6.

There has been a royal house by the Thames at Windsor since the time of Edward the Confessor. Near to this original house, on a chalk hill, William I built a castle, with a ward (bailey†) either side of a low motte†. In the time of Henry I the court moved here from the old Saxon palace which, in time, became known as Old Windsor as the present town of Windsor grew up at the castle gate.

When first built, about 1070, the castle's motte was ringed with a timber palisade and probably had a central timber tower. In time the palisade was replaced by a stone wall—a 'shell keep'—within which, in the later C12, a second shell keep was built as subsidence caused problems to the first. At much the same time it appears that Henry II built masonry defences around the Upper Ward, and part of the Lower. By 1216 the castle was sufficiently strong to withstand a siege by forces opposed to King John.

Under Henry III (1216–72), one of England's greatest builder-kings, Windsor was transformed. The defences were completed in stone and towers added, the 'king's house' in the Upper Ward was remodelled, while in the Lower (which seems to have housed the garrison) a great hall and chambers were added. In the earlier C14 Edward III (1328–77) remodelled a number of the key buildings, enhancing their magnificence. St George's Hall, in the Lower Bailey, was extended to eighteen bays, making it the largest royal hall in England after Westminster. Under Edward a cult of chivalry flourished, and in 1344 he held a great tournament at Windsor, during which he announced the creation of a new order of the Round Table. In the event it was founded in 1348 as the Order of the Garter, which is today the world's oldest order of chivalry. To serve as the Order's chapel a collegiate church† dedicated to St George was established. Then, during the last twenty years of his life, Edward engaged in what became the most expensive secular building campaign in medieval England. The Round Tower was remodelled, and then ranges of new buildings in the perpendicular style were erected around the Upper Ward to provide better accommodation and perhaps to enhance the castle's skyline. By 1377 Windsor was the largest palace in

England. What is generally regarded as its architectural high point, St George's Chapel, was added a century later; it occupies much of the Lower Ward. Begun about 1475 it was completed some fifty years later, and was funded partly by the royal purse and partly by Knights of the Garter whose arms figure in its fan vaulting. It contains a number of tombs, some royal; among details of especial note are the elaborate iron gates intended for the tomb of Edward IV (d. 1483).

Despite remodellings under later rulers, notably Charles II (after 1674) and George IV (after 1824) the castle remains, outwardly at least, much as it was left at the end of the Middle Ages.

B. Kerr, Windsor Revealed: New Light on the History of the Castle (English Heritage, 1997).

Woodchester, Gloucestershire Roman villa

ST 840030. N of the village of North Woodchester N from the Stroud–Nailsworth road (A46). The villa lies partly below a small cemetery approached by minor no-through road.

Although no longer visible, this is the site of one of the grandest villas in Gloucestershire, perhaps the country residence of some high-ranking official. Excavated in part by Samuel Lysons in 1793–6, the villa, comparable in scale to that at FISHBOURNE, contains at least sixty-four rooms arranged in three courts. The centrepiece was a hall opening off a courtyard containing the famous 15 m. square Orpheus pavement. One of the most superior mosaics found in Britain, this has concentric circles of birds and animals. The original is buried but a full size replica is occasionally exhibited.

G. Clark, 'The Roman Villa at Woodchester', Britannia, 13 (1982), 197–228.

Wotton-under-Edge, Gloucestershire Medieval lynchets†

ST 763940. 14 km. SE of Stroud on B4058, E of M5 with access from junction 14. Figure 129.

In the Middle Ages, the expanding population of the C12 and C13 caused ever more marginal (poor) land to be brought into cultivation. In steeply hilly areas sloping ground, never cultivated before or since, was put under the plough, the ox teams labouring along the contour on flights of narrow cultivation terraces called lynchets. On the Cotswold Edge there are many fine flights of lynchets, as on the sloping grasslands around the market town of Wotton-under-Edge, especially on Wotton Hill at the north-west end of the town and on Coombe Hill to the north-east, above the B4058 to Nailsworth. Several footpaths give access, including one off a sharp bend on Coombe Road (the B4058) on the town edge. As you climb the footpath through the lynchets you begin to realize the scale of the enterprise, with some of the steps between

▲ **Fig. 129.** Wotton-under-Edge, Gloucestershire: lynchets (Photograph: Paul Stamper)

lynchets being of 2 m. or more. Sometimes it is argued these formed naturally through successive ploughings along the hillside; however, a degree of initial construction seems more probable. Woodland names on the wold-top above preserve the name 'Conygre', indicating a conigree or warren, probably of post-medieval date, where rabbits were bred in artificial linear mounds kept by a warrener.

C. Taylor, Fields in the Landscape *(Dent, 1975).*

9 London

This region includes the county and unitary authorities of Greater London.

Modern London may seem a hopeless place to see any archaeology, but it is surprising just how much has survived. Prior to the C1 AD the area now covered by Greater London was settled by communities living along the banks of the Thames and its main tributaries and associated gravel terraces. Roman settlement in the area north of the Thames between Ludgate and Aldgate first triggered the development of an urban centre at London, followed up by the emergence of the City of London and numerous smaller nodes that were towns in their own right before being drawn into the larger conurbation that is now London in post-medieval and modern times.

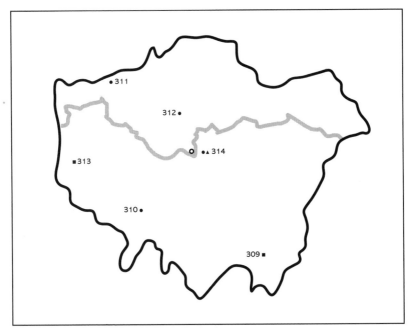

▲ **Fig. 130.** Map of Region 9

309 **Caesar's Camp (Keston), Greater London**
310 **Caesar's Camp (Wimbledon), Greater London**
311 **Grim's Ditch, Greater London**
312 **Hampstead Heath, Greater London**
313 **Heathrow Airport, Greater London**
314 **London (*Londinium*)**

Caesar's Camp, Keston, Mark, Greater London Iron Age hillfort†

TQ 422639. E of A233 5 km. S of Bromley town centre. Within small country park with parking and picnic facilities.

A roughly oval hillfort originally about 17.5 ha. but now partly levelled. The boundary defences comprise an internal bank, outer ditch, and small counterscarp bank† outside the ditch. They remain upstanding on the north and west sides, and are just traceable on the south side. On the west, the basic boundary is enhanced by the addition of two further banks. The entrance is to the north-west and can be seen today as slightly in-turned banks. Excavations have shown a period of occupation spanning the C4 BC through to C1 BC.

N. Piercy Fox, 'Caesar's Camp, Keston', ACant, 84 (1969), 185–99.

Caesar's Camp, Wimbledon Common, Greater London
Iron Age hillfort†

TQ 224711. At S end of Wimbledon Common, W of Camp Road and S of Horse Ride. Crossed by footpaths.

A more or less circular hillfort of 4.5 ha. with a flattened side to the north-west following the contour of the hill slope. The boundary earthworks comprise a bank and ditch separated by a berm†.

Excavations in 1937 revealed a ditch nearly 4 m. deep and 12 m. wide and a bank with timber revetting on both sides. Pottery dating to the C5 was recovered. Sadly, the earthworks are less impressive today, not least because a local builder reduced them. The basic plan can still be seen, however, and there are traces of the original entrance on the west side about 30 m. north of the footpath through the middle.

A. Lowther, 'Caesar's Camp, Wimbledon, Surrey: The Excavations of 1937', Arch J, 102 (1945), 15–20.

Grim's Ditch, Harrow and Stanmore, Greater London Prehistoric and later linear earthwork†

TQ 134923. On the E edge of Grim's Dyke golf course, NW of Old Redding off Oxhey Lane (A4008).

Grim's Ditch is a linear earthwork that has been traced for more than 8 km. between Pinner Green (TQ 114923) and Brockley Hill (TQ 174937) where it comes to within 200 m. of the line of the Roman Watling Street. The best surviving length is at Old Redding (TQ 134923) where it can be seen from the road. There is also a section in the grounds of the Grim's Dyke Hotel.

Throughout its length, Grim's Ditch consists of a V-shaped ditch with a bank on the north side, which in places reaches a height of 3 m.

Limited excavations in 1953 and 1955 found Iron Age pottery suggesting a construction date in the C1 BC or early C1 AD, a view confirmed by more recent excavations. As a boundary, however, its use probably continued through into medieval times.

R. Ellis, 'Excavations at Grim's Dyke, Harrow, 1979', TLMAS 33 (1982), 173–6.

Hampstead Heath, Hampstead, Greater London Bronze
Age round barrows†

TQ 273865. Set in parkland, N of Parliament Hill and halfway between Hampstead and Highgate Ponds. Best approached from Millfield Lane along the path towards the Vale of Health.

Once known as Boadicea's Grave, this circular mound resembles a Bronze Age round barrow. A visible ditch still runs round the edge of the mound. Excavations in 1894 failed to find any traces of a burial or grave goods within the mound or ditch.

The position of the mound and the local place name Parliament Hill raises the possibility that it is a moot mound forming a local assembly place in early medieval times. Since such assemblies were often held at prominent, well-established, and historically significant places it is quite possible that a prehistoric barrow was used as a moot. The excavations showed that the mound had been enhanced with soil from the cutting of the ditch in modern times. A clump of fir trees were planted, probably in the mid-C18 AD.

C. Read, 'Account of the Opening of the Tumulus on Parliament Hill, Hampstead', PSAL, 2nd ser., 15 (1984), 240–5.

Heathrow Airport, Heathrow, Greater London Iron Age
enclosure and ritual site

TQ 0876. Beneath the eastern end of the main northern runway at Heathrow Airport. No access. Figure 131.

Few passengers arriving into London's Heathrow Airport realize that they are touching down into an area rich in archaeological remains. Excavations in advance of the construction of the main runways in 1944 revealed a site known as Caesar's Camp. This proved to be a long-lived site that began in the Neolithic, continued into the later Bronze Age, and then into the middle Iron Age, when a square enclosure was constructed.

The enclosure is about 100 × 110 m. in size, bounded by a ditch, flanked on the inside by a low bank. Within the enclosure on the north side were at least six circular houses. To the south the interior appears to have been rather empty except for a timber building 4 × 5 m. Concentrically set around the central building was a palisaded fence or enclosure, with an entrance to the east. This structure is interpreted as a

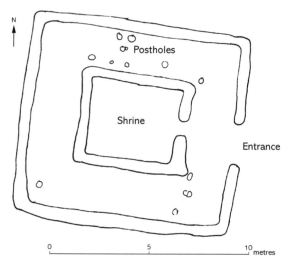

▲ **Fig. 131.** Plan of the Iron Age shrine under the eastern end of the main runway at Heathrow Airport, Heathrow, Greater London (after Grimes & Close-Brooks)

shrine or temple typical of examples constructed during the last few centuries BC.

W. Grimes and J. Close-Brooks, 'The Excavation of Caesar's Camp, Heathrow, Harmondsworth, Middlesex, 1944', PPS 59 (1993), 303–60.

London (*Londinium*), Greater London   Roman, medieval, and later city   ★★

TQ 3080. The Museum of London, London Wall, has a superb set of galleries and is a good starting point. Figures 132 and 133.

The Roman city of *Londonium* lies under the heart of the modern City, in the area of St Paul's Cathedral. Founded probably soon after AD 43, at the lowest bridging point of the river Thames, the settlement became a focal point for the developing road system in south-east England. Excavations have provided much information about the early city and have identified several key buildings. The first London had a brief beginning, being one of the towns burnt by Queen Boudicca. It was rebuilt and became the centre of government for the province. In the C2 Britain was divided into two provinces and London remained capital of Britannia Superior (Upper Britain). A century later when Britain was further divided into four provinces London became capital of *Maxima Caesariensis*. Throughout, London remained the financial centre for all Britain and the Imperial treasury was still there at the end of Roman rule. A mint was established by the Emperor Carausius in AD 288.

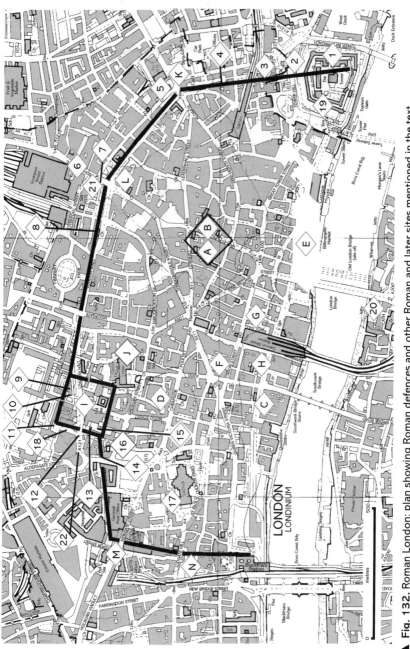

▲ Fig. 132. Roman London: plan showing Roman defences and other Roman and later sites mentioned in the text

▲ **Fig. 133.** St. John's Chapel, Tower of London (after Clark)

In the AD 70s when the settlement was rapidly expanding, a substantial public building was built on high ground east of the Walbrook (**A**). In the late C1 the centre of the town was replanned and this building replaced by a great basilica† and forum† stretching from Lombard Street on the east to Lime Street on the west (**B**). Other public buildings included bath-houses in Upper Thames Street (**C**) and Cheapside (**D**) and a temple of Mithras on the east bank of the Walbrook (**E**). An imposing official building constructed on the bank of the Thames (G), now partly under Cannon Street Station (**F**) may have been the governor's headquarters. London was a port and a sequence of waterfronts, quays, and warehouses developed along the north bank of the Thames. The riverbank in the mid-C1 lay north of modern Lower and Upper Thames Street some 100 m. from the present river edge (**H**).

A large rectangular military fort was built on the north-west edge of the town (**I**) probably in the early C2. It was served by four gates and the lower part of the northern half of the west gate is preserved under the double carriageway of London Wall. Parts of the fort wall, with foundations of an intermediate turret, and the turret at the south-west corner, can be seen to the west of Noble Street.

The amphitheatre was recently discovered under the Guildhall Yard (**J**). Excavations have shown the earlier timber phase to date to AD 70 with a masonry rebuild around 125. Part of its outline is marked out.

In about 200 *Londinium* was enclosed with a massive defensive stone wall which extended round the east, north, and west sides of the Roman city, from the site of the Tower of London to Blackfriars. Where the Roman roads left London at Aldgate, Bishopsgate, Newgate, and Ludgate, gatehouses were built (**K–N**). Large sections of the Roman wall were repaired or rebuilt in medieval times. Surviving fragments of the Roman and later wall can be seen at several different locations between the Tower of London and the Museum of London. This is laid out as a Wall walk (guides available); the circuit is 2.8 km. long and each point is marked by a panel.

Starting from the Tower of London a section of Roman wall with a semicircular bastion lies immediately east of the White Tower (**1**). The bastion was rebuilt in the C13. Next to Lanthorn Tower are the remains of the massive riverside wall as revealed by excavation. At Wakefield Gardens, Tower Hill (**2**) a section of Roman masonry survives to 4.4 m. below the medieval stonework. Following the defences round, Roman remains, comprising the typical red tile and ragstone, can be seen at Cooper's Row (**3**) and about 45 m. north of Tower Hill underground station (**4**). The red sandstone plinth at the base marks the Roman ground level. The base of one of the towers added to the wall in the C4 can also be seen. Aldgate (**5**) was the location of one of the Roman gates into the City, rebuilt in medieval times but demolished in the C18.

Excavations in 1977 for a subway cut through the Roman wall at Duke's Place (**6**) now marked by a mosaic mural. Bishopsgate Street (**7**) preserves the line of Ermine Street (London to York), entering the City by a gate that probably survived until the Middle Ages. The line of the City Wall continues round following the back walls of the shops fronting onto Wormwood Street (**8**). All Hallows Church (**9**) was first built against the Roman City Wall. The churchyard wall lies on top of the City Wall. The vestry on the north side of the church is built over the semicircular foundations of a Roman tower. In the crypt are the remains of a Roman house with two tessellated floors.

At St Alphege (**10**) the City Wall originally formed the northern wall of the Roman fort. In the C11 a church dedicated to Alphege was built with the City Wall as its northern side. The church was demolished in the C16. Just outside Temple Court in Queen Victoria Street (**11**) is a reconstruction of the Temple of Mithras discovered nearby in 1954. Old Street, Cripplegate (**12**) marks the original northern entrance to the Roman fort, subsequently rebuilt in medieval times. The medieval tower at the north end of the gardens by the east side of the Museum of London (**13**) marks the north-west corner of the Roman and medieval defences. The west gate of the Roman fort was discovered during excavations at Bastion House (**14**). The northern tower, originally a guardroom, is still visible. The base of the Roman City Wall is also visible at the north end of Noble Street (**15**) supporting a C19 brick wall. The outer wall is the foundation of the west wall of the Roman fort with a small square turret on the inner face. When the fort became incorporated into the City defences the wall was thickened and part of the core of this thickening still survives parallel to the fort wall. At the south end of Noble Street (**16**) is the south-west corner of the fort with the foundations of a rectangular corner watch-tower. A new gate of military design was constructed at Aldersgate, probably during the C4 when the city defences were strengthened against possible barbarian attack. The gate continued into medieval times but was finally demolished in the C18.

West of the walled city on the south bank of the Thames, further Roman remains are known in Greenwich Park. Until recently these comprised a fenced off mound with a small patch of visible tesserae. Archaeological work, the most recent of which has been by Channel 4's Time Team, has confirmed the presence of an important Roman building, probably a temple complex.

The story of what became of London after the end of Roman rule in the C5 has mainly come from archaeology. This has shown that the Roman city was abandoned (although some elite functions may have continued there, as St Paul's Cathedral (**17**) was founded in 604 and there may have been a royal hall in Cripplegate (**18**)), the focus of activity shifting to a new trading centre 3 km. to the west, around what is now Covent Garden. In 886, after Viking raids, King Alfred refounded the city within the protective Roman walls and the old town, or 'Aldwych', was abandoned.

At the conquest in 1066 it was naturally to the capital that William marched after victory at Hastings. Against the south-east corner of the Roman city wall he built a wooden fort, and then between 1075 and 1095 had his aide-de-camp, Gundulf of Bec, bishop of Rochester, build a great keep-palace of Caen stone (**19**). Known as the White Tower since the C13, when it was whitewashed, this has three storeys over a basement, and includes the two-storey chapel of St John (Fig. 133) whose apsidal east end breaks forward of the wall line. The outer circuit of defences, lined with towers, moated, and with a river entrance (Traitor's Gate) under St Thomas's Tower, were developed in a rather piecemeal fashion in the mid- to late C13.

The Conqueror's choice of location for his stronghold was determined by security considerations, and lay about 4 km. along the Thames from Westminster, fairly recently established as the seat of government. A great new hall was built here by the Conqueror between 1095 and 1100, replaced in 1394 by the present structure, Westminster Hall, designed for Richard II. Its most impressive feature is the hammerbeam roof, which leaves the hall floor unencumbered by columns. The rest of the Palace of Westminster was badly damaged in a fire of 1834.

There had been an abbey at Westminster since the C7. In the mid-

C11 Edward the Confessor began to rebuild it in the Norman style, but this project was incomplete at his death in 1065. The following year William I emphasized his royal legitimacy by being crowned here and helping to complete the abbey. The Conqueror's church was replaced by the abbey we see today, a product of Henry III's wish to have in a single building church, royal burial place, and private chapel. Stylistically influenced by major French churches such as Rheims and Amiens, work began in 1245 at the east end, but only five bays had been completed by the time Henry died in 1272. Nothing happened for a century, then building recommenced in the same style, finally reaching the west end in the mid-C16 (although it was left to Christopher Wren to complete things in the C17). At the east end late medieval additions include a chapel added by Henry VII between 1503 and 1512 to enshrine his predecessor, Henry VI, and legitimate his own authority. It is one of the finest late Perpendicular buildings in the country. Overall, the church (admission charge) is astonishing. So too are Henry III's eight-sided chapter house, and the cloisters (later C13 and C14). The Abbey has a huge number of treasures, and tombs of the royal and great; one of the most exotic features is the Cosmati cosmographical mosaic pavement of 1268 in the sanctuary east of the crossing. Further Cosmati work lies east of the high altar on the floor of the Confessor's Chapel and on the base of Henry III's own tomb with its effigy by William Torel (1291). Other royal tombs include those of Eleanor of Castle (also 1291); Richard II and Anne of Bohemia (about 1395); and Henry VII and his wife and mother (about 1512–18).

Two great general calamities befell London's medieval buildings. One was the great fire of 1666, the other the Second World War blitz. Even so, far too much survives to allow more than an invidious selection. Of churches, Southwark Cathedral (**20**) was founded as an Augustinian† priory, and its church was rebuilt in cruciform plan after a fire of about 1212; the Temple church in the Inns of Court has a round nave consecrated in 1185 which is modelled on that of the Knights Templar in Jerusalem; St Helen's, Bishopsgate (**21**), has two naves and the best collection of tombs of any of the City churches; and St Bartholomew the Great, West Smithfield (**22**), which was founded as a hospital in Henry I's time and to which an Augustinian priory attached soon after, has a choir and ambulatory† of about 1120.

Of London's palaces other than Westminster, St James's Palace, Marlborough Road, was begun in 1531 by Henry VIII when he was already at work enlarging Whitehall and Hampton Court. It is especially notable for its gatehouse and slightly later (1540) chapel. Further out from central London are Eltham Palace (English Heritage), with Edward IV's hall of about 1475–80 and Henry VIII's chapel of 1528–30; Lambeth, an episcopal palace (Church of England, tours by appointment), the gateway to which, of 1480, is the capital's earliest brick building of substance; and Hampton Court, originally ecclesiastical but enlarged by Henry VIII (Historic Royal Palaces), with its successive courts and early Renaissance detailing.

The visitor can always take a break in one of London's several parks, such as Hyde Park. Requisitioned in 1536 from Westminster Abbey by Henry VIII to serve as one of his many deer parks, Hyde Park has been open to the public since the time of James I.

G. Milne, Roman London *(Batsford and English Heritage, 1995)*; J. Hall and R. Merrifield, Roman London *(HMSO and Museum of London, 1993)*; E. Harwood and A. Saint, London *(HMSO, 1991)*; CA *has published two special London issues: 11/24 (1991), and 14/158 (1998).*

10 The Weald and downland of south-east England

This region includes the counties and unitary authorities of Kent, East Sussex, West Sussex, Surrey, Hampshire, Isle of Wight, Southampton, Portsmouth, Brighton and Hove, and Medway.

Two areas of chalk downland dominate this region. From east Kent to northern Hampshire run the North Downs, chalk ridges, low hills, and plateau land that attracted settlement from prehistoric times. Several major rivers cut through the North Downs, flowing northwards to the Thames, among them the Len, Medway, Mole, and Wey. Each has its own character; the Medway, for example, with its wide lush valley and broad estuary has been an agriculturally rich area since at least the fifth millennium BC when Neolithic communities built distinctive kinds of long barrows† there.

The South Downs run westward from Beachy Head on the south coast to join the North Downs around Andover. The South Downs are narrower and higher than their northern counterparts, broken into discrete blocks by a series of deeply incised valleys carrying the Cuckmere, Ouse, Adur, and Arun. Between Beachy Head and Worthing the coastline is punctuated with impressively high chalk cliffs. These downs have some of the most impressive causewayed enclosures† and hillforts† in southern England.

The North Downs have a steep escarpment on the south side, the South Downs an escarpment on the north side. Between is the Weald, an area of mixed topography and geology. In the centre, around Tunbridge Wells, is a ridge of sandstone hills, but all around is relatively low-lying clayey land. Much of this was occupied during early postglacial times, but the dense woodland and heavy soils were not cleared until later prehistory. One prompt for this may have been the availability of iron ore, one of few sources in lowland England; it certainly spawned major industries here during Roman and medieval times.

West and south of the chalk is the New Forest and Hampshire basin. Sandy heaths interspersed with clay vales are normal here, the lighter soils being heavily used to the point of exhaustion by early prehistoric communities and more or less abandoned from about 700 BC onwards. The New Forest became was a favourite royal hunting ground; William Rufus was killed here in AD 1100.

Since the formation of the English Channel about 10,000 BC, the south coast has been important for contact with the Continent. The

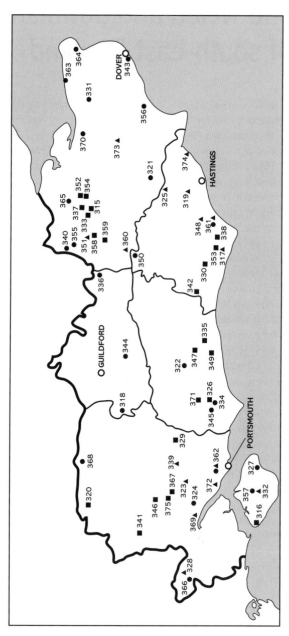

▲ Fig. 134. Map of Region 10

coast is eroding by up to 1 m. per year in parts of the region, whilst new land is forming in places such as Romney marsh and Dungeness.

Addington Park, Addington, Kent Neolithic long barrow† ★

TQ 654592. N of A20 10 km. NW of Maidstone. W of Addington, cut by minor road leading to Wrotham Heath. Figure 135.

Addington is the larger of two adjacent long barrows overlooking a tributary of the Medway. The mound is 60 m. long by 14 m. wide at the east end. Traces of a peristalith† and the remains of a chamber at the eastern end are visible.

About 100 m. north-west is the CHESTNUTS LONG BARROW.

B. Philp and M. Dutto, The Medway Megaliths, *2nd edn (Kent Archaeological Trust, 1985).*

▼ **Key to Fig. 134**

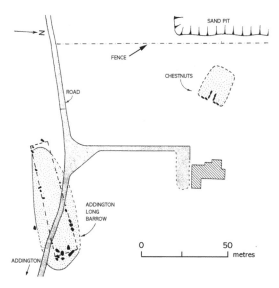

▲ **Fig. 135.** Plan of the Medway style long barrows at Addington Park and The Chestnuts, Kent (after Philp & Dutto)

Afton Down, Isle of Wight Bronze Age round barrow† cemetery

SZ 352857. 3 km. SE of Freshwater between A3055 and B3401. Best viewed from the Tennyson Trail from Freshwater Bay (off-road parking) or the B3399 between Brook Hill and Shalcombe (limited parking). National Trust.

The Tennyson Trail passes three groups of barrows in contrasting situations. At the west end, the **Afton Down** group has fourteen round barrows and a long barrow, in a ragged row broadly east to west (SZ 353858), at the foot of a gentle slope. The most westerly barrow is a large fine bowl barrow. Moving east is a long barrow, followed by a disc barrow reshaped as a golf tee. Two bowl barrows are next, then a bell barrow. Another bowl barrow separated it from a second bell barrow which contained a central cremation burial. Finally, there are three small low contiguous bowl barrows.

East of the Afton Down group is the **East Afton Down** group (SZ 365857), three bowl barrows in a row roughly north–south across the axis of a ridge.

Eastwards again is the **Five Barrow** group on the top of Brook Down, probably the best group of barrows on the island. It comprises eight mounds of the early second millennium BC. The biggest is the bell barrow at the west end. In the middle are six bowl barrows, while to the east is a disc barrow with a low central mound in the centre of a round ditched enclosure. The hollows in the barrow tops indicate unrecorded excavations.

L. Grinsell and G. Sherwin, 'Isle of Wight Barrows', PIWNHS 3 (1941), 179–222.

Alfriston, East Sussex   Medieval priest's house

TQ 521029. 4 km. NE of Seaford. National Trust; restricted opening hours. Admission charge.

In 1896 the Clergy House became the first house to be purchased by a new body called the National Trust. Despite its then ruinous state, it was appreciated was that here was a fine and complete example of a C14 timber-framed house. It is similar to Kent's Wealden dwellings, with a central, open hall (that is, open from floor to rafters) with crown post roof and two-storeyed ranges to either end.

The house was presumably built for a priest of St Andrew's, which it adjoins. The shingle-spired church has much of interest.

Other later medieval timber-framed buildings of note in the village include two inns, the George and the Ship.

Alfriston Clergy House (The National Trust, 1995) (Site Guidebook).

Alice Holt Forest, Surrey   Roman pottery kilns

Centred SU 405805. The most extensive concentration of kilns can be found on E side of the Blacknest tributary of the river Slea about 2 km. within Alice Holt Forest. Parking at Visitor centre (SU 415810); cross over A325 and follow forest footpaths through to Goose Green Inclosure and Straits Inclosure.

This area was well known in Roman (and later) times for its pottery industry. Roman production spanned the C1 to C5 and vessels were marketed across southern England. Numerous dumps of waste pottery exist, some visible as low mounds alongside the forest rides near to the stream. When the vegetation is low humps and bumps indicate other traces of activity such as clay pits, water leats, and ponds.

M. Lyne and R. Jefferies, The Alice Holt/Farnham Roman Pottery Industry, Council for British Archaeology Research Report 30 (1979).

Battle, East Sussex   Battlefield and medieval abbey

TQ 749157. The town of Battle is 9 km. NW of Hastings. Battlefield and abbey ruins English Heritage; restricted opening hours. Admission charge. Figure 136.

On 14 October 1066 Harold, king of England, was hacked down by a mounted Norman knight. Already wounded in the face by an arrow, Harold dropped dead or dying. The English were beaten, and on 25 December the victorious William, the 'Conqueror', was crowned William I in Westminster Abbey.

The chain of events which was to end at Hastings began ten months

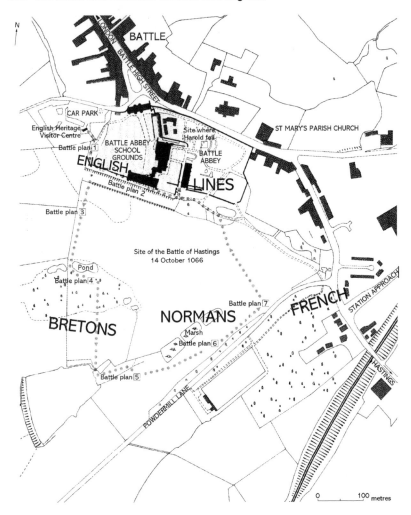

▲ **Fig. 136.** Battle, East Sussex, showing the armies' dispositions on 14th October 1066 (after English Heritage)

earlier with the death of King Edward the Confessor. For fifteen years William, duke of Normandy, had been his heir presumptive. On his deathbed, however, Edward named as his successor Earl Harold of Wessex, his wife's brother and commander of the army. Thus, it was to seize what he saw as rightfully his—the English throne—that William sailed with his invasion force.

The battlefield, inland from Hastings and 13 km. north-east of William's landing place at Pevensey, remains much as it was. The main difference is that the English position, along the crest of a shallow valley,

The Battle of Hastings: the fleeing Saxons rally

'The duke [William] who was following the victorious standards did not turn from his course when he saw these enemy troops rallying. Although he thought that reinforcements had joined his foes he stood firm. Armed only with a broken lance he was more formidable than others who brandished long javelins. With a harsh voice he called to Eustace of Boulogne, who with fifty knights was turning in flight, and was about to give the signal for retreat. This man came up to the duke and said in his ear that he ought to retire since he would court death if he went forward. But at the very moment when he uttered the words Eustace was struck between the shoulders with such force that blood gushed out from his mouth and nose, and half dead he only made his escape with the aid of his followers. The duke, however, who was superior to all fear and dishonour, attacked and beat back his enemies. In this dangerous phase of the battle many Norman nobles were killed since the nature of the ground did not permit them to display their prowess to full advantage.'

William of Poitiers, writing about 1070, *EHD* ii. 228–9

is occupied by Battle Abbey, founded by William to commemorate his victory and to honour the dead. The battle is well documented, not least because of its depiction in the Bayeux Tapestry.

The high altar of Battle Abbey's church (now only foundations) marked the spot where Harold fell. Other parts of the Abbey complex are better preserved. Now occupied by Battle School, the abbot's great hall is usually open during the summer. The Abbey site, an English Heritage property, has a museum in the gatehouse of 1338, which stands between the Abbey and Battle town's market place.

J. Coad, Battle Abbey *(English Heritage, 1994) (Site Guidebook).*

Beacon Hill, Burghclere, Hampshire Iron Age hillfort† ★

SU 458573. 9 km. S of Newbury, W of A34(T) within a small country park. Parking, picnic area, and viewpoint signposted from the A34. A footpath leads uphill from car park to the fort.

Set on the northern edge of the Hampshire downs, Beacon Hill commands fine views northwards with defences utilizing the local topography to good effect. An entrance with hornworks lies in the south-east corner, and traces of a second, blocked, entrance midway along the west side.

At least sixty round houses have been found in the interior along with two short sections of bank and ditch, indicating an earlier enclosure. In the south-west corner is the grave of Lord Carnarvon, sponsor of Howard Carter's excavations of the tomb of Tutankhamen.

Nearby is the **Seven Barrows** round barrow† cemetery beside and cut by the A34 south of Beacon Hill (SU 462553) and the unfinished hillfort and round barrows beside the Wayfarer's Walk on **Ladle Hill** (SU 478568).

B. Eagles, 'A New Survey of the Hillfort on Beacon Hill, Burghclere, Hampshire', Arch J, 148 (1991), 98–103.

Benenden, Iden Green, Kent Roman ford

TQ 802323. Access via footpath opposite entrance to Benenden School off B2086 (1 km.). Marked on OS map and located just S of the track leading to Stream Farm.

Stone slabs (now destroyed) mark where the Roman road running north to south once crossed the stream. The minor road south of Iden Green follows the line of the Roman road towards the A268.

C. Lebon, 'The Roman Fort at Iden Green, Benenden', ACant, 101, 1984 (1985), 69–81.

Bignor, West Sussex Roman villa   ★★

SU 988147. 7 km. SW of Pulborough, E of Bignor village. Privately owned. Open March to October. Admission charge. Figure 137.

Occupation on the villa site close to Stane Street began in the C1 AD with a small timber farmstead set within a ditched enclosure. During the early

▼ **Fig. 137.** A mosaic from the dining room, Bignor Roman villa, West Sussex. It shows an eagle carrying off Ganymede from Mount Ida, where he tended sheep, to become a cup-bearer to the Gods (Photograph copyright: Trustees of Bignor Roman villa)

C3 this was replaced by a simple four-roomed stone house, later modified and extended. A bath block was started behind the west wing but not completed, being replaced by a more elaborate block at the east end of a new south wing. The complete complex, including an aisled barn and various outbuildings, was walled. The agricultural buildings were demolished during the C3 so that the north wing of the main villa and the baths could be extended. At the same time a porticus (covered walk) was built to link the east ends of the north and south corridors, effectively forming an impressive courtyard villa. New rooms continued to be added and existing rooms provided with hypocausts†. Fine mosaics were laid depicting mythical and classical scenes. Prominent among these is Ganymede being carried off by an eagle; the mosaic of the six dancing girls (or maenads, followers of Dionysus) with flying veils; and Venus and the gladiator. The bath block has a mosaic depicting Medusa.

S. Frere, 'The Bignor Roman Villa', Britannia, 13 (1982), 135–95.

Bishop's Waltham, Hampshire Medieval palace

SU 552173. In the town of Bishop's Waltham. English Heritage; restricted opening. Admission charge. Figure 138.

In the Middle Ages Winchester was England's richest bishopric, with a vast landed estate. Many bishops held office as officials and ministers of government and their lifestyle reflected this status. Country residences such as Bishop's Waltham were designed to accommodate the bishop and his household as well as powerful guests and their retinues.

Surrounded by a broad moat, the palace buildings are arranged around a great inner court. The complex is dominated by the west tower, a stone keep-like structure constructed by Henry of Blois (bishop 1129–71), nephew of Henry I. Originally of three storeys, the tower provided private accommodation for the bishop. The tower was remodelled in the late C15 and the great hall rebuilt. This was transformed into a magnificent first-floor state room, lit by a range of windows filled with decorative glass. Further C15 additions include the bakehouse, brewhouse, a fourth storey to the west tower, a new chapel, and down the north range of the courtyard an 80 m. long range of timber-framed lodgings; part of the last survives, housing the ticket office and a small exhibition.

West of the palace were fishponds, while south and east are brick turrets of about 1500 (no admittance) on the wall around the huge kitchen garden. South of the garden was a deer park, while east of the palace the town of Bishop's Waltham's rectilinear grid-plan suggests planned development.

J. Hare, Bishop's Waltham Palace (English Heritage, 1990) (Site Guidebook).

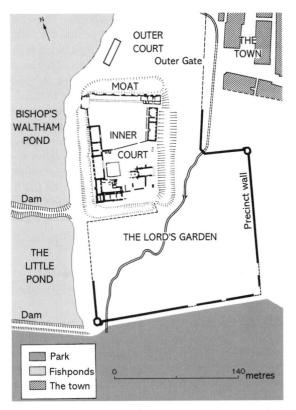

▲ Fig. 138. Bishop's Waltham, Hampshire (after English Heritage)

Bitterne (*Clausentum*), Southampton Roman settlement

Centred SU 435134. From Southampton centre take the A3024 across Northam Bridge to E side of river Itchen. Immediately after bridge, by Bitterne Manor House (flats) drive, a public footpath gives access to the river. The fort wall is visible through the fence looking towards the flats. See Figure 155.

Although an important Roman settlement, set on a promontory enclosed on three sides by the river Itchen, little is visible today. Originally a fort, a small port developed here in the later C1 and C2. The fourth side of the promontory was defended with earthwork defences, the approximate outer line of which follows Rampart Road. New fortifications constructed in the C4 were probably connected with Theodosius' reorganization of the Saxon Shore defensive system.

M. Cotton and P. Gathercole, Excavations at Clausentum, *Ministry of Works Archaeological Reports 2 (HMSO, 1958).*

Bodiam, East Sussex Medieval castle ★

TQ 782256. 15 km. N of Hastings. National Trust. Restricted opening. Admission charge.

Bodiam is the most perfect and unspoilt of the Hundred Years War castles. It was built largely between 1386 and 1388 and was intended to deter French coastal raids.

Outwardly it is impressive: quadrangular, with round corner towers and intermediate square ones, and a twin-towered gatehouse on the north side. The defences concealed accommodation for a great household. In the east range, with private access to the great hall and chapel in the south range, were the personal chambers. At the west end of the hall were buttery, pantry, and kitchen. The servants had their own common hall and kitchen in the west range of the central court, while the garrison was placed next to the great gate in the north-west corner. The extensive extended household of retainers occupied private lodgings in the towers, each with its own fireplace and garderobe†.

The region has some of the best of Henry VIII's coastal forts: Calshot, Hampshire (SU 488025); Hurst, Hampshire (SZ 319898); Camber, East Sussex (TQ 922185); Deal, Kent (TR 378521); and Walmer, Kent (TR 378501). All are managed by English Heritage.

P. Everson, 'Bodium Castle, East Sussex: A Fourteenth-Century Designed Landscape', in D. Morgan Evans et al. (eds), The Remains of Distant Times (Boydell Press, 1996), 66–72.

Boxgrove, Chichester, West Sussex Palaeolithic activity area

SZ 9208. Immediately below steep southern slope of the South Downs east of Boxgrove village. Within the gravel pit: no public access, but view from A285 on Halnaker Hill.

Boxgrove gravel pits north-east of Chichester saw the discovery in 1994 of the oldest human remains yet found in northern Europe—a male tibia.

Excavations between 1983 and 1996 revealed buried land surfaces which date back 500,000 years with a buried chalk cliff, in front of which was a flat plain extending down to the coast. Veins of flint eroded out of the cliff provided an accessible source of raw material for tool-making.

The people who lived and hunted nearby belonged to a species known as *Homo erectus*, the first hominid species to colonize Europe.

M. Pitts, Fairweather Eden (Century, 1997).

Brading, Isle of Wight Roman villa ★★

SZ 599 863. S of Brading, off the A 3055. Signposted. Owned privately. Admission charge. Car park. Open March–November. Site museum. Figure 139.

A classic courtyard villa with fine mosaic floors. The west wing with the

▲ **Fig. 139.** Brading Roman villa, Isle of Wight, as first illustrated in October 1880 (Copyright: Isle of Wight County Council)

main house is displayed under cover. The complex uncovered dates to around AD 300 although there were probably buildings here in the C1 AD. The main house faced east towards the main gate with an aisled farmhouse to the north and a range of farm buildings to the south. There were two bath-houses, one in the farmhouse, the other south of the courtyard. The mosaics depict a range of fabulous creatures, gods, and heroes, including the four seasons, Orpheus playing a lyre, Perseus and Andromeda, an astrologer, and a Medusa head.

D. Tomalin, Roman Wight *(Isle of Wight County Council, 1987).*

Breamore, Hampshire Anglo-Saxon church
SU 153188. 13 km. S of Salisbury. Figure 140.

St Mary's, beyond the village green, is a large, late Saxon church of advanced cruciform design. Of especial note structurally is the double-pyramid tower roof, a form known otherwise only from descriptions of towers later demolished. Many of the Saxon windows survive. Inside, a carved inscription, meaning 'here the covenant is explained to thee', is thought to date to about 1020. Also of note is the carved Saxon rood over the south door of the nave (now inside the C12 porch).

H. and J. Taylor, Anglo-Saxon Architecture *(Cambridge University Press, 1965), i. 94–6.*

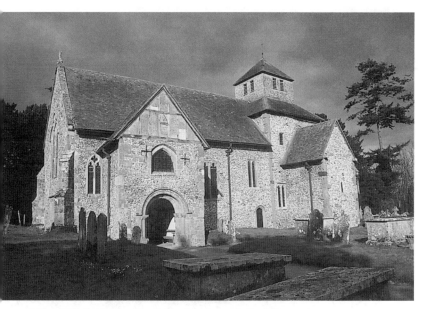

▲ Fig. 140. Breamore, Hampshire (Photograph: Paul Stamper)

Butser Hill, Petersfield, Hampshire Reconstruction Iron Age
farm and experimental archaeology centre ★★

SU 7120. W of A3(T) 5 km. S of Petersfield, 20 km. N of Portsmouth. Signposted footpath from car park in Queen Elizabeth Country Park, or from car park on S side of Butser Hill (SU 711201). Open afternoons Easter to end of September.

Set high on the chalk downs of Hampshire, the Butser Hill Iron Age farm provides a vivid impression of life in Iron Age times. Fields and paddocks are stocked with authentic species of plants and animals. Depending on the time of year you may see ploughing, sowing, or harvesting, and other craft activities.

P. Reynolds, Iron Age Farm (Colonnade Books, 1979). See also: www.skcldv.demon.co.uk/iafintro.htm

Caburn Hill, East Sussex Iron Age hillfort†

TQ 444089. N of A27(T) 4 km. SE of Lewis. Approached by track from Glynde. A footpath from Glynde to Lewis over Mount Caburn passes just N of the fort.

Set high on a steep-sided hill, this fort dominates the Ouse valley. Excavations suggested three main phases. Earliest is a C6 BC unenclosed settlement. About 300 BC the first defences were built, a bank and ditch enclosing about 1.1 ha. The defences were strengthened in the C1 BC, perhaps in response to the Roman threat. A second line of revetted ramparts was built, with a broad shallow ditch, best seen on the east and south-east side. Inside are slight traces of 140 or so pits. At the invasion Roman troops fired the timber gate. The fort was then abandoned but later Roman activity and perhaps some C12 AD refortification shows its strategic value.

A. Wilson, 'Excavations at The Caburn, 1938', SAC 80 (1939), 193–213.

Canterbury (*Durovernum Cantiacorum*), Kent   Roman

★

civitas† capital and medieval cathedral city

TR 1457. 88 km. E of London. A 'time walk' can be experienced at Canterbury Heritage, Stour Street. Finds: Roman Museum, Butchery Lane (1); Royal Museum and Art Gallery, High Street. Figure 141.

▼ **Fig. 141.** Canterbury, Kent: modern street plan showing the location of known Roman sites

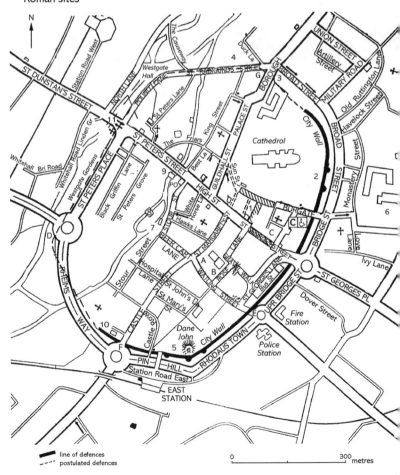

Canterbury, one of the first Roman *civitas* capitals, was tribal capital of the *Cantiaci*. Located at an important river crossing it was an extensive Iron Age trading settlement. The early planned Roman town comprised mainly timber buildings. Various public buildings were added from the Flavian period on. A theatre was discovered at the junction of St Margaret's Street and Watling Street (**A**). A public bath-house was located in the same street (now the Marlowe car park) (**B**). Several private houses have been discovered, a particularly well-appointed one lying under Butchery Lane, now a Roman museum (**1**). A private bath-suite was investigated in St George's Street (**C**). The C3 walled defences, enclosing 48 ha., have an irregular plan with external bastions; the circuit (**2**), subsequently reused in the C13, is now perpetuated by the modern ring road. Four gates have been identified, London Gate (**D**) and Riding Gate (**E**) set on Watling Street, Worth Gate (**F**) at the south end of Castle Street on a route leading to LYMPNE, and Quenin Gate (**G**) set astride the road to RICHBOROUGH. Both London Gate and Quenin Gate were blocked in medieval times. Quenin Gate, now in a car park off Broad Street (**3**), is the only gate where Roman masonry is visible. In St Radigund's Street the Roman wall was incorporated into the north wall of the church of St Mary Northgate (**4**). The wall stands to about 8.8 m. and the crenellations are visible in the medieval masonry. Several cemeteries have been investigated outside the town. The mound of Dane John, now landscaped into gardens (**5**), may have been a Roman burial mound. Recent excavations have shown there to be a Norman motte† and bailey† here but whether an extant mound was reused is at present unresolved.

The cathedral priory of Christ Church gained everlasting notoriety when, in 1170, Archbishop Thomas Becket was hacked to his death by four knights. The murder shocked Christendom, and Canterbury became England's major centre of pilgrimage: it was of course the destination of Chaucer's pilgrims. Such visitors brought money which paid for lavish building works. Good estate management played its part, too, and Thomas Chillendon, prior from the 1390s, leased out the priory lands within months of taking up office. It was this income which financed the reconstruction of the nave. Architecturally there is considerable contrast between this, built by the celebrated architect Henry Yevele, and the lavish east end where Becket is buried. Between them, at the crossing, is the fan-vaulted 'Bell Harry', completed in 1503. The Martyrdom in the North-West Transept marks the site of his murder, although the shrine itself was destroyed in the mid-C16. Here, too, is the tomb of the Black Prince, eldest son of Edward III.

Entrance to the Cathedral Close is guarded by Christ Church Gate, probably built about 1507 as a memorial to Prince Arthur, Henry VII's eldest son.

Long before the C12 Canterbury had been a centre of Christianity, and the destination of Augustine's mission of conversion to the English in 597. The remains of St Augustine's Abbey (**6**) (English Heritage), founded in 598, lie east of the cathedral.

The city still has many early buildings, and the centre retains much of its medieval plan and scale; timber-framed buildings stand behind many of the later façades. Of specific note is a C13 building off Stow Street built as a home for retired clergy (now Canterbury Heritage (**7**)). Close by, beside the river Stour, is the Greyfriars (**8**), the remains of the Franciscan Friary founded about 1220. Near the junction of High and Stour Streets is Eastbridge Hospital (**9**), of C12 date, one of many institutions providing pilgrim accommodation. The remains of the Norman castle lie at the south end of Castle Street (**10**), and the West Gate, built about 1380 marks the end of St Peter's Street (**11**).

M. Lyle, Canterbury *(Batsford and English Heritage, 1994)*.

Carisbrooke, Isle of Wight Medieval castle

SZ 486877. 2 km. SW of Newport. English Heritage; restricted opening. Admission charge. Car park. Figure 142.

Whoever held Carisbrooke controlled the Isle of Wight. The Normans built their castle on a site fortified earlier by the Saxons—a *burh*†—against the Vikings. It may also have been built over a Roman fort. Putative Roman walling can be observed either side of the Great Gatehouse facing the Lower Enclosure or Bowling Green. On the east side part of a typical later Roman rounded bastion and part of an in-turned entrance are exposed at the base of the Norman motte†.

▼ **Fig. 142.** Carisbrooke Castle, Isle of Wight (after Saunders)

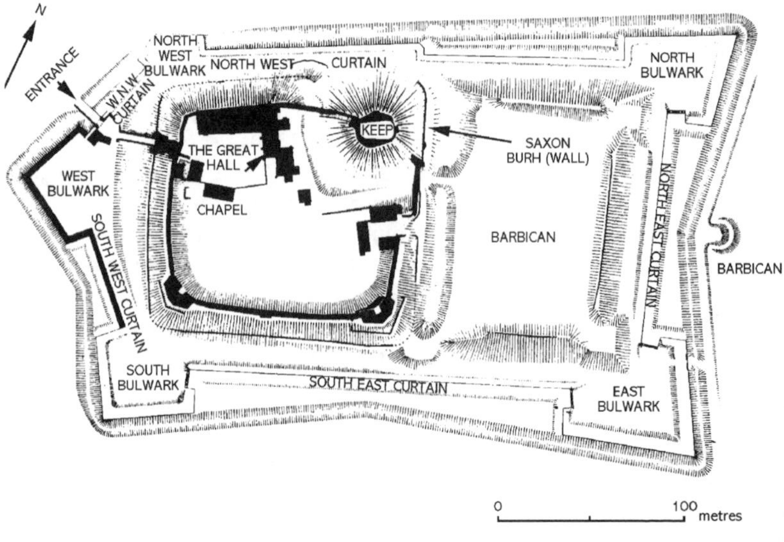

The motte and bailey† was probably begun about 1080, and by 1136 the castle had stone walls. The twin-towered gatehouse through which the castle is entered was added about 1335 to an earlier gateway, with the upper parts of the towers with their gunports and machicolations† being added about 1470. Beyond the gateway, steps lead to the walk around the curtain walls. From here can be seen the castle's outer defences with their angular, Renaissance-style artillery bulwarks added about 1600 by an Italian engineer against the threat posed by Spain. The Lord or captain of the castle was an important figure, and the domestic buildings reflect this. The great hall, incorporating a chapel, was begun in the C13; today it houses the Museum. Among the other buildings is a well-house of 1587 over the 49 m. deep castle well.

R. Chamberlin, Carisbrooke Castle *(English Heritage Site Guidebook, 1985)*.

Chestnuts Long Barrow, Addington, Kent Neolithic long barrow†

TQ 652592. 10 km. NW of Maidstone. W of Addington in the garden of a private house called Rose Alba beside minor road to Wrotham Heath. Addington is best approached by turning N off the A20. Permission to visit should be sought from house. See Figure 135.

The more northerly of a pair of long barrows west of Addington (see above ADDINGTON PARK) and a classic example of the Medway style of long barrow with its rectangular mound and simple stone-built end chamber.

The now reduced mound was originally about 20 m. long by 15 m. wide. The eastern end has an imposing façade of four large upright stones with a simple rectangular chamber opening from the middle. A possible capstone† lies to one side. Excavations found at least nine cremations, and late Neolithic artefacts. It is likely, however, that the monument was constructed earlier between 3800 BC and 3000 BC.

J. Alexander, 'The Excavation of the Chestnuts Megalithic Tomb at Addington, Kent', ACant, 76 (1961), 1–57.

Chichester (*Noviomagus Regnensium*), West Sussex Roman town and medieval cathedral city

SU 865047. County town on south coast. Finds: Chichester District Museum, 29, Little London. Figure 143.

The site of a walled Roman town with probable military origins. An important inscription, now under the portico of the Assembly Rooms, North Street (**1**) dedicates a temple jointly to Neptune and Minerva on the authority of Tiberius Claudius Cogidubnus, who himself is described as 'Great King of Britain'. The inscription suggests that the

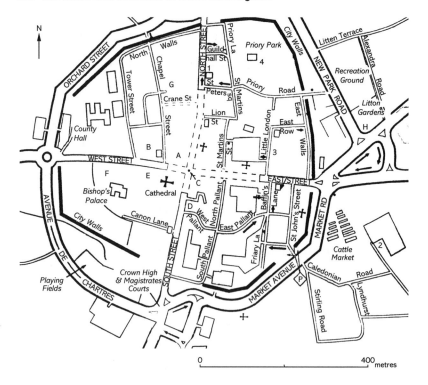

▲ **Fig. 143.** Chichester (*Noviomagus Regnensium*), West Sussex: modern street plan showing location of known Roman sites

area, occupied by the *Regnenses*, was a client kingdom in early Roman times ruled by Cogidubnus (see also FISHBOURNE).

The settlement developed into a planned Roman town from early Flavian times. The forum† probably lies at the intersection of West Street and North Street (**A**). An inscribed plinth for a statue or column of Jupiter was found on the site of the post office (**B**). The modern North, South, East, and West Streets meeting at the Tudor Market Cross (**C**) probably perpetuate the line of Roman roads. Excavations have located other public buildings including a public bath-house, and possibly a theatre or temple near All Saints Church (**D**). Building remains have been found near the Cathedral (**E**), Bishops Palace (**F**), and Chapel Street (**G**) including several mosaic floors. A mosaic panel can be seen in the Cathedral. A large cemetery exists outside the Eastgate alongside Stane Street (**H**). About 5 m. south-east of the Eastgate beyond the town defences, in Whyke Lane North, is the amphitheatre (**2**). It is now a hollow surrounded by a low bank in a recreation area. The earthen town defences, following a polygonal plan, were converted to stone in the C3 enclosing some 40 ha. The Roman walls were later incorporated into the medieval walls and the gateways probably perpetuated.

Chichester's was another of the great churches where rebuilding began in the Romanesque style after the Norman Conquest. Work began about 1091 and the church was consecrated in 1184. Little is later: the east end (mainly C13), the cloisters (about 1400), and the spire (C15). It has the only remaining detached bell-tower (1375–1430) of any English cathedral.

J. Wacher, The Towns of Roman Britain (Batsford, 1995), 255–71.

Cissbury Ring, Findon, West Sussex. Neolithic flint mines and Iron Age hillfort†

TQ 137079. 5 km. N of Worthing, E of A24 on the town outskirts. Signposted car park on W side of hill, footpath to hilltop. National Trust.

The earliest features at Cissbury are 100 or more flint mine shafts on the western side of the hilltop, visible as hollows up to 6 m. in diameter and up to 3 m. deep. In the C19, when nearly thirty examples were excavated, they were variously interpreted as cattle pens, huts, reservoirs, or 'druidical recesses'.

When flint was reached the miners cut a series of radiating galleries out from the shaft to follow the seam. The work was done with antler picks, levers, and bone shovels. Stone lamps provided light. Some of the galleries had incised lines cut into the wall, perhaps tally marks, or identification symbols. One set of carvings depicted the head of a red deer and a short-horned bull. In shaft 27 the skeleton of a woman was found buried, apparently from a roof fall. Radiocarbon dates indicate activity from about 3600 BC onwards through the Neolithic.

Overlying the flint mines is a roughly oval-shaped, 24 ha. Iron Age hillfort. The single rampart, comprising a massive inner bank, a berm†, a deep flat-bottomed ditch, and a small counterscarp bank†, was probably first constructed about 400 BC. There are two entrances, one facing east, the other south.

During Roman times the interior of the hillfort was cultivated; traces of lynchets† can be seen towards the east side. In late Roman times, the site was refortified by adding a turf capping to the bank. Some of the small enclosures within the fort may also date from this period, although one on the north-west side may be Neolithic.

E. Curwen and R. Ross Williamson, 'The Date of Cissbury Camp', Ant J, 11 (1931), 14–36.

Clacket Wood Service Station, M25, Surrey Roman villa

TQ 545405. Service station on M25 between junctions 5 and 6. Small display.

When the Service Station was constructed, excavations investigated the

Roman road near where it passes a Roman building at Titsey, perhaps a villa or, more likely, a temple. Medieval pottery kilns were also discovered.

G. Hayman, 'The Excavation of Two Medieval Pottery Kiln Sites and Two Sections through the London–Lewes Road at Clacket Lane, near Titsey, 1992', SuAC 84 (1997), 1–87.

Coldrum Long Barrow, Trottiscliffe, Kent   Neolithic long barrow†

TQ 654607. NE of Trottiscliffe village. Accessible along signposted lanes from Trottiscliffe or Ryarsh. National Trust.

This well-preserved Medway long barrow, sits on a low ridge in the shadow of the North Downs. The mound is slightly wedge-shaped, about 20 m. long, and edged with a peristalith† of rounded sarsen† boulders. The chamber at the east end, partly restored, survives as four upright stones forming three sides of a simple box-like structure. Excavations located at least twenty individuals inside the chamber. Today the east end of the site has been truncated.

E. Filkins, 'Excavations at Coldrum', Ant J, 8 (1928), 356–7.

Coombe Hill, Willingdon, Eastbourne, East Sussex   Neolithic causewayed camp

TQ 574021. On hilltop W of Willingdon, 5 km. NW of Eastbourne. Footpath N from car park at TQ 580016, approached by lane from Willingdon.

This causewayed camp is clearly visible as low earthworks in the grassland. There are two roughly concentric circuits of ditches. It is oval in plan, but incomplete on the north side because of the slope.

Excavations revealed that the inner ditch was U-shaped in cross-section, about 4 m. across and 1 m. deep. Pottery, flint tools, arrowheads, and quernstones (for grinding cereals) were found. A radiocarbon date suggests it was occupied about 3200 BC.

West of the camp is a large bowl barrow; while to the east there are two round barrows†, a disc, and a bowl barrow.

R. Musson, 'An Excavation at Combe Hill Camp, near Eastbourne, August 1949', SAC 89 (1950), 105–16.

Corhampton, Hampshire   Anglo-Saxon church

SU 610203. 6 km. NE of Bishop's Waltham.

St Mary's is an excellent example of a simple two-cell church, little changed since constructed in the C10 or C11. A remarkable survival east of the south door is a Saxon sundial, divided into eight for the eight tides into which the Saxons divided the day. Inside, the most striking feature is the Saxon chancel arch, with its through stones (up the sides), imposts (off which the arch springs), and through-stone voussoirs forming the arch itself.

Internally the church contains late C12 or early C13 wall paintings showing the story of St Swithun, the first bishop of Winchester, an altar stone, and a possibly C13 stone seat; and in the nave an early medieval font. A massive yew in the churchyard is said to be more than 1,000 years old.

H. and J. Taylor, Anglo-Saxon Architecture *(Cambridge University Press, 1965), i. 176–9.*

Crofton, Orpington, Kent Roman villa

TQ 454659. Immediately W of Orpington railway station. Limited opening during April to October. Admission charge. Site museum.

Set in the valley of the river Cray, part of a small Roman villa has been excavated. Occupation dates from the C1 AD. The remains of ten rooms from a modest building can be seen under cover. Much of the villa complex was destroyed by C19 building works and the construction of the railway.

B. Philp, 'The Roman Villa at Orpington', KAR 78 (1984), 196–9.

Danebury, Stockbridge, Hampshire Iron Age hillfort† ★

SU 323377. 9 km. SW of Andover, 3 km. E of Middle Wallop, SE of the A343. Situated within a signposted country park with parking. Self-guided trail.

Excavated between 1969 and 1994 Danebury is the most completely investigated hillfort in England. Occupation dates back to the C7 or C8 BC when 16 ha. of the hill was enclosed by a single circuit of ditch. This was part of a massive 2 km. linear boundary†, which subdivided the region into two distinct blocks. An inner enclosure and some four-post storage structures may belong with the first enclosure, and a hoard of bronze tools and weapons was deposited here about 600 BC.

The first hillfort proper was built in the C5 BC: a simple univallate structure with a single defensive rampart. There were gates to the south-west and east linked by a road. Inside, the northern area was used mainly for storing agricultural produce, the southern for houses and storage structures.

The hillfort was elaborated by the addition of an annexe and defensive outworks at the south-western entrance in the C4 BC. Further changes were made about 300 BC when the south-western entrance was blocked and the eastern entrance strengthened.

The interior of the developed hillfort was well planned. A network of roads provided access and subdivided the space available. In the centre was a series of rectangular shrines or sanctuaries. Most of the houses were set around the inside of the rampart, mainly in the northern sector. A population of 200–300 could have been accommodated. Storage remained a major aspect of life within Danebury, but in the later life of the fort was mainly confined to the southern sector.

The agricultural base of the settlement was a mixed economy dominated by sheep and cattle husbandry and wheat cultivation. Horses, pigs, and dogs were also kept. Evidence of various craft industries—woodworking, weaving, and metalworking—was found within the fort.

The latest occupation dates to about AD 20, by which time the inhabitants were importing Roman commodities including wine.

B. Cunliffe, Danebury: An Iron Age Hillfort in Hampshire, vol. vi: A Hillfort Community in Perspective, Council for British Archaeology Research Report 102 (1995).

Ditchling Beacon, East Sussex Iron Age hillfort†

TQ 332131. 9 km. N of Brighton, E of A273. Car park and viewpoint signposted from minor road between Westmeston and Claydon. National Trust.

Situated on the northern scarp of the South Downs, the hill is crowned by a roughly rectangular enclosure of 5.5 ha. defined by a single bank and ditch. Constructed in the C5 or C4 BC, it is possible that the enclosure was used as a seasonal corral for livestock grazing the downs.

Several other hillforts and enclosures can be seen along the northern edge of the South Downs. West of Ditchling is **Wolstonbury Hill** (TQ 284138) and **Devil's Dykes** (TQ 260111), while to the east is the later Bronze Age settlement of **Plumpton Plain** (TQ 385122).

D. Rudling, 'Trial Excavations at Ditchling Beacon, East Sussex, 1983', SAC 123 (1985), 251–4.

Dover (*Dubris*), Kent Roman town; Saxon Shore fort; Roman
lighthouse; medieval castle   ★★

TR 3141. The Painted House, in New Street. Restricted opening hours. Admission charge. The Castle and Roman lighthouse are E of the town (TR 326416). English Heritage. Restricted opening hours. Admission charge. Figures 144 and 145.

Dover was one of the bases of the fleet of the *Classis Britannica*. The fort (now under the inner relief road) was constructed around 130 and occupied until the mid-C3. In the later C3 a new fort was built as part of the Saxon Shore defensive system. During excavations north of Market Street the fort wall was found cut through a partly demolished Roman town house with preserved painted walls. An earlier house, also with painted walls, existed on the site in the C2. Now partly preserved under cover, the **Painted House** has one of the largest expanses of Roman wall-plaster visible *in situ* in Britain.

The **Roman lighthouse** (*pharos*) was one of a pair of C2 lighthouses

▲ **Fig. 144.** The Roman lighthouse (*pharos*), Dover (*Dubris*), Kent (Photograph: Jane Timby)

set on the cliffs either side of the river estuary. Only the eastern one, now in the grounds of Dover Castle, survives. The octagonal plan structure, unique in Britain, still stands to 19 m., although the upper 5.8 m. are a medieval rebuild. It was modelled on the C3 BC *pharos* in Alexandria and would have had a beacon on the top. Reused Roman building materials can be seen in the walls of the adjacent Saxon church.

Dover Castle overlooking the town stands within and utilizes the defences of a massive late Iron Age hillfort†. The first medieval castle dates to 1066, when the army of William the Conqueror moved from Hastings to London. The great square keep at the heart of the castle was added almost a hundred years later for Henry II. The keep is entered through a defensive forebuilding within which there are two chapels. The two floors lie over basement storerooms and each forms a separate suite of accommodation with a hall and chamber divided by a spine

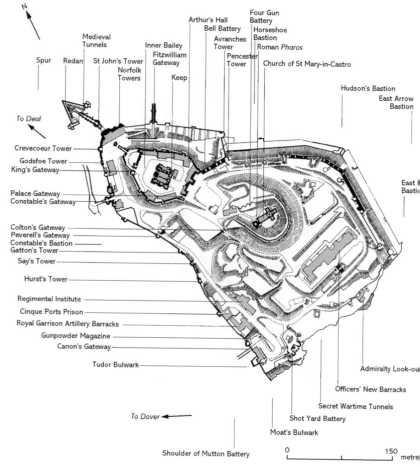

N

Four Gun
Battery
Arthur's Hall
Bell Battery   Horseshoe
Medieval   Avranches Bastion
Tunnels   Tower   Roman *Pharos*
Spur   Redan   St John's Tower   Inner Bailey   Pencester
                        Fitzwilliam   Tower
                Norfolk   Gateway   Church of St Mary-in-Castro
                Towers   Keep

Hudson's Bastion
East Arrow
Bastion

To Deal

Crevecoeur Tower

Godsfoe Tower
King's Gateway

East
Bastic

Palace Gateway
Constable's Gateway

Colton's Gateway
Peverell's Gateway
Constable's Bastion
Gatton's Tower

Say's Tower

Hurst's Tower

Regimental Institute

Cinque Ports Prison

Royal Garrison Artillery Barracks

Gunpowder Magazine

Canon's Gateway

Tudor Bulwark

Admiralty Look-ou

Officers' New Barracks

Secret Wartime Tunnels

To Dover

Shot Yard Battery

Moat's Bulwark

Shoulder of Mutton Battery

0   150
                        metre

▲ Fig. 145. Dover Castle, Kent (after English Heritage)

wall. Around these the exterior walls and towers are honeycombed with passages, stairs, chambers, and services.

The keep stands within an inner bailey†, also of the 1180s, called the Keep Yard, the walls of which are set with fourteen towers. C18 barrack buildings now line the walls; all incorporate medieval fabric, most notably the hall built for Henry III in 1240.

The outer bailey is huge. As completed in the C13 by Henry III, Dover's walls comprise the earliest example of concentric defences in Western Europe: carefully planned walls and towers provide overlapping fields of fire. The Battlements Walk allows the exploration of the numerous towers along the wall's length.

The castle is entered via the Constable's Gateway (1220s), a most elaborate entrance, with D-plan towers facilitating flanking fire. Additional security measures included a drawbridge and tunnels which led to St John's Tower forward of the main gateway.

There is much to see at Dover Castle. Although it declined in importance after the C16 its defences were extended in the 1750s, during the Napoleonic Wars, and later in the C19. In May 1940 it was from the naval headquarters deep beneath the castle that the evacuation of the British army from Dunkirk was organized and directed. Many of these later military works can be seen, including secret wartime tunnel systems.

B. Philp, The Excavation of the Roman Forts of the Classis Britannica at Dover 1970–1977 (Kent Archaeological Rescue Unit, 1981); B. Philp, The Roman House with Bacchic Murals at Dover (Kent Archaeological Rescue Unit, 1989); J. Coad, Dover Castle (Batsford and English Heritage, 1995).

Farley Heath, Surrey Roman temple

TQ 051450. Between Farley Green and Shamley Green adjacent to parking area. Information board.

Modern foundations outline the plan of a Roman temple excavated in the C19. This was a typical Romano-Celtic temple set inside a larger *temenos*†, built before AD 100 and probably remaining in use up to the C5. The temple occupies an elevated position and was approached via a spur road leading off Stane Street. Bronze fittings thought to come from a priestly headdress were found.

A. Lowther and R. Goodchild, 'Excavations at Farley Heath, Albury, during 1930', SAC 48 (1943), 31–40.

Fishbourne, West Sussex Roman palace ★

SU 839905. 2 km. W of Chichester and signposted from A27. Car-parking. On-site museum. Restricted opening hours. Admission charge. Figure 146.

Fishbourne is one of Britain's earliest and most palatial Roman buildings. The first buildings, of timber, were military granaries. By the 60s a large, masonry courtyard house had been built, colonnaded and provisioned with a bath-suite and an ornamental garden. This was perhaps the residence of Cogidubnus, king of the *Atrebates*, who was known to be pro-Roman. After AD 75 an impressive palace was built incorporating the early house in its south-east corner. The interior decoration was sumptuous with marble veneers, moulded stucco friezes, painted walls, and some remarkable mosaic floors, some of which survive. After several modifications and alterations, the palace was eventually destroyed by fire around 285 and thereafter abandoned. Another unusual feature at Fishbourne was the discovery of large formal gardens within the courtyard and in front of the palace, now partly reconstructed.

B. Cunliffe, Fishbourne Roman Palace (Tempus Publishing, 1998).

▲ **Fig. 146.** Fishbourne Roman palace, West Sussex. The garden under excavation showing the original bedding trenches. The pipes supplied water to marble basins and fountains. The garden has been replanted in a Roman style (Photograph: Sussex Archaeological Society)

Flowerdown Barrows, Winchester, Hampshire Bronze
Age round barrows†

SU 459320. At Littleton on NW outskirts of Winchester. Signposted access. English Heritage.

Two round barrows are the last survivors of a once substantial cemetery. Nearest the road is a bowl barrow of modest proportions; to the north is a well-preserved disc barrow. A ditch with an outer bank defines a circular platform about 30 m. in diameter. On the platform are two mounds which, although never excavated, were probably built about 1600 BC.

L. Grinsell, 'Hampshire Barrows I', PHFCAS 14/1 (1938), 9–40.

Harrow Hill, Findon, West Sussex Neolithic flint mines and
Bronze Age enclosure

TQ 081100. 4.5 km. S of Storrington, approached by footpath from car park on South Downs Way at TQ 086119. Figure 147.

Harrow Hill is an isolated and conspicuous hill rising to 150 m. above sea level. Near the top of the hill is a rectangular ditched early Iron Age enclosure with two entrances, perhaps a stock enclosure.

Pre-dating the Iron Age enclosure by over 2000 years was an extensive flint mine complex. The part-filled mines south of the enclosure show as simple hollows, while those to the east have doughnut-shaped mounds of spoil and waste around the central hollow. In all about 160 probable flint mines have been identified, ranging in diameter from 6 m. to over 15 m. across, and up to 4 m. deep before excavation.

Each hollow is the partly infilled remains of an extraction pit or mine shaft cut through the chalk to reach seams of flint below. Up to four such seams exist in the chalk on Harrow Hill but not all were exploited in each quarry. The upper seam exposed on the hillside was quarried using open-cast pits on the northern and southern sides. In all, five shafts have been excavated at Harrow Hill, ranging from 3 m. to 6.75 m. deep. Examination of a substantial flint-working floor nearby found that flint axes were being made alongside other implements. A radiocarbon date shows that the mine is early, operating by about 3700 BC.

G. Holleyman, 'Harrow Hill Excavations, 1936', SAC 78 (1937), 230–51.

Herstmonceux Castle, East Sussex Medieval great house

TQ 646104. 8 km. E of Hailsham off the A271. Visitor centre. Figure 148.

Herstmonceux, one of several so-called castles built in the mid-C15 for men of substance, is more of a country house. It stands in open countryside outside Herstmonceux village.

Herstmonceux was built in the 1440s for Sir Roger Fiennes, one of a group of wealthy nobles who became high officials at court after campaigning in France with Henry V and John duke of Bedford. For it he chose to use brick, still in the mid-C15 an attention-drawing novelty as a building material. Rising from the moat, what most impresses the visitor is the castle's size, its symmetry—four-square and with a central gatehouse (its gunports and machicolations† more for show than potential use)—and the number of towers. Those at the corners are largest: octagonal, battlemented, and splaying markedly outward from top to bottom. What also impresses is the completeness of the building, which had in fact been a ruin for 150 years before sympathetic restoration early in the C20.

The interior of the castle, which houses a college, is not open to the public.

M. Thompson, The Decline of the Castle (Cambridge University Press, 1987), 83–5.

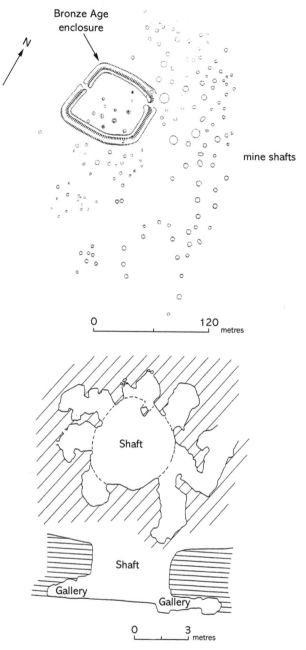

▲ **Fig. 147.** Plan of the enclosure and flint mines on Harrow Hill, West Sussex (after Holleyman)

▲ **Fig. 148.** Herstmonceux Castle, East Sussex (after Parker)

Highdown Hill, Ferring, Worthing, West Sussex Iron Age enclosure

TQ 092043. 4 km. NW of Worthing, approached by footpath from car park at Highdown Tower signposted N from A259 from Worthing to Littlehampton. National Trust.

This imposing little hill, overlooking Worthing and the coastal plain, has repeatedly attracted settlement. A late Bronze Age farmstead stood here, and a hoard of tools and weapons found nearby were perhaps hidden during times of unrest. Nothing now remains of this occupation.

The earliest visible features are the grass-covered ramparts of a small Iron Age hillfort†. Excavations revealed a steep-sided ditch separated from the bank by a narrow berm†. The rampart was of chalk rubble secured by timber posts front and back. Little is known about the Iron Age occupation, but the site was certainly reoccupied in the late C3 and C4 AD, and in Saxon times a cemetery was established within the ramparts.

A. Wilson, 'Report on the Excavations at Highdown Hill, Sussex, August 1939', SAC 81 (1940), 173–204.

Holtye, East Sussex Roman road

TQ 462388. A lay-by on A264 400 m. E of White Horse Public House marks where a Roman road running NNW–SSE crosses the modern road. Follow public footpath S for 400 m. to exposed section of road. Information board.

Of historical interest is the fact the road here was excavated by I. Margary in 1939, known for his pioneering work on the Roman road system. The road is unusually constructed of compacted iron slag. It probably linked the iron-smelting industries based in the Ashdown Forest with Watling Street.

I. Margary, Roman Roads in Britain *(John Baker, 1975).*

Ightham Mote, Kent Medieval moated manor house ★

TQ 584535. 6 km. E of Sevenoaks. National Trust; restricted opening. Admission charge.

Ightham Mote, at Ivy Hatch, is a picturesque medieval moated manor. It is of various dates, principally from the mid-C14 to the early C16. The moat was probably dug soon after 1300 and is crossed by a stone bridge leading to a crenellated gatehouse of about 1450. From this the main courtyard is entered.

The ground floor hall is part of the north range, its arch-braced roof tree-ring dated to the 1330s. Its windows have geometric tracery in the Decorated style, with rebates for hinged shutters. Off its north-west end are two timber-framed private ranges and a first-floor chapel. Called the New Chapel, this formed part of improvements at Ightham by Richard Clement, a Tudor royal servant, who bought it in 1521. It retains its original stalls, screen, and pulpit, while its four-centred barrel-vault roof is painted with Tudor badges including the pomegranate motif of Catherine of Aragon and the Tudor, York, and Lancaster roses. All pay homage to Henry VIII. It superseded an older chapel with vaulted crypt off the solar.

N. Nicolson, Ightham Mote *(The National Trust, 1998) (Site Guidebook).*

Kit's Coty House, Blue Bell Hill, Aylesford, Kent Neolithic long barrow† ★

TQ 745608. E of A229 2 km. S of junction 3 on M2. 3 km. NE of Aylesford, signposted from the A229 and accessible by footpath from minor road N from Aylesford where the Pilgrim's Way and Rochester Road meet. English Heritage. Figure 149.

Kit's Coty was apparently named by a shepherd who used to live in the stone chamber, 'coty' meaning a tiny house in local dialect. Originally the chamber stood at the east end of a mound some 70 m. long by 15 m. wide, now largely disappeared. At the west end there was a large stone, the General's Tombstone, blown to bits in 1867 because it hampered cultivation. This was probably the last remains of a peristalith† around the mound.

Today only the stone chamber survives. Typical of the Medway group of long barrows, it comprises three large uprights supporting a single massive capstone†.

About 500 m. south, beside the road to Aylesford, is another tomb, known as LITTLE KIT'S COTY.

R. Jessup, The Archaeology of Kent *(Methuen, 1930), 66–70.*

▲ **Fig. 149.** Kit's Coty House, Blue Bell Hill, Aylesford, Kent (Photograph by Timothy Darvill)

Little Kit's Coty, Aylesford, Kent Neolithic long barrow†

TQ 745604. Under trees within railings W of A229, 2.5 km. S of junction 3 on the M2 at Blue Bell Hill. 2.5 km. NE of Aylesford, signposted access by minor roads NE of Aylesford. English Heritage.

Sometimes known as the Countless Stones, this jumbled group of twenty-one boulders represents the collapsed chamber and façade of a Medway-style long barrow, originally similar to COLDRUM or THE CHESTNUTS.

R. Jessup, The Archaeology of Kent *(Methuen, 1930), 79–81.*

Long Man of Wilmington, Wilmington, East Sussex Ancient hill-figure

TQ 543035. 1 km. S of Wilmington on N face of the South Downs. Figure 150.

The Long Man is the tallest hill-figure known in England at 70 m. from

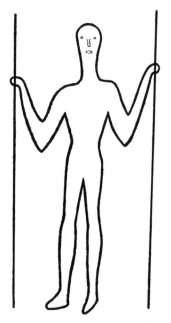

▲ **Fig. 150.** The Long Man of Wilmington, Wilmington, East Sussex (after Marples)

head to toe; the two uprights held one in each hand either side are slightly taller at 72 m. Traditionally assumed to be male, although not definitely so, the figure is defined in the turf by a single white line.

The two uprights have been variously interpreted as spears, agricultural tools, or symbols of office. Alternatively it may represent a person standing between two uprights (?posts), a doorway, or some other structural feature.

The original date of the hill-figure (extensively restored 1874) is unknown. Like both the UFFINGTON WHITE HORSE and the CERNE ABBAS GIANT, the Long Man lies in an area rich in Neolithic and Bronze Age monuments. One site, the Windover Hill long barrow†, lies immediately above the Long Man.

P. Newman, Lost Gods of Albion: The Chalk Hillfigures of Britain *(Sutton Publishing, 1997), 126–50.*

Lullingstone, Kent Roman villa ★★

TQ 529651. 1 km. SW of Eynsford off A225. Signposted. English Heritage; restricted opening. Admission charge.

Lullingstone villa is one of seven known in the Darent valley. Initially constructed as a winged corridor timber building in the C1 AD, it was later rebuilt in masonry and a large bath-suite added. Abandoned in the C3 it was rebuilt in the C4. The C4 building was richly decorated with mosaic floors and wall paintings. The floors include scenes depicting the Rape of Europa and Bellerophon killing the Chimaera.

In the latest phase of occupation a chapel was built within the house. Christian iconography on the decorated wall-plaster, including two chi-rhos and six figures with arms outstretched in prayer, suggests that the owners were ardent Christians.

G. Meates, The Roman Villa at Lullingstone, *vol. i:* The Site, *Kent Archaeological Society Monograph 1 (1979).*

Lympne (*Portus Lemanis*), Kent · Roman Saxon Shore fort

TR 117342. Lympne village is 6 km. W of Folkestone. The ruins (known as Stutfall Castle) lie in a field S of the village, via footpath for the 'Church and Castle'.

This former coastal Saxon Shore fort now stands 2.4 km. inland overlooking Romney marsh. The site, probably a base for the British fleet in the C2, became part of the coastal defensive system in the C3. Tiles stamped by the Roman fleet, *Classis Britannica* (CLBR), have been found here along with an altar dedicated to Neptune, erected by a commander of the fleet dating to the earlier phase of occupation. Excavations suggest that the fort had been abandoned by the mid-C4.

The fort was probably originally square in plan with semicircular bastions. Unstable soil conditions have resulted in collapse and movement of the stone walls, which are now considerably displaced from their original positions. C19 excavations identified various internal buildings including the *principia†*, and a bath-suite in the south-east corner. The fort was linked directly by road to CANTERBURY, LONDON, and probably DOVER.

B. Cunliffe, 'Excavations at the Roman Fort at Lympne', Britannia, 11 (1980), 227–88.

Newport, Isle of Wight · Roman villa

SZ 501885. Located on Cypress Road, in the suburbs of Newport just off the A3056. Street parking. Admission charge. Restricted opening.

A delightfully presented villa of the winged corridor type built in the late C3 over earlier occupation. It was richly appointed with a bath range, mosaic flooring, and underfloor heating. Artefacts on display. Behind the building is a reconstructed Roman garden.

D. Tomalin, Newport Villa and Roman Wight (Isle of Wight County Council, 1975).

Oldbury Hill, Ightham, Sevenoaks, Kent · Iron Age hillfort†

TQ 582561. N of A25 5 km. E of Sevenoaks, 2 km. E of Ightham. Access by footpath from picnic area on W side of site. National Trust. Figure 151.

Oldbury Camp, the largest Iron Age fort in south-east England, covers some 50 ha. It is bounded by a single bank and outer ditch, which follows the edge of a steep-sided plateau, with entrances to north and south.

Excavations have revealed that the site, built in the early C1 BC, was originally of simple construction with a bank and ditch. The defences were greatly strengthened just before the Roman Conquest. Piles of sling stones were found in the interior, presumably reserves that were never used. The site was never intensively occupied and may have been a place of refuge for people and livestock at times of unrest or danger from invasion. A spring near the centre of the site would have provided a

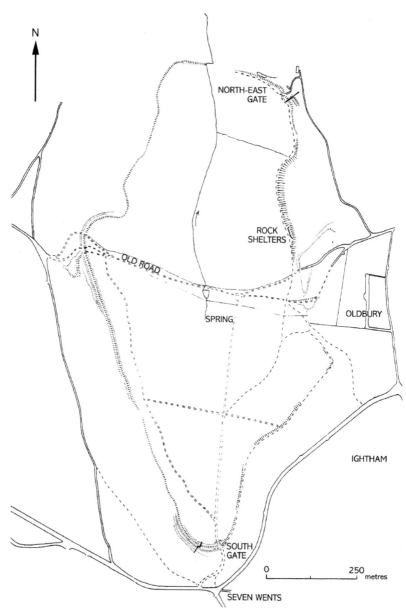

N

NORTH-EAST
GATE

ROCK
SHELTERS

OLD ROAD

SPRING

OLDBURY

IGHTHAM

SOUTH
GATE

0   250 metres

SEVEN WENTS

▲ **Fig. 151.** Plan of Oldbury Hill, Ightham, Sevenoaks, Kent (after Thompson)

constant source of water. On the east side of the site are the OLDBURY ROCK SHELTERS.

F. Thompson, 'The Iron Age Hillfort of Oldbury, Kent: Excavations 1983–4', Ant J, 66 (1986), 267–86.

Oldbury Rock Shelters, Kent Palaeolithic and later rock shelters

TQ 585562. On E side of OLDBURY CAMP. Access through Oldbury Camp (see above). National Trust.

The steep eastern side of the greensand plateau on which Old Camp stands was once the edge of a river valley. High on the side of the valley is a band of hard stone (Oldbury Stone), below which softer rock has eroded out leaving overhangs and rock shelters along the base of the cliff. Although altered by modern quarrying, traces of these shelters still survive. Excavations have recovered several flint handaxes of Mousterian type to the east of the rock shelters, suggestive of Middle Palaeolithic occupation around if not within the shelters.

The importance of the area in Palaeolithic times is emphasized by the fact that only 19.5 km. north of this site is the **Barnfield Gravel Pit, Swanscombe** (TQ 598746), now a nature reserve, where numerous Acheulian flint tools and the bones of Swanscombe Man (who probably lived during Middle Palaeolithic times) were discovered in the 1930s.

D. and A. Collins, 'Cultural Evidence from Oldbury', BIA 8–9 (1970), 151–76.

Penshurst Place, Kent Medieval great house

TQ 527439. 7 km. NW of Tunbridge Wells.

About 1340 Sir John de Pulteney, a London merchant and financier and four times mayor of London, constructed a splendid house of Wealden sandstone. Of traditional H-plan, it comprises a Great Hall flanked by, at the one end, a residential range with private chamber over undercroft† and, at the other, a kitchen and service range. The hall remains open to its 18 m. high, sweet chestnut roof, which is of kingpost construction with wooden corbels carved as human figures, said to represent people who worked on the manor.

At first, Penshurst was apparently undefended, but about 1392 a square, stone-walled enclosure, with corner and interval towers, was constructed around the house. Even if not a response to the Peasants' Revolt of 1381, these defences represent a wealthy family's unease at living in 'a society starved of law'.

Penshurst church is the burial place of the Sidneys, including Sir William (d. 1554), commander of the right of the English line at Flodden in 1513. It also contains a fine late C13 tomb, a shallow relief carving of a woman in anguished prayer, locked in her coffin by a foliated cross.

J. Newman, The Buildings of England: West Kent and the Weald (Penguin, 1980).

Pevensey Castle (*Anderida*), Sussex Roman Saxon Shore fort

TQ 645048. 10 km. NE of Eastbourne on A259. English Heritage; restricted opening. Admission charge.

Pevensey was one of the six south-coast Saxon Shore forts. The late C3 Roman walls were reused as the outer bailey† of a Norman castle. Unlike some of the other shore forts Pevensey has a slightly irregular oval shape, fitting the local terrain. The projecting bastions are drum-shaped, built of stone laced with horizontal bonding courses of red tile. The walls are 3.7 m. thick and enclose about 4 ha. A pair of machine-gun posts was built in 1940 in the collapsed ruins of the Roman wall, while a pillbox set into the north-west bastion was disguised to look like the fort.

J. Goodall, Pevensey Castle *(English Heritage, 1999) (Site Guidebook).*

Portchester Castle (*Portus Adurni*), Hampshire Roman Saxon Shore fort and medieval castle

SU 625046. S of Portchester off A27, junction 11 on M27. English Heritage. Restricted opening to the castle. Admission charge. Parking. Figure 152.

Portchester Castle stands on a promontory at the head of Portsmouth harbour. The first major structure was a 3.4 ha. late Roman military shore fort. Occupied until the late C3, the fort was reoccupied in the mid-C4 when barbarian attacks threatened. In the late C3 a massive masonry wall fronted by a double-ditch system was constructed, enclosing a series of metalled roads and buildings. Details of the internal layout have been discovered through excavation, although nothing remains visible today. The Roman walls can be seen and were originally

---

The 'Saxon Shore'

The term Saxon Shore or *litus saxonicum* comes from a document known as the *Notitia Dignitatum* which dates from the end of the C4 AD. This lists the country's military installations and the principal commands, amongst which there is a count (*comes*), of the Saxon Shore. It is likely that a system of defences was established around the south and east coasts in the early C3 in response to barbarian raiders. The earliest forts were probably at BRANCASTER and RECULVER. In the late C3 several other forts were constructed including BURGH, DOVER, RICHBOROUGH, LYMPNE, and PEVENSEY. In total ten forts are known. The later Roman defences adopted many new designs; the shore forts are less symmetrical compared to earlier forts and the walls are free-standing with no internal ramparts. Many have external bastions and gates with rectangular, semicircular, or polygonal towers.

▲ **Fig. 152.** The north wall of the Roman fort, Portchester (*Portus Adurni*), Hampshire, showing the projecting D-shaped bastions (Photograph: Jane Timby)

3.1 m. wide and 6.1 m. high with four gates and twenty forward-projecting D-shaped bastions, of which fourteen survive.

Occupation continued throughout Saxon times, and in the C11 the Roman enclosure was reused as the bailey† of a castle built by Henry I. The east and west gates were remodelled and the two postern gates on the north and south walls blocked in the C11. Much of the stone used in the Norman castle was robbed from the Roman fort.

B. Cunliffe, Excavations at Portchester Castle, *vols i–iv, Reports of the Research Committee of the Society of Antiquaries of London 32, 33, 34, and 43 (vol. iv with J. Mumby) (1975–85).*

Reculver (*Regulbium*), Kent Roman Saxon Shore fort

TR 228694. 5 km. E of Herne Bay. Car park. English Heritage.

Originally a C1 fort enlarged in the early C3, as one of the early Saxon Shore forts. Only the rubble core of the walls remains. Originally 2.4 m. thick with rounded corners, these enclosed an area of around 3.2 ha. Recent coastal erosion has removed much of this. Beyond the walls are two steep ditches. Excavations identified a street grid with houses, barracks, and other buildings.

Inside the walls are the twin towers of a C13 church with Saxon origins.

B. Philp, The Roman Fort at Reculver *(Kent Archaeological Rescue Unit, 1970).*

Richborough (*Rutupiae*), Kent   Roman military base and Saxon Shore fort   ★★

TR 324602. 2 km. N of Sandwich off A257. English Heritage, restricted opening. Admission charge. Site Museum.

Traditionally thought to be where the Romans landed in AD 43. A marble-faced monument erected inside the fort in about 80 is thought to commemorate the completion of the conquest. An alternative interpretation is that it represented a formal entrance to and exit from Britain. Although Richborough is now some 3 km. from the sea, in Roman times it was an island in the river Wantsum with direct coastal access. The main road (Watling Street) to Canterbury and thence London runs from the west gate. There is little to see of the early Claudian defences apart from a short length of parallel ditches inside the later walls, near the west gate along the road line. Timber granaries alongside the road, of about 44–85, are marked out on the ground. All that remains of the marble-faced monument is a massive cross-shaped plinth of flint and pebbles, which supported a four-way arch.

During the later C3 an earth fort with a triple line of ditches was constructed. In the late C3 the site was levelled, including the triumphal arch, and a larger Saxon Shore fort constructed in stone, the walls of which now dominate the site. Other visible remains from this period include a four-roomed bath-house in the north-east corner over the earlier *mansio†*.

Later elements include the chapel of St Augustine at Fleet in the north-east corner, traditionally where the saint arrived in Kent in AD 597. Near the north-west corner of the fort lie the remains of a hexagonal, Roman baptismal font, evidence of a church pre-dating the C6 chapel.

B Cunliffe, Richborough V, *Reports of the Research Committee of the Society of Antiquaries of London 23 (1968); S. Johnson,* The Roman Forts of the Saxon Shore *(Elek, 1976), 48–51.*

Rochester (*Durobrivae*), Kent   Roman town and medieval cathedral city

TQ 426686. Access via the M2/A2 and M20 motorways. Figure 153.

A 9 ha. defended Roman town set where Watling Street crosses the river Medway. The original earthen defences were replaced in the C2 by a

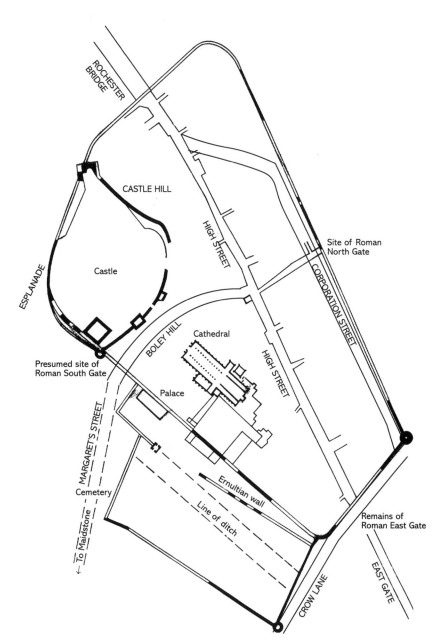

▲ **Fig. 153.** Rochester (*Durobrivae*), Kent: modern street plan showing the location of the Roman defences and other sites

wall, traces of which can be seen below the Norman walls of the castle along the Esplanade (**1**). Further traces of the wall, still 3 m. high, can be seen in a public garden in Eagle Court (**2**) (follow an alleyway south of the High Street adjacent to the Eagle Tavern, leading to the YMCA). A further glimpse can be gained below some modern brickwork down Free School Lane (**3**). There has been little archaeological work but buildings have been glimpsed in the High Street (**A**), beneath the Cathedral (**B**) and in the Northgate area (**C**). Cemeteries are known outside the south gate at Boley Hill (**D**), at Borstal, and at Strood.

The cathedral is largely of the later C12 and C13 (see especially the C13 transepts and crypt). The castle keep is early C12.

B. Burnham and J. Wacher, The Small Towns of Roman Britain *(Batsford, 1990), 76–81.*

Rockbourne, Hampshire Roman villa

SU 120170. Off B3078 5 km. NW of Fordingbridge. Signposted. Restricted opening. Admission charge. Site museum.

A local antiquarian excavated some sixty-six rooms of a villa, occupied from the C2–C5. The house, built over an Iron Age round house, was extended in the mid-C2 and a detached bath-house added. Around AD 150 the villa was demolished for a larger building. Further ranges and ancillary buildings were added during the C3 creating a courtyard villa. An unusual under-floor heating system was found where curved roof tiles (*imbrices*) were used rather than stacks of *pilae* bricks. Mosaic floors were laid including one with a 'wheel' motif.

RCHME, 'West Park Roman Villa, Rockbourne, Hampshire', Arch J, *140 (1983), 129–50.*

St Catherine's Hill, Winchester, Hampshire

Iron Age hillfort†

SU 484276. 2 km. SE of Winchester, N of M3. Access by footpath from minor roads leading E from St Cross on the edge of Winchester.

Situated high on a chalk knoll towering over the river Itchen, and with fine views over Winchester, this hillfort, enclosing about 7.6 ha., was defended by a single rampart, ditch, and a small counterscarp bank†. The entrance on the north-east side is marked by in-turned ramparts.

The hillfort underwent at least four major phases of rebuilding, starting in the C6 BC, but in the middle part of C1 BC it was attacked, overrun, and burnt.

On the hilltop is the site of a medieval chapel to St Catherine, partly set within a rectangular earthwork enclosure; to its east is a turf-cut maze said to be C18.

C. F. C. Hawkes, 'St Catherine's Hill, Winchester: The Report of 1930 Reassessed', in D. Harding (ed.), Hillforts *(Academic Press, 1976), 59–75.*

Silchester (*Calleva Atrebatum*), Hampshire Roman *civitas*†
capital ★

SU 643624. 1.5 km. E of Silchester village. Car park on NW edge. Town walls and amphitheatre: English Heritage. A public footpath crosses the site. Small museum on W side. Waymarked wall walk, leaflets at main car park. Figure 154.

Silchester, originally a large Iron Age settlement, later became a major defended Roman town. Unlike most Roman towns it was eventually abandoned and is today fields. Through excavations of 1890 to 1909 and aerial photography, the later town plan is known in considerable detail. It was established shortly after the conquest with the laying of a street grid, and the construction of public buildings, including an amphitheatre to the immediate north-east of the town. About AD 100 the town was surrounded by a ditch and a gravel rampart with masonry gates. In the later C3 this was replaced with stone walls, which still partly survive. A ditch, originally 14 m. wide, ran outside the walls.

The elliptical amphitheatre could have seated between 4,500 and 9,000 spectators. In medieval times the arena was occupied by a timber hall, with the seating banks forming simple defences.

M. Fulford, Calleva Atrebatum *(Calleva Museum, 1987).*

▼ **Fig. 154.** View of the 1998 excavations in Insula IX, Silchester (*Calleva Atrebatum*), Hampshire, showing the foundations of a Roman house (Photograph: Jane Timby)

Southampton, Southampton Saxon trading port and medieval town

SU 4514. Access via the M3 and M27. Figure 155.

Three successive settlements have stood at the head of Southampton water where a peninsula juts between the rivers Test and Itchen. On the east bank of the Itchen was Roman *Clausentum*. In the C7, Hamwih, a middle Saxon trading port, was founded on the east side of the peninsula. In the C10 the present town was established on the south-west corner of the peninsula. A major port, it witnessed the embarkation of voyagers including medieval crusaders, and in 1620 the Pilgrim Fathers.

Southampton's city walls are among the best. Begun about 1202 in earth and timber, they were rebuilt in stone in 1260, added to after a

▼ **Fig.·155.** Southampton: showing the location of the Roman settlement of *Clausentum*, the Saxon settlement of Hamwih and the Medieval town (after Pelham)

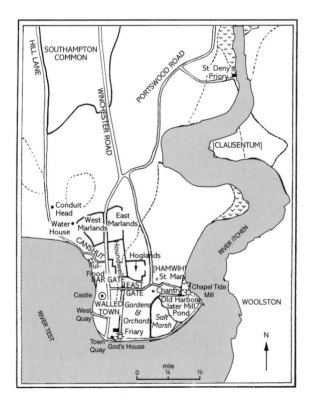

destructive French raid of 1338, while later in the C14 a further French threat led to the construction of a wall along the west side which, for expediency, incorporated the seaward walls of existing houses, still to be seen.

Several gates and towers stand along the walls. The Bargate, at the north end of High Street and the main entry to the walled town, is a complex structure with a C12 core, twin drum towers of about 1300, to which the façade with its civic heraldry was added about a century later. At the south-east corner is God's House Gate and Tower (archaeology museum), largely C14 and C15, which guarded the town sluice controlling the flow of water into the moat around the town walls. It incorporated accommodation for the Town Gunner, evidence of adaptation to the threat of artillery in the late Middle Ages with its gunports which punctuate the defences. The West Gate is a plain gate tower of the mid-C14. Of the castle, in the north-west quarter of the walled town, there is little to see.

Various civic, commercial, and domestic structures emphasize the town's role as a leading medieval port. Fronting onto the Town Quay, at the south end of Bugle Street, is the late C14 woolhouse (Maritime Museum). To the east, in Porter's Lane, are remains of six medieval houses. The best-surviving examples of merchants' houses are the Duke of Wellington (Bugle Street; C15), the Red Lion (High Street; C15), and most notably 58 French Street, early C14 and perhaps England's earliest complete medieval town house.

Holyrood Church, fronting High Street was blitzed in the Second World War. St Michael's, on the west side of the walled town, and with work of 1070 is Southampton's oldest building. It has a C12 Tournai marble font.

C. Platt, Archaeology in Medieval Southampton (Henry Stone, 1973).

Stone-by-Faversham, Kent Roman mausoleum

TQ 992614. Access via footpath 30 m. N of Watling St (A2), 2.4 km. W of Faversham and opposite turning signposted Newnham and Doddington. English Heritage.

A C4 square Roman mausoleum was later incorporated in an ecclesiastical building. The stone ruins of the Saxon or medieval chapel still remain and the Roman masonry comprising stone and tile bonding can be seen on the west part of the chancel. The nave was originally timber. A small Roman settlement lies close by with Watling Street about 30 m. to the south.

H. Taylor and D. Yonge, 'The Ruined Church at Stone-by-Faversham: A Reassessment', Arch J, 138 (1981), 118–45.

Titchfield Abbey, Hampshire Medieval abbey converted to

country house

SU 541067. On W side of Fareham. English Heritage; restricted opening. Admission charge. Figure 156.

Titchfield Abbey, founded in 1232 for Premonstratensian† canons, had an unremarkable history, and what makes the site worth visiting are the remains of the country house contrived out of it after its dissolution in 1537. This Palace House was built for Thomas Wriotesley, a subordinate of Thomas Cromwell's, and was complete by about 1542. The monastic church was converted into a gatehouse range by demolishing its tower and transepts and raising instead a twin-towered Caen stone gateway. The fabric shows how stone and brick were used to block old windows while other windows were roughly inserted. Behind the gatehouse, around the monastic cloister, there were similar conversions, the whole façade being topped with a bombastic row of crenellations

▼ **Fig. 156.** Titchfield, Hampshire, with Wriotesley's conversion superimposed on the monastic plan (after Howard)

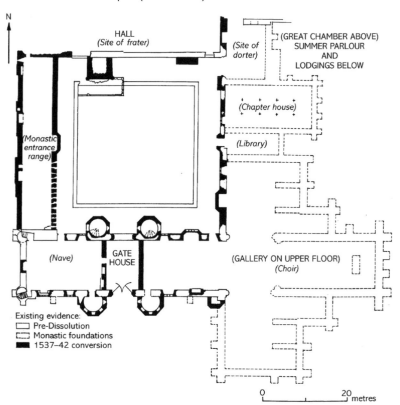

(battlements). The house apparently saw few changes before its partial demolition in 1781.

Another Dissolution conversion to a country house took place at **Netley Abbey** (English Heritage) a few kilometres to the west (SU 453089).

R. Graham and S. Rigold, Titchfield Abbey *(English Heritage, 1985) (Site Guidebook).*

The Trundle, Singleton, Chichester, West Sussex Neolithic causewayed enclosure† and Iron Age hillfort† ★

SU 877111. 5.5 km. N of Chichester. Access by footpath from car park at SU 872110 on minor road S of Singleton, or from the E by footpath from car parks overlooking Goodwood racecourse.

The Trundle is one of the most dominant hills along the western part of the Sussex Downs. In the centre of the hill are the slight remains of one of the most elaborate Neolithic causewayed enclosures in England. The inner circuit of the Neolithic ditches encloses an area 122 m. across, covering about 1.2 ha. Slight traces of the bank and segmented ditch can be seen in the grass. A second circuit, sometimes referred to as the spiral ditch, appears to encircle the inner enclosure one and a quarter times, fading out in the north-west. Traces of a third circuit possibly link to the spiral ditch. A bank and ditch across the spur of the hill on the north side (SU 874114) may also be connected with the Neolithic enclosure.

Radiocarbon dates show construction started around 4200 BC. Pottery, animal bones, marine shells, and some disarticulated human remains were found in ditch fills.

The name 'The Trundle' refers to a C3 and later Iron Age hillfort that partly overlies the causewayed enclosure. The obvious ramparts comprising a bank and outer ditch are probably of two phases, and enclose about 4 ha. There are in-turned entrances to the east and west.

E. Curwen, 'Excavations in the Trundle, Second Season, 1930', SAC *72 (1931), 100–50.*

Westwell, Kent Medieval parish church

TQ 9947. 6 km. NW of Ashford.

Apart from the C16 porch, St Mary's is largely C13, comprising west tower, aisled nave, chancel, and chapels. Most exceptional is the stone-vaulted chancel with its stone chancel screen with three tall and narrow openings. Fixtures include a triple *sedilia*† (three seats inset in the south wall for priest, deacon and subdeacon), while the central east lancet window contains a complete Jesse Tree (the upper part C13, the lower put together from scraps in 1960).

J. Newman, The Buildings of England: North-East and East Kent *(Penguin, 1983).*

Winchelsea, East Sussex Failed medieval new town

TQ 905175. 12 km. NE of Hastings. Some National Trust. Figure 157.

Many 'new towns' were founded in the early Middle Ages by landowners keen to profit from increased rent and tolls. Not all were a success. Old Winchelsea, at the mouth of the river Brede, was finally swallowed by the sea in 1287 after suffering for decades from coastal erosion. Eight years earlier Edward I had been persuaded to help resite the borough, and by 1283 his town planners had laid out a grid of streets on a hilltop at a place called Iham. These streets defined thirty-nine quarters for a town—New Winchelsea—intended to include a market, three churches, a friary, stone defences, and 700 houses.

▼ **Fig. 157.** Winchelsea, East Sussex. The new town plan based on a 1292 rental (after Brandon, and Beresford & St Joseph)

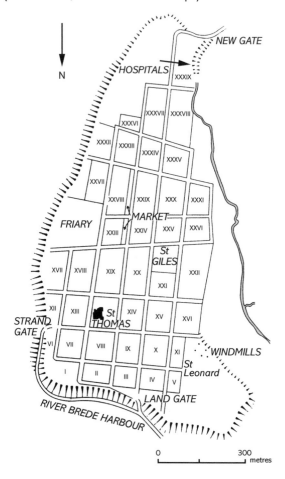

Over-ambition and a declining economy left the planners' ambitions unfulfilled. Of the main church, St Thomas's, probably only the aisled chancel was completed. This stands in its own quarter, and is very grand: in the Decorated style, and containing elaborate wall tombs commemorating successive Admirals of the Cinque Ports. New Winchelsea was larger in the early C14 than it is today—the grass fields on its southern edge were then built over—but the town was already in trouble, and the Black Death of 1348–9 and French raids ended hopes of real urban success. As well as the street plan and St Thomas's the visitor can see the town's Strand (north-east) and New (south) gates as well as the undercrofts† of some of its larger houses.

M. Beresford and J. St Joseph, Medieval England, 2nd edn (Cambridge University Press, 1979), 238–41.

Winchester (*Venta Belgarum*), Hampshire   Roman *civitas*†
capital and medieval cathedral town   ★

SU 488829. 19 km. N of Southampton. Ancient capital of Wessex. Winchester City Museum. The Square. Admission free.

Although the tribal capital of the *Belgae* and later a substantial defended Roman town, there are few remains visible. Earthworks at Oram's Arbour on the west side of the town date to the C1 BC. A large public building complex north of the cathedral was probably the forum basilica†. The medieval walls follow the line of their Roman predecessors which enclosed 58 ha. The only surviving wall fragment is on the west side of the river Itchen by City Bridge. A large C4 cemetery was excavated at Lankhills outside the north gate.

After the collapse of Roman authority in the early C5 Winchester apparently retained some important role in the region. About 648 King Cenwalh (642–73) founded the Old Minster, the church of an episcopal see transferred from Dorchester on Thames. The outlines of its excavated walls have been laid out beside the nave of the cathedral. The original Minster church grew east and west, acquiring towers, apsidal chapels, and, in 974, incorporated in pride of place the remains of Bishop Swithun (d. 861). Also buried here was King Alfred (reigned 871–99) in whose time, and following a Viking raid in 860, Winchester became a *burh*† with refurbished defences and a new—the present—street plan. His son Edward the Elder (reigned 889–925) founded two further major churches: the New Minster, alongside the Old Minster and thereafter the burial place of kings including Cnut (d. 1035); and (for holy women) the Nunnaminster (see remains of church in Abbey Passage beside the Guildhall).

The cathedral was begun in 1079–80 by William I. While the crypt is original and preserves the plan of the Norman apse, the rest of the structure is largely later. The tower and transepts are early C12, while the nave and west window, begun about 1350, represent one of the first major building campaigns in England in the Perpendicular style.

Other major projects of the early Middle Ages were the bishop's palace at Wolvesey in the south-east corner of the city (English Heritage), and St Cross Hospital east of the city. By 1148 there were around fifty-seven churches in the city and its suburbs. Of these, and of the various monasteries, chapels and so on, only seven now stand; some have C12 or C13 work.

There is little to see of Winchester's Norman castle (south of the West Gate) with the notable exception of the aisled Great Hall of the 1220s. Hanging within is the top of the extraordinary Round Table made for Edward I in the late C13, a deliberate echo of the table around which the legendary King Arthur's gallant knights gathered. The painted scheme with its equally propagandist Tudor Rose is of about 1516.

Later medieval structures include, in the southern suburbs, Winchester College founded in the 1380s; the West Gate (largely late C14); and the Market Cross (or Buttercross) in the High Street (early C15).

T. James, Winchester *(Batsford and English Heritage, 1997).*

11 Wessex and the west country

This region includes the counties and unitary authorities of Dorset, Wiltshire, Somerset, North Somerset, Bath and North-East Somerset, Bristol, South Gloucestershire, Swindon, Poole, and Bournemouth.

Wessex embraces a great diversity of landscapes and archaeology. In the extreme south-east are the sandy heaths of the New Forest and Dorset coast, with acid soils and scrubby vegetation. Where they reach the coast there are low cliffs and sandy beaches. Crossing these landscapes are the meandering valleys of the rivers Avon, Stour, and Frome that link the south coast with the interior heartland of southern England.

West and north of the heaths lie the interconnected blocks of chalk downland so typical of central southern England: the Marlborough Downs overlooking the upper Thames valley; Salisbury Plain, now extensively used for military training; Cranborne Chase; the North Dorset Downs centring on Cerne Abbas; and the South Dorset Downs south of Dorchester. These last areas comprise the Wessex of Thomas Hardy.

North and west of the chalkland is the hill and vale country that separates the lowlands of southern England from the more rugged terrain of the west. In the north part of the region, in Avon and north Wiltshire, are the southern limits of the Cotswold hills with their fine limestones so prized for building. Further south in Somerset are the steep-sided Mendip hills, the Quantocks, the Blackdown hills, the Brendon hills and, in the far west, Exmoor.

Between these uplands are low flat plains and valleys, the most extensive of which is the Somerset Levels extending to more than 100 square kilometres south of the Bristol Channel.

Such a rich diversity of landscape is also reflected in the range of archaeological sites in the area. The chalk downs in particular have attracted the attention of antiquarians and archaeologists since the C17 and as a result the area is comparatively well explored.

The central south coast of England has been one of the main areas of cross-channel trade since early prehistoric times. Fine natural harbours abound, most notably around Poole and Christchurch on the coast of Dorset.

Ackling Dyke, Dorset Roman road

SU 022178 to ST 967032. Visible in places. Figure 159.

One of the main Roman roads crossing Dorset running from Exeter, via Dorchester, Old Sarum, Silchester, and Staines to London. It enters modern Dorset at Bokerley junction where it passes through BOKERLEY DYKE running straight to BADBURY RINGS where it just clips the outer earthworks. Much of the route from Gussage St Michael to the county border can be walked. Parts of it are still up to 12 m. wide and 1.5 to 2 m. high with visible side ditches. At OAKLEY DOWN it cuts through two earlier Bronze Age disc barrows, and on Handley Hill (SU 010152) it cuts the Neolithic Dorset cursus†. Beyond DORCHESTER the road is less straight and obvious.

I. Margary, Roman Roads in Britain *(John Baker, 1973).*

Avebury, Wiltshire Neolithic henge† and stone circles†   ★★

SU 103700. 10 km. W of Marlborough, N of the A4. Signposted access to car parks via the A4361. National Trust and English Heritage. Museum. World Heritage Site. Figures 4 and 160.

Avebury is the largest and finest henge monument in Britain. Set on a flat plain east of the river Kennet it is relatively low-lying but surrounded by hills. Approaching the site from the car park, the most immediately visible feature is the great enclosure earthwork formed by a bank and inner ditch; you can walk the entire circumference, a distance of 1.3 km.

Avebury has an external diameter of 427 m. between the top of the

▼ **Fig. 158.** Map of Region 11

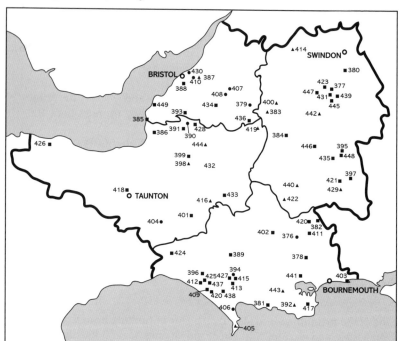

banks. It is not precisely round, but given its overall size, its geometry is impressive.

There are four entrances, all used by modern roads. The south-east and south-west entrances were approached by stone-lined avenues connecting the henge to its wider landscape. The Beckhampton Avenue to the south-west has largely disappeared, but the West Kennet Avenue to the south-east remains, partly reconstructed in the 1930s (SU 103697

▲ **Fig. 159.** View of Ackling Dyke, looking north, near Gussage All Saints, Dorset (Photograph: Jane Timby)

to SU 118680). The Avenue has a double row of standing stones† placed in pairs about 15 m. apart at intervals of 25 m. The stones were probably chosen for their shapes, tall narrow pillars alternating with squat diamond-shaped slabs perhaps reflecting sexual symbolism. Burials have been found at the foot of some stones. The Avenue formed a processional way linking Avebury with THE SANCTUARY some 2.4 km. to the south-east.

Inside Avebury is a series of stone settings. The largest is the outer circle of ninety-eight sarsen† stones. With a diameter of 331.6 m. this is the largest stone circle in Britain. Pairs of larger stones flank the entrances.

Within the outer circle are the remains of two smaller circles. The southern circle in the south-east quadrant originally had twenty-nine stones. Near the centre was a tall standing stone now marked by a concrete obelisk, adjacent to which was a short straight line of stones which may have formed one side of a square around the central upright.

In the north-east quadrant was a second circle, although little survives. Its focus was a setting of three or four stones known as the Cove.

Avebury was built between about 2900 and 2600 BC. The stone circles were probably constructed by beaker-using people, and may have been an addition to the basic earthwork structure.

C. Malone, Avebury *(Batsford and English Heritage, 1989).*

▲ Fig. 160. Aerial view of Avebury henge, Wiltshire (CUCAP CA-208)

Badbury Rings, Wimborne, Dorset Iron Age hillfort† and

Roman settlement ★

ST 964030. 12 km. N of Bournemouth, 6 km. NW of Wimborne Minster. Access from car park N of B3082. National Trust.

This 7.2 ha. Iron Age hillfort has three circuits of massive ramparts. Entrances open to the east and west. The west entrance is unusual in having a rectangular projection from the middle rampart. The east entrance is simpler, staggered to corner attackers with the ramparts in-turned to create an entrance passage.

Badbury Rings later lay at the junction of two Roman roads; a length of ACKLING DYKE survives as a low mound on the north-west side of the hillfort. Slight traces of a small Roman settlement lie south-west of the modern car park. Also visible are three Bronze Age round barrows†

450 m. west of the hillfort. Other barrows can be seen at the north-east end of the car park.

RCHME, An Inventory of Historical Monuments in the County of Dorset, vol. v: East Dorset (HMSO, 1975), 61–3.

Barbury Castle, Wroughton, Wiltshire Iron Age hillfort

SU 149763. Within Barbary Castle Country Park 10 km. S of Swindon. Signposted via minor roads S from the B4005.

Bisected by the Ridgeway along the northern edge of the Marlborough downs and with views over the upper Thames valley, this large oval hillfort of 4.6 ha. was strongly defended by two lines of massive ramparts. Aerial photography has revealed huts and storage pits in the interior.

About 6.5 km. to the east is another Iron Age hillfort **Liddington Castle** (SU 209797).

M. MacGregor and D. Simpson, 'A Group of Iron Objects from Barbury Castle, Wiltshire', WANHM 58 (1963), 394–402.

Bath (*Aquae Sulis*), Bath and North East
Somerset Roman baths, temple, and museum ★★

ST 751647. Roman baths and temple precinct are below the city centre Pump Room. Museum. Admission charge. Baths virtual tour: www.romanbaths.co.uk/. Figures 161 and 162.

Like their Regency successors, the Romans exploited the curative properties of three natural hot springs at Bath. The Roman name, *Aquae Sulis*, suggests the springs were presided over by the Celtic goddess Sulis (equivalent to the Roman Minerva). The springs were the focus of a simple bathing facility in the C1, but became increasingly aggrandized later. The main bath measures 22 × 8.8 m., and was entirely lead-lined.

A magnificent classical temple was erected to Sulis Minerva. Several fragments of its pediment were discovered when the C18 Pump Room was built. They show Minerva's shield supported by winged Victories standing on globes. On the shield is the Bath Gorgon, a Medusa mask perhaps representing a water god. The Roman baths were abandoned in the C5 and, except for a mention in an Anglo-Saxon poem entitled *The Ruin*, were forgotten until the C18.

Bath's Norman abbey was replaced after 1499 by the present Perpendicular structure. In the early C18 Bath became a popular resort and its warm-toned Bath Stone buildings reflect the style of that era.

B. Cunliffe, Roman Bath (Batsford and English Heritage, 1995).

▼ Fig. 161. Bath (*Aquae Sulis*): modern street plan showing the location of the Roman defences and other sites (after Burnham & Wacher)

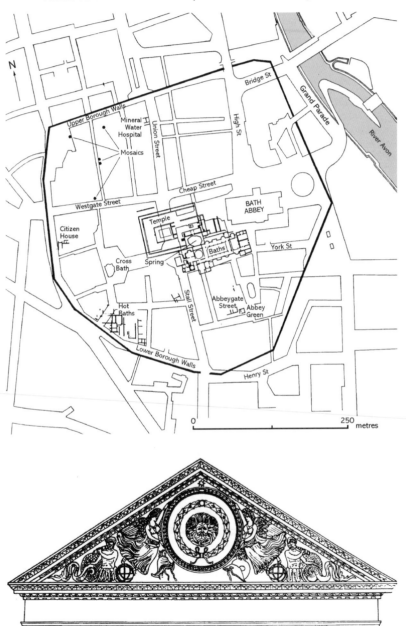

▲ Fig. 162. Bath (*Aquae Sulis*): reconstruction of the Roman temple pediment (after Cunliffe)

Roman baths

To the Romans the public baths were not just a place to get clean but a place for social intercourse, eating and drinking, taking exercise, and playing games. The Roman bath-house was based on the same principle as a Turkish bath with a series of rooms of graduated heat. Outside the building there was usually an exercise yard (*palaestra*). Clothes were left in the changing room (*apodyterium*) from which you entered the first cold room (*frigidarium*). Having washed off the worst dirt you passed into the warm room (*tepidarium*) and finally ended up in the steamy atmosphere of the hot room (*caldarium*). The sweat was wiped off with a curved bronze instrument known as a strigil and oils were rubbed onto the body. The system could be short-circuited by going straight to the *laconicum* which had intense dry heat. The warm rooms were heated by furnaces and under-floor hypocausts.

Many of the richer villas such as BIGNOR and LULLINGSTONE had their own private bath-houses.

Bindon Hill, West Lulworth, Dorset Iron Age hillfort†

SY 835803. 6 km S of Wool, E of Lulworth Cove. Access via the Dorset Coast Path from car park beside B3070 at Lulworth Cove. Figure 163.

Bindon Hill is a low chalk ridge overlooking the English Channel. The hillfort is defined by an earthwork nearly 2.8 km. long from the cliffs west of Worbarrow Bay to a curved butt above Lulworth Cove. Most of this can be followed on the ground as it defines and encloses most of the ridge and the flat low-lying platform to the south, an area of about 114 ha. Pottery suggests a construction date in the mid-first millennium BC.

Follow the Dorset Coast Path east of Bindon Hill, past Arish Mell, to **Flowers Barrow Fort** (SY 864805), an enclosure defined on three sides by a double rampart with an original entrance to the south-east.

R. Wheeler, 'An Early Iron Age Beach-Head at Lulworth, Dorset', Ant J, 33 (1953), 1–13.

▼ **Fig. 163.** Plan of the hillfort at Bindon Hill, West Lulworth, Dorset (after RCHME)

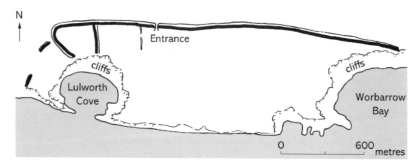

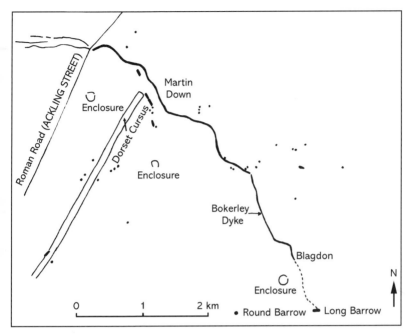

▲ Fig. 164. Plan of Bokerley Dyke, Dorset (after Bowen)

Bokerley Dyke, Dorset   Prehistoric and later linear boundary†

SU 033200–SU 063168. 15 km. SW of Salisbury on NE side of Cranborne Chase. Access from N end via A354. Figure 164.

Bokerley Dyke is not so much a linear earthwork as a spinal zone used as a boundary over several millennia. Hence, the archaeological evidence comprises numerous broadly parallel features spread over 6 km.

One of the best sections is from Martin Down (SU 034199) to Blagdon Hill (SU 055180). Here the main dyke has a sinuous course in part following the topography but elsewhere weaving between pre-existing features. The dyke has a bank to the south and a ditch up to 9 m. wide and 3.6 m. deep to the north. Visible breaks are modern.

In later prehistory the dyke was probably a tribal boundary between the *Atrebates* to the north-east and the *Durotriges* to the south-west.

H. Bowen, The Archaeology of Bokerley Dyke (HMSO, 1990).

Bradford-on-Avon, Wiltshire   Anglo-Saxon church, medieval barn, and bridge   ★

ST 824609. 8 km. SE of Bath. Figure 165.

Bradford-on-Avon has numerous fine historic buildings, many in Bath oolitic limestone. Especially notable is St Laurence's, one of England's

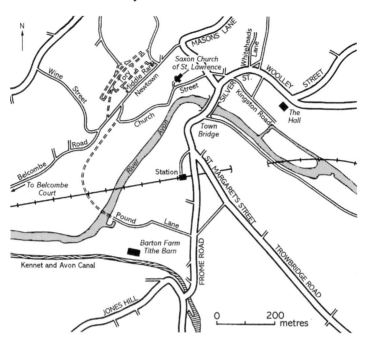

▲ **Fig. 165.** Bradford-on-Avon, Wiltshire (after Clifton-Taylor)

most complete Saxon chapels. It adjoins the later Norman church. It comprises a nave 7.6 m. long and a chancel half that, with north and south side-chapels or *porticus*, the exact function of which is unknown. All survive except the south *porticus*. Externally the coursed limestone walls are decorated with blind arcading and pilaster strips (vertical bands). Its date is uncertain. Traditionally associated with Aldhelm, an early C8 saint, on architectural grounds it is mainly C10 or C11.

A short walk from the church, on the south side of the town (ST 824604), is a 51 m. long Cotswold limestone barn of the mid-C14 (English Heritage), once part of Shaftesbury Abbey's Barton Farm. The fourteen-bay barn is impressive with its ashlar walls and stone-tiled roof.

A. Clifton-Taylor, Six More English Towns (BBC Books, 1981), 139–65.

Bratton Camp and the Westbury White Horse, Bratton, Wiltshire Neolithic long barrow†, Iron Age hillfort†, and hill-figure

ST 900516. 2 km. E of Westbury, 1 km. W of Bratton village. Access (signposted) from minor road SW of Bratton to Westbury Hill. English Heritage.

On a promontory overlooking the upper Avon valley, this roughly rect-angular hillfort encloses about 10 ha. It has a double bank and ditch except on the east where there is only a single line of defences. An entrance is visible on the south side with a rather good outwork for added protection. The modern road probably passes through a second entrance.

Inside the fort is a fine Neolithic long barrow still nearly 4 m. high. It was built in the earthen long barrow tradition, trapezoidal in outline with a timber chamber at the east end. Excavations revealed two adult inhumations. Traces of the side ditches can be seen.

West of the camp is the oldest of Wiltshire's white horses, the **Westbury White Horse**. It was recut by Lord Abingdon in AD 1778, but its earlier history is not known.

P. Newman, The Lost Gods of Albion (Sutton Publishing, 1997), 36–45.

Brean Down, Somerset   Prehistoric field-system† and Roman temple

ST 2959. 4 km. SW of Weston-super-Mare, 3 km. N of Brean village. Footpath from parking area on minor road N from Brean village. National Trust.

In the central part of Brean Down, a promontory jutting into the Bristol Channel, are slight traces of late prehistoric or Romano-British field-systems, visible as low banks. One block, to the south-west, has three Bronze Age barrows or cairns† within the fields. A second, towards the east end above the present beach, also contains small cairns together with the site of an excavated C4 Romano-Celtic temple. At the east end is a small promontory fort, probably Iron Age.

M. Bell, Brean Down. Excavations 1983–87, HBMCE Archaeological Report 15 (English Heritage, 1990).

Brent Knoll, Burnham on Sea, Somerset   Iron Age hillfort†

ST 341510. W of M5, 1 km. SW of East Brent, W of A370. Accessible by footpath from East Brent or Brent Knoll village.

Crowning a distinctive conical hill, this hillfort has extensive views over the Bristol Channel and Somerset Levels.

The fort is triangular and covers about 1.6 ha. The builders took advantage of the natural shape of the hill, artificially steepening an already precipitous slope on the west and south sides. The single line of ramparts, thickest to the west, is broken by an entrance on the east side where additional outworks and additional scarping can be seen. The interior has been damaged by quarrying. Finds suggest Roman reuse of the defences.

I. Burrow, 'Hillforts and Hilltops 1000 BC–1000 AD', in M. Aston and I. Burrow (eds), The Archaeology of Somerset (Somerset County Council, 1982), 83–98.

Bristol City, Bristol Medieval port

ST 593727. S of the M4 and W of the M5, 185 km. from London.

Bristol stands on the Avon, where a bridge was erected and a *burh*†
founded in the years around 1000 AD. The town developed rapidly in the
C12 as the export trade grew in Cotswold cloth, tanned hides, lead, tin,
and alabaster carvings, and with it an import trade in Bordeaux wine,
Gascon woad, Spanish and Portuguese iron, and foodstuffs such as
honey, almonds, and Madeira sugar. Later, in the C15, it became an
important cod fishery. Christopher Columbus came here in the 1480s to
talk to Atlantic fishermen about their experiences sailing west, while in
1497 John Cabot embarked here for his historic voyage to Newfound-
land. A replica of his vessel, *The Matthew*, stands next to Brunel's SS
Great Britain in the Floating Harbour.

Before its Dissolution in 1542, Bristol cathedral was the church of St
Augustine's Abbey, founded in the C12. The east end and the choir (see
stained glass, and niches with statues of C15 abbots) are of 1298–1330,
the central tower of about 1500, while the nave was not completed until
1868. The Chapter House is one of the finest Norman rooms in England.

In Park Street is the Lord Mayor's Chapel, the surviving part of St
Mark's Hospital, set up in the C13 to feed a hundred poor every day. The
east end of the Chapel was rebuilt and the tower erected in the late C15,
and it contains several high-quality medieval tombs and Spanish floor
tiles, further evidence of Bristol's mercantile contacts.

On Whitsun Street is the gate of St James's Priory, founded about
1130; of medieval date are the west front and the aisle piers. The
Dominican Friary stood in Quaker's Friars; part of its timber roof survives, the oldest in Bristol. Not far away, Castle Park occupies the site of
Bristol's castle.

Bristol's medieval prosperity is reflected in its churches. St Nicholas's, at a gateway in the walls near the Floating Harbour, was probably
where Cabot worshipped. The upper part of the church is an C18 rebuild,
but the lower church, or Crypt, is C14, with the 5 m. thick town wall
forming its southern wall. Bombed in 1944, the church is now a museum
of Bristol's ecclesiastical and medieval history. In the C14 Temple
Church, in Temple Street, are the foundations of the earlier circular
church of the crusading Knights Templar†. On Redcliffe Hill is St
Mary's, a largely late medieval structure. This was a wealthy suburb in
the Middle Ages; the church contains tombs of benefactors including
William Cannynges (d. 1474) and Philip Mede (d. 1471), and many fine
brasses.

L. Keen (ed.), 'Almost the Richest City' *(British Archaeological Association, 1997).*

Cadbury Camp, Clevedon, North Somerset   Iron Age

hillfort†

ST 454725. E of M5, 5 km E of Clevedon. Approached by footpath along Ticken-ham Hill from minor road N from B3130 in Tickenham Village. National Trust.

On a ridge overlooking the eastern shore of the Bristol Channel, this oval 2.5 ha. hillfort is defined by two concentric lines of ramparts and ditches. There is also an outwork on the west side about 150 m. from the fort, perhaps to defend this relatively easy approach. To the north is an elaborate entrance. There is a third bank on the defensive circuit at this point.

I. Burrow, 'Hillforts and the Iron Age', in M. Aston and R. Iles (eds), The Archaeology of Avon *(Avon County Council, 1985), 40–51.*

Cerne Abbas Giant, Dorset   Ancient hill-figure   ★★

ST 667016. 1 km. NE of Cerne Abbas village. Access by footpath from N side of village. Best view from (signposted) lay-by on E side of A352 Dorchester to Sherborne road 1 km. N of village. National Trust.

The Cerne Giant is the 55 m. high image of a naked male wielding a large club in his right hand. The Giant's features are depicted by natural chalk rammed into a narrow trench. The left arm is outstretched and there is some suggestion that he originally held something in this hand too, perhaps a cloak, animal skin, or a human head.

Controversy surrounds his date. The earliest reference is C17, but it is almost certainly older. Stuart Piggott argued that the figure is the Roman god Hercules cut in the late C2 AD. Others have seen the figure as the Celtic Jupiter. Without detailed investigations the precise date cannot be determined.

T. Darvill et al., The Cerne Giant: An Antiquity on Trial, *Bournemouth University School of Conservation Sciences Occasional Paper 5 (Oxbow Books, 1999).*

Charterhouse-on-Mendip, Somerset   Roman lead mines and

settlement

ST 500565. In Ubley Warren Nature Reserve off B3134 between Burrington Combe and Castle of Comfort Inn, 5 km. N of Cheddar. Figure 166.

An important lead and silver mining area worked during Roman and later times. The mines were under Imperial control until around 170, then became private. The nature reserve is covered with quarry pits, grooves, and mines resulting from Roman and later workings. The remains of a small amphitheatre and three rectangular enclosures, possibly Roman, can be seen in fields beside the road. Vestiges of a street plan can sometimes be seen on ploughed land north-east of the amphitheatre. There are traces of a Roman road from the site

▲ **Fig. 166.** An inscribed lead pig from Blagdon, Mendip Hills, Somerset (after British Museum)

south-east through Green Ore and along the ridge of the Mendips to Old Sarum.

B. Burnham and J. Wacher, The Small Towns of Roman Britain *(Batsford, 1990), 208–11.*

Cheddar Gorge and the Mendip Caves,
Somerset Prehistoric occupied caves and rock shelters ★

ST 4653. 4 km. E of Axbridge, Cheddar Gorge is followed by B3135. Part National Trust. Restricted opening for some caves and facilities.

Cheddar Gorge is a deeply incised valley on the south side of the Mendip hills. The caves and rock shelters along its limestone cliffs are well known for their use in Upper Palaeolithic times between about 25,000 BC and 12,000 BC.

Most famous is **Gough's Cave** (ST 466539), now with a small museum in the entrance. This was extensively occupied in late Upper Palaeolithic and early Mesolithic times. In 1903 the bones of 'Cheddar Man' were discovered. This unaccompanied inhumation of a young adult dates to about 8000 BC and belongs to the main period of occupation in the cave during early post-glacial times.

Occupied caves in the Mendips are not confined to Cheddar Gorge. To the east is another important group open to the public at **Wookey Hole** (ST 533478) where Middle and Upper Palaeolithic tools were discovered.

In Burrington Combe on the north side of Mendip is **Aveline's Hole** (ST 476586) which again contained late Upper Palaeolithic flint tools, harpoons, and human burials.

R. Jacobi, 'Ice Age Cave-Dwellers 12000–9000 BC', in M. Aston and I. Burrow (eds), The Archaeology of Somerset *(Somerset County Council, 1982), 11–13.*

Corfe Castle, Dorset Medieval castle and town

SY 959824. On A351 Wareham to Swanage road. National Trust; restricted opening. Admission charge. Visitor centre on A351 N of village.

Corfe's hilltop castle commands the only broad gap through the Purbeck hills. Although slighted in 1645–6 its ruins are still impressive.

At its heart, in the Inner Ward, is a C12 square keep, modernized in the C16. Adjoining it are the ruins of La Gloriette, a residential hall complex built by King John (1199–1216). He was also responsible for the curtain wall of the west bailey† with its polygonal Butavant Tower. The defences were completed in the C13.

Corfe town gained borough status in 1572. Between its two broad main streets stands its church, with a C15 tower. There are many high-quality buildings of local stone and with stone slate roofs, many dating from the period of prosperity it enjoyed in the C16 and early C17.

Corfe Castle (The National Trust, 1985) (Site Guidebook).

Dolebury, Churchill, North Somerset Iron Age hillfort†

ST 450589. 1 km S of Churchill, 15 km. E of Weston-super-Mare on NW side of Mendip Hills E of A38. Access by footpath from Churchill.

Probably the finest hillfort on Mendip, with extensive northward views. The single line of defences comprise a massive 6 m. high stone-built inner bank, a ditch, and a large counterscarp bank†. Outer defences run across the ridge to the east.

Inside the fort, badly disturbed by C19 lead-mining, are four long narrow pillow mounds, part of a C17 or later rabbit warren. Remains of the warrener's house lie within a circular earthwork in the north-east corner.

C. Dymond, 'Dolebury and Cadbury', PSANHS 29 (1883), 104–16.

Dorchester (*Durnovaria*), Dorset Roman town

SY 6990. 12 km. N of Weymouth. Dorchester County Museum, High West Street contains archaeological material. Colliton Roman town house lies adjacent to the Council Offices. Figure 167.

The *civitas*† capital of the *Durotriges*, Dorchester became a walled Roman town in the C3. The defences are best seen in the south-west corner in Bowling Alley Walk. The wall stood on the edge of the grass verge with its bank extending across the path into the hospital grounds. Outside the wall were triple ditches. A small wall fragment survives south of the Top o'Town roundabout.

Within the walls, several town houses have been investigated, including one at Colliton Park found during the construction of County Hall. The remains of this C4 building, including a rare splayed window opening and mosaic flooring, have been preserved. A large public bath-house was excavated at Wollaston House.

Outside the walls is the amphitheatre (see MAUMBURY RINGS). Roman Dorchester was served by an aqueduct†. Its channel can be seen at Fordington Bottom where it is about 2 m. wide and 1 m. deep, and at POUNDBURY.

J. Wacher, The Towns of Roman Britain (Batsford, 1995), 323–35.

▲ **Fig. 167.** The remains of the Roman house at Colliton Park, Dorchester, Dorset (Photograph: Jane Timby)

Durrington Walls, Durrington, Wiltshire Neolithic henge†
enclosure

SU 150437. 1.5 km. N of Amesbury, cut by A345. Best viewed from NE of WOOD-HENGE visitor car park. Within a World Heritage Site. Figure 168.

In a dry-valley overlooking a bend in the river Avon, this henge enclosure comprises a large sub-oval enclosure with an external diameter of 446 × 479 m. The ditch and external bank are separated by a berm†. The internal area is 321 × 387 m. There are entrances to the north-west and the south-east. The latter opens to the river Avon a few metres beneath.

Overlooking the site from the south it is possible to make out the line of the earthwork bank, especially on the east side the A345, and occasionally it is possible to see parts of the now-silted inner ditch. The position of the enclosure is very clear, as too its relationship with the river.

Excavations revealed a series of massive circular timber buildings each over 30 m. in diameter. The enclosure earthworks were constructed about 2600 BC and continued in use until about 1900 BC. Since domestic and ritual activity were closely entwined there is good reason to see the

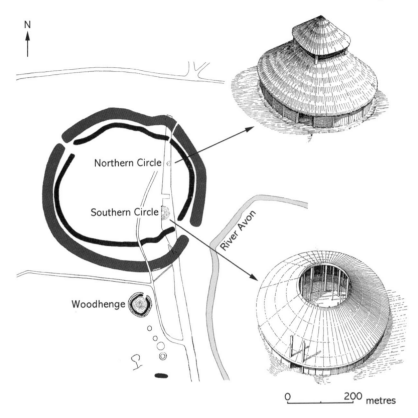

N

Northern Circle

Southern Circle

River Avon

Woodhenge

0　　　　　200 metres

▲ **Fig. 168.** Plan of Durrington Walls and Woodhenge, Wiltshire (after Wainwright & Longworth)

site as a large enclosed settlement with areas set aside for communal or ceremonial purposes.

About 100 m. south of Durrington Walls is WOODHENGE.

G. Wainwright and I. Longworth, Durrington Walls: Excavations 1966–68, *Reports of the Research Committee of the Society of Antiquaries of London 29 (1971).*

Eggardon Hill, Powerstock, Dorset Iron Age hillfort†

SY 542947. 15 km. W of Dorchester, N of A35(T). Access via signposted footpath from minor road between Askerwell and Toller Porcorum. National Trust.

Situated on a spur on the western edge of the Wessex downs, Eggardon overlooks undulating valley land. Roughly D-shaped in plan and covering about 14.5 ha., the defensive circuit of twin ramparts and ditches can be fully traced. Two entrances can be seen, the eastward having staggered gaps in the ramparts and in-turned rampart terminals.

Prehistoric houses

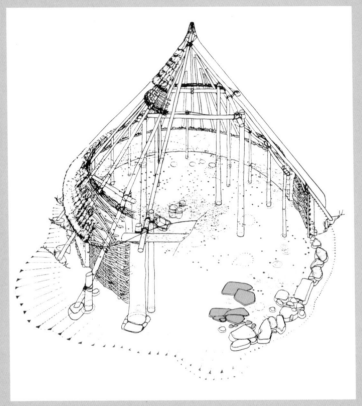

▲ **Fig. B.** Cut-away reconstruction of a Bronze Age house excavation at Trethellan Farm, Newquay, Cornwall (after Nowakowski)

'Where did people live?' is always one of the most important questions that archaeologists ask of an ancient culture, but it is sometimes one of the most difficult to answer. Amongst many early communities houses were insubstantial, and thus now difficult to find after millennia of erosion and decay. To make matters worse, many were built wholly or substantially of wood, which does not survive well for long periods.

The earliest houses known in England date to the later Mesolithic and early Neolithic. They are generally rectangular or oval in plan, with a central hearth, walls of timber posts, and pitched roofs covered in thatch or turf.

From the later Neolithic onwards the majority of houses are round in plan, the main exceptions being a few later Bronze Age and early Iron Age houses such as can be seen in outline at Crickley Hill. The round-house tradition begins with the massive timber lodges found at late

Neolithic henges and henge enclosures such as Durrington Walls and Woodhenge. Through the Bronze Age more modest structures dominate, most between 4 m. and 10 m. in diameter. In upland areas, where stone is widely available, the remains of these structures usually comprise a circular stone wall foundation (rather pejoratively called 'hut circles') and a slight platform where the structure has been built into a slope. When excavated, such houses are often found to have a conical roof structure that extends beyond the line of the wall to provide a storage area under the edge of the roof and make them more weatherproof. In lowland areas there are no surface traces of houses except, occasionally, slight hollows or platforms. Here the walls were of wattle and daub. There are reconstructed examples at Flag Fen.

The basic form of prehistoric house continued from the Bronze through into the Iron Age, although in the course of time an increasing range of sophistication is added: drainage gulleys around the eaves-drip to keep the interior drier and elaborate porches around the doorways are the most common. Some rather good reconstructions of Iron Age houses can be seen at Butser Hill, Hampshire, and the Somerset Levels and Peat Moors Centre, Shapwick, Somerset.

Inside the fort are two round barrows†, both rather denuded, and over 500 small depressions, collapsed pits.

RCHME, An Inventory of the Historical Monuments in the County of Dorset, vol. i: West Dorset (HMSO, 1952), 13–15.

Figsbury Ring, Salisbury, Wiltshire   Iron Age hillfort†

SU 188338. 6 km. NE of Salisbury. Access by footpath from signposted car park N of A30. National Trust.

Strategically positioned overlooking the river Bourne, this C4 or C5 BC hillfort is roughly circular. It is unusual in that its outer bank and ditch are separated by a wide flat space from an inner ditch that has no bank. This, which is 13 m. to 16 m. across and 1.5 m. to 4 m. deep, may have been a quarry for material to build or enhance the outer rampart. Equally, it may be the remains of an earlier enclosure, perhaps even a Neolithic causewayed camp† or henge†.

The outer ramparts show at least two phases of construction. Two entrances are visible: east and west. The east has traces of an outwork, perhaps a hornwork.

M. Cunnington, 'Figsbury Rings: An Account of the Excavations in 1924', WANHM 43 (1925), 48–58.

Glastonbury, Somerset   Medieval town

ST 5039. E of M5, access from junction 23. Tribunal and Fish House are English Heritage; the Tribunal has restricted opening hours. Figure 169.

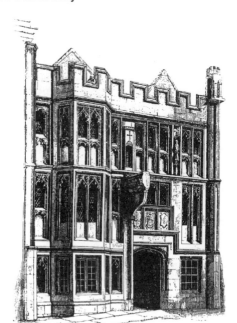

▲ **Fig. 169.** Glastonbury, the George inn, Somerset (Parker)

Glastonbury is rich in history, legend, and myth. The Benedictine†
abbey, founded about AD 700, was one of the country's richest; that
wealth is shown by the size of the abbey church, and the exquisite chapel
of St Mary, built after a disastrous fire of 1184. Most interesting is the
later C14 abbot's kitchen, square and complete. It has a steeply pitched
octagonal roof, drawing smoke and steam upwards from the great corner fireplaces to an elaborate central louvre. The site museum and visitor
centre makes clear how in the Middle Ages the abbey drew pilgrims (and
hence income) to the reputed grave of King Arthur, discovered here—
perhaps conveniently—during the late C12 rebuilding campaign.

Other legendary delights continue to call the religious and curious to
Glastonbury, notably the Chalice Well and the Holy Thorn. This last
supposedly blossomed from the staff of St Joseph of Arimathaea when
he came here in AD 60. Other places of interest include the medieval
George and Pilgrim Inn, the C15 abbey courthouse (the Tribunal), St
John's Church with its late C15 tower, and St Benedict's, rebuilt by
Abbot Bere about 1520. The superb tithe barn, of about 1360, was part
of the abbey estate.

Fish was important in the monastic diet, and 6.5 km. north-west
of the town is the C14 **Meare Fish House** (ST 459418). The huge

adjoining lake was drained in the C18. The Fish House was used to store nets and tackle, and perhaps to process the catch.

Finally, climb **Glastonbury Tor** (ST 511386) for a panoramic view of the town and the Somerset Levels. St Michael's Chapel, of which the C13 tower remains, is presumed to be a pilgrims' chapel. Excavations showed there had been monastic occupation on the Tor since the C7, perhaps a hermitage or retreat.

P. Rahtz, Glastonbury *(Batsford and English Heritage, 1993).*

Glastonbury Lake Village, Somerset Iron Age lake village

ST 492409. 1.5 km. NW of Glastonbury, W of A39, visible from a minor road leading N from B3151 towards Godney. Small information sign at site. Figure 170.

Deep in the low-lying Somerset Levels, the Glastonbury lake village was discovered by Arthur Bulleid in 1892; eleven years' digging followed. The site was important because of the quality of preservation; being water-logged the wood used for dwellings, structures, and artefacts was well preserved.

What Bulleid first saw, partly still visible, were low mounds representing house platforms. Glastonbury was a small village of between four and a dozen family units living on a partly artificial island created in a swampy wetland between about 250 BC and 50 BC.

Some houses and structures have been reconstructed at the Peat

▼ **Fig. 170.** Reconstruction of a Glastonbury Iron Age house at the Somerset Levels and Peat Moors Centre, Shapwick (Photograph: Paul Stamper)

Moors and Levels Visitor Centre next to the Willows Garden Centre, Shapwick (ST 425414).

J. Coles and S. Minnitt, Industrious and Fairly Civilized: The Glastonbury Lake Village *(Somerset County Museum Service, 1995).*

Great Chalfield Manor, nr. Melksham, Wiltshire Medieval

manorial complex

ST 860630. 4 km. SW of Melksham off B3107 via Broughton Gifford Common. National Trust. Restricted opening. Admission charge.

The late medieval Chalfield Manor complex is built of yellowish-grey Corsham stone. The main H-plan building dates to about 1480, with central hall (with mural of its builder Thomas Tropenell) flanked by kitchens and service rooms to one side, and to the other a two-storey solar wing with private rooms. Other structures within the moat include a gatehouse and All Saints' Church, the latter basically C13 but with a south chapel rebuilt by Tropenell.

Great Chalfield *(The National Trust, 1980) (Site Guidebook).*

The Grey Mare and Her Colts, Kingston Russell, Dorset Neolithic long barrow†

SY 584871. 2 km. N of Abbotsbury, 1 km. E of KINGSTON RUSSELL *stone circle. Signposted footpath from SY 589867.*

This long barrow has a rectangular mound 25 × 10 m. with a peristalith† around the edge. It is orientated south-east to north-west, and, unusually for a long barrow in this area, has a stone chamber at the south-east end. The chamber, originally roofed by a large capstone†, now fallen, opened directly onto the front of the barrow. It is possible to see the outline of a concave façade and shallow forecourt.

S. Piggott, 'The Chambered Cairn of "The Grey Mare and Colts"', PDNHAS 67 *(1945), 30–3.*

Hambledon Hill, Child Okeford, Dorset Neolithic

causewayed enclosure† complex and Iron Age hillfort†   ★

ST 845126. 7 km. NW of Blandford Forum, N of A357, W of A350, accessible by footpaths running N from minor road to Child Okeford W of A350. Figure 171.

This hilltop overlooking the Vale of Blackmore has a long history of occupation starting in middle Neolithic times when two causewayed camps and two long barrows were erected.

On the Stepleton spur was a small causewayed camp, possibly a settlement, although nothing remains to be seen of it. A bank and ditch ran north-west towards the main camp on the central knoll near the trig point. This enclosure, difficult to see but still preserved, had a single

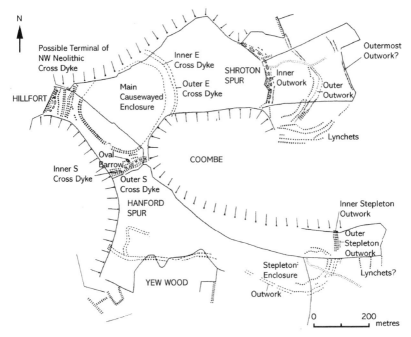

▲ **Fig. 171.** Plan of the Neolithic enclosures and Iron Age hillfort on Hambledon Hill, Dorset (after Mercer)

circuit of causewayed ditches, and may have been a ceremonial site in which bodies were exposed before being buried in long barrows†. A small long barrow or oval barrow (now destroyed) lay immediately south of the main enclosure, while another, clearly visible as a grassy mound 68 m. long, lies within the hillfort on the north-west spur of the hill.

The most impressive earthworks are those of the Iron Age hillfort. Standing on a sinuous ridge, the builders of this hillfort sculpted it onto the natural shape of the hill with remarkable skill. Probably of several phases, it covers 12.5 ha. and is bounded by two lines of ramparts. Inside, numerous hut-platforms can be seen as scoops of 5 m. to 14 m. in diameter.

About 1.6 km. south of Hambledon Hill is **Hod Hill** (ST 856106), another major Iron Age fortress with impressive defences and the outline of a Roman fort in the north-west corner.

R. Mercer, Hambledon Hill: A Neolithic Landscape *(Edinburgh University Press, 1980).*

Ham Hill, Yeovil, Somerset Iron Age hillfort†

ST 485165. 9 km. W of Yeovil, S of A3088. Partly within Ham Hill Country Park near Montacute and Stoke Sub Hamdon. Figure 172.

N

STROUDS HILL

QUARRIED
AREA

0   1000
                                                          metres

▲ Fig. 172. Plan of the hillfort on Ham Hill, Yeovil, Somerset (after G. Smith)

Well known as a source of fine honey-coloured limestone for building, the top of Ham Hill is crowned by an 84 ha. L-shaped hillfort, amongst the largest in Britain. Although badly mutilated by quarrying, some of the defences can still be traced, especially on the north and north-west sides. The defences consist of two banks each with external ditches. However, on the more level ground at the south-west and extreme north-west they are triple. The only original gateway is to the north-west where there is an in-turned entrance. Occupation spanned much of the later first millennium BC. Continued use, or reuse, in Roman times is also attested.

G. Smith, 'Excavations at Ham Hill, 1983', PSANHS 134 (1990), 27–45.

Hengistbury Head, Bournemouth Later prehistoric
settlements, cemeteries, and trading port

SZ 164910. 1 km S of Christchurch on S side of Christchurch harbour, 9 km. E of Bournemouth town centre. Signposted from B3059.

Now a coastal promontory this site has been a focus of settlement and trade for over 12,000 years. Throughout Iron Age times Hengistbury Head was an important port for ships crossing the English Channel or voyaging along the south coast. From about 150 BC communities living here became involved in international trade; supplies to support the chieftains and petty kings living in southern Wessex. Imports included wine and oil *amphorae* from the Mediterranean, glass, fine pottery, and jewellery. The inhabitants of Hengistbury minted coins, and were engaged in metalworking, shaleworking, and glassworking.

About 700 BC a double rampart was set across the neck of the promontory to protect some 80 ha. The double ramparts are over 40 m. wide and the inner bank rises more than 7 m. above the base of its adjacent ditch.

B. Cunliffe, Hengistbury Head, Dorset, *vol. i:* The Prehistoric and Roman Settlement, 3500 BC–AD 500, *Oxford University Committee for Archaeology Monograph 13 (1987).*

Ilchester (*Lindinis*), Somerset Roman town

ST 520226. At the junction of A37 and A303.

Ilchester was the second *civitas*† capital of the *Durotriges* in later Roman times. Nothing is visible, although much information has been collected from excavations. The Fosse Way is joined by Roman roads from the Polden hills and Dorchester in the middle of the town.

B. Burnham and J. Wacher, The Small Towns of Roman Britain *(Batsford, 1990),* 62–70.

Isle of Portland, Dorset Medieval field-system†

SY 9681. 4 km. S of Weymouth; access via A354 S from Weymouth.

Either side of the road to the Coastguard Station at Portland Bill is one of England's few remaining areas of open field landscape. While much consolidation of the allotment-like strips of arable land has gone on, groups (and some single examples) of curved strips, up to 300 m. long, survive. Some are separated by grass baulks, others by stone walls.

The fields drop steeply to the sea, and some are terraced. Encroaching into them are quarries, which still yield the Portland limestone so prized by medieval and later builders.

M. Beresford and J. St Joseph, Medieval England, *2nd edn (Cambridge University Press, 1979), 42–3.*

Jordan Hill, Weymouth, Dorset Roman temple

SY 698 821. 3 km. NE of Weymouth, signposted off A353 at Overcombe. Roadside parking. English Heritage.

Site of a C4 Romano-Celtic temple, the outer foundations of which are laid out. Excavations show that it consisted of a classic square *cella*†surrounded by a verandah. A well or shaft in the south-east corner contained a possibly ritual deposit of birds and coins.

C. Drew, 'The Excavations at Jordan Hill, 1931', PDNHAFC 53 (1932), 265–76.

Keynsham East (Somerdale), Bath and North-East Somerset Roman building

ST 656690. Within Cadbury's Somerdale Factory. Access during business hours.

The visible remains comprise a small Roman building with four main rooms and a bath-suite, excavated in 1922. They were moved here when the chocolate factory was built.

M. Fitter, 'A Roman Well at Keynsham', PSANHS 135 (1991), 166–7.

Keynsham West, Bath and North-East Somerset Roman villa

ST 645693. Cut by A4 just W of Keynsham; masonry fragments behind mortuary chapel in Keynsham cemetery.

The site of a large courtyard villa with over fifty rooms, some with fine mosaics. Architectural fragments including stone guttering remain in the modern cemetery.

A. Bulleid and D. Horne, 'The Roman House at Keynsham, Somerset', Archaeologia, 75 (1926), 109–38.

Kingston Russell, Abbotsbury, Dorset Neolithic stone circle†

SY 577878. 12 km. W of Dorchester, 2.5 km. N of Abbotsbury, approached by footpath from pull-in on minor road between Abbotsbury and Martinstown at SY 589867. English Heritage.

Although all the stones in this circle have fallen, its rather flattened shape (27.7 × 20.6 m.) is clear. Local sarsen† and conglomerate was used as pillars, the largest stones being those on the north side.

The approach from the east passes a Neolithic long barrow† known as THE GREY MARE AND HER COLTS.

S. and C. Piggott, 'Stone and Earth Circles of Dorset', Antiquity, 13 (1939), 138–58.

Kings Weston, Bristol Roman villa

ST 534776. 3 km. NW of Sea Mills. On N side of King's Weston Hill close to W end of Long Cross. Key obtainable from Blaise Castle House Museum, Henbury, Bristol.

A villa built in the late C3, altered several times, and abandoned in the late C4. It has two wings linked by a corridor and porch. The back wall of the corridor was arched and looked out onto a gravelled court, around which other rooms were ranged. Beside the west wing was a bath-suite of which three rooms are now visible. Room 6 houses a mosaic from a villa excavated at Brislington, Bristol in 1899. Room 7 contains a poorly executed late C3 geometric mosaic.

G. Boon, 'The Roman Villa in Kingsweston Park', TBGAS 69 (1950), 5–58.

Knowlton, nr. Cranborne, Dorset   Neolithic henges† and
Bronze Age round barrows†   ★

SU 024100. 4 km. SW of Cranborne, 10 km. N of Wimborne Minster. Accessible along a signposted minor road W of B3078. English Heritage. Figure 173.

▼ **Fig. 173.** Plan of Knowlton, Dorset (after RCHME)

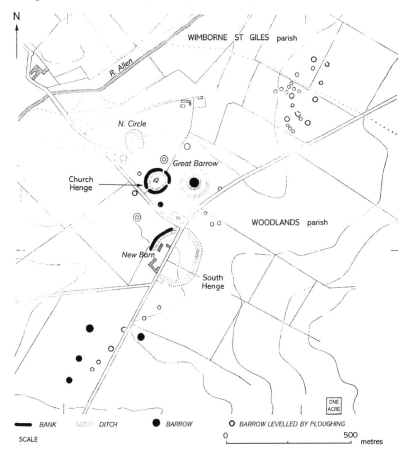

The little-explored complex of Neolithic and early Bronze Age monuments at Knowlton lies in a major river valley. The ceremonial significance of the place may have been perpetuated into medieval times and a Christian church stands in the centre of the monuments.

The focus of the Knowlton complex is the Church Henge, so called because it is dominated by the ruins of a Norman church abandoned in the late C18. The earthworks of the Neolithic henge comprise a 2 m. high bank with a 2 m. deep ditch.

North-east of the Henge is the Great Barrow. Tree-covered, this mound is 40 m. in diameter and over 6 m. high; it is the biggest round barrow in the region. Two other now-flattened enclosures stand north-west of the Church Henge.

South of the Church Henge is the Southern Circle, lying at the foot of a gentle slope and cut by the modern road (B3078). A small section of bank and ditch survives behind New Barn Farm visible from the road under trees. The enclosure had a diameter of about 228 m.

RCHME, An Inventory of Historical Monuments in the County of Dorset, vol. v: East Dorset (HMSO, 1975), 113–16. See also: http://csweb.bournemouth.ac.uk/consci/text_kn/knhome.htm

Long Bredy, Litton Cheney, Dorset Neolithic bank barrow

SY 572912. 12 km. W of Dorchester, immediately S of A35 E of turning to Litton Cheney.

A classic bank barrow of about 3500 BC, nearly 200 m. long and 21 m. wide. It is orientated north-east to south-west, and is slightly higher at the north-east end. The sides are roughly parallel and there are flanking side ditches.

R. Bradley, 'The Bank Barrows and Related Monuments of Dorset in the Light of Recent Fieldwork', PDNHAS 105 (1983), 15–20.

Maiden Castle, Dorset Neolithic causewayed enclosure† and long mound; Iron Age hillfort†; and Romano-British temple ★★

SY 670885. 2.5 km. SW of Dorchester town centre. Accessible by footpath from car park (signposted) at end of a minor road W of A354 on the outskirts of Dorchester. English Heritage. Figures 174 and 175.

Maiden Castle is the largest and most impressive developed hillfort in Britain. It lies on a chalk knoll, its natural topography having been sculptured and modelled through successive phases of construction and reconstruction.

The first occupation dates to about 3800 BC and comprised a causewayed enclosure on the eastern end of the hill. When abandoned around 3400 BC, a long mound was constructed over the earlier defences. This earthen mound, over 540 m. long, runs along the spine of the hill.

▲ **Fig. 174.** Aerial view of Maiden Castle, Dorset (CUCAP AY 5)

▲ **Fig. 175.** The Romano-Celtic temple on Maiden Castle, Dorset (Photograph: Jane Timby)

In the early Bronze Age the hill was turned over to grazing. Burial monuments were constructed and some can be seen adjacent to the car park.

Around 600 BC the hill was reoccupied on a large scale and the first major fortification constructed. This comprised an enclosure of 6.5 ha. bounded by a single rampart and ditch on the eastern summit, more or less over the site of the Neolithic camp. In plan, the fort was of angular shape defined by five straight stretches of boundary.

In the C5, the fort was extended and rebuilt as a massive developed hillfort nearly three times bigger (45.2 ha.). The defences comprise four concentric glacis-style ramparts on the south side and three on the north, with intervening ditches, which completely surround the hill and also cover its sides from top to bottom. The ramparts were repeatedly rebuilt and modified.

There were two opposed entrances, east and west, both different but both having pairs of gates side by side. At the east end the main ramparts stop to form a funnel-shaped entrance which contains an inner and an outer ditched hornwork, which would have broken the line of approach. At the massive western entrance the main ramparts continue round the end of the hill but have been interrupted in a staggered fashion so that anyone approaching has to twist and turn several times before reaching the two gates through the inner rampart. For added protection a fifth, outer, line of rampart and ditch was added to the fort's western end.

Towards the north-east corner of the site there was a shrine which later became the site for a small Roman temple. The foundations of this are visible on the ground, a classic Romano-Celtic structure comprising a *cella*, approximately 5 m. square surrounded by a verandah.

By the early C1 AD the hillfort seems to have been in decline and occupation small scale. Mortimer Wheeler, who excavated here in the 1930s, made much of the Roman conquest of the site by Vespasian in AD 43. Among the most vivid finds was a young man with a Roman ballista† bolt in his spine, one of fifteen burials showing violence.

N. Sharples, Maiden Castle (Batsford and English Heritage, 1991).

Malmesbury, Wiltshire Medieval abbey and town

ST 9387. 20 km. SW of Cirencester.

Malmesbury had a monastery from the C7, and by the C14 the church was so large that it resembled a cathedral. All, however, could have been destroyed at the Dissolution had not William Stumpe, a wealthy clothier, given the nave of the abbey church for use as the parish church. Other buildings housed his looms and weavers, but in time these buildings disappeared, leaving what is to be seen today. This is a medieval master-work. The church is entered via a Norman south porch with a door of eight continuous orders, alternate bands of which are carved with biblical scenes. It dates to around 1170.

Inside the Abbey, apart from the vaulted roof, which is early C14, the main features are mainly C12: squat piers supporting pointed arches (as at DURHAM), with an arcade above with typical Norman decoration, predominantly zigzag work. There is a gallery behind this, and on the south side an oratory, the purpose of which is uncertain.

In the town note especially the Market Cross built about 1500 and Abbey House, the mansion built for William Stumpe.

A. Brodie, 'Malmesbury Abbey', Arch J, 145 (1988) (Supplement), 31–5.

Maumbury Rings, Dorchester, Dorset Neolithic henge† and Roman amphitheatre

SY 691899. On S edge of Dorchester town, beside main road S to Weymouth. English Heritage.

During the C17 Civil War the grass-covered banks became a fort to defend the town. Ramps were constructed to allow canon to be hauled up onto the banks, whose outer face was scarped back, and a parapet added to the crest.

Mentally stripping these relatively recent changes away, the main visible earthworks were used in Roman times as an amphitheatre. The arena is still visible as an oval-shaped flat area with its entrance to the north. As many as 13,000 people could have been accommodated on the banks, and certainly 10,000 were present in AD 1705 for the public execution of Mary Channing.

The amphitheatre made use of still earlier structures, principally a late Neolithic henge monument. Unusually, the henge ditch of the henge comprised a more or less continuous cut about 2 m. deep, in the base of which was a series of shafts, in some cases extending down to a depth of 11 m. deep. Their purpose is not known.

R. Bradley, 'Maumbury Rings, Dorchester: The Excavation of 1908–1913', Archaeologia, 105 (1975), 1–97.

Nether Adber, and Marston Magna, Somerset

Medieval settlement

ST 5922. 8 km. NE of Yeovil, E of A359. Somerset County Council.

The earthworks of Nether Adber form one of the best examples of a deserted medieval village in Somerset. North and south of Thorny House fields contain the banks and ditches of house plots (crofts) laid out around a triangular village green. Perhaps in the later Middle Ages, some crofts were combined into larger holdings, occasionally with barn or byre as well as a farmhouse. Other crofts were replaced between the 1150 and 1350 by a manorial complex with L-shaped moat connected to a fishpond to the north. Of the chapel mentioned in 1351 there is no sign. The village's shrinkage continued in the C16, and by 1537 there were only three messuages (perhaps farmhouses) and one cottage here.

Footpaths lead to another site in public ownership, **Marston Magna**, 2 km. to the north-east, where broad moats delimit the site of the medieval manorial complex. The southernmost moat is continued by the earthworks of a straight, rectangular fishpond, almost 100 m. long, which supplied fish for the manorial table. The field to the south shows undulating medieval ridge and furrow†. North-east of the manor site is St Mary's Church; the chancel is Norman, the rest of the fabric late medieval, in the Perpendicular style.

M. Aston and C. Lewis (eds), The Medieval Landscape of Wessex (Oxbow Books, 1994), 255–69.

Nine Barrows, Nine Barrow Down, Corfe, Dorset Bronze
Age round barrow† cemetery

SY 995816. 5 km. NW of Swanage, N of A351. Access either by track W from SZ 018812 on minor road between New Swanage and B3351 or S from SY 995819 on B3351. National Trust.

Strung out along Nine Barrows Ridge this cemetery comprises a long barrow† and seventeen round bowl barrows.

L. Grinsell, Dorset Barrows (Dorset Natural History and Archaeological Society, 1959).

The Nine Stones, Winterbourne Abbas, Dorset Neolithic
stone circle†

SY 611904. In woodland beside S side of A35, 7 km. W of Dorchester. Parking difficult. English Heritage.

This unusual small stone circle stands in a narrow valley. It measures 9.1 × 7.9 m., is a slightly elliptical circle, and has nine upright stones. It resembles the KINGSTON RUSSELL stone circle; both have a north–south axis with the largest stones to the north. Like most Dorset stone circles this was probably built around 1700 BC.

S. and C. Piggott, 'Stone and Earth Circles', Antiquity, 13 (1939), 138–58.

Norton Fitzwarren, Taunton, Somerset Later prehistoric
enclosures

ST 195263. N of Blackdown View in Norton Fitzwarren village on W side of Taunton. N of A361(T); some signposting to a car park. Somerset County Council.

Overlooking the Vale of Taunton Deane, this Bronze Age enclosure and Iron Age hillfort is best seen by following the self-guided trail from the car park in Blackdown View. Leaflets available from County Hall in Taunton.

About 1300 BC a rampart was constructed enclosing an area of 2 ha. Part of this can be seen as a grassy mound on the eastern side of the hill (point 10 on the trail). Excavations show that the enclosure was an important meeting place for local communities and among the finds was a hoard of eight finely made bronze bracelets and three axes.

Later, about 500 BC, the hilltop was refortified. The ramparts of this Iron Age hillfort are still visible as substantial banks, with an entrance on the north-east side (point 8).

Like many hillforts in south-west England, Norton Fitzwarren continued to be occupied after the Roman conquest of the area about AD 50.

P. Ellis, 'Norton Fitzwarren Hillfort: A Report on the Excavations by Nancy and Philip Langmaid between 1968 and 1971', PSNHAS 133 (1989), 1–74.

Norton St Philip, Trowbridge, Somerset   Medieval inn

ST 772558. On A366 between Radstock and Trowbridge, W of A36(T).

Gloucestershire and Somerset have some of England's finest medieval inns, most built by monasteries. The provision of hospitality within the monastery itself was in some cases becoming a considerable burden in the C14 and C15; building an inn removed travellers from the precinct and, furthermore, secured an income. The George, at Norton, is among the earliest of such hostels. It was built by the Carthusian† monks of Hinton Charterhouse for merchants attending Norton's two great annual fairs where wool and cloth were sold, en route to the Italian and Flemish markets. It comprises a substantial main range fronting the street, with an arched gateway and mullioned bay windows. Inside, in the bars, are moulded ceiling beams and carved fireplaces. The core of the building is C14; the upper floors were given their present jettied front about 1500 during remodelling after a fire. To the rear is a court-yard with what were originally stabling and storage ranges.

E. Williams et al., 'The George Inn', Arch J, 144 (1987), 317–27.

Oakley Down, Handley, Dorset   Neolithic and Bronze Age
barrow cemetery

SU 007154. 18 km. SW of Salisbury, 15 km. NE of Blandford Forum. S of A354 between Woodyates and Handley Down. Figure 176.

Oakley Down in the heart of Cranborne Chase is one of the largest and most visually impressive round barrow cemeteries in central southern England. It contains at least thirty-one separate barrows spanning over a thousand years from the middle Neolithic to the end of the early Bronze Age. The line of the Roman Road linking Badbury Rings with Old Sarum runs along the east side of the cemetery, clipping some of the barrows.

The original focus of the cemetery was probably **Wor Barrow**, a

▲ **Fig. 176.** Aerial view of Oakley Down round barrow cemetery, Dorset (CUCAP AQ-11)

middle Neolithic oval barrow, the excavated remains of which can still be seen in the field north of the A354 (SU 012173).

In the early Bronze Age attention moved slightly to the south-east. Several different types of round barrow† are represented. Twenty are simple bowl barrows with central mounds surrounded by ditches, the rest are collectively known as 'fancy barrows': two bell barrows; one saucer barrow; six disc barrows; and two which defy classification.

RCHME, An Inventory of the Historical Monuments in the County of Dorset, *vol. v:* East Dorset *(HMSO, 1975), 102–4.*

Oldbury Camp, Cherhill, Wiltshire Iron Age hillfort†

SU 049693. 5 km. E of Calne, 4 km. W of Beckhampton. S of, and visible from, the A4. Access by signposted track and footpath running S of A4. National Trust.

This roughly triangular 6 ha, down-land hillfort is bounded by a pair of well-preserved ramparts and accompanying ditches. The entrance was on the east side and the in-turned rampart terminals are visible. There may have been a second entrance to the south-east. A low bank and shallow ditch divides the interior of the fort, but is probably not con-temporary with the use of the fort. Excavations allow the site to be dated to the earlier Iron Age, perhaps the C5–C3 BC. Flint-digging has damaged the interior. Within the camp is the Lansdowne Monument erected in 1845 to commemorate Sir William Petty, a C17 economist.

North of the camp is the **Cherhill White Horse** cut in 1780 by Dr Christopher Alsop of Calne in the style of the artist Stubbs.

H. Cunnington, 'Oldbury Camp, Wiltshire', WANHM 28 (1871), 277.

Old Sarum, Salisbury, Wiltshire Iron Age hillfort† and medieval town

SU 138327. 3 km. N of Salisbury town centre, access (signposted) from the A345. Car park. English Heritage; part of the site has open access; the castle has restricted opening. Admission charge. Figure 177.

Old Sarum lies on a prominent hill overlooking the river Avon; it is the forerunner of modern SALISBURY and has a complicated history spanning the period from 400 BC to AD 1220.

The earliest visible remains on the hill are the ramparts of an Iron Age hillfort. Oval in plan, covering about 20 ha., this fort was bounded by a single bank and ditch with an entrance where cars now drive in. Little is known about the later prehistoric occupation, although in Roman times it was called *Sorviodunum.*

Soon after the Norman Conquest William I founded a castle here, within the Iron Age hillfort, whose ditch was deepened to form an outer defence. The site was made the seat of county government.

Between the castle and the ramparts was a zone about 100 m. wide. In one quarter a cathedral was established in the later 1070s as the English Church was reorganized by the Normans. A town, perhaps never hugely populous, was also founded. A century and a half later the need for defence had gone and in the 1220s the site was largely abandoned in favour of New Sarum, the modern Salisbury.

RCHME, Ancient and Historical Monuments in the City of Salisbury (HMSO, 1980), 1–24.

Old Wardour, Wiltshire Medieval castle

ST 939263. 6 km. NE of Shaftesbury. English Heritage; restricted opening. Admission charge. Figure 178.

Old Wardour was built in the 1390s for Lord Lovel, clearly influenced by what he had seen in France during the Hundred Years War. Although squat and powerful, it is more lordly residence than military stronghold, its clever, integrated, room plan probably due to William Wynford, one of England's finest architects (he remodelled the nave of WINCHESTER cathedral). In plan it is hexagonal, the regularity broken only by the two towers which flank the entry, above which is the great hall. Service rooms and a kitchen lay at one end of the hall, and at the other the lord's private apartments. The rest of the hexagon was devoted to chambers for

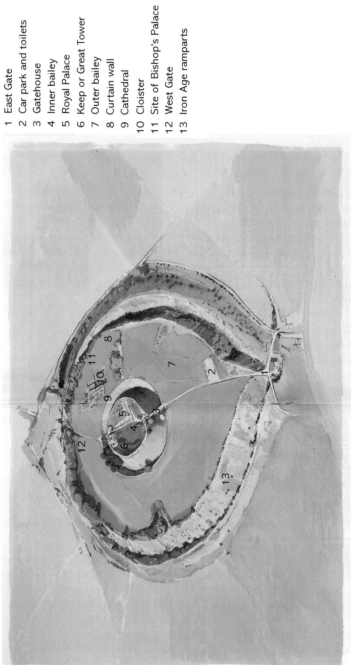

1 East Gate
2 Car park and toilets
3 Gatehouse
4 Inner bailey
5 Royal Palace
6 Keep or Great Tower
7 Outer bailey
8 Curtain wall
9 Cathedral
10 Cloister
11 Site of Bishop's Palace
12 West Gate
13 Iron Age ramparts

▲ Fig. 177. Old Sarum, Salisbury, Wiltshire (after English Heritage)

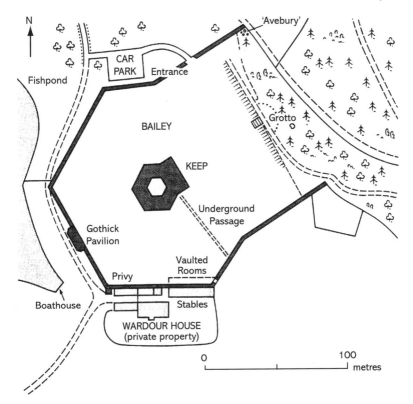

▲ **Fig. 178.** Old Wardour Castle, Wiltshire (after English Heritage)

the household and guests. After 1570 another leading architect, John Smythson, modernized the house and added classically inspired fronts to the entrance and to the grand entrance to the hall.

The keep stood within a walled enclosure, again hexagonal, originally with stables, additional accommodation, and probably storage buildings.

Today the castle is ruinous, having twice been besieged in the 1640s during the Civil Wars.

A. Saunders and R. Pugh, Old Wardour Castle *(English Heritage, 1991) (Site Guidebook).*

Pilsden Pen, Broadwindsor, Dorset Iron Age hillfort

ST 413013. 7 km. W of Beaminster, 5.5 km. SW of Broadwindsor. N of B1364. Access via footpath N of B1364 from Lob Gate car park. National Trust.

Occupying the highest hill in Dorset at 277 m. above sea level, this oval 3 ha. enclosure utilizes the naturally steep hill slopes in its defences on all but the north-west side. The massive boundary earthworks comprise two banks and ditches, with a small counterscarp bank† beyond.

Three entrances can be recognized. At the south-east entrance the outer bank stops short of the entrance gap to form an oblique line of approach. At the south-west entrance there is a platform between the ramparts.

The half-dozen or so low cigar-shaped mounds are pillow mounds relating to a more recent rabbit warren.

P. Gelling, 'Excavations at Pilsdon Pen, Dorset, 1964–71', PPS 43 (1977), 263–86.

Poor Lot, Black Down, Kingston Russell, Dorset Bronze Age round barrow† cemetery

SY 588907. 10 km. W of Dorchester, 3 km. W of Winterbourne Abbas. Mainly S of A35(T), but with some examples and parking N of road. English Heritage. Figure 179.

One of the finest groups of barrows in southern Wessex comprising at least forty-four barrows of which twenty-four are bowl barrows, seven bell barrows, eight disc barrows, and five pond barrows. The range of types here is wide; so is the distribution, which extends from the hilltop south of the A35, down into the valley along which the modern road runs, and up the slopes north of the road. The accessible barrows are mainly on the lower ground.

Like many barrow cemeteries, Poor Lot started around 3500 BC with two 100 m. long earthen long barrows† south of the road. Both are well preserved. North of the road is a Neolithic oval barrow, later elaborated by the addition of three round mounds, which may represent a second early focus and account for the wide distribution of barrows.

RCHME, An Inventory of the Historical Monuments in the County of Dorset, vol. ii: South-East (HMSO, 1970), 461–3.

Porlock, Exmoor, Somerset Neolithic stone circle†

SS 845447. S of A39, 4.5 km. SW of Porlock. On open moor immediately beside (W) of minor road running S from A39 towards Exford.

Ten standing stones† and stumps together with eleven fallen stones in a ring about 25 m. in diameter are all that remain of this once-impressive stone circle constructed about 2000 BC.

All the stones are local sandstone, undressed, and, in common with other circles on Exmoor, are fairly small in size, the largest only 1 m. long.

A small round barrow† lies a few metres to the north-east of the circle. Other stone circles on Exmoor include the **Withypool Stone Circle** (SS 838343), and **Almsworthy Stone Circle** (SS 847416).

H. St G. Gray, 'The Porlock Stone Circle, Exmoor', PSANHS 74 (1929), 71–7.

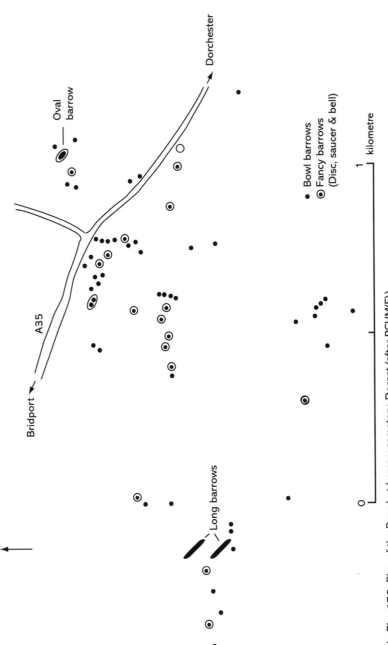

▲ Fig. 179. Plan of the Poor Lot barrow cemetery, Dorset (after RCHM(E))

Poundbury, Dorchester, Dorset Iron Age hillfort†

SY 683912. On the NW side of Dorchester. Public access from minor road to Bradford Peverell.

This rectangular, 6 ha. fort is bounded by two lines of ramparts and ditches, except on the north where one of the banks is dispensed with. The inner rampart was probably built in the C6 BC and comprised a chalk rubble core revetted in front with a timber face. Immediately in front was a narrow berm†, beyond which was a V-profile ditch. The outer bank and ditch were added about the C1 BC. At the same time the inner rampart was widened and heightened, and a parapet added.

A Bronze Age round barrow stands inside the fort. Around the north and eastern sides of the fort is a flat terrace just below the defences. This carries an aqueduct† bringing water from a reservoir south of Frampton to the town of *Durnovaria*, probably built in the C1 AD.

Poundbury was also the site of Roman occupation and notably of a major late Roman cemetery with probable Christian connotations.

D. Farwell and T. Molleson, Excavations at Poundbury 1966–8, vol. ii: The Cemeteries, *Dorset Natural History and Archaeological Society Monograph 11 (1993).*

Priddy Circles and Nine Barrows, Priddy,
Somerset Prehistoric enclosures and Bronze Age round barrow†
cemeteries

ST 538518. 5 km. W of Chewton Mendip, 8 km. E of Cheddar. The circles are between the B3134 and B3135. The barrows S of B3135. Parking for both sites beside B3135 at ST 540524. Visible from the road.

This group of enclosures and barrows stands under pasture on the high windswept plateau of the Mendip hills.

The four **Priddy Circles** are round enclosures, each about 183 m. in diameter and bounded by a small bank and external ditch. The circles are arranged in a line roughly north to south, the northernmost circle standing a little apart from the others. Excavations in the southern circle revealed a U-shaped ditch and the bank was revetted with timber uprights and faced with dry-stone walling. The circles probably date to the late Neolithic or early Bronze Age.

East of the Circles are two groups of round barrows. **Priddy Nine Barrows** (ST 538516) is a cluster of seven large and conspicuous barrows with two outliers to the north-east. All seem to have contained cremation burials.

Nearby is the **Ashen Hill Barrow Cemetery** (ST 539514), with eight equally large barrows arranged in a row. The barrows have yielded cremations in pits, urns, and cists†.

E. Tratman, 'The Priddy Circles, Mendip, Somerset: Henge Monuments', PUBSS 11 (1967), 97–125.

Salisbury, Wiltshire Medieval cathedral city ★

SU 143295. 35 km. NW of Southampton.

Resiting the castle and town of OLD SARUM in 1219 to where major roads from London, Exeter, Winchester, Southampton, and elsewhere crossed the river Avon paid off, and by the early C14 Salisbury ranked with England's wealthiest provincial centres.

The Avon's meadows offered ample flat building ground. Work on the cathedral began almost immediately; the Lady Chapel was consecrated in 1225, and the cathedral as a whole in 1258. The speed of building gives Salisbury an architectural unity emphasized by the use throughout the interior of dark and slender marble shafts, which contrast strongly with the pale yellow limestone of the main fabric. The only major addition to the original church, about 1300, was a heightened tower surmounted by a 123 m. high spire. Inside the spire its wooden scaffolding still survives. Also witness to the builders' abilities, and to problems with the weight of the spire, are the iron strapping put around the uppermost part of the tower in the C14 and the curving strainer arches built in the crossing about 1450. The cathedral has many fine tombs, Britain's oldest working clock (1386), and one of only four original copies of the Magna Carta.

Beyond the close, cleared about 1800, is a bustling city, still occupying the grid of streets laid out by the bishop's planners almost 800 years ago. Along with streets and house plots a huge market place was laid out, and is still impressive, although later encroached upon (Butcher Row, Fish Row, etc.). At its west end is the stone Poultry Cross, first mentioned in 1335, the one survivor of four shelters where specific trades or goods were on offer. To the west is St Thomas's Church, founded in 1269 but rebuilt by wool merchants in the C15. St Edmund's was founded later as the population grew. St Martin's pre-dates the new town and probably served the village of Milford.

P. Brimacombe, A Tale of Two Cathedrals: Old Sarum–New Salisbury *(English Heritage, 1997)*

The Sanctuary, Avebury, Wiltshire Neolithic timber structure
and stone circle†

SU 118679. On Overton Hill 2.5 km. SE of AVEBURY. Lay-by car-parking. English Heritage. Within a World Heritage Site.

At the south-eastern end of the West Kennet Avenue (see above AVEBURY) was a series of structures culminating in the construction of a stone circle. Totally destroyed by the C18, this site was rediscovered by aerial photography in 1930, and subsequently excavated.

Controversy surrounds interpretation, but two main phases can be recognized. First was a timber structure. Around 2500 BC, after the wooden posts had rotted or been removed, two concentric rings of sarsen† stones were set up. It was then that the monument became linked to Avebury by the Avenue which leads off the outer stone circle at the Sanctuary.

Today the positions of posts and stones are marked by concrete blocks.

Six round barrows of 1500 BC to 2500 BC lie either side of the A4 next to the Sanctuary; other barrows are scattered across the downs, many marked by tree clumps

J. Pollard, 'The Sanctuary, Overton Hill, near Avebury: A Re-examination', PPS 58 (1992), 213–26.

Sea Mills (*Portus Abonae*), Bristol Roman military harbour, port, and settlement

ST 551759. At S side of Portway (A4), at its junction with residential road Roman Way in Bristol suburbs 5 km. W of city centre.

A small settlement located on the Bristol Channel at Avonmouth. Excavations in 1934 uncovered a C3–C4 building, the foundations of which are visible. This would have been a major redistribution centre for the lead and silver workings on the Mendips (see CHARTERHOUSE).

P. Ellis, 'Sea Mills, Bristol: The 1965–1968 Excavations on the Roman Town of Abonae', TBGAS 105 (1987), 15–108.

Silbury Hill, Avebury, Wiltshire Neolithic mound   ★

SU 100685. 1.5 km. S of Avebury. Beside A4 between West Kennet and Beckhampton, very clearly visible. Parking and viewing area on W side. English Heritage. Within a World Heritage Site. Figure 180.

Probably the most enigmatic site in the Avebury area, Silbury Hill is reputedly the largest prehistoric man-made mound in Europe.

Its present shape is a 37 m. high, truncated cone with a base area of 2.1 ha. The flat top is 30 m. in diameter. The chalk to build this mound was quarried from a surrounding ditch, now partly silted up. Excavations in 1968–70 showed that **Silbury I** comprised a flat circular area about 20 m. in diameter, enclosed by a wattle fence. In the centre was a clay mound, covered in soil and turfs. Over this was piled earth and stones to form a mound 36 m. in diameter and 5.4 m. high.

Silbury II. Some time after 2600 BC the mound was enlarged with chalk to form a mound 73 m. in diameter.

Silbury III. Around 2200 BC the mound was extended to a diameter of about 158 m. The new mound seems to have been built in stages producing the effect of a stepped cone. Each stage was constructed with dumps of chalk within retaining walls. Finally, the mound was given the smooth profile seen today.

▲ Fig. 180. View of Silbury Hill, Wiltshire (Photograph by Timothy Darvill)

Silbury's purpose is not known. No burials have been discovered within it, although some may exist in unexplored portions.

The hill was used as a fortification in the C11 and C12 AD. It was then that the terrace near the top of the hill was created.

A. Whittle, Sacred Mound, Holy Rings. Silbury Hill and the West Kennet Palisade Enclosures: A Later Neolithic Complex in North Wiltshire *(Oxbow Books, 1997).*

Somerset church bench ends, Somerset Medieval church fittings

Until about 1400 a church served much like a modern village hall, as a general purpose meeting room. Thereafter, as the feeling grew that churches should be used only for sacred purposes, church rooms began to be constructed, and by 1500 almost all Somerset parishes had one. As there was now less need for the nave to be a general-purpose open space, and as preaching became commoner, churches began to fill up with pulpits, lecterns, screens, and benches. Somerset has one of England's richest collections of elaborately carved medieval church woodwork, and some of the most charming work is on bench ends. Some show trades: at **Bishops Lydeard** (ST 1629) a windmill, at **Spaxton** (ST 2237) a fuller, and at **Kingston St Mary** (ST 2229) a weaver's shuttle. Rural life appears at **Barwick** (ST 5613) (bird shooting) and **Lyng** (ST 3329) (wrestling, and courting), while at **South Brent** (ST 3350) the fox and goose cartoon appears.

R. Dunning (ed.), Christianity in Somerset (Somerset County Council, 1976), 15–17.

South Cadbury Hillfort, Little Cadbury, Somerset Iron Age hillfort†

ST 628251. 9 km. W of Wincanton 11 km. NE of Yeovil. S of A303(T), accessible by footpath SW from South Cadbury church.

Overlooking the valleys of the Yeo and Brue, this hillfort is unusual in having a water supply, King Arthur's well, at the north-east corner. Excavations 1966–70 revealed much about the history of settlement on the hill.

In the C5 BC work began on the hillfort whose ramparts dominate the hill. The first phase was an impressive structure, especially from the outside, and highly defensible too. There were two entrances, one to the south-west, the other to the north-east.

Around the C3 BC, the defences were expanded outwards with the addition of three outer banks and ditches and the entrances elaborated to create the developed hillfort seen today.

Inside the fort were numerous houses and other structures, and in the centre was a shrine of the type known at other hillforts and HEATH-ROW AIRPORT. There is some evidence for an attack during the Roman Conquest; Roman military equipment and a military building have been found.

Archaeological evidence shows that during a sub-Roman C6 AD phase the inner rampart was refurbished and a timber 'feasting hall' built. Imported eastern Mediterranean pottery suggests an owner of rank and power. Some have suggested that the legendary King Arthur occupied the site, which accordingly was Camelot. Whatever the reality, the site was certainly important, and a mint was established here by King Ethelred the Unready in the C10.

L. Alcock, 'By South Cadbury, is that Camelot' (Thames & Hudson, 1972).

Stanton Drew, Stanton Drew, Bath and North-East Somerset Neolithic stone circles† ★

ST 598633. 10 km. S of Bristol, 2 km W of Pensford. Signposted access from Stanton Drew village. Part English Heritage. Figure 181.

Just above the floodplain of the river Chew is a group of late Neolithic ceremonial monuments set in lush meadows. At the centre is the **Great Circle**, a huge ring of stones, 112 m. in diameter, with twenty-seven remaining uprights of local limestone. From this circle an avenue of stones leads north-eastwards towards the river for 88 m. Geophysical

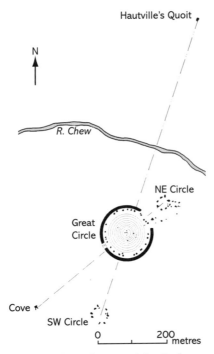

▲ **Fig. 181.** Plan of Stanton Drew, Somerset (after Burl)

surveys revealed the stone ring stands on the inner lip of a circular ditch with a single entrance to the north-east. This arrangement is very similar to that at AVEBURY. Here, however, the stone circle seems to have replaced a timber structure with nine concentric rings of upright timber posts. Analogies can be found at WOODHENGE.

Two other circles lie nearby. The **North-East Circle**, 29.5 m. in diameter, has four stones remaining, and an avenue extending eastwards towards the river. The **South-West Circle**, 44 m. in diameter, has ten stones remaining.

A line projected from the centre of the North-East Circle, through the centre of the Great Circle, aligns with the cove. This is next to the church in the back garden of the Druid's Arms public house. It comprises two upright stones and a third, now fallen. Again there are analogies with arrangements at Avebury.

A line projected from the centre of the South-West Circle, again passing through the centre of the Great Circle and continuing northwards across the river Chew, lines up with the final element in the complex—**Hautville's Quoit**. This is a large standing stone†, now fallen, beside the B3130 (ST 601638).

A. Burl, The Stone Circles of Britain, Ireland and Brittany (Yale University Press, 2000),. 148–9. See also: www.engh.gov.uk/archaeometry/stantondrew

Stonehenge, Amesbury, Wiltshire Neolithic and Bronze Age
ceremonial centre and stone circles†   ★★

SU 123422. 4 km. W of Amesbury signposted from the A303(T) N of Amesbury.
English Heritage and National Trust. Restricted opening hours. Admission charge.
Audio-tape guides. Within a World Heritage Site. Figure 182.

Stonehenge stands high on the chalk downs of Salisbury Plain, but what first attracted people here is not known. Perhaps the special character of the place was signalled by ceremonial activities here about 7000 BC. Concrete discs at the western end of the modern car park mark the positions of three massive timber posts aligned on what might have been a large and long-established tree (unmarked).

The familar stone structure of Stonehenge represents part of a long-lived and complicated monument spanning nearly fifteen centuries from about 2950 BC through to 1500 BC. Three main constructional phases have been identified.

Stonehenge 1 comprises the circular earthwork enclosure, 97 m. in diameter, constructed around 2950 BC. The ditch was modest in scale and the spoil was used to construct an internal bank about 1.8 m. high. There was an external bank around at least some of the enclosure, and this can be seen in places. One entrance opened to the north-east, a second to the south, a third to the south-west. The ditch was used for special ceremonies, and cattle skulls were placed either side of the entrances. Inside the bank was a circle of fifty-six holes (the Aubrey Holes—so-called after the antiquary who discovered them), which probably held upright posts (some marked by concrete discs).

Stonehenge 2 dates to between 2900 BC and 2400 BC, the late Neolithic. During this phase the ditch continued to fill up and the posts in the Aubrey Holes decayed or were removed. New timber settings were constructed in the north-eastern entrance and in the central area. Some may have been buildings. Towards the end of Phase 2 the site was used as a cremation cemetery. Deposits of burnt human bone were inserted into pits in the bank and ditch, and into the tops of some of the abandoned Aubrey Holes. Aubrey Burl has argued that during phases 1 and 2, the users of the site were interested in the movements of the moon and that standing in the circle and looking out through the north-east entrance allowed a view of the minor and major risings of the moon as its rising positions moved back and forth across the horizon over the 18.61 years of the lunar cycle.

Stonehenge 3 dates to between 2550 BC and 1600 BC. It is subdivided into a number of sub-phases, during the first of which, Phase **3i**, the earliest stone structure was built, probably about 2500 BC. This comprised two concentric rings of bluestone pillars that had been brought over 220 km. from the Presely mountains of south-west Wales.

External stone settings were introduced at this time too. Immediately

N

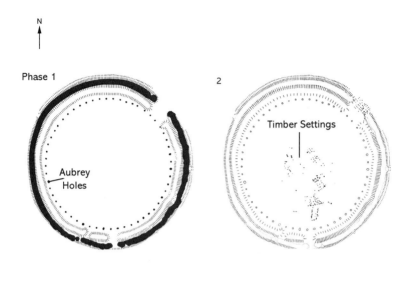

Phase 1

Aubrey
Holes

2

Timber Settings

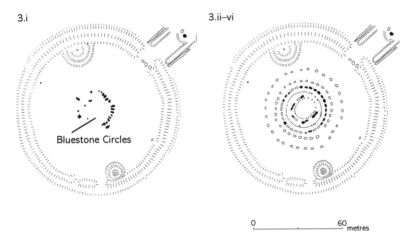

3.i

Bluestone Circles

3.ii–vi

0   60
                                  metres

▲ **Fig. 182.** Plans of the main phases of Stonehenge, Wiltshire (after Cleal, Walker & Montague)

outside the north-east entrance two stones were erected. One (the Heel Stone) still stands. The second (later removed) lay west of the Heel Stone. Together they formed a sort of gun-sight for viewing the horizon from the centre of the circle, marking the point on the north-eastern horizon where the midsummer sun rose. This new axis also incorporated other solar events, for example the setting of the midsummer sun and the rising and setting of the midwinter sun. Four 'station stones' set at the corners of a rectangle just inside the inner toe of the surrounding bank were also set up. Two still stand.

The Phase 3i monument was short-lived; it was dismantled and a new structure begun: **Stonehenge 3ii–3vi** represented by the structures which dominate the site today.

In **Stonehenge 3ii** a horseshoe-shaped setting of five large trilithons, each made from three local sarsen† blocks dressed and worked to shape, was set up in the centre of the enclosure with its open end aligned on the midsummer rising sun. The tallest of the five trilithons, 7.7 m. high, was to the south-west, opposite the entrance, the pairs on either side being of decreasing height. Three trilithons are complete, the other two are part fallen. Around the central horseshoe was a ring of thirty upright shaped sarsen blocks, their tops joined with lintel slabs. Sixteen uprights remain standing. Additionally, parts of two of the trilithons, and pieces of the sarsen circle, are collapsed on the ground. Rock art comprising images of axes and daggers was engraved into some of the trilithons and other sarsen stones.

Outside the main circles, the stone next to the Heel Stone seems to have been removed, and a ditch dug around the Heel Stone. Ditches may also have been dug round two of the station stones making them look like small round barrows. Having made the sighting stones useless, a new setting was constructed as a sort of passage defined by a pair of stones and two single stones. One of the pair, now prostrate beside the entrance, is known as the Slaughter Stone.

In **Stonehenge 3iii** and **Stonehenge 3iv** the structure was elaborated with the addition of a succession of bluestone rings between and within the existing settings. A straight Avenue 530 m. long and 12 m. wide comprising parallel banks and exterior ditches was constructed to perpetuate the main axis of the monument on the rising midsummer sun.

Stonehenge 3v is the most elaborate form. Several bluestones in the central oval were removed so that the remaining eleven formed a horseshoe imitating the trilithon setting. Overall, the structure in Phase 3v comprised (from the centre out): bluestone horseshoe with the Altar Stone at its focus, trilithon horseshoe, bluestone circle, sarsen circle. The main axis of the monument remained the same as previously. Observers standing at the Altar Stone at sunrise on midsummer's morning would have seen the light from the rising sun appear to shine up the avenue, through the settings at the entrance, between the uprights in the sarsen

The Druids

A number of classical authors writing between the C4 BC and C3 AD refer to the fact that amongst the societies outside the Greek and Roman worlds in northern Europe there was a male priesthood of some kind which they referred to as Druids (Greek: *druidai*; Latin: *druidae*). They were portrayed in different ways by different authors, but may be visualized as priests, magicians, seers, law-givers, and tutors of the community. They were widely recognized as powerful and, to the eyes of classical writers at least, dangerous. They held assemblies in sacred places, at least some of which were natural shrines such as woodland groves or springs. They were believed to have indulged in human sacrifice and divination.

The Druids and the religion they represented were, by the early C1 AD, made the object of successive measures of repression by the Roman authorities. They, and the beliefs they stood for, had effectively been eradicated by the C2 AD if not before.

Druids appear at Stonehenge on midsummer morning clad in white robes greeting the sun. But these are modern-day druids and have no direct link with their prehistoric namesakes.

circle, between the pillars of the bluestone circle, into the open end of the sarsen and bluestone horseshoes and on to strike the Altar Stone at the very heart of the monument. Exactly what ceremonies were enacted on midsummer's morning, or whenever, is not known. One glimpse, however, may be provided by the find of an adult male buried in 2200 BC in the ditch on the north-west side having been shot in the back with arrows.

Altogether, the construction and use of Stonehenge spanned at least 1,500 years, and new features were still being planned when it was finally abandoned about 1500 BC. During its life there were two successive cosmological systems informing the layout, first based on lunar events, later on solar events. But Stonehenge was not built primarily as an observatory or a giant calculator. Rather it was a place where people came to engage in ceremonies and events.

Around Stonehenge there are many related monuments. Most notably, a fine bell barrow stands immediately to the east. Footpaths help the visitor explore the wider setting of Stonehenge, and a self-guided trail leaflet can be bought at the ticket office. Note especially the **Stonehenge cursus**, a long narrow enclosure over 3 km. in length to the north of Stonehenge (SU 109429 to SU 137433) constructed about 2800 BC; the **New King Barrow Ridge** barrow cemetery (SU 135423); the **Cursus Barrow Cemetery** (SU 116427); and the **Winterborne Stoke Crossroads Barrow Cemetery** (SU 101417).

R. Cleal et al., Stonehenge in its Landscape: Twentieth-Century Excavations, *English Heritage Archaeological Report 10 (1995). See also:* www.intel.com.cpc/explore/stonehenge/index.htm

Stoney Littleton, Wellow, Bath and North East Somerset Neolithic long barrow†

ST 735573. 7 km. S of Bath. Access by footpath from car park at Stoney Littleton, signposted from Peasedown St John on A367. English Heritage.

A fine Neolithic long barrow constructed in the Cotswold–Severn tradition about 3700 BC. The cairn†, edged by a dry-stone wall, measures about 30.5 × 15.2 m. At the front are two projecting horns† flanking a forecourt, at the back of which is the entrance to the chambers. Look for an ammonite fossil on the left-hand door jamb; the stones of the chamber and passage were carefully chosen and some came from outcrops more than 8 km. away. The burial chambers open from a central passage—three on each side and an end chamber. These chambers originally contained heaps of bones representing many individuals.

A Bulleid, 'Notes on Some Chambered Long Barrows of North Somerset', PSANHS 87 (1941), 56–71.

Tisbury, Wiltshire Medieval manor and church

ST 9429. 8 km. W of Wilton.

During the Middle Ages a farm belonging to the Benedictine† nuns of Shaftesbury Abbey was run from Place Farm. On the road is the gatehouse, with pedestrian gate and a double cart entrance. Beyond, an inner gatehouse leads to the farmhouse, of medieval date, and a 60 m. long, thirteen-bay C15 thatched cruck barn. Within Tisbury itself is its cruciform church, C12 with C14 and C15 additions. It has several good memorials to the Arundells including Catherine Howard's sister, Lady Blanche, defender of Wardour during the Civil War. Rudyard Kipling, too, lies here.

N. Pevsner and B. Cherry, The Buildings of England: Wiltshire (Penguin, 1975), 520–3.

Upton Park, Poole, Dorset Reconstructed Roman farmhouse

SY 996926. Within Upton Park Country Park beside A35 W of Poole. For opening times and activity days contact Poole Waterfront Museum. Figure 183.

Several Roman farms and salt-working sites have been found around Poole harbour. One farmhouse has been reconstructed, the details based on excavated evidence. The structure is timber-framed, with a thatched roof.

B. Putnam, Roman Dorset (Dovecote Press, 1993).

▲ **Fig. 183.** The reconstructed Roman house, Upton Park, Poole, Dorset (Photograph: Jane Timby)

Wansdyke, Wiltshire Medieval frontier dyke

Across southern and western England are several linear dyke systems of the later first millennium AD, which delineate or defend territorial boundaries. Wansdyke is one the largest systems, a 14 km. long western section (West Wansdyke) in Somerset and a 20 km. long eastern section (East Wansdyke) in Wiltshire, the two being separated by a gap of 30 km. Its bank and ditch face north, apparently to defend lands to its south. Its date is about AD 500 and may thus have been built either by the residual British population against Anglo-Saxons, or as a frontier after the Anglo-Saxon advance was stopped.

One of the best parts of the eastern section is at Tan Hill, All Cannings, Wiltshire, south of Avebury (SU 090646).

B. Yorke, Wessex in the Early Middle Ages *(Leicester University Press, 1995), 26–7.*

Wareham, Dorset Anglo-Saxon burh†

SY 9287. 10 km. W of Bournemouth, on W side of Poole Harbour. Figure 184.

Wareham stands between the rivers Frome and Piddle on Poole harbour, a position of great natural strength; by the early C8 it was a cross-channel port. In the reign of Alfred (king of Wessex 871–99) Wareham became a *burh*, one of the fortified places established against the Vikings.

▲ **Fig. 184.** Wareham, Dorset: St Martin's church (Photograph: Paul Stamper)

It has massive earthen bank and ditch defences, and within them a regular grid of streets. During the Second World War the defences were rescarped against tank attack.

The town has two churches. The older foundation, **Our Lady of St Mary**, was established in the C8 as a minster church. Unfortunately the Anglo-Saxon fabric was demolished in C19 when the church was rebuilt. It has five apparently Christian tombstones or memorials of perhaps C8 date, a lead font, and two good C12 knight effigies. The other Saxon church, **St Martin's**, stands at the north gate. It is probably late C11, and is England's earliest reasonably complete urban parish church. It comprises a tall, square chancel and nave, both late Saxon, with a C13 north aisle. Inside is the original chancel arch, with later squints to either side, and wall paintings of about 1100 in the chancel. The church contains the effigy of T. E. Lawrence (Lawrence of Arabia), killed nearby in 1935.

Just inside the south-west corner of the *burh* defences is a motte†, all that remains of Wareham's castle. Trinity Lane preserves the line of the bailey†.

In the later Middle Ages the harbour silted up, and Wareham became a market town. Much of its character is the result of rebuilding after a fire of 1762.

D. Hinton, Discover Dorset: Saxons and Vikings *(Dovecote Press, 1998), 46–7, 54–7, 64–7.*

Wells, Somerset Medieval cathedral†

ST 551459. 18 km. S of Bristol, E of M5 off junctions 22 and 23. Figure 185.

Wells has had a church since at least the early C8 and a cathedral since 909. The present structure was begun about 1189, and the nave† (all but the three western bays), transepts†, and first three bays of the choir†, all completed by 1200, are an especially early example of the Gothic architectural style. The nave was extended west, and the statuary-festooned west front constructed, after 1239. After 1300 the choir was lengthened, the eastern chapels and chapter house added, and the central tower completed. The last is supported by strainer arches, introduced about 1330 to counteract its hugely increased weight. Slightly later are the western towers, cloisters, and the Chain Gate, the last a bridge over the roadway to the Vicars' Choral Hall.

South of the cathedral is the Bishop's Palace. This dates in part from 1230, its fortifications and moat from the 1340s.

▼ **Fig. 185.** Wells, Somerset: the cathedral and moated Bishop's Palace (Devon/Somerset County Councils)

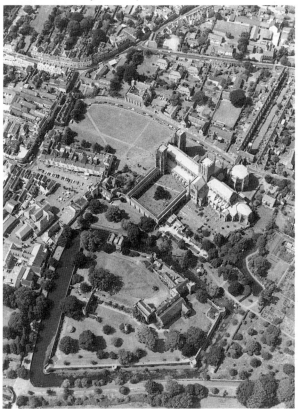

On the north side of the cathedral is the Vicars Close, a complete street of terraced houses built about 1360 to provide accommodation for the Vicars Choral, lay brethren who sang the cathedral services. No 22 shows the original appearance of a house. Closing the street at one end is the C14 chapel with C15 library above. The Hall at the south end of the street, with pulpit for reading during meals, is of about 1350.

J. Sampson, Wells Cathedral West Front: Construction, Sculpture and Conservation *(Sutton Publishing, 1998).*

West Kennet Long Barrow, Avebury, Wiltshire Neolithic
long barrow† ★

SU 104677. 2 km. S of AVEBURY. *Access by footpath from lay-by on A4. English Heritage. Within a World Heritage Site.*

This long barrow, the biggest in southern England at more than 100 m. long, was constructed in the Cotswold–Severn style. The mound is of chalk rubble quarried from two side ditches.

At the eastern end is the chamber of transepted plan. Two pairs of chambers open from the passage and there is a fifth chamber at the far end. When first constructed the tomb was entered from a small forecourt, later filled with stones. When in use, about 3800 BC, it would have been dark and the floor strewn with decaying bodies. Excavations found around forty-six individuals, not all complete, accompanied by pottery and personal ornaments.

About 3300 BC the tomb fell out of use and was blocked up. Soil was dumped in the chambers, and three enormous stones, which still partly block the entrance, were erected across the front.

S. Piggott, The West Kennet Long Barrow: Excavations 1955–56, *Ministry of Works Archaeological Reports 4 (1962).*

White Barrow, Tilshead, Wiltshire Neolithic long barrow†

SU 023468. Among trees 1 km. S of Tilshead. Access by footpath/track SW from A360 at SU 036474. National Trust.

This well-preserved long barrow was constructed in the earthen long barrow tradition. It is 76 m. long, widest at the east end where it is over 2 m. high. There are well-defined berms† on either side of the mound and clear traces of the side ditches.

E. Crittall (ed.), The Victoria History of the Counties of England: Wiltshire I.2 *(Institute of Historical Research, 1973), 284–332.*

Windmill Hill, Avebury, Wiltshire Neolithic causewayed
enclosure† and Bronze Age round barrows†

SU 086714. 2 km. NW of AVEBURY. *Access by footpath north from Avebury Trusloe. National Trust. Within a World Heritage Site.*

Overlooking the headwaters of the river Kennet, this is one of the largest causewayed camps in England. Covering about 8.5 ha., the boundary earthworks were begun about 3600 BC and comprise three roughly concentric rings of interrupted ditches originally flanked by internal banks. All the enclosure ditches contained considerable quantities of domestic rubbish. Evidence of recutting suggests the ditches were periodically cleared out. Burials (mostly infants) lay on the ditch floors, and human bones were scattered throughout the ditch fills.

How Windmill Hill was used is uncertain. Perhaps it was a periodic meeting place for the inhabitants of the surrounding downland for seasonal festivals and ceremonies.

The four large round barrows on the hill were built in the second millennium BC long after the causewayed camp had been abandoned.

A. Whittle et al., The Harmony of Symbols: The Windmill Hill Causewayed Enclosure *(Oxbow Books, 1999).*

Woodhenge, Durrington, Wiltshire Neolithic henge†

SU 151434. 1.5 km. N of Amesbury, 200 m. SW of DURRINGTON WALLS. Car park (signposted) W of A345 towards Larkhill. English Heritage. Within a World Heritage Site.

Woodhenge, immediately outside DURRINGTON WALLS is a classic class I henge monument comprising an earthwork enclosure formed by a bank and internal ditch with a single north-east entrance. The external diameter is 85–8 m.

Woodhenge was fully excavated in 1926–8. In contrast to STONE-HENGE, this monument comprised a slightly oval wooden building represented by six concentric rings of postholes† (now marked by concrete pillars). The building is similar to the south circle inside Durrington Walls, and one possibility is that Woodhenge was a shrine or temple adjacent to a settlement inside the larger henge enclosure. The long axis of the structure at Woodhenge points to the entrance into the henge; like Stonehenge, the whole site is orientated towards the rising midsummer sun.

M. Cunnington, Woodhenge *(Devizes: privately published, 1929).*

Worlebury, Weston-super-Mare, Avon Iron Age hillfort††

ST 314625. On Worlebury Hill on N side of Weston-super-Mare.

This notable hillfort overlooking the Bristol Channel at the mouth of the river Severn has a pair of ramparts separated by a great ditch on the east side, a single rampart on the south, and is defended by steep natural slopes on the north and west. Outer defences lie to the east. The ramparts, stone-built with well-laid masonry faces inside and out, are now tumbled and obscured by woodland.

The main entrance is on the south-east side at the junction of the single and multiple ramparts; here it is possible to see the in-turned ramparts creating an entrance gap.

C. *Dymond and H. Tomkins,* Worlbury, an Ancient Stronghold in the County of Somerset *(Bristol: privately published, 1886).*

12 The south-west peninsula

This region includes the counties and unitary authorities of Devon, Cornwall, Isles of Scilly, Plymouth, and Torbay.

Deceptively long, the triangular block of land forming this region has a distinct identity, and the increasingly rugged coastline encloses a bewildering range of landscapes.

Most distinctive are the upland massifs. Dartmoor, now a National Park, is the largest; a granite dome cut into slices by the rivers radiating out from its centre. Exmoor, also a National Park, on the north Devon coast and spilling eastwards into Somerset, is smaller but no less exposed. West of Dartmoor is Bodmin Moor; the valley of the river Tamar separating Devon from Cornwall runs between the two. Throughout, the uplands contain abundant monuments of later Neolithic and Bronze Age date, emphasizing that this was a time when the climate favoured dense occupation of the high ground where only bracken and gorse now flourish. Stone circles and stone rows are a distinctive feature of these areas. In the extreme south-west, on the heaths of West Penwith, land-divisions and fields set out in later prehistory still form the framework of today's countryside.

Little work has been carried out in the major river valleys of the south-west. The Roman presence in the area west of Exeter was weak, and in much of the extreme south-west prehistory essentially continued down to the early Christian era. All around the coast, however, are distinctive sites of later prehistoric and Romano-British date such as cliff castles and hillforts. Some continued in use well into the first millennium AD, and were perhaps amongst the first settlements encountered by the incoming early Celtic saints.

Coastal and maritime factors have inevitably been influential. Contacts with northern France and Spain date back to the Neolithic. Defence has featured large as the peninsula projects well into the western approaches, providing an important first line of defence against coastal shipping entering the English Channel from the west. The medieval and later castles are especially impressive.

In the far south-west are the Isles of Scilly, an archipelago that until the Bronze Age was a larger land mass that has slowly drowned as the sea level has risen so that now only the former hills are habitable.

Ballowall (Carn Gluze) Barrow, St Just, Cornwall Neolithic round barrow†

SW 354313. Under grass 1 km. W of St Just. Access via minor road from St Just to Cape Cornwall via New Downs. English Heritage. Figure 187.

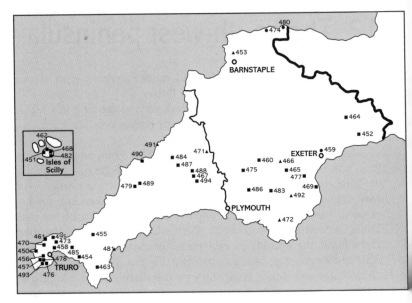

▲ **Fig. 186.** Map of Region 12

450 Ballowall, Cornwall
451 Bant's Carn, Isles of Scilly
452 Blackbury Camp, Devon
453 Braunton, Devon
454 Breage Church, Cornwall
455 Carn Brea, Cornwall
456 Carn Euny, Cornwall
457 Chun Castle, Cornwall
458 Chysauster, Cornwall
459 Exeter (*Isca Dumnoniorum*), Devon
460 Grimspound, Devon
461 Gurnard's Head, Cornwall
462 Halangy Down, Isles of Scilly
463 Halliggye Fogou, Cornwall
464 Hembury, Devon
465 Horridge Common, Devon
466 Houndtor, Devon
467 Hurlers, Cornwall
468 Innisidgen, Isles of Scilly
469 Kent's Cavern, Torquay
470 Lanyon Quoit, Cornwall
471 Launceston, Cornwall
472 Leigh Barton, Devon
473 Man-an-Tol, Cornwall

474 Martinhoe, Devon
475 Merrivale, Devon
476 Merry Maidens, Cornwall
477 Milber Down Camp, Devon
478 Nine Maidens, Cornwall
479 Nine Maidens, Cornwall
480 Old Burrow, Devon
481 Pendennis, and St Mawes,
     Cornwall
482 Porth Hellick Down, Isles of Scilly
483 Riders Rings, Devon
484 Roughtor, Cornwall
485 St Hilary, Cornwall
486 Shaugh Moor and Upper Plym Valley,
     Devon
487 Stripple Stones, Cornwall
488 Stowes Pound, Cornwall
489 The Longstone, Cornwall
490 The Rumps, Cornwall
491 Tintagel, Cornwall
492 Totnes, Devon
493 Tregiffian, Cornwall
494 Trethevy Quoit, Cornwall
495 Zennor Quoit, Cornwall

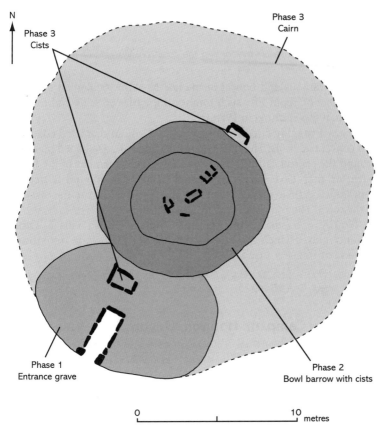

▲ **Fig. 187.** Plan of the Ballowall (Carn Gluze) Barrow, St Just, Cornwall (after Barnatt)

This strange round barrow is several monuments in one. Discovered under mining waste, it was excavated in the 1870s. Four main stages of construction can be discerned. The earliest, of later Neolithic date, is an entrance grave on the seaward side, a simple rectangular chamber set in a cairn†. Second, a small cairn was built next to the entrance grave on the landward side. This contained two or three cists†. In the third phase, around 1700 BC, two more cists were added, one in the back of the entrance grave and another against the outer wall of the small cairn. The structures were then covered by a substantial cairn, essentially a bowl barrow. Some care is needed in picking out these phases because the excavator built an additional inner wall in order to allow the barrow to be viewed more easily.

W. Borlase, 'Typical Specimens of Cornish Barrows', Archaeologia, 49 (1886), 181–98.

Bant's Carn, St Mary's, Isles of Scilly. Neolithic entrance grave

SV 911124. Under grass overlooking the coast on NW side of the Island near Halangy Point. English Heritage.

The most famous and typical of the late Neolithic Scillonian entrance graves. One of about fifty such tombs on the Isles of Scilly and in West Penwith, it was restored in 1970.

It has a roughly circular cairn†, about 12 m. in diameter, edged by two concentric walls. The outer forms the edge of a D-shaped platform around the central cairn. It may represent an enlargement of the initial cairn, or may have been constructed to give the mound a stepped appearance. A boat-shaped stone slab chamber opens from the east side of the cairn. The roof is formed by large capstones†.

Nearby is a small Iron Age and Romano-British village. Other entrance graves which can be visited on St Mary's include INNISIDGEN and PORTH HELLICK DOWN.

P. Ashbee, 'Bant's Carn, St Mary's, Isles of Scilly: An Entrance Grave Restored and Reconstructed', CoA 15 (1976), 11–26.

Blackbury Camp, nr. Honiton, Devon   Iron Age hillfort†

SY 188924. In woodland 8 km. S of Honiton. Access (signposted) from minor road linking Swetcombe (B3174) and Hangman's Stone (A3052). English Heritage.

A splendid oval 2 ha. hillfort bounded by a single rampart and ditch. An original entrance on the south side has out-turned rampart terminals forming an entrance passage 54 m. long. To this was added a triangular outer defence, or barbican†. Other gaps are recent.

A. Young and K. Richardson, 'Report on the Excavations at Blackbury Castle', PDAES 5 (1955), 43–67.

Braunton, Devon   Medieval field-system†

SS 475360. 7 km. NE of Barnstaple.

Braunton has an unenclosed arable field, one of few remnants of the open fields of the Middle Ages left in England. Dispersed arable strips in the Great Field are documented in the 1320s, and their origins may pre-date the Norman Conquest.

P. Weddell, 'Braunton Great Field', Arch J. 157 (2000), 440–45

Breage Church, Cornwall   Roman marker stone

SW 618285. Church of St Breaca, located in centre of Breage village immediately N of A394, 5 km. W of Helston.

A granite marker stone or milestone is preserved in Breage church. An inscription suggests that it was originally erected to the Emperor Postumus (AD 258–68).

R. Collingwood and R. Wright, The Roman Inscriptions of Britain I: Inscriptions on Stone *(Sutton Publishing, No. 2232, 1995).*

Carn Brea, Redruth, Cornwall Neolithic enclosures and settlement site

SW 686407. On a prominent hill 1.5 km. SW of Redruth. Access by track from Carnkie on S side, or by footpath from any of the surrounding villages. Figure 188.

Carn Brae has three summits separated by two saddles. The eastern summit supports a medieval castle while the middle summit has a monument of 1836 to Sir Frances Basset, a local mine owner.

The early settlement lies on the eastern summit, within an enclosure defined by a discontinuous tumbled stone wall and ditch over 320 m. in length. This enclosure, constructed of stones and boulders, was used about 3000–3500 BC; it took approximately 30,000 hours' work to build.

The enclosure is joined to, and partly enclosed within, a more extensive set of ramparts, now under bracken. The arrangement forms a complicated whole with an inner heavily defended enclosure, an outer less well-delimited area to the west, with the extreme western end further delimited as if to give special emphasis to the central summit. Perhaps 150–200 people lived here at any one time. Some 35 per cent of all flint and stone implements recovered were leaf-shaped arrowheads, a clear sign of the defensive nature of the site.

R. Mercer, 'Excavations at Carn Brea, Illogan, Cornwall, 1970–73: A Neolithic Fortified Complex of the Third Millennium bc', CoA, *20 (1981), 1–204.*

Carn Euny, Sancreed, Cornwall Iron Age and Romano-British courtyard house village, and fogou†

SW 402289. 2 km. W of Sancreed. Access by signposted track between Brane and Grumbla. English Heritage.

This hamlet was occupied between the C5 BC and the C4 AD. Initially it comprised wooden houses, later replaced in stone, some traces of which survive. From the C2 AD onwards, the settlement comprised the three large interlocking courtyard houses similar to CHYSAUSTER.

A large fogou can also be seen on the site with an unusual circular side chamber with a corbelled roof. It is probably pre-Roman. The purpose of this and other fogous in the area is uncertain; they may have been for defence (as hideaways), or for the cool storage of agricultural produce. Possibly they were a shrine or ceremonial place, each a sort of private chapel where the villagers worshipped their gods.

P. Christie, 'The Excavation of an Iron Age Souterrain and Settlement at Carn Euny, Sancreed, Cornwall', PPS *44 (1978), 309–434.*

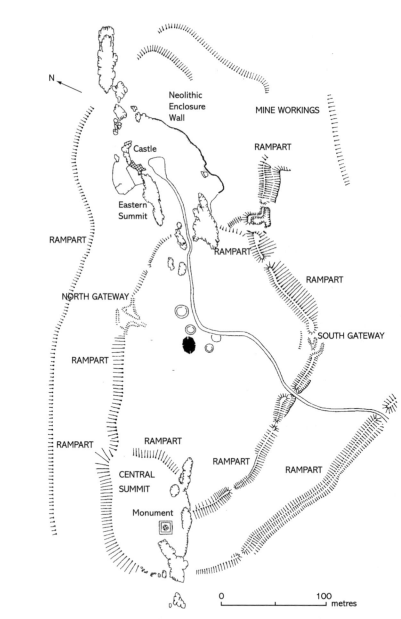

▲ **Fig. 188.** Plan of the Neolithic enclosures on Carn Brea, Redruth, Cornwall (after Mercer)

Chun Castle, St Just, Cornwall Iron Age enclosure

SW 405339. On open moorland 7 km. NW of Penzance. Access by track and footpath from minor road to Little Bosullow.

This circular hillfort lies in a spectacular position, defended by two concentric stone walls. There is a staggered entrance to the south-west. Parts of the gateway remain, including a pair of stone gateposts.

Inside are several enclosures defined by low walls radiating out from the centre. Most have foundations of circular buildings about 5 m. in diameter. There is a well in the northern part of the interior. The site was occupied from C3 BC through into the C4 AD.

About 300 m. west is **Chun Quoit** (SW 402400), a Neolithic portal dolmen† tomb of about 4000 BC. What remains is a simple box-like chamber comprising four inward-sloping upright slabs topped by a massive capstone. A slight cairn† surrounds it.

E. Leeds, 'Excavations at Chun Castle, in Penwith, Cornwall (second report)', Archaeologia, 81 (1931), 33–42.

Chysauster, Gulval, Cornwall Iron Age village   ★★

SW 473350. On side of Carnaquidden Downs 7 km. SW of St Ives. Signposted access from minor road running N from B3311 to Chysauster and Bosulval. English Heritage. Restricted opening. Admission charge. Figure 189.

Chysauster is the best-preserved courtyard house settlement (see also CARN EUNY). Mostly it is C2–C4 AD, the remains of a village of up to eight substantial dwellings with garden plots, fields, and paddocks. Within the modern stone walls are partly reconstructed structures.

A street or path leads through the centre of the village, four houses on each side, articulating the houses and linking them to the surrounding landscape. Two or three outlying houses are presumably part of the same settlement.

The houses share a common plan. The entrances point east or north-east away from the prevailing wind and lead via a passage into a space or courtyard typically 7 m. or 8 m. across, where animals may have been kept. The area left of the entrance is often recessed and may have had a lean-to roof as a shelter for livestock. Opposite the entrance, across the courtyard, is a roughly circular room, which may have had a conical roof of turf or thatch. Right of the entrance is a long narrow room, and there is sometimes a small circular room as well. The houses were probably occupied by single extended families.

A fogou or underground passage lies 130 m. to the south. Its floor is nearly 2 m. below ground level. Two massive lintel-stones remain in place; a third has fallen.

H. Hencken, 'An Excavation by H M Office of Works at Chysauster, Cornwall, 1931', Archaeologia, 83 (1933), 237–84.

▲ **Fig. 189.** Chysauster, Cornwall. View from the courtyard within House 6 looking east showing the entrance to the Round Room (right) and the Long Room (left) (Photograph: Jane Timby)

Exeter (*Isca Dumnoniorum*), Devon Roman legionary fort, *civitas*† capital, and medieval city

Centred SX 919925. Located at S end of M5 at mouth of the river Exe. Figure 190.

Although Exeter was founded by the Romans, little evidence survives above ground. A legionary fortress, subsequently incorporated into the basilica†, was discovered by excavation in Cathedral Green. After the withdrawal of the army Exeter became the administrative centre of the *Dumnonii*. In the later C2 the town was provided with earthwork defences, rebuilt in stone in the C3. Sections of the walls can still be seen, much altered or rebuilt in medieval times, in particular to the west of South Street. The south gate Roman tower is marked out on the pavement in South Street opposite Holy Trinity Church.

There was a minster church at Exeter from the 670s, and the see was transferred here from Crediton in 1050. A new cathedral† was begun in the early C12, of which the two transept† towers survive. In the later C13–C14 the cathedral was largely rebuilt. Inside note especially the remains of painting on stonework; the arcaded stone pulpitum of 1324 beneath the organ case of 1665; the stepped *sedilia*† in the choir; the bishop's throne of 1313–16; and the forty-eight C13 misericords†, England's earliest set.

Much of the medieval town was destroyed by bombing in 1942 and

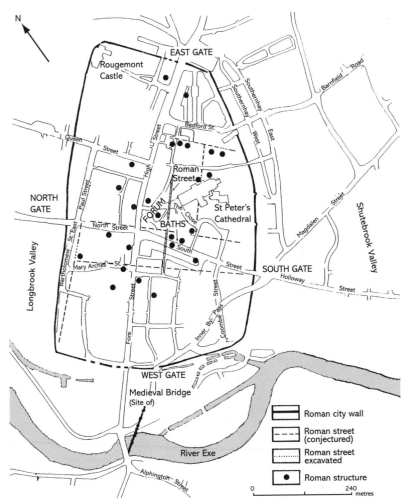

▲ Fig. 190. Exeter (*Isca Dumnoniorum*), Devon: modern street plan showing the location of the Roman defences and other sites

later redevelopment. At the north corner of the medieval town (Rougemont) is the gate-tower of the Norman castle. Three reminders of civic prosperity are the Guildhall (High Street), of 1330 and remodelled in 1468–9, and 1593–6 when the porticoed frontage was added; Tucker's Hall (Fore Street), the hall of the Guild of Weavers, Fullers, and Shearsmen founded in 1489; and the remaining arches of the Exe Bridge, built about 1200 as the main west entry to the city. On West Street is a good jettied house, moved here in 1961. Among ecclesiastical buildings see St Nicholas's Priory, in an alleyway called the Mint between Fore Street and Bartholomew Street East, where there is a Norman undercroft† with C15 guest hall above.

J. Wacher, The Towns of Roman Britain (Batsford, 1995), 335–43.

Grimspound, Dean Prior, Devon Bronze Age enclosed settlement ★

SX 701809. On open moorland 7 km. SW of Moretonhampstead. Footpath access from car park beside minor road running S from B3212 at Shapley Common to Jordan. English Heritage. Within Dartmoor National Park. Figure 191.

Grimspound, the best-known middle Bronze Age enclosed settlement on Dartmoor, lies in open moorland within a sheltered shallow valley. When occupied, between about 1600 BC and 1200 BC, the climate was warmer.

Partly restored in C19 the site is enclosed with a wall of granite

▼ **Fig. 191.** Aerial view of Grimspound, Dean Prior, Devon (CUCAP ANM-37)

boulders. The perimeter wall, up to 2.75 m. thick, encloses an irregular quadrilateral area of about 1.59 ha. A single original paved entrance opens to the south, marked by massive upright stones forming the portals. Two other gaps in the boundary are recent.

Within the enclosure are twenty-four small house foundations of which eighteen were excavated. One particularly dominant structure near the centre has higher walls and a porch protecting the entrance. At least five pens or small compounds are attached to the inside of the enclosure wall on the west side; presumably gardens, stock pens, or storage areas. Open areas within the enclosure are probably communal areas.

Grimspound, like the other Bronze Age nucleated settlements on Dartmoor, was probably connected with a pastoral economy. The orientation of the entrance suggests that the focus of attention for the occupants was the surrounding high open moorland.

A. Fox, 'Grimspound, Manaton', Arch J, 114 (1957), 158–9.

Gurnard's Head, Cornwall Iron Age cliff castle†

SW 433385. On a coastal promontory 8 km. W of St Ives. Access by track and footpath N from Treen on B3306. Also accessible from the Cornwall Coast Path. National Trust.

This narrow headland was defended as a cliff castle with three stone ramparts across its neck. The innermost, now visible as a grassy bank, was originally a formidable stone wall 5 m. wide at the base and over 2 m. high. The middle bank is now topped by a modern stone wall. The outer defences comprise only a V-shaped ditch across the headland. The staggered entrance runs through the middle of all three lines of defences.

Inside are two groups of house foundations on the east side. Sixteen possible circular house platforms can be identified, up to 10 m. in diameter with central hearths.

Construction of the fort probably began in the C2 BC, continuing into the early first millennium AD. Like other cliff castles, it may have been a ceremonial site rather than a settlement.

A. Gordon, 'The Excavation of Gurnard's Head, an Iron Age Cliff Castle in Western Cornwall', Arch J, 97 (1940), 96–111.

Halangy Down, St Mary's, Isles of Scilly Iron Age Settlement

SV 911124. Beside the coast at the foot of Halangy Down on NW side of the Island, immediately below BANT'S CARN. English Heritage.

A small hamlet occupied for more than 500 years from the middle Iron Age until early Romano-British times. Excavations revealed a complex of intercutting stone-built houses, perhaps the successive homes of a single extended family.

The earliest complete structure visible is the oval house on the north-west side of the site. This has a central hearth and stone walls representing internal divisions. It overlies earlier structures, and ovens used for drying corn. The whole group overlies a much earlier cultivation terrace, the edge of which is marked by a stone wall north-west of the structures.

The most prominent feature is a courtyard house south-east of the oval house, partly overlying it. Like the courtyard houses at CARN EUNY and CHYSAUSTER, it has thick walls, a single entrance to the south-west, and a series of chambers leading off the central courtyard.

On the upper hill slope are extensive remains of a field-system†, visible mainly as terrace edges, and some Bronze Age round houses.

P. Ashbee, 'Excavations at Halangy Down, St Mary's, Isles of Scilly, 1969–70', CoA 9 (1970), 69–76.

Halliggye Fogou, Cornwall Iron Age fogou†

SW 714239. In a farmyard 1 km. S of Mawgan. Access via signposted track from Garras. English Heritage. Figure 192.

This well-preserved fogou, provisionally dated to later Iron Age and Romano-British times, lies on the edge of a settlement enclosure bounded by a double rampart. The enclosure has gone, but the fogou remains.

It is T-shaped in plan and partly follows the line of enclosure rampart, being dug underneath it. One entrance (now blocked) opened from the northern arm of the top-stroke of the T into what would have been the ditch. The upright of the T is slightly curved, and set on an east

▼ **Fig. 192.** Plan of the Halliggye Fogou, Cornwall (after Maclean)

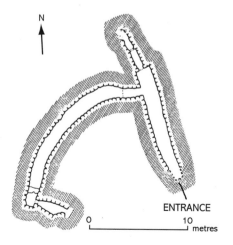

N

ENTRANCE

0   10
        metres

to west axis. The modern entrance brings visitors into this section of the underground passage. A torch is useful when visiting this site.

The fogou is built with large heavy lintels and supports for the relatively small doorways. Smaller masonry is used for the walls and the roof of the main passage. At the west end of the main passage is a small side chamber on the south side. Close by is a ridge or stumble-trap across the main passage.

Like similar fogous at CARN EUNY and CHYSAUSTER, the purpose of this structure is not precisely known.

R. Maclean, 'The Fogou: An Investigation of Function', CoA 31 (1992), 41–64.

Hembury, Honiton, Devon

Neolithic causewayed camp† and Iron Age hillfort†

ST 113030. On a partly wooded prominent hill 5.5 km. NW of Honiton. Footpath access from A373 immediately S of site.

Hembury occupies a low flat-topped ridge overlooking the valley of the river Otter. The earliest defences date from about 4000 BC, and, while the full plan of the enclosure is unknown, there was a causewayed ditch across the ridge about midway along its length to defend the southern end. Other earthworks enclosed the northern end. All the ditches were substantial although no traces remain today. There was a gateway on the western side and a timber building immediately behind the enclosure boundary. Evidence of extensive occupation has been found dating to about 4000 BC.

Hembury was abandoned before 2500 BC, and not reoccupied until the mid-first millennium BC. Initial refortification involved constructing a box rampart around the edge of the hilltop enclosing about 3 ha. Later, this was replaced by a dump rampart 8.9 m. wide. This is the upper rampart visible today, one or two other ramparts being set on the side of the hill to provide a wide band of defences. There were two entrances.

Occupation ended in the early C1 AD, before the Roman Conquest. After the conquest, the fort was probably reused as a garrison for Roman troops.

M. Todd, 'Excavations at Hembury (Devon), 1980–83: A Summary Report', Ant J, 64 (1984), 251–68.

Horridge Common/Mountsland Common, Ilsington, Dartmoor, Devon Bronze Age field-system† and settlements

SX 756747. On open moorland 7 km. SW of Bovey Tracey. Access from S using minor roads and track leading NW from A38(T) at Bickington via Owlacombe Cross, or from N by footpath S from Rippon Tor. Within Dartmoor National Park. Figure 193.

One of the most extensive and complete Bronze Age field-systems in

▲ **Fig. 193.** Aerial view of the field-system at Mountsland Common, Ilsington, Dartmoor, Devon (CUCAP BMC 50)

England. Although now desolate open moorland, when it was first built, about 1700 BC, it must have been a bustling piece of agricultural land.

The field boundaries are stone walls (reaves) originally faced on both sides, about 1 m. high, and probably supporting a hedge. Although now tumbled, the reaves at Horridge Common are complete except where cut by modern tracks and woods.

The dominant axis of the field-system is represented by a series of long boundaries running up and down the slope about 50 m. apart known as parallel reaves. The strips between the parallel reaves are subdivided by transverse-reaves which define the upper and lower limits of rectangular fields.

Droveways lie alongside some fields, in most cases leading to buildings. Some of these were dwellings but others were probably stores or animal shelters.

Horridge Common is typical of Dartmoor as a whole. It has been suggested that the pattern represents a system of neighbourhood groups in which there would be between six and fifteen buildings, forming small farming units. The field-system is part of the much larger Rippon Tor reave system which covers some 3,300 ha. It is known as a coaxial field-system because of the arrangement of the axial reaves. Its upper boundary is marked by a larger-than-average reave, known as a terminal reave, beyond which was open grazing land.

It was in the open areas above the reaves that ritual and ceremonial monuments lay; several cairns† can be seen around Rippon Tor. Within the field-system, cultivation was probably mainly confined to the areas around the settlements while the larger fields further away were used for grazing. A deterioration in climate in the early first millennium BC contributed to the abandonment of such upland areas.

A. Fleming, The Dartmoor Reaves *(Batsford, 1988).*

Houndtor, Devon   Deserted medieval village

SX 746788. 7 km. W of Bovey Tracey. 1 km. walk from Hound Tor car park. Within Dartmoor National Park. English Heritage.

High on the east side of Dartmoor in the lee of the granite outcrop from which it took is name are the foundations of a deserted medieval settlement. Although its early history and origins remain obscure, people were living here permanently by the C13. Throughout the C13, a deterioration in the climate made agriculture at such a high altitude increasingly less tenable. Houses became barns as people moved away, and by the mid-C14 Houndtor was deserted.

The buildings were constructed with low, granite boulder walls, still 1 m. high. Grouped closely together are the remains of four long-houses, four smaller houses, a shed, and, on the north-west edge of the settlement, three barns with internal crop-drying ovens. Small banked and walled enclosures are associated with some of the houses, perhaps pens for animal husbandry. The long-houses are a typical medieval house type with access via opposed doors in the long sides of the dwelling, between which there was a cross passage. On the drier, uphill side there was the main living room, with a central open fire. At the far end of the room there was sometimes an inner chamber, perhaps a bedroom. On the downhill side was a byre with central drain leading out through a hole in the gable-end wall. Here animals would be over-wintered.

Between the hamlet and the Tor slight earthworks show the traces of irregularly shaped fields, some of which were given over to arable cultivation in strips. Sheep farming may also have been important.

About 370 m. north-west are the foundations of a contemporary farmstead known as Houndtor 2. This comprises a house and two barns (one, again, with drier), built within a prehistoric stone pound and making use of the remains within of hut circles.

G. Beresford, 'Three Deserted Settlements on Dartmoor', MA 32 (1988), 175–83.

Hurlers, Minions, Bodmin Moor, Cornwall Neolithic stone circles†

SX 258714. On open moorland 500 m. NW of Minions. Access (signposted) from small parking area beside the track leading NW from Minions village. English Heritage.

Once thought to be people turned to stone for dancing on the sabbath, this group of stone circles was actually a late Neolithic ceremonial centre probably constructed about 2000 BC.

Partly restored in 1936, the three main circles lie in a roughly straight line south-west to north-east. The most south-westerly circle is the first encountered. Almost exactly circular in plan, nine pillars of local granite remain standing with a further four visible as shallow pits.

The central circle is egg-shaped in plan, and has seventeen pillars standing. Five of these were re-erected in 1935–6. At the same time fourteen markers were placed to indicate where other missing stones had once been. Near the centre is a recumbent stone, re-erected to mark the position of an original centre stone. Excavations revealed a spread of quartz in the central part of the circle.

The north-eastern circle has thirteen stones remaining. When excavated the interior was found to be partly paved with granite slabs.

Two upright stones known as **The Pipers** lie about 120 m. west-south-west of the central circle. Legend records that these represent the musicians playing for the dancers when the group was turned to stone. A few upright stones to the north-east of the north-eastern circle may represent a fourth circle.

The surrounding area is rich in prehistoric sites, including many barrows, enclosures, stone circles, and a stone row. Of particular note is the **Rillaton Barrow** about 450 m. north of the Hurlers, and very visible on the skyline. When excavated in 1818, the barrow contained a skeleton accompanied by a gold beaker, pottery, a bronze dagger, and some beads (now in the British Museum).

J. Barnatt, Prehistoric Cornwall (Turnstone Press, 1982), 180–7.

Innisidgen, St Mary's, Isles of Scilly Neolithic entrance grave

SV 921127. Beside the coast on N side of the Island overlooking Crow Sound. English Heritage.

Two entrance graves—Innisidgen and Lower Innisidgen—form a pair near the northern shore of the Island, although when the graves were built the sea level was much lower and these monuments would have been well inland.

Innisidgen is in very good condition with a round cairn† 8 m. in diameter revetted by a kerb of coarse walling, and a partially infilled chamber. The chamber walls are of coursed stone and it has five capstones†.

Lower down the slope is the more ruinous **Lower Innisidgen**. The round mound incorporates natural outcrops of rock. The kerb† is incomplete. There is a trapezoidal chamber with an original south entrance.

P. Ashbee, Ancient Scilly (David & Charles, 1974), 70–119.

Kent's Cavern, Torquay Palaeolithic occupied cave ★

SX 934641. On E side of Torquay accessible from Ilsham Road, off Babbacombe Road. Well signposted with free car park.

Now a 'show cave', with a display inside the entrance and more in the Museum of the Torquay Natural History Society, Babbacombe Road.

The cave has two main chambers, with a series of galleries and chambers leading off them. Two main phases of occupation have been recognized: the first dates to the early Upper Palaeolithic, about 30,000 BC, and is associated with Solutrian-style flintwork including some very fine laurel leaf points. Bone harpoons, a bone sewing needle, and a rod of ivory also belong to this period. The second belongs to the later Upper Palaeolithic, about 10,000 BC, and includes Creswellian style flintwork. Animals such as hyenas and wolves also used the caves.

J. Campbell and C. Sampson, A New Analysis of Kent's Cavern, Devonshire, England, University of Oregon Anthropological Papers 3 (1971).

Lanyon Quoit, Morvah, Cornwall Neolithic chambered tomb

SW 430337. In moorland immediately N of minor road from Madron to Trevowhan. National Trust. Figure 194.

A particularly dramatic site with a great cover slab supported 1.5 m. off the ground by three upright stones. This is in fact a C19 reconstruction, the authenticity of which is unknown. Human bones were found within the chamber. Careful scrutiny of the ground around the chamber reveals that it stands at the northern end of a long low mound some 25 m. in length and 12 m. wide. There is some suggestion that the southern end of the mound contained side chambers or cists†, but these have now gone.

J. Barnatt, Prehistoric Cornwall (Turnstone Press, 1982), 121–4.

Launceston, Cornwall Medieval castle and town

SX 3384. 14 km. SW of Okehampton beside A30(T) on the Devon–Cornwall border. Castle: English Heritage with restricted opening. Admission charge.

▲ **Fig. 194.** Lanyon Quoit, Morvah, Cornwall (Photograph: Timothy Darvill)

Launceston castle was probably constructed in 1067–8 by the Conqueror's half-brother Robert, count of Mortain (earl of Cornwall), as the Norman army moved south-west to put down a Saxon revolt. It was placed to guard a major ford, and controlled the whole of the countryside between Bodmin Moor and Dartmoor.

The castle's buildings and defences were frequently upgraded, and in the later C12 the present circular stone shell keep was built around the motte† top. In the mid-C13 the High Tower was constructed from the local black volcanic polyphant stone within the shell keep and rising above it. Joist holes show how the intervening space was roofed over. The principal room took up the first floor of the high tower. Access to the motte across the deep C13 ditch separating it from the bailey† was, and is, via a bridge. Originally the bridge and steps up the motte were covered in with a tunnel-like lead-roofed passageway.

Until 1838 Launceston was the county town of Cornwall. Walled in the mid-C13 (the south gate remains) its principal building is the church of St Mary Magdalene. Apart from its west tower this was rebuilt in granite from 1511; the east and south walls are intricately carved with religious symbols and secular heraldry. Inside is a carved and painted pre-Reformation pulpit. As in Totnes, many of the town's buildings are slate-hung against the weather.

A. *Saunders*, Launceston Castle *(English Heritage, 1998) (Site Guidebook).*

Leigh Barton, Devon   Medieval buildings

SX 721467. At Leigh, 3 km. N of Kingsbridge, visible from an unclassified road leading N off B3194.

Standing isolated in a valley is an impressive group of late medieval buildings of outwardly manorial character. What is curious is that it is not known who built it, when and why. Tradition associates it with Buckfast Abbey and with a family called Leigh who were freeholders here, but although the monastery held land in the parish, there is no contemporary evidence it had a grange. Nevertheless, the buildings indicate something unusual, and it seems possible that the abbey built a retreat for the abbot or other members of the abbey alongside the Leighs' farmhouse.

A stone gatehouse (*c.*1450) fronts onto a lane from Kingsbridge to Aveton Giffard. Above the arched entrance, and reached via a newel stair, is a single chamber. Although there are short lengths of wall to either side the complex was apparently otherwise unenclosed.

On the far side of a courtyard is a farmhouse, largely C17 but with some earlier fabric. There are also fragments of a richly decorated early C16 screen, which once divided an open hall. Behind the farmhouse is an L-shaped range of similar date to the gatehouse. Its ground floor was once a great kitchen.

H. Gordon Slade, 'Leigh Barton', Arch J, 147 (1990) (Supplement), 112–14.

The Longstone, St Breock, Cornwall   Neolithic standing stone†

SW 968683. On the highest point of St Breock Downs W of A39(T) 9 km. W of Bodmin. Access by track NW of minor road from Rosenanhon to Burlawn. English Heritage.

Known as 'Men Gurta' – the name means 'place of waiting' – this is the heaviest standing stone still upright in the region at an estimated 16.8 tons. It stands 3.05 m. tall and comprises a block of roughly dressed feldspar standing on a low mound of quartz.

About 500 m. to the east is another standing stone, and the whole of St Breock Downs from the Camel valley to St Eval is covered in scatters of cairns† and bowl barrows.

A. Saunders, 'St Breock Beacon Longstone', PWCFC 2/3 (1959), 111–12.

Man-an-Tol, Morvah, Cornwall   Neolithic standing stones†

SW 427349. On moorland 1 km. NE of Little Bosullow. Footpath access across the moor from a farm track leading NE from minor road between Madron and Trevowhan at SW 419344.

This strange and unique monument now comprises three stones set in a straight line. The central stone is pierced by a round hole. How much of the monument has been lost, and whether the stones remain in their original positions, is unclear. What remains may be part of a stone circle†, a stone row†, or the chamber of a long barrow†. Children apparently used to be passed through the pierced stone as a cure for rickets.

A. Preston-Jones, 'The Men an Tol Reconsidered', CoA 32 (1993), 5–16.

Martinhoe, Devon   Roman fortlet

SS 663493. Take the minor road to Martinhoe village off the A39 6.5 km. W of Lynton. At NW end of village follow track N and then take right footpath across two fields to the fortlet. Figure 195.

An early Roman fortlet sited to observe the Bristol Channel and South Wales. It comprises a square inner enclosure enclosed with a roughly circular outer rampart and ditch, the entrance to the outer being on the landward side and that to the inner on the seaward side, for added security. It was built in the Neronian–early Flavian period (AD 58–75) and contained wooden barracks adequate for the accommodation of 65–80 troops under a centurion. The fort was abandoned about 75 when the founding of the legionary fortress at Caerleon rendered it no longer necessary.

A. Fox and W. Ravenhill, 'Early Roman Outposts on the North Devon Coast: Old Burrow and Martinhoe', PDAS 24 (1966), 3–39.

▼ **Fig. 195.** Plan of Martinhoe Roman fortlet, Devon (after Saunders adapted from Fox)

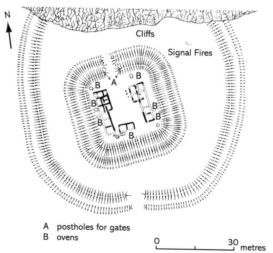

A   postholes for gates
B   ovens

0 — 30 metres

Merrivale, Devon   Neolithic and Bronze Age stone rows†

SX 553746. On open moorland S of B3357 7 km. E of Tavistock. Car park at the hilltop E of site. Although it is easily accessible from the road, the ground is rough and sometimes boggy. Within the Dartmoor National Park. English Heritage.

The focus of this partly restored group of early and middle Bronze Age ceremonial monuments is a pair of double stone rows. The northern row runs east to west, is 181.3 m. long, and has 186 stones. At each end there are substantial terminal stones; at the east end there is some evidence of a circular cairn† to the north of the terminal. About midway along the course of the row is a small cairn and cist† set around with a setting of four or five stones. Another, rather larger cist lies in moorland south of the row.

The southern parallel row is 263.6 m. long. The eastern end is marked by a large triangular-shaped stone. There is a small cairn near the centre of the row, from where a single line of upright stones extends south-westwards for about 43 m. A river runs between the two rows, perhaps suggesting that the juxtaposition of the two sites relates to two topographically defined territories.

To the south are a stone circle, a cairn, two standing stones, and a large burial cist. North of the stone rows, on both sides of the main road, are numerous Bronze Age hut circles.

Stone rows were among the last major ceremonial monuments to be built in prehistoric Britain. How such rows were used is not exactly known, but their structure in guiding lines of sight and the movements of people approaching them or moving along is probably significant.

A. Burl, From Carnac to Callanish (Yale University Press, 1993).

Merry Maidens, St Buryan, Cornwall Neolithic stone circle†

SW 432245. On farmland S of B3315 5.5 km. SW of Newlyn.

Otherwise known as the Stone Dance, this is an impressive stone circle. Restored between 1862 and 1869, the circle today comprises nineteen pillars of local granite in a ring 24 m. in diameter. The stones are graded in height with the tallest to the south-south-west.

Two standing stones† north of the circle are called **The Pipers**, while one to the west is **The Fiddler**. A legend common to many west-country stone circles records that nineteen maidens and their musicians were turned to stone here for dancing on a Sunday.

The destroyed Boleight stone circle stood a short distance to the south-west, and the TREGIFFIAN entrance grave lies a little beyond.

J. Barnatt, Prehistoric Cornwall (Turnstone Press, 1982), 155–9.

Milber Down Camp, Watcombe, Devon Iron Age hill-slope enclosure

SX 884699. Partly in woodland 2 km. SE of Newton Abbot, cut by the road towards Coffinswell. Access by footpath from the road.

A typical hill-slope enclosure of the kind found throughout Devon and eastern Cornwall. It comprises four roughly concentric and widely spaced ramparts with outer ditches. The outer rampart is turned inwards in its north-west sector, and is continued inwards to meet the third rampart and thus define an entrance passage between two parallel ramparts. It is thought that the entrances through the other ramparts were destroyed when the road was built.

Excavations date the construction of the enclosure to the C2 BC and its abandonment around the Roman Conquest. Among the finds were some bronze figurines including bird, duck, and stag.

Hill-slope enclosures may have been occupied by livestock herders who used the gaps between the ramparts to corral animals. The presence of low banks between the first and second ramparts, which could have formed pens, provides further support for this.

A. Fox et al., 'Report on the Excavations at Milber Down, 1937–8', PDAES 4 (1950), 27–66.

Nine Maidens, Boscawen-un, Cornwall Neolithic stone circle†

SW 412274. In a walled enclosure surrounded by farmland 5 km. W of Newlyn. Access along lane S from A30 past Boscawen-noon farm.

A restored stone circle with nineteen upright pillars around its circumference and a single central stone. In general, the stones are graded in height towards the west, the exceptions being three blocks added in C19. One stone to the west-south-west is white quartz, a stone that attracted special attention in the later Neolithic.

Recognized in late medieval times as one of the three main Druidic meeting places in Britain, in 1928 the Gorsedd of the Bards of Cornwall was inaugurated in the circle; modern bardic circles are used in much the same way in Wales. The association between this and other stone circles and the Druids is, however, quite erroneous.

J. Barnatt, Prehistoric Cornwall (Turnstone Press, 1982), 159–62.

Nine Maidens, St Columb Major, Cornwall Neolithic stone row†

SX 937676. On grassland E of A39(T) 4.5 km. N of St Columb Major, accessible by footpath from the road.

A typical stone row, comprising a line of upright stone slabs, constructed about 2000 BC as a ceremonial site. Ten stones are now visible, one being a recent addition. Sadly, only six of the stones remain upright. About 500 m. to the north-east is another stone, possibly part of the same structure, known as the 'Old Man' or 'Magi Stone'.

J. Barnatt, Prehistoric Cornwall (Turnstone Press, 1982), 221–3.

Old Burrow, Devon Roman fortlet

SS 788493. A39 Minehead to Lynmouth road—by first path on the N of road 0.75 km. after crossing the Somerset–Devon border at County Gate (from Minehead direction).

A well-preserved, bleakly situated early Roman fortlet. It was built around AD 48 to enable a watch on the *Silures*, South Wales. It comprises an inner and outer enclosure with an entrance to the outer on the landward side, and the inner to seaward. It was abandoned about 52 after the defeat of Caractacus and the *Silures*.

A. Fox and W. Ravenhill, 'Early Roman Outposts on the North Devon Coast: Old Burrow and Martinhoe', PDAS 24 (1966), 3–39.

Pendennis, and St Mawes, Cornwall Henrician castles ★

Pendennis (SW 24318) 2 km. SE of Falmouth; St Mawes (SW 842328) in St Mawes on A3078. English Heritage. Restricted opening. Admission charge. Figure 196.

Standing either side of Falmouth haven are two castles built by Henry VIII along England's south coast between 1539 and 1545. They formed part of a package of improvements to coastal defences in response to an alliance entered into between France and Spain with the intention of invading England and re-establishing papal authority.

Both castles were designed to be spare and functional military buildings. Their sole function was to provide an effective platform for artillery, with basic accommodation for the captain and his gunners. St Mawes, east of the estuary, remains much as built. It has a squat, central tower with four floors: a basement kitchen; an entry-level floor apparently given over to mess rooms and other accommodation; an upper gun deck, where the gunners probably slept; and the main, flat roof. The last formed the main gun deck, while other cannon were mounted on the lower, semicircular lunettes (outer towers) set around the tower's exterior.

At Pendennis, west of the estuary (foot ferry available), the core is again a low, central tower. Of 1540–5 this has a similar internal plan to St Mawes, with roof level and upper gun decks. Almost immediately this was surrounded by a lower battery providing fourteen further gun positions, while about 1550 a battlemented entrance block was built containing the governor's lodgings. Far more than St Mawes, which it soon eclipsed, Pendennis saw periodic modernization. In 1597 the Spanish threat lead to the enclosure of the whole castle within a massive outwork which includes seven angle bastions; this was sufficiently strong for a Royalist garrison to hold out at Pendennis in 1646 for five months against Fairfax's Parliamentary army. Later structures include an early

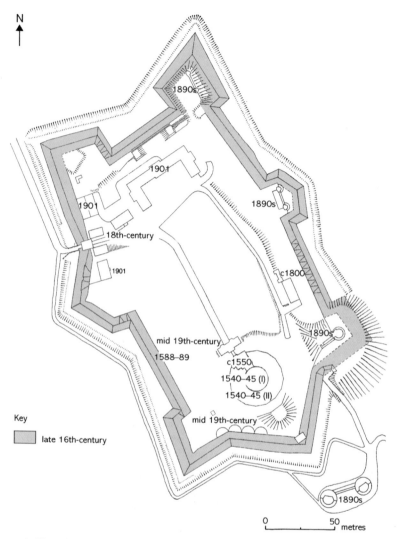

N

Key

late 16th-century

1890s

1901

1901

18th-century

1901

1890s

c1800

1890s

mid 19th-century
1588–89

c1550
1540–45 (I)
1540–45 (II)

mid 19th-century

1890s

0   50
|_____| metres

▲ **Fig. 196.** Pendennis Castle, Cornwall (after English Heritage)

C13 storehouse, barracks of 1901, and a Second World War observation point. Both castles house cannon and later artillery of various types and have displays and demonstrations.

B. Morley, The Castles of Pendennis and St Mawes *(English Heritage, 1988) (Site Guidebook).*

Porth Hellick Down, St Mary's, Isles of Scilly Neolithic

entrance graves and cairns†

SV 929108. On farmland on E side of the Island N of Porth Hellick Point. English Heritage.

Seven entrance graves and two cairns are scattered across the down over about 300 m. The largest is **The Great Tomb**, excavated in 1899. Today the monument consists of a large platformed cairn retained by a kerb† of coursed walling. It contains a simple chamber with four massive capstones† and, rather unusually, an entrance constricted by a projecting jambstone. An unroofed section of passage, also rare in these tombs, gives access to the chamber entrance. The line of a second, outer, kerb is visible as a low bank 2.7 m. from the inner kerb.

Of the remaining six entrance graves, four have large capstones visible in the top of the mounds and sections of the chamber walls projecting out. The other two are so ruinous that their chambers are now only central depressions. The associated cairns are harder to find and comprise very low flat-topped platforms.

C. Thomas, Exploration of a Drowned Landscape *(Batsford, 1985), 134–7.*

Rider's Rings, Brent Moor, Buckfastleigh, Devon Bronze

Age hilltop enclosure

SX 680645. On open moorland 5 km. NW of South Brent. Footpath access over rough terrain from car park at Shipley bridge on minor road N from South Brent. Within Dartmoor National Park.

Rider's Rings stands at an altitude of 350 m. above sea level on a slope overlooking the river Avon. Two main elements to the enclosure are visible, both bounded by ruined walls of granite blocks. The small roughly square enclosure, known as the south compound, is probably the earliest, the long rectangular northern compound being appended to the south-east side of the original structure.

The enclosure wall was originally 2 m. wide with two entrances, one into each compound. That to the southern compound opens to the north-west and is between two house platforms attached to the perimeter wall about halfway along its length. The entrance to the northern compound opens to the south-east and can be seen about halfway along the southern boundary. Other gaps are more recent.

Inside the enclosures are thirty-six house foundations, some free-standing, others attached to the perimeter walls. Many have doorways opening to the south-east. Some of those around the perimeter lie adjacent to small pens, probably small gardens or livestock shelters.

Some later features are visible: parallel to the north side of the compounds is a post-medieval leat embanked on the downslope side. Within the northern compound is a rectangular structure, probably a post-medieval sheepfold.

J. St Joseph, 'Air Reconnaissance: Recent Results 9', Antiquity, *41 (1967), 60–1.*

Roughtor, Camelford, Cornwall Neolithic enclosure and Bronze Age ceremonial sites

SX 1480. On open moorland 5 km. SE of Camelford. Footpath access from minor road SE from Camelford to Poldue Downs. Part National Trust. Figure 197.

The Roughtor area is extremely rich in well-preserved later Neolithic and Bronze Age monuments. At the north-west end is **Showery Tor** (SX

▼ **Fig. 197.** Plan of the enclosure and related features at Roughtor, Camelford, Cornwall (after Johnson & Rose)

N

Standing Stone

Showery Tor

Little Rough Tor

Rough Tor

Rough Tor Moors

Stone Circle

● Round barrows/cairns
ᗭ Hut circles
⳹ ⳹ Blanket bog/marsh

0   1 kilometre

149814), a natural granite outcrop (tor) which became the focus of a burial cairn† arranged as a ring of stones all around the tor. The use of stones in this way is not uncommon from the early Neolithic onwards and it has been speculated that the living rock was itself held sacred by early farming communities.

Rough Tor (SX 145806) forms the highest point of an elongated hill. Around the edge of the hill and joining Roughtor to Little Roughtor is a series of tumbled stone walls, in places forming a double line. They are identifiable as spreads of rough stones linking natural outcrops and steep slopes into a single boundary. Close inspection reveals that the walls were built with orthostats† faces and a rubble core. Overall, the area enclosed is about 350 m. by 210 m. There are several possible entrances marked by an increase in the number of walls. One on the north side is marked by the outward extension of the stone walls. Within the enclosure cleared areas on the north side represent house platforms. The site is undated, but analogies with CARN BREA suggest that it may be Neolithic. On the top of Roughtor are the remains of the chapel of St Michael, licensed in AD 1371 to act as a guide to travellers across the moor.

On the southern slopes on **Roughtor Moors** (SX 145802) are numerous groups of round stone house foundations typical of the second millennium BC. More than 250 have been recorded, some connected together by low stone walls. At the extreme southern end is a stone circle† (SX 144799). Further groups of house foundations and prehistoric boundaries are visible on the west and north slopes.

N. Johnson and P. Rose, Bodmin Moor: An Archaeological Survey, *vol. i (RCHME, English Heritage, and the Cornwall Archaeological Unit, 1994), 46–8.*

The Rumps, Pentire Head, St Minver, Cornwall Iron Age

cliff castle† ★

SW 934810. On the coast NW of Pentire Point, 10 km. NW of Wadebridge. Access along the Cornwall North Coast Path from Pentireglaze or New Polzeath, or by footpath from track leading from Pentireglaze to Pentire farm. National Trust.

A late Iron Age cliff castle, occupied between about 200 BC and AD 70, perched high on a rocky promontory jutting out into the Atlantic Ocean.

Three lines of ramparts, not all necessarily contemporary, cut off the neck of the promontory and provide the main defences. The entrance was defended by a gatehouse.

Inside are several flat platforms which when excavated showed evidence for timber-framed houses. Finds included pottery, spindle whorls, grindstones, querns, thatch weights, various glass and metal ornaments, and imported Mediterranean wine *amphorae*. The animal bones indicated that large quantities of sheep were kept, with some cattle and pig. Other cliff castles in Cornwall worth visiting are: **Treryn Dinas**, Treen (SW 397222), and **Trevelgue Head** (SW 827630).

B. Brooks, 'The Excavation of the Rumps Cliff Castle, St Minver, Cornwall', CoA 13 (1974), 5–50.

St Hilary, near Marazion, Cornwall   Roman marker stone

SW 550314. In the church in St Hilary village approached via a minor road leading N from B3280 2 km. from its junction with the A394 to the S at Goldsithney.

A well-preserved rectangular granite stone, known as the 'Constantine stone', now in the south aisle of the church. It was found in 1854 built into the C14 foundations of the chancel. It was erected in AD 306–7 'To the Emperor Caesar Flavius Valerius Constantinus Pius, most noble Caesar, son of the deified Constantius Pius Felix Augustus'.

R. Collingwood and R. Wright, The Roman Inscriptions of Britain, vol. i: Inscriptions on Stone (Sutton Publishing, No. 2233, 1995).

Shaugh Moor and Upper Plym Valley, Yelverton, Devon   Prehistoric settlements, field-systems†, and ceremonial monuments

SX 5765. On open moorland N of china clay workings, 18 km. NE of Plymouth, 5 km. E of Yelverton. Footpath access from Cadover Bridge on minor road running NE from Shaugh Prior. English Heritage and National Trust. Within Dartmoor National Park.

Along the valley of the river Plym are numerous groups of round stone house foundations, small stone enclosures, field-systems, cairns†, stone circles†, and stone rows†, mainly of Bronze Age date. Overlying the prehistoric remains are some medieval field-systems and settlements, mainly of the C12–C14, when again the climate was better.

On east side of the valley **Trowlesworthy Warren** (SX 575645) is particularly worth visiting, where there are six small enclosures each containing between five and ten round houses.

West of the river two areas demand attention: **Legis Tor** (SX 573654) comprises four interlinked pounds and a series of houses. The pounds appear to have developed organically around a core pound, which is probably the second smallest in the middle of the south edge of the group. Originally the walls of these pounds would have been 2–3 m. high. They would have been ideal for containing livestock during harsh conditions on the higher moor.

Ditsworthy Warren (SX 590668) on the north-west part of the area includes numerous cairns and a stone row.

A. Fleming, 'The Prehistoric Landscape of Dartmoor. Part 1. South Dartmoor', PPS 44 (1978), 97–124.

Stowes Pound, Minions, Bodmin, Cornwall Neolithic

enclosure and Bronze Age settlement

SX 257726. On open moorland on the top of Stowes Hill, 1 km. N of the HURLERS, *1.5 km. N of Minions. Footpath access across moorland N from Minions. Figure 198.*

Rich in archaeological remains the area north of Minions is physically dominated by Stowes Hill, on the top of which are two connected enclosures; a larger enclosure at the north end of the hill is joined to a smaller one above the disused Cheesewring Quarry.

The 5 ha. north enclosure is defined by stone walls, now tumbled, originally 2–3 m. high. The main entrances to the northern enclosure are on the east and west sides, elaborated and defined by antennae walls running outwards from the main enclosure walls to form elongated entrance passages. These antennae walls double back on themselves to enclose the whole hill at a lower level than the main enclosure. Inside the northern enclosure are more than 100 round-house foundations, visible where the natural stone clitter has been cleared away. The 1 ha. small enclosure to the south has a more substantial wall and three simple entrances. There are no house platforms in the interior, but the wall does enclose the Cheesewring, a rather impressive natural tor.

Like ROUGHTOR, the enclosures at Stowe's Pound shares many features in common with CARN BREA and may be of Neolithic date.

N. Johnson and P. Rose, Bodmin Moor: An Archaeological Survey, vol. i (RCHME, English Heritage, and the Cornwall Archaeological Unit, 1994), 46–8.

▼ **Fig. 198.** Stowes Pound, Minions, Bodmin, Cornwall (after Johnson & Rose)

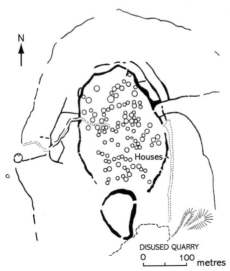

Stripple Stones, Bodmin, Cornwall   Neolithic henge† and
stone circle†

SX 144752. On open moorland on Hawkstor Downs, NW of A30(T), 24 km. SW of Launceston, 12 km. NE of Bodmin. Access by footpath from minor road NW from A30 at SX 136737. This path passes the Trippet Stones.

The Stripple Stones is the most south-westerly henge monument known in England. It comprises a ring of fifteen pillars, four standing and nine fallen. In the centre is a large recumbent stone. Around the circle is a ditched enclosure with an outer bank. An entrance is to the south-west. Overall the henge has a diameter of 68.5 m.

The **Trippet Stones** (SX 131750) is an almost perfectly round stone circle, 33 m. in diameter, and easy to appreciate from the eight leaning and four fallen stones even though these represent only half the original number. The central pillar is a modern boundary stone.

H. St G. Gray, 'The Stone Circles of East Cornwall', Archaeologia, 61 (1905), 1–60.

Tintagel, Cornwall   Legendary site, and medieval castle. Roman
marker stone

SX 048891. On the N Cornish coast, 25 km. W of Launceston. Park in village, and follow the signposted steep 600 m. long footpath with steps. English Heritage site and visitor centre. Restricted opening. Admission charge. Figure 199.

▼ **Fig. 199.** Tintagel, Cornwall: the spectacular cliff-top setting (Photograph: Paul Stamper)

Legendary associations, which made Tintagel the birthplace of King Arthur, vie with its spectacular coastal setting. The most obvious feature is the stone castle, which occupies two quite distinct rock outcrops. On the mainland are the Upper and Lower Wards, while on Tintagel Island are the ruins of a hall and residential block. The complex was probably built soon after 1236 by Henry III's younger brother Richard, earl of Cornwall. Its design is as curious as its siting is precipitous, and it may have been built as a lordly seaside residence. After Richard's death in 1272 the castle's maintenance was neglected, and by 1540 it was ruinous.

At least 170 other buildings have been found on the island, many exposed for the first time by a fire in 1983. Excavations have found imported Mediterranean wine and oil jars and fine red tableware of C5–C6 date. They have also found early slate-lined graves in the churchyard of the Norman church, which stands apart from the present village. The evidence suggests a high-status site of post-Roman date. The discovery in 1998 of a stone inscribed with the Latinized name 'Artognou' in an early C6 context provides a dramatic twist to the story. Although variants of the name 'Arthur' were common in post-Roman Britain the secular Latin inscription, which translated reads 'Arthnou, father of a descendant of Coll, had this made', used language common to individuals of the highest status. It can probably never be proved that Tintagel was the residence of a king named Arthur; but neither can such claims now be dismissed.

In the church of **St Materiana, Tintagel** (SX 051884) is a Roman marker stone, a rectangular slate pillar. The lettering is interpreted as a dedication to Caius Flavius Valerius Licinius, Emperor between 308 and 324. A Roman camp was sited nearby on the cliff.

In the nursery gardens near **St Piran's Chapel**, Genver Lane, Trethevey, 3 km. east of Tintagel (SX 077892) is another such stone dating to the mid-C3. The worn inscription translates as 'To the Emperor Caesara our Lords Gallus and Volusianus'.

C. Morris, 'Tintagel', CA 14/159 (159) (1988), 84–8.

Totnes, Devon   Medieval castle and town

SX 8060. 16 km. SW of Exeter, 4 km. W of Torbay, SW of A38(T) on A381 S of Newton Abbott. Castle: English Heritage with restricted opening. Admission charge.

The Saxon town of Totnes was part of the south-western estates granted by William the Conqueror to Juhel, one of his commanders. He probably built the first castle here, a motte† and bailey† overlooking the town at its gates. Today the castle's bailey stands empty; originally it would have contained accommodation and stabling. Modern steps curve up the side of the motte (the castle mound), one of the largest in the country. It is crowned with a stone shell keep of about 1300, which replaced a timber predecessor.

The town was a Domesday borough, at the highest navigable point and lowest bridging place on the river Dart. The line of its defences is followed by North and South Streets, while High Street bisects the town, leading from the castle to Totnes Bridge. The medieval cloth and tin trades brought prosperity, and in the 1520s Totnes ranked fifteenth in wealth among England's provincial towns. Something of this success is reflected in the town's buildings, most notably around the Butter Walk in High Street, where the upper storeys of the houses are supported on stone pillars. In all sixty-six of its houses, many slate-hung against the rain, pre-date 1700. Public buildings include St Mary's Church and the Guildhall of about 1553, which incorporates granite piers from the fruit market of 1611.

Another of Devon's historic towns, Okehampton, lies on the north edge of Dartmoor. The Norman castle (SX 584942) is an English Heritage property.

S. Brown, Totnes Castle *(English Heritage, 1998) (Site Guidebook).*

Tregiffian, St Buryan, Cornwall Neolithic entrance grave

SW 430245. On the roadside S of B3315 6 km. SW of Newlyn, 2.5 km. SE of St Buryan. Partly cut by the road. English Heritage.

Situated near the valley bottom, this site has very restricted views. It was restored following excavations in 1967–8.

The circular mound, of which just over half survives, is 15 m. in diameter with a stone kerb. The rectangular chamber lies within the south sector of the cairn†. Rectangular in plan, 4.47 m. long by 1.82 m wide, it is constructed in the usual fashion with vertical slabs infilled with dry-stone walling. The entrance is flanked by two jambs. The eastern jambstone is decorated with a series of thirteen simple cup-marks† and twelve oval marks made from pairs of cups joined together.

A. ApSimon, 'Tregiffian Barrow', Arch J, *130 (1973), 241–3.*

Trethevy Quoit, St Cleer, Cornwall Neolithic portal dolmen† ★

SX 259688. In farmland 1 km. NE of St Cleer. Signposted access from minor road between Tremar and Darite. English Heritage. Figure 200.

This Neolithic tomb on the edge of Bodmin Moor is one of the largest and most impressive in Cornwall. It stands over 3 m. high and is constructed of massive slabs of local stone.

The distinctive design, with six (originally seven) upright slabs forming the walls of the chamber and a single very large sloping capstone† forming the roof, shows that it is part of the portal dolmen tradition of tomb-building.

Traces of an oval mound are visible, but it probably never covered the chamber. As with other portal dolmens, access was through the gap between the side walls and the capstone.

▲ **Fig. 200.** Trethevy Quoit, St Cleer, Cornwall (Photograph: Timothy Darvill)

Today, the upright stone forming the back of the chamber has collapsed inwards, and a hole in one corner of the portal slab allows access into the chamber.

J. Barnatt, Prehistoric Cornwall *(Turnstone Press, 1982), 131–4.*

Zennor Quoit, Zennor, Cornwall Neolithic portal dolment

SW 469380. On moorland on N side of Amalveor Downs, 1.5 km. SE of Zennor. Access by footpath S from B3306.

This fine burial chamber constructed in the portal dolmen tradition is situated in a rather desolate spot. The most arresting feature is a large cover slab, now partly collapsed. Originally, this was supported on five stones, three set in classic H-shaped formation to the east, with back-stones behind. This arrangement formed the main chamber. East of the H-setting are two large flat upright slabs with a narrow gap between forming a kind of façade.

The stone setting is central to a low circular platform about 12 m. in diameter. C19 excavations discovered Neolithic pottery and a perforated whetstone.

About 300 m. north-east of Zennor Quoit is **Sperris Quoit** (SW 470382), a second portal dolmen on the hill. Sadly, there is little to see beyond a single upright and three fallen stones.

C. Thomas and B. Wailes, 'Sperris Quoit: The Excavation of a New Penwith Chambered Tomb', CoA 6 (1967), 9–23.

Chronology

The rounded dates are estimates, but precise dates are derived from historical records. The reigns and names of principal rulers, emperors, kings and queens are shown in bold.

BC

500,000	Earliest known human communities (*Homo erectus*) move into Britain
120,000	*Homo neanderthalis* occupation in Britain characterized by the Mousterian tool-making traditions
40,000	*Homo sapiens sapiens* (modern humans) appear in Britain
30,000	Beginning of the last main period of glaciation to affect England (Devensian)
10,000	Resettlement of Britain after the last Ice Age. Conventionally the late upper Palaeolithic (LUP) and early Mesolithic
7000	Britain becomes separated from the Continental mainland with divergence of tool-making traditions and economies. 6000–4500 BC is conventionally the later Mesolithic
4500	Earliest agriculture and start of monument construction. Conventional start of the Neolithic
3000	Major discontinuity with abandonment of enclosures and long barrows, development of new classes of ceremonial monuments. Peterborough and Grooved Ware pottery extensively used
2500	Beaker style pottery appears alongside existing forms before coming to dominance
2200	Earliest metalworking (copper, gold and bronze). Start of the Bronze Age
2000–1500	Warrior elites represented in rich burials especially in southern and central England
1700	Appearance of food vessels and collared urns in graves and on domestic sites
1500	Round houses become predominant and extensive field-systems set out in many parts of England, including upland areas
1200	Climatic optimum with the maximum extension of settlement during prehistoric times
1100	First wheeled vehicles
c.1000	Climatic deterioration with the start of upland abandonment
750	Earliest use of iron. Start of the Iron Age
700	Many settlements fortified and hillfort construction begins in central and western parts of Britain
300	Consolidation of territorial units and development of small-scale kingdoms and tribal groupings
100	Intensification of trade with the classical world. The Roman Empire reaches the northern coast of Gaul

55	First campaign in southern England by Julius Caesar
54	Second campaign in southern England by Julius Caesar
C1	First identifiable petty kings and rulers in southern England; some issued their own coinage

AD

41–52	Claudius
43	Roman invasion of southern England—Claudian invasion led by Aulus Plautius
49	Foundation of Colchester as a *colonia*
*c.*50	Foundation of London
54–68	Nero
60–1	Suetonius Paulinus attacks Anglesey, Boudiccan revolt, destruction of Colchester, London and Verulamium
69–79	Vespasian
71–4	Petilius Cerealis conquers the *Brigantes*. Legionary fortress at York
78–4	Gnaeus Julius Agricola, Governor of *Britannia*. Campaigns in northern Britain
79–81	Titus
81–96	Domitian
90–6	Foundation of *colonia* at Lincoln
96–8	Nerva
*c.*96–8?	Foundation of *colonia* at Gloucester
98–117	Trajan
98–117	Legionary fortresses rebuilt in stone
117–38	Hadrian
122	Hadrian visits Britain
122–33	Construction of Hadrian's Wall. Revival of public building in cities
138–61	Antoninus
139–43	Construction of Antonine Wall from the Firth of Forth to the Firth of Clyde
155–8	Rebellions in north Britain
158/63	Hadrian's Wall reoccupied
161–80	Marcus Aurelius
180–92	Commodus
180s	Earthwork defences provided for many unwalled British towns
193–211	Septimius Severus
196–7	Clodius Albinus, governor of *Britannia*, takes troops to Gaul to seize power. Hadrian's Wall over-run and forts destroyed
197–208	Hadrian's Wall reestablished and forts rebuilt
208–11	Severus arrives in Britain
211	Septimius Severus dies in York
211–17	Caracalla
*c.*212	Britain divided into two provinces: *Britannia Superior* centred on London and *Britannia Inferior* centred on York

237	York made a *colonia*
253–68	Gallienus
259–74	Britain becomes part of Gallic Empire ruled by usurpers
270–5	Aurelian
270s	Establishment of Saxon Shore fortification system
275–87	Saxons raiding in the south-east and south coast
284–305	Diocletian
286–305	Maximian
287–93	Carausius, commander of the British fleet, seizes Britain and Gaul
293–4	Carausius murdered and replaced by Allectus
296	Constantius defeats Allectus and regains Britain. Barbarian attacks lead to reoccupation of Hadrian's Wall.
*c.*310	Britain becomes a civil diocese of four provinces: *Britannia Prima* administered from Cirencester, *Britannia Secunda* administered from York, *Maxima Caesariensis* administered from London, and *Flavia Caesariensis* administered from Lincoln
305–6	Constantius
306	Constantius dies in York
305–11	Galerius (co-emperor)
307–37	Constantine I
313	Edict of Milan grants acceptance of Christian Church
314	British bishops at Council of Arles
337–50	Constans
343	Constans visits Britain
337–40	Constantine II
337–63	Constantius II
360–3	Julian
360–3	Official revival of paganism in empire
364	Intensive raiding by Picts, Scots, Attacotti and Saxons
364–75	Valentinian I
367–83	Gratian
367	Barbarian invasion. Hadrian's Wall overthrown
369	Count Theodosius sent to restore order. Defensive system rebuilt and signal stations established
379–95	Theodosius
383	Magnus Maximus, commander in Britain, seizes power in Britain, Gaul and Spain
391	Theodosius bans pagan worship
395–423	Honorius
395	Stilicho (commander-in-chief of western armies) tries to re-establish order in Britain
410	Honorius advises *civitates* of Britain to look to their own defences. Sometimes taken as the end of Roman administration in *Britannia*
420/30	Regular circulation of coinage ceases. Large pottery industries collapse
425–55	Valentinian III

440/50	Traditional date for the end of Romano-British society and start of increasing Saxon dominance in the east of England
450–600	Anglo-Saxon settlement expansion in southern, midland, and eastern England. Establishment of tribal groupings and local kingdoms: Northumbria, East Anglia, Mercia, and the West Saxons. Early Saxon period
597	St Augustine's mission sent from Rome by Pope Gregory reaches England. Re-establishment of Christianity in some areas
c.620	King Redwald of East Anglia dies, and possibly buried in one of the grave-mounds at Sutton Hoo
631	The Venerable Bede completes work on his *Historia Ecclesiastica*
650	Conventional start of the middle Saxon period
700	Pagan burial practices end. Coastal trading places (*wics*) develop on the south and east coasts, for example Ipswich, Hamwic (Southampton), and Sandwich
789	First raid by Scandinavians on the south coast
793	Viking raid on Lindisfarne and the east coast
800	Conventional start of the late Saxon period in southern England and the Viking Age for northern areas
865	Danish 'Great Army' arrives in East Anglia, captures York in 866, and seizes territory in Northumbria, Mercia, and East Anglia
871–99	Alfred the Great
878	Defeat of the Viking army at Edington by Alfred the Great. Treaty of Wedmore establishing the Danelaw territory of eastern England
927–39	Athelstan
927	Wessex, Mercia, and Northumbria unified as England by Athelstan
980s	Renewed Scandinavian raids, culminating in an invasion by the Danish king Svein Forkbeard in 1013
C10–C11	Revival of urban life. Replanning of villages and open field systems. Churches built in many settlements
1042–66	Edward the Confessor
1066	Battle of Hastings. Norman Conquest of England. End of Anglo-Saxon England. Construction of castles begins on a large scale
1066–87	**William I** (William the Conqueror)
1086	Compilation of the Domesday Book
1087–1100	William II
early C12	Arrival of reforming monastic orders such as the Cistercians and the Augustinians
1100–35	Henry I
1135–54	Stephen
1154–89	Henry II
1189–99	Richard I (The Lion Heart)
1199–1216	John
1216–72	Henry III
early C13	Establishment of friaries in towns
later C13	Continued agricultural expansion and urban growth

1272–1307 Edward I
1280s Decorated architectural style appears
1283 Final conquest of Wales by Edward I
c.1300 Population levels peak
1307–27 Edward II
1315–22 Agricultural crisis
1327–77 Edward III
1340s Perpendicular architectural style appears
1348–9 First outbreak of the Black Death in southern England, spreads
northwards
1377–99 Richard II
1399–1413 Henry IV
c.1400 First use of gunpowder for munitions. Prompts a response in the
architectural development of defensive works and fortifications
1413–22 Henry V
1422–71 Henry VI
1455–87 Wars of the Roses
1461–83 Edward IV
1483 Edward V
1483–5 Richard III
1485 Battle of Bosworth Field
1485–1509 Henry VII
1509–47 Henry VIII
1536–40 Dissolution of the monasteries
1549 Publication in English of the Book of Common Prayer. Reformation of the English Church

Glossary

abbey: a monastery in the charge of an abbot or abbess.

agger: the raised embankment on which a Roman road was built.

alien priory: in the early Middle Ages a monastery subsidiary to one abroad, especially in France. Suppressed by the Crown in 1414 during the Hundred Years War.

almshouse: in the Middle Ages and later, a charitable foundation housing and caring for the poor, especially the elderly.

ambulatory: a processional space running around the east end of a major church in the Middle Ages, often leading from the ends of the aisles. Also used for the walkway surrounding a Romano-Celtic temple.

amphitheatre: an oval or round unroofed space surrounded by tiers of seats used for entertainment in the Roman period.

amphora **(pl. *amphorae*):** a large handled ceramic container used in the Roman period for transporting commodities such as olive oil, wine, or fish sauce (*garum*)

apodyterium: a changing room in a Roman bath-house.

apse: the half-round or polygonal easternmost projection of churches and chapels. Especially popular in the C12.

aqueduct: an artificial channel for conveying water.

Atrebates: a tribe whose territory lay, for the most part, south of the Thames, the area now covered by Sussex, Surrey, Hampshire, Wiltshire, and Berkshire. The late Iron Age *oppidum* at Silchester (*Calleva Atrebatum*) subsequently became the *civitas* capital for the northern Atrebatic region.

Augustinians: regular canons (priests) who lived in communities to the Rule of St Augustine of Hippo (354–430). Known as the Black Canons, they espoused poverty, celibacy, and obedience.

aumbry: cupboard in the north wall of a church's chancel.

auxiliary: a Roman soldier in a unit other than a legion.

avenue: two parallel lines of standing stones, or a pair of parallel banks, defining a pathway or line of approach to a ceremonial monument. Possibly a processional way.

bailey: a defended enclosure containing most of a medieval castle's buildings. First appears in the motte and bailey castles introduced by the Normans.

ballista: a large military catapult which could throw iron bolts or stone balls for up to 365 m. The bastions added to the late Roman Saxon shore forts were designed to house these weapons.

bank barrow: long low bank of soil and stones, sometimes with side ditches, of late Neolithic date. Possibly the focus of ceremonies which involved walking up and down the length of the monument.

baptistery: a room or building wherein Christian baptism took place. Well before the end of the Saxon period infants were being baptized in fonts within the body of the church.

barbican: in later medieval castles, an outer tower or fortification connected by walls to the main structure.

basilica: a rectangular, usually aisled hall to be found in Roman fort *principiae* or town fora, which formed the administrative centre.

bay: in a building, the space between two of its main structural subdivisions such as piers or aisle posts.

***Belgae*:** Caesar referred to the invasion and subsequent settlement of people from Belgic Gaul into Britain. Several writers have identified the immigrants with the Aylesford-Swarling culture of Kent, Essex, and Hertfordshire. It is alternatively suggested that they were based in the Solent area of Hampshire where the name of Winchester (*Venta Belgarum*) refers to the market of the *Belgae*.

Benedictines: the largest of England's monastic orders, followers of the Rule of St Benedict (d. 543).

berm: flat area between a ditch and an adjacent earthwork.

Black Death: the pandemic plague which swept much of the world in the 1340s. In England it killed at least a third of the population in 1348–9.

***Brigantes*:** a large northern tribe who probably occupied the Pennines and adjacent areas. The settlement at Stanwick lies deep in Brigantian territory.

***burh*:** a fortified strongpoint or settlement, the main network of which was established in the late C9 as England was reconquered from the Vikings.

cairn: heap of stones, often covering a burial, either gathered specially to build a mound or incidentally as a result of clearing fields.

capstone: a slab of stone forming the top of a burial chamber or similar structure.

Carthusians: a monastic order (the Poor Brothers of God and the Charterhouse) whose way of life was modelled on that of early Christian desert hermits. Monks lived separately, and largely silently.

cathedral: the main church of a diocese and containing the bishop's throne or *cathedra*.

causewayed camp/causewayed enclosure: Neolithic settlement and/or ceremonial site bounded by one or more rings of discontinuous ditches with a continuous bank on the inside broken only by entrances.

***cella*:** the main chamber of a Roman temple containing the cult statue; some temples have more than one.

chancel: the east part of a church, including its main altar. Before the Reformation usually divided from the nave by a rood screen.

chantry chapel: a private chapel which, until the dissolution of such in 1548, contained an altar where masses were said for the souls of the founder's family. Chantries were also endowed by guilds and fraternities.

chevaux de frise: a series of upright pointed stones set across possible lines of attack in order to impede access.

chi-rho: Christian symbol composed of the first two letters of the Greek name for Christ.

choir: that part of a church set aside for the sung portion of the service.

cist: a slab-lined stone burial chamber constructed in the ground. Usually rectangular or polygonal in plan.

Cistercians: members of the reforming Benedictine order founded at Cîteaux in Burgundy in 1098. The Cistercian ideal espoused a frugal, meditative, and devotional life; large numbers of lay brothers undertook farming and industrial work to support the monks. Popularly known (from the colour of their habits) as the White Monks.

civitas: an administrative centre with its surrounding territory the boundaries of which are usually based on those of pre-Roman communities.

clerestory: the uppermost storey in a high building such as a church, often projecting above side aisles (hence 'clear storey'), pierced with windows to light the body of the building.

cliff castle: settlement set on a coastal promontory which is defended on the seaward side by high cliffs and on the landward side by earth or stone ramparts.

clinker construction: in shipbuilding, where planks overlap, being held together by clench nails.

collegiate church: a church served by a community or 'college' of priests.

colonia: the highest rank of Roman chartered town in which all the inhabitants became Roman citizens.

concentric castles: as developed in the later C13 under Edward I, castles where the towers and wall lines are carefully designed to give multiple, overlapping, fields of fire.

corbelling: method of roofing which involves making successive layers of stone project forward over the preceding course until a only a small gap is left which can be covered by a single slab to complete the roof.

Cornovii: A tribe occupying the area now covered by Shropshire extending into Staffordshire, Herefordshire, Worcestershire, parts of Cheshire and Flintshire. The *civitas* capital was based at Wroxeter.

counterscarp bank: small bank on the outer (downslope) edge of a defensive ditch.

cove: setting of upright stones, usually forming three sides of a square, found inside late Neolithic henges or near stone circles.

croft: the long back garden behind a medieval village house.

crop-mark: a difference in crop-growth owing to buried features. Usually best visible from the air, but sometimes at ground-level too.

cup-mark/cup and ring mark: small pecked hollow in a natural rock surface, in some cases surrounded by a single ring or set of concentric rings.

cursus: long narrow rectangular enclosure bounded by a bank and external ditch. Middle and late Neolithic in date. Used for ceremonial activities, possibly including processions.

Decorated style: the elaborately ornate architectural style popular in later C13 and earlier C14 England.

Dissolution: that part of the mid-C16 Reformation which between 1536 and 1540 saw the abolition of monasteries (and in 1548 chantries) and the confiscation of their lands and possessions by the Crown.

Dobunni: an Iron Age tribe whose territory was focused on Gloucestershire, extending into north Somerset, north and west Wiltshire, Oxfordshire, west of the Cherwell, and much of Worcestershire. The territory is defined by the distribution of *Dobunnic* coinage. The *civitas* capital was at Cirencester.

Dumnonii: the Iron Age tribe occupying the south-west peninsula.

Durotriges: a confederacy of smaller tribal units based on modern Dorset.

excarnation: the exposure of human bodies to the elements to facilitate the decomposition of the flesh before the bones are gathered up for burial or disposal.

fabrica: a Roman workshop.

false entrance: a false or symbolic doorway built into the front of a Neolithic long barrow.

fell: an area of open moorland or hill-land with generally sparse vegetation, exposed scree, and rock outcrops.

field-system: a group of fields arranged for convenience of use, usually accessible from one another via gateways or droveways.

fogou: a stone-lined underground passage.

forecourt: semicircular area at the higher, wider end of long barrows in which rituals were performed.

forum: the main central square of a Roman town; a market place.

friars: Franciscans (or Grey Friars) founded 1209, and the Order of Preachers (Dominicans, or Black Friars) founded about 1214 were monks who lived in friaries, usually urban, spreading the gospel by preaching.

frigidarium: an unheated room in a Roman bath-house containing a cold bath.

fulling mill: a water mill powering wooden tilt-hammers which beat newly woven cloth to cleanse and shrink it.

garderobe: a medieval lavatory, usually a seat in a wall chamber above a chute dropping to a pit or to water.

glacis rampart: defensive earthwork typically bounding a middle or late Iron Age hillfort comprising a bank and ditch constructed so as to present an unbroken slope from the crest of the bank to the bottom of the ditch.

granary: a building for grain storage, and hence needing to be dry and vermin proof. Often elevated on posts or props.

Guild: a medieval fraternity based on a town trade or church, devoted to the physical and spiritual welfare of its members and their families.

henge: a roughly circular Neolithic earthwork monument comprising a ditch and external bank normally with one or two entrances. Sometimes enclosing a stone circle, setting, or timber structure.

hillfort: settlement situated on a hilltop which is defended by one or more lines of ramparts constructed from earth and stone. Hillfort construction began in the north and west of Britain about 800 BC, and continued down to the Roman Conquest.

horns: projections sticking out from the end of a long barrow, usually from the higher, wider end flanking the forecourt.

horrea: a granary.

hut circle: stone foundations of a round house or building. These foundations usually supported a wooden superstructure.

hypocaust: the hot air under-floor heating system found in Roman bath-houses or the living rooms of well-appointed town houses or villas.

Iceni: the territory of the Iron Age tribe of the *Iceni* as defined by their coinage centred upon Norfolk stretching west to the Nene valley. The *civitas* capital was established at Caistor-by-Norwich (*Venta Icenorum*). In the early Roman period the tribe was ruled by the famous Queen Boudicca.

infirmary: in a monastery, the room or building where its sick and infirm were cared for.

insula: a square or rectangular block within a Roman town plan with streets on each side.

keep: the main tower of a medieval castle, a mixture of principal residence and strongpoint.

kerb: stone or wooden edging to a barrow or cairn.

knight: in the Middle Ages, a man who held his land in return for military service.

Knights Templar: the military order founded in 1119 to protect pilgrims to the Holy Land. In 1312 its possessions were transferred to the Knights Hospitaller.

laconicum: a room in a Roman bath-house with a hot dry atmosphere.

Lady chapel: a chapel dedicated to the Virgin Mary, usually part of the retrochoir or ambulatory.

lavabo: a basin, sometimes of considerable elaboration, for the ritual washing of hands before mass by priests and monks.

lay brothers, or sisters: usually illiterate members of a monastic community who lived under vows doing its manual work.

legion: the elite troops of the Roman army. A legion comprised some 6,000 men including many specialist craftsmen.

linear earthwork: substantial bank and ditch forming a major boundary between two adjacent landholdings. Most are of late Bronze Age and Iron Age date.

long barrow: roughly rectangular or wedge-shaped mound of earth and/or stones, sometimes bounded by a dry-stone wall or **peristalith**, which contains one or more stone or wooden chambers in which human bodies were buried. Mostly middle Neolithic in date, a number of regional traditions of long barrow building can be identified: Cotswold–Severn tradition, the earthen long barrow tradition, etc.

lynchets: horizontal cultivation terraces constructed as a means of cultivating steep hillsides where flat arable land was in short supply. Of various dates, from prehistoric to C13 or C14.

macellum: a small Roman market.

machicolations: sometimes called 'murder holes', these are the openings in overhanging parapets at the top of the walls of castles, town gates and the like, which enabled missiles to be directed on to the heads of attackers. Only in popular tradition was boiling oil employed.

manor: an estate, typically owned by a lord resident in a manor house. His tenants held their lands in return for specific rents, and sometimes 'labour services' on the lord's land such as work at harvest time.

mansio: a Roman guest house used for official visitors.

mass: the principal act of Christian worship and the greatest sacrament. Also called Holy Communion or the Lord's Supper.

megalith: literally, a large stone. Hence megalithic tomb: constructed using large stones.

midden: place where domestic rubbish and refuse was dumped.

milecastle: a small walled fortlet incorporating gateways to north and south provided at approximate intervals of one Roman mile along the length of Hadrian's Wall.

milefortlet: small turf-and-timber fortlets provided at mile intervals along a stretch of the Cumberland coast west of Hadrian's Wall's western end.

minster: a major church of the Saxon period served by a community of priests. These preached the gospel over the surrounding area.

misericord: a small bracket, on which an elderly cleric could half sit, on the underside of a medieval choir stall. Often carved with ornate scenes, whether spiritual, domestic, or bestial.

monastery: the buildings of a religious community, usually monks or friars.

motte: the mound, usually conical, forming the stronghold of a later C11 and C12 motte and bailey castle.

multivallate: having several concentric rings of defences; usually used with reference to the ramparts around Iron Age hillforts.

municipium: a Roman town with self-governing privileges.

natatio: a swimming pool usually found in the *palaestra* of a large Roman bath-house.

nave: the western part of a church, and where the congregation worships.

Notitia Dignitatum: A document usually dated to *c.* AD 395 which lists the principal civil and military officials of the Empire. It includes details of each military command and its garrison.

nymphaeum: Roman shrine dedicated to nymphs, semi-divine beings associated with water or trees.

open field-system: the later Saxon and medieval system of cultivation whereby a settlement's arable land was divided into two, or more typically, three great fields. Although largely without physical subdivisions, these were subdivided into hundreds of long, thin, strips which were shared out among the lord and his tenants.

oppidum: large, regularly organized settlement of late Iron Age date, sometimes bounded by substantial earthworks but usually situated on or near a trading route (e.g. a river or port) rather than in a highly defensible position.

orthostat: a large stone set upright in the construction of a wall round a burial chamber or other similar structure.

palaestra: an exercise ground often attached to Roman public baths.

palisade: fence or wall made of upright wooden posts set in the ground.

palstave: small-bladed axe blade bound to a wooden haft.

parclose screen: a screen separating a chapel or tomb from the body of a medieval church.

parish: the defined territory around a church from which its parishioners come. In the Saxon and medieval periods its priest was supported by the parishioners' tithe payments—nominally a tenth of all they produced.

Parisii: a tribe occupying the area now covered by eastern Yorkshire which in the Iron Age is well known for its chariot burials and square-ditched barrow cemeteries. The Roman *civitas* capital was based at Brough.

peristalith: ring of standing stones round a burial-mound, usually forming a monumental kerb.

Perpendicular: the light and airy architectural style popular in England from the mid C14 to the C16.

pilasters: stone strips (sometimes 'lesenes'), usually vertical, on Saxon churches. While undoubtedly decorative, they also add vertical strength.

pillar: an upright stone, either selected or shaped for the purpose, used in the construction of a stone circle.

piscina: in a church, a basin, usually in the wall to the south of the altar, where the mass or communion vessels were washed.

portal dolmen: small early Neolithic tomb comprising a rectangular chamber defined by three uprights set in an H-shaped formation at the front, a single upright at the back, and a large capstone supported by the uprights. A low circular mound sometimes surrounded the chamber.

posthole: a hole dug to support a wooden post. In excavations usually encountered as a hole filled with a darker soil marking where the base of a post has rotted away.

praetorium: the house of the Roman commandant of a fort.

Premonstratensians: an order of regular canons (priests) founded in France in 1120 and modelled on the Cistercians.

presbytery: sometimes sanctuary, that part of the east end of a major church normally reserved for the clergy and containing the high altar.

principia: the headquarters building in a Roman fort or fortress.

priory: a monastery or nunnery in the charge of a prior or prioress. Nominally of lower rank than an abbey.

prospect mound: a raised mound which gave a view over a garden and across the landscape beyond. A typical feature of larger gardens in the C16 and C17.

rector: originally the incumbent of a parish who was supported by all of its tithes and fees. His house would be the rectory.

rampart: defensive bank or wall built of soil and/or stone, usually with a ditch on the outside. Sometimes, rampart banks had a timber frame for added strength.

Regni: the southern part of the Atrebatic tribe administered in the Roman period from Chichester (*Noviomagus Regnensium*).

revetment: a facing, usually of turf, wood or stone, designed to prevent the collapse of a mound or bank.

ridge and furrow: broad and low 5–15 m. wide corrugations found in permanent pasture and representing the deliberate ridging for drainage of arable land in the Middle Ages and later. Usually marks former open field land.

ring cairn: an low unbroken bank of stones surrounding a circular area in the centre which was used for burial. Early Bronze Age in date.

ringwork: fortification, usually of the later C11 or C12, with a circular, banked, enclosure surrounded by a ditch or moat

rood screen: screen, usually wooden and with the figures of Christ on the cross, the Virgin Mary, and St John the Evangelist, which separated the nave and chancel in a medieval church. Most such screens were removed at the Reformation.

round barrow: circular mound of earth and/or stone covering one or more burials (inhumations or cremations). Late Neolithic and Bronze Age in date. Sometimes called a 'tumulus' on Ordnance Survey maps.

sarsen: kind of sandstone found as large boulders on the chalklands of Wessex.

sedilia: three seats in the south wall of a medieval church's chancel for priest, deacon, and subdeacon.

See (or diocese): the territory of a bishop. From the Latin *sedes*, 'seat'—that is, bishop's chair.

simple passage grave: small circular mound of earth and/or stones covering a small stone chamber accessible from the outside of the mound via a short passage. The chamber was used to contain burials. Early to middle Neolithic in date.

small town: term used to define a lower-status Roman settlement below that of a town or city which can be distinguished in legal, functional, and morphological terms but of higher status than sites which are primarily agricultural.

standing stone: large block of stone, usually roughly rectangular in cross-section, set upright to mark a cemetery or, when associated with stone circle, a significant alignment of some kind. Mostly early to middle Bronze Age in date.

stone circle: ring of upright stones used for ritual and ceremonial purposes. Mostly late Neolithic and early Bronze Age in date. Some regional variations in design can be recognized.

stone row: line of three or more upright stones. Probably used to mark significant alignments or ceremonial way.

temenos: the sacred precinct or enclosure around a Roman temple, usually demarcated by a wall or ditch.

tepidarium: a room of moderate heat lying between the *caldarium* and the *frigidarium* in a Roman bath-house.

tithe: the tenth share of usually agricultural produce assigned in the Middle Ages for the support of the local parish church.

toft: the plot on which a medieval house stood.

transept: a projection north or south from the nave of a church. Typically both occur, giving a cruciform church plan.

triclinium: the dining room of a Roman house.

Trinovantes: see Catuvellauni.

undercroft: a cellar-like room beneath a medieval hall or chamber.

vicar: effectively a deputy for a rector, resident in a vicarage.

vicus: usually used to describe civilian settlements outside Roman forts.

Viking: Scandinavian raiders, traders and settlers whose first documented appearance in England was in 789.

villa: a Roman country house, normally part of a working farm usually divided into the residential quarters and the farm buildings.

Museums

A number of national museums, and most local authority museums, display archaeological material from their catchment area. Increasingly, some local authorities, local societies, trusts, and charities are creating and running heritage interpretation centres of various sorts. The following are particularly worth visiting:

Northumbria

Bowes Museum, Barnard Castle, Co. Durham DL12 8NP. [Tel.: +(0)1833 690606]. Archaeological finds from the southern part of County Durham including material from the Stainmore Pass military sites.

Museum of Antiquities, The Quadrangle, The University, Newcastle-upon-Tyne NE1 7RU. [Tel.: +(0)191 2328511]. Collections representing all periods from early prehistory through to medieval times. The main museum for Hadrian's Wall. Includes a reconstruction of the Temple of Mithras.

Lake District and the North West

Carlisle Museum and Art Gallery, Tullie House, Castle Street, Carlisle, Cumbria CA3 8TP. [Tel.: +(0)1228 34781]. Important displays of pre-historic and Roman material from Cumbria.

Lancaster City Museum, Market Square, Lancaster LA1 1HT. [Tel.: +(0)1524 64637]. Archaeological material from the region, strong on Roman and medieval Lancaster.

Liverpool Museum, William Brown Street, Liverpool L3 8EN. [Tel.: +(0)151 207 0001]. Archaeology galleries display material from local sites.

Yorkshire and the Humber Basin

Doncaster Museum and Art Gallery, Chequer Street, Doncaster DN1 2AE. [Tel.: +(0)1302 4287]

Jorvik Centre, Coppergate, York YO1 1NT. [Tel.: +(0)1904 643211]. See site entry for YORK.

Sheffield City Art Gallery, Surrey Street, Sheffield S10 2TP. [Tel.: +(0)1742 27226]. Extensive displays of archaeological finds from the Peak District. Includes the Bateman Collection of finds from C19 barrow digging in the area.

Yorkshire Museum, Museum Gardens, York YO1 2DR. [Tel.: +(0)1904 29745]. Good archaeological displays rich in Roman, Anglo-Saxon and Viking material from York and the surrounding area.

East Midlands

Castle Museum, Nottingham NG1 6EL. [Tel.: +(0)1602 411881]. Extensive exhibitions of archaeological material from the area.

Derby Museum and Art Gallery, The Strand, Derby DE1 1BS. [Tel.: +(0)1332 31111]. Exhibits dealing with Roman and medieval Derby.

Jewry Wall Museum, St Nicholas Circle, Leicester. Excellent archaeological displays of prehistoric, Roman and medieval material from Leicestershire. See also site entry for LEICESTER.

Lincoln City and County Museum, Broadgate, Lincoln, Lincolnshire LN2 1EZ. [Tel.: +(0)1522 26866]. Extensive displays of archaeological material from the region.

The Midlands Plain and Welsh Borders

Avoncroft Museum of Buildings, Stoke Heath, Bromsgrove, Worcestershire B60 4JR. [Tel.: +(0)1527 31886]. A selection of historic buildings rebuilt and preserved in this open-air museum.

Birmingham City Museum and Art Gallery, Chamberlain Square, Birmingham B3 3DH. [Tel. +(0)121 235 3890]. The local history and archaeology galleries include much material from the west Midlands area.

Grosvenor Museum, 27 Grosvenor Street, Chester, Cheshire CH1 2DD. [Tel.: +(0)1244 216163]. Excellent displays of Roman material from Chester and Cheshire.

Rowley's House Museum, Barker Street, Shrewsbury, Shropshire SY1 1QT. [Tel.: +(0)1743 61196]. A timber-framed building dating back to the C16 with extensive displays of archaeological finds from Shropshire, including a section devoted to material from WROXETER.

Worcester City Museum and Art Gallery, Foregate Street, Worcester WR1 1OT. [Tel.: +(0)905 25371]. Extensive displays of archaeological material focusing on the Roman and later settlement of the area.

East Anglia

Castle Museum, The Castle, Norwich NR1 3JU. [Tel.: +(0)1603 611277]. Strong on medieval material, also including an exhibition of links between Norfolk and the rest of Europe since later prehistoric times.

Colchester and Essex Museum, The Castle, Colchester, Essex CO1 1TJ. [Tel.: +(0)1206 712481]. See site entry for COLCHESTER.

Ipswich Museum, High Street, Ipswich, Suffolk IP1 3QH. [Tel.: +(0)1473 213761]. Strong archaeological displays including Roman and Saxon finds and exhibitions.

University Museum of Archaeology and Anthropology, Downing Street, Cambridge CB2 3DZ. [Tel.: +(0)1223 337733]. Substantial collection of archaeological material from the Cambridge region.

The Chilterns and Northampton Uplands

Buckinghamshire County Museum, Church Street, Aylesbury, Buckinghamshire. [Tel.: +(0)1296 82158]. Large collections of prehistoric, Roman and
medieval material from the Chilterns, including finds from the Roman
villa at Hambledon.

Hertford Museum, 18 Bull Plain, Hertford, Hertfordshire SG14 1DT. [Tel.:
+(0)1992 52686]. Extensive archaeological displays, including a good
selection of Palaeolithic axes.

Northampton Museum and Art Gallery, Guildhall Road, Northampton
NN1 1DP. [Tel.: +(0)1604 34881]. The Northamptonshire Rooms include
archaeological finds from the region, mainly later prehistoric through to
Anglo-Saxon.

Verulamium Museum, St Michael's, St Albans, Hertfordshire AL3 4SW. [Tel.:
+(0)1727 54659]. See site entry for ST ALBANS.

Cotswolds and Upper Thames Valley

Ashmolean Museum, Beaumont Street, Oxford OX1 2PH. [Tel.: +(0)1865
278000]. The oldest museum in England, opened in AD 1683, with abundant exhibitions of archaeological material from central England and further afield too. Presented in refreshingly traditional galleries.

Corinium Museum, Park Street, Cirencester GL7 2BX. [Tel.: 01285 5611].
Good coverage of local prehistory and medieval remains; excellent displays of Roman material from Cirencester and other sites in the Cotswolds. Reconstruction Roman rooms and a small garden.

Gloucester City Museum and Art Gallery, Brunswick Road, Gloucester,
Gloucestershire GL1 1HP. [Tel.: +(0)1453 24131]. Extensive prehistoric,
Roman and medieval exhibitions. Includes material from the Iron Age
Birdlip Grave. The Museum is built over part of the Roman city wall.

Oxfordshire County Museum, Fletcher's House, Woodstock OX7 1SP. [Tel.:
+(0)1993 811456]. Extensive displays on local archaeology including
Neolithic tombs and Saxon settlements.

Reading Museum and Art Gallery, Blagrave Street, Reading RG1 1QH. [Tel.:
+(0)1734 55911]. Extensive archaeological displays that are very strong on
the Roman period and particularly on SILCHESTER.

London

British Museum, Great Russell Street, London WC1B 3DG. [Tel.: +(0)171 636
1555]. Extensive displays of British Archaeology, including much
from England. The Romano-British gallery opened in 1998 is particularly
fine.

Museum of London, London Wall, the Barbican, London EC2Y 5HN. [Tel.:
+(0)171 600 3699]. Extensive and excellent displays of archaeological
material and reconstructions relating to London and its surroundings.

The Weald and Downlands of South-East England

Folkestone Museum and Art Gallery, Grace Hill, Folkestone, Kent CT20 1HD. [Tel.: +(0)1303 57583]. Wide-ranging displays of prehistoric, Roman, Saxon and medieval finds from the area.

God's House Tower Museum, Winkle Street, Town Quay, Southampton. [Tel.: +(0)1703 220007]. C15 defensive tower that now houses an extensive display of archaeological material from the town spanning the Roman period through to post-medieval times.

Museum of the Iron Age, Church Street, Andover SP10 1DP. [Tel.: +(0)1264 66283]. Excellent display based on material from the excavations at Danebury, but in the context of southern England as a whole.

Museum of Sussex Archaeology, Barbican House, High Street, Lewes, East Sussex BN7 1YE. [Tel.: +(0)1273 474379]. The museum occupies a C16 timber framed building and has excellent displays of material from important archaeological sites in Sussex.

Weald and Downland Open Air Museum, Singleton, nr. Chichester, West Sussex PO18 0EU. [Tel.: +(0)24363 348]. A collection of medieval and later buildings rescued from destruction and re-erected on the site.

Winchester City Museum, The Square, Winchester, Hampshire. [Tel.: +(0)1962 68166]. Wide selection of archaeological material from the town and its environs. Rich collections from later prehistory through to medieval times.

Wessex and the West Country

Roman Baths Museum, Pump Room, Stall Street, Bath BA1 1LZ. [Tel.: +(0)1225 61111]. See entry for BATH.

Bristol City Museum and Art Gallery, Queen's Road, Clifton, Bristol BS8 1RL. [Tel.: +(0)1272 299771]. Extensive archaeological displays showing material from the region, including the Tormarton burials with a Bronze Age spear embedded in a man's back.

Dorset County Museum, West High Street, Dorchester DT1 1XA. [Tel. 01305 62735]. Major archaeological collections covering prehistory through to medieval times in the Dorchester region. Includes displays on Maiden Castle and Mount Pleasant.

Glastonbury Lake Village Museum, The Tribunal, High Street, Glastonbury, Somerset BA6 9DP. [Tel.: +(0)1458 32949]. Displays of finds and related material from excavations at the Glastonbury Lake Village and other sites in the Somerset Levels.

Salisbury and South Wiltshire Museum, The Close, Salisbury, Wiltshire SP1 2EN. [Tel.: +(0)1722 332151]. Excellent displays covering the prehistory of Wessex, including Stonehenge and Durrington Walls, and the pioneering archaeological work of Lieut. Gen. Pitt Rivers.

Somerset County Museum, Taunton Castle, Taunton, Somerset TA1 4AA. [Tel.: +(0)1823 255504]. A C12 and later building housing extensive displays of archaeological material from Somerset.

Waterfront Museum, Poole Quay, Poole BH15 1BW. [Tel.: +(0)1202 683138]. Modern displays focusing on the later prehistoric, Roman and medieval settlement of Poole and the surrounding area. Includes displays of the Studland Bay Wreck.

Wiltshire Archaeological and Natural History Society Museum, Long Street, Devizes, Wiltshire SN10 1NS. [Tel.: +(0)1380 77369]. First-rate galleries covering the prehistory of Wessex; includes a display about the Bush Barrow.

The South-West Peninsula

Cornwall County Museum, The Royal Institution of Cornwall, River Street, Truro, Cornwall TR1 2SJ. [Tel.: +(0)1872 72205]. Displays include material relating to the prehistory and early history of Cornwall.

Plymouth City Museum and Art Gallery, Drake Circus, Plymouth, Devon PL4 8AJ. [Tel.: +(0)1752 668000]. Archaeological displays include prehistoric and later material from Dartmoor.

Royal Albert Memorial Museum, Queen Street, Exeter EX4 3RX. [Tel.: +(0)1392 265858]. Good displays of archaeology from the south-west.

Further reading

The archaeological literature is vast and widely scattered through books, journals, and collections of edited papers. The following listing is intended only as a starting point.

General

For the novice with a growing interest in archaeology a fun place to start is Paul Bahn's *Archaeology: A Very Short Introduction* (Oxford University Press, 1996). The standard textbook-style introduction to modern archaeology is *Archaeology: Theories, Methods and Practice* by Colin Renfrew and Paul Bahn, 2nd edn (Thames & Hudson, 1996). This provides a highly authoritative background to almost all aspects of the discipline. For a more particularly British perspective *Archaeology: An Introduction* by Kevin Greene, 3rd edn (Batsford/Routledge, 1996) is supported by additional material on the Internet at www.staff.ncl.ac.uk/kevin.greene/wintro/. *The Archaeology of Britain*, ed. John Hunter and Ian Ralston (Routledge, 1999) provides an up-to-date introduction to recent work from the upper Palaeolithic through to the Industrial Revolution.

Environmental background

The prehistoric environment is systematically explored in a series of papers edited by Ian Simmons and Michael Tooley as *The Environment in British Prehistory* (Duckworth, 1981). The prehistoric and later environment is covered by Martin Jones in *England before Domesday* (Batsford, 1986), and by John Evans in *The Environment of Early Man in the British Isles* (Elek, 1975). Farming in prehistoric times is well covered by Francis Pryor in *Farmers in Prehistoric Britain* (Tempus, 1998). For the environment of medieval England see Grenville Astill and Annie Grant's edited volume *The Countryside of Medieval England* (Blackwell, 1988) and Oliver Rackham's *The History of the Countryside* (Dent, 1986).

Prehistory

The European setting to British prehistory is well covered in a series of papers edited by Barry Cunliffe as *The Oxford Illustrated Prehistory of Europe* (Oxford University Press, 1994). *An Introduction to British Prehistory* ed. J. V. S. Megaw and D. A. Simpson (Leicester University Press, 1979) provides a very detailed account of the British evidence by a variety of expert authors, while *Prehistoric Britain* by Timothy Darvill (Routledge, 1998) provides an overview by a single author. *Prehistoric Britain from the Air* by Timothy Darvill (Cambridge University Press, 1996) presents a thematic review illustrated with aerial photographs.

   Detailed accounts of the Palaeolithic are provided for the whole of Europe by Clive Gamble in *The Palaeolithic Settlement of Europe* (Cambridge University Press, 1986); for the earlier periods by Derek Roe in *The Lower and Middle Palaeolithic Periods in Britain* (Routledge, 1981) and John Wymer in *Lower Palaeolithic Archaeology in Britain* (John Baker, 1968); and the later phases by John Campbell in *The Upper Palaeolithic of Britain* (Clarendon Press, 1977) and Nicholas Barton in *Stone Age Britain* (Batsford/English Heritage, 1997).

The Mesolithic is well covered by Christopher Smith in *Late Stone Age Hunters of the British Isles* (Routledge, 1992). A highly readable summary account is provided by John Wymer's *Mesolithic Britain* (Shire Archaeology, 1991).

Neolithic Britain is still well served by Stuart Piggott's book *The Neolithic Cultures of the British Isles* (Cambridge University Press, 1954), updatable by reference to Alasdair Whittle's *The Earlier Neolithic of Southern England and its Continental Background* (British Archaeological Reports, 1977), and Julian Thomas's *Understanding the Neolithic* (Routledge, 1999). A good short introduction is provided by Joshua Pollard in *Neolithic Britain* (Shire Archaeology, 1997)

The later Neolithic and Bronze Age are covered by Colin Burgess in *The Age of Stonehenge* (Dent, 1980) and Michael Parker Pearson in *Bronze Age Britain* (Batsford/English Heritage, 1993).

Later prehistory is given a European context by John Collis in *The European Iron Age* (Routledge, 1984). *Iron Age Britain* by Barry Cunliffe (Batsford and English Heritage, 1995) provides a good summary account of the period that is explored in more detail in his *Iron Age Communities in Britain*, 3rd edn (Routledge, 1991).

Roman Britain

There are numerous general introductions to Roman Britain. The standard texts are dominated by heavy-weight volumes, notably Peter Salway's *Roman Britain* (Clarendon Press, 1993). More fully illustrated, and rather easier to read, are Peter Salway's *The Oxford Illustrated History of Roman Britain* (Oxford University Press, 1993), and G. D. B. Jones and D. Mattingly's *An Atlas of Roman Britain* (Oxford University Press, 1990).

The Roman invasion and its aftermath are considered by John Wacher in *The Coming of Rome* (Routledge, 1979); Romanization is discussed in Martin Millett's *The Romanization of Britain* (Cambridge University Press, 1990) and the papers in *Research on Roman Britain 1960–1989* ed. Malcolm Todd (Society for the Promotion of Roman Studies, 1989).

Roman military archaeology has a diverse literature. On the army useful starting points include I. P. Stephenson's *Roman Infantry Equipment, the Later Empire* (Tempus, 1999) and Eric Birley's *The Roman Army* (Gieben, 1998). A good introduction to the forts and defences is David Breeze's *Roman Forts in Britain* (Shire Archaeology, 1983), while a detailed listing of recorded examples can be found in Vivian Swan and Humphrey Welfare's *Roman Camps in England: The Field Archaeology* (HMSO, 1995).

Standard works on the northern frontier include David Breeze and Brian

Dobson's *Hadrian's Wall* (Penguin, 1987), David Breeze's *The Northern Frontiers of Roman Britain* (Batsford, 1982), and Jim Crow's *Housesteads* (Batsford/English Heritage, 1995).

The Roman landscape is well illustrated by S. S. Frere and J. K. St Joseph's excellent and wide ranging *Roman Britain from the Air* (Cambridge University Press, 1983), towns being comprehensively treated by John Wacher in *The Towns of Roman Britain* (Routledge, 1997) and John Wacher and Barry Burnham, *The Small Towns of Roman Britain* (Batsford/Routledge, 1990). General views of rural settlement include A. L. F. Rivet's *Town and Country in Roman Britain*, 2nd edn (Hutchinson, 1964) and Richard Hingley's more recent *Rural Settlement in Roman Britain* (Seaby, 1989).

Villas and related structures are described by David Johnson in *Roman Villas* (Shire Archaeology, 1983), while more detailed treatments include John Percival's *The Roman Villa: An Historical Introduction* (Batsford, 1976). Mosaics are reviewed by Peter Johnson in *Romano-British Mosaics* (Shire Archaeology, 1982).

Other aspects of the archaeology of Roman Britain are covered by Guy de la Bédoyère's *The Finds of Roman Britain* (Batsford, 1988), Richard Reece's *Coinage in Roman Britain* (Seaby, 1987), Paul Tyers's *Pottery in Roman Britain*, 2nd edn (Batsford, 1995), Martin Henig's *Religion in Roman Britain* (Batsford, 1985) and the same author's *Art in Roman Britain* (Batsford, 1995).

Later Roman Britain and the role of communities outside the Empire is the subject of Malcolm Todd's *The Northern Barbarians 100 BC–AD 300* (Hutchinson, 1975), while events within the northern Empire from the later C3 are usefully covered by Stephen Johnson's *The Roman Forts of the Saxon Shore* (Elek, 1976), Guy de la Bédoyère's *The Golden Age of Roman Britain* (Tempus, 1999), and Charles Thomas's *Christianity in Roman Britain to AD 500* (Batsford, 1981). The end of Roman Britain is dealt with by Simon Esmonde Cleary's *The Ending of Roman Britain* (Batsford, 1989), and Nick Higham's *Rome, Britain and the Anglo-Saxons* (Seaby, 1992).

Medieval England

For the Anglo-Saxon period James Graham Campbell's *The Anglo-Saxons* (Penguin Books, 1991) provides a good overview, while for more detail Martin Welch's *Anglo-Saxon England* (Batsford/English Heritage, 1992) covers the earlier part of the period and Julian D Richards's *Viking Age England* (Tempus, 2000) and Andrew Reynolds's *Late Anglo-Saxon England* (Tempus, 1999) together review the later stages.

General surveys of the post-Conquest period abound. From an archaeological perspective Colin Platt's *Medieval England* (Routledge, 1978), John Steane's *The Archaeology of Medieval England and Wales* (Croom Helm, 1984), and David Hinton's *Archaeology, Economy and Society* (Seaby, 1990) stand out. For the growing political, administrative, and social complexity of life in the Middle Ages see *The Oxford Companion to British History*, ed. John Cannon (Oxford University Press, 1997).

Churches are well covered in the county-by-county volumes in the *Buildings of England* series conceived, edited, and initially largely written by Sir

Nikolaus Pevsner (Penguin, 1951–). For parish churches Warwick Rodwell's *Church Archaeology* (Batsford/English Heritage, 1989), Richard Morris's *Churches in the Landscape* (Dent, 1989), and Colin Platt's *The Parish Churches of Medieval England* (Secker & Warburg. 1981) complement each other nicely. For monasteries three modern surveys are J. Patrick Greene's *Medieval Monasteries* (Leicester University Press, 1992), Michael Aston's *Monasteries in the Landscape* (Tempus, 2000), and Glyn Coppack's *Abbeys and Priories* (Batsford/English Heritage, 1990).

Colin Platt's *The Architecture of Medieval Britain* (Yale, 1990) is a magisterial survey. A well-illustrated introduction to humbler buildings is Anthony Quinney's *The Traditional Buildings of England* (Thames & Hudson, 1990). For other subjects the following are all accessible surveys: N. J. G. Pounds, *The Medieval Castle* (Leicester University Press, 1990); Colin Platt, *The English Medieval Town* (Secker & Warburg, 1976); Patrick Ottaway, *The Archaeology of British Towns* (Routledge, 1992); and John Blair and Nigel Ramsey's edited volume *English Medieval Industries* (Hambledon Press, 1991). Medieval rural settlement is explored in Christopher Taylor's *Village and Farmstead* (George Philip, 1983), while Christopher Dyer's *Standards of Living in the Middle Ages* (Cambridge University Press, 1989) gets to grips with peasant life from diet to underwear!

Useful addresses and Internet sites

Archaeology is a big international subject with a long history. There are many organizations involved, more than 500 in Britain alone. Only a few can be mentioned here but with the increasing development of the Internet, and access to it, finding out what is going on gets easier and easier as time goes by. Most English counties have an established county archaeological society that publishes, more or less annually, a volume of transactions with articles of local and/or regional interest. Sets of these volumes can usually be found in the local public reference library or records office.

National societies

Council for British Archaeology. Established in 1944, the Council for British Archaeology is an independent charity which works to advance the study and practice of archaeology in Great Britain and Northern Ireland. Personal and institutional membership is possible. Members receive a magazine entitled *British Archaeology*. Bowes Morrell House, 111 Walmgate, York YO1 2UA. Tel.: +(0)1904 671417. There is an Internet site at www.britarch.ac.uk

Royal Archaeological Institute. Founded in 1844 the RAI is a membership-based society that plays a lead role in stimulating research and interest in the past. Publications include the *Archaeological Journal*. For details of how to join contact the RAI, c/o Society of Antiquaries of London, Burlington House, Piccadilly, London W1V 0HS.

Young Archaeologists' Club. The YAC is the only national club of its kind for anyone between the ages of 9 and 16. Membership includes a pin badge and a card that entitles members to free or discounted entry to centres around the country. Members also receive the Club's quarterly magazine *Young Archaeologist*. YAC also arranges field study holidays and a range of other activities. All enquiries to: The Young Archaeologists' Club, c/o Council for British Archaeology, Bowes Morrell House, 111 Walmgate, York YO1 2UA.

Heritage organizations

English Heritage. English Heritage was established in 1984 as the principal government agency charged with the preservation and management of England's archaeological heritage and stock of historic buildings. English Heritage is responsible for more than 400 archaeological sites and historic monuments. There is a membership scheme allowing free admission to English Heritage monuments. For details of the membership scheme contact: English Heritage Membership Department, PO Box 1BB, London

W1A 1BB. Tel.: +(0)20 7973 3434. There is also information on the Internet at www.english-heritage.org.uk

The National Trust. The National Trust for England, Wales and Northern Ireland was created in 1895 to preserve places of historic interest or natural beauty for the enjoyment of the nation. Anyone can become a member of the Trust and enjoy free access to all Trust properties. Further information from: The National Trust, Freepost MB1438, Bromley, Kent. BR1 3BR. Tel.: +(0)870 458 4000. See also its Internet site at www.ukindex.co.uk/nationaltrust

Period societies

Prehistoric Society. For details contact: Hon. Secretary, Prehistoric Society, University College London, Institute of Archaeology, 31–34 Gordon Square, London WC1H 0PY. www.britarch.ac.uk/cba/prehist

Society for Medieval Archaeology. For further details contact: The Society for Medieval Archaeology, PO Box YR7, Leeds LS9 7UU. www.britarch.ac.uk/cba/medieval

Society for the Promotion of Roman Studies. For further details contact: Hon. Secretary, Society for the Promotion of Roman Studies, Senate House, Malet Street, London WC1E 7HU. Tel.: +(0)20 7862 8727 www.sas.ac.uk/icls/roman/

Magazines and journals

Current Archaeology. Published six times a year, provides lively accounts of recent discoveries, excavations, technical advances, book reviews, and notice of events. An annual supplement entitled *Directory of British Archaeology* lists details of over 500 organizations concerned with archaeology in the British Isles. Available by subscription only. For details contact: Current Archaeology, 9 Nassington Road, London NW3 2TX. There is an Internet site at www.archaeology.co.uk

Antiquity. A quarterly magazine which is the main international journal for the archaeological community and anyone with a serious interest in archaeology. Available by subscription only. For details contact: Antiquity Subscriptions Department, The Company of Biologists, Bidder Building, 140 Cowley Road, Cambridge CB4 4DL. http://intarch.ac.uk/antiquity

Archaeology on the Internet

A number of indexes to archaeologically relevant Internet resources exist and the following addresses will take you to some of the more useful, comprehensive and easy to navigate listings and virtual libraries—happy surfing!

http://archnet.unconn.edu/

http://csweb.bournemouth.ac.uk/consci/arkylink/links.html

http://odur.let.rug.nl/arge/

http://web.idirect.com/~atrium/commentarium.html

Index of sites

Star-rated sites ★ *and* ★★
Sites mentioned within substantive entries are marked +

Illustrations– Acknowledgements

Photographs are © the authors, apart from the following which are reproduced by kind permission:

2, 6 Cambridge University Collection of Air Photographs: © reserved; **8** © The British Museum; **9** © Colchester and Essex Museums; **12** © St Albans Museum; **33, 35, 38** Cambridge University Collection of Air Photographs: © reserved; **44** © National Trust Photographic Library; **46, 47** Cambridge University Collection of Air Photographs: © reserved; **49** © Leeds Museum and Galleries; **51** © Alan Sorrel; **55** Cambridge University Collection of Air Photographs: © reserved; **62** © York Archaeological Trust; **68** © Michael Jones, City Archaeologist, City of Lincoln Council; **69** Cambridge University Collection of Air Photographs: © reserved; **79** Brian William, © Crown copyright. NMR; **81** © Clwyd-Powys Archaeological Trust 85–16–29; **98** © A. P. Baggs; **105** © St Albans Museum; **112** © National Photographic Library/Ian Shaw; **127** Cambridge University Collection of Air Photographs: © reserved; **137** Reproduced with the kind permission of the Tupper family, Bignor Roman Villa, West Sussex; **139** © The Illustrated London News Picture Library; **146** © D. Baker/ Sussex Archaeological Society; **160, 174, 176** Cambridge University Collection of Air Photographs: © reserved; **185** © F. Griffith, Devon County Council; **191, 193** Cambridge University Collection of Air Photographs: © reserved.